USING

VERSION

Simply 8.0 Accounting®

for Windows™: An Integrated Simulation

M. PURBHOO • D. PURBHOO

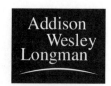

Addison
Wesley
Longman

Toronto

Canadian Cataloguing in Publication Data

Purbhoo, Mary, 1949-
  Using Simply Accounting version 8.0 for Windows: an integrated simulation

Issued also as trade ed. under the title: Teach yourself Simply Accounting version 8.0 for Windows. Includes index.

ISBN 0-201-71690-9 (college)
      0-201-73014-6 (trade)

1. Simply Accounting for Windows (Computer file). 2. Accounting-Computer programs. I. Purbhoo, D. (Dhirajlal). II. Title. III. Title: Teach yourself Simply Accounting version 8.0 for Windows.

HF5679.P894 2001   657'.0285'5369   C00-932394-5

Simply Accounting® is a trademark of ACCPAC INTERNATIONAL, INC.
Windows™ is a trademark of Microsoft Corporation.

0-201-71690-9 (college)
0-201-73014-6 (trade)

Vice President, Editorial Director: Michael Young
Acquisitions Editor: Samantha Scully
Marketing Manager: James Buchanan
Developmental Editor: Laurie Goebel
Production Editor: Marisa D'Andrea
Copy Editor: Dawn Hunter
Production Coordinator: Patricia Ciardullo
Page Layout: Mary Purbhoo
Art Director: Mary Opper
Cover Design: Anthony Leung
Cover Image: EyeWire Images

This edition is also published as Teach Yourself Simply Accounting Version 8.0 for Windows: An Integrated Simulation.

1 2 3 4 5   05 04 03 02 01

Printed and bound in Canada.

Bound to stay open

Preface

Version 8.0B of the Simply Accounting program was used to create the data files and the screen illustrations in this book. Any Simply Accounting program, version 8.0 or later, should allow you to use this book. For versions other than 8.0B, there may be some screen changes. In addition, since each version uses different payroll tax tables, your Payroll amounts may be slightly different from the amounts we show.

Using Simply Accounting Version 8.0 for Windows: An Integrated Simulation updates our previous books with all the new features of the software and two extended simulations in modular form. In each chapter, a new topic, setup or set of journals is introduced with detailed keystroke instructions and screen illustrations, allowing you to build the Play Wave Plus company, the main simulation, as you learn the software. To avoid a long delay between the introduction of new concepts and the opportunity to practise, we also present Live Links, the practice simulation, at the end of each chapter. Live Links parallels and reinforces the introduction of the new material in Play Wave Plus and builds in the same modular form.

After an introductory chapter, we introduce Play Wave Plus and the software with the General Ledger and Journal, in order to simplify the setup and to begin journal entries as early as possible. To avoid beginning a new company with adjusting entries, we initially use the General Journal for all transactions. Since the General Journal is modelled after manual accounting methods, this helps users to appreciate the ease of using subsidiary journals as they are added. Except for a few General Journal entries in Chapter 3, each journal is used only for its intended types of transaction.

Chapters 2 to 18 add ledgers, journals and features of the software as the business grows over time. After starting as a service business that contracts out payroll services, Play Wave Plus grows to become a fully integrated company with international vendors and customers, administering its own payroll, selling inventory and developing budgets and projects for additional financial control. By completing the accounting transactions for six months — two complete business cycles — there is also opportunity to close the books, enter adjustments and begin a new fiscal period. We have even created Web sites and e-mail addresses specifically for the simulations in this book to illustrate and teach these features of the software.

The last two chapters, Kindred Kitchenwares and Anderson Farm, provide comprehensive simulations for further practice. Anderson Farm also has realistic source documents for additional challenge.

Chapter 1 stands apart from the other simulations. This hands-on chapter has its own sample data file to encourage users to explore all aspects of the software without concern about damaging their own files or making mistakes.

We have also added a number of appendices for further reference: an introduction to Windows, using the mouse and copying files; instructions for installing the Simply Accounting program; a complete reference guide to GST and PST; illustrations for correcting errors after posting (with screens showing the original and the reversing entries); a detailed description of setting and using passwords for security; and, finally, keystroke instructions for exporting data to a number of independent programs. The data CD also includes a review of basic accounting theory that you may print for reference. This supplement is provided in two formats: MS Word 97 and Acrobat 4.0. Refer to the ReadMe file on the CD for instructions.

The Data Disk now includes data files for both extended simulations on a chapter-by-chapter basis for those users who prefer to work through the text in a non-sequential manner (read the Data Disk section).

Users familiar with our previous books will see that we have retained many of the features that we considered essential: business simulations that we try to bring to life with realistic background information; a comprehensive variety of accounting transactions and tax situations; complete, detailed and easy-to-follow keystroke instructions with many screen illustrations to help you learn all the features of the software; and many opportunities to practice and reinforce earlier work. To this, we have added Web site and e-mail links for the simulations and chapter review questions.

Our sequential presentation of information and transactions is modelled after a realistic business situation. The accounting transactions are presented in order of natural business occurrence. Therefore, each chapter has transactions for all of the journals already introduced, providing continual reinforcement of all concepts, not just the new ones. For example, Chapter 7 introduces the two Receivables journals, but users also complete purchases, payments and adjusting entries. In any business, payroll, sales, payments, receipts and purchases all occur on the same day, and in a small business, a single individual enters all this information. Accounting transactions are not pre-sorted according to the journal they belong to. Journal entries should be posted for the date of the transaction to maintain a proper journal sequence and audit trail. An important part of learning to use accounting software, therefore, is deciding which journal is appropriate for each type of transaction. Presenting transactions sequentially, as we do, encourages this ability to analyze transactions and make decisions.

Acknowledgments

Authors can learn a great deal from the instructors and students who use their texts, as well as from reviewers and surveys. Input from multiple levels helps us to maintain our high standards, and we appreciate the feedback that we receive from these different sources. Instructors and independent users who call us for assistance show us where we need to clarify our presentation. Surveys that point out a preference for one approach over another lead us to apply different strategies for ordering the topics and to increase our Data Disk support to achieve more independence among the chapters. Reviewers who tell us what they like about our books, and where their classroom challenges lie in teaching Simply Accounting, also lead to further improvements. Whenever it is feasible, we incorporate their suggestions and try to develop our texts to assist with these classroom challenges.

We would like to thank Louise Connors at Nova Scotia Community College, Gordon Holyer at Malaspina University College, Frank Mensink at Conestoga College, Graham Hughes at British Columbia Institute of Technology, Shirley Connolly at College of the North Atlantic and Cynthia Lone at Red River College, whose review of a previous edition of this text provided helpful suggestions for this version.

Keystroke instructions and transactions were checked by a number of people. Both authors performed this task several times. We were fortunate once again to have the assistance with this task from Joanna Severino-Souto, a teacher with the Toronto District Board of Education and director of Compu-Smart Kids, and Irene Mota, teacher with the Dufferin-Peel Catholic District School Board. By independently checking the accuracy of all keystroke instructions and transactions details, they have been an important part of our quality control team on several projects. It is a pleasure to work with these professional teachers who pay careful attention to details and are able to work within very tight deadlines.

Attention to detail is necessary to produce a book that is both correct and professional in appearance. We were impressed with the ability of Dawn Hunter, the copy editor, who found many little mistakes, as well as some big ones, in early drafts of the text. Her corrections contributed to both the accuracy and readability of the text.

The friendly support from the editorial team at Pearson Education, especially Samantha Scully, Laurie Goebel and Marisa D'Andrea, also helped to make this entire project run smoothly.

Over time, we have developed a comfortable and collaborative relationship with Mary Watson and Tyler Lee at ACCPAC International, who generously and professionally provide updated product information and troubleshooting advice.

We also give a heartfelt thank you to the Andersson family — Krister, Anna Karin, Maria, Malin and Tomas — whose warmth and hospitality contributed to one of our most memorable vacations. Their farm in Sweden served as the inspiration for the Anderson Farm simulation in Chapter 20 of this book.

And finally, to the group of North York physicians, Dr. Colapinto, Dr. Baron and Dr. Rappaport, who made it possible for this project to be finished, we thank you and dedicate this book to you.

Using This Book

The Play Wave Plus simulation progresses in a sequential manner, with each ledger added in a new chapter followed by the journals for that ledger in the next chapter. Within each chapter, information is also presented sequentially. The data or transactions to be entered are presented as they occur, in a sequence of time or data input. Keystroke instructions are interwoven with these transactions or data to continue the concept of an integrated approach.

Design Aids

We have added some key design elements to make sure that you can easily follow the flow of information. The following key designs are used throughout the book to help you identify elements that are different from regular text information. (This paragraph is typed as regular text.)

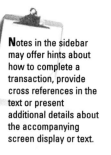

Notes in the sidebar may offer hints about how to complete a transaction, provide cross references in the text or present additional details about the accompanying screen display or text.

◆ Keystroke statements: Instructions that include detailed and specific steps for working through new material. You must complete these steps. If there is a word or key that you must click or press, it is presented in boldface type. Text that you must type or key in is presented as boldface text in the Courier font, for example,

◆ Click **Proceed**, or ◆ Type `Memo 13`

☐ Source Documents: Accounting transactions that you must enter to complete the simulation. Each one has a check box on the left for you to mark the transaction after completing the entry.

☑ Accounting transactions for which we provide keystroke instructions have a ✓ added to the check box.

Reference material: Extended explanations for accounting procedures, alternative methods of completing transactions or detailed descriptions of input fields for a Simply Accounting screen are presented on a grey background with a typeface that is different from the regular text. If you want to proceed quickly using the specific steps of entering transactions, you can return later to this information. **Key words** are presented in boldface type so that you can scan the section to find the details you need.

SETUP DATA

Data that you must input as part of a company setup, such as Charts of Accounts, vendor lists, etc., is generally presented as boxed information.

Bookmark

Use the bookmark to hold the page containing the source document while you work through keystroke instructions. Use the page index on the bookmark to quickly find a keystroke section for review while you are entering source documents in later chapters.

The Data Disk

We have developed the simulations with the intention that all users will work through the book in order by completing all the ledger setups and transactions. The journal entries in each chapter are linked to transactions in the previous journal chapter (e.g., payments linked to purchases). However, many of the chapters may be completed in a different sequence. Refer to the section "An Alternative Chapter Sequence" later in this section for details.

We hope that the Data Disk will not be used as an alternative to following the keystroke instructions that introduce new types of transactions and setups.

Theoretically, a Data Disk is not needed. Users can create their own data files and build on them from one chapter to the next. With regular backups, users should be able to continue smoothly, perhaps returning to an earlier backup copy if serious mistakes are made. A great sense of satisfaction results from working through the material on your own and getting it right; for example, having the bank account reconciled each month, with no unresolved amounts. The setup chapters involve creating records, entering balances and finishing the history for a ledger. The ability to finish the history correctly is an important check on the accuracy of your work and understanding of the software. For example, finishing the history for the General Ledger to prepare for journal transactions requires an understanding of account types, account numbering and the structure of the Balance Sheet and Income Statement, as well as the ability to enter account balance amounts correctly.

However, we also learn when we make mistakes and try to understand what went wrong. We recognize that mistakes are made, that disk and file errors occur and that some users may not need to complete all the transactions in order to master the concepts. Some errors are difficult to recover from because they are not discovered until much later. Therefore, we provide the Data Disk, which offers entry points at the start of each chapter for the two principal simulations.

You can check your work as you proceed by printing the journal entries from the files for Chapter 18. This report will show all transactions except for those in Chapter 18.

Data Disk Files

The Data Disk files are organized by chapter. Chapter 1 has a stand-alone data file. There is no file for Chapter 2 because the starting point is the creation of company data files from scratch. The files for Chapter 3 have the setup from Chapter 2 completed and are ready for the journal entries in Chapter 3. The files for Chapter 4 have all the journal entries in Chapter 3 completed and the files are ready for the Payables Ledger setup in Chapter 4. And so on. The Chapter 1 files are somewhat different. We have provided an independent sample company for practising and exploring the features of the program.

The chart of data files on the next page shows the link between chapters in the book and Data Disk files.

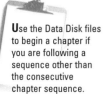
Use the Data Disk files to begin a chapter if you are following a sequence other than the consecutive chapter sequence.

Anderson Farm may be completed any time after Chapter 10. Kindred Kitchenwares may be completed any time after Chapter 15.

For... Use:	Folder\File name	Session Date	Folder\File name	Session Date
Chapter 1	Ch01\overview.sdb	Apr. 30/01		
	Play Wave Plus simulation		**Live Links simulation**	
Chapter 2	create your own files for this chapter			
Chapter 3	Ch03\play\playch03.sdb	Mar. 15/02	Ch03\links\linkch03.sdb	Jul. 8/02
Chapter 4	Ch04\play\playch04.sdb	Mar. 31/02	Ch04\links\linkch04.sdb	Jul. 31/02
Chapter 5	Ch05\play\playch05.sdb	Mar. 31/02	Ch05\links\linkch05.sdb	Jul. 31/02
Chapter 6	Ch06\play\playch06.sdb	Apr. 14/02	Ch06\links\linkch06.sdb	Aug. 8/02
Chapter 7	Ch07\play\playch07.sdb	Apr. 14/02	Ch07\links\linkch07.sdb	Aug. 8/02
Chapter 8	Ch08\play\playch08.sdb	Apr. 30/02	Ch08\links\linkch08.sdb	Aug. 31/02
Chapter 9	Ch09\play\playch09.sdb	May 14/02	Ch09\links\linkch09.sdb	Sep. 14/02
Chapter 10	Ch10\play\playch10.sdb	May 14/02	Ch10\links\linkch10.sdb	Sep. 14/02
Chapter 11	Ch11\play\playch11.sdb	May 31/02	Ch11\links\linkch11.sdb	Sep. 30/02
Chapter 12	Ch12\play\playch12.sdb	May 31/02	Ch12\links\linkch12.sdb	Sep. 30/02
Chapter 13	Ch13\play\playch13.sdb	May 31/02	Ch13\links\linkch13.sdb	Sep. 30/02
Chapter 14	Ch14\play\playch14.sdb	Jun. 1/02	Ch14\links\linkch14.sdb	Oct. 1/02
Chapter 15	Ch15\play\playch15.sdb	Jun. 1/02	Ch15\links\linkch15.sdb	Oct. 1/02
Chapter 16	Ch16\play\playch16.sdb	Jun. 30/02	Ch16\links\linkch16.sdb	Oct. 31/02
Chapter 17	Ch17\play\playch17.sdb	Jul. 31/02	Ch17\links\linkch17.sdb	Nov. 30/02
Chapter 18	Ch18\play\playch18.sdb	Aug. 14/02	Ch18\links\linkch18.sdb	Dec. 14/02
Kindred Kitchenwares (Chapter 19)	create your own files for this simulation			
Anderson Farm (Chapter 20)	create your own files for this simulation			

An Alternative Sequence

We know that some of our users prefer a multi-simulation approach with stand-alone chapters that may be completed in a sequence different from the one we provide. By using the Data Disk files, the integrated simulation chapters may also be completed as independent exercises.

For example, some prefer Account Reconciliation to be introduced earlier, while others prefer to delay it. We have tried to strike a balance by delaying it until the end of the first fiscal quarter, so that reconciliation procedures for three months are completed in a single chapter. This delay provides more immediate practice. This topic may be taught at any time after Chapter 3 has been completed. Closing Routines (Chapter 13) is another topic that can be completed any time after Chapter 3 because it includes only General Journal entries. By using the Data Disk for these topics, they may be taught later or earlier than we present them.

In our Version 6 book, Account Reconciliation was covered in Chapter 4. In Version 8, it is covered in Chapter 11.

The practice simulation at the end of each chapter, Live Links, may be completed on a chapter-by-chapter basis after finishing the Play Wave entries, or it may be delayed. We present it at the end of the chapter to provide immediate reinforcement of newly learned material.

Ledger setup is another topic that some prefer to learn later, others earlier. If you want to postpone the coverage of ledger setups, you can complete all (or some) of the journal chapters first.

The only restriction is that journal chapters must be completed in sequence, since each chapter includes journal transactions that are explained in previous chapters.

The following chart shows how the chapters may be used more independently. In brackets, we show the chapters that must be completed before beginning a new chapter or topic.

If you skip Account Reconciliation in Chapter 11, you should also skip the Account Reconciliation transactions at the end of Chapters 15, 16 and 18. Use the Data Disk to resume with the following chapter and then return to your own files later to do the reconciliation.

JOURNAL ENTRY CHAPTERS	LEDGER SETUP CHAPTERS	OTHER
Complete in sequence (complete this chapter first)	(May be completed at any time after chapter in brackets)	(May be completed at any time after chapter in brackets)
Chapter 1 Introduction		
	Chapter 2 (after Ch 1) General Ledger	
Chapter 3 (after Ch 1) General Journal	Chapter 4 (after Ch 2) Accounts Payable	Chapter 11 (after Ch 3) Account Reconciliation
		Chapter 13 (after Ch 3) Closing Routines
Chapter 5 (after Ch 3) Payables Journals	Chapter 6 (after Ch 2) Accounts Receivable	
Chapter 7 (after Ch 5) Receivables Journals		Chapter 12 (after Ch 7) Graphs
		Chapter 20 (after Ch 7) Practice (Anderson Farm)
Chapter 8 (after Ch 7) Additional A/P & A/R	Chapter 9 (after Ch 2) Payroll Ledger	
Chapter 10 (after Ch 8) Payroll Journals	Chapter 14 (after Ch 2) Inventory Ledger	
Chapter 15 (after Ch 10) Inventory Journal Transactions		Chapter 19 (after Ch 15) Practice (Kindred Kitchenwares)
Chapter 16 (after Ch 15) Budget		
Chapter 17 (after Ch 16) Project		
Chapter 18 (after Ch 17) Dual Currency		

Instructor's Support Package

We have created a support package for instructors using this book. The package includes a solutions disk and a printed document.

The solutions disk contains the Simply Accounting files for the four simulations with all transactions completed. For both the Play Wave Plus and Live Links simulations, we provide two sets of files — one for the end of the first quarter and one for the end of the second quarter. From these files, instructors may print or display any reports for the simulations with any report date, thus providing the printed solutions or reports that are suitable for their own classroom circumstances. **Use the Simply Accounting software program to access these files and print the reports.**

The printed document includes suggested answers to the end-of-chapter review questions as well as additional instructional aids.

Additional testing materials, including simulations suitable for hands-on testing, are also available.

Contents

INTRODUCTION TO SIMPLY ACCOUNTING

Objectives

- **start the Simply Accounting program**
- **access data files**
- **understand the Home window screen icons and menus**
- **describe the purpose of each ledger and journal**
- **use Simply Accounting Help features**
- **use the View menu to change the appearance of the program**
- **save files and make backups**
- **exit the program**

Introduction

In this chapter, you will use a sample data file to explore the Simply Accounting software. Because this file is not connected in any way with the work in the remaining chapters, you can make changes to this file without affecting your ability to complete the simulations correctly. You may even want to use this file in later chapters as a test for other aspects of the program. For example, if you are unsure about how the program will handle a transaction, you can enter the same transaction in two different ways to see the effects.

Simply Accounting Overview

This chapter provides a quick introduction to the Simply Accounting program. If you are already familiar with Windows programs, you can work through the chapter quickly. Otherwise, you can use the sample data file to explore the program fully by opening and closing the ledger and journal windows, and viewing the reports, ledger settings, accounts and records.

The screen illustrations in this book were captured while running Simply Accounting under Windows 98.

Starting the Simply Accounting Program

◆ Click **Start** on the task bar at the bottom of the desktop window.

◆ Point to **Programs** to expand the list of available programs.

◆ Point to **Simply Accounting** to expand its program list as shown:

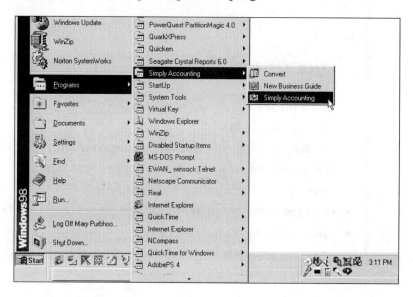

Cascading Menus

The Start menu, the Programs menu and the Simply Accounting menu in the illustration above are examples of cascading or expanding menus. When you point to a menu option with an arrow beside it (▶), a second level of menu options or programs will open. Many of the menus in Simply Accounting are cascading menus.

◆ Click **Simply Accounting** to open the Simply Accounting – Select Company window:

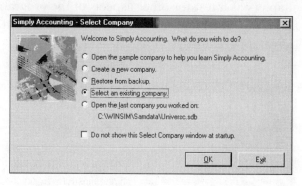

In the screen illustrations, the Winsim folder has been installed directly in C: instead of in the default Program Files folder.

From this opening window, you can choose to work with one of the sample companies that came on the program disk, create a new company from scratch or from a template, restore a backup file, select some other data files or choose the same files you worked with the last time. If you are starting the Simply Accounting program for the first time, the Select Company window will not include the option to Open the last company you worked on, as in the previous screen illustration. Instead, you will see the following screen:

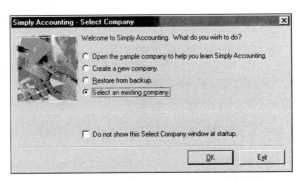

If you want to skip this window, you can click Do not show this Select Company window at startup. Bypassing the Select Company window will place you in the Open Company window as the first screen.

◆ Click **Select an existing company.**

◆ Click **OK** to access the Simply Accounting – Open Company window:

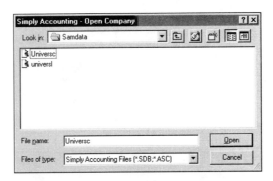

By default, the last file you worked on is listed in the File name field. If this is the first time you are using the program, the default folder set up on your computer system will appear. The Samdata folder, inside the Winsim folder, is shown above. All Simply Accounting data files within the selected or open folder are listed in the large centre text area of the window.

WARNING! Back up Your Data Disk First

Before you use the data that comes with this text, make a copy of the folders on the CD-ROM Data Disk and place the original in a safe place. You must open data files from a drive that you can write to, so you will be unable to start the Simply Accounting program from data files on the CD-ROM.

To copy the data folders, double click the My Computer icon on the windows desktop. Double click the CD-ROM icon to select it. Choose the Edit menu and click Select All. Choose the Edit menu and click Copy. Click the Back button to return to the My Computer window. Double click the drive and then double click the folder you want to use to store the data, for example, the Data folder in the Winsim folder. You will need to double click the folder at each successive level — (C:), then Program Files, then Winsim and finally Data — in order to open the final folder. Choose the Edit menu and click Paste. Then change the file properties to remove the Read-Only restriction. Refer to Appendix A for complete instructions on copying disks and files and changing file properties.

CD-ROM files are Read-Only files. You must remove this restriction before Simply Accounting can open the files. Refer to Appendix A if you need help with this step.

◆ Click Samdata (or My Documents, or the folder named in the Look in field) or its drop-down list arrow ▾ to see the list of available drives for your computer:

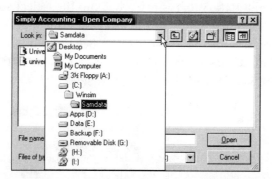

To access the data file you need, you must open the folder at each level in turn. Using the drop-down list in the Look in field, you can use the following sequence from any folder.

◆ Click **(C:)** in the drop-down list. (Double click Program Files if you used the default location when you installed the program.)

◆ Double click the **Winsim folder** in the text area.

◆ Double click the **Data folder**:

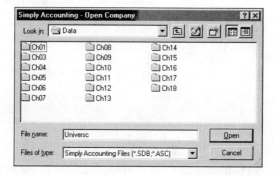

Folder Ch01 has the practice file for this chapter. The folders Ch03 to Ch18 each have subfolders named Play and Links for the two simulations in these chapters. The files you need to work through the exercises in this text are contained in their respective chapter and company folders.

◆ Click **Ch01** to select this folder.

◆ Click **Open** to list the available Simply Accounting files in the Ch01 folder:

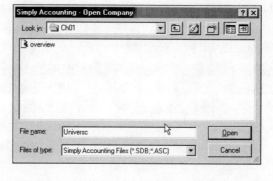

4

A single file is listed. Notice that the Files of type field shows Simply Accounting Files (*.SDB, *.ASC). Only the files with these extensions are listed because Simply Accounting recognizes these tags. The second file in the same folder is part of the same data set. You can see the list of all files with the Windows Explorer program. All the files for a company must be in the same folder and must be intact before you can access the data. Therefore, it is very important when you copy files to be sure that you have included both files from the folder.

◆ Click **overview** to select it.

◆ Click **Open** to access the file.

If you have not removed the Read-Only file properties, you will see the following message about Read-Only files:

◆ Click **OK**. You will need to change the file properties before proceeding. Refer to Appendix A, page 622 for instructions on removing the Read-Only restrictions and then try to open the file again.

If you see a message advising you to update the Federal Claim amounts, click Done to avoid seeing the message again.

You will see the Session Date dialog box:

The date of the previous working session is entered and highlighted for editing. April 30, 2001 (04/30/2001), is the date in the illustration. If your display is different (for example, if the day or year are placed before the month) refer to the section on Display Date Formats at the end of this chapter.

Session Dates

Simply Accounting allows you to move Session dates backwards as well as forwards within the fiscal period for a company.

In large companies, accounting entries are made daily, and the **Session date** would be the date that the transactions occurred and were entered. In a smaller company, the transactions that occurred might be entered once a week, so the Session date would be advanced by one week at a time. The new Session date must be between the start and the end of the fiscal period. The drop-down list arrow in any date field provides you with the range of eligible dates for the company. The first date of the next fiscal period is the last date in the drop-down list. You cannot go beyond this date until you close the books. Simply Accounting allows you to work with dates up to the year 2027. In our practice simulations, we use dates that relate to the transaction dates and not the actual calendar date. In this way, we can tell you what dates to use for journal entries and reports.

Since there are no journal transactions in this chapter, you can accept the Session date.

◆ Click **OK** to display the Home window, Simply Accounting – OVERVIEW.SDB.

The Simply Accounting Home Window

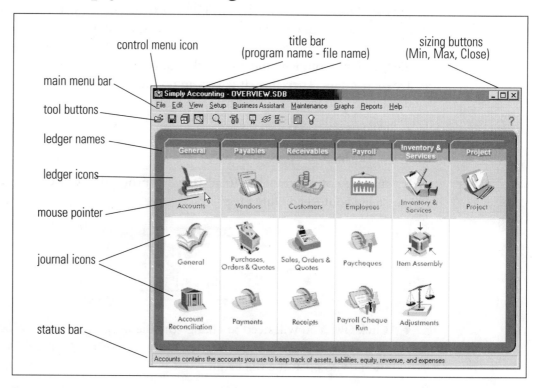

The Home Window

The Home window is the starting point for working with the data files for a company and provides access to all the ledgers and journals.

The **title bar** at the top of the Home window is like the title bar in other Windows programs, with the control menu icon in the far left corner, the program and file names beside the control menu icon, and the sizing and Close buttons at the right. The **control menu icon** has a pull-down menu for controlling window size and location.

The **sizing buttons** at the right are alternatives to the pull-down menu commands. They are **Minimize** ⬓ (to a task bar button), **Maximize** ⬜ (to full screen size) or **Restore** ⧉ (if the window has been maximized, the Restore button replaces the Maximize button) and **Close** ☒ (to exit the program — Simply Accounting automatically saves any changes you made during the work session).

The next line, the **main menu bar**, contains a number of menu items, each with its own pull-down menu of several options. The menu bar changes from one window to the next, as do the pull-down options, although often there are common items. Many of the menu options have cascading menus. When you point to the arrow ▶ beside an option, a second level of options will appear. The Home window menu bar includes the following:

File Menu

New Company: Create a new set of data files for a new company.

Open Company: Open a different data file and close the one you are working on.

Save: Save all changes made and keep the file open.

Save As: Save a working copy of the data file under a different file name. Keeps the newly saved file open.

Backup: Make a backup copy of the currently open file (in a special format).

Refer to Appendix A and your Windows Help and reference books if you need a more complete introduction to using Windows.

The Close button closes the window that it is part of. If you choose a Close button that is part of another open window, you will close that window instead.

Restore: Restore a file that was previously saved using Backup (creates a working copy).

Import General Journal Entries: Import data into the General Journal from another program.

Import Transactions: Import sales orders from customers or quotes from vendors.

Import Online Statements: Import bank statements downloaded from the bank's Web site on the Internet.

Export to Microsoft Access: Export data in Microsoft Access program format.

Export GIFI: Export reports in GIFI format (Canada Customs and Revenue Agency income tax report format).

Exit: End your work session and automatically save any changes you made.

Edit Menu

Find: Provide quick access to the records in the ledger selected from the secondary cascading menu.

DDE: Use Dynamic Data Exchange to send data from the ledger selected (in the secondary cascading menu) to another program.

View Menu

Status Bars: Turn on (or off) the display of an information line that describes the function of the field or icon at the position of the mouse pointer.

Automatic Advice: Turn on (or off) the display of warning and advisory messages about good accounting practice and potential errors.

To-Do Lists: Turn on (or off) the automatic display of reminder lists.

Checklists: Turn on (or off) the automatic display of reminder checklists of periodic business routines.

Account Numbers: Choose whether to include account numbers with account names in reports and journal entries.

Modules: Hide or display the icons for an individual module selected from the cascading menu.

Icon Windows: Open the ledgers with or without the record icons as the initial window. If the icon window is not included, the first ledger record is displayed when you open the ledger.

Setup Menu Options

Wizards: Help you to modify Settings for a company file, for Linked Accounts or for General Ledger Accounts by walking you through the changes step by step.

Company Information: Store background information for a company (name, address, fiscal dates, etc).

Names: Change names for some payroll fields, the project ledger and taxes.

Reports & Forms: Choose printers for various printing jobs and enter settings for printing forms and reports.

Settings: Customize the way you use the program for your company (e.g., tax rates, discounts).

Credit Cards: Set up credit cards with linked accounts and transaction fees for sales and purchases.

Shippers: Set up shipping companies used for automatic tracking of shipments via Internet access.

Currencies: Set up a second currency with exchange rates and linked accounts.

Import Duty Information: Track duty on imported goods.

Customize: Change the background appearance of windows and hide unused journal fields.

Linked Accounts: Choose accounts for the ledger selected from the cascading menu to link with the General Ledger.

Set Security: Set up passwords for different users to restrict access to data.

Business Assistant Menu

To-Do Lists: Display lists that remind you when you may want to post certain transactions.

Checklists: Display reminder lists of periodic routines that should be completed.

Business Advice: Display guidelines for good business practice for all modules.

New Business Guidelines: Display checklists for starting different types of businesses.

Maintenance Menu

Change Session Date: Change the date of a work session within the fiscal period.

Start New Year: Advance the Session date to the beginning of the next fiscal year or period.

Automatically Clear Data: Set up which data will be cleared automatically at year-end.

Clear . . . : Make room on your data disk by clearing historical information no longer needed. You can clear any or all of the following: journal entries, paid vendor and customer invoices, GST reports, account reconciliation data, inventory tracking data or invoice lookup data. Always back up data files and print appropriate reports before clearing data.

Check Data Integrity: Check ledger and journal entries for completeness and accuracy. Debits should equal credits and unpaid invoices should equal the receivables and payables account balances.

Database Utilities: Repair security (clear all passwords) and compact database to conserve disk space.

Graphs Menu

Display, print or export various graphs created from company data.

Reports Menu

Display, print or export a variety of financial reports and labels for your company. Report lists are presented in cascading menus.

Help Menu

The Help menu is described on page 12.

Home Window Tool Buttons

Tool buttons offer alternative access to functions that correspond to common menu items listed above. When a keyboard command alternative is available, it is displayed with the tool button label. The Home window tools are:

Open Company closes the file you are working on and provides the Open Company window.

Save the current file.

Backup starts the Simply Accounting backup Wizard to back up the current data file.

Export to Microsoft Access. Starts a Wizard to select data and then create a file in Access format.

Find ledger record in the selected ledger or open the Select Record Type screen.

Setup allows you to enter linked accounts if a journal is selected, or ledger settings if a ledger is selected.

Change the Session date.

To-Do Lists opens the To-Do Lists windows.

 Checklists opens the Checklists windows.

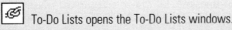 Display list for the ledger selected, or journal report for a selected journal or the Select Report screen if no icon is selected.

Advice opens the Simply Accounting Advice screen. Choose General Advice or Management Reports.

Help opens the Simply Accounting main Help window. If an icon is selected, you get help for that item.

Ledgers and Journals

The main part of the Home window contains ledger and journal icons for the six ledgers or modules. Ledger icons appear in the first row of icons, below the ledger name. Each one has a specific purpose. Ledgers contain records of accounts, while journals are used to enter accounting transactions. Journal icons appear in the two rows below the corresponding ledger icons.

Each account in a ledger is on a separate ledger page and shows the current balance in the account. Ledger records for vendors and customers also include address details and payment terms. The General Ledger is the main ledger, with accounts that link to the other subsidiary ledgers. For example, the balance in the *Accounts Receivable* account in the General Ledger is the total of all amounts owed by customers. The outstanding balances for individual customers are held in the Receivables Ledger records. Each time a customer transaction takes place, the customer record is updated and the *Accounts Receivable* balance is also updated. When you post a journal entry in a computerized accounting system, the program automatically updates all the subsidiary ledgers. In a manual system, ledger entries are recorded separately from journal entries.

Home Window Ledger and Journal Icons

The **General Ledger** contains information about the accounts. The General Ledger **Accounts icon** is used to enter new accounts, edit account names and numbers and delete accounts that are not needed. Before finishing the history, you also enter historical account balances through the Accounts ledger. The General Ledger includes two journals — General and Account Reconciliation. (See Chapter 2.)

The **General Journal** is used to record individual accounting transactions that cannot be recorded in any of the other journals. These are usually adjusting entries such as depreciation, adjustments for supplies used, for prepaid expenses that have expired, other accruals, bank loans and transactions involving capital accounts (investments, dividends, etc.). These transactions have a number of things in common. They do not involve customers, vendors or payments by cheque. If you choose not to use the subsidiary ledgers, you could enter all accounting transactions in the General Journal. The General Journal is modelled after the manual double-entry accounting system of entering debits and credits. (See Chapter 3.)

The **Account Reconciliation Journal** is used to match the transactions on the bank statement with transactions in the General Ledger bank account or accounts. Any automatic transactions, such as service charges or interest on bank loans can also be processed through the Account Reconciliation Journal. For these items, the bank statement is the source of information that the transaction has occurred. Other accounts with regular statements may also be set up for account reconciliation. When the Account Reconciliation Journal is not used, these transactions are recorded in the General Journal. (See Chapter 11.)

The **Payables Ledger** is used to store and record information about vendors or suppliers and any transactions with them. You can access the ledger through the **Vendors icon** to enter new vendors, edit information about existing vendors and delete vendor records. Before finishing the history, you also enter historical balances for vendors through this ledger. Vendor information includes name, address, contact person, options for payment terms and foreign currency transactions, and historical balances. The balance owing to all vendors combined is the amount shown in the *Accounts Payable* account. (See Chapter 4.)

The two journals for the Payables Ledger are Purchases (Purchases, Orders & Quotes) and Payments. Use the **Purchases Journal** to record credit purchases of goods and services from vendors, to record cash purchases (the payment accompanies the purchase), to record and fill purchase orders, to record or pay tax liabilities to government agencies, and to record and fill purchase quotes. Use the **Payments Journal** to make a payment by cheque against credit purchases that you entered previously, to make cash purchases, to record tax remittances, to pay credit card accounts and to make prepayments to vendors. The cheque numbering sequence can be set up to advance automatically. In other words, whenever you are writing a cheque in payment that is not payroll related, you should be using the Payables journals for the entry. By using these journals, the vendor records and the General Ledger accounts are kept up to date. In the manual system, you would enter the transaction in the General Journal and then update the General Ledger and the subsidiary Payables Ledger as separate steps. (See Chapter 5.)

The **Receivables Ledger** mirrors the Payables Ledger but represents the customer side. Through the **Customers icon**, you can enter information for new customers, edit the records for existing customers or delete customer records and enter historical transactions for the customers involving sales and payments. You can record the customer's name, contact person, address, telephone and fax numbers, credit limits, payment terms and historical balances. The balance owed by all customers is automatically recorded in the *Accounts Receivable* account. (See Chapter 6.)

The Accounts Receivables journals are Sales (Sales, Orders & Quotes) and Receipts. Use the **Sales Journal** to record the sale of goods or services to customers, both credit sales and sales that include immediate payment. Sales Orders and Sales Quotes are also entered and filled in the Sales Journal. When the customer makes a payment against a credit sale, use the **Receipts Journal** to enter the payment. Customer deposits may also be entered in the Receipts Journal. When you use the Receivables Journals, Simply Accounting automatically updates customer records and related General Ledger accounts. (See Chapter 7.)

In the **Payroll Ledger**, you can store employee information. The **Employees icon** provides access to the Payroll Ledger records. Name, address, social insurance number, date of birth, rates and amounts for income, deductions and tax claims are included, as is the historical information about the employee. You can add new employees, edit information about employees or delete employee records through the Employees icon. (See Chapter 9.)

Use the **Payroll Journal** (Paycheques) to make employment-related payments to an employee or the **Payroll Cheque Run Journal** to pay more than one employee in a single transaction. This may include regular wages, overtime wages, salaries, bonuses, commissions, vacation pay or payroll advances. The program automatically calculates tax deduction amounts and liabilities that result from these. Again, the employee records and all the related General Ledger accounts are updated each time you make a Payroll Journal entry. (See Chapter 10.)

The **Inventory & Services Ledger** stores information about inventory items, whether goods or services, that the company offers for sale. The Inventory Ledger records the names, units, prices and quantities for each item, as well as historical costs and transactions. Through the **Inventory & Services icon**, you can add new inventory, edit and delete inventory records, and enter costs and historical sales. Prices for a second currency and import duties are also stored in the ledger. The Inventory Ledger has two journals, Item Assembly and Adjustments. (See Chapter 14.)

The **Item Assembly Journal** is used to move inventory items from one category to another. For example, if you combine several items to sell as a group or to assemble into a different inventory item, you can transfer the individual items to a single new group item. You can also re-classify inventory from one asset group to another by moving it to a new item in the new asset group.

The **Adjustments Journal** is used when you need to account for lost, damaged or recovered inventory items. You would also use the Adjustments Journal to take out an inventory item for store use (not available for sale). Sales of inventory items are entered in the Sales Journal and inventory purchases are recorded in the Purchases Journal. (See Chapter 15.)

The **Project Ledger** does not have journals. Projects are used when you want to allocate amounts to different departments, divisions or projects. For example, an employee might spend half of the time working in one department and half in another. You can distribute the wage expenses equally between the two departments to get a better picture of the expenses that each group incurs. Use the **Project icon** to access the Ledger to add, modify or delete projects. The actual distribution information is entered as part of a regular journal entry before posting. Whenever an account is set up to allow allocations, you can distribute the amount by clicking the Allocate column or tool in the journal. (See Chapter 17.)

Simply Accounting Help
Status Bar

Simply Accounting provides different forms of help. The most immediate form is the status bar. When you point to a menu option or a Home window icon, the status bar at the bottom of the screen describes the function of the command, option or icon. Many of the screens in Simply Accounting include this status bar and you should read the message any time you use a feature of the program for the first time. Reading the status bar is a quick way to explore a window and its menu options.

◆ Click **File** on the menu bar in the Home window. The menu options appear.

◆ Point to **Backup**, but do not click.

The status bar should read "Makes a backup copy of the currently open data file."

◆ Click a blank portion of the Home window to close the File menu without executing a command.

◆ Point to the **Accounts icon** and read the status bar.

◆ Right-click the **Accounts icon** to select it. (The ledger name, Accounts, changes colour. The account book opens when you point to the icon.)

◆ Now point to the **Payments Journal icon** in the Payables column, but do not click. Read the status bar again.

Notice that the status bar message refers to the position of the mouse pointer on the Payments icon and not to the position of the insertion point or cursor, which is on the selected Accounts icon.

◆ Now point to [icon] (the first tool button, the one that looks like an open file folder).

◆ Hold the mouse on it for a few seconds to see its label pop open — "Open Company (Ctrl + O)" — the label and the alternative keyboard command.

◆ Point to a blank portion of the window; the status bar remains empty.

◆ Point to the remaining icons and click other menu names to see their functions displayed in the status bar.

Help Menu and Tools

The Help menu and tools provide more extensive information to help you use the program effectively. Sometimes different routes lead to the same information. The Help menu is easy to use. The Help menu list is shown here:

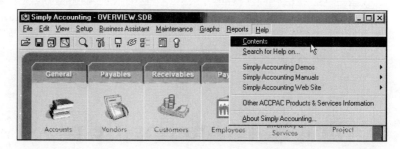

The Help Menu

The Help menu has information about how to use the Simply Accounting program, about accounting procedures and about the program.

Contents: Leads to the same screen as the Help tool [?] . Provides access to all parts of Simply Accounting Help. Includes a complete alphabetical index of accounting and Simply Accounting terms and procedures and provides access to the glossary of accounting terms.

Right-click means to click the button on the right-hand side of the mouse.

Search for Help on: Leads to the same screen as the Help tool 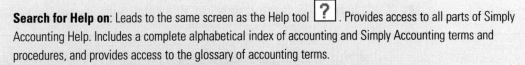. Provides access to all parts of Simply Accounting Help. Includes a complete alphabetical index of accounting and Simply Accounting terms and procedures, and provides access to the glossary of accounting terms.

Simply Accounting Demos: Provides access to demo programs that can be downloaded from the Web.

Simply Accounting Manuals: Contains the program manuals, if you have installed them from the program CD.

Simply Accounting Web Site: Provides access to the Simply Accounting Web site with information about the program, updates, and so on.

Other ACCPAC Products: Provides brief descriptions of other products from the same company.

About Simply Accounting: Shows the version number and serial number of the active program.

◆ Click the **Help tool** [?] in the Home window or click the **Help** menu and then click **Contents** to open the main Help window:

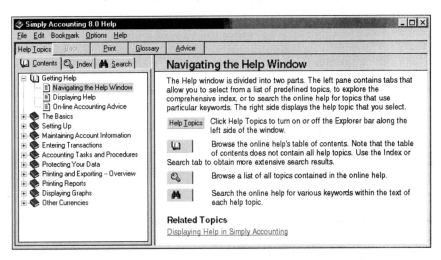

The left side of the window contains the list of topics and the right side has the help information for the selected topic. The contents are organized into books of related topics. When you open a book, you will see a list of subtopics.

◆ Double click **The Basics**, the second book on the list, to open the subtopics list.

◆ Click **Toolbar Buttons** to display this topic.

◆ Click the **Index tab**.

You can move down the entry list to "ledgers" in three ways:

◆ Click the down scroll arrow ▼ till you reach the entries starting with "l", or

Click any index entry and press   to move down the list till you reach the l entries, or

Type the letter l (the cursor is already in the input field above the lists).

◆ Click **ledgers, definition** to select this entry and display the definition on the right side of the window:

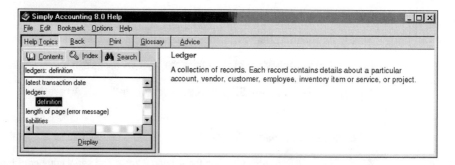

The Help window has additional options. You can access General Advice from the Advice button or a Glossary (dictionary definitions) of accounting and program terms. You can also print the on-screen information, return to the Help Contents or Index, or start a new Search. The Back button will return you to the previous Help window if you have viewed more than one help entry.

◆ Click **Glossary** to open the Glossary window.

◆ Click **J** in the alphabet buttons at the top of the window to advance to the entries beginning with J.

◆ Click **Journal Entry** to see a bubble open with a definition for the chosen term. Click on another entry to see its definition.

◆ Click ☒ to close the Glossary window to return to the Index explanation for ledgers, definition.

◆ Click the **Search tab.** If this is the first time you are using Search, you will start the Find Setup Wizard:

The screen that follows was created with the default setting, Minimize database size.

◆ Click **Next**.

◆ Click **Finish** to begin creating an alphabetized list of terms and accounting procedures.

When the Wizard is finished, you will see the Search window:

Your previous help information remains on the right side of the window until you request a new topic.

◆ Type **accounts** in the data entry field (number 1). The Help window now looks like the one shown below:

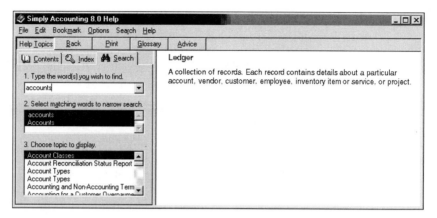

As you begin typing, Simply Accounting matches the letters already typed, so you may not have to type the entire term, and then creates a list in the central field (number 2) that you can use to narrow the search. Two items appear in the second field. The ledger definition remains on the right side of the window.

◆ Double click a topic in the third field to see its explanation on the right.

◆ Double click **accounts** (in the first field) to begin a new search.

◆ Type **closing routines**

◆ Now both fields 2 and 3 are blank because no match was found.

◆ Choose the **Search menu** and click **Options**.

Notice the settings. We were searching for topics containing all the words and the search process was continuous with each keystroke. The program tried to make a match each time we added a letter to the search term.

◆ Click **At least one of the words you typed** as the setting for Scarch topics.

◆ Click **OK**.

Now there are three entries in the third field. If you are not satisfied with the extensiveness of the search, you can rebuild the database. Choose the Search menu and click Rebuild to begin the Find Wizard again.

◆ Click **Closing the books** because this is the closest match to our search terms.

◆ Change the Options setting back to Search for topics containing All the words you typed. (Choose the Search menu, click Options, click this selection, then click OK.)

◆ Double click the current entry in field one and type the letter **a**

The third field now lists all topics so you can choose a topic directly from it or use any word starting with "a" listed in the second field to narrow the search.

◆ Double click an entry to see the information available on the topic selected.

◆ Search for help on additional topics of your choice.

◆ Close any Help display windows that are open (click ☒) to return to the Home window.

Simply Accounting Advice

The advice topics generally include information about good accounting practices rather than definitions and how-to procedures.

◆ Choose **Business Assistant**, then choose **Business Advice** and click **All Modules** as shown:

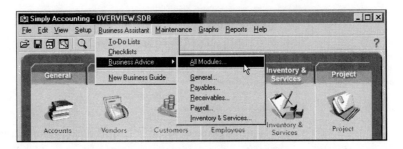

◆ The display includes the topics you have requested:

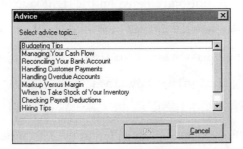

If an icon is selected, you will see advice related to the selected ledger.

◆ Click **Handling Overdue Accounts** to select this topic.

◆ Click **OK** to display the information. The display advises you on the steps to follow for handling customer accounts that are overdue.

◆ Close the display to return to the Home window.

◆ Click the **Advice tool** 💡 to open the Advice screen:

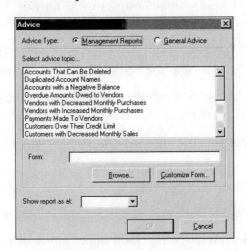

This screen provides access to two kinds of advice, the General Advice we saw earlier from the Help menu and the Management Reports. The list of Management Reports is shown as the default selection. Whereas General Advice provides information about accounting practices in general, the Management Reports give information for the data file that is open. To access the Management Reports, you must install Crystal Reports from the program CD-ROM. You can use the default forms, choose other forms for the reports or customize your own.

♦   Click **Accounts That Can Be Deleted**.

♦   Click **OK**.

The report lists three accounts that can be deleted because they are unused or have no journal entries.

♦   Close the report to return to the Home window.

The View Menu

The Home window and other windows can be modified in a number of ways from the View menu. The View menu also controls the display of other aspects of the program.

Changes to the Home Window

Status Bars

The first option in the View menu is the inclusion of status bars. Initially, and by default, the status bars are on. There is a ✓ beside the menu option.

♦   Choose the **View** menu and click **Status Bars** to remove the ✓ and the status bars will not be displayed.

♦   Choose the **View** menu and click **Status Bars** again to turn them on.

Hiding Modules

Sometimes a business uses only some of the modules in the Simply Accounting program. For example, if there are no employees, the Payroll Ledger and Payroll journals are not needed. Their icons can then be removed from the Home window or hidden. This is different from restricting access to the modules by setting passwords. (See Access Symbols later in this chapter.)

If you are not using a module, you must hide it before you can finish the history for the remaining modules.

The following Home window shows only three modules:

The Payables, Payroll and Project modules are hidden. To change your Home window so that these modules are hidden,

◆ Choose the **View** menu, then choose **Modules** and click **Payables**.

◆ Choose the **View** menu, then choose **Modules** and click **Payroll**.

◆ Choose the **View** menu, then choose **Modules** and click **Project**. Your View Modules menu should now look like the one below with only two ✓ remaining:

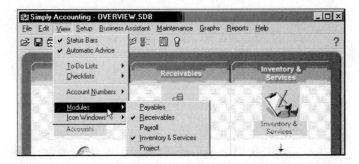

There is a ✓ beside Receivables and Inventory & Services but not beside the other three modules. You cannot hide the General Module.

◆ Repeat the same steps to show the modules again.

Changes to Other Screens

Automatic Advice

You can choose to include Automatic Advice or leave it out. Again, the default setting is to include advice. The automatic advice includes such details as advising you that a customer is about to exceed a credit limit, or that year-end is approaching and it is time to prepare for it. You should leave the option selected because the information can help to prevent you from making transaction errors.

Some Advisor windows look like this:

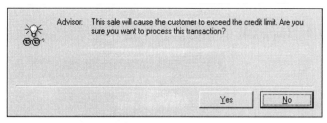

The warning gives you a chance to take a different action, such as not proceeding with the sale or asking for a deposit so that the customer stays within the credit limit. Click No to return to the Sales Invoice or click Yes to accept the sale with the customer exceeding the limit.

Other Advisor windows provide information that you should be aware of, like the following warning on Payroll Journal adjustments:

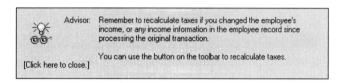

To return to the journal entry, click on the advice screen where indicated.

To-Do Lists and Checklists

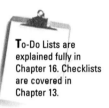

To-Do Lists are explained fully in Chapter 16. Checklists are covered in Chapter 13.

To-Do Lists provide reminders about upcoming events such as recurring transactions, payments that are due, discounts that are still available and customer accounts that are due. They can simplify some of these day-to-day transactions by providing direct access to the relevant journal entry. From the View menu, you can select whether you want the To-Do Lists to appear automatically or not.

Checklists offer a set of routines such as printing reports, clearing data and making backups that you should perform at critical times, such as end-of-month or end-of year. You can add your own items to these checklists as well.

Viewing Account Numbers

Simply Accounting offers you the choice of including account numbers with the account names in reports and transactions. If you omit account numbers in transactions, account lists will be displayed in alphabetical order. We will display a General Journal report with and without the account numbers.

◆ Choose the **Reports** menu, then choose **Journal Entries** and click **All** to open the report options screen (click Reports, then point to Journal Entries and click All):

◆ Click the **Start date field list arrow** 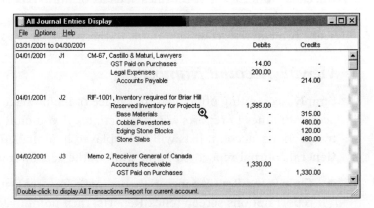▼ and click the first date displayed, March 31, 2001.

◆ Click **OK** to display the report:

```
┌─────────────────────────────────────────────────────────────────────┐
│ ▌ All Journal Entries Display                              _ □ ×     │
│ File  Options  Help                                                   │
│ 03/31/2001 to 04/30/2001                        Debits      Credits   │
│ 04/01/2001   J1     CM-67, Castillo & Maturi, Lawyers            ▲   │
│                     2670  GST Paid on Purchases    14.00        -     │
│                     5200  Legal Expenses          200.00        -     │
│                     2200    Accounts Payable         -       214.00   │
│                                                                       │
│ 04/01/2001   J2     RIF-1001, Inventory required for Briar Hill       │
│                     1500  Reserved Inventory for Projects  1,395.00 - │
│                     1360    Base Materials           -       315.00   │
│                     1380    Cobble Pavestones        -       480.00   │
│                     1400    Edging Stone Blocks      -       120.00   │
│                     1460    Stone Slabs              -       480.00   │
│                                                                       │
│ 04/02/2001   J3     Memo 2, Receiver General of Canada               │
│                     1200  Accounts Receivable   1,330.00        -    ▼│
│                     2670    GST Paid on Purchases    -      1,330.00   │
│ Double-click to display Vendor or Customer Aged Report or Employee Report │
└─────────────────────────────────────────────────────────────────────┘
```

Notice that the first line of each journal entry has descriptive reference details, including the date, journal entry number, invoice number and description. The second and subsequent lines have the accounts and amounts. The number is displayed beside each account name.

◆ Click ☒ to close the report and return to the Home window.

◆ Choose the **View** menu, then choose **Account Numbers** and click **In Reports** to change the setting — turn off the display of numbers (remove the ✔).

◆ Choose the **Reports** menu, then choose **Journal Entries** and click **All** to open the report options screen (click Reports, then point to Journal Entries and click All):

◆ Click the **Start date field list arrow** ▼ and click the first date displayed, March 31, 2001.

◆ Click **OK** to display the report:

```
┌─────────────────────────────────────────────────────────────────────┐
│ ▌ All Journal Entries Display                              _ □ ×     │
│ File  Options  Help                                                   │
│ 03/31/2001 to 04/30/2001                        Debits      Credits   │
│ 04/01/2001   J1     CM-67, Castillo & Maturi, Lawyers            ▲   │
│                     GST Paid on Purchases          14.00       -     │
│                     Legal Expenses                200.00       -     │
│                       Accounts Payable               -       214.00   │
│                                                                       │
│ 04/01/2001   J2     RIF-1001, Inventory required for Briar Hill       │
│                     Reserved Inventory for Projects  1,395.00  -     │
│                       Base Materials                 -       315.00   │
│                       Cobble Pavestones              -       480.00   │
│                       Edging Stone Blocks            -       120.00   │
│                       Stone Slabs                    -       480.00   │
│                                                                       │
│ 04/02/2001   J3     Memo 2, Receiver General of Canada               │
│                     Accounts Receivable         1,330.00       -     │
│                       GST Paid on Purchases          -      1,330.00 ▼│
│ Double-click to display All Transactions Report for current account.  │
└─────────────────────────────────────────────────────────────────────┘
```

Notice that account numbers are omitted from the report. The remaining information is the same.

◆ Click ☒ to close the report. We find account numbers helpful and prefer to include them in all reports and transactions.

If you choose not to include account numbers in transactions, lists of accounts will appear in alphabetical order instead of numerical order.

◆ Choose the **View** menu, then choose **Account Numbers** and click **Reports** to change the setting again — turn on the display of numbers (add the ✓).

You can change this setting any time and it will be applied immediately. Because the accounts are numbered logically according to their position in the financial statements, we always include account numbers in the simulations in this book.

Icon Windows

Choosing to include Icon windows for the ledgers does not change the appearance of the Home window. The Icon windows are the ones that appear whenever you open one of the ledgers. They show a list of all accounts (or customers, vendors, employees, inventory items or projects) for the ledger. Depending on the setting chosen, the Icon window may have the accounts displayed by name or by icon. If you skip this window, you will go directly to the first ledger record when you open the ledger. Again we will show both settings, with and without the icon window.

◆ Click the **Customers icon** to open the Customers icon window.

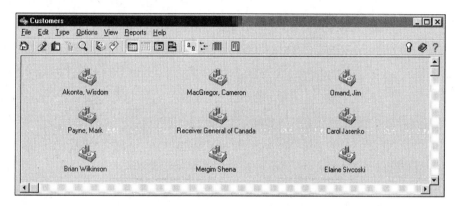

There is one icon for each customer on record. The icons are not in alphabetical order, and each icon can be moved to any position by dragging. As you create new customers, their icons are added to the bottom of the icon window.

◆ Choose the **Options** menu, then click **Re-sort Icons** in the Customers window to place the icons in order.

◆ Now choose the **View** menu, then click **Name** in the Customers window to display the customers by name instead of by icon. Notice that account balances, total sales for the year and credit limits are added to the display.

◆ Choose the **View** menu, then click **Icon** again to restore the original view.

◆ Double click the **icon for Akonta, Wisdom** to open the record for this customer.

◆ Click ☒ to close the ledger record.

◆ Click ☒ to close the Customers icon window and return to the Home window.

◆ Choose the **View** menu, then choose **Icon Windows** and click **Customers** to remove the ✓ and the icon window for the Receivables Ledger.

◆ Click **Yes** to continue past the warning.

The software will warn you that the program will remove information about Customers icon positions. Click Yes to continue.

◆ Click the **Customers icon** to open the Receivables Ledger for Akonta:

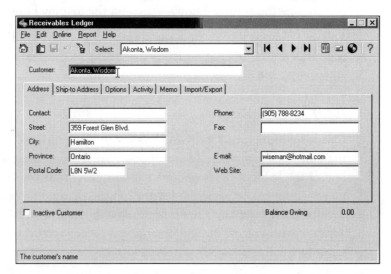

◆ Click ⊠ to close the Receivables Ledger window to return to the Home window.

◆ Choose the **View** menu, then choose **Icon Windows** and click **Customers** to restore the ✓ and the icon window for the Receivables Ledger.

Icon windows are especially helpful when you are setting up a ledger initially and entering all the records or accounts. Because you can see all the accounts at once, it is easy to see which records you have entered already, or in the case of accounts, which numbers you have already used. The view by name is easier to use during setup because the names are always in order and account balances are added.

Access Symbols in the Home Window

In the Overview data files, all the journals and ledgers are accessible. You can open any of them to enter or to edit information. If a ledger or journal is not available, it will have a restricted access symbol. There are three symbols that you should be familiar with.

 If a ledger has not been set up and the history is not finished, you will see a **Not Finished (Open History** or **quill pen)** symbol beside the ledger icon.

 If access has been restricted by passwords, you will see an additional icon beside the ledger or journal icon that is restricted. If you see a report with an X above it, you have editing access but not viewing access — you can enter transactions and ledger records but cannot display reports.

 A pencil icon with an X above it indicates that you have viewing access but do not have editing access. You can display reports but cannot enter transactions or edit ledger records.

No Icon   If you have hidden a module from the View menu, there are no icons for it in the Home window. You can restore the hidden icons from the View menu.

In addition, if you have neither editing nor viewing access to a ledger, the icon for the restricted portion will be removed from the Home window. You can restore these icons only by changing the access from the Set Security option, not from the View menu. (See Appendix E.)

Saving and Backup Procedures

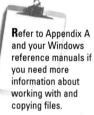
The Save As command from the Home window File menu makes a working backup copy. However, because of the large file sizes, we recommend using the Backup command regularly to conserve disk space.

You can save files and make backups of Simply Accounting data files in a number of ways. You can, of course, copy the files using the Copy and Paste procedure in Windows Explorer or the My Computer window. To be certain that all files for a company are copied together, you should copy the folder with its entire contents. There are also several alternatives in Simply Accounting. Your work is automatically saved to your file each time you display reports or compile information in any way. The program also saves your work when you exit the program properly.

The first and most direct way to save your work is with the Save command.

◆ Click the Save tool 💾 or choose the **File** menu and click **Save** in the Home window.

The Save feature ensures that your most recent work is moved from the computer's temporary storage to permanent storage, adding it to the current data file.

However, sometimes the primary data file is damaged or lost. In this case, you need to have a duplicate copy of your file to continue working without re-entering data.

Refer to Appendix A and your Windows reference manuals if you need more information about working with and copying files.

The Backup command or tool creates a compressed version of the current data file. The program guides you through the steps with easy-to-follow screens. Backup copies created in this way cannot be opened or used directly by the Simply Accounting program. You must restore them first. The Restore command (File menu or Select Company screen) activates a Wizard to make the restoration easy to complete. Simply Accounting has a setup option (in the Setup menu, Settings option, System tab) for reminding you to make backups on a regular schedule, such as daily or weekly. We provide instructions in Chapter 2 for adding this setting to all your data files to encourage you to make regular backups of your work. The program also provides reminders to back up your work each time you are about to complete a step that cannot be reversed, such as finishing the history for a ledger or advancing to a new fiscal year and removing the old year's data.

Backup procedures using the backup command are also covered in Chapter 2.

◆ Choose the **File** menu and click **Backup** or click the Backup tool 🗗 to start the backup procedure:

The Backup procedure keeps track of your backups by numbering them and you can choose your own file name, folder and comment. Use the Browse button to find an existing folder, or create a new folder. If you name a new folder, the program creates it for you.

◆ Click **Cancel** to return to the Home window.

Continue to work with the Overview data file if you want to examine other aspects of the Simply Accounting program.

When you are finished, you should close the file and exit the program.

Exiting the Program

Whenever you finish your work session properly by closing the data file, opening another company file or exiting the program, Simply Accounting automatically saves your work again. You do not have to use the Save command separately.

As usual, there are different ways to finish the work session:

◆ Choose the **File** menu and click **Exit**, or

Click the **Close button** ☒ , or

Choose the **control menu icon** and click **Close** to return to the Windows desktop.

The control menu is part of the main program window so it closes the program. In general, the Close command from the control menu icon for any window will close the window. Using the control menu Close command for a window is the same as using ☒ , the Close button for the window. The File menu in the Home window has the Exit command as well, which exits or closes the program to return you to the Windows desktop.

The keyboard command for closing the selected or active window is *alt* + *f4*.

Date Display Formats

The format for dates in Windows programs is controlled by the Windows settings. We show all dates in this book with month first, followed by day and then year. Your computer may be set up with the day preceding the month in dates. In this case, some dates that you enter by following our instructions will create errors because the day and month will be reversed. For example, 05-06 (May 6) will be interpreted as June 5, while other dates such as 04-30 are unambiguous and the program will input them correctly. You should check your date settings before beginning the simulations.

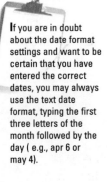

If you are in doubt about the date format settings and want to be certain that you have entered the correct dates, you may always use the text date format, typing the first three letters of the month followed by the day (e.g., apr 6 or may 4).

◆ Point to **Start** on the task bar, then choose **Settings** and click **Control Panel** as shown:

This will open the Control Panel window:

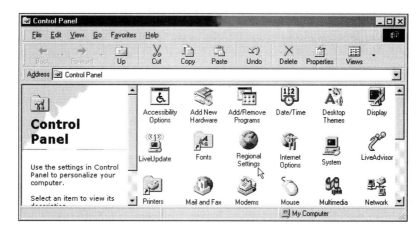

◆ Double click the **Regional Settings icon** to open its window:

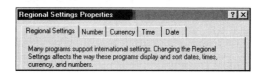

◆ Click the **Date tab** to open the screen for changing date formats:

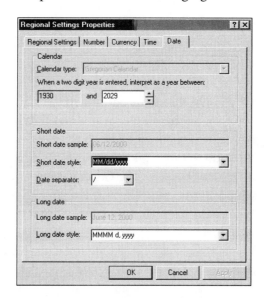

You can see that there are fields for choosing a short date format, a date separator symbol and a long date format. We will view the alternatives for a short date style because these are the ones that are used most frequently in Simply Accounting.

◆ Click the **Short Date Style field list arrow** to see the list of format styles:

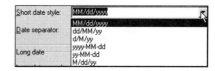

The choices include showing the month first with two-digits for month, day and year or with a single digit, omitting the leading zeros for day and month. You can also

Your choices may be different from those we show. You can add a format to this list if you want to.

choose to place the day first or to place the year first. You can also display a three-letter abbreviation for the month or a four-digit year.

◆ Click on any **month first** option for this book (M is the first character). Choose a four-digit year option so that you will be certain that the dates are for the year 2002 and not for 1902.

◆ From the **Long Date Style** list, click one of the month-first options.

◆ Type a date separator symbol in the appropriate field if you want to change the symbol. You can use any non-numeric keyboard character you like. In the illustrations on the previous page, we used / as the date separator character.

◆ Click **OK** to save the changes and return to the Control Panel window.

◆ To see the changes, open the Regional Settings Date tab screen again. The new formats should appear.

◆ Close the Regional Settings screen and then close the Control Panel screen to return to the desktop. The next time you start the Simply Accounting program, your date formats will be changed.

Review Questions

1. What is the difference between Save and Save As (in the File menu)?
2. How does Simply Accounting Help differ from Simply Accounting Advice?
3. What are the roles of the ledger and journal icons in the Home window?
4. What purpose do the tool buttons in the Home window serve?
5. Why might the status bar line in a Simply Accounting window be blank? How do you turn on the status bar if it is off? Why should you leave it turned on?
6. How do you open or access a Simply Accounting company data file?
7. What does it mean if the icons for a ledger are missing from the Home window?
8. If you have selected the General Journal icon, and you point to the Vendors icon, what will the status bar line tell you?
9. What happens if your date format is set up as day-month-year? How can you change it?
10. If you are unsure of the date format settings, how can you enter a date to be certain that it is interpreted correctly?

CHAPTER 2

GENERAL LEDGER SETUP

Objectives

- **create new data sets**
- **enter descriptive company information**
- **customize program settings for the General Ledger**
- **create new accounts**
- **edit accounts**
- **define linked accounts for the General Ledger**
- **make backup copies**
- **finish the history for the General Ledger**
- **display and print General Ledger reports**
- **restore files from backup**

Introduction

In this chapter, we will set up the company files and General Ledger for Play Wave Plus to prepare for making General Journal entries. This involves customizing the program for the business. In this chapter, we will enter only the settings we need for the General Ledger — printers, address information, accounts and historical balances. When we add the remaining ledgers in the following chapters, we will also add vendors, customers, employees, inventory, tax and payroll information, as well as the settings for these ledgers. Setting up each ledger prepares it for the journal entries that will be introduced in the following chapter.

Play Wave Plus Company Information

PLAY WAVE PLUS COMPANY PROFILE

Play Wave Plus is owned and operated by Kerwin Child in the new Megacity in Ontario. His primary source of revenue is from contracts with parks, schools, day care centres and private residences to design, build and install playgrounds. Occasionally, he repairs existing playgrounds. Child began to plan his business over the winter months, preparing some designs to show to potential customers.

On March 1, he officially started the business. He had arranged some contracts and purchased the office equipment, supplies and building materials he needed for the first jobs. He had accounts with a few suppliers and, in some cases, he had arranged discounts for early payment of the accounts.

He hired one full-time employee and a part-time architectural design student to assist him. Casual Contractors, an employment agency that also provides payroll services, manages the payroll for Child for a small monthly fee. Casual Contractors also makes all the required payroll remittances for Child.

Because the playgrounds are installed as fixtures on the properties, they are designated as real property and the installation service is exempt from retail sales taxes (PST). Play Wave Plus, therefore, has PST exempt status for purchases of raw materials and manufacturing equipment. The customers pay GST on the playgrounds and the installation services they buy from Play Wave. Play Wave uses the regular method of calculating GST and makes quarterly remittances equal to the GST collected minus the GST paid on purchases.

Initially, Child will set up only the General Ledger in Simply Accounting to record his business transactions. This will give him additional time to become familiar with the software program and will simplify the setup. His computer system is equipped with Internet and e-mail access and, in time, he expects to use these functions to interact with both suppliers and customers.

By March 15, 2002, he had completed two contracts and was ready to enter the accounting information. He used the manually prepared Trial Balance and Balance Sheet to get started.

PLAY WAVE PLUS: TRIAL BALANCE

As at March 15, 2002

Bank Account: Chequing	$ 15 430	
Accounts Receivable	5 420	
Supplies: Fibreglass & Plastics	2 500	
Supplies: Lumber	2 500	
Supplies: Hardware	2 500	
Supplies: Office	1 000	
Portable Computer System	3 000	
Machinery & Tools	8 000	
Shop	100 000	
Truck	30 000	
Yard	150 000	
Accounts Payable		$ 3 745
GST Charged on Services		490
GST Paid on Purchases	1 775	
Mortgage Payable		200 000
Kerwin Child, Capital		110 890
Revenue from Contracting		7 000
	$322 125	$322 125

PLAY WAVE PLUS: BALANCE SHEET

As at March 15, 2002

Current Assets			Current Liabilities		
Bank Account: Chequing	$ 15 430		Accounts Payable	$ 3 745	
Accounts Receivable	5 420		GST Charged on Services	490	
Supplies: Fibreglass & Plastics	2 500		GST Paid on Purchases	−1 775	
Supplies: Lumber	2 500			$ 2 460	
Supplies: Hardware	2 500				
Supplies: Office	1 000		**Long Term Liabilities**		
	$29 350		Mortgage Payable	$200 000	
Plant & Equipment				$200 000	
Portable Computer System	$ 3 000				
Machinery & Tools	8 000		**Total Liabilities**	**$202 460**	
Shop	100 000				
Truck	30 000				
Yard	150 000		**Equity**		
	$291 000		Kerwin Child, Capital	$110 890	
			Net Income	7 000	
				$117 890	
			Total Equity	**$117 890**	
Total Assets	**$320 350**		**Liabilities and Equity**	**$320 350**	

GST Paid on Purchases has a debit balance because equipment and supplies were purchased for the business startup.

General Ledger Setup

Setting up the General Ledger involves the following stages:

- Creating the data files
  creating company files
  adding company information

- Customizing the settings
  setting up printers
  changing default settings

- Creating the General Ledger Chart of Accounts
  creating accounts
  entering historical account balances
  verifying data entry

- Identifying linked accounts

- Making backup copies

- Finishing the history for the Ledger

Creating Company Files

◆ Start the Simply Accounting program to access the Select Company screen:

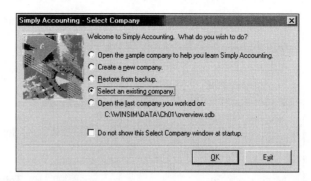

◆ Click **Create a new company**.

◆ Click **OK** to proceed to the Setup Wizard screen:

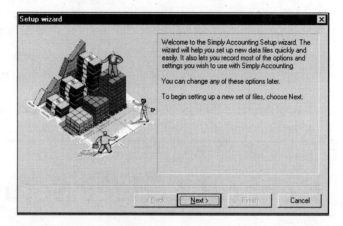

The **Setup Wizard** allows you to enter and choose settings for most ledgers. However, not all the menu options appear, and the Wizard sequences them differently. Since you should be familiar with all the options and their locations, we will use the menus to complete the setup. If you want to use the Setup Wizard, click Next and follow the instructions. You can return to a previous setup screen by choosing Back, leave the Wizard and save your changes by clicking Finish or leave without saving the changes by clicking Cancel.

◆ Click **Cancel** to bypass the Wizard and access the Create Company window:

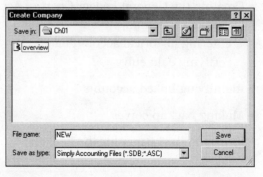

The Create Company window shows the folder you worked with most recently. In the File name field you will see the name NEW or NEW.sdb as the default new file name.

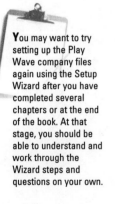
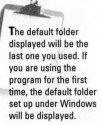

We show the Ch01 folder inside the Data folder under the main program folder, Winsim, that was created at the time of installation.

Refer to Appendix A if you need additional help with creating new folders or if you want to see different methods of creating folders.

◆ Open the drive and folder you want to use for your new data files.

◆ Click the **Up one level tool button** to go to the Data folder or click the Save in field list arrow to access the list of drives and click the one you want.

◆ Click the **Create New Folder tool button** to create a new folder.

◆ Type **Play** to replace the highlighted folder name (New Folder).

We recommend that you create a folder for each simulation, then create separate subfolders for each chapter and the backups for that chapter.

◆ Click the **Play folder icon** (using the left mouse button) to save the new name and select the new folder.

◆ Click **Open** to open the new folder. Check that Play is named in the Save in field. If you skip this step, you will be in the main folder for the drive, in this case C:.

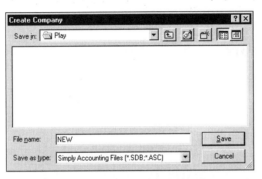

If a folder is selected, the Open button replaces Save. If a file is selected, the Save button appears.

◆ Double click **NEW**, (or NEW.sdb), the name displayed in the File name field.

◆ Type **play** to name the new data files.

Simply Accounting will create the appropriate file extension for you. If you type another extension, Simply Accounting will add its own extension as well. You may use a longer file name, but we will continue to use shorter file names to ensure maximum flexibility.

◆ Click **Save** to see the following Company Dates dialog box:

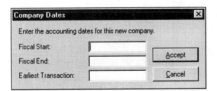

Company Dates or fiscal dates are extremely important. The fiscal period is the period during which a business calculates its income — total revenue earned during the period minus total expenses. At the beginning of the period, **Fiscal Start**, the income is zero. During the fiscal period, revenue and expense amounts are accumulated continually. At the end of the fiscal period, **Fiscal End**, the revenue and expense amounts are reset to zero by transferring the balances to the capital account to prepare for the next period. This is called closing the books. The third date, the **Earliest Transaction**, is the day on which the business begins to use the computerized accounting system, converting from the manual accounting system. Anything that happened before the earliest date is historical data, so complete financial records should already exist for this period. After the conversion date, or the Earliest Transaction date, accounting transactions are entered as journal entries. The Earliest Transaction date must be on or after the Fiscal Start date and must be before the Fiscal End.

A company normally has a fiscal period of one year for income tax purposes. Some small businesses may be required to use the calendar year as the fiscal year. However, a company that wants to report more frequently may choose to close its books more frequently, perhaps using quarters to report for more frequent feedback on performance. Play Wave will close its books quarterly, so a fiscal period of three months will be entered.

The format for entering dates is the same for all Simply Accounting date fields. Month is entered first, followed by day and year. If you type 02 for the year and the year displays as 1902, re-enter the year as 2002. If the Fiscal End date changes to 31/05/2002, you should change the system date settings. Refer to pages 24–26 for further details on setting date formats for your computer.

The cursor is in the Fiscal Start field. This is the only stage at which you must include the year as part of the date. You may use almost any non-numerical character or a space to separate the day, month and year. The separator character you see on-screen will be the one from the date format settings.

◆ Type **Mar 01 02**

◆ Press ⬚tab⬚. The date changes to match your setting format and the cursor advances to the Fiscal End field.

◆ Type **05-31-02**

◆ Press ⬚tab⬚ to advance to the Earliest Transaction date field.

◆ Type **03-15-02**

Check the dates you have entered. If they are correct,

◆ Click **Accept**. After a brief delay, you will see the Home window for Play Wave. (If you see a reminder about Payroll updates, click Done to close the message.)

We will show alternative formats for entering dates throughout the book.

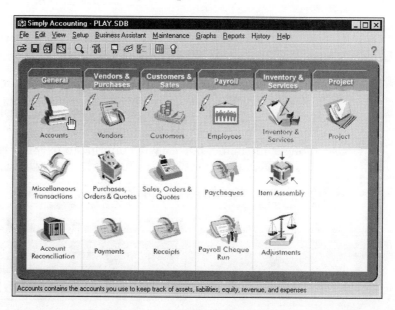

Although you can make journal entries before finishing the history, you must complete some setup steps first.

The new file name, PLAY.SDB, appears in the title bar. The **Open History symbol** has been added for each ledger to indicate the ledger setup is incomplete. Review Chapter 1 if you are not familiar with the Home window. Initially the Home window uses non-accounting terminology. Thus, Miscellaneous Transactions replaces the General Journal label.

Adding Company Information

The first step is to add the basic company information summarized here:

COMPANY INFORMATION

Company Name:	Play Wave Plus
Address:	7310 Recreation Court
	Megacity, Ontario M5E 1W6
Telephone:	(416) 832-4521
Fax Number:	(416) 832-1234
GST (business number):	34567 9876 RT

◆ Choose the **Setup** menu and click **Company Information** in the home window to open the Company Information screen:

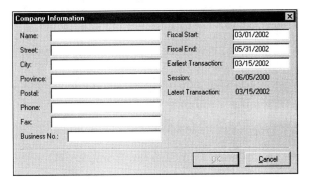

Company Information Screen

Notice that the **fiscal dates** you entered earlier appear on this screen. If you need to change them, this is where you can do so, as long as the history is not finished. Fiscal End is the only date that you can change later.

The **Name** you enter in this screen will appear on all reports you print from this data set. So, if you want to customize your own data set, you can easily include your name with the company name.

The address fields — **Street**, **City**, **Province** and **Postal code** — are straightforward. Simply Accounting corrects the postal code format for all Canadian postal codes, so you can enter them without capitals or spaces. Similarly, the program corrects the format for **Telephone** and **Fax** numbers, and you do not need to type the hyphens or brackets. However, this time-saving feature spoils you when you are entering postal codes or phone numbers in other programs where you still need to enter them in the correct format.

The program will add the company address to the cheques and invoices that you print, unless you have preprinted forms. The city and province will be added as defaults for customer, vendor and employee records because most often these are located in the same city as the business, thus saving data entry time. The default information can be accepted or changed.

All businesses must use a single **Business Number** for tax reporting purposes. For most businesses, the nine-digit GST number became the Business Number. Different letter and number extensions are added to the base number if the company files different reports (e.g., GST and Payroll).

Until the new settings are saved, the **Session date** is set as the current calendar date. When you save and re-open the data files, the Earliest Transaction date becomes the Session date until you change the Session date. The **Latest Transaction date** is the latest date used for posting transactions and therefore shows if you have any postdated transactions.

◆ Type `Play Wave Plus - Purbhoo` (substitute your own name for Purbhoo).

◆ Press ⌨tab to move to the Street field and enter the company's street address.

Historical transactions must fall between the Fiscal Start date and the Earliest Transaction date.

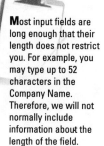
- ◆ Type **7310 Recreation Court**
- ◆ Press ⟨tab⟩ to move to the City field.
- ◆ Type **Megacity**
- ◆ Press ⟨tab⟩ to move to the Province field.
- ◆ Type **Ontario**
- ◆ Press ⟨tab⟩ to move to the Postal code field.
- ◆ Type **m5e1w6**
- ◆ Press ⟨tab⟩ to correct the format and move to the Phone field.
- ◆ Type **4168324521**
- ◆ Press ⟨tab⟩ to correct the telephone number format and advance the cursor.
- ◆ Type **4168321234** to enter the fax number.
- ◆ Press ⟨tab⟩ to move your cursor to the Business No. field.
- ◆ Type **34567 9876 RT**
- ◆ Click **OK** to return to the Home window.

Setting up Printers

- ◆ Choose the **Setup** menu and click **Reports & Forms** to see the printer settings:

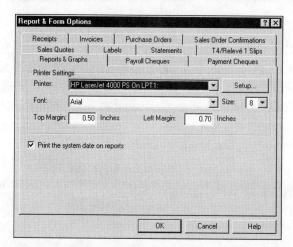

By default, the **printer settings** for Reports & Graphs appear first — its tab is in front. Many input screens are subdivided by tabs that resemble the tabs on file folders. The open folder tab is in the front row and the tab appears as full size, as if it is in front of the other folders. Normally the default Windows printer will be selected already. All of the printers you installed in Windows are shown in the pull-down list beside Printer.

From this initial Printer Settings screen, you can change the **font, size** and **margins** of your printed outputs. You may need to experiment with these settings to find the combination that gives you the best printing results. If your printed reports are difficult to read, you may have a non-text default font selected. You can change the font from this screen at any time. The option to **Print the system date on reports** will add the current date set up on your PC to all your printed reports. You should leave this option selected.

If the printer you need is not selected,

◆ Click the **Printer field drop-down list arrow** to see the printers installed.

◆ Click the **printer** you will use to print reports and graphs. You can set the printers for the remaining printouts, such as labels, invoices and cheques, later, as needed.

◆ Click **Setup** to access the options that control your printing jobs.

Additional Printer Settings

For the HP LaserJet 4000 printer, the number of copies, paper size and page orientation are set from the Paper tab. Each printer will have different options and tab labels. You should click on each tab to view the settings for your own printer. Once you choose the settings, including paper size and number of copies, the settings will apply to all your Simply Accounting data files. However, you must select a printer for each type of report or form. For example, changing the printer for Reports will not change the printer for Invoices.

◆ Click **Cancel** to return to the Report & Form Options window without changes.

◆ Click **OK** to return to the Home window.

Changing Default Settings
Display Settings

◆ Choose the **Setup** menu and click **Settings** to see the Display settings. Be sure that no Home window icon is selected (has its label in a different colour):

Click the Display tab if you see a different Settings screen at this stage.

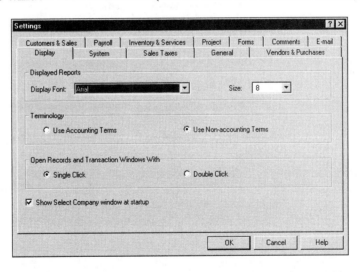

Other appearance settings, in the View menu, were described in Chapter 1. Do not change any of the View menu default settings. We want to show the icon windows, the status bar and ledgers. We also want to leave the automatic advice turned on and include account numbers.

Display Settings

Display settings refer to the appearance of the screens in Simply Accounting. You can change the **Display Font** and **Size** of the on-screen reports by selecting from the drop-down lists. Check this setting if you are having difficulty displaying your reports and seeing as much information as you want.

You can choose to display icons and reports with accounting **Terminology** or with non-accounting terminology.

The program offers the option of **Opening Records** (ledgers) **and Transaction Windows** (journals) with a single or a double click. If you choose single click to open the windows, you can select an icon by clicking with the right mouse button (right-click). If you open windows with the double click option selected, clicking the left mouse button once will select that icon.

The final choice, to **Show Select Company Window at Startup**, refers to the opening screen that you see when you start the program. See pages 2–3 to review this window.

The **Help** button in each Settings screen provides brief descriptions of the settings options in that screen.

◆ Click the **Help button** to see descriptions of the Display Settings options.

◆ Click **Use Accounting Terms** to select this option. You can change these settings at any time by returning to this menu.

System Settings

◆ Click the **System tab** at the top of the Settings screen to display the next group of settings:

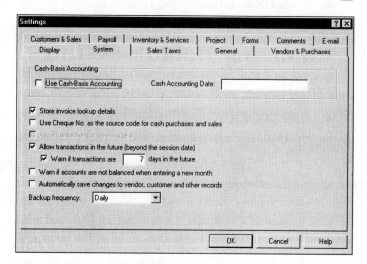

System Settings

The System settings include several practical features. The first option, **Cash Basis Accounting**, involves the timing for recording accounting transactions. Cash Basis Accounting records a transaction when cash is received or payments are made, regardless of when the revenue is earned (services delivered or goods sold) or the expense is incurred. Nonprofit organizations are the most common users of this method because there is frequent uncertainty about the receipt of funds and about the link between specific expenditures and revenue. For example, memberships are often not renewed, and one-time expenses related to a fundraising campaign may not generate any revenue or may generate an income stream for several years. If you use the Cash Basis method, you must enter the date at which the alternative method is to begin so that the computer can keep track of the appropriate timing details, like waiting to record a revenue until the customer makes the payment.

Most businesses use the accrual method of accounting, the default setting for the Simply Accounting program. Revenue is recognized when it is earned and expenses are recognized in the period that they were used to produce revenue according to the matching principle. A detailed example illustrating cash versus accrual based accounting is presented at the end of this reference section.

Refer to the document on the data CD named Basic Accounting for a brief review of basic accounting theory and principles. You may print this document or view it on-screen.

With **Store invoice lookup details** selected, you can look up Payables and Receivables invoices to view, store and print invoices after they have been posted, making it easier to verify details related to vendor or customer inquiries and to make corrections. You can use the program to adjust or correct invoices that were posted in error without making reversing entries only when Invoice Lookup is activated. We strongly recommend that you always use this option.

The feature to **Use Cheque No. as the source code for cash purchases and sales** instead of the invoice number applies when you use account reconciliation. Again, leave this option selected for the later chapters when you will add the account reconciliation feature.

You can control whether or not to allow transactions outside the normal range of dates. If you have data for more than one fiscal period, the option to **Allow transactions in the previous year** becomes available. When you post to a previous fiscal period, you are warned that the transaction will affect the previous year's balances. This option can be useful if you have in fact forgotten to include some transactions before moving to the next fiscal period. However, you should be aware of the effect of posting these transactions. You may also **Allow transactions in the future**, beyond the Session date and add a **Warning** if they are entered more than a specified number of days in advance. You may choose to enter a series of postdated payments or receipts or other recurring transactions during the same work session.

Simply Accounting permits journal transactions before entering all the history. You should select **Warn if accounts are not balanced when entering a new month** if you choose to proceed with unfinished history.

When you make changes to accounting records, you can allow the program to **Automatically save changes** when you close the record, or you may let the program prompt you to save the changes. When you see the prompt, the program will again offer the choice of saving automatically and changing the default setting.

The **Backup frequency** refers to how often you want the software to remind you to back up your data set. Normally, you should make a new backup at the end of each work session. You can choose a regular frequency from one of the drop-down list choices (Daily, Weekly, Semi-monthly, Monthly, Other or Never). When you choose Other, type a specific number of days such as 5 or 10 in the new Number of Days field. The program's backup feature makes backing up easy so you should use the reminders.

Cash versus Accrual Basis Accounting Example

The following example illustrates the differences between cash basis and accrual basis accounting.

A contract for $4 000 was signed on Dec. 1 for work to be completed over two months. The customer paid $500 on Dec. 1 on signing the contract and $3 500, the remaining balance, on completion of the project on January 31. Materials costing $1 000 were used evenly throughout the project but paid for completely when the work was started on Dec. 2. On Dec. 31, the year-end for the business, the project was half finished.

Cash Basis Accounting Journal Entries

Dec. 1/01	Cash	500	
	Revenue		500
Dec. 2/01	Material Expenses	1 000	
	Cash		1 000
Jan. 31/02	Cash	3 500	
	Revenue		3 500

PARTIAL INCOME STATEMENT

Cash Basis Method	Dec. 2001	Jan. 2002
Revenue from Contracts	$ 500	$3 500
Material Expenses	1 000	0
Net Income (Loss)	**$ (500)**	**$3 500**

Accrual Basis Accounting Journal Entries

Date	Account	Debit	Credit
Dec. 1/01	Cash	500	
	Unearned Revenue		500
Dec. 2/01	Materials Inventory	1 000	
	Cash		1 000
Dec. 31/01	Material Expenses	500	
	Materials Inventory		500
Dec. 31/01	Unearned Revenue	500	
	Accounts Receivable	1 500	
	Revenue		2 000
Jan. 31/02	Cash	3 500	
	Accounts Receivable		1 500
	Revenue		2 000
Jan. 31/02	Material Expenses	500	
	Materials Inventory		500

PARTIAL INCOME STATEMENT

Accrual Method	Dec. 2001	Jan. 2002
Revenue from Contracts	$2 000	$2 000
Material Expenses	500	500
Net Income (Loss)	**$1 500**	**$1 500**

The goal for the System settings is to maximize control without losing flexibility. Some of the default System settings are correct. We are not using cash basis accounting and we want to Store invoice lookup details. We will allow transactions up to seven days in the future without a warning. We will set the backup frequency to weekly because we usually advance the Session date one week at a time and we will add warnings and save record changes automatically.

◆ Click **Warn if accounts not balanced when entering new month.**

◆ Click **Automatically save changes to vendor, customer and other records.**

◆ Click the **Backup frequency field list arrow** as shown here:

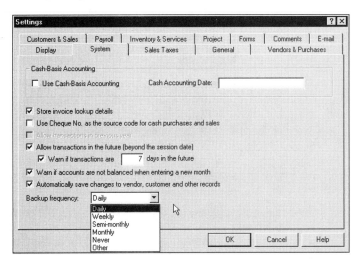

The Number of Days field opens when you choose Other as the Backup frequency.

◆ Click **Weekly** to select this frequency. Now the software will remind you each time you advance the date by one week that it is time to back up your files again.

The next tab in the Settings window allows you to define relevant sales taxes. We will set them in Chapter 4 because they are used for the Payables and Receivables ledgers.

General Ledger Settings

◆ Click the **General tab** at the top of the Settings screen to see the options for the General Ledger settings:

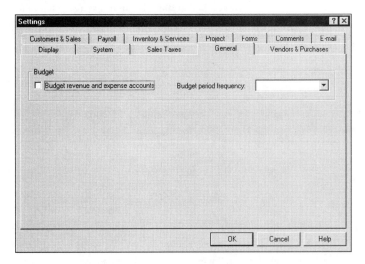

In the General settings, the **Budget** feature allows you to store budget amounts for all revenue and expense accounts. We will activate the budgeting feature when we set up and start to use budgets in Chapter 16.

◆ Do not change the default settings. You will activate budgeting later.

The remaining Settings tabs refer to the other ledgers. They will be introduced with those ledgers in later chapters.

◆ Click **OK** to save the new settings and return to the Home window.

Creating General Ledger Accounts

Before creating accounts for Play Wave, look at how the accounts are organized.

STRUCTURE OF THE CHART OF ACCOUNTS

Assets (Section Heading)
Group Heading (H) — Non-postable account
Group Account (G) — Postable account
Subgroup Account (A) — Postable account
Subgroup Account (A) — Postable account
Subgroup Total (S) — Non-postable account
Group Total (T) — Non-postable account

Group Heading
Postable accounts
•
•
Group Total

Liabilities (Section Heading)
Group Heading
Postable accounts
•
•
Group Total

Equity (Section Heading)
Group Heading
Postable accounts
•
•
Current Earnings account (X)
Group Total

Revenue (Section Heading)
Group Heading
Postable accounts
•
•
Group Total

Expense (Section Heading)
Group Heading
Postable accounts
•
•
Group Total

Simply Accounting organizes accounts into five sections, **Assets**, **Liabilities** and **Equity sections** from the Balance Sheet, and **Revenue** and **Expense** from the Income Statement. Each section is assigned a group of four-digit account numbers so that the program will know where to place the accounts you create, and how to interpret the balance amounts.

Accounts are numbered as follows:

Assets	1000 – 1999
Liabilities	2000 – 2999
Equity	3000 – 3999
Revenue	4000 – 4999
Expense	5000 – 5999

Thus, the program can handle up to 5000 separate ledger accounts.

The name or heading of each section is added automatically by the program to your reports. You cannot change these names. The program also automatically calculates a total for each section: Total Assets, Total Liabilities and Total Equity for the Balance Sheet, and Total Revenue and Total Expense for the Income Statement. In addition, the program calculates two more amounts automatically: Total Liabilities and Equity for the Balance Sheet and Net Income (Loss), or Total Revenue minus Total Expense, for the Income Statement, because these amounts are normally shown on these statements.

Accounts may be either postable or non-postable. Postable accounts can have an account balance and may be used in journal entries. Non-postable accounts do not have a balance and cannot be used to make journal entries. They are used to further organize the financial statements. The non-postable account types are **Group Headings (H)**, **Group Totals (T)** and **Subgroup Total (S)** accounts. Postable account types include only **Group Accounts (G)** and **Subgroup Accounts (A)**. In addition to these five account types that you can create, there is a single **Type X** account that the program creates, the *Current Earnings* account. This non-postable account automatically calculates the net income for the business from changes in revenue and expense accounts. You must assign an account type to each account when you create it.

Simply Accounting requires that the accounts be in a logical order as defined by the account number and type. For example, each section must have a Group Heading account at the beginning and a Group Total at the end. There must be at least one postable account between the Heading and Total. You can have more than one group (Group Heading, postable accounts, Group Total) within each section to subdivide the section. If you want a subtotal within a group, between two totals, you must place together all the accounts that should be subtotalled as Subgroup accounts. They will appear in a separate column to the left of the other postable accounts. The subtotal, the Subgroup Total will be placed in the right column with the remaining postable accounts, the Group accounts. The Group Totals will be calculated automatically by adding all Group accounts and Subgroup accounts that appear after the previous Group Total. All Group Totals within a section are added together to create the section total.

The following Liabilities section for Play Wave at the end of March illustrates the different account types.

Number	Name			Type
	LIABILITIES			Section Heading
2000	CURRENT LIABILITIES			(H) Group Heading
2200	Accounts Payable		$3 745.00	(G) Group Account
2640	PST Payable		0.00	(G) Group Account
2650	GST Charged on Services	1 015.00		(A) Subgroup Account
2670	GST Paid on Purchases	−1 951.40		(A) Subgroup Account
2750	GST Owing (Refund)		−936.40	(S) Subgroup Total
2790	TOTAL CURRENT LIABILITIES		$2 808.60	(T) Group Total
2800	LONG TERM LIABILITIES			(H) Group Heading
2850	Mortgage Payable		199 900.00	(G) Group Account
2890	TOTAL LONG TERM LIABILITIES		$199 900.00	(T) Group Total
	TOTAL LIABILITIES		$202 708.60	Section Total

The order of accounts in all statements is numerical and all accounts have numbers. Thus, the headings and totals and subtotals that you use to further organize your financial statements are also classified as accounts and must have numbers assigned to them for the program to place them in the correct order.

Account Class Options

Accounts can be further classified within a section according to the account class. Account classes are explained in Chapter 4. Generally you can accept the default class assigned by the program.

Creating the Chart of Accounts

You are now ready to create the Chart of Accounts. To do this you will need the Chart of Accounts from the manual system. Each account has been assigned a number, following the guidelines given above, and the account type is indicated in brackets beside each account.

We have added Group Headings, Group Totals, Subgroup Total accounts and account numbers to the Balance Sheet accounts on page 29. We have also added the revenue and expense accounts that Play Wave will need.

PLAY WAVE
CHART OF ACCOUNTS

Assets
1000 CURRENT ASSETS (H)
1080 Bank Account: Chequing (G)
1200 Accounts Receivable (G)
1300 Supplies: Fibreglass & Plastics (A)
1320 Supplies: Lumber (A)
1340 Supplies: Hardware (A)
1360 Supplies: Office (A)
1380 Total Supplies (S)
1395 TOTAL CURRENT ASSETS (T)

1500 PLANT & EQUIPMENT (H)
1520 Portable Computer System (G)
1540 Machinery & Tools (G)
1640 Shop (G)
1660 Truck (G)
1690 Yard (G)
1790 TOTAL PLANT & EQUIPMENT (T)

Liabilities
2000 CURRENT LIABILITIES (H)
2200 Accounts Payable (G)
2640 PST Payable (G)
2650 GST Charged on Services (A)
2670 GST Paid on Purchases (A)
2750 GST Owing (Refund) (S)
2790 TOTAL CURRENT LIABILITIES (T)

2800 LONG TERM LIABILITIES (H)
2850 Mortgage Payable (G)
2890 TOTAL LONG TERM LIABILITIES (T)

Equity
3000 OWNER'S EQUITY (H)
3100 Kerwin Child, Capital (G)
3600 Net Income (X)
3800 UPDATED CAPITAL (T)

Revenue
4000 GENERAL REVENUE (H)
4020 Revenue from Contracting (G)
4390 TOTAL GENERAL REVENUE (T)

Expense
5000 OPERATING EXPENSES (H)
5180 Hydro Expense (G)
5200 Maintenance Expense (G)
5230 Propane Gas Expense (G)
5250 Telephone Expense (G)
5260 Truck Expenses (G)
5390 TOTAL OPERATING EXPENSES (T)

ACCOUNT TYPES Shown in ( )
H = Group **H**eading
G = **G**roup Account
A = Subgroup **A**ccount
S = **S**ubgroup Total
T = Group **T**otal
X = Current Earnings

Notice that we have left spaces between the numbers of adjacent accounts. This is essential so that you can add new accounts later between the existing accounts while preserving the logical order of groups and subgroups. The single letter abbreviations for account types (H, G, A, S, T and X) are the codes used by the software and will appear when you display the Chart of Accounts.

To begin, you should be in the Home window. You can access the ledger accounts from the Accounts icon as shown:

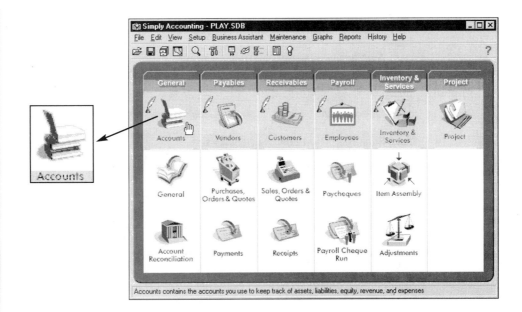

♦ Click the **Accounts icon** to open the Accounts icon window:

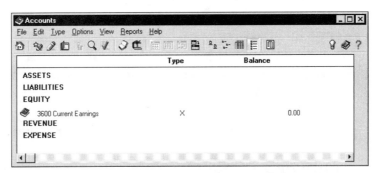

You can see that at present there is only one account in the window, *3600 Current Earnings*. This account represents net income (loss). We will discuss this account further and rename the account *Net Income* later in this chapter.

The Accounts Icon Window Tools and Menus

Bring the Home window to the front of the other windows.

Use **Modify Accounts Wizard** to create, edit or remove an account.

Edit the selected account.

Create a new account.

Remove the selected account.

Find an account using the Find Account window.

Check the validity of accounts for errors in account sequences.

Open the **General Journal**.

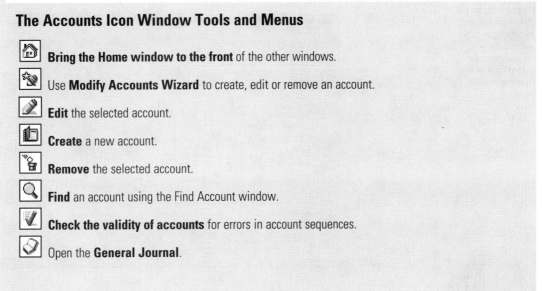

Open the **Account Reconciliation Journal**.

Auto arrange the icons in the Icon window.

Arrange icons in the Icon window (place the icons in straight rows).

Re-sort icons in the Icon window to restore alphabetical order.

Restore Icon **window** to its default size.

Display accounts in the Icon window **by icon.**

Display accounts in the Icon window **by small icons**. More icons will fit on the screen.

Display accounts in the Icon window **by name.** Accounts appear in numerical order with balances.

Display accounts in the Icon window **by type.** Accounts appear in order with balances and types.

Select a report for the Ledger from the available list.

Advice about the Ledger.

Help contents as available from the Home window Help menu.

Help about the icon window.

Except for one additional **Edit** menu option, **DDE**, the Accounts window menu options duplicate the tool buttons. DDE, Dynamic Data Exchange, allows interaction with other software programs with links that continually update the information in the secondary program. (See Appendix F.) The **File** menu contains the options to Create, Remove and bring the Home window to the front. The Edit menu also has the Wizard, Edit, Check Validity and Find options. The **Type** menu provides access to the General Ledger journals. Auto arrange, Arrange icons, Re-sort icons and Restore window appear in the **Options** menu. The **View** menu has the four display options. The **Reports** menu accesses General Ledger reports and the **Help** menu has the three help options.

Creating an Account

The next step is to create the remaining accounts in the Chart of Accounts.

◆ Click the **Create tool button** 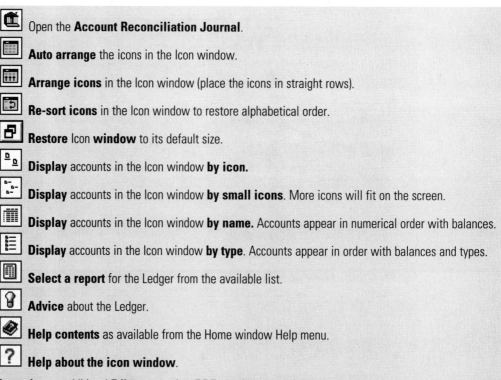 or choose the **File** menu and click **Create** to see the new ledger account window:

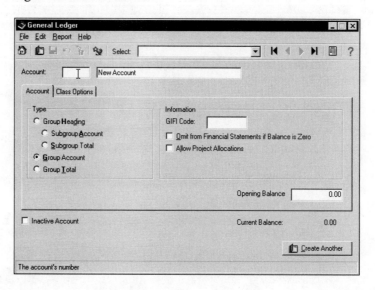

The program may enter an account number and type as a best guess of the next account you want to enter based on your cursor position in the Accounts window.

The General Ledger Input Form

Most **Tools** (the Modify Accounts Wizard is relabelled Start Account Wizard) are the same as those in the Accounts window. The Display Report tool (beside Help) provides immediate access to the Chart of Accounts. The remaining tools permit you to go immediately to the account ledger record indicated:

⏮ Go to the First account in the list.

◀ Go to the Previous account.

▶ Go to the Next account.

⏭ Go to the Last account in the list.

From the list in the **Select** field, you can access the ledger window for any account that you have already created. Click the list arrow to see the list.

Account Tab Input Fields

Account: The first and second account fields contain the four-digit account number and the account name, respectively. All accounts have numbers, not just the postable accounts. This numbering is necessary so that the program can organize the Chart of Accounts properly into the various sections and groups, and place the headings and totals in the correct place as well. The account name or description field may contain up to 35 characters, allowing for fully descriptive names.

Type: The five account types were explained on pages 40–41. The sixth account type, Current Earnings (X), is not listed because you cannot create this type yourself.

GIFI (General Index of Financial Information) Code: This is the Canada Customs and Revenue Agency code for the account to make the financial statements consistent with the electronic filing forms.

Omit from Financial Statements if Balance is Zero: You may choose to omit the account from financial statements if its balance is zero, that is, not print this account in the financial statements if the account balance is zero. For most accounts this may be appropriate, but you should always print the Cash account balances.

The **Allow Project Allocations** switch opens the allocation field in journals for the selected account. The setting is turned on by default for revenue and expense accounts.

Opening Balance: The balance in the account from the Trial Balance as at the date that you are converting from the manual system. Once you finish the ledger history, the opening balance is removed but the **Current Balance**, updated from journal entries, is always shown on the ledger page.

The first account in the Chart of Accounts is account *1000 CURRENT ASSETS*, the Group Heading. We will enter it first.

The cursor is in the account number field where you enter the four-digit account number.

◆ Type **1000**

◆ Press (tab) to advance to the account name or description field.

◆ Type **CURRENT ASSETS**

◆ Press (tab).

Notice that a new tab is added to the form — the Account Reconciliation tab. Because this is an asset account, it may be used as an account that is set up for account

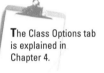

The Class Options tab is explained in Chapter 4.

Accounts may be marked as inactive and then included in reports or omitted.

We always capitalize the names of Group Heading and Group Total accounts to help set them off from other accounts in the financial statements. Simply Accounting also follows this practice in the Chart of Accounts in the template files.

reconciliation. You will set up the Account Reconciliation feature in Chapter 11. When you have activated the Budgeting feature, postable revenue and expense accounts will have a Budgeting tab beside the Account tab. These features apply only to postable accounts, not to headings and totals.

◆ Click **Group Heading** as the Account Type. Notice that the balance field disappears because headings are non-postable accounts and cannot have a balance. Your completed account ledger form should look like this:

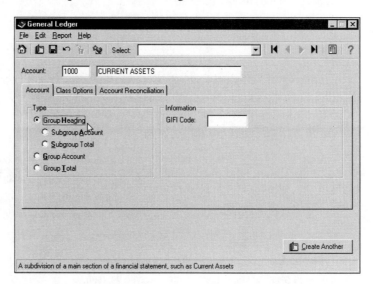

You can obtain more information about GIFI from the Canada Customs and Revenue Agency Web site <www.ccra-adrc. gc.ca>.

◆ Click **Create Another** to save the new account. A new ledger form appears. The next account to enter is the Cash account, *Bank Account: Chequing*. The cursor should be in the Account number field (if it is not, click the Account number field).

◆ Type **1080**

◆ Press tab .

◆ Type **Bank Account: Chequing**

◆ Press tab .

Do not enter account balances yet. We will enter them in the next stage.

The cursor advances to the Type section. The default account type, Group Account, is correct, so you should leave it.

Now you must choose whether you want to Omit printing of this account in the financial statements if the account balance is zero. Since you should always print bank account balances, leave the option to Omit from Financial Statements unchecked. Omitting zero balances for other accounts is a matter of personal preference. We will use the project allocations feature only for revenue and expense accounts (Chapter 17), so you can accept the default settings.

Account classes are a further way of organizing accounts. They will be discussed in Chapter 4. We can accept the default classes assigned by the program at this stage.

◆ Check your work carefully and correct mistakes in text by highlighting incorrect information and re-typing the correct details. Correct the account Type by clicking the correct type.

◆ Click **Create Another** to save the account and see a new ledger account form.

There are now three accounts. Each time you create an account, Simply Accounting creates an icon or entry for it in the Accounts window for easy reference. To see these account entries in the Accounts window,

◆ Click the **Accounts task button** on the task bar at the bottom of the Windows desktop to make it the active window:

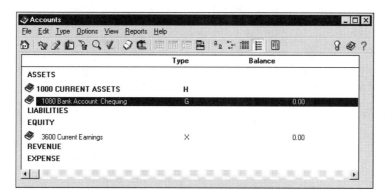

Notice that *CURRENT ASSETS*, the Group Heading, is on the list too. There are no account balances at this stage because we have not entered them yet.

◆ Click the **General Ledger task button** on the task bar at the bottom of the Windows desktop to restore it.

◆ Continue to enter the remaining accounts from the Chart of Accounts on page 42. Remember that the program has created account 3600, so you do not need to create this account. After creating the last account, remain in the ledger window.

If you want to take a break at this stage, close the Ledger window, close the Accounts window and close the Home window. To resume with the next step, open the Play data files. Accept (or type) March 15 as the Session date. Click the Accounts icon to open the Accounts window. Click the Create tool to prepare for the next step.

Entering Opening Account Balances

If you close the General Ledger window before adding all account balances, or if the total debits and credits are not equal, the Trial Balance will be out of balance. Simply Accounting will enter an adjusting amount to an account of your choice to force the Trial Balance to balance.

Since you could finish the history and be unable to correct opening balance errors, we want to minimize these adjustments. That is why we leave the balances at zero until all accounts are created, and enter opening account balances as a separate step.

We will use a separate account to track these adjustments, so that it will be easy to check the final Trial Balance against the original. If all amounts are entered correctly, the *Test Balance* account will have a zero balance.

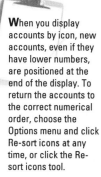

Open windows appear on the task bar as icons in Windows 98 when the task bar is at the minimum size. It may be difficult to distinguish the different Simply Accounting windows. You can increase the height of the task bar by dragging its top frame to see program names on the task bar.

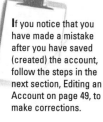

When you display accounts by icon, new accounts, even if they have lower numbers, are positioned at the end of the display. To return the accounts to the correct numerical order, choose the Options menu and click Re-sort icons at any time, or click the Re-sort icons tool.

If you notice that you have made a mistake after you have saved (created) the account, follow the steps in the next section, Editing an Account on page 49, to make corrections.

◆ Create the Group account *1010 Test Balance*.

The following Trial Balance shows the opening balance amounts for each account at the time of conversion to the computerized system.

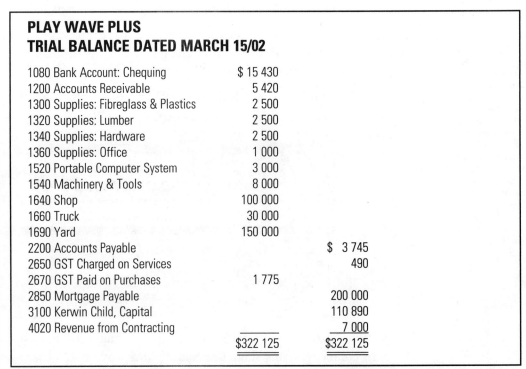

PLAY WAVE PLUS
TRIAL BALANCE DATED MARCH 15/02

Account	Debit	Credit
1080 Bank Account: Chequing	$ 15 430	
1200 Accounts Receivable	5 420	
1300 Supplies: Fibreglass & Plastics	2 500	
1320 Supplies: Lumber	2 500	
1340 Supplies: Hardware	2 500	
1360 Supplies: Office	1 000	
1520 Portable Computer System	3 000	
1540 Machinery & Tools	8 000	
1640 Shop	100 000	
1660 Truck	30 000	
1690 Yard	150 000	
2200 Accounts Payable		$ 3 745
2650 GST Charged on Services		490
2670 GST Paid on Purchases	1 775	
2850 Mortgage Payable		200 000
3100 Kerwin Child, Capital		110 890
4020 Revenue from Contracting		7 000
	$322 125	$322 125

◆ Click the **Select field** and click *Bank Account: Chequing* to open the ledger.

The General Ledger form you completed looks like this:

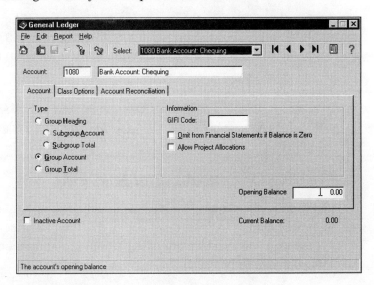

◆ Double click the **Opening Balance field.**

It is important that you understand when to enter the **account balance** as a positive amount and when to enter it as a negative amount. The rule is simple. Normally accounts have a positive balance. Accounts that usually have debit balances, assets and expenses, have debit balances entered as positive amounts. When you enter a negative amount for the same account by adding a minus sign to the number, the program will enter this as a credit amount. This usually occurs when you have a contra-account, but it may be that the bank account is overdrawn, or the receivables show cash advances from customers. Liability accounts normally have a credit balance, so credit balances are entered as positive amounts and debit balances as negative. Equity and revenue accounts also normally have credit balances. On the Balance Sheet, negative balance amounts are printed with a minus sign.

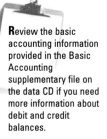

Review the basic accounting information provided in the Basic Accounting supplementary file on the data CD if you need more information about debit and credit balances.

- Type **15430** (the amount from the Trial Balance).

- Click the **Go to next account tool** to open the ledger for *Accounts Receivable*.

- Double click the **Opening Balance field** and type the amount.

If you need to interrupt your work before entering all balances or you have entered amounts incorrectly, you will see a message like the one shown here when you close the Ledger window:

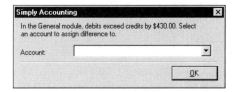

- Click the **drop-down list arrow** and select the *Test Balance* account, the one we created for these temporary adjustments. Click **OK** to close the warning.

- Continue to enter the balances for the remaining accounts from the Trial Balance.

- Close the Ledger window to return to the Accounts window.

Remember to enter the GST Paid balance as a negative amount (–1 775) because the contra-liability account has a debit balance.

- Click the **Check validity of accounts tool** to check sequence of account types (e.g., for missing totals or headings). Your first error will be identified. An example of an error message is shown below:

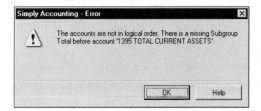

Follow the instructions below to correct the error and then check the validity of accounts again until you see the message that the accounts are in logical order.

Editing an Account

Notice that in our chart of accounts, account 3600 is named *Net Income*. We need to edit the account name to make it consistent with the chart. There are different ways to access a specific account. You can use the Select field in any ledger record window. From the Accounts window you can double click the account name directly.

Accessing Accounts from the Ledger Window

- Open the Ledger window for *Test Balance* or any other account if you do not already have a Ledger window open.

◆ Click the **Select field drop-down list arrow** to see the accounts currently set up:

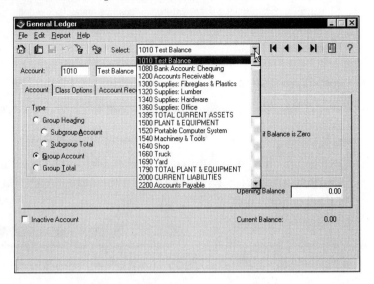

◆ Type **3** to advance to the first 3000 level account. Scroll down the list if necessary until you see account 3600.

◆ Click *3600 Current Earnings*, the account name, to bring forward the ledger form for this account.

Alternative Methods of Accessing a Ledger Record

Accessing Accounts Directly from the Accounts Window

From the Accounts window, scroll through the list if necessary until you see account *3600*. Click account *3600 Current Earnings* to select it.

Click the Edit tool  (or choose the Edit menu and click Edit) or double click account *3600 Current Earnings* to open the ledger window.

Using Find in the Accounts Window

From the Accounts window, click the Find tool button [🔍] or choose the Edit menu and click Find to open the Find Account screen. Type 3 to advance to the first 3000 level account. Scroll to advance to the *Current Earnings* account. Click Find to open the ledger window for the account.

Using the Find Tool in the Home Window

From the Home window, click the Find tool to open the Select Record Type window. Choose Accounts, the module or ledger you need, from the drop-down list and then click Select. Click *3600 Current Earnings*, the account you want to open. Click Find to access the record.

Using the Find Menu Option in the Home Window

From the Home window, choose the Edit menu, then choose Find and click Accounts, the type of record you want. Click Select. Click *3600 Current Earnings*, the account you want to open. Click Find to access the record.

The Find tool and menu option in the Home window allow you to access the records for all ledgers.

Using the Home Window Menu

In the Home window, choose the Reports menu, then choose Lists and click Chart of Accounts.

Displaying the Chart of Accounts from the Accounts Window Menu

From the Home window, click the Accounts icon 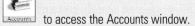 to access the Accounts window.

Choose the Reports menu and click Display Chart of Accounts.

Using the Tool Button in the Accounts Window

From the Home window, click the Accounts icon to open the Accounts window.

Click the Select a Report tool button to display the Select a report window.

The Chart of Accounts is first on the list so it is already selected. The remaining reports on this list include all reports related to the General Ledger. Click Select.

The Select a Report tool in the Accounts window provides access to all reports for the General Ledger.

Trial Balance

We will use the Trial Balance to verify that we entered the amounts correctly.

From the Home window,

◆ Choose the **Reports** menu, then choose **Financials** and click **Trial Balance** as shown:

You will see the following Report Options window:

Sort and Filter options cannot be used for the Trial Balance.

You must enter a date for the Trial Balance. The default date is the only one available at this setup stage so you should accept it.

◆ Click **OK** to display the report.

Your displayed report should match the Trial Balance shown on page 48 except that the Trial Balance report includes all postable accounts, even those with zero balances.

◆ Choose the **File** menu and click **Print** in the displayed report window to print the Trial Balance.

◆ Close the displayed report to return to the Home window.

Displaying the Trial Balance from the Accounts Window

From the Accounts window, you can access the Trial Balance by choosing the Reports menu and clicking Trial Balance. You can also click the Select a Report tool and then choose Trial Balance from the drop-down list.

◆ Make corrections to account names, numbers, types and opening balances if necessary by following the instructions for Editing an Account on page 49.

Defining Linked Accounts

Before Simply Accounting can perform its automatic functions, you must identify the accounts that it should use.

Linked Accounts

Linked accounts are used by the Simply Accounting program to complete some of the automatic accounting processes. They also integrate the different ledgers. There are two linked accounts for the General Ledger:

• the Current Earnings account that we renamed *Net Income*
• a capital account or Retained Earnings account.

Changes in revenue and expenses are automatically recorded in the **Current Earnings** (*Net Income*) account, with revenues increasing the balance and expenses decreasing the balance. You do not post these journal entries as you do in a manual accounting system, in fact, you cannot because the Current Earnings (*Net Income*) account is not available as a postable account. The Current Earnings (*Net Income*) balance appears on the Income Statement.

The second General Ledger linked account is used at the end of each fiscal period when it is time to "close the books." All revenue and expense account balances are closed into the appropriate capital account, zeroing these accounts. This is a two-step process manually — first closing these accounts into the Current Earnings account and then closing the Current Earnings (*Net Income*) account into the **Retained Earnings** account. The revenue and expense account balances are reset to zero to prepare for the income calculations in the next fiscal period. Simply Accounting performs these closing routines automatically as soon as you begin working with dates following the Fiscal End date. Obviously you should make a backup of the data files before taking this step.

The Setup tool works much like the Display tool. If you select an icon first, you access the function directly. If you do not, you access a selection list. If you select a journal icon and then the Setup tool, you see the linked accounts for the ledger. If you select a ledger icon first, you see the Settings screen for the ledger.

Using the Setup Tool to Access Linked Accounts

You should be in the Home window.

◆ Right-click the **General Journal icon** (just below the Accounts icon). The underlined General label means the icon is selected.

◆ Click the **Setup tool** . If another journal or ledger is selected, you cannot access the General Linked accounts using the Setup tool button.

You will see the General Linked Accounts window:

Alternative Methods of Accessing the Linked Accounts Screen

Setup Tool Method without Selecting an Icon First

If no journal or ledger icon is selected in the Home window when you click the Setup tool, you will access the Select Setup screen. Click the drop-down list arrow to see the list of ledgers and journals.

Scroll down the list and click General. Click Select to access the General Linked Accounts screen.

Using the Home Window Setup Menu

From the Home window, choose the Setup menu. Point to Linked Accounts so that the secondary menu opens and then click General. You will see the General Linked Accounts window.

Notice that the Current Earnings linked account is predefined. You cannot change it, although you can edit the account name and number as we did in the General Ledger. (See Editing an Account.) The Retained Earnings account is still undefined. At year-end, we want the net income to be posted to the capital account, *3100 Kerwin Child, Capital*.

◆ Click the **drop-down list arrow** beside the Retained Earnings field to see all the accounts that arc available for this linking function:

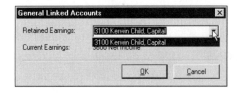

Because you can select only a postable capital account, the list is restricted to these accounts. At present, 3100, the one we want, is the only postable capital account.

◆ Click *3100 Kerwin Child, Capital*.

◆ Click **OK** to save the linked accounts.

You will see an advisory message that the account class has changed to Retained Earnings because of the linked account designation:

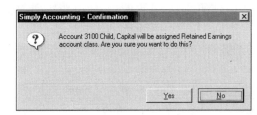

If you are using Version 8.0A, the confirmation screen shows an OK button. Click OK instead of Yes.

◆ Click **Yes** to accept the change and return to the Home window.

Once an account is defined as a linked account, you cannot delete it from the Chart of Accounts until you unlink it or remove the linked setting. A linked setting is an integrating feature.

To delete the linked setting, open the Linked Accounts window. Click the account you want to unlink. Press ⌧. (You can now remove the account from the Accounts window.) Then choose a new account or leave the field blank if the linked account is not required. Both linked accounts for the General Ledger are required.

Preparing for Journal Entries

You have now entered all the background information you need to prepare for journal entries. However, in the Home window, all the Ledger icons still have the Open History symbol. To prepare for making journal entries, the ledger histories should be finished. Finishing the history for a ledger is not reversible, so you must make a backup copy of your work before you proceed.

Working with an Unfinished History

Simply Accounting permits you to enter current journal transactions before the history is finished and balanced. In this way, you can keep the journal records current and enter the historical details later when there is time available to do so, or the setup may be completed later by a different individual.

However, you must complete some elements before making journal entries. You must create and define essential linked accounts before you can use the subsidiary journals. Historical customer and vendor invoices must be entered before you can enter payments for them, and invoices must have the correct payment terms and dates. You may enter new accounts from the General Journal as they are needed, and you may enter opening account balances later from the Accounts tab. From a control point of view, it is preferable to enter all historical information first so that you do not confuse the historical and current data or work with accounts that are incorrect in some way. You cannot change an account number after the account is used in journal entries so some corrections may be difficult to make later.

The balance on the General Ledger Accounts tab is the opening historical account balance. Your Trial Balance and Accounts window will always display current balances that change as you post new journal entries. Therefore, you cannot use these reports to check your historical account balances after you make journal entries. You must go to the ledger records to see the opening balances.

You can perform a number of checks to increase the accuracy of your work. You should compare your reports carefully with the charts given in this application and make corrections. Pay particular attention to correct account numbers. Check the validity of accounts by using the Edit menu option or tool.

Warning!

Since there is much more flexibility regarding editing the accounts before we finish the history, having a backup of the files in the not finished stage allows you to return to them without starting from scratch. Certain restrictions apply once you have finished the ledger history. For example, you cannot change account balances. Having a not finished version of the file will save you the time it would take to re-enter all of the setup information if you have incorrect account balances. In the not finished stage, you can simply edit the balances.

Simply Accounting also has some safeguards that prevent you from proceeding with major errors in your files. If linked accounts are not defined or if your accounts are not in order (e.g., a Subgroup Total is missing), you will receive the appropriate error message when you try to finish the history. However, you may still have mistakes that cannot be detected by the program.

Backing up Your Data Files

Different methods of backing up files result in different types of files and different methods of accessing them. Refer to page 23 for details.

The Backup feature creates a compressed version of the data set. You cannot access it using the Open Company window. The file must first be restored using the Restore feature. You can restore backups from the File menu in the Home window with a file open or from the Select Company window.

To begin the backup, the file must be open and you should be in the Home window.

◆ Choose the **File** menu and click **Backup** to see the Backup screen:

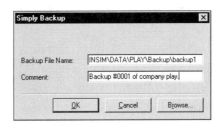

Warning!
Do not attempt to apply the Copy command to the Save As window because you will copy only the single .SDB file and not the complete data set.

Simply Accounting has added the file name and folder for you by default in the same drive and folder where your previous working copy is located. You can edit these names. You can click Browse to find the folder you need. We will replace the file name "backup" with a descriptive label, but use the new Backup folder.

◆ Drag through the second **backup** (after the final backslash) to highlight it.

◆ Type **nfplay** to replace the highlighted part of the Backup File Name.

If you use floppy disks for your backup files, you must use a blank formatted disk for each backup file or overwrite the previous backup.

◆ Press ⌨tab to advance to the Comment field and highlight it.

◆ Type **Not finished version of play**

◆ Click **OK**.

If you have entered a new folder name, you will see the following message:

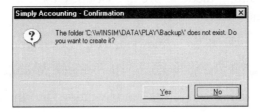

Since you want to create the folder, you should proceed.

◆ Click **Yes**.

Although you can make a working backup copy of the company data files using Windows Copy and Paste commands or the Simply Accounting Save As command (Home window, File menu) we do not recommend this approach for frequent backups because the data files are very large. The Backup command creates a compressed file so you can store many backups using minimal disk space.

Simply Accounting displays the message that the backup is in progress and that the files are being compressed. The program will confirm that the backup has been completed.

◆ Click **OK** to continue.

Once you have made the backup copy, it is safe to proceed with finishing the ledger history.

Finishing the General Ledger History

From the Home window,

◆ Choose the **History** menu and click **Finish Entering History** as shown:

You will see the following message advising you have not defined some essential linked accounts for the unused ledgers:

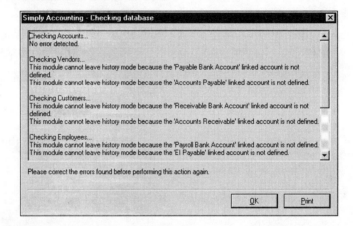

These messages indicate that the General Ledger is free of errors but that the remaining modules are not set up. We must hide the ledgers that are not used until we are ready to set them up.

◆ Click **OK** to acknowledge the warning and close the message.

◆ Click the **View** menu, then choose **Modules** and click **Payables**.

You will return to the Home window, but the icons for the Payables Ledger have been removed.

◆ Click the **View** menu, then choose **Modules** and click **Receivables**. (Notice that Payables no longer has a ✓ beside it.)

◆ Now repeat this step to hide the remaining modules, Payroll, Inventory and Project, until your Home window looks like the one shown:

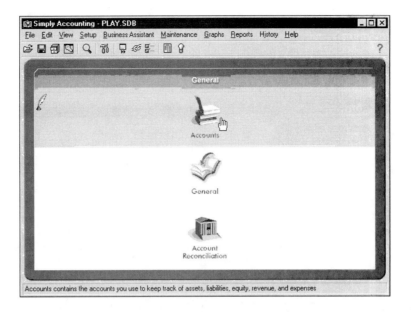

Accounts contains the accounts you use to keep track of assets, liabilities, equity, revenue, and expenses

◆ Choose the **History** menu and click **Finish Entering History**.

At this stage you may see another screen listing errors that relate only to the General Ledger. For example, the following screen shows common General Ledger errors:

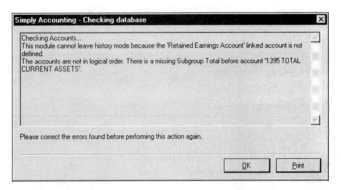

If you see a screen like the one above, you have not finished the history. Click Print so that you can use the message as a guide for making corrections. Click OK to return to the Home window. You must correct your errors before you can finish the history and before you begin making journal entries.

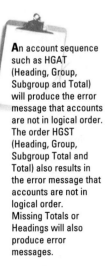

An account sequence such as HGAT (Heading, Group, Subgroup and Total) will produce the error message that accounts are not in logical order. The order HGST (Heading, Group, Subgroup Total and Total) also results in the error message that accounts are not in logical order. Missing Totals or Headings will also produce error messages.

Finishing History Errors

A number of common errors will prevent you from finishing the history. When you select the Finish Entering History menu option, Simply Accounting will create a status report listing all the errors so that you can correct them. You can print this report for reference while you make the corrections.

Click OK. Correcting these errors in the above list requires

- placing the accounts in logical order, that is, adding the missing Subgroup Total account after the Subgroup accounts, changing the account type for *1380 Total Supplies* to Subgroup Total or adding this account if it is missing.
- defining the Retained Earnings linked account.

Make the corrections and then select the History menu and click Finish Entering History again.

When all the information is complete and correct, Simply Accounting will allow you to proceed with finishing the history, warning you that this action cannot be reversed.

WARNING! Do not proceed to the journal transactions in Chapter 3 until you see the following screen:

If you see any other messages at this point, you still have mistakes and you must correct them. Also be sure that you have made a backup.

◆ Click **Proceed**.

Your updated Home window will be restored after a brief period. The Open History symbol is removed from the Accounts Ledger icon as shown:

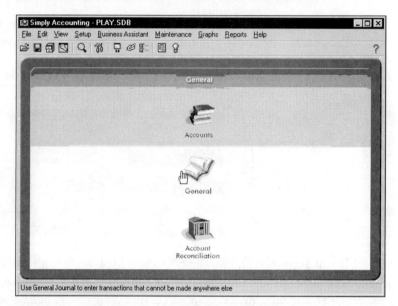

◆ Choose the **File** menu and click **Exit** or click ☒ to exit the program and save your work.

Restoring a File from Backup

Start the Simply Accounting program. You will see the Simply Accounting – Select Company window.

◆ Click **Restore from Backup**

◆ Click **OK** to see the Restore information window.

Or, with any Simply Accounting data file open,

◆ Choose the **File** menu and click **Restore** to see the Restore information window:

If you have not made a backup copy yet, you can do so now by clicking Backup. This will access the Backup feature described above. (Cancel will return you to the Home window without finishing the history.)

Although you may begin to post journal entries with historical errors and before finishing the history, you should not do so. If you want to continue with the next chapter, use the data files from the data CD to begin the next chapter and then try to find your own errors later. Being able to set up your own data files correctly is an important part of learning to use the Simply Accounting program.

You may remove the Test Balance account once you have finished the ledger history. Click the Accounts icon to open the Accounts window. Click the Test Balance account to select it. Click the Remove tool or choose the File menu and click Remove. Click Yes to confirm the account's removal.

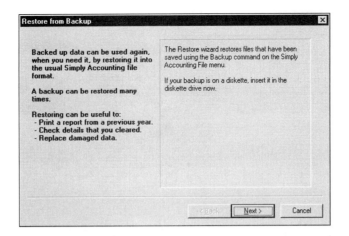

◆ Click **Next** to access the Backup Wizard:

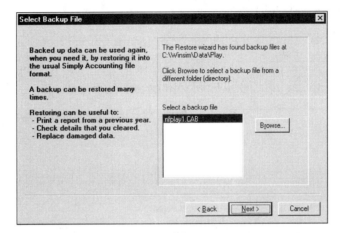

All the backup files in the currently selected folder are listed. If you need to select a different folder, click browse and find the folder you need.

◆ Click **Next** to proceed, following the on-screen instructions.

The program asks you to confirm your choices:

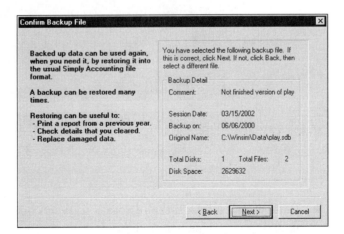

◆ Click **Next** to proceed.

The next screen asks for the name of the new restored file:

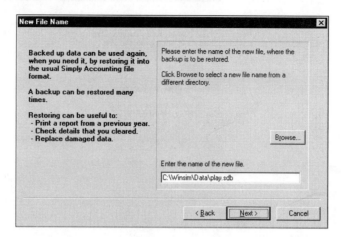

By default, the program enters the name of the original file you backed up.

◆ Change the file name or location if necessary and then click **Next** to proceed.

If you do not change the name, and choose to replace the original file, the program warns you before making the substitution:

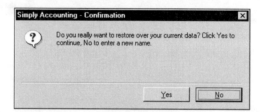

◆ Click **Yes**. If the original file is damaged, you should replace it.

After choosing the files, the program provides another opportunity to change the settings:

The program will ask you to confirm that you want to replace the original file if you are using the same file name. If the original file is damaged, you should replace it.

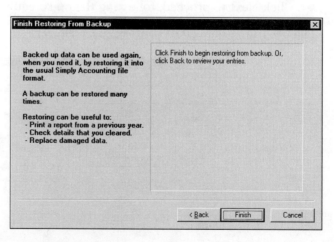

◆ Click **Finish** to begin the restoration. When it is finished, you will see the Session date screen for the restored file.

◆ Click **OK** to accept the Session date and open the Home window for the new file, the not finished version.

◆ Close the data file so that you can create a new company file for Live Links.

Practice: Live Links

The Live Links simulation parallels the Play Wave Plus simulation. At the end of each chapter, you will have a chance to reinforce the material you learned in the chapter by setting up the same ledgers or using the same journals for transactions for this second company. Thus the Live Links simulation runs throughout the workbook and builds in the same modular fashion as the Play Wave Plus company.

In this chapter, you will set up the General Ledger for Live Links.

COMPANY PROFILE

Live Links is a computer services company owned and operated by Helen Lively in Burnaby, British Columbia. Lively graduated from the University of British Columbia's computer science program eight years ago and has held jobs for several different companies. In 2002, she started her own business, bringing her vast experience and business contacts with her. By July 1, she has set up her office, purchased supplies and equipment and arranged the first contracts. Lively and her two assistants provide a wide range of computer-related training and informational workshops to companies of all sizes. As expert computer technicians, they also offer repair and upgrading services to the same businesses. Their service projects range from basic installation of extra memory to more complex data recovery services. To assess the profitability of these various sources of income, Lively has created separate revenue accounts for consulting work, workshops, including training, and other services that include disk duplication, computer upgrades and repair work.

Lively has registered her company for GST using the regular method. She is also registered for PST so that some of her purchases will be exempt. She charges GST on all services and sales, including the workshops and training. Her customers pay PST on repairs and upgrading work, but not on workshops or training. She remits GST quarterly and PST monthly. She plans to close her books quarterly.

Her two assistants are paid monthly through the bank's payroll services. Accounts have been set up with regular suppliers, some of whom offer discounts if the account is settled early. Lively offers early payment discounts to some of her account customers as well.

General Ledger Setup

Instructions

1. Close any other data files you have open.

2. Create a new folder named **Links** to store the new files. Create a new company file, naming it **Links**.

3. Enter the company's fiscal dates:

   Fiscal Start: July 1, 2002
   Fiscal End: September 30, 2002
   Earliest Transaction: July 8, 2002

4. Enter the company information:

> **COMPANY INFORMATION**
>
> Company Name: Live Links Computer Services
> Address: 20300 Silicon Valley Rd. North
>   Burnaby, British Columbia   V5B 3A2
> Telephone: (604) 372-7199
> Fax Number: (604) 372-8144
> Business Number: 74120 7654

5. Enter display and system settings:

> **SETTINGS**
>
> **Display**:   Use Accounting Terms
> **System**:   Backup frequency: semi-monthly
>   Warn if accounts not balanced when starting a new month
>   Automatically save changes to vendor, customer & other records
> **General**:   No changes

6. Create the accounts in the Chart of Accounts.

7. Enter account balances from the Trial Balance on the following page. Remember to enter the balance for GST Paid on Purchases as a negative amount. If your Trial Balance is not balanced when you close the ledger, choose the *Test Balance* account.

8. Edit the Current Earnings account: Change the name to Net Income.

9. Enter General linked accounts:

> **Retained Earnings**:   3100 Helen Lively, Capital
> **Current Earnings**:   3600 Net Income

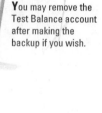

You may remove the Test Balance account after making the backup if you wish.

10. Check your work by printing the Chart of Accounts and Trial Balance. Make corrections if necessary.

11. Back up your work.

12. Hide all modules (except the General module).

13. Finish entering the General Ledger history.

14. Close the file and exit the program.

LIVE LINKS COMPUTER SERVICES: CHART OF ACCOUNTS

Assets
1000 CURRENT ASSETS (H)
1010 Test Balance (G)
1080 Bank Account: Chequing (G)
1200 Accounts Receivable (G)
1220 Memory Chips (A)
1240 Supplies: Computer (A)
1260 Supplies: Office (A)
1280 Net Supplies (S)
1390 TOTAL CURRENT ASSETS (T)

1500 PLANT & EQUIPMENT (H)
1520 Computers & Peripherals (G)
1540 Custom Tools (G)
1560 Data Recovery Equipment (G)
1580 Duplication Equipment (G)
1600 LCD Projection Unit (G)
1680 Motor Vehicle (G)
1800 TOTAL PLANT & EQUIPMENT (T)

Liabilities
2000 CURRENT LIABILITIES (H)
2100 Bank Loan (G)
2200 Accounts Payable (G)
2640 PST Payable (G)
2650 GST Charged on Services (A)
2670 GST Paid on Purchases (A)
2750 GST Owing (Refund) (S)
2790 TOTAL CURRENT LIABILITIES (T)

Equity
3000 OWNER'S EQUITY (H)
3100 Helen Lively, Capital (G)
3200 Helen Lively, Drawings (G)
3600 Net Income (X)
3800 UPDATED CAPITAL (T)

Revenue
4000 GENERAL REVENUE (H)
4020 Revenue from Consulting (A)
4040 Revenue from Services (A)
4060 Revenue from Workshops (A)
4200 Net Sales (S)
4390 TOTAL GENERAL REVENUE (T)

Expense
5000 OPERATING EXPENSES (H)
5010 Advertising & Promotion (G)
5050 Hydro Expense (G)
5100 Telephone Expense (G)
5120 Vehicle Expenses (G)
5300 Wages (G)
5950 TOTAL OPERATING EXPENSES (T)

LIVE LINKS COMPUTER SERVICES: TRIAL BALANCE
DATED JULY 8/02

Account	Debit	Credit
1080 Bank Account: Chequing	$ 8 400	
1200 Accounts Receivable	2 140	
1220 Memory Chips	2 400	
1240 Supplies: Computer	300	
1260 Supplies: Office	400	
1520 Computers & Peripherals	5 600	
1540 Custom Tools	2 000	
1560 Data Recovery Equipment	7 500	
1580 Duplication Equipment	4 000	
1600 LCD Projection Unit	1 200	
1680 Motor Vehicle	32 000	
2200 Accounts Payable		$ 1 570
2650 GST Charged on Services		140
2670 GST Paid on Purchases	3 800	
3100 Helen Lively, Capital		66 030
4020 Revenue from Consulting		2 000
	$69 740	$69 740

Review Questions

1. Why is it important to add non-postable accounts to your Chart of Accounts?
2. Why should you leave spaces between account numbers when you create the Chart of Accounts in Simply Accounting?
3. What is the backup frequency setting? How do you change it?
4. What does it mean if a field, menu option or tool on your input screen is dimmed?
5. Describe two ways to access the General Ledger record for an account.
6. How are the Earliest Transaction date and Session date different?
7. What does the Open History symbol on the Accounts icon indicate? How do you remove it?
8. What is the difference between postable and non-postable accounts?
9. How are Subgroup accounts different from Group accounts? Why is it important to use Subgroup accounts?
10. Why is it important to make a backup copy of your data files before you finish the history for the General Ledger?
11. What types of errors can prevent you from finishing the history? What kinds of errors might go undetected?
12. What does it mean if the Session date is July 10 and the Latest Transaction date is July 31?
13. Why is it helpful to create a separate "test balance" account? If you did not have this account, how could you determine whether your Trial Balance amounts were correct?
14. When might you use the feature of allowing future transactions? Can you foresee any problems with allowing future transactions? What controls might you want to place on the use of future transactions?

CHAPTER 3

GENERAL JOURNAL

Objectives

- *explain General Journal entry screen components*
- *distinguish between Session date and posting date*
- *complete General Journal transactions*
- *review, display and correct General Journal transactions*
- *store recurring entries*
- *adjust journal entries after posting*
- *advance the Session date*
- *complete additional entries for practice*
- *display and print General Ledger reports*

Introduction

Initially, Play Wave will not use the subsidiary ledgers (Payables, Receivables, Payroll and Inventory), and you will enter all accounting transactions in the General Journal. As the remaining ledgers are set up in the following chapters, you will make the transition to completing only adjusting entries in the General Journal.

If you have not completed the General Ledger setup in Chapter 2 or have history errors in your file, you can use your copy of the file from the Data Disk — Ch03\play\playch03 — to begin this chapter. You can check your work by printing the journal entries from the Data Disk files for later chapters.

PlayWave
Plus

The General Journal

The General Journal is modelled after the manual double-entry accounting system of entering debits and credits. For this reason, all types of transactions can be entered through the General Journal. Small businesses may choose to use only the General Ledger module of the program. This enables them to take advantage of many features of a computerized accounting software and still produce a variety of reports. When all the ledgers in the Simply Accounting program are used, the General Journal is used to record individual accounting transactions that cannot be recorded in any of the other journals. These are usually adjusting entries such as depreciation, adjustments for supplies used or for prepaid expenses that have expired, other accruals, bank loans and transactions involving capital accounts (investments, dividends, etc.). These transactions have a number of things in common. They do not involve customers, vendors or payments by cheque.

Adjusting Entries

Refer to the Basic Accounting supplement on the data CD for a more detailed review of basic accounting procedures and principles.

Adjusting entries always involve one balance sheet account and one income statement account. They are always recorded in the General Journal at the end of a period (month or quarter or year.) There may be no external document to trigger the transaction. For example, when a portion of the prepaid insurance expires, the accountant must make an entry to record the expense even though there is no document at that time to remind him or her. In other cases, there may be a document, such as for the physical count of supplies on hand at the end of the period to determine how much has been used. All adjusting entries fall into one of four categories.

Notice that all adjusting entries use accrual basis accounting and adhere to the recognition and matching principles.

1. **Prepaid expenses and Capital Expenditures**: When an expenditure is made for something that will extend beyond the accounting period, the purchase is initially recorded as an asset. When a portion of the asset has expired or been used, the portion used or expired must be recorded as an expense. This category includes prepaid expenses such as for insurance or rent, supplies used and depreciation. Depreciation is calculated only on fixed assets, capital expenditures, plant and equipment. Supplies are written off as expenses as the supplies are used.

    Machinery that is purchased and expected to last for 10 years is recorded with the following entry:

    | Mar. 1 | Machinery | 60 000 | |
    | | Accounts Payable | | 60 000 |

    One month's depreciation on this machinery would be $500 ($60 000/120 months) using the straight-line method of calculating depreciation. The adjusting journal entry records the depreciation:

    | Mar. 31 | Depreciation Expense | 500 | |
    | | Accum Depreciation: Machinery | | 500 |

    When rent is prepaid for six months at the rate of $1 400 per month, the initial journal entry to record the prepayment is:

    | Mar. 1 | Prepaid Rent | 8 400 | |
    | | Accounts Payable (or Bank Account) | | 8 400 |

    The following adjusting journal entry would be made at the end of each month for the six-month period of prepayment:

| Mar. 31 | Rent Expense | 1 400 | |
| | Prepaid Rent | | 1 400 |

The Accounts Receivable account is used in Simply Accounting to record the unearned revenue or advance so that the advance will become part of the customer's ledger account. This is explained further in Chapter 8.

2. **Unearned revenue**: Sometimes a business receives payment from customers before the work is completed or before the merchandise is delivered. Advances, deposits and down payments are common examples of this situation. Subscriptions also fall into this category because the goods will be delivered in the future but payment is made in advance. At the end of the period, the adjusting entry should show the amount of revenue that has been received but not yet earned. When a customer provides an advance, the advance is recorded as shown:

| Mar. 1 | Bank Account | 1 000 | |
| | Accounts Receivable (Unearned Revenue) | | 1 000 |

At the end of the period, if half of the work is completed, the adjusting entry is made:

| Mar. 31 | Accounts Receivable (Unearned Revenue) | 500 | |
| | Revenue | | 500 |

3. **Unrecorded expenses**: Regular payments for expenses do not often correspond with the timing of the reporting for the accounting period. For example, loan payments may be made on the 20th of each month while the last day of the month is the end of the accounting period. At the end of the month, 10 days of unpaid interest has accumulated. To match this expense with the period of revenue, an adjusting entry is required for the amount that is owing at the end of the month. Interest on loans and mortgages, and wages payable are common unrecorded expenses requiring end-of-period adjusting entries. For example, if monthly salaries amounting to $4 800 will be paid in the middle of January, the following adjusting entry is needed at the end of December before the business closes its books:

| Mar. 31 | Salaries Expense | 2 400 | |
| | Salaries Payable | | 2 400 |

4. **Unrecorded revenue**: The final category involves work that is partially completed at the end of the period but for which payment has not been received. For example, work projects are rarely completed exactly at the end of a period. If a contract for $6 000 is three-quarters finished at the end of the period, the completed portion represents earned revenue for the past period and must be recorded in an adjusting entry:

| Mar. 31 | Accounts Receivable | 4 500 | |
| | Revenue | | 4 500 |

Accessing the General Journal

The first transaction we must enter is the purchase of building supplies from The Buildex Corp. The following purchase invoice accompanied the goods received:

The Buildex Corp.			
Sold to: Play Wave Plus 7310 Recreation Court Megacity, ON M5E 1W6		**Date** March 16, 2002	**Invoice #** BC-456
Qty	**Item**	**Unit Price**	**Amount**
	Fibreglass & Plastics		$1 000 00
	Lumber		$1 000 00
		GST (7%)	$140 00
Terms: 2/10, net 30		**Amt due**	$2 140 00

◆ Open your working copy of the data files for Play Wave. You will see the Session
Date screen:

Session Dates, Transaction Dates and Posting Dates

The **Session date** refers to the date of your work session, the date that you are making the entries on the
computer. In this book, we will provide the Session date that you should enter. In an actual business setting,
you would enter the current or calendar date as the Session date. After you start making journal entries, and
advancing the Session date, the most recent Session date you entered will appear on this screen.

In Simply Accounting, there are several important dates. During setup, you entered the Fiscal Start and End
dates and the Earliest Transaction date. As the first Session date, the program enters the Earliest Transaction
date from your setup. When recording transactions, the Session date becomes the default date for all entries
and reports. You can and usually must change this default to enter the transaction date instead. The **transaction
date** is the date that the business transaction occurred. Journal entries are **posted** with the transaction date you
entered in the journal. You can enter a transaction date between the Earliest Transaction date and the Fiscal
End if you allow future transactions (see page 36).

The Session date for the first group of transactions is March 22, 2002. The previous
Session date is already highlighted for immediate editing. Although we always use
month followed by day in date entries, we show alternate formats for entering dates.

◆ Type **3-22-02**

◆ Click **OK**. (Close any other windows that may appear before the Home window.)

You will access the Home window for Play Wave:

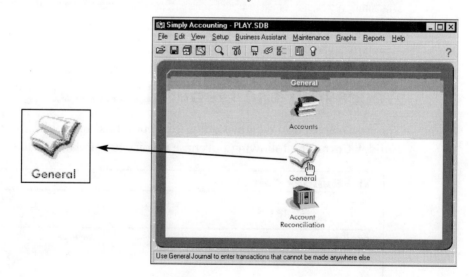

The Open History symbol no longer appears on the Accounts Ledger icon. The other
ledgers have not yet been set up, so their icons are hidden. You will set up all ledgers
in the following chapters. You are now ready to enter the General Journal
transaction.

Remember that in Chapter 2 we chose to open journals with a single click.

◆ Click the **General Journal icon** to open the General Journal input screen:

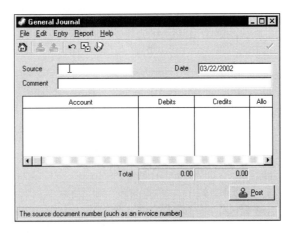

General Journal Window

The General Journal resembles a manual journal entry form with a wide single column for accounts in addition to the debit and credit columns. (The fourth column is used for allocating amounts to projects.) The journal has its own menu and tool bars with choices that are relevant to this journal. Hold the mouse briefly over each tool button, menu option and journal input field and read the status bar description to become familiar with the various fields and options. Dimmed tools and menu options are unavailable.

Journal Menu Options Found in All Simply Accounting Journals

File	Printer Setup	Choose printers and control printer settings.
	Print	Print a copy of the current entry, cheque or invoice.
	Bring the Home window to the front.	
Edit	Undo Entry	Delete the entire journal entry, but leave the journal window open.
	Cut	Remove selected text and place it on the Windows clipboard.
	Copy	Place a copy of the selected text on the clipboard without deleting the original text.
	Paste	Place a copy of the text from the clipboard at the cursor position. A copy remains in the clipboard until you cut or copy another selection of text to replace it.
	Insert Line	Add a blank line to the invoice above the selected line so you can add information.
	Remove Line	Delete the selected line on the current invoice or journal.
	Restore Window	Restore the size of the window to the preset, default size if it has been changed.
	Customize Journal	Remove fields that are not needed in journals.
Report	Display ... Journal Entry	Display the current journal entry.
Help	Contents	Display table of contents for help.
	... Journal	Display help information for the journal currently open.
	Advice	Display advice relevant to the journal that is open.

Menu Options Found Only in General Journal

Entry	Store	Save a copy of the current journal entry that will be repeated regularly.
	Recall	Bring to the screen the entry that you stored so that you can post it again for the new date without re-entering all the details.
	Adjusting Entry	Recall a posted entry and make corrections.
	Allocate	Divide amounts among different projects.
	Post	Save a permanent record of the transaction and update the ledger.

Tool Buttons in the General Journal

The tool buttons duplicate the menu options.

 Bring the Home window to the front.

 Store as recurring transaction (found in all journals except Account Reconciliation).

 Recall recurring transaction (found in all journals except Account Reconciliation).

 Undo current transaction (found in all journals).

 Customize journals by removing unused fields.

 Adjust previously posted entry (not found in Account Reconciliation, Adjustments and Item Assembly).

 Allocate amounts to projects (not found in Account Reconciliation and Item Assembly).

 Post (found in all journals).

General Journal Input Fields

Source: Source refers to the original reference number from the invoice or document you are using to record the transaction. The document may be an invoice, a cheque, a bank memo, an internal memo or some other form. Most of these have a reference number as part of the control information. In the first transaction, the purchase invoice number is the source document. You may use up to 13 characters in the Source field.

Date: In the Date field, you should enter the date on the invoice, memo or other source document — the date that the transaction occurred. This date becomes the posting date. The date format is the same as used earlier: month-day-year. The format shown on-screen is the format selected in your Windows Control Panel.

Comment: The descriptive comment you enter here becomes part of the permanent journal entry, making it easier to trace through historical information to check its accuracy. You can enter fairly detailed comments because the field allows up to 39 characters.

Account Column: The number and name of the account that is affected by the transaction. Each account may be used only once in a single General Journal entry. Only postable accounts may be selected.

Debits Column: The amount that is debited to the account on the same line. If the account is credited, the debit column remains blank.

Credits Column: The amount that is credited to the account on the same line. If the account is debited, the credit column remains blank.

Allo (Allocate) Column: If you allow allocations for an account, you may choose to allocate or distribute the amount for that account among projects or other divisions.

Total: The program calculates the total of all debit and credit amounts in the columns and shows the total in the Total fields. You cannot post an entry until the debits and credits have the same non-zero total.

Entering a General Journal Transaction

Now you can enter the source document shown on page 69. We show the transaction again here in summary form. This is the format we will use throughout most of the book for our source documents. In the Anderson Farm simulation in Chapter 20, all documents are shown in realistic source formats.

> ✔ Purchase Invoice #BC-456
> Dated Mar. 16/02
> From The Buildex Corp., $1 000 for fibreglass and $1 000 for lumber plus $140 GST
> paid. Invoice total $2 140. Terms: 2/10, n/30.

The checkmark (✔) in the source document check box indicates that we provide keystroke instructions for the transactions in the text that follows.

The cursor, the flashing line insertion point, is in the Source field.

◆ Type **BC-456**

◆ Press ⟨tab⟩ to complete the source entry, advance the cursor to the Date field and highlight the present contents, the Session date.

In the Date field, you should enter the date on the purchase invoice using the format month-day-year.

◆ Type **mar 16**

◆ Press ⟨tab⟩ to complete the date entry and advance to the Comment field.

◆ Type **Buildex purchase (terms: 2/10, n/30)**

◆ Press ⟨tab⟩ to move the cursor into the Account field.

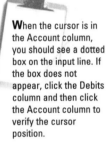

When the cursor is in the Account column, you should see a dotted box on the input line. If the box does not appear, click the Debits column and then click the Account column to verify the cursor position.

Finding the Correct Account

There are different ways of entering account information in this field. You may type the account number directly if you know it or from looking it up in the Chart of Accounts. Or you may use the program's Select Account feature to list the available postable accounts. Press ⟨enter⟩ or double click when the cursor is in the Account field to reach the Select Account list, the list of postable accounts. If you type the first digit of the account number, the list will advance to that section. A typical journal entry starts with the debit portion, so enter this part first. If you need to debit an expense account, type 5 to advance the list to the 5000 level accounts. You can access the Select Account list from all Simply Accounting journal entry Account fields in the same way.

◆ Type **1**

◆ Press ⟨enter⟩ to view the selection list. Notice that the list has 1080 highlighted because this is the first postable asset account beginning with 1:

We have deleted the Test Balance account.

◆ Click *1300 Supplies: Fibreglass & Plastics.* (This account should be in view.)

If you want to return to the journal without selecting an account, choose Cancel. To add the highlighted account to your journal form,

◆ Click **Select** or press (enter).

You will return to the journal form and the account number and name have been added. Check that you added the correct account. If you did not, click the incorrect account, press (enter) again to return to the Select Account list, and reselect.

The cursor is in the Debits column. (For a review of Debits and Credits refer to the Basic Accounting supplement on the data CD.) Enter the asset or expense portion (plus any PST paid on the purchase) for the purchase in this field. Amounts are entered the same way as you entered historical balances in the General Ledger setup. Do not type dollar signs. Do not type decimals for whole numbers.

◆ Type **1000**

◆ Press (tab) to advance to the next line in the account column. Your partially completed journal entry now looks like the one shown here:

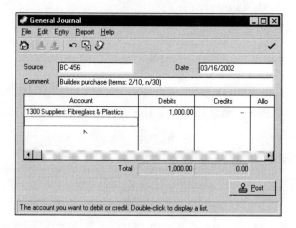

The next account is another asset account, *1320 Supplies: Lumber.*

◆ Double click to display the Select Account list.

You will notice that account 1300 is not included in the list displayed. Each account can be used only once in a single General Journal entry so 1300 cannot be selected again.

◆ Click *1320 Supplies: Lumber* to select it.

◆ Press (enter) or click Select.

The second account is added to the form and the program has advanced to the Credits column. By default, Simply Accounting will always enter an amount that will balance the amounts that you have entered already. A credit of $1 000 will balance the entry at this stage, but this is incorrect.

◆ Press (del) to remove the highlighted amount.

◆ Click **line 2 of the Debits column** (below 1,000.00), or press (shift) + (tab).

◆ Type **1000**

When a purchase includes PST, the PST amount is included directly as part of the asset cost or expense. PST paid on purchases is not refundable. Purchases of raw materials, inventory and equipment used in manufacturing are generally PST exempt.

The program will interpret 1000 and 1000.00 and 1000. in the same way, and will print 1,000.00 for all of them. If you type other characters in number fields, the program ignores them. The program does not print dollar signs in journal screens or reports.

◆ Press ⌗tab⌗ to advance to the third line in the account column.

The next account is a GST liability account, a 2000 level account.

◆ Type **2**

◆ Press ⌗enter⌗.

◆ Scroll down and then click *2670 GST Paid on Purchases* to highlight the account.

◆ Click **Select** or press ⌗enter⌗.

The GST account is added to the form and the program has advanced to the Credits column again. Because a credit of $2 000 will now balance the entry, the program enters this amount. Again we need another debit amount.

◆ Press ⌗del⌗ to remove the highlighted amount.

◆ Press ⌗shift⌗ + ⌗tab⌗ or click **line 3 in the Debits column**.

◆ Type **140**

◆ Press ⌗tab⌗ to enter the amount and advance to the next account line.

◆ Choose *2200 Accounts Payable* as the final account for this entry.

Notice that the credit amount now has changed to 2 140, because this will balance the entry. It is correct so you can accept it. The total in the Credits column is still zero.

◆ Press ⌗tab⌗ to accept the default credit amount and to update the totals.

Your completed entry should look like the following:

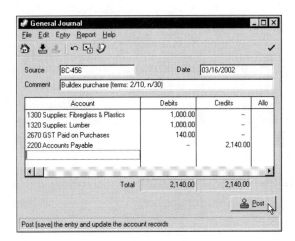

Notice that the Store, Undo and Post tool buttons are available (no longer dimmed) because the entry is complete and balanced.

The Recall tool is unavailable because there is no stored entry that can be recalled. Allocate is dim because no account is selected. As soon as you store an entry, the Recall tool is available for that journal. When you select a line with an account for which you have allowed allocations, the Allocate tool is available. Project distributions will be covered in Chapter 17. The Allo column refers to these distributions.

Before posting the entry to save it permanently, you should review the journal entry.

◆ Choose the **Report** menu and click **Display General Journal Entry** as shown:

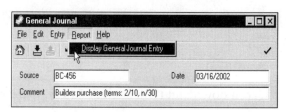

You will see the journal entry that will be posted if you make no further changes:

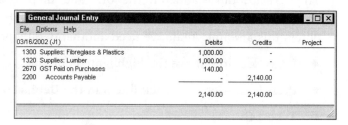

It is important to check the display carefully. If you post an entry that is incorrect, you cannot change it without making an adjusting entry.

◆ Click ⊠ to close the display window and return to the General Journal.

Making Corrections before Posting

It is important to make the corrections before posting the transaction. To correct an error in the Source, Date, Comment or Amount, highlight the incorrect information and type the correct information. Change an account number by double clicking it to reach the Select Account list. Click the correct account and press (enter). After making a change, press (tab) to ensure that the change is registered. Pressing (tab) will move you to the next field. Pressing (shift) and (tab) together will move you back to a previous field. Sometimes it may be easier to remove a complete line from the journal entry. To do this, click the line you want to remove. Then choose the Edit menu and click Remove Line. You can also delete the entire transaction by choosing the Edit menu and clicking Undo Entry (or click the Undo tool ⟲).

No Erasers Allowed!

The inability to change a posted entry is an important internal control feature of the Simply Accounting program. An accountant or bookkeeper is not allowed to change an entry after it is posted so that the auditor can state with reasonable certainty that the information has not been falsified.

Making Corrections after Posting

If you have posted a General Journal entry incorrectly, you must make a reversing entry to restore all balances to their pre-transaction balances. You can do this with the Simply Accounting Adjust Entry feature (see page 80). To do this manually, prepare a journal entry with an appropriate Source number and Comment to clearly identify the correcting entry. Use all the accounts that you used in the original incorrect entry, but switch the debits and credits. In other words, if you entered an amount as a credit in the original transaction, enter it as a debit in the correcting one. If the original was a debit, enter it as credit. Then complete a new journal entry with the correct information. (See Appendix D.)

◆ Make corrections if you find any errors.

Posting creates a permanent record of the accounting transaction.

◆ Click **Post** [🔨 Post] to save the entry.

A new blank journal form appears. Notice that the default date is now March 16, the date of your previous transaction. After you close and re-open the journal, the Session date becomes the default again.

◆ Now enter the following transaction in the General Journal.

☐ Sales Invoice #102
Dated Mar. 16/02
To Central Nursery Schools, $5 000 plus $350 GST charged for contract negotiated
in February. Invoice total for work completed is $5 350. No deposit was requested
because the owner is a personal friend. Terms: 2/10, n/30.

Adding New Accounts from a Journal

In the previous chapter, you learned to enter new accounts from the Accounts ledger.

Any time you need to add an account, you may do this through the General Ledger. From the General Journal,

Click the Home window tool [🏠] to return to the Home window.

Click the Accounts icon [Accounts] to open the Accounts window.

Click the Create tool [🗐] to access a new account ledger form.

The ledger window is the same as shown in Chapter 2, except that the Opening Balance field is unavailable. Once the Ledger history is finished, account balances can be changed only by making journal entries.

Sometimes, however, you may be part way through the journal entry when you realize that you need a new account. When this happens, you can add an account directly from the Journal, as illustrated in the following keystrokes.

The next transaction requires an account that is not yet in the Chart of Accounts.

☑ Cash Purchase Invoice #CIBC-22113
Dated Mar. 16/02
From CIBC Insurance, $1 200 for six-month insurance policy to cover business
premises. Issued cheque #101 in full payment.

☑ New account required: 1280 Prepaid Insurance (G)

◆ You should still be in the General Journal. Begin the journal entry by entering the Source, Date and Comment. Click the Account field to position the cursor.

Hint: Remember to display your journal entry to review it before you post. Your sales invoice should include the following entries: Accounts Receivable — 5,350 (Debit), GST Charged on Services — 350 (Credit), Revenue from Contracting — 5,000 (Credit).

◆ Double click the **Account field** to open the Select Account window as shown:

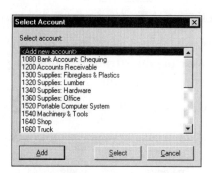

The first line on the account list is <Add new account> and an Add button appears below the list.

◆ Click **Add** (or click Add new account and click Select) to begin the Account Wizard:

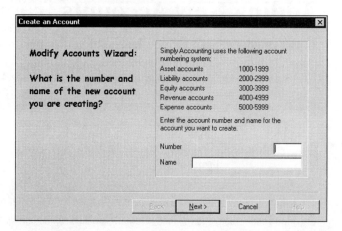

The Wizard walks you through the account creation with explanations about each part of the account information form. The first screen requires the account number and name. The cursor is in the Account Number field.

◆ Type **1280**

◆ Press ⟨*tab*⟩ to advance to the Account Name field.

◆ Type **Prepaid Insurance**

◆ Click **Next** to proceed to the next step. For the remaining Wizard screens, you may accept the default settings by clicking Next until you reach the final screen.

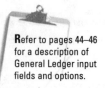

Refer to pages 44–46 for a description of General Ledger input fields and options.

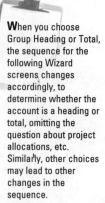

When you choose Group Heading or Total, the sequence for the following Wizard screens changes accordingly, to determine whether the account is a heading or total, omitting the question about project allocations, etc. Similarly, other choices may lead to other changes in the sequence.

Create an Account Wizard Screen Sequence

The Wizard screens cover all the input fields and options that are found in the Ledger screens.

Type the **Account Number** and **Name**. These fields must be completed.

Enter a **GIFI code** for filing electronic returns. This field may be left blank.

Is the account a **Heading or a Total**, that is, a non-postable account? The default selection is No, that is, defining it as a postable account, one whose balance is affected by processing entries. Usually you will be adding postable accounts while you are entering transactions. *Prepaid Insurance* is a postable account.

Choose the **type** of postable account. You would select Yes if the account is a Subgroup account and No if it is a Group account, not part of a subgroup. *Prepaid Insurance* is not part of a subgroup. The default is No to indicate a Group account.

Choose a **class option** for the account. In most cases, you can accept the default, the Section name.

Indicate whether you want to **allow project allocations** for the new account. For Revenue and Expense accounts, you should select Yes. For other accounts, leave the setting at No.

Decide whether you want to **omit the account from financial statements** if it has a zero balance. Click Yes to omit the account with a zero balance.

If you have selected Bank or Credit Card as the class option for a new account, you will see an additional setup screen asking whether you want to **set up the account for reconciliation** with bank statements. Account reconciliation is explained in Chapter 11.

The information you entered is summarized on the left. If you have made a mistake, click Back to return to a previous step, or click Cancel and begin again. The final screen allows you to check your work:

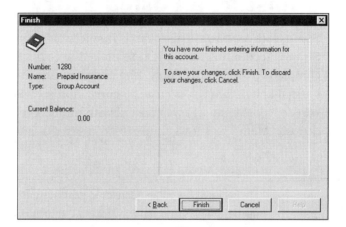

- Click **Finish** to save the new account and return to the General Journal. Notice that the new account is added to the journal form, but the cursor has not advanced, in case you want to choose a different account.

- Press (tab) to advance to the Debits column.

- Complete the journal entry by entering the debit amount and the credit portion of the transaction. Review your work carefully by displaying the journal entry. When you are certain that it is correct,

- Click **Post** [🖈 Post] .

- Enter the following transactions in the General Journal.

  ☐ Memo #1
  Date Mar. 17/02
  The bank statement for February included $10.50 in bank charges and $38.50 in interest earned resulting in a net deposit to Bank Account: Chequing of $28.00. Add two new Group accounts 5170 Bank Charges and 4250 Interest Revenue using the Add New Account Wizard.

You may also correct account information by editing the account in the General Ledger after you enter the account. Refer to page 84. Account numbers may not be changed once the account has been used in a journal transaction, so you should cancel (undo) the the transaction if you have made a mistake in the account.

☐ Sales Invoice #103
   Dated Mar. 19/02
   To Vindri Estates, $2 500 plus $175 GST charged for custom treehouse built on the estate. Invoice total $2 675. Terms: net 1 day.

☐ Cash Receipt #2
   Dated Mar. 20/02
   From Vindri Estates, cheque #147 for $2 675 in full payment of account. Reference invoice #103.

☐ Cash Purchase Invoice #VM-100
   Dated Mar. 21/02
   From Vincent Meade, $200 plus $14 GST paid for maintenance services rendered in shop and yard, and for inventory maintenance. Invoice total $214. Issued cheque #102 in full payment.

Adjusting a Posted Entry

Sometimes an error is discovered in a journal entry after the entry has been posted. Simply Accounting allows you to make the correction by adjusting the entry without completing a reversing entry. The program fills in the reversing and correcting journal entries after you post the correction so that the audit trail is complete. The bank entry (Memo #1) was posted with an incorrect amount for bank charges and net deposit. Memo #2 shows the correct information.

 Memo #2
   Date Mar. 21/02
   The bank charges on the February statement were $18.50 in bank charges, and the net deposit was $20. The entry for this transaction was posted incorrectly. The interest amount is correct. Adjust Memo #1 to make the correction.

The General Journal should still be open.

◆ Click the **Adjust a previously posted entry** tool (or choose the Entry menu and click Adjusting Entry) to open the Select Entry To Adjust screen:

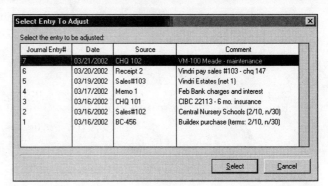

All journal entries are listed with the most recent one at the top of the list.

◆ Click **Memo 1** (Journal entry # 4) to select it.

◆ Click **Select** or press (enter) to open the journal entry as it was posted:

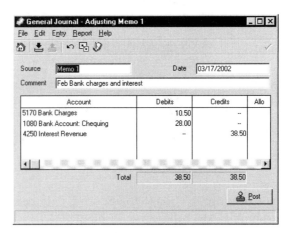

All fields may now be edited, just as if you have not yet posted the transaction.

◆ Click **10.50**, the amount in the Debit column for *Bank Charges* to select it for editing.

◆ Type **18.50** to correct the amount.

◆ Click **28.00**, the amount in the Debit column for *Bank: Chequing Account*.

◆ Type **20** to replace the incorrect amount.

◆ Press (tab) to update the totals.

We will also modify the source so that this entry is recognized as the correction for Memo #1.

◆ Click the **Source field** before the current entry (before the M in Memo 1).

◆ Type **(COR)**

◆ Review the entry to see the correct transaction and close the display.

◆ Make corrections if necessary.

◆ Click **Post** [🖈 Post].

When you review the General Journal, you will see three entries for the bank memo. The original incorrect entry, an adjusting entry created by the program (ADJMemo 1) and the correct entry (COR) Memo 1. Thus a complete audit trail exists for the transaction and the correction.

Changing the Session Date

When the transaction date falls after the Session date, you should advance the Session date to enter these later transactions. You must be in the Home window to change the Session date.

◆ Click ☒ to close the General Journal.

◆ Back up your data files.

◆ Click the **Change session date tool** 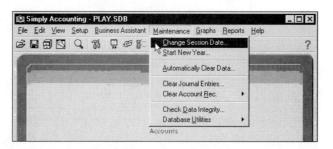 or choose the **Maintenance** menu and click **Change Session Date** as shown:

If you attempt to change the Session date before backing up your files, you may see a warning like the following:

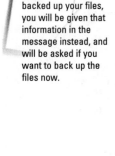
If you have never backed up your files, you will be given that information in the message instead, and will be asked if you want to back up the files now.

◆ Click **Yes** if you have not made a backup yet. You will go directly to the backup screen. If you choose not to make a backup at this time, click No.

The Change Session Date window appears with the current Session date highlighted, ready to be edited:

Although it is possible to move the Session date back, we will follow the conventional practice of only advancing the date.

◆ Type 03-30

◆ Click **OK**. This will allow you to enter transactions up to and including March 30.

Since you are advancing the Session date by more than one week you will see the following warning screen:

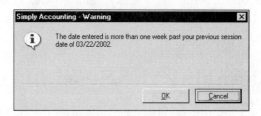

◆ Click **OK** to proceed if you have entered the correct date. If you have entered an incorrect date, click Cancel and type the date again.

After a brief delay, you will see the Checklists window:

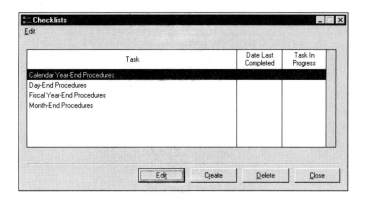

We will introduce the Checklists feature, and the following To-Do Lists window, in later chapters.

◆ Click Close to close the Checklists window and show the To-Do Lists window.

◆ Click Close to close the To-Do Lists window.

Since we will not use the Checklists and To-Do Lists in the next few chapters, we will turn them off. To avoid showing the lists each time you change the Session date,

◆ Choose the **View** menu, then choose **Checklists** and click **After Changing Session Date** to turn off the option.

◆ Choose the **View** menu, then choose **To-Do Lists** and click **After Changing Session Date** to turn off the option. To be sure that the checkmarks are removed, choose the View menu again and point to Checklists and then point to To-Do Lists.

You should be in the Home window again to enter the General Journal transaction.

◆ Enter the following transactions in the General Journal.

☐ Cheque Copy #103
Dated Mar. 23/02
To The Buildex Corp., $2 097.20 in full payment of account, including $42.80 purchase discount taken for early payment. Reference invoice #BC-456. Add the new account 5100 Purchase Discounts (G) using the Add New Account Wizard.

☐ Cash Purchase Invoice #OH-147211
Dated Mar. 24/02
From Ontario Hydro, $80 for hydro services plus $5.60 GST paid. Invoice total $85.60. Issued cheque #104 in full payment.

☐ Cash Purchase Invoice #BC-452941
Dated Mar. 24/02
From Bell Canada, $180 for installation and $60 for telephone services plus $16.80 GST paid and $19.20 PST paid. Invoice total $276. Issued cheque #105 in full payment. (The Telephone expense portion is $259.20 with PST included.)

◆ Close the General Journal to return to the Home window.

◆ Back up your work.

◆ Change the Session date to March 31, 2002.

◆ Create the following new accounts. They are needed for the remaining transactions for March. Allow project allocation for all postable Expense and Revenue accounts. (Click the Accounts icon in the Home window. Click the Create tool to open a new ledger form. Refer to pages 44–46 for a review if necessary.)

☐ 5050 Fibreglass & Plastics Used (G)
   5060 Lumber Used (G)
   5070 Hardware Used (G)
   5120 Depreciation: Computer (G)
   5130 Depreciation: Mach & Tools (G)
   5140 Depreciation: Shop (G)
   5150 Depreciation: Truck (G)
   5190 Insurance Expense (G)
   5210 Mortgage Interest Expense (G)
   5220 Office Supplies Used (G)
   5295 Contracted Payroll Expenses (G)

◆ Close the Ledger window after creating the last account. Leave the Accounts window open.

Editing Accounts

To record depreciation for the fixed assets at the end of the month, we want to show each asset as part of its own group with accumulated depreciation and followed by a subtotal showing the net book value of the asset. The assets are currently recorded as Group accounts. To make them part of a subgroup, we need to change the account type to Subgroup. The first asset to be edited is *1520 Portable Computer System*.

From the Accounts window,

◆ Click account *1520 Portable Computer System*.

◆ Click the **Edit** tool 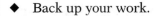 or choose the Edit menu and click Edit.

◆ Click **Subgroup Account** as the account type.

◆ Click the **Next account button** ▶ to find the next account you want to edit or choose the account from the Select account list.

◆ Now change the account type from Group to Subgroup for the following accounts.

☐ 1540 Machinery & Tools (A)
   1640 Shop (A)
   1660 Truck (A)

The next step is to create the accumulated depreciation account and Subgroup Total for each depreciable asset. By creating a separate subgroup for each type of plant and equipment, the Balance Sheet will show both net and undepreciated amounts for each item.

◆ Click the **Create** tool 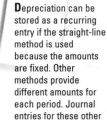 in any ledger window or in the Accounts window to add the following new accounts.

☐ 1530 Accum Deprec: Computer (A)
1535 Net Computer (S)
1550 Accum Deprec: Mach & Tools (A)
1555 Net Mach & Tools (S)
1650 Accum Deprec: Shop (A)
1655 Net Shop (S)
1670 Accum Deprec: Truck (A)
1675 Net Truck (S)

If you see a message that the accounts are not in logical order, you have made an error in one of the account numbers or types. Correct your errors before continuing.

◆ Close the Ledger window and the Accounts window. Display the Chart of Accounts to check that you have made the changes correctly. Open the General Journal and continue entering the remaining transactions for March.

☐ Cash Purchase Invoice #CC-69
Dated Mar. 31/02
From Casual Contractors, $1 600 for subcontracted payroll expenses for the MegaCity Parks and Recreation project. Issued cheque #106 in payment.

☐ Cash Receipt #3
Dated Mar. 31/02
From Central Nursery Schools, cheque #121 for $5 350 in full payment of account. Reference invoice #102.

☐ Bank Debit Memo #632147
Dated Mar. 31/02
From Royal Trust, $2 000 preauthorized withdrawal for mortgage payment. This amount consists of $1 900 interest and $100 for reduction of principal.

☐ Memo #3
Dated Mar. 31/02
Based on the end-of-the-month count of supplies remaining, it was determined that the following quantities of supplies were used during March. Make the necessary adjusting entry to account for the supplies used.

Fibreglass & Plastics	$2 500
Lumber	$2 500
Hardware	$1 500
Office Supplies	$100

Recurring Transactions

Frequently a business repeats the same transaction on a regular basis. For example, insurance payments may be made through automatic monthly withdrawals, supplies may be purchased weekly with a standing order, rent is paid monthly, and so on. Simply Accounting permits you to store these repeating entries and then recall them as needed to save the time required to re-enter the complete transaction. The

Depreciation can be stored as a recurring entry if the straight-line method is used because the amounts are fixed. Other methods provide different amounts for each period. Journal entries for these other methods should not be stored as recurring entries.

adjusting entry for prepaid insurance that has expired is a recurring monthly entry. By setting up the transaction as a recurring entry, you will enter it once and recall it each month afterwards. You will then not need to enter it from scratch each time.

◆ Complete the following journal entry as usual but **DO NOT POST IT**.

> Memo #4
>
> Dated Mar. 31/02
>
> One month of prepaid insurance, $200, has expired. Prepare an adjusting entry to debit Insurance Expense and credit Prepaid Insurance for this amount. Since this entry will be repeated at the end of each month, store it as a recurring monthly entry.

Keystrokes for Recurring Transactions

Once the transaction is correct and ready for posting (do not post it yet),

You must store a transaction before you post it!

◆ Click the **Store as recurring entry transaction** tool 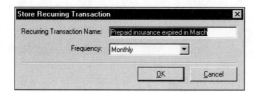 to open the Store Recurring Transaction screen:

We want to make the name of the entry generic by removing the reference to March. In the selected Recurring Transaction Name field,

◆ Type **Prepaid insurance expired** (or delete the words "in March").

Monthly, the frequency selected by default, is correct in this case.

> Several **frequency periods** are available for the entry. You can see the options by clicking Monthly (the Frequency field) or its arrow. Then click the period you need. The frequency options are: Random (the Session date is used for the transaction because it recurs on an irregular basis), Weekly, Bi-Weekly (every 2 weeks or 14 days), Semi-Monthly (twice per month), Monthly, 13-period (every 4 weeks), Bi-Monthly (every 2 months), Quarterly (every 3 months), Semi-Annually (every 6 months) and Annually.

◆ Click **OK** to save the entry and return to the General Journal.

The only change in the General Journal now is that the Recall tool is not dimmed. You can now post the entry.

◆ Click the **Post** tool ⌞ 🔒 Post ⌟ .

◆ Click the **Recall recurring transaction tool** 🔼 to see the Recall Recurring Transaction screen:

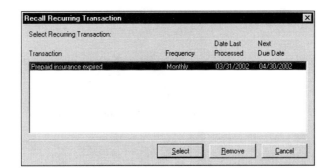

The transaction we stored is listed with its next due date in the right-hand column, exactly one month past the previous date for the transaction. When we recall it at the end of April, the date will be correctly entered. From this screen, you may select an entry that you have stored, remove an entry that is no longer required or cancel to return to the General Journal without choosing the transaction.

◆ Click **Cancel** to return to the General Journal.

◆ Enter the remaining transaction to record depreciation for March using the straight-line method in the General Journal and store the entry to recur monthly.

Depreciation is calculated on a straight-line basis from the following asset values. The computer system has a three-year life expectancy and $300 scrap value. Machinery & Tools are expected to last for five years and have a scrap value of $500. The Shop has a 30-year life expectancy and a scrap value of $10 000. The Truck will last for five years. Its scrap value is $6 000.

☐ Memo #5
Dated Mar. 31/02
Depreciation is calculated and recorded monthly for all depreciable assets. Prepare the adjusting depreciation entry to record the following depreciation amounts:

Portable Computer System	$75
Machinery & Tools	$125
Shop	$250
Truck	$400

Since the depreciation is calculated at a fixed straight-line rate, this entry will be repeated at the end of each month. Store it as recurring monthly entry then post it.

◆ Close the General Journal.

General Ledger Reports

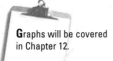

Graphs will be covered in Chapter 12.

You can display all the reports described below from either the Home window or from the Accounts window.

General Journal Report

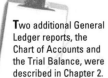

Two additional General Ledger reports, the Chart of Accounts and the Trial Balance, were described in Chapter 2.

The General Journal Report lists the journal entries in full detail for the requested period. The General Journal provides an audit trail, a detailed record of journal entries that can be checked for accuracy by an independent auditor.

You should be in the Home window.

◆ Choose the **Reports** menu, then choose **Journal Entries** and click **General** as shown:

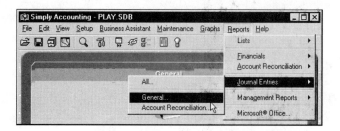

You will see the General Journal Options screen:

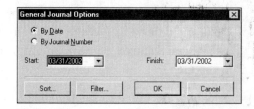

The **Journal options** are quite simple. You must select whether to report the journal transactions by the posting date or by the journal number. The Simply Accounting program assigns a number, in sequence, to each journal entry you post. When you choose to report by number, journal numbers replace the Start and Finish date fields. The Session date is the default for both dates and the By Date option is selected initially.

For the dates, you may type in the first and last posting date that you want to include in the report or you may select one of the dates in the drop-down lists. Any dates between the ones in the list, the Earliest Transaction date and the Session date are valid dates for the report.

You can sort and filter the report by date, journal entry number, source or comment.

The Start date is selected so that you may edit it immediately.

◆ Type **03-15-02**

◆ Press ⌨*(tab)* to advance to the Finish field if you need to change it. Normally you would accept the Session date as the Finish date unless there are postdated entries.

◆ Type **03-31-02**

◆ Click **OK** to display all the transactions you have entered as shown here:

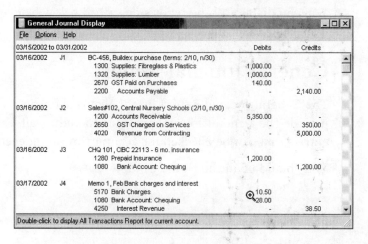

When you postdate journal entries, the Latest Transaction date will be the last date on the drop-down list of dates for all reports.

You can see that the journal includes all the details you entered in the General Journal input screen, along with the journal entry number assigned by the program.

Drill-Down Reports

You will see the cursor change to a magnifying glass  as you move the mouse over various details in a displayed report. This symbol indicates that a secondary, or drill-down, report is available directly at this stage. The status bar tells you what secondary or drill-down report you can access. When you pass over an account name or its balance, you can access the General Ledger (All Transactions) report for that account. If the cursor is over a name, you can access the corresponding vendor, customer or employee report, if there is one. Once you are in the second level of the report, you can drill-down further to additional reports if they are available. When you close the drill-down report, you will return to the previous report.

◆ Double click *1200 Accounts Receivable* in the second journal entry. You will see the General Ledger or All Transactions report for the account.

◆ Choose the **File** menu and click **Print** to print the General Ledger report.

◆ Close the General Ledger Display to return to the General Journal report.

◆ Choose the **File** menu and click **Print** to print the General Journal report.

Once you have displayed any report, you may print it from the File menu as explained in Chapter 2. You may also export the report as explained in Appendix F.

Filtering Reports

Sometimes you want to see only a portion of a report. You can use the report sorting and filtering options to vary the final report. You can access the sort and filter options from the opening report options screen by clicking the appropriate button. You can also sort or filter the report after displaying it. We will filter the report to show only the transactions for the bank charges and the corrections. All these entries were posted on March 17, so we can use that as the selection criterion.

◆ Choose the **Options** menu and click **Filtering** to see the Report Filter window:

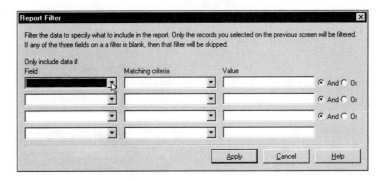

Journal reports may be sorted or filtered according to date, journal number, source and comment. You can filter by several fields or just one. The criteria are combined using the normal logic meanings for And and Or. Use And when both criteria must be satisfied, and use Or when either one must be met to add the item to the report. We will use the Date as the criterion.

◆ Click the first **Field list arrow**.

◆ Click **Date**.

◆ Click the first **Matching criteria list arrow**.

◆ Click **Is equal to**.

- ◆ Click the first **Value field**.

- ◆ Type `3-17-02`

- ◆ Click **Apply** to display the report with only three bank-related journal entries.

The filter options remain in effect until you reset them, so we will restore the original values.

- ◆ Choose the **Options** menu and click **Filtering** again. To remove a filter, you must replace the field entries with blanks.

- ◆ From the **Date** list, choose the **Blank entry** (the top entry on the list).

- ◆ From the **Matching criteria** list, choose the **Blank entry**.

- ◆ Double click **2002/3/17**, the date in the Value field, and press *del*.

- ◆ Click **Apply** to see the normal journal display.

Sorting Reports

Sorting allows you to change the order of the information in a report by applying your own sorting criteria.

- ◆ Choose the **Options** menu and click **Sorting** to open the Sort Report window:

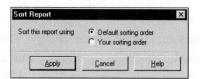

- ◆ Click **Your sorting order** to expand the window and see the sorting options.

- ◆ Click the **first Sort by list arrow** to see the sorting options for the Journal report:

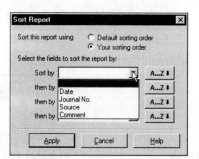

We will display the report in reverse order from the most recent journal entry to the earliest.

- ◆ Click **Journal No.**

- ◆ Click **A...Z**. This button acts as a switch and the label changes to Z...A to indicate that the order is reversed.

- ◆ Click **Apply** to see the journal displayed in reverse order.

- ◆ Choose the Options menu and **Sorting** again so that you can restore the default selection.

◆ Click **Default sorting order**. This will leave the sorting criteria we selected available until we delete the entries as we did for the filter. However, the sort will not apply because we have chosen the default.

◆ Click **Apply** to restore the report.

◆ Close the General Journal Display to return to the Home window.

Accessing the General Journal Report

There are four other methods of accessing the General Journal report:

- Click the Accounts icon in the Home window to open the Accounts window.
  Choose the Reports menu and click Display General Journal in the Accounts window.

- Click the Accounts icon in the Home window to access the Accounts window.

  Click the Select a report tool  in the Accounts window.

  Choose Display General Journal from the list. Click Select or press (enter).

- Click the Display tool  in the Home window.

  Choose General Journal from the list. Press (enter).

- Right-click the General Journal icon in the Home window to select it.

  Click the Display General Journal tool  to open the report options screen. The name of the tool changes to correspond to the selected icon.

The General Journal for individual transactions is also available as a drill-down report from several other displayed reports. You should routinely point the mouse across any report on-screen. Then see which secondary reports are available by reading the status line information.

Balance Sheet

You can also view the Balance Sheet and all other General Ledger reports from the Reports menu or the Select a Report tool in the Accounts window.

The Balance Sheet describes the financial position of a business at a specific point in time. The Balance Sheet may be prepared for any date between the Earliest Transaction date and the Latest Transaction date.

From the Home window,

◆ Choose the **Reports** menu, then choose **Financials** and click **Balance Sheet** to display the report options:

The Sort and Filter options are available for many reports. The procedure for using these options is the same for all reports. However, you cannot sort or filter any of the financial statement reports.

Balance Sheet Options

Report Type: ☐ Comparative Balance Sheet

As at: [03/31/2002 ▾]

[Sort...] [Filter...] [OK] [Cancel]

At this stage you can choose to display the Balance Sheet at a single point in time or to display two Balance Sheets simultaneously so that they can be compared. The date field drop-down list shows the earliest and latest dates that you can choose.

◆ Click **Comparative Balance Sheet** to expand the report options:

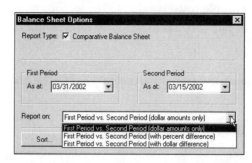

Now there are two date fields for the two Balance Sheets — the Earliest Transaction date and the Session date — and a drop-down list of comparative items to report on. The Report on list has been expanded in the screen above.

◆ Edit the date in either date field if necessary (03-31-2002 and 03-15-2002 are the dates required).

◆ Click the **Report on field** or its arrow to show the three comparison options as illustrated in the preceding screen.

◆ Click **First Period vs. Second Period (with percent difference)**.

◆ Click **OK** to display the report.

The report has the amounts for two Balance Sheets for the dates we entered, as well as an additional column that calculates the difference between them as the percentage change from the earlier (second) to the later (first) period.

Comparative Report Types

The three reports provide different ways of comparing the two Balance Sheets. **First Period vs. Second Period (dollar amounts only)**, the first option, shows only the actual dollar balance amounts for both dates. No additional calculations are included. **First Period vs. Second Period (with percent difference),** the second type, shows the dollar balance amounts for both dates as well as the percentage change from the earlier to the later period. The percentage is calculated using the formula

$$\frac{(Period\ One - Period\ Two)}{Period\ Two} \times 100\%$$

Positive percentages indicate that the balance amounts have increased, negative percentages indicate decreases. **First Period vs. Second Period (with dollar difference)**, the final option, again provides the dollar balance amounts but also calculates the change from period two to period one as a dollar amount only (Period One – Period Two).

The additional information from the comparative reports allows a business to assess its performance over time.

Drill-Down Reports

To view the General Ledger (All Transactions) report for any account on the Balance Sheet, double click the account name or its balance amount. Closing the drill-down report will return you to the previous report.

◆ Choose the **File** menu and click **Print** to print the report.

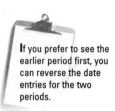

If you prefer to see the earlier period first, you can reverse the date entries for the two periods.

◆ Close the display when you are finished.

Income Statement

The Income Statement describes the change in financial position of a business over a period of time. In Simply Accounting, you can display the Income Statement for any period between the Fiscal Start date and the Latest Transaction date. The program automatically calculates Net Income as the difference between Revenue and Expenses.

From the Home window,

◆ Choose the **Reports** menu, then choose **Financials** and click **Income Statement** to see the Income Statement report options:

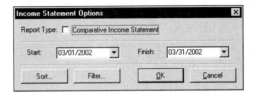

◆ Click **Comparative Income Statement** to see the expanded options. There are now two sets of Start and Finish dates, one set for each Income Statement.

◆ Click the **Report on field** to see the list:

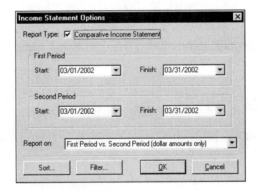

The comparative report types are the same as those described for the Balance Sheet. They permit a business to assess whether it performed better or worse in one period relative to the other. Since we have only one month of transactions, we will report only the single Income Statement.

◆ Click **Comparative Income Statement** again to close the Comparative Report Options and return to the single statement options.

The dates are correct, the beginning of the fiscal period is the default Start date and the latest Session date is the Finish date. If you need to change a date, you can click the default date and type in the date you want.

◆ Click **OK** to see the report.

Drill-Down Reports

To view the General Ledger report for any account on the Income Statement, double click the account name or its balance amount. When you close the drill-down report, you will return to the previous report.

◆ Choose the **File** menu and click **Print** to print the report.

◆ Close the display when you have finished printing and viewing the report.

Trial Balance

The Trial Balance report shows all postable accounts with their dollar amounts as either a debit or credit balance. Both Balance Sheet and Income Statement accounts are included. The Trial Balance is usually prepared before closing the books at the end of a fiscal period because it shows the amounts that will be transferred from the revenue and expense accounts to the capital account (retained earnings). Simply Accounting can display the Trial Balance for any date between the Earliest Transaction date and the Latest Transction date. Refer to page 53 for instructions on displaying the Trial Balance.

Cash Flow Projection

The Cash Flow Projection offers a projection of cash flow for the requested future period based on recurring entries, payment commitments and customer receipts expected according to the payment terms for purchases and sales that have already been made. It does not include other sources such as cash purchases and sales or future purchases and sales. Since this statement will be more relevant once you begin to use the Payables and Receivables ledgers, we will delay its introduction.

General Ledger Report

The General Ledger report may be prepared for one or more postable accounts. The report includes the opening balance and any journal entries posted to the account as well as the closing balance for the period selected for the reports.

From the Home window,

◆ Choose the **Reports** menu, then choose **Financials** and click **General Ledger** to see the report options:

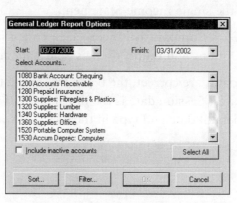

Inactive accounts, as defined in the ledger records, may be included in reports by clicking the option to include them. By default, they are omitted from reports.

◆ Type **03-15-02** in the Start date field to replace the highlighted default Session date.

The Finish date, the current Session date, is correct, so you can leave it.

◆ Press ⌃ and click the following accounts. Each one will remain highlighted:
1080 Bank Account: Chequing
1280 Prepaid Insurance
2650 GST Charged on Services
2670 GST Paid on Purchases
4020 Revenue from Contracting

If you select an account incorrectly, press ⌃ and click it again to deselect it. To select all accounts at once, click Select All.

◆ Click **OK** to view the report.

Drill-Down Reports

If the cursor is over a date or a name in the comment portion of the journal entry, you can double click to access the corresponding vendor, customer or employee report, if there is one. Double click any other detail to see the journal entry for the transaction. When you close the drill-down report, you will return to the previous report.

◆ Choose the **File** menu and click **Print** to print the report.

◆ Close the display when you have finished printing and viewing the report.

◆ Close the Play Wave data file.

Practice: Live Links

For the first month, all journal transactions are entered in the General Journal. GST only and no PST is charged on workshops and training. Both GST and PST are charged on other services. The PST rate in British Columbia is 7 percent. The GST rate is 7 percent.

General Journal Entries
Instructions

If you have not completed the General Ledger setup in Chapter 2 or have history errors in your file, you can use your copy of the file from the Data Disk — Ch03\links\linkch03 — to continue this chapter. You can check your work by printing the journal entries from the files for later chapters.

1. Open the data file for Live Links.

2. Enter **July 15, 2002,** as the first Session date.

3. Turn off the Checklists and To-Do Lists from the View menu in the Home window.

4. Complete the following transactions for Live Links for the month of July. You may choose to enter new accounts from the Accounts Ledger or from the General Journal window.

☐ New accounts required: 1300 Prepaid Rent (G)
                            1620 DLP Projection Unit (G)
                            5020 Bank Charges (G)
                            5070 Loss on Sale of LCD Projector (G)

☐ Sales Invoice #102
Dated July 9/02
To Prolegal Services Inc., $2 000 plus $140 GST charged and $140 PST charged for data recovery services. Invoice total $2 280. Terms: net 30 days.

☐ Cash Purchase Invoice #MR-0206
Dated July 9/02
To Massey Realty, Landlord, $6 000 plus $420 GST paid for rent on business premises prepaid for six months. Invoice total $6 420. Issued cheque #10 in full payment.

☐ Purchase Invoice #2345
Dated July 10/02
From Visual Technologies, $4 800 plus $336 GST paid for new digital light projector (DLP) with 500 ANSI lumens and true SVGA. Invoice total $5 136. Terms: n/10 days.

☐ Bank Credit Memo #346792
Dated July 10/02
From The Learnx Bank, a three-month demand loan for $6 000 at 10 percent interest. Loan and interest payable at the expiration of the loan period.

☐ Bank Debit Memo #432714
Dated July 10/02
From The Learnx Bank, $20 for bank charges for bank services required for June (previous month).

☐ Sales Invoice #103
Dated July 11/02
To Prince College, $1 500 plus $105 GST charged for workshops presented. Invoice total $1 605. Terms: payment on completion of workshop.

☐ Cash Receipt #1
Dated July 11/02
From Prince College, cheque #4622 for $1 605 in full payment of account. Reference invoice #103.

☐ Cheque Copy #11
Dated July 12/02
To Visual Technologies, $5 136 in full payment of account. Reference invoice #2345.

☐ Sales Invoice #104

Dated July 13/02

To Elsie Cordeiro, $1 000 plus $70 GST charged and $70 PST charged for old LCD Projection Unit. Invoice total $1 140. Terms: cash on receipt. Since the old projector had a book value of $1 200, you must recognize $200 as the loss on the sale.

☐ **Advance the Session date to July 22, 2002**

☐ Cash Receipt #2

Dated July 16/02

From Elsie Cordeiro, cheque #212 for $1 140 in full payment of account. Reference invoice #104.

☐ Cheque Copy #13

Dated July 17/02

To Helen Lively, $100 for personal use. (Cheque #12 was damaged and voided.)

☐ Cash Purchase Invoice #BD-5524

Dated July 19/02

From Business Depot, $100 plus $7 GST paid and $7 PST paid for office supplies. Invoice total $114. Issued cheque #14 for $114 in full payment. (Remember to add the PST paid to the asset portion of the journal entry.)

☐ **Advance the Session date to July 29, 2002**

☐ Cash Receipt #3

Dated July 26/02

From Prolegal Services, cheque #821 for $2 280 in full payment of account. Reference invoice #102.

☐ Cash Purchase Invoice #PU-1142

Dated July 28/02

From Promo Uno, $60 plus $4.20 GST paid and $4.20 PST paid for advertising flyers. Invoice total $68.40. Issued cheque #15 in full payment.

☐ Cash Purchase Invoice #34214

Dated July 28/02

From Petro Partners, $200 plus $14 GST paid and $14 PST paid for vehicle maintenance services. Invoice total $228. Issued cheque #16 in full payment.

☐ Cash Purchase Invoice #BCT-1131

Dated July 28/02

From BC Telephone, $80 plus $5.60 GST paid and $5.60 PST paid for telephone services. Invoice total $91.20. Issued cheque #17 in full payment.

Remember to add the amount for PST paid to the expense portion of the journal entry.

☐ Cash Purchase Invoice #BCH-1421

Dated July 28/02

From BC Hydro, $50 plus $3.50 GST paid (no PST paid) for hydro services. Invoice total $53.50. Issued cheque #18 in full payment.

☐ Cash Sales Invoice #105

Dated July 28/02

To Metro Credit Union, $1 500 plus $105 GST charged for in-service training (workshops). Invoice total $1 605. Received cheque #4102 for $1 605 in full payment on completion of workshop.

☐ **Advance the Session date to July 31, 2002**

☐ Edit these asset accounts. Change the account type from Group account (G) to Subgroup account (A) to prepare for adding Accumulated Depreciation accounts and Subgroup Totals.

> 1520 Computers & Peripherals
> 1540 Custom Tools
> 1560 Data Recovery Equipment
> 1580 Duplication Equipment
> 1620 DLP Projection Unit
> 1680 Motor Vehicle

☐ New accounts required for depreciation entries and end-of-month adjustments. Allow project allocations for all new expense accounts:

> 2220 Interest Payable (G)
> 5290 Payroll Services (G)
> 5060 Interest Expense (G)
> 5072 Depreciation: Computers (G)
> 5074 Depreciation: Custom Tools (G)
> 5076 Depreciation: Data Recovery Equip (G)
>
> 5078 Depreciation: Duplication Equipment (G)
> 5080 Depreciation: DLP Projection Unit (G)
> 5082 Depreciation: Motor Vehicle (G)
> 5090 Supplies Expense: Computer (G)
> 5092 Supplies Expense: Office (G)
> 5094 Memory Chips Used (G)
>
> 5098 Rent Expense (G)
> 1530 Accum Deprec: Comp & Peri (A)
> 1535 Net Computers & Peripherals (S)
> 1550 Accum Deprec: Custom Tools (A)
> 1555 Net Custom Tools (S)
> 1570 Accum Deprec: Data Recovery Equip (A)
> 1575 Net Data Recovery Equip (S)

Be careful to distinguish between the new account DLP Projection Unit and the old account LCD Projection Unit when you are making journal entries.

1590 Accum Deprec: Duplication Equip (A)
1595 Net Duplication Equipment (S)
1630 Accum Deprec: DLP Projection Unit (A)
1635 Net DLP Projection Unit (S)
1690 Accum Deprec: Motor Vehicle (A)
1695 Net Motor Vehicle (S)

☐ Bank Debit Memo #452142

Dated July 30/02

From Learnx Bank, monthly payroll and payroll services for administrative assistant.

Wages	$3 000.00
Payroll Services fee	40.00
GST Paid @ 7%	2.80
Total	$3 042.80

Amount withdrawn from bank account as authorized by contract #3322888.
Store as recurring monthly entry.

☐ Memo #1

Dated July 31/02

Based on the end-of-the-month count of supplies remaining, it was determined that the following quantities of supplies were used during July. Make the necessary adjusting entry to account for the supplies used.

Office Supplies	$200
Computer Supplies	$100
Memory Chips	$600

☐ Memo #2

Dated July 31/02

One month of prepaid rent, $1 000, has expired. Prepare an adjusting entry to debit the Rent Expense account for this amount. Since this entry will be repeated at the end of each month, store it as a recurring monthly entry.

☐ Memo #3

Dated July 31/02

Although the bank loan interest will not be paid until the end of the loan period, one month's interest expense has accrued and should be recognized. Prepare an adjusting entry to recognize $50 as Interest Payable for the month of July. Store this entry as a recurring monthly entry because the entry will be repeated until the loan is repaid.

☐ Memo #4

Dated July 31/02

Depreciation is calculated and recorded monthly for all depreciable assets. Prepare the adjusting depreciation entry to record the following depreciation amounts*:

Computers & Peripherals	$150
Custom Tools	$50
Data Recovery Equipment	$200
Duplication Equipment	$100
DLP Projection Unit	$125
Motor Vehicle	$500

Since the depreciation is calculated at a fixed rate using the straight-line method, this entry will be repeated at the end of each month. Store it as a recurring monthly entry.

*Depreciation Information for Equipment

Computers & Peripherals: purchased for $5 600, depreciated over 3 years, scrap value $200

Custom Tools: purchased for $1 200, depreciated over 2 years, scrap value $0

Data Recovery Equipment: purchased for $7 500, depreciated over 3 years, scrap value $300

Duplication Equipment: purchased for $4 000, depreciated over 3 years, scrap value $400

DLP Projection Unit: purchased for $4 800, depreciated over 3 years, scrap value $300

Motor Vehicle: purchased for $32 000, depreciated over 5 years, scrap value $2 000

5. Close the General Journal and print the following reports to check your work:

General Journal for July 8 to July 31, 2002
Balance Sheet as at July 31, 2002
Income Statement for July (July 1 to July 31, 2002)
Trial Balance as at July 31, 2002

6. Close the Simply Accounting program.

Review Questions

1. How is the posting date different from the Session date?
2. How does Simply Accounting help provide a complete audit trail?
3. Why would you not enter adjustments for supplies used as recurring transactions?
4. What are some of the advantages of entering transactions in Simply Accounting over using a manual accounting approach? Are there any disadvantages?
5. Describe two methods of creating new accounts once the General Ledger history is finished.
6. What are the limits on entering new Session dates? On entering Transaction dates?
7. What date appears as the default in journals? In reports?
8. How is a General Journal entry in Simply Accounting different from a manual accounting journal entry?
9. Describe the procedure for correcting a journal entry after posting.
10. What does it mean if the Post tool button (or menu option) is dim?

CHAPTER 4

PAYABLES LEDGER SETUP

Objectives

- **explain the components of the Payables Ledger entry screens**
- **enter settings for the Payables Ledger**
- **set up a bank account for cheque numbering sequence**
- **understand and identify Payables Ledger linked accounts**
- **enter address information and payment terms for vendors**
- **enter historical invoices and payments for vendors**
- **enter additional vendors for practice**
- **display and print Payables Ledger reports**
- **finish Payables Ledger history**

Introduction

Play Wave Plus will now begin to use the Payables Ledger, recognizing that journal entries will be easier and that the continual ledger updates will provide useful management information. In this chapter, you will set up the Accounts Payable Ledger — the ledger that deals with the vendors or suppliers. This involves changing the settings for the Payables Ledger, identifying the accounts that link the Payables entries to the appropriate General Ledger accounts, creating the vendor account ledgers, and adding the historical purchase information for vendors with outstanding invoices. The *Accounts Payable* control account connects the Payables and General Ledgers — it shows the total owing to all vendors and this balance is divided among the individual vendor accounts.

If you have not completed the journal transactions in Chapter 3 and want to continue working on Chapter 4, you can use your copy of the file from the Data Disk — Ch04\play\ playch04 — to begin this chapter.

The Accounts Payable Ledger

The Payables Ledger contains all the information about individual vendors and suppliers. Information cannot be entered in the Payables Ledger separately from the General Ledger because the ledgers work in a linked or integrated manner. In a manual accounting system, the Payables Ledger, a subsidiary ledger, is separate from the General Ledger. Essentially you need to enter information twice, once in the General Ledger and then again in the Payables Ledger. In large companies, these steps are often completed by separate people or departments. The accountant makes the regular General Journal entries and then the payables clerk adds the invoice details to the individual vendor records and also records the payments made. Because the ledgers in Simply Accounting are integrated, making journal entries in one ledger directly updates the others through the linked accounts, without the need to enter the information twice.

Changing Default Settings
Payables Ledger Settings

In the same way that you defined the default settings for the System and General Ledger, you must enter defaults for the Payables Ledger.

◆ Start the Simply Accounting program and open your working copy of the Play Wave Plus data set.

◆ Click **OK** to accept March 31, 2002, as the Session date.

You should be in the Home window. Before setting up the Payables Ledger, we must restore its icons.

If the To-Do List and Checklist appear, close these windows. Turn off the lists from the View menu. (See page 83.)

◆ Choose the **View menu**, then choose **Modules** and click **Payables.** The Home window now has icons for the two ledgers we are using:

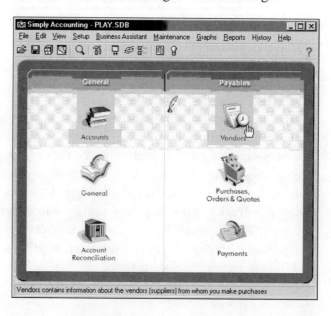

◆ Click the **Setup tool** button  to display the Select Setup screen:

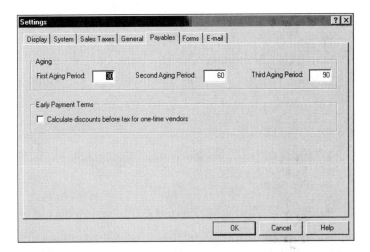

◆ Click **Vendors** from the drop-down list.

◆ Click **Select** to display the Payables Settings options:

Accessing Payables Settings

There are other ways to access the Payables Settings screen from the Home window:

• Choose the Setup menu and click Settings and then click the Payables tab.

• Right-click the Vendors icon. Then click the Setup tool button or choose the Setup menu and click Settings.

Payables Settings

The first Payables Settings option refers to **Aging** periods. These settings will be used to age the accounts in your payables reports and graphs. The default settings are 30, 60 and 90 days because these are commonly used in business. Usually you would select periods that fit most of your vendors' payment terms. If vendors expect net payment in 15 days, and charge interest on accounts over 30 days, you would want to enter these periods to help monitor your payments due and to manage your cash flow. If some offer a discount for early payment, you probably want to enter this period as your current period. Check the vendor accounts listed on pages 112 and 123 — some vendors offer discounts, and most expect net payment within 30 days.

The second option requires knowledge of how your vendors **calculate discounts** and how sales taxes are calculated when discounts are involved. Generally, when a discount is offered at the time of the sale, the full invoice amount is reduced. Thus the tax is also reduced. One-time vendors are in this position. It may be necessary to make an adjusting entry for taxes to allocate part of the discount as a portion of the taxes. Discounts will be discussed later in the chapter. Refer to Appendix C for a complete discussion of sales taxes. The examples that follow illustrate how the program calculates the discount and tax in both situations.

Always contact your provincial and federal tax offices for detailed and current tax information for your own business to be certain that you are applying the rules correctly.

A 2% discount calculated **before tax** on a $1 000 purchase with $70 GST

Mar. 15	Supplies: Lumber	$1 000.00	
	GST Paid on Purchase	70.00	
	Purchase Discounts		20.00
	Bank Account: Chequing		1 050.00

A 2% discount calculated **after tax** on the same purchase as above

Mar. 15	Supplies: Lumber	1 000.00	
	GST Paid on Purchases	70.00	
	Purchase Discounts		21.40
	Bank Account: Chequing		1 048.60

We will change the aging periods. Periods of 15, 30 and 60 days will more closely match the different vendor discount and net payment periods. Discounts for one-time vendors are calculated on the full after-tax amount, so the default is correct.

The first aging period entry, 30 is already selected, ready for editing.

◆ Type **15**

◆ Press ⌧tab⌧ to advance to the second period and highlight it.

◆ Type **30**

◆ Press ⌧tab⌧ to advance to the final aging period and highlight the entry.

◆ Type **60**

Sales Tax Settings

Now you are ready to enter Sales Tax information. Play Wave pays GST on most purchases and PST on some. We want to enter the rates as defaults so that the program can automatically calculate the amounts.

You can access all Settings screens directly from any one Settings screen by clicking the appropriate tabs.

◆ Click the **Sales Taxes tab** to access the Sales Taxes settings:

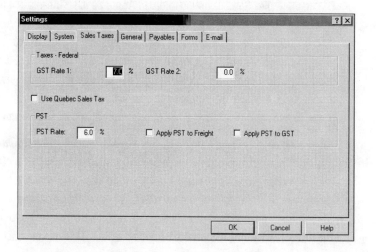

Sales Taxes

The Sales Taxes settings include both federal and provincial taxes. The **Federal sales tax**, GST, is set at 7 percent throughout most of Canada. In Nova Scotia, New Brunswick and Newfoundland, the federal and provincial taxes are combined or harmonized at a single rate of 15 percent. The tax can be renamed HST (Harmonized Sales Tax) in the Names options under the Setup menu (see page 255). A second GST rate field is available in case the government chooses to add a different tax rate for a special group of goods or services. You might also use this field to set the rate for interprovincial sales when you need to charge 15 percent in some provinces and 7 percent in others.

The **PST (Provincial Sales Tax)** rates and rules vary from one province to another. In Ontario, the rate is 8 percent and applies to most goods sold at the retail level to the end user of the goods. In Prince Edward Island, the rate is 10 percent, and Alberta has no Provincial Sales Tax, so its rate is zero. Because some provinces charge PST on freight while others do not, you can indicate the setting for your own province on this Settings screen. In addition, provincial taxes may be applied to a price that includes GST, as in Prince Edward Island, or not, as in Ontario and British Columbia.

If Quebec is the province of business, you must **Use Quebec Sales Tax**. When you check this option, a QST Registration number field opens, and two QST rate fields replace the PST fields. For a discussion of sales taxes, refer to Appendix C.

At present the single PST rate for Ontario, the province in our simulation, is 8 percent so the default setting is incorrect.

◆ Click the **PST Rate field** to highlight 6.0, the default entry.

◆ Type **8**

PST is not applied to GST or to freight charges in Ontario, so leave these boxes unchecked.

Forms Settings

Payables journal entries include mailing payments and writing cheques. Even if you do not use the computer to generate the cheques, invoices and purchase orders, you can use the software to number them automatically, providing a way of checking the manual work. To set up this feature, you must indicate the next number in each sequence. Some of this information is entered in the settings for Forms.

◆ Click the **Forms tab** to open the Forms Settings screen:

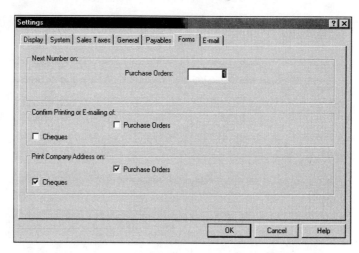

Only the Forms settings related to the Payables Ledger appear because the other Ledgers are still hidden.

The Forms screen provides the settings for numbering sequences as well as the control over printing of various forms. When you input the **Next Number**, the program can update the sequence automatically as you enter further transactions. You can also use these numbers as a control or check of your manual records. When you choose to **Confirm Printing**, the program will warn you to print before posting a transaction. You can turn on the warning for any forms that you print through the computer. If you are not using the computer to print invoices, cheques and forms, you should leave the option turned off. **Printing the Company Address** on various forms is another option. If you are using preprinted forms that already include this information, you should leave the option turned off. If you are using generic unprinted forms, you should include the address. For tutorial purposes, if you have blank paper, you should also print the address. The forms and settings that refer to the Receivables Ledger will be added and explained in Chapter 6.

Play Wave has had no purchase orders yet, so the purchase orders will begin with number 20001. The purchase order number field contents are highlighted.

◆ Type **20001** to enter the revised purchase order sequence number.

◆ Click **OK** to save the changes and return to the Home window.

The next step is to enter the next cheque number for payments. From the source documents (Chapter 3, page 85), you can see that Cheque #106 was the last cheque written. Therefore cheque numbering should begin with 107.

Cheque numbers are recorded in the ledger for the bank account, so we must edit the record for *Bank Account: Chequing*.

◆ Click the **Accounts icon** to open the Accounts window.

◆ Scroll to move to the top of the account list.

◆ Double click *1080 Bank Account: Chequing* to open the ledger record. Notice that the account number is dimmed because the account has journal entries. The current balance is updated from these journal transactions.

◆ Click the **Class Options tab** to open the Class window:

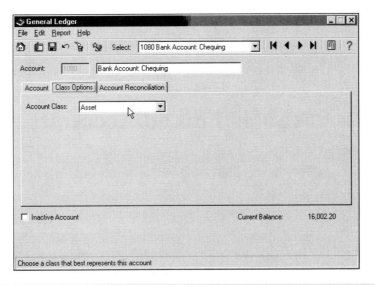

Class Options are a further way of organizing accounts. When you first assign an account number, Simply Accounting applies the Section class to the account based on the first digit, that is, Assets, Liabilities, Equity, Revenue or Expense. Some accounts must be further classified for the program to link account information. If you want to assign a class, click the Account Class list arrow to see the options for that account. The class options for assets include Asset, Bank, Credit Card, Receivables, Accounts Receivable, Inventory, Current Asset, Capital Asset and Other Asset. Most of the necessary classes are assigned automatically once you select a special purpose for an account. Bank accounts, however, must be given the Bank classification by the user.

You must enter class information for bank accounts so that they may be set up as linked accounts with automatic cheque numbering sequences.

◆ Click the **Account Class list arrow** to open the list.

◆ Click **Bank** to add the bank-related input fields to the screen.

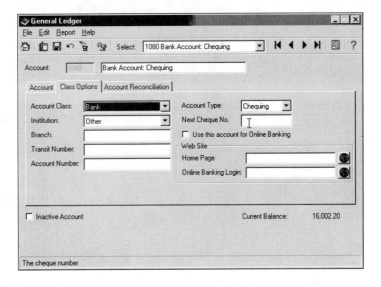

The Bank information fields allow you to enter details about the account and the bank for online banking. The default Chequing Account Type is correct.

◆ Click the **Next Cheque No. field**.

◆ Type **107**

◆ Choose the **File** menu and click **Save** to record the change.

◆ Click the **Account tab** to return to the main General Ledger window.

Leave the Ledger window open for the next step, creating an additional account.

Payables Linked Accounts

In order for the Payables Ledger to be linked with the General Ledger, you must identify the accounts that perform this linking role so that the program will automatically update the appropriate General Ledger accounts.

When we entered a credit purchase in the General Journal, we had to indicate each account that was involved, the expense or asset account, the *Accounts Payable* account and the *GST Paid on Purchases* account. If freight was charged, you would also debit that account. Many of these accounts, *Accounts Payable* and *GST Paid on Purchases*, are common to all credit purchases. Similarly, when you make a payment on account, the same two accounts are always involved, *Bank Account: Chequing* and *Accounts Payable*. When you make these same entries directly through the Payables Journals, the program takes care of these common entry components. Therefore you must identify these common accounts as linked accounts. All the accounts we will need to link exist already, except the account for freight expense.

☐ Create a new account in the General Ledger: 5080 Freight Expense (G)

◆ Close the Ledger and Accounts windows to return to the Home window.

◆ Choose the **Setup** menu, then choose **Linked Accounts** and click **Payables** to access the linked accounts for the Payables ledgers:

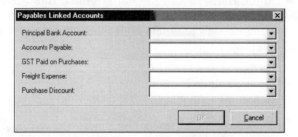

Payables Linked Accounts

Principal Bank Account: Simply Accounting allows you to define separate bank accounts for payments to vendors, cash receipts from customers and for payroll transactions. You may also define a single bank account for all of these transactions.

The Payables Bank account is the default postable asset account, type Group or Subgroup, to which all cash payments to vendors for purchases are credited automatically by the Simply Accounting program. Cash purchases are credited to this bank account at the time that the purchase invoice is posted from the Purchases or Payments Journals. Payments for credit purchases are processed through the Payments Journal. Again, the bank account is credited automatically when the cheque is issued and the payment is posted. All cheques issued for purchases should be processed through this account. In the journals, you may still choose a different bank account, as long as it is defined as a Bank class account.

When you use a second currency, you can also define a linked bank account as the default for payment and receipt transactions using this currency.

Accounts Payable: You must choose a liability account. All credit purchases from vendors are automatically credited to the *Accounts Payable* control account. When a business makes payments on account, this account is automatically debited for the amount of the payment entered in the Payments Journal. The balance in this account reflects the sum of all amounts owed to all vendors. You can view individual vendor balances in the ledger pages for the individual vendors or in the vendor reports.

Although this is a postable account, you cannot post directly to it from any of the journals when the Payables Ledger is used. It is selected by default by the Simply Accounting program whenever you enter credit purchases in the Purchases Journal or payments in the Payments Journal. The *Accounts Payable* account portion of these journal entries is created automatically by the software.

GST Paid on Purchases: If business-related purchases have GST applied to them, the amount of GST entered in the GST fields in the Purchases Journal is automatically debited to this linked account for purchase transactions. It is a contra-liability account because it normally has a debit balance — it reduces the amount of GST owing. *GST Paid on Purchases* is a postable account that you can define as an asset or as a liability account, although you should use the same category as the *GST Charged on Services* account. It is preferable to use a liability account because most of the time a business will owe GST to the Receiver General. Furthermore, if you choose Subgroup Account as the type, the subtotal of this account and the other GST liability accounts will show the total amount of GST owing.

To make the GST remittance, make an Other Payment in the Payments Journal. GST paid is entered as a negative amount to debit the *Accounts Payable* for the Receiver General of Canada and reduce the amount owing.

Refundable QST Paid: This linked account appears only when the **Use Quebec Sales Tax** option is selected (Settings for Sales Taxes from the Setup menu). It operates very much like the *GST Paid* account but applies to any Quebec (Provincial) Sales Tax paid for purchases that qualify (i.e., they are refundable). The QST paid on some purchases will be non-refundable. Again, when the settings are entered correctly, the Simply Accounting program automatically debits the account for the amount of refundable tax paid. Like the *GST Paid* account, the *Refundable QST Paid* account is a postable account that you can define as an asset or as a liability account. Again, it is preferable to use a liability account (contra-liability) because most of the time a business will owe QST to the Minister of Revenue. Furthermore, you should choose Subgroup as the account type, and subtotal this account with other QST liability accounts to show the total amount owing. When a remittance is made, through the Payments Journal, the amount of *Refundable QST Paid* is entered as a negative amount to credit it and to decrease or debit the *Accounts Payable* balance.

Freight Expense: If vendors charge for delivery and these expenses cannot reasonably be assigned to individual inventory items as part of the cost of goods sold, they are debited automatically to a separate *Freight Expense* account whenever a freight amount is entered in the freight field of the Purchases Journal. You must choose a postable expense account for *Freight Expense*, type Group or Subgroup.

Purchase Discount: Although you may choose either a revenue or an expense account for the *Purchase Discount* linked account, it is more common to use an expense account (a contra-expense, to be exact). The discount is related to the expenses of conducting business — it reduces the cost of purchases — it is not a true source of income or revenue. This is a postable account and may be a Group or Subgroup account.

When a vendor offers a discount for early settlement of an account, the amount of the discount is calculated automatically if the payment terms are included with the invoice and the payment is made before the discount offer expires. When the payment is posted, the discount amount is credited to the *Purchase Discount* linked account, and the *Accounts Payable* account is debited for the full invoice amount — the amount of the payment plus the amount of the discount. The Payables Bank account is credited for the amount of the payment.

You must define the Principal Bank account and Accounts Payable linked accounts before you can finish the Payables Ledger history.

If you have entered a rate for GST, you must define the GST Paid linked account before you can open the Purchases Journal. If you are using Quebec Sales Tax, you must also define the QST linked account.

If you do not define the Freight Expense linked account, the freight fields in the Purchases Journal will be unavailable. Thus, if freight is charged, you must define its linked account.

If you do not define the Purchase Discount linked account, and you enter a discount rate in the Purchases Journal, you cannot post the journal entry. The debits and credits are not equal because of the missing credit for the discount.

Deleting Linked Accounts

To delete a linked account when it is no longer required, you must be in the linked accounts screen. Click on the account you do not need. This will select the account. Press ⟨*del*⟩ and click OK to save the changes. You must remove the linked account, that is, unlink it, before you can remove the account from the General Ledger.

Play Wave Plus has one bank account that is used for all the ledgers.

◆ Click the **Principal Bank Account field arrow** to see the accounts that can be selected. Only Bank class accounts are included in the list.

◆ Click *1080 Bank Account: Chequing* to select it.

◆ Press ⟨*tab*⟩ to advance to the Accounts Payable field.

◆ Click *2200 Accounts Payable* from the drop-down list to select it. Notice that you can choose only a liability account.

◆ Press ⟨*tab*⟩ to advance to the GST Paid on Purchases account field.

◆ Click *2670 GST Paid on Purchases* from the drop-down list of assets and liabilities. Linked accounts previously selected are unavailable.

◆ Press ⟨*tab*⟩ to advance to the Freight Expense account field.

◆ Click *5080 Freight Expense* from the list of expense accounts.

◆ Press ⟨*tab*⟩ to advance to the Purchase Discount account field.

◆ Click *5100 Purchase Discounts* from the list of accounts.

◆ Click **OK** to save the new linked account settings:

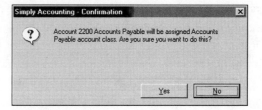

This message advises you that the account class for *Accounts Payables* will be changed because we have identified it as the linked Payables account.

◆ Click **Yes** (or OK in Version 8.0A) to accept the change and return to the Home window.

Entering Vendor Records

Accounts Payable vendor records are entered in the Payables Ledger, accessed with the Vendors icon as shown:

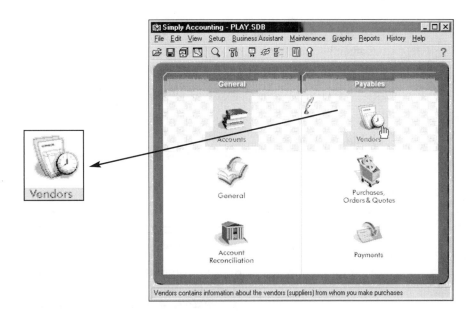

◆ Click the **Vendors icon** to open the Vendors account window:

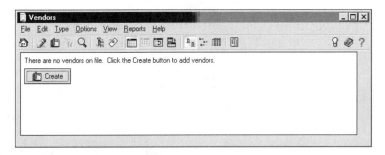

The Vendors Window Tools

The tool buttons in the Vendors window should be familiar by now. Most of them are the same as those in the Accounts window (page 43). The report and advice tools refer specifically to the Payables Ledger. All Payables Ledger reports are available from the Select a report tool and from the Reports menu. The two Payables Journal tools replace the two journal tools in the Accounts window. You can access the journals by clicking the tool buttons or by selecting the journals from the Type menu.

 Purchases Journal (including Orders & Quotes) opens the journal.

 Payments Journal opens the journal.

The opening screen advises you that there are no vendor records yet and provides instructions about creating these records. The first vendor we want to add is Groundfos Machinery, to record the purchase of excavation equipment in early March. Play Wave made one payment towards the invoice but still has an outstanding balance. Complete details for the company, including historical transactions follow.

Vendor (Contact)	Address	Phone, Fax, Tax ID	E-mail, Web, Terms, Total Purchases
Groundfos Machinery (Wanda Hammer)	23 Drilling St. Thornhill, ON L3G 4M1	Tel: (905) 881-5432 Fax: (905) 881-5566 Tax ID: 3875 61992	E-mail: groundfos@diggers.ca Web: www.groundfos.diggers.ca Terms: 1/20, n/30 (before tax) YTD Purchases: $4 280

Historical Information

Date	Invoice/Cheque #	Terms	Pretax Amount	Tax	Total
Mar. 13/02	GM-961	(1/20, n/30)	$4 000.00	280.00	$4 280.00
Mar. 13/02	Chq #100				1 070.00
				Balance	$3 210.00

◆ Click the **Create button** [Create] (or click the Create tool [ ], or choose the File menu and click Create) to open the Payables (vendor) Ledger window:

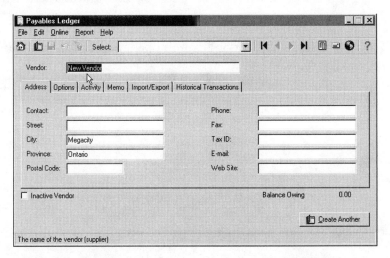

The ledger has several parts that are accessed with the tabs. The first part contains address or contact information.

Payables Ledger

Menu and Tools

File — The File menu options are the same as those in the General Ledger.

Edit — Most of the Edit options are the same as those in the General Ledger. The Modify Accounts Wizard is removed and Insert Line, Remove Line and Restore Window are added.

Online — The E-mail and Web site options provide direct access to the e-mail message screen or the Web site if Internet access is set up.

Report — Vendor List is the only report available from the Payables Ledger screen.

Help — Information related to the Payables Ledger is directly available from this Help menu.

The Create and Remove tool buttons are the same as those in the Accounts window described on page 43. The Help tool provides information about the Payables ledger, the Display tool provides the Vendor List report and the Select list allows you to select any other vendor record. The four tools, first, previous, next and last vendor allow you to move through the vendor records quickly to find the one you want, just as they do in the General Ledger. The new icons for Web site access and e-mail messaging require Internet access.

Send an **E-mail** message to the vendor. Click the tool, then type and send an e-mail to the vendor.

 Go to the Vendor's Web site. Click the tool to go directly to the Web site if you have Internet access.

Two fields appear at the bottom of all ledger windows. Checking the box for **Inactive Vendor** allows you to keep vendors on record but exclude them from lists and reports. The **Balance Owing** is calculated by the program from the historical invoices. The balance field is not available for input.

Address Tab Input Fields

Vendor: Enter the business name of the vendor or supplier.

Contact: Enter the name of the individual or department you will contact for details about purchases and invoices. If the address is very long, the Contact field may be used as an additional street address line.

Address: Details include Street, City, Province and Postal Code. The address is used to create mailing labels for vendors. By default, the program enters the city and province that you entered as Company Information (Setup menu). You can edit this information if it is incorrect for the vendor.

Phone and Fax Numbers: The program corrects the formats for both postal codes and telephone numbers, so you can type them without brackets or hyphens.

Tax ID: The Business tax/GST registration number for the vendor.

E-mail and Web Site: If you have Internet access and you know the vendor's Internet address, you can enter them here. You can then link directly with the vendor's Web site from the Ledger record and e-mail orders from the Purchases Journal while entering transactions.

Vendor Address Details

Check your work very carefully as you proceed and make corrections if necessary by selecting the text you need to change and typing the correction.

Initially the Vendor name field is selected, so you can begin to edit it immediately.

- ◆ Type `Groundfos Machinery`
- ◆ Press `tab` to advance to the Contact field.
- ◆ Type `Wanda Hammer`
- ◆ Press `tab` to advance to the Street address field.
- ◆ Type `23 Drilling St.`
- ◆ Press `tab`.
- ◆ Type `Thornhill` to replace the default information because it is incorrect for this vendor.
- ◆ Press `tab`.
- ◆ Press `tab` again to skip the Province field.
- ◆ Type `l3g4m1`
- ◆ Press `tab`.
- ◆ Type `9058815432` in the Phone field.

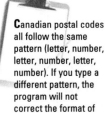
Canadian postal codes all follow the same pattern (letter, number, letter, number, letter, number). If you type a different pattern, the program will not correct the format of the postal code.

- ◆ Press tab.

- ◆ Type **9058815566**

- ◆ Press tab to advance to the Tax ID field.

- ◆ Type **387561992**

- ◆ Press tab to advance to the E-mail field.

- ◆ Type **groundfos@diggers.ca** (type the e-mail address exactly as you would enter it from your Internet account).

- ◆ Press tab.

- ◆ Type **www.groundfos.diggers.ca** (type the Web site address exactly as you would enter it from your Internet account).

Vendor Options

- ◆ Click the **Options tab** to see the next group of input fields:

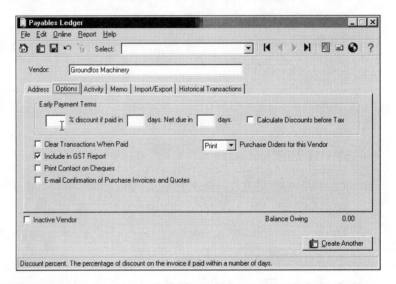

Options Tab Screen

Early Payment Terms: Some vendors offer discounts for prompt payment of accounts. Others expect net payment within a defined period and may charge interest on overdue accounts. When you enter the payment terms for a vendor in the ledger, they will be added automatically to the Purchases Journal when you select that vendor. Applicable discounts will also be calculated automatically. The terms for individual invoices may be changed in the Purchases Journal if necessary.

Calculate Discounts before Tax: This option is the same as the one in the Payables Settings for One-time vendors. Vendors may calculate the discount on the pretax amount only or on the full invoice amount. GST is payable by the vendor on the full purchase price when the discount is taken after the sale. PST in Ontario is payable on the discounted amount. Tax rules may be different for discounts that are taken at the time of a purchase and discounts that are offered later for early payments, and may vary from province to province.

Clear Transactions When Paid: Only if disk storage space is very limited might you choose to clear invoices as soon as they are paid. Normally, you would want to retain them until closing maintenance routines are performed, so that you will have as complete a history of the transactions with the vendor as possible and you can adjust invoices to correct errors. Unpaid invoices cannot be removed.

Include in GST Report: Checking this option produces important results. GST fields are available for purchase invoices when you choose the vendor so that you can enter correct GST codes. If you do not include the vendor in GST reports, only the non-taxable and exempt GST codes are available. The GST codes and the linked account information permit the program to calculate GST amounts automatically and post them to the appropriate accounts. The GST Reports will then include the information for this vendor. You should therefore leave this option checked for all vendors who supply taxable goods and services. Some Payables Ledger accounts, such as the Receiver General, Minister of Finance, municipal tax offices or insurance providers do not supply taxable services. These vendors should not be included in the GST report. Clicking the box or option will remove the checkmark. In this way, you cannot accidentally add GST to the balances owing to these agencies. Clicking the option again restores the checkmark and includes the vendors in GST reports. For most vendors, the default setting, to include in GST reports, is correct.

Print Contact on Cheques: If the Contact field contains address information or a department name, it should be included on the cheque. If it contains the name of an individual, it should not be printed on the cheque.

E-mail Confirmation of Purchase Invoices and Quotes: Send an e-mail message automatically upon receipt of purchase invoices or quotes if the box is checked.

Print or E-mail Purchase Orders for this Vendor: If you have an e-mail address for the vendor and if the vendor accepts orders by e-mail, you can send the purchase order directly from the Purchases Journal window when you choose this option. If you must print and mail (or fax) the order, you can choose the Print option. You can override the default setting in the purchase order screen.

Groundfos Machinery offers the terms 1/20, n/30 — a discount of 1 percent is available if the account is settled within 20 days and net payment is due in 30 days. Discounts are calculated before tax.

◆ Click the **%** **discount field** of the Early Payment Terms section to move the cursor.

◆ Type **1** to enter the percentage amount of the discount.

◆ Press (tab).

◆ Type **20** to enter the discount period.

◆ Press (tab).

◆ Type **30** to indicate that net payment is due in 30 days.

◆ Click **Calculate Discounts before Tax**.

The remaining default settings are correct for the vendor. We want to retain paid invoices. Because the Contact field does not contain address details, it should not be printed on cheques. The vendor supplies taxable goods and must be included in GST reports. Groundfos does not accept purchase orders by e-mail.

Historical Activity

◆ Click the **Activity tab** to advance to the next group of vendor details:

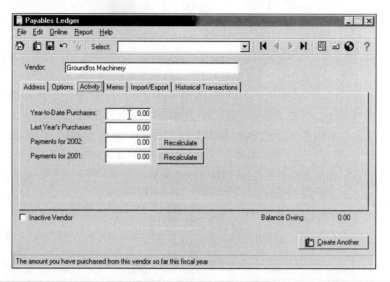

Activity Tab Screen

The program updates information for transactions with this vendor in the current year and in the past year based on historical and current invoices and payments. The information is also added to the inventory tracking reports. At the end of a fiscal year, the program automatically transfers the totals for the current year to the past year.

Four totals are calculated: **Year-to-Date Purchases** — the total amount of all purchases from this vendor in the current fiscal year; **Last Year's Purchases** — the total amount of all purchases from this vendor in the previous fiscal year; **Payments for 2002** — the total of all payments made in the current year; and **Payments for 2001** — the total of all payments made in the previous year. The reference years are updated from the company's fiscal dates.

Since Play Wave has been operating for only one month, there are no purchases for the previous year. The year-to-date (YTD) purchases consist of the purchase for $4 280 that we will record later as a historical invoice.

◆ Click the **Year-to-Date Purchases field.**

◆ Type **4280**

Vendor Memos

◆ Click the **Memo tab** to advance to its screen:

The total purchases made before using the Purchases Journal should be entered manually on the Activity tab screen. Payments that are not recorded as historical payments must also be added to the Activity screen in the Payments for 2002 field.

When there are no historical invoices to record, click Create Another to save the record and open a new Ledger window after completing the Activity tab fields.

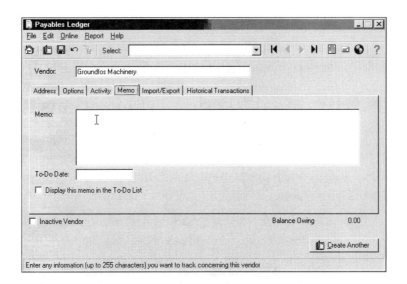

Memo Tab Screen

The **Memo** field allows you to write a note about the vendor or about a purchase as a reminder to yourself. You can indicate a date for the reminder and include this memo with the To-Do List so that it will appear automatically. For example, you might have a standing order that requires a one-time change. The memo can be dated to remind you about the change before you post the recurring entry. To add a memo, type the message in the Memo field. Enter the date that you want to be reminded about the memo in the **To-Do Date** field and click the option to **Display this memo in the To-Do List**. To-Do Lists are used in Chapter 16.

There are no memos required for this vendor.

◆ Click the Import/Export tab to show the next information screen:

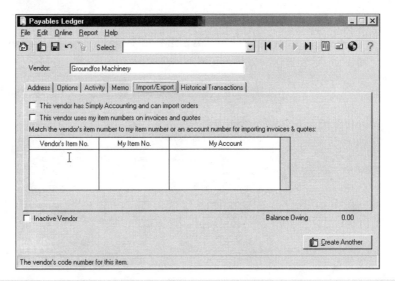

Import/Export Tab Screen

From this screen, you can match the vendor's inventory codes to the codes of your own business. If the vendor also uses the Simply Accounting program, then invoices can be imported or exported directly. The vendor may use the same or different inventory numbers, or the vendor's inventory may be placed directly into an asset or expense account. When invoices are received or sent, the program will translate the vendor's inventory numbers to those of your own business automatically, or vice versa. Refer to Appendix F for further information.

No importing or exporting of invoices will take place at this stage.

To check the vendor information, click each tab in turn to read the information and make corrections if necessary.

Historical Vendor Transactions

Historical transaction dates must be between Fiscal Start and Earliest Transaction date (March 1 to March 15 for Play Wave) so we will enter only the ones that occurred before starting to use Simply Accounting, not the ones entered in the General Journal because they occurred after March 15.

◆ Click the **Historical Transactions** tab to move to the final stage of setting up the vendor record. You will see the following warning:

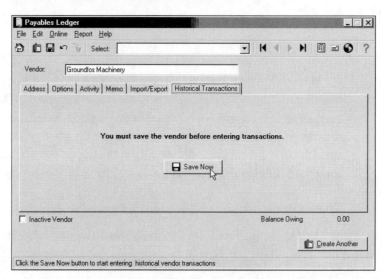

◆ Click **Save Now** to save the information, create a vendor account icon in the Vendors window and access the input screens for invoices and payments:

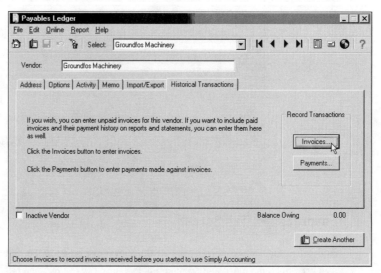

Notice the Invoices and Payments buttons added to the ledger. These are used to add purchases and payments that you want to keep on record. You must enter all outstanding invoices. Simply Accounting uses the open-invoice method of tracking invoices.

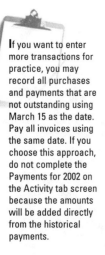
If you want to enter more transactions for practice, you may record all purchases and payments that are not outstanding using March 15 as the date. Pay all invoices using the same date. If you choose this approach, do not complete the Payments for 2002 on the Activity tab screen because the amounts will be added directly from the historical payments.

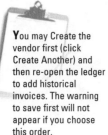
You may Create the vendor first (click Create Another) and then re-open the ledger to add historical invoices. The warning to save first will not appear if you choose this order.

Open-Invoice Accounting

The open-invoice accounting approach records and retains individual invoices, and payments are made against individual invoices. The alternative keeps track only of the totals owing to vendors (or by customers), and when a payment is made, the total owing is reduced without connecting it to any specific invoice. Accommodating discounts for early payments requires the open-invoice accounting method because of the need to track the separate invoices to see if they are paid on time. Fully paid invoices may be removed as they are paid or they may be retained and then deleted periodically. (See Payables Ledger, Options tab screen.)

Historical Vendor Invoices

◆ Click **Invoices** to open the Historical Invoices form:

The Historical Invoices Screen

Vendor: Groundfos Machinery, the vendor's name, appears so that you can be certain you are entering information for the right vendor.

Invoice No.: The actual invoice number from the purchase invoice.

Date: Replace the default date, the Earliest Transaction date, with the actual invoice date. Historical invoices must be dated between the Fiscal Start date and the Earliest Transaction date.

Terms: You can edit the terms that appear by default from the vendor record information if the terms for this invoice are different.

Pre-Tax Amount and **Tax**: The first amount is the amount of the invoice before taxes and second one is the tax amount. The discount is calculated on the first amount, the pretax amount when you have set the vendor option to calculate discounts before tax. The program completes the Invoice Total field automatically by adding the two amounts. This total amount will be included in the Balance field of the vendor ledger. The total of all amounts owing to all vendors (all outstanding balances) must match the balance in the *Accounts Payable* control account.

When the discounts are calculated after tax, a single amount field is available for the full amount of the invoice as shown here:

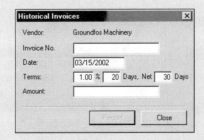

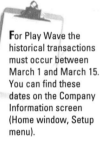

For Play Wave the historical transactions must occur between March 1 and March 15. You can find these dates on the Company Information screen (Home window, Setup menu).

The purchase from Groundfos Machinery, invoice #GM-961 for $4 280, took place on March 13. The cursor is in the Invoice Number field. The default payment terms are correct.

Simply Accounting does not allow duplicate source numbers for purchase invoices.

◆ Type GM-961

◆ Press (tab) to advance to the Date field and highlight the Session date.

◆ Type Mar 13

◆ Click the **Pre-Tax Amount field** to move the cursor and skip the Terms fields.

◆ Type 4000

◆ Press (tab) to advance to the Tax field.

◆ Type 280

◆ Check your work carefully before recording (storing) either historical invoices or payments.

◆ Click **Record** to save the invoice and to open a new invoice form for the next purchase entry. The previous invoice date is now the default date.

You must click Record to save the invoice. If you click Close before you click Record, you will not save the invoice.

If there are other invoices to record, enter the information for each one separately and record them. There are no more invoices from this vendor. After all the invoices are recorded,

◆ Click **Close** to indicate that there are no more invoices to record. You will return to the vendor ledger Historical Transactions screen.

Notice that the balance owing is $4 280 because of the invoice you have just recorded.

Historical Vendor Payments

◆ Click **Payments** to open the Historical Payments screen:

The Historical Payments Screen

Vendor: Again, the Vendor's name appears for reference.

Number: The cheque number from the cheque used to pay the vendor.

Date: The date of the payment or the date on the cheque. All historical payments must be dated between the Earliest Transaction date, the default date on the payment screen, and the Fiscal Start date.

The next part of the form contains a separate line of information for each historical invoice recorded.

Invoice column: The number from the invoice so you can indicate which invoices were paid. All the invoices that you entered for the vendor should appear.

Amount column: The amount owing from the original invoice.

Disc. (Discount) Available column: If a discount is available for early payment and the discount period has not expired, the program will calculate the amount of the discount and enter it in this column, based on the date of the invoice, the date of the payment and the payment terms. The discount will become unavailable as soon as the date of payment passes the discount period. Simply Accounting keeps track of these dates for you.

Disc. (Discount) Taken column: If the discount is still available, clicking this column will show the discount amount. Generally discounts are available only when full payment is made before the discount period expires. The discount amount can be deleted by pressing ⌈del⌉.

Amount Paid column: The lesser of the amount of the cheque and the amount of the invoice. By default the full invoice amount appears. You can edit this figure but you cannot enter an amount greater than the balance owing.

Invoice #GM-961 was partially paid on March 13, using cheque #100. No discount will be taken because the full amount is not yet paid. If the Session date is beyond the discount period, then no discount will show as available.

◆ Click the **Number field** to move the cursor to the cheque number field.

◆ Type **100**

◆ Press ⌈tab⌉ to advance to the Date field.

◆ Type **03-13** (the date on the cheque).

◆ Press ⌈tab⌉ to accept the date.

◆ Click the **Amount paid field** for the first invoice line to skip the discount and highlight the full amount $4 280.

◆ Type **1070** to enter the amount of the cheque.

◆ Press ⌈tab⌉ to accept the amount.

When a discount is taken, or other invoices are paid with the same cheque, click the Discount Taken and Amount paid fields for these invoices. Accept the defaults when the invoice is paid in full. If an amount is entered for the discount taken, and the invoice is not paid in full, delete the discount for these partial payments. Invoices paid with separate cheques should be recorded as separate payments.

◆ Check your work carefully. Correct any errors before recording the payment.

◆ Click **Record** to save the payment and open a new payment form with the amount owing reduced to $3 210 by the previous payment.

◆ Click **Close** to indicate that there are no further payments to record.

You will return to the Payables Ledger record. The balance owing is updated by the payment and is now $3 210.

◆ When you have finished, click **Create Another** to open a new ledger form.

Check the Payments for 2002 on the Activity tab screen to see that the payment has been added by the program.

- ◆ Click the **Address tab** to return to this input screen.
- ◆ Now add the remaining vendors and balances from page 123.
- ◆ Close the Payables Ledger window after entering the last vendor to return to the Vendors window.

Correcting Vendor Information

You can correct any vendor Ledger field by accessing the record, highlighting the incorrect information and typing the new information to replace it.

Accessing the Vendor's Record

As soon as you save the record, by choosing Create Another or Save Now, the program will add an icon for the new vendor in the Vendors window. From now on, when you need to edit vendor information, you can open the vendor record from the Vendors window. Just double click the vendor's icon. Most of the information in the ledger can be edited any time, even after you have added journal entries. The historical and balance fields, however, are updated directly from journal entries and cannot be edited.

You can choose from many ways to access the record for an individual vendor. From the Vendors window,

- Click the vendor's icon and then click the Edit  tool or choose the Edit menu and click Edit.
- Choose the Edit menu. Click Find to open the Find Vendor screen. Click the vendor's name. Click Find.
- Click the Find tool 🔍 to open the Find Vendor screen. Click the vendor's name and then click Find.
- From any open Payables Ledger record, click the Select list arrow and then click the vendor's name.

You can also access the vendor's record from the Home window.

- Click the Find tool 🔍 to access the Select Record Type screen. Click Vendors and then click Select to open the Find Vendor screen. Click the vendor's name and then click Find.
- Right-click the Vendors icon to select it. Click the Find tool 🔍 to access the Find Vendor screen. Click the vendor's name and then click Find.
- Choose the Edit menu, then choose Find and click Vendor to access the Find Vendor screen. Click the vendor's name and then click Find.

Delete vendor records from the Vendors window. Select the vendor icon and click the Remove tool 🗑 (or choose the File menu and click Remove). Confirm that you want to delete the vendor. Before you can delete a vendor, you must pay all outstanding invoices and clear the paid transactions.

You can also remove a record while the ledger for that vendor is open. Click the Remove tool or choose the File menu from the Ledger and click Remove.

Correcting Historical Invoices after Recording

Before you can finish the Payables Ledger history, the total of all outstanding balances must match the General Ledger *Accounts Payable* control account balance. If you discover a mistake in one of the historical invoices or payments after recording them, you can correct the error by paying and then removing the invoice as follows:

- Make a payment against the outstanding invoice for the full amount still owing.
- Choose The Maintenance menu, then choose Clear Paid Transactions and click Clear Paid Vendor Transactions.
- From the list of vendors, click the name of the vendor for whom you made the mistake.

- Enter March 15 as the date on or before which you want to remove paid transactions.
- Click OK to remove the invoices, then click Yes when asked to confirm your choice.
- Open the vendor's ledger record and click the Activity tab. Click the Payments for 2002 entry and press <kbd>del</kbd> to reset the amount to zero.
- Re-enter the correct historical invoices and payments.

- **D**o not clear paid transactions for any vendors
- **C**hoose to print purchase orders.
- **D**o not include contact on cheques.
- **D**o not calculate discounts before tax.

If information for an address field is missing, you can leave the field blank. Press <kbd>tab</kbd> to skip a field and leave it blank. Do not omit any of the outstanding invoices.

You can restore the alphabetical order of vendor icons in the Vendors window. Choose the Options menu and click Re-sort Icons or choose the Re-sort icons tool. To view the vendors by name, choose the View menu and click Name or click the Display by name tool. Vendor balances are included when you display vendors by name.

VENDOR ACCOUNTS

Vendor (Contact)	Address	Phone, Fax, Tax ID	E-mail, Web, Terms, YTD Totals
Bell Canada (Orrel Caller)	900 Nexus Blvd. Megacity, ON M8B 3C3 Include in GST Reports	Tel: (416) 522-7166 Fax: (416) 522-8700	E-mail: Bell.Can@sympatico.ca *Web: www.bell.ca Terms: net 1 YTD Purchases: $276.00 2002 Payments: $276.00
Casual Contractors (Mannie Temps)	33 Resource Cr. Megacity, ON M6G 4F3 Do **NOT** include in GST Reports	Tel: (416) 921-7101 Fax: (416) 922-7000 Tax ID: 421357533	E-mail: mtemps@casual.con.ca Web: www.for.people.com Terms: net 1 YTD Purchases: $1 600.00 2002 Payments: $1 600.00
CIBC Insurance (Mosely Safer)	10 Protector Ave. Oshawa, ON L4F 9D1 Do **NOT** include in GST Reports	Tel: (905) 577-3982 Fax: (905) 577-3900	Web: www.insure.cibc.ca Terms: net 1 YTD Purchases: $1 200.00 2002 Payments: $1 200.00
Meade, Vincent	11 Honeywell Ct. Megacity, ON M2V 2M2 Include in GST Reports	Tel: (416) 823-4192	Terms: net 1 YTD Purchases: $214.00 2002 Payments: $214.00
Ontario Hydro (Serge Lektrik)	450 Water St. Megacity, ON M5T 5H5 Include in GST Reports	Tel: (416) 393-0921 Fax: (416) 393-9900	*Web: www.torontohydro.com Terms: net 1 YTD Purchases: $85.60 2002 Payments: $85.60
The Buildex Corp. (Sheeta Plastik)	340 Synthetics Lane Richmond Hill, ON L5T 3D5 Include in GST Reports	Tel: (905) 577-2727 Fax: (905) 577-7120 Tax ID: 532894429	E-mail: 705124.5421@cs.com Web: www.builditall.com Terms: 2/10, n/30 (after tax) YTD Purchases: $2 140.00 2002 Payments: $2 140.00
Swede Steel Co. (Sven Svenske)	55 Husqvarna Rd. Megacity, ON M3S 7S7 Include in GST Reports	Tel: (416) 466-2372 Fax: (416) 466-3000 Tax ID: 765456644	E-mail: SSCo@interlog.com Web: www.forged.steel.ca Terms: 2/15, n/30 (after tax) YTD Purchases: $535.00

Swede Steel Co.: Historical Information

Date	Invoice	Terms	Pretax Amount	Tax	Total
Mar. 2/02	SC-4211	2/15, n/30 (after tax)			$535.00

| | | | **Accounts Payable Total** | | **$3 745.00** |

WARNING!

After you enter the historical invoices for Swede Steel Co. and if you have entered all amounts correctly up to this point, the program may display the following message:

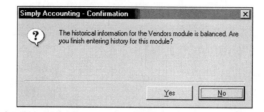

The total of outstanding balances for individual vendors now matches the *Accounts Payable* account opening balance and the program is providing a shortcut to finishing the history for the ledger.

◆ Click **No** so that you can continue adding historical information. Check your work carefully, and make a backup before losing the opportunity to enter or change historical details. There may be errors that you need to correct before finishing the ledger history.

Payables Ledger Reports
Vendor List

Use the Vendor List to check the address and contact details for the vendors you entered. From the Vendors window:

◆ Click the **Select a report** tool , click **Display Vendor List** and click **Select** (or choose the Reports menu and click Display Vendor List).

From the Home window,

◆ Choose the Reports menu, then choose **Lists** and click **Vendors**. The vendor address list is displayed immediately. (Or click the Display tool, choose Vendor List and then Select. Or right-click the Vendors icon and click the Display Vendor List tool.)

◆ Print the list or check your work from the on-screen display. Close the display.

Vendor Aged Detail Report

Use the Vendor Aged Detail report to check the historical invoices and payments.

◆ Choose the **Reports** menu, then choose **Payables** and click **Vendor Aged** in the Home window (or, from the Vendors window, choose the Reports menu and click Vendor Aged) to display the report options:

Having a backup in the not finished stage means that you can edit historical information for a vendor if you have made an error. For example, if an invoice date is incorrect, the discount will not be calculated correctly. This type of error will not be detected by the program.

The Display/Report tool label changes when you select a Home window icon first.

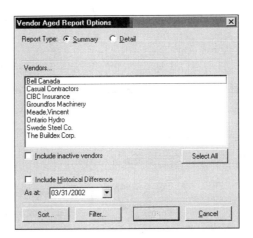

The Vendor Aged Report can be shown in **Summary** or **Detail** form. The Summary option lists only the total outstanding balance for each vendor, in aged columns according to the aging periods entered for the Payables Settings. The Detail Report provides the details for individual invoices and payments, again in aged columns. You can select one or more vendors to include in the report. To include a vendor, press *ctrl* and click the name. By default, the Session date is given for the report, but you may choose any date after the Earliest Transaction date up to the Session date. You may include payment terms as part of the Detail report. To check the accuracy of the historical data for all vendors at the Session date, you should include all the details, including terms. Including Historical Difference also tells you whether the total of all invoices matches the *Accounts Payable* account balance. To add all these details,

Press *ctrl* and click individual vendor names to add them to a report. Once vendors are selected, pressing *ctrl* and clicking the names again will deselect them.

◆ Click **Detail**. The option to Include Terms (payment terms) is added to the bottom of the report options window.

◆ Click **Select All** to include all the vendors in the report.

◆ Click **Include Terms**.

◆ Click **Include Historical Difference**.

The date is correct.

◆ Click **OK** to display the report.

The total owing in the Vendor Aged Detail report should be $3 745, the balance for the Accounts Payable account on March 15.

Drill-Down Reports

From the Vendor List you can display the Vendor Aged Report for the selected vendor when you double click any item of information for that vendor.

From the Vendor Aged Summary Report, you can go to the Vendor Aged Detail Report for a vendor by double clicking any of the information for the vendor you want. From the Vendor Aged Detail Report you can view the vendor record by double clicking the vendor's name. Double clicking an entry line or invoice information in the Detail reports will drill down to Invoice Lookup, showing a copy of the original journal invoice if the entry was recorded in the Payables journals. Invoice Lookup is explained in Chapter 8.

◆ Print the report from the display by choosing the File menu and clicking Print.

◆ Close the display when finished.

Finishing the History for the Payables Ledger

◆ Back up your data files before finishing the history for a ledger. In this way, if you have made a mistake in one of the historical invoices, you can remove the incorrect details (see page 122). Otherwise, you must start from scratch or with your most recent not finished version.

There are additional ways to verify the accuracy of your data.

◆ Choose the **Maintenance menu** and click **Check Data Integrity** to see a summary:

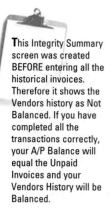

This Integrity Summary screen was created BEFORE entering all the historical invoices. Therefore it shows the Vendors history as Not Balanced. If you have completed all the transactions correctly, your A/P Balance will equal the Unpaid Invoices and your Vendors History will be Balanced.

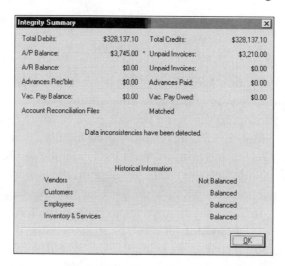

The Historical Difference in the Vendor Aged Detail Report also provides information about whether the ledger is balanced.

The above screen shows the data integrity check **before** entering the invoice for Swede Steel. Therefore, the Payables Ledger is not balanced — the *Accounts Payable* account balance exceeds the total unpaid invoices.

◆ Click **OK** to return to the Home window.

◆ Choose the **History** menu, then choose **Enter Historical Information** and click **Payables**.

If you have made errors in the historical invoices or payments, or have omitted a linked account, you will see messages describing your errors. **Do NOT begin the journal entries in Chapter 5 if you see any of these error messages.**

Finishing History Errors

Errors are detected sequentially for a ledger. The first message refers to a missing essential linked account:

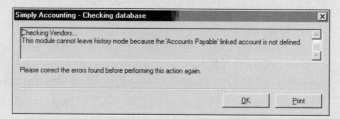

Click OK to return to the Home window. Add the missing linked accounts and try finishing the history again.

If all linked accounts are defined, the program checks for a match between the total of the individual outstanding vendor balances and the *Accounts Payable* account balance in the General Ledger. If you have entered amounts incorrectly, you will receive an error message like the following:

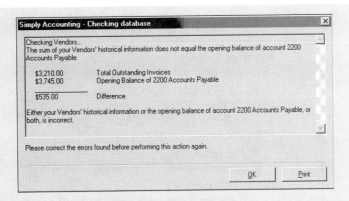

Click OK. You will return to the Home window. Check the individual vendor historical entries again by examining the Vendor Aged Detail Report including historical difference. Refer to page 122 for help with correcting historical invoices. Try finishing the ledger history again.

Once your history is balanced and all linked accounts are defined, you should be allowed to finish the history.

◆ Choose the **History** menu, then choose **Enter Historical Information** and click **Payables**. Simply Accounting will display the warning:

◆ If you have **backed up** your files already, click **Proceed**.

◆ Close the Play Wave data file so that you can set up the Payables Ledger for Live Links.

Practice: Live Links

In this practice section, you will add the Payables Ledger for Live Links so that they can begin using the Payables journals in the next chapter. The historical invoices are those that occurred before using the General Journal. In British Columbia, the PST rate is 7 percent and applies to the sale of most goods and some services.

Payables Ledger Setup
Instructions

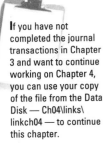

If you have not completed the journal transactions in Chapter 3 and want to continue working on Chapter 4, you can use your copy of the file from the Data Disk — Ch04\links\ linkch04 — to continue this chapter.

1. Open the Live Links data file and accept July 31 as the Session date.

2. Restore the icons for the Payables Ledger (Home window, View menu, Modules, Payables).

3. Set up the Payables Ledger with the following settings:

> **Payables Settings:**
>   Aging Periods: 15, 30 and 60 days
>   Do NOT calculate discount before taxes (leave the box unchecked)
> **Sales Taxes:**
>   GST Rate 1 is 7%, GST Rate 2 is 0%
>   Do not Use Quebec Sales Tax
>   PST rate is 7%
>   Apply PST to Freight; do not apply PST to GST.
> **Forms Settings:**
>   Next Number on Purchase Orders: 1
> **1080 Bank Account: Chequing**
>   Change account class to Bank. Next Number on Cheques: 19

4. Create the required new General Ledger accounts and then enter the linked accounts for the Payables Ledger:

> **New Accounts:**
> Create two new accounts required as Payables Ledger linked accounts
>   5200 Freight Expense (G)
>   5135 Purchases Discounts (G)
>
> **Linked Accounts for the Payables Ledger:**
>   Principal Bank Account: 1080 Bank Account: Chequing
>   Accounts Payable: 2200 Accounts Payable
>   GST Paid on Purchases: 2670 GST Paid on Purchases
>   Freight Expense: 5200 Freight Expense
>   Purchase Discount: 5135 Purchases Discounts

5. Enter the following vendor accounts and historical purchases and payments:

VENDOR ACCOUNTS

All vendors in this list are to be included in GST reports. Do not clear paid transactions.

Vendor (Contact)	Address	Phone, Fax, Tax ID	E-mail, Web, Terms, Total Purchases
BC Hydro (Sol Powers)	7000 Coalport Rd. Vancouver, BC V9S 4G5	Tel: (604) 491-0900 Fax: (604) 491-8102	*Web: eww. bchydro.ca Terms: net 1 YTD Purchases: $53.50 2002 Payments: $53.50
BC Telephone (Ting A. Ling)	555 Ring Road Vancouver, BC V6B 3E1	Tel: (604) 255-2355	E-mail: tingling@bcnet.ca *Web: www.bell.ca Terms: net 1 YTD Purchases: $91.20 2002 Payments: $91.20
Business Depot (N. Graves)	35 Graphics Ave. Vancouver, BC V8G 2F5	Tel: (604) 288-8235 Fax: (604) 288-7819 Tax ID: 6433 57882	E-mail: NGraves@stargate.com Web: www.business.graphics.com Terms: net 15 YTD Purchases: $114.00 2002 Payments: $114.00

VENDOR ACCOUNTS CONTINUED

Vendor (Contact)	Address	Phone, Fax, Tax ID	E-mail, Web, Terms, Total Purchases
Massey Realty (Kalina Massey)	100 Real Estates Rd. Richmond, BC V6R 4J8	Tel: (604) 488-9012 Fax: (604) 485-0987 Tax ID: 3876 47665	E-mail: kalinam@pathcom.com Web: www.massey.houses.com Terms: net 1 YTD Purchases: $6 420.00 2002 Payments: $6 420.00
Petro Partners (Hi Octayne)	299 Fewell Dr. Burnaby, BC V9J 4H3	Tel: (604) 249-2486 Fax: (604) 248-9712	Terms: net 1 YTD Purchases: $228.00 2002 Payments: $228.00
Promo Uno (M. Press)	100 Adze Rd. Vancouver, BC V7R 3D9	Tel: (604) 444-7777 Fax: (604) 444-2091 Tax ID: 4589 64223	E-mail: mpress@promo.uno.ca Web: www.promotions.com Terms: net 30 YTD Purchases: $68.40 2002 Payments: $68.40
Visual Technologies (C. Kleerly)	210 Sightview St. North Vancouver, BC V5E 9U4	Tel: (604) 643-5431 Fax: (604) 667-6129 Tax ID: 8978 45661	Terms: net 10 YTD Purchases: $5 136.00 2002 Payments: $5 136.00
Acculink Memory Inc. (Mimi Forget)	622 Recall Blvd. Vancouver, BC V6K 3V7	Tel: (604) 441-6201 Fax: (604) 442-7228 Tax ID: 2827 49126	E-mail: mforget@watergate.ca Web: www.recall.accurate.com Terms: 2/15, n/30 (before tax) YTD Purchases: $1 070.00
CyberTek Inc. (X. Celle)	44 Keyes Blvd. Vancouver, BC V5R 9B1	Tel: (604) 555-1234 Fax: (604) 554-4321 Tax ID: 1998 20012	E-mail: xc@intergate.bc.ca Web: www.cybertek.products.ca Terms: net 30 YTD Purchases: $856.00

Historical Invoices

Date	Invoice/Cheque #	Terms	Pretax Amount	Tax	Total
Acculink Memory Inc.:					
Jul. 5/02	AC-32	2/15, n/30 (before tax)	$1 000.00	$70.00	$1 070.00
CyberTek Inc.					
Jul. 4/02	536	net 30			$856.00
Jul. 4/02	Chq #9				$356.00
				Balance Owing	$500.00
			Accounts Payable Total		**$1 570.00**

The total Accounts Payable balance for all vendors should be $1 570, the balance in the Accounts Payable account.

6. Print the Vendor List and Vendor Aged Detail Report to check your work.

7. Back up your data files.

8. Finish the Payables Ledger history.

9. Close the Live Links data file.

Review Questions

1. What steps are involved in preparing the Payables Ledger for journal entries?
2. What must you do if you record an incorrect historical invoice for a vendor?
3. What amounts must be equal before you can finish the Payables Ledger history?
4. What is the purpose of entering historical invoices and payments for vendors?
5. What changes can you make to a vendor's ledger record before finishing the Payables Ledger history? after finishing the ledger history?
6. If the bank issued you a new series of cheques using a different numbering sequence, how would you enter the change in Simply Accounting?
7. Simply Accounting does not update alphabetical characters in the numbering sequence for forms. If your purchase orders are pre-numbered PW-1001, PW-1002, etc., how could you use the computer to track these numbers automatically?
8. Where do you enter the rates for sales taxes?
9. What role do linked accounts serve?
10. What reports should you print before finishing the Payables Ledger history to check that you entered the vendor information correctly? What information does each of these reports provide?
11. How would you add a second chequing account so that you could make payments from it?
12. Why are cheque number sequences added in the account's ledger rather than in the Forms settings?

CHAPTER 5

PAYABLES JOURNALS

Objectives

- **understand when to use the Payables journals**
- **complete credit and cash purchase transactions**
- **prepare and fill purchase orders**
- **make payments to vendors**
- **enter discounts on purchases**
- **make adjustments to purchase invoices**
- **add new vendor records from journals**
- **make sales tax remittances**
- **display and print Payables Ledger reports**

Introduction

In this chapter, you will begin to enter transactions in the Purchases and the Payments Journals for Play Wave. Because these journals are part of the Payables Ledger, using them for transactions allows you to keep the account information for all vendors up to date at all times. At the same time, the General Ledger is automatically kept up to date through the linked accounts we defined for the Payables Ledger. You will continue to use the General Journal for any transactions that are traditionally entered in the General Journal. Just as in a normal business, these General Journal entries would be interspersed with the Payables transactions from day to day.

If you have not completed the Payables Ledger setup in Chapter 4 and want to continue working on Chapter 5, you can use your copy of the file from the Data Disk — Ch05\play\playch05.sdb — to begin this chapter.

The Payables Journals

The Payables Ledger has two journals, one for entering purchase transactions, including purchase orders and quotes, and one for entering payments to vendors for previous purchases made on account. Any time that *Accounts Payable* is involved in a transaction, you must use the Purchases or the Payments Journal to enter the transaction. In fact, once the Payables Ledger is set up, you cannot choose *Accounts Payable* directly as a postable account. *Accounts Payable* does not show up on the Select Account list that you get from the Account fields. It can only be updated directly by the program through Purchases and Payments Journal entries. You must also use one of these two journals whenever a cheque is written to pay for a purchase or to settle a vendor account.

Payables Journal Entries
Entering Purchase Orders

◆ Open your working copy of the Play Wave file.

◆ Type **04-07-02** as the Session date.

The first transaction for April is a purchase order:

> ☑ Purchase Order #20001
> Dated Apr. 1/02
> Shipping date Apr. 4/02
> From The Buildex Corp., $1 500 for plastics and fibreglass and $1 500 for lumber plus $210 GST paid. Invoice total $3 210. Order is to be shipped within 3 days.
> Terms: 2/10, n/30 days.

Purchase Orders

Companies often use purchase orders as an internal control. The purchase order authorizes the purchase to be made without further permission. The form then also serves as an internal check against the future delivery of the goods ordered since the order may not by completely filled with the first shipment of goods. Comparing the order form with the invoice attached to the shipment shows the difference.

Purchase Orders are entered in the Purchases Journal (Purchases, Orders & Quotes icon) as shown here:

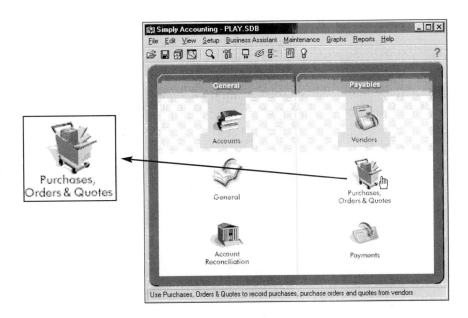

♦ Click the **Purchases, Orders & Quotes Journal icon** (the Purchases Journal icon) to open the Purchases Journal – Purchase Invoice:

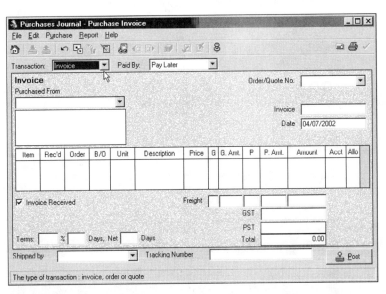

The Purchases Journal

The Purchases Journal input form resembles a purchase invoice more than a journal entry. By completing the invoice, however, you provide the details that Simply Accounting requires to complete a journal entry, and you have invoice details for future reference.

The invoice contains a number of tools that were in the General Journal — Home window, Store, Recall, Undo, Customize Journal, Allocate and Post. The remaining tools are new:

Remove the current purchase order or quote.

Adjust invoice, order or quote (for editing after posting).

Look up an invoice (to review, store or adjust an invoice after posting).

Most of the Purchases Journal fields can be removed with the Customize Journal option. We will use all the fields in later chapters.

Look up the previous invoice (when you are in the lookup screen).

Look up the next invoice (when you are in the lookup screen).

Track shipments if shipping information was part of the invoice.

Fill backordered quantities (fill purchase order).

Cancel backordered quantities.

Use (select) the same vendor automatically for the next transaction after posting the current transaction.

E-mail the purchase order to the vendor if the vendor accepts purchase orders by e-mail.

Print the purchase order.

Most of the menu options are the same as those in the General Journal. In addition, E-mail is a new option under the File menu and the **Purchase menu** duplicates the tool button options — Store, Recall, Remove Purchase Order or Quote, Adjust Invoice, Look up Invoice, Previous Invoice, Next Invoice, Track Shipments, Fill Purchase Order, Cancel Backordered Items, Use the Same Vendor Next Time, Allocate and Post.

The purchase invoice is designed to accommodate both inventory and non-inventory purchases.

Transaction: Choose invoice, purchase order or purchase quote from the drop-down list.

Paid By: Choose the method of payment from the drop-down list. **Pay Later** purchases are normal credit purchases. The amount is added to the balance owing in the account you have with the vendor. *Accounts Payable* is credited for the purchase. **Cash** and **Cheque** selections involve payment at the time of purchase. Payment for the goods is made by cheque or in cash for the full purchase amount and *Bank Account: Chequing* is credited. When **Credit Cards** are set up, they are also on the Paid By list.

Purchased From: Select the vendor from whom the purchase is made from a list of all vendors on record.

Order/Quote No.: The next purchase order number in sequence from the automatic numbering in the Forms Settings or the vendor's quote number. Previous order numbers may not be used as quote numbers.

Invoice: The vendor's invoice number from the invoice received with the purchase from the vendor.

Date: The date of the transaction or invoice. The default is the Session date or the date of the previous entry.

Item: Inventory code or item number.

Rec'd: The quantity, number of units of the item received, usually for inventory purchases. For non-inventory purchases, the quantity is usually one.

Order: The quantity or number of units ordered. Fractional quantities are allowed, up to four decimal places.

B/O: The quantity that is backordered, not yet received.

Unit: Again for inventory, the unit of measurement for the item purchased (e.g., kit, dozen, tonne, each).

Description: The inventory item name or description, or a description that you type for the goods purchased.

Price: The price per unit for the goods.

G: The GST code that applies to the purchase.

G. Amt.: The amount of GST applied to the purchase. GST is calculated automatically by the program based on the GST rate entered in the Sales Taxes settings, the code and the amount of the purchase.

Credit cards are covered in Chapter 8.

P: The Provincial Sales Tax rate that applies to the purchase, as a percentage.

P. Amt.: The amount of PST applied, calculated automatically by the program (rate times amount). Since PST is not refundable, the program adds this amount directly to the cost of the asset or the expense.

Amount: If you have entered a quantity and a unit price, the software calculates a total amount before taxes for the invoice line and enters it in this column.

Acct: The account that is to be debited for the purchase, normally an asset or an expense account. The program automatically credits *Accounts Payable* (or *Bank Account: Chequing* for cash purchases). Sometimes you will debit a liability account, such as when you remit sales taxes or payroll taxes to the government. To credit an account, as for returns, you must enter a negative amount. The program will then debit *Accounts Payable* or *Bank Account: Chequing*.

Allo: If you are using project costing, you can use this column to allocate or distribute an expense (or revenue) among the projects. Projects are discussed in Chapter 17.

Freight: There are five freight fields. They contain, in order, the GST code that applies to the freight amount, the amount of GST paid on the freight charge, the PST rate that applies to freight, the amount of PST, and the amount of freight charged by the vendor, before taxes.

GST: The total GST on the entire purchase invoice. The program adds up all of the GST amounts on the invoice and automatically debits *GST Paid on Purchases* . If the amount is negative, as for returns, *GST Paid on Purchases* will be credited.

PST: The total amount of PST paid on the purchase. The program automatically adds this amount to the asset cost or expense amount.

Total: The program automatically adds all the amounts to calculate the total. The total is automatically credited to *Accounts Payable* (or *Bank Account: Chequing*). For negative amounts, *Accounts Payable* is debited.

Invoice Received: A check box to confirm that the invoice was received or was included with the purchase.

Terms: The payment terms for this vendor, according to the entry in the vendor's ledger record. You can edit the terms for an individual invoice if they are different from the default terms.

Shipped By: Choose a shipping service from the drop-down list, if appropriate. Shippers and their tracking Web sites are entered from the Setup menu in the Home window. Shipment tracking is covered in Chapter 8.

Tracking Number: Enter the shipper's tracking number for the delivery, if appropriate.

Since this is not a purchase, we need to change the transaction type.

◆ Click the **Transaction field**, or its list arrow, to see the drop-down list of types:

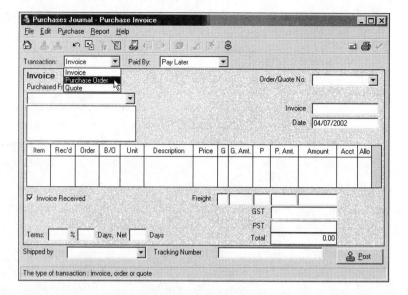

Transaction Types

You can enter three different types of transactions in the Purchases Journal.

Invoice: A normal purchase. The goods are received with the invoice.

Purchase Order: The merchandise is ordered from the vendor for delivery at some future date.

Quote: The vendor offers a price for merchandise. Businesses often receive quotes from a number of vendors for the same merchandise. At some later date, a quote may be turned into a firm purchase order or a purchase.

◆ Click **Purchase Order** to select this type and to modify the invoice form:

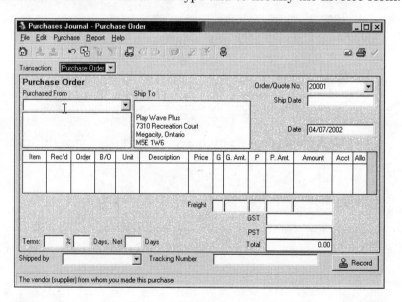

A Ship To field is added to the form and the next automatic purchase order number from the Forms Settings is added to the Order/Quote number field. By default, the business name and address appear as the shipping destination. The address may be edited if there is another business location.

◆ Click the **Purchased From field arrow** to see the list of vendors. (In this case you must click the arrow to see the list. If you click the field instead, you will add a text insertion point because you can type a name in this field.)

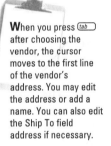

If you type the first letter of the vendor's name, you will advance to the part of the list beginning with that letter. This can save time if you have many vendor records. If only one vendor on the list begins with that letter, the vendor's name is added directly when you type the first letter.

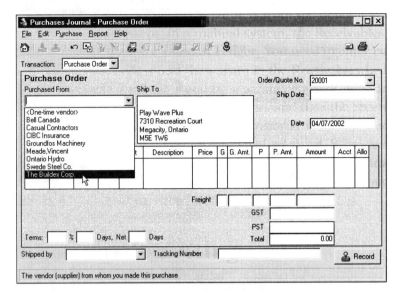

◆ Click **The Buildex Corp.**, the vendor for this purchase.

The vendor's name, address and payment terms are now added to the order form.

When you press ⟨tab⟩ after choosing the vendor, the cursor moves to the first line of the vendor's address. You may edit the address or add a name. You can also edit the Ship To field address if necessary.

◆ Click the **Ship Date field** to move the cursor because the shipping address is correct.

◆ Type **April 4** (the date that you expect to receive the merchandise).

◆ Press ⟨tab⟩ to advance to the Date field.

◆ Type **4-1** to replace the Session date with the transaction date, April 1.

◆ Click the **Order field**. You must enter an order quantity on a purchase order.

◆ Type **1**

◆ Press ⟨tab⟩. The program fills in the B/O field with the order quantity. The entire order is therefore backordered. The Unit field does not apply to this purchase.

◆ Click the **Description field**.

◆ Type **Fibreglass & plastics**

◆ Press ⟨tab⟩ to advance to the Price field.

◆ Type **1500** (the price of the first item on the purchase order before taxes).

◆ Press ⟨tab⟩ to advance to the G field.

◆ Double click or press ⟨enter⟩ to see the set of GST codes:

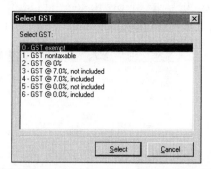

GST Codes

Purchases may be exempt from GST, be non-taxable or be zero-rated — codes 0, 1 and 2, respectively. GST may be included in the purchase price, as in many entertainment businesses and small restaurants (code 4) or not included in the prices, the usual business practice (code 3). In addition, if there are two separate GST rates for different types of goods or in different provinces, codes 5 and 6 may be used as well. The GST rates entered in the Sales Taxes Settings screen will appear on the Select GST list. If your screen shows only codes 0 and 1, check that you have selected a vendor for the purchase order and that you have activated the option to Include in GST Report for the vendor. Refer to Appendix C for more information about GST.

The Buildex Corp. does not include the GST in its prices. The rate is 7%.

◆ Click **3 - GST @ 7.0%**, not included.

◆ Click **Select** to add the code to your screen.

The program advances to the G. Amt. field and enters the GST amount. It also calculates the purchase amount as the price times the number of units ordered. The purchase is PST exempt, so we can skip the PST rate and amount columns.

◆ Click and then double click the **Acct field** to move the cursor and display the Select Account list.

◆ Click *1300* to select the *Supplies: Fibreglass & Plastics* account.

◆ Click **Select** to add the account to the invoice.

Enter the order for lumber on the following line by repeating the steps above. The quantity ordered is one, the description is Lumber, the GST code is 3, the price is $1 500, and the account number is *1320 Supplies: Lumber*. If there are additional items from the same vendor, enter them on the following lines, one item for each line.

The default vendor terms are correct, and there is no freight charge or shipping information, so the form is complete. Check your work carefully. Your order should look like the following:

If you have chosen not to include the vendor in GST reports in the vendor record, only codes 0 and 1 will be displayed. GST codes are also not available before you select a vendor for the order or purchase. If all codes are not available, check the vendor's ledger record to be sure that the vendor is included in the GST reports. Also make sure that the linked account for GST Paid is defined.

Notice that you can add a new account from the Purchases Journal too. In fact, this option is available in any Account field in the journals. You can also use the same account number more than once in the Purchases Journal.

We cannot display the journal entry for orders. Because no transaction has taken place, no journal entry is created.

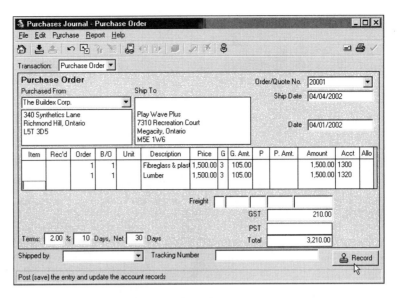

The Total and the GST have been added to the invoice.

Correcting the Purchase Order

You can edit all the fields on the Purchase Order directly by highlighting the incorrect information and retyping the correct details. If you want to change a GST code or account number, double click the incorrect item to view the Select list. Make the correct selection in the usual way. When you return to the order, the new information replaces the old. When you change an amount or quantity, press (tab) after making the correction to update the totals. You can change vendors by reselecting from the vendor list.

To insert a line, place the cursor on the order form line below the new one, choose the Edit menu and click Insert Line. For example, to insert a line between line one and two, click any part of line 2 and choose Insert Line. To remove a line, click anywhere in the line, choose the Edit menu and click Remove Line.

If you want to start over, choose the Edit menu and click Undo (or choose ⌹). Confirm that you want to delete the current transaction.

To make **corrections after posting** the order, you must first remove the incorrect order. Open the Purchases Journal and choose Purchase Order as the transaction type. Choose the purchase order you want to remove from the Order/Quote field list. Press (tab) to bring the order to the screen.

You can now choose ⌹ or choose the Edit menu and click Remove Purchase Order. Confirm that you want to remove the purchase order. Enter a new purchase order carefully with the correct information. The purchase order number will be updated to the next number in the sequence.

◆ Click **Record** ⌹ Record to save the order. A new blank order form appears.

◆ Close the Purchases Journal to return to the Home window because the next source document is a payment.

Entering Payments to Vendors

The Payments Journal is used to pay for previous credit purchases. Any unpaid purchases that were entered in the Vendor records as historical invoices, or Purchases Journal invoices that are still outstanding will appear in the Payments Journal.

The next transaction describes a payment for purchases made on account, including a discount for early payment.

✔ Cheque Copy #107
Dated Apr. 2/02
To Groundfos Machinery, $3 170 in full payment of account, including $40 discount
(before tax) for early payment. Reference invoice #GM-961.

Payments are entered in the Payments Journal indicated here:

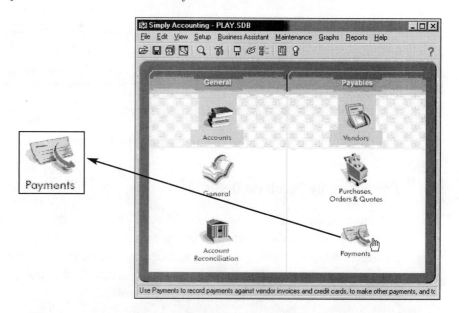

◆ Click the **Payments icon** to open the Payments Journal:

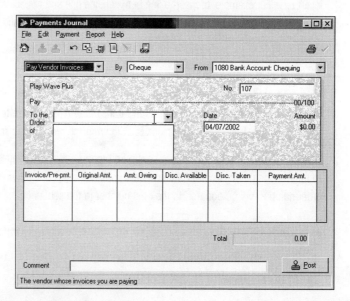

The Payments Journal Input Form

The upper portion of the Payments Journal resembles a cheque, while the lower segment looks like a statement. Most of the Payments Journal tools, Home window, Store, Recall, Undo, Customize, Lookup, Print, Allocate and Post, are the same as those in journals discussed earlier. If you have turned on the option to confirm printing (Forms Settings), the program will warn you to print when you try to post the payment before printing. Most of the menu items are also familiar.

There are two new tools:

 Enter prepayments or advances to vendors as deposits on purchases.

 Include fully paid invoices in the list of invoices. Normally these are not included. You should choose this option when you need to make a reversing entry. Any paid invoices that have not been cleared will be listed. Unpaid or outstanding invoices are always displayed.

There are three drop-down lists at the top of the journal input screen. **Pay** provides three options: Pay Vendor Invoice to make a payment against an outstanding invoice; Pay Credit Card Bill to make a payment to reduce the balance owing on a credit card (when these are set up); and Make Other Payment to make a cash purchase from a vendor. The second list, **By**, offers Cash and Cheque as payment methods. The final list, **From**, includes all bank accounts that were defined as Bank class and to which a payment may be credited.

Many of the input fields should also look familiar from the historical vendor payments input screen.

No.: The number of the cheque issued in payment of the account. Simply Accounting enters the next cheque number for the selected bank account based on the information provided in the account's ledger. The numbers are updated each time a payment is posted. You can edit the cheque number if necessary, as for NSF cheques, so that you do not affect the numbering sequence. The principal linked bank account is selected by default.

Pay: The cheque amount — completed by the program.

To the Order of: Select the vendor's name from the drop-down list, or the credit card being paid.

Date: As usual, this is the transaction date, the date on the cheque. The Session date is entered by default.

The statement portion contains six columns. The first four are completed automatically by the program and cannot be edited. All unpaid invoices for the selected vendor appear after you enter the vendor's name. Each invoice appears on a separate line of the statement.

Invoice/Pre-pmt.: The vendor's invoice number (from the Number field in Historical Invoices or the Invoice field in the Purchases Journal), or the reference number for a prepayment.

Original Amt.: The total amount of the original invoice, before any payments.

Amt. Owing: The balance still owing, or the amount that is unpaid.

Disc. Available: If the vendor's terms include a discount for early payment, the amount of the discount will appear in this column if the applicable period has not expired. The program automatically calculates the discount as a percentage of the total invoice. If the discount period has passed, based on the invoice date and the cheque date, the discount available column will show 0.00 as the discount.

Disc. Taken: If the discount is still available, and the full amount of the invoice is paid within the discount period, the amount in this field will be the full discount available. If a partial payment is made, the discount will not be taken. The amount in this column can be edited as any other input field.

Payment Amt.: By default, the program enters the amount owing as the payment amount, taking into account the discount. Again, you can edit the amount if a partial payment is made. For reversing entries, you can enter a negative amount. You may pay more than one invoice with a single cheque. The program will enter the total of the payment amounts on the Pay line of the cheque portion and in the Total field of the statement portion.

Comment: Enter a descriptive comment for the transaction, especially if this is a prepayment or other payment. The comment will become part of the journal entry.

The Enter prepayments and the Include fully paid invoices tools act as switches that stay on until you click them again, even if you close the journal. Therefore, you should turn them off before closing the journal.

The default selections for Pay, By and From are correct. We are paying a normal vendor invoice by cheque from *Bank Account: Chequing*.

◆ Click the **Vendor field (To the Order of) arrow** to access the vendor list.

◆ Click **Groundfos Machinery** to select this vendor and add the name to the invoice:

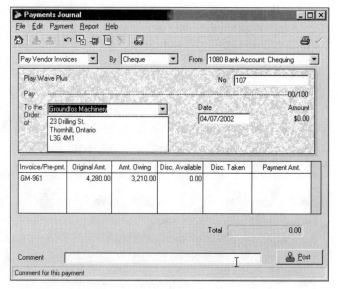

Notice that the one unpaid invoice appears in the statement portion of the journal. When there are other outstanding invoices, each one appears on its own line. You may choose to pay one or more invoices, partially or fully, with the same cheque.

◆ Double click the **Date field** and highlight the default date.

◆ Type **4-2-02**

◆ Press ⟨tab⟩ to advance to the Invoice field.

Notice that once you changed the date, the discount became available because the date of the cheque fell within the applicable discount period. Since the full invoice is paid, the discount will be taken. The discount is 1% of $4 000, the original full invoice amount before taxes.

◆ Click the **Disc. Taken column** for the first invoice line to enter the discount amount.

◆ Press ⟨tab⟩ to advance to the Payment Amt. column.

The total amount owing is entered and highlighted as the default. The amount can be edited if the invoice is not paid in full. Notice that the Total is not yet entered.

◆ Press ⟨tab⟩ to accept it. The amount is now added to the Total field and the Pay line of the cheque.

> **O**nce the cursor is in the Invoice column, you can press ⟨tab⟩ repeatedly to advance and accept the remaining default information as you move through the columns.

Partial Payments

If you need to enter a partial payment, just type the actual amount of the payment to replace the highlighted default amount. If the discount amount is not taken, you can press ⟨del⟩ when the discount amount is highlighted to remove the entry. The full discount will continue to be available until the invoice is paid in full or until the discount period has expired, whichever comes first.

The payment is complete and should now look like the following:

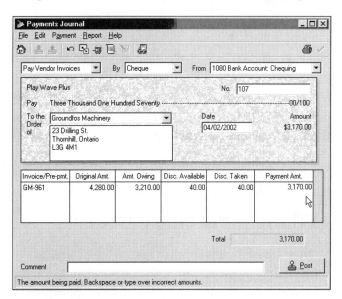

Before posting the transaction, you should review the journal entry.

◆ Choose the **Report** menu and click **Display Payments Journal Entry** to see the journal entry that will be posted:

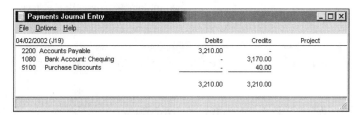

Even though you did not enter any account numbers, you will notice that the program has automatically debited *Accounts Payable* and credited *Bank Account: Chequing*. Remember that these were the accounts identified as the Payables linked accounts. In addition, *Purchase Discounts* has been correctly credited. By using the Payments Journal, which is linked to the General Ledger, the appropriate accounts are updated automatically. The vendor ledger record is also updated automatically. The balance owing is reduced by the payment. You can see that it is much easier to enter a payment in the Payments Journal than in the General Journal. It is harder to make a mistake because the program clearly identifies the vendor and prevents you from overpaying an account. In addition, you cannot enter an incorrect account number as you might in a General Journal entry.

◆ Close the journal entry to return to the Payments Journal.

Correcting the Payments Entry

Edit the text in any field by highlighting the incorrect information and typing over it. To change the vendor, reselect from the vendor list. Confirm that you want to discard the transaction.

You can also discard the transaction by clicking [icon] or by choosing the Edit menu and clicking Undo Entry. Again, you must confirm this action.

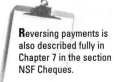

Reversing payments is also described fully in Chapter 7 in the section NSF Cheques.

After posting the payment, you may want to display the Vendor Aged Detail Report for Groundfos Machinery to see the payment recorded in the ledger.

To make **corrections after posting**, select the vendor and click the Include fully paid invoices tool ▤ to show the invoice that was incorrectly posted. Type negative amounts in the Amount field (and Disc. Taken field) to replace the positive amounts you entered incorrectly. Display the journal entry to be sure that it reverses the incorrect one. Post the entry. This will restore the invoice to its original level.

◆ Click **Post** 🖳 **Post** to save the transaction and update all the accounts.

A new blank Payments Journal window appears. Notice that the date of the previous cheque is now the default date.

◆ Close the Payments Journal to return to the Home window because the next transaction is not a payment.

Filling a Purchase Order

Once ordered merchandise arrives, the purchase order for it should be marked as filled, and replaced with a purchase invoice to create an *Accounts Payable* entry for the vendor. The next source document describes this transaction.

> ✔ Purchase Invoice #BC-612
> Dated Apr. 4/02
> From The Buildex Corp., to fill purchase order #20001, $1 500 for plastics and fibreglass and $1 500 for lumber plus $210 GST paid. Invoice total $3 210. Terms: 2/10, n/30 days.

Purchase orders are filled in the Purchases Journal.

◆ Click the **Purchases Journal** icon in the Home window (Purchases, Orders & Quotes) to open the Purchases Journal.

The default transaction type is correct as Invoice.

◆ Click the **Order/Quote No. field arrow** to display the list of orders and quotes on record. The only entry right now is purchase order number 20001:

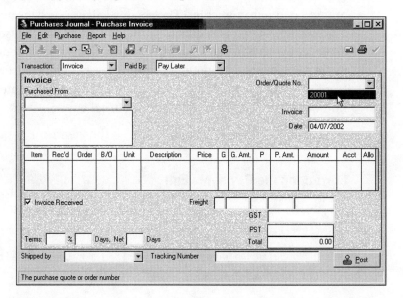

◆ Click **20001** to select it.

◆ Press ⌨tab. The purchase order is partially entered on the form:

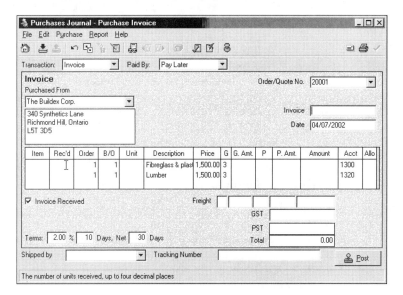

◆ Click the **Fill backordered quantities tool** 🔲 (or choose the Edit menu and click Fill Purchase Order) to complete the invoice.

The backordered quantity becomes the quantity received. Only the invoice number is missing because it was not on the order. The date also needs correcting.

◆ Click the **Invoice field**.

◆ Type **BC-612**

◆ Press ⌨tab to move to the Date field and select the default date.

◆ Type **4-4** to replace the Session date. The completed journal entry is shown here:

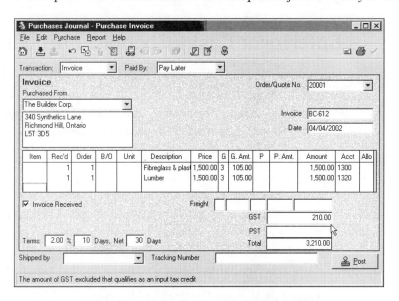

Before posting the transaction you should review your work.

◆ Choose the **Report** menu and click **Display Purchases Journal Entry**:

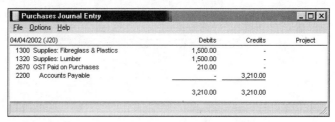

Notice that although only the two supplies accounts appear on the invoice form, *GST Paid* and *Accounts Payable* are also updated. These accounts link the Payables and the General Ledger because we defined them as the linked accounts. The balance owing in the vendor record is updated as well by the entry. The discount period will begin with the transaction date.

◆ Close the journal entry to return to the Purchases Journal.

Make corrections if necessary, as you made corrections to the purchase order.

◆ Click **Post** [Post] to save the transaction and update all accounts. The program displays the following message:

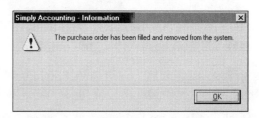

The purchase order has been removed because it is filled. This purchase order will no longer appear on the list of purchase orders/quotes in the journal.

◆ Click **OK** to return to the Purchases Journal.

◆ Close the Purchases Journal.

Entering a Cash (Cheque) Purchase

The next transaction shown is a cash purchase. That is, the payment by cheque or cash accompanies the purchase and the *Accounts Payable* balance does not change. Cash purchases may be entered in the Payments Journal as Other Payments or in the Purchases Journal as invoices paid by cheque. We will use the Payments Journal.

> ✔ Cash Purchase Invoice #VM-120
> Dated Apr. 7/02
> From Vincent Meade, $200 plus $14 GST paid for maintenance services rendered in shop and yard, and for inventory maintenance. Invoice total $214. Issued cheque #108 in full payment. Store this invoice as a recurring monthly entry.

◆ Click the **Payments Journal icon** [Payments] to open the journal.

◆ Click **Pay Vendor Invoices** as shown:

After posting the purchase, you may want to display the Vendor Aged Detail Report for The Buildex Corp. to see the purchase recorded in the ledger.

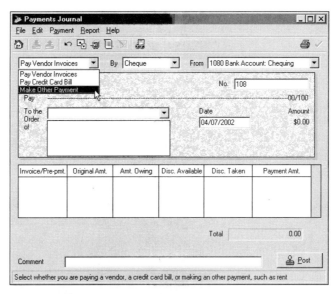

◆ Choose **Make Other Payment** to add the journal fields required for the invoice:

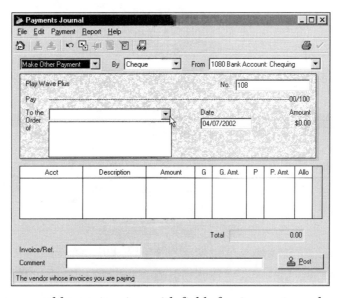

The journal now resembles an invoice, with fields for Account number, taxes and invoice number. The inventory fields of the Purchases Journal are removed. The cheque number is updated automatically for the bank account and is correct. The Session date is correct for this transaction.

◆ Choose **Vincent Meade** (or Meade, Vincent) from the To the Order of drop-down list as the vendor.

◆ Click the **Account field**.

◆ Type **5** and double click to open the Select Account list and advance to the first 5000 level account. Scroll down until 5200 is in view.

◆ Double click *5200 Maintenance Expense*. The cursor is in the Description field.

◆ Type `Maintenance services` as a description of the service received.

◆ Press `tab` to advance to the Amount field. As usual, enter amounts before tax.

◆ Type **200**

◆ Press ⌈tab⌋ to move to the G field (GST code).

◆ Press ⌈enter⌋ to see the list of GST codes.

◆ Double click **3 - GST @ 7% not included** to add the GST code and amount to the invoice.

Because this is a service, there is no **PST** paid. You can skip these fields.

◆ Click the **Invoice/Ref. field** to move the cursor.

◆ Type **VM-120** and press ⌈tab⌋ to advance to the Comment field.

◆ Type **VM-120, shop and yard maintenance**

The entry is complete as shown here:

Since the Comment is included in Journal Reports but the Invoice/Ref number is not, we repeat the invoice number in the Comment field.

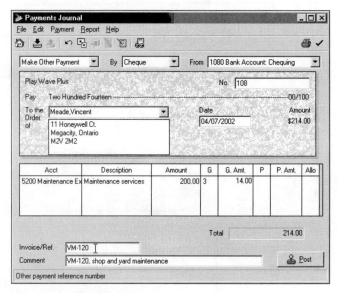

You are now ready to review the entry.

◆ Choose the **Report** menu and click **Display Payments Journal Entry**:

If other bank accounts are set up and defined as Bank class, you may use them instead of the principal linked bank account for payments.

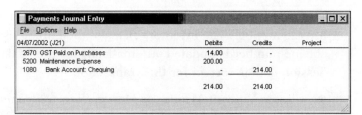

The journal entry is similar to the previous Purchases Journal entry with one important difference. *Bank Account: Chequing* is credited instead of *Accounts Payable* because immediate payment was made by cheque. *Bank Account: Chequing* is the bank account identified as the linked bank account for the Payables Ledger. After you post the invoice, the transaction will be recorded in the vendor's ledger as Other with a Payment recorded on the same day. Thus, the year-to-date total purchase and payments (Ledger record Activity tab) are updated and the transaction is added to the Vendor Aged Detail Report.

◆ Close the displayed entry to return to the Payments Journal. Make corrections to the invoice if necessary.

Since this is a recurring transaction, we need to store it before posting.

◆ Click **Store recurring transaction** 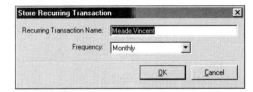 to see the Store Recurring Transaction screen that is familiar from the General Journal:

The Store Recurring Transaction screen is the same for all journals, with a Name and Frequency field. Both are correct so we need only to save the entry.

◆ Click **OK** to return to the journal. Notice that the Recall tool is now available.

◆ Click **Post** [🖊 Post] to save the transaction.

◆ Close the Payments Journal.

Entering Cash Purchases in the Purchases Journal

To enter the transaction for Meade using the Purchases Journal,
- Open the Purchases Journal.
- Choose Invoice as the type of Transaction and Paid by Cheque as the payment method. This adds a Cheque number field to the invoice. The number is updated for the selected bank account and should be correct.
- Select the vendor and add the invoice number and date.
- Enter a Description, GST code, Amount and Account as in any other invoice.
- Review the entry. If this is a recurring entry, store it. Post.

Using the Purchases Journal to enter a transaction like the one above will provide exactly the same journal entry and ledger updates as the Other Payment entry. Both journals also provide the options of paying by cash and credit card. To recall or adjust an entry, you must begin from the same journal that you used for the entry.

Adjusting an Invoice

The next transaction shows a correction or adjustment to an invoice previously posted. Since we have the Invoice Lookup feature turned on, we can adjust the invoice without making a complete reversing entry.

 Memo #6
Dated Apr. 7/02
From Manager: Purchase Invoice #BC-612, dated Apr. 4/02 from The Buildex Corp. included a freight charge of $40 plus $2.80 GST on the invoice. The invoice must be adjusted to add the freight charge. The new invoice total is $3 252.80.

◆ Click the **Purchases Journal** icon  to open the Purchases Journal.

You can adjust purchase orders or quotes in the same way as purchases. When you select the appropriate transaction type, the Adjust menu option changes to purchase order or quote accordingly. To adjust an Other Payment in the Payments Journal, first select Make Other Payment and then click the Adjust tool.

◆ Click the **Adjust invoice tool**  (or choose the Purchase menu and click Adjust Invoice) to access the Adjust an invoice screen:

In the Adjust an invoice window, you can enter the search parameters for finding the invoice you need to correct. Choose a range of dates or choose a vendor. You can even enter a specific invoice number if you know it.

The Adjust an Invoice Screen

The fields in this screen define how widely or narrowly you want to search for the required invoice. You can search a single journal entry date or a range of dates and you can search through invoices for all vendors or for a single vendor. If you have posted a large number of invoices, narrowing the search parameters will make it easier to find the right invoice quickly.

Start: The Start field may be blank or may contain the current calendar date. Enter a starting date that you are certain will precede the required entry. You may choose a date from the drop-down list.

Finish: The date at the end of the range or the final journal entry date. The Session date is the default. Choose a date that you are certain will come after the required entry.

Vendor Name: You can search through the invoices for all vendors or for a single vendor selected from the drop-down list.

Invoice Number: You may enter the invoice number that you want if you know what it is. When you enter an invoice number, the OK button becomes available.

We will search through all invoices entered in April.

◆ Click the **Start field**.

◆ Type **04-01-02**

The Finish date, the Session date, is appropriate since there are no entries past that date. The default selection, Search All Vendors, is the one we want.

◆ Click **Browse** to open the list of all invoices that fall within the designated range:

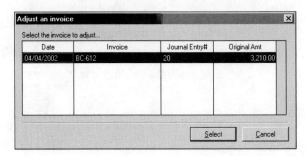

When there are several invoices on the Adjust an invoice list, you can click anywhere on the line for an invoice to select it.

The Adjust an invoice window includes all the requested invoices. Only invoices entered through the Purchases Journal will be included, so the cash purchase from Meade is not on the list. Invoice #BC-612 is the one we want and it is selected.

◆   Click **Select** to open the Purchases Journal – Adjusting Invoice window:

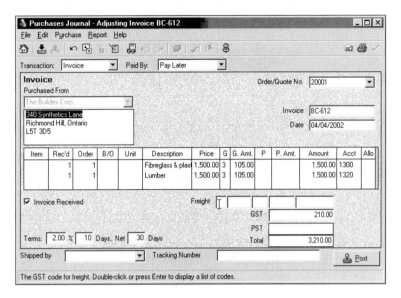

This is a copy of the original invoice that you can edit as required. All fields are available for editing except the Vendor field. If you have posted an invoice for the wrong vendor, you must complete a reversing entry (see Appendix D). The only change required is to add freight.

Use the status bar information to guide you through the freight fields.

Reviewing the Freight Fields

There are five freight fields. In the first field, enter the GST code that applies to the freight amount. The program calculates the amount of GST paid on the freight charge and places it in the second Freight field. In the third field, enter the PST rate that applies to freight, if PST is charged on freight in the province. The program calculates the amount of PST and enters it in the fourth field if the rate is not zero. Freight is not taxable in all provinces. In the final field, enter the amount of freight charged by the vendor, before taxes. In the Freight amount field, enter only freight charges that are not included as part of the cost of the goods purchased.

◆   Double click the **first Freight field**, the smallest box on the left beside the word Freight, the GST code field, to access the Select GST list.

◆   Double click code **3 – GST @ 7% not included** to select and add this code to the invoice.

◆   Click in the **last Freight field**, the freight amount field furthest to the right.

◆   Type **40**

◆ Press ⌨tab to enter the amount and update all the totals as shown here:

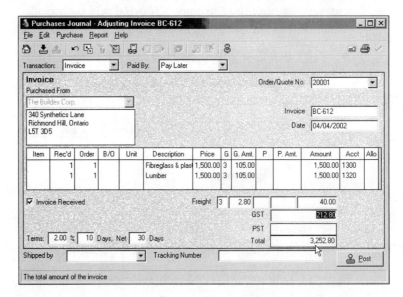

Notice that the GST on the freight amount is entered. The GST and Total are also updated to include the freight.

◆ Choose the **Report** menu and click **Display Purchases Journal Entry** to view the new journal entry.

The single correct journal entry is displayed:

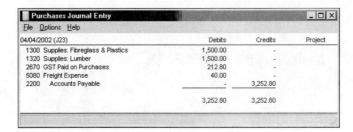

The entry is now correct. What you cannot see at this stage is that the program has created two entries at the same time — the one in the display and one that reverses the original entry. The original entry is not removed, just as you would not remove it in a manual accounting system, so that you maintain a complete audit trail.

◆ Close the display. When you are certain that the adjusted entry is correct,

◆ Click **Post** 🖳 Post .

To see the updated journal, display the Purchases Journal for the first week of April.

◆ Close the Purchases Journal window to return to the Home window.

Purchases Journal Report

◆ Choose the **Reports** menu, then choose **Journal Entries** and click **Purchases** to see the report options:

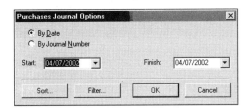

This screen is just like the General Journal Options screen in Chapter 3. All journal options screens look the same and include Sort and Filter options for the same fields. You may also display the report by posting date, the date of the transactions you entered, or by journal number, the journal entry sequence that the program creates according to the order in which you enter the transactions. Journals may be printed for any range of dates between the Earliest Transaction date and the Session date. The range of dates permitted can be seen in the drop-down lists for the dates. By default, the Session date is provided as both the start and finish dates and the Start date is highlighted for editing. You can also sort and filter the report by date, journal entry number, source or comment.

◆ Click **By Journal Number** to change the option.

The numbers displayed as the Start and Finish will depend on your previous actions. From the journal display on page 146, we see that the original Buildex transaction was J20. This is the first number we need to include.

◆ Click the **Start number field** on your display.

◆ Type **20** to replace the highlighted start number.

◆ Click **OK** to display the report:

In addition to the original purchase entry, the journal includes the reversing or adjusting entry (Journal entry #22), the opposite of entry #20, which was posted incorrectly. Notice the explanatory comment for the reversing entry. The final entry, J23, is the correct one.

◆ Close the display when you have finished viewing it.

Enter J1 if you are in doubt about the actual journal entry number. Displaying the journal in reverse order (sorting by Journal Number and reversing the order) will also make it easier to see the recent entries.

In the Vendor Aged Detail Report, only the final correct invoice will be recorded. Because the cash purchase from Meade was recorded in the Payments Journal it will be part of the Payments Journal Report, not the Purchases Journal Report

Sales Tax Remittances

The next transaction involves two new features, remittance of sales taxes and the addition of a new vendor. New vendors can be added directly from the Purchases or Payments Journal.

A business like Play Wave is classified as a manufacturing contractor — they make goods and they also install them as part of "real property." Although the customer does not pay PST on the contracted work, the business still has a tax obligation equal to 8 percent of the manufactured cost of the installed goods. In essence, the business becomes the final customer for these products and it is the final customer who must pay the retail sales tax.

Retail Sales Tax Calculation

The rules regarding PST vary from province to province and for different types of products and services.

Most retail businesses charge their customers PST on sales. When Play Wave sells uninstalled playground equipment products directly to customers, as in Chapter 15, the customers will pay PST on the sale. The business remits this full amount, recorded in the *PST Payable* account, to the Minister of Finance. The service to install the goods is, however, not taxable when the goods become part of real property (e.g., houses). A business that manufactures and installs these kinds of products is classified as a manufacturing contractor. Retailers do not pay PST on merchandise that will be resold to customers. The manufacturing contractor is similarly exempt from paying PST on the raw materials and tools used to manufacture goods. However, manufacturing contractors still have a retail sales tax obligation. They must pay PST on the manufactured cost of the goods that they install. The manufactured cost is basically the cost of all raw materials used in making the goods plus the cost of labour to manufacture the goods. The customer's final contract price includes this manufactured cost plus the cost of the labour to install the goods on the customer's property and any additional markup to ensure a profit. The PST or Retail Sales Tax is therefore calculated on less than the full contract price.

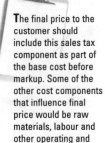

The final price to the customer should include this sales tax component as part of the base cost before markup. Some of the other cost components that influence final price would be raw materials, labour and other operating and overhead expenses.

For a retailer, the amount of PST Payable is simply the balance in the *PST Payable* account, 8 percent of revenue. The manufacturing contractor must calculate the PST owing based on the calculated manufactured cost of goods installed during the previous month, and then record the liability in a separate General Journal entry. By debiting the expense account *Sales Tax on Manufactured Cost*, the tax is recognized as a part of the total operating expenses. The *PST Payable* account is credited to record the liability.

Thus, to prepare for making the actual remittance in the Purchases Journal, the first step is to calculate and record the tax liability on manufactured cost. Two new accounts are needed for the sales tax remittance transactions.

◻ Create 2 new Group accounts: 5240 Sales Tax on Manufactured Cost (G)
                                   4280 PST Compensation (G)

◻ Memo #7
  Dated Apr. 7/02
  The manufactured cost of all goods sold in March is calculated to be $8 100. The PST at 8% is $648. Record $648 as the PST Payable for March 2002. (Complete a General Journal entry to debit the new expense account Sales Tax on Manufactured Cost, and credit PST Payable.)

◆   Close the General Journal.

◆ Change the Session date to April 14, 2002. (Click 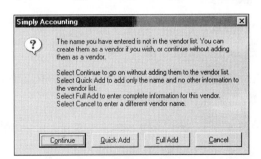 or choose the Maintenance menu and click Change Session Date. Type 04-14-02. Click OK.)

Adding a New Vendor

◆ Open the **Payments Journal**.

◆ Choose **Make Other Payment** from the Pay drop-down list.

The following transaction makes the payment to the Minister of Finance. Because the Minister is a new vendor, complete record details are provided.

> ✔ Memo #8
> Dated Apr. 8/02
> Pay the PST amount owing for March 2002 to the Minister of Finance. This liability is reduced by the sales tax compensation of 5% of the PST account balance. Issue cheque #109 in payment.

> ✔ Vendor: Minister of Finance
> Address: Mowat Block, 800 Bay St.
>   Megacity, ON M3R 2F2
> Tel: (416) 592-1000
> *Web site: www.gov.on.ca
> Do not include in GST reports.
> Memo: PST remittance is due. Date May 15. Display memo in To-Do List.

Remember that the * before the Web address indicates a real site address.

◆ Click the **To the Order of field**.

◆ Type **Minister of Finance**

◆ Press `tab`.

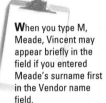

When you type M, Meade, Vincent may appear briefly in the field if you entered Meade's surname first in the Vendor name field.

As you type in the new name, the program tries to find a match in the existing vendor list. The program recognizes that you have entered the name of a vendor that is not yet on record and gives you the opportunity to add a record for the vendor:

> **Simply Accounting**
>
> ? The name you have entered is not in the vendor list. You can create them as a vendor if you wish, or continue without adding them as a vendor.
>
> Select Continue to go on without adding them to the vendor list.
> Select Quick Add to add only the name and no other information to the vendor list.
> Select Full Add to enter complete information for this vendor.
> Select Cancel to enter a different vendor name.
>
> [Continue] [Quick Add] [Full Add] [Cancel]

If you have typed a name incorrectly, choose Cancel to return to the To the Order of field on the Payments Journal Invoice. If you do not want to add this vendor to your mailing list, you may choose Quick Add. The vendor's name becomes part of your ledger records, but no other information is included for the vendor. If you do not want the vendor on your lists or in the Vendor Aged Detail Reports, you would choose Continue. This is appropriate for Cash Purchase transactions from one-time vendors. For the Quick Add and Continue selections, you will return to the Payments Journal.

The final option is to add the full vendor record. We want a complete record for the Minister of Finance because we will make regular payments and we need to modify some options for the vendor. Therefore, we will add the full record.

◆ Click **Full Add** to show the Payables Ledger form for the new vendor:

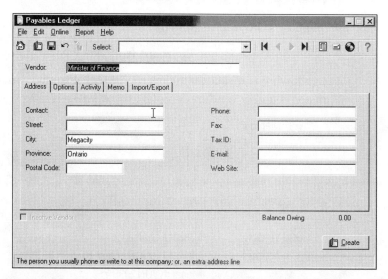

The vendor's name is already added from the Payments Journal entry. The Address tab appears first.

◆ Enter the address information on the ledger page. Use the Contact field to enter Mowat Block as part of the address.

◆ Click the **Options tab**.

◆ Click **Include in GST Report** to remove the checkmark.

GST does not apply to Provincial Sales Tax remittances so the Minister of Finance should not be included in GST reports and the GST codes can be removed from the journals for this vendor.

◆ Click **Print Contact on Cheques** so that Mowat Block will be included with the address.

Skip the Activity tab screen. There are no previous transactions for this vendor.

◆ Click the **Memo tab**.

We can add program reminders to remit sales tax on a monthly basis and add the memo to the To-Do List.

◆ Type **PST remittance is due** (in the Memo field).

◆ Click the **To-Do Date field**.

◆ Type **05-15-02**

◆ Click the option **Display this memo in the To-Do List**.

◆ Click **Create** to save the vendor record and return to the Payments Journal.

Retail Sales Tax Remittances

To make the remittance, use the *PST Payable* account balance as the amount to be remitted. The relevant journal entry will debit *PST Payable* to reduce the liability and credit *Accounts Payable* (or *Bank Account: Chequing* if the entry is completed as a cash purchase).

The final step will recognize the sales tax compensation. A business making PST remittances in Ontario can withhold 5 percent of the total amount of tax as compensation for collecting and remitting the payment to the Minister of Finance before the due date assigned to the business. Enter this amount on the second line of the Journal with a minus sign in the amount field and choose the *PST Compensation* revenue account. The minus sign provides the necessary credit to the revenue account instead of a normal debit, and a debit to *Accounts Payable* (or *Bank Account: Chequing*) rather than the usual credit. Neither the *PST Payable* amount nor the *PST Compensation* should have GST applied.

Sales taxes must be remitted by the due date assigned to the business in order to avoid late payment penalties and to be eligible for the sales tax compensation. Payments may be made monthly, quarterly or annually depending on the total annual sales for the business. Play Wave's PST remittances are due on the 15th of each month.

◆ Enter April 8 as the invoice date and press (tab).

◆ Press (enter) and choose *2640 PST Payable* from the Select account list.

◆ Type an appropriate description in the Description field and press (tab).

◆ Type **648** and press (tab).

◆ Double click the **G column** to see the available GST codes.

Notice that only the non-taxable codes, 0 and 1, are listed. This is the result of choosing not to include the vendor in GST reports.

◆ Double click Code 1 to add the non-taxable code or click Cancel to leave the GST code field blank. Both options are acceptable.

Use the next invoice line to record the sales tax compensation (5% of $648 is $32.40).

◆ Click the **Account field** on the next invoice line and press (enter).

◆ Choose *4280 PST Compensation* as the account. Press (tab).

◆ Type an appropriate description and press (tab).

◆ Type **-32.40** in the Amount column and press (tab).

◆ Press (enter) and double click **GST code 1**.

◆ Type **Memo 8** in the Invoice/Ref. number field and in the Comment field.

◆ Choose the Report menu and click **Display Payments Journal Entry** to review the journal entry:

You may want to add a further description to the Comment field, such as PST remittance for March.

Payments Journal Entry				
File Options Help				
04/08/2002 (J25)		Debits	Credits	Project
2640	PST Payable	648.00	-	
1080	Bank Account: Chequing	-	615.60	
4280	PST Compensation	-	32.40	
		648.00	648.00	

Observe the journal entry carefully. Notice that *Bank Account: Chequing* is credited for the *PST Payable* amount minus the sales tax compensation. If you had chosen to enter the transaction as a Purchase Invoice with the Pay Later option, you would make an additional separate Payments Journal entry.

◆ Close the display.

When you are certain that the entry is correct,

◆ Click **Post** [🏬 Post] to save the transaction.

◆ Enter the following purchase and purchase order:

> ☐ Purchase Invoice #SC-5019
> Dated Apr. 8/02
> From Swede Steel Co., $2 000 for nuts, bolts, steel bars and other hardware plus
> $140 GST paid. Invoice total $2 140. Terms: 2/15, n/30.

> ☐ Purchase Order #20002
> Dated Apr. 8/02
> Shipping Date: Apr. 30, 2002
> From Groundfos Machinery, $12 000 for hydraulic ground drill plus $840 GST paid.
> Invoice total $12 840. Terms: 2/20, n/30. (Edit the payment terms discount rate.)
> Using the Account Wizard from the Account field, create a new Subgroup account
> for the new drill — 1580 Hydraulic Drill (A). (Remember to change the account type.)

◆ Close the Purchases Journal to return to the Home window.

◆ Create two more General Ledger accounts to complete the drill Subgroup of accounts and maintain the logical order of accounts:

> ☐ 1590 Accum Deprec: Hydraulic Drill (A)
> 1595 Net Hydraulic Drill (S)

Payables Ledger Reports

Vendor Lists and Vendor Aged Reports were described in the previous chapter. The Purchases Journal was described earlier in this chapter.

Payments Journal

◆ Choose the **Reports** menu, then choose **Journal Entries** and click **Payments** to see the report options:

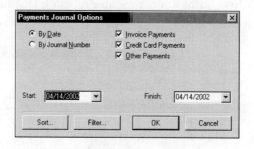

Remember to edit the payment terms for this purchase order. Then edit the payment terms in the vendor's ledger record.

You can access all Payables Ledger reports from the Reports menu or from the Select a report tool in the Vendors window.

To see the journal entries for all journals in a single report, go to the Home window. Choose the Reports menu, then choose Journal Entries and click All.

You can include all types of payments made in the journal or choose to report on only one or two types. By default, all are selected. The remaining report options are the same as those for the Purchases Journal. You can sort and filter, and report by posting date or by journal entry number. The Session dates are the defaults for both Start and Finish dates. We want to print the journal for the first week of April, because that will include all the payment entries to date and we need to include all types of payments.

◆ Type **04-01-02**

◆ Press ⌧ to advance to the Finish date to highlight it for editing.

◆ Type **04-08-02**

◆ Click **OK** to display the report.

Drill-Down Reports

The same drill-down reports are available from both the Purchases Journal Report and the Payments Journal Report. Double click the journal entry number, the date or the invoice number to access the Invoice Lookup window for the journal entry with the usual lookup options. Lookup is available only for transactions entered in the Purchases or Payments Journals. The General Journal transactions for March will not be available. When you double click the vendor name, the Vendor Aged Detail Report appears for the selected vendor. Double clicking the account number, account name or the amount will lead you to the General Ledger (All Transactions) report for the selected account. The date range for the drill-down report will match the dates for the journal report. You may print the drill-down report. When you close the drill-down report, you will return to the journal report window.

Invoice Lookup is introduced in Chapter 8.

◆ Close the display when you arc finished viewing it.

Alternate Methods of Accessing Journal Reports

There are several ways to access the Purchases and Payments Journal Reports, both from the Home window and from the Vendors window.

The label for the Display tool changes when you have an icon selected in the Home window.

• From the Home window, click the Display tool button. Choose Purchases Journal or Payments Journal from the Select Report screen to indicate the report you want. Click Select to display report options.

• From the Home window, right-click the Purchases Journal icon to select it. Then click the Display Purchases Journal tool to display the Purchases Journal Report options. To see the Payments Journal Report options, right-click the Payments Journal icon and then click the Display Payments Journal tool.

• From the Vendors window, click the Select a report tool. Then choose Display Purchases Journal or Display Payments Journal to indicate the type of report you want and to display the report options. All Payables Ledger reports are included in this selection list.

• From the Vendors window, choose the Reports menu and click Display Purchases Journal or Display Payments Journal to display the corresponding report options. All Payables Ledger reports are included in this Reports menu.

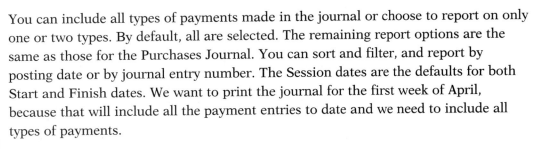

Aged Overdue Payables Report

◆ Choose the Reports menu, then choose **Payables** and click **Aged Overdue Payables** in the Home window to see the report options:

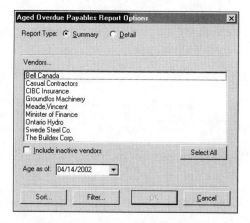

The Aged Overdue Payables Report and its options are very similar to the Vendor Aged Report discussed in the previous chapter. You may print the report for one or more vendors or for all vendors. Press _ctrl_ and click the name of each vendor to include in the report or click Select All to include them all.

The Detail and Summary options allow you display only the total owing in each aging period, the Summary option, or the individual invoices in each aging period, the Detail option. If there are overdue accounts, they will be listed in a separate column, based on the vendor terms. The report also includes due dates for invoices. If there are no outstanding invoices for a vendor, that vendor is omitted from the report.

To display the Detail report for all vendors up to the Session date,

◆ Click **Detail**.

◆ Click **Select All**.

◆ Click the **Date field** (Age as of) to move the cursor and prepare the field for editing.

◆ Type **04-14-02** if this date does not appear.

◆ Click **OK** to display the report. The Swede Steel Co. invoice is overdue.

Drill-Down Reports

From the Detail report, double click the vendor's name to display the Vendor Aged Report. Double click any other item in the report to access the Invoice Lookup window for the journal entry and all of the usual lookup options.

From the Summary report, double click any item on the line for a vendor to see the Aged Overdue Detail Report for the same vendor.

You may print the drill-down report. When you close the drill-down report, you will return to the previous report.

◆ Choose the **File** menu and click **Print** in the **Report** window to print the report.

◆ Close the display when you are finished viewing and printing the report.

Vendor Purchases

Only the vendor purchases that you entered in the Purchases Journal or as Other Payments in the Payments Journal are listed in the Vendor Purchases Report. The Detail Report lists the number of units purchased, the cost per unit and the total cost. The Summary Report shows the total cost and the number of transactions for each vendor. Although the report can include both inventory and other purchases as well as freight, it is primarily an inventory report. Therefore, it will be explained in Chapter 15 when the Inventory Reports are introduced.

Pending Purchase Orders

The Pending Purchase Orders Report shows all purchase orders that have not been filled as at the Session date.

◆ Choose the Reports menu, then choose **Payables** and click **Pending Purchase Orders** in the Home window to see the report options:

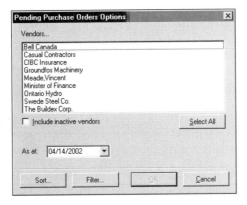

Press ⌃ctrl⌄ and click the name of each vendor you want to include in the report.

Again, you can include one or more vendors or all vendors. Only vendors with outstanding orders will actually be added to the report. Others are omitted.

◆ Click **Select All**.

◆ Click **OK** to display the report.

Although there is one outstanding purchase order at this time, it is not included in the report because the shipping date is later than the report date. Display the report for April 30 to display the purchase order. The report includes the purchase order number, the vendor, the purchase order and shipping dates, and the total order amount.

Drill-Down Reports

Double click the vendor's name to display the Vendor Aged Report. Double click any other item in the report to view the purchase order. The order is in Lookup format and cannot be adjusted from this window. When you close the drill-down report, you will return to the previous report.

◆ Choose the **File** menu and click **Print** in the report window to print the report.

◆ Close the display when you are finished viewing and printing the report.

Printing Mailing Labels

If you have printer label forms, you can use the Simply Accounting program to prepare mailing labels for one or more vendors. Be certain that your print options are set up correctly for the label paper you are using.

Setting the Printer for Labels

For practice, you can use ordinary paper to see how the labels will be printed. It is also good practice to print a sample of a few labels on ordinary paper to make sure that your margin and font settings are appropriate.

The following instructions will print two columns of labels on ordinary paper.

◆ Choose the **Setup** menu and click **Reports & Forms**.

◆ Click the **Labels tab** to display the Labels settings screen:

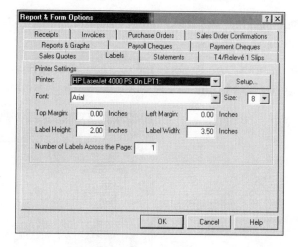

◆ Choose one of your printers from the list of printers in the Printer list.

◆ Choose a font from the Font list and print size from the Size list.

◆ Enter .5 in the Top Margin field.

◆ Enter .5 in the Left Margin field.

◆ Enter 2 in the Label Height field.

◆ Enter 3 in the Label Width field.

◆ Enter 2 in the Number of Labels that are printed Across the Page field.

◆ Click **OK** to save the settings and return to the Home window.

Printing Labels

◆ Choose the **Reports** menu, then choose **Mailing Labels** and click **Vendors** in the Home window to see the options:

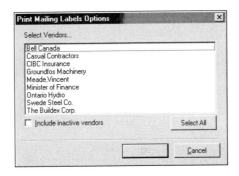

You can include one or more vendors in the list by pressing ⌜ctrl⌝ and clicking the names.

◆ Click **Select All** to print labels for all vendors.

◆ Click **OK** to print the labels. Printing will begin immediately.

Management Reports

Management Reports are the Simply Accounting Advice reports that are customized for your data files. If you have the Crystal Reports program installed (from the Simply Accounting installation disk) you can further modify the reports to suit your needs.

◆ Choose the **Reports** menu, then choose **Management Reports** and click **Payables** in the Home window to see the options:

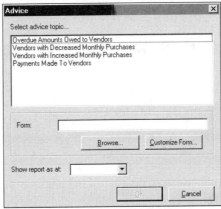

The advice topics include reports that management can use to make decisions about which vendors to pay first, or to analyze purchase patterns over time. The Browse button allows you to find a report form file, while the Customize button allows you to modify a selected report form.

◆ Click **Payments Made To Vendors** as the advice topic.

◆ Click **OK** to see the report showing all vendors and the total payments for the current and previous year.

◆ Click the **Print tool** 🖶 to print the report.

◆ Close the report when finished.

The report forms are in the Forms folder under Winsim. You can install them by installing the Crystal Reports program from the program CD.

Before starting the practice for Live Links,

◆ Make the payment to Swede Steel Co. for the overdue account.

> ☐ Cheque Copy #110
> Dated Apr. 8/02
> To Swede Steel Co., $535 in payment of account. Reference invoice #SC-4211.
> There is no discount because the discount period has ended.

◆ To follow good management practice, we recommend printing the following reports:

> Journal Entries: All Journals (April 1 to April 8)
> Trial Balance: As at April 8
> Income Statement: from March 1 to April 8
> Balance Sheet: As at April 8

◆ Close the Play Wave files to prepare for making journal entries for Live Links.

Practice: Live Links

In this chapter, you will begin to make journal entries for Live Links using the two Payables Journals. As in any normal business, you will continue to use the General Journal for entries that require the use of the General Journal.

Payables Journal Entries
Instructions

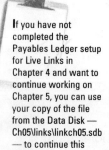

If you have not completed the Payables Ledger setup for Live Links in Chapter 4 and want to continue working on Chapter 5, you can use your copy of the file from the Data Disk — Ch05\links\linkch05.sdb — to continue this chapter.

1. Open the data file for Live Links.

2. Enter **August 8, 2002,** as the Session date.

3. Enter the following transactions for Live Links using the appropriate journals. Remember to make regular backups of your data files.

> ☐ Add the following new accounts
> 1640 Laser Colour Printer (A)
> 1650 Accum Deprec: LC Printer (A)
> 1655 Net Laser Colour Printer (S)
> 4220 Sales Tax Compensation (G)

> ☐ Add the following two new vendors:
>
> | | |
> |---|---|
> | Name: | Minister of Finance, BC |
> | Address: | 100 Ruling Court |
> | | Victoria, BC V8R 3R3 |
> | Tel: | (250) 654-7829 |
>
> Do not include in GST reports.

Name: Tektronics Inc.
Contact: Lin Tran
Address: 75 Lazer Ave.
Vancouver, BC V2T 6H2
Tel: (604) 446-0127
Fax: (604) 448-9114
Tax ID: 5566 44553
E-mail: LTran@tektronics.nettwerk.ca
Web site: www.tektronics_lasers.com
Terms: 2/5, n/30 (after tax)
Include in GST reports.

☐ Purchase Order #1
Dated Aug. 1/02
Shipping date Aug. 4/02
From Tektronics Inc., $7 500 plus $525 GST paid for new high-resolution colour
laser printer. A freight charge of $40 plus $2.80 GST will be added to the invoice.
Invoice total $8 067.80. Printer is to be shipped within 3 days. Terms: 2/5, n/30 days.

☐ Cheque Copy #19
Dated Aug. 2/02
To Acculink Memory Inc., $1 070 in full payment of account. There is no discount
because the early payment period has passed. Reference invoice #AC-32.

☐ Purchase Invoice #TI-663
Dated Aug. 3/02
From Tektronics Inc., to fill purchase order #1, $7 500 plus $525 GST paid for new
high-resolution colour laser printer. Freight charges of $40 plus $2.80 GST are
added. Invoice total $8 067.80. The printer is expected to last for 3 years with a
scrap value of $300. Terms: 2/5, n/30 days.

☐ Cheque Copy #20
Dated Aug. 6/02
To CyberTek Inc., $500 in full payment of account balance. Reference invoice #536.

☐ Memo #5
Dated Aug. 7/02
Helen Lively, owner, invested an additional $10 000 in the business from her
personal funds. She deposited the money directly into the bank account in lieu of
securing an additional bank loan to purchase the laser colour printer.

☐ Cheque Copy #21
Dated Aug. 8/02
To Tektronics Inc., $7 906.44 in full payment of account, including $161.36 discount
taken for early payment. Reference invoice #TI-663.

Memo #6
Dated Aug. 8/02
Use the General Ledger account balance for PST Payable on July 31, 2002, to record the PST liability owing to the Minister of Finance, BC. The PST Payable liability of $210 is reduced by $6.93, the sales tax commission of 3.3% of the PST account balance. Issue cheque #22 for $203.07 in payment. (Record as an Other Payment.)

Purchase Invoice #BD-6972
Dated Aug. 8/02
From Business Depot, $90 plus $6.30 GST paid and $6.30 (7%) PST paid for copy paper to prepare workshop handouts. Invoice total $102.60. Terms: net 15 days. (Enter 7 in the P field for the PST rate at 7%, enter 90 in the Amount field and allow the program to allocate the tax payment automatically to the expense account.)

Purchase Quote #PUQ-222
Dated Aug. 8/02
Shipping date Aug. 25/02
From Promo Uno, $450 plus $31.50 GST paid and $31.50 (7%) PST paid for design, printing and lamination of posters to advertise workshop series. Invoice total $513. Terms: net 30 days. Quote will remain valid for 15 days.

Purchase Quote #BDQ-773
Dated Aug. 8/02
Shipping date Aug. 31/02
From Business Depot, $550 plus $38.50 GST paid and $38.50 (7%) PST paid for design, printing and lamination of posters to advertise workshop series. Invoice total $627. Terms: net 15 days. Quote will remain valid for 15 days.

4. Print the following reports:
Journal Entries: All journals for August 1 to August 8
Trial Balance: As at August 8
Income Statement: From July 1 to August 8
Balance Sheet: As at August 8
Vendor Aged Detail Report: For all vendors as at August 8

5. Close the data file for Live Links to prepare for setting up the Receivables Ledger for Play Wave Plus.

Review Questions

1. How would you enter a purchase on account that includes a partial payment?
2. How is entering a purchase invoice in the Purchases Journal different from entering it in the General Journal?
3. How is a cash purchase different from a purchase that is paid later?
4. What reasons may there be for the message "there is no data to report" when you request a report?
5. What happens when you post a purchase invoice? What linked accounts are affected and how are they affected?

6. How do you change a purchase quote into a purchase order?

7. What must you do to post a transaction to the *Accounts Payable* account?

8. If you forgot to add sales tax to an invoice, how could you make the correction?

9. What information is included in the Payments Journal Report? How would you get the Purchases and the Payments Journal entries in a single report? Why might you want separate reports?

10. How do you make corrections to a purchase invoice after posting? What do you enter? What does Simply Accounting do?

11 Describe two methods of adding a new vendor once you have finished the Payables Ledger history. Explain the differences between Quick Add, Full Add and Continue.

12. If you accidentally prepared and posted an invoice that filled a purchase order, but forgot to use the purchase order, what corrections would you make?

CHAPTER 6

RECEIVABLES LEDGER SETUP

Objectives

- *explain the components of the Receivables Ledger entry screens*
- *enter settings for the Receivables Ledger*
- *understand and identify Receivables Ledger linked accounts*
- *enter address information and payment terms for customers*
- *enter historical invoices and payments for customers*
- *enter additional customers for practice*
- *display and print Receivables Ledger reports*
- *finish the Receivables Ledger history*

Introduction

Play Wave Plus will begin to use the Receivables Ledger at this stage to simplify the journal entries and increase the amount of management information available about customers. In this chapter, you will set up the Receivables Ledger to prepare for entering transactions in the Sales and Receipts Journals. Setting up the Receivables Ledger — the ledger that deals with all customer information — is very similar to setting up the Payables Ledger. You must change the ledger settings, identify the accounts that link the Receivables and General Ledgers, create customer accounts and add historical sales information for all customers. The *Accounts Receivable* control account is the primary account that links with the General Ledger. It shows the total of all amounts owed by customers.

If you have not completed the journal entries in Chapter 5 and want to continue working on Chapter 6, you can use your copy of the Data Disk file — Ch06\play\playch06.sdb — to begin this chapter.

The Accounts Receivable Ledger

The Receivables Ledger contains all the information about individual customers. You cannot work with the Receivables Ledger separately from the General Ledger as you can in a manual accounting system. In a manual system, the Receivables Ledger is a subsidiary ledger separate from the General Ledger. You need to enter customer transactions in the General Ledger and then again in the Receivables Ledger. In large companies, these steps are often completed by separate people or departments. The accountant makes the regular General Journal entries and then the receivables clerk adds the invoice details to the individual customer records and also records the receipts. In Simply Accounting, the ledgers are fully integrated. Whenever you enter information through the journals of the Receivables Ledger, the program automatically updates the corresponding General Ledger accounts through the linked accounts, without the need to enter the information twice.

Changing Default Settings
Receivables Ledger Settings

You can set the defaults for the Receivables Ledger to customize further the program for the company data files.

◆ Start the Simply Accounting program if you have not already done so and open the file for Play Wave Plus. The Session date should be April 14, 2002.

◆ Click **OK** to accept the Session date.

You should be in the Home window. Before we can set up the Receivables Ledger, we must restore its icons.

◆ Choose the **View menu**, then choose **Modules** and click **Receivables**.

◆ Click the **Setup tool** button 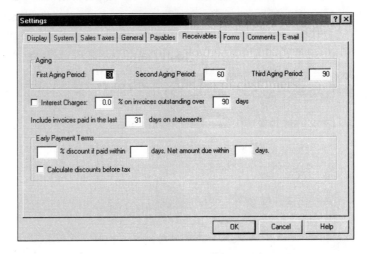 to display the Select Setup screen.

◆ Click **Customers** from the drop-down list.

◆ Click **Select** to display the Receivables Settings options:

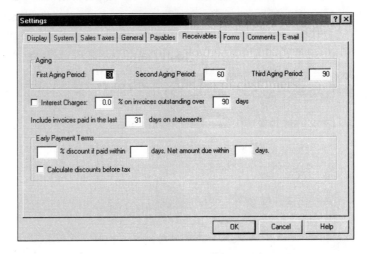

Accessing Receivables Settings

There are other ways to access the Receivables Settings screen from the Home window:

• Choose the Setup menu and click Settings. Click the Receivables tab in the Settings screen.

• Right-click the Customers icon. Then click the Setup tool button or choose the Setup menu and click Settings.

Receivables Settings

Like the Payables Ledger, the Receivables Settings include an option for **Aging** periods. These settings will be used to age the accounts in your receivables reports and graphs. Again, the default settings are the commonly used 30, 60 and 90 days. The periods entered should match the payment terms provided to customers. If there is a discount period, it may be helpful for the reports to show this as the first aging period. If interest is charged on overdue accounts, this will provide a useful second aging period.

To encourage prompt payments, a business may adopt a policy of charging interest on overdue accounts. The business policy terms for **Interest Charges** (interest rate and number of days) are entered as defaults for the Receivables Ledger so that they will apply to all customers. Although the program automatically calculates interest charges and prints them on the customer statement, you must create a separate sales invoice to record the accounting entry for the interest charges. Play Wave charges 1.5% interest, calculated monthly on the outstanding balance, on accounts over 30 days.

The next setting refers to the customer statements. You have the option to **Include Paid Invoices** for a designated period. All unpaid invoices are included automatically. Normally you will want to include paid invoices for the length of the billing cycle so that customers will have a record of their payments. Thus, if statements are sent monthly, you would include paid invoices for 31 days.

For most customers, Play Wave offers a 2 percent discount for payment within 10 days and requests net payment in 30 days. These terms are entered in the **Early Payment Terms** section of the screen and they will be the default terms applied to all sales invoices. You can edit the terms for individual customers or invoices.

The final option is to **Calculate the discount before or after taxes**. This option was described for vendor discounts in Chapter 4, page 103, and the calculations are made the same way. GST charged is calculated on the full pre-discount amount. PST is calculated on the discounted amount in Ontario. It may be necessary to adjust *PST Payable* and *GST Owing* amounts when remittances are made to reflect these policies.

PST rates and policies vary from one province to another. Always check with the provincial Ministry of Finance for the rules in your own province.

We need to add the discount terms (2 percent in 10 days, net in 30 days) to the default settings and modify the aging periods to reflect these terms. The monthly billing cycle matches the default of 31 days so paid invoices in this period will be included in the statement. Discounts are calculated before taxes and interest at 1.5% per month is charged on unpaid accounts over 30 days.

The first aging period is selected so it can be edited immediately.

◆ Type **10**

◆ Press (tab) to advance to the second period and highlight it.

◆ Type **30**

◆ Press (tab).

◆ Type **60**

◆ Click **Interest Charges** to add a ✓ to the check box and activate the option.

- ◆ Press (tab) to advance to the % field.

- ◆ Type 1.5

- ◆ Press (tab) to advance to the days over field.

- ◆ Type 30

- ◆ Click the % **field** (the first Early Payment Terms field in the last section on the Settings screen) to move the cursor.

- ◆ Type 2

- ◆ Press (tab) to advance to the Days field.

- ◆ Type 10

- ◆ Press (tab) to advance to the Net Days field.

- ◆ Type 30

- ◆ Click **Calculate discount before tax** to turn on this option.

These default settings will apply as the default to all customer invoices but you can change the terms for any individual customer or for an individual invoice.

Forms Settings

- ◆ Click the **Forms tab** to access the Forms Settings screen:

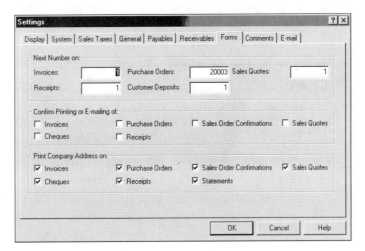

This, of course, is the same screen we used for the Payables Ledger Forms settings, but additional number fields are added for the Receivables Ledger. Notice that the Purchase Orders number has been updated to include the transactions in the previous chapter.

Forms Settings

The Forms screen is divided into three sections. The first one, **Next Number on**, allows us to indicate the next number in sequence for most of the forms that can be printed. The automatic numbering sequence is an easy form of internal control because the program automatically updates the sequence and provides a warning when you try to use a duplicate number or when you skip a number. In addition to updating the numbers for purchase orders, you can enter a starting or next number for Sales Invoices, Sales Quotes, Receipts and Customer Deposits. Only numeric sequences can be updated automatically. If you want to use alpha-numeric invoice numbering (e.g., PW-202), you can have PW preprinted on the invoice form and allow the program to update the numeric portion, 202.

The middle section is used when you print invoices, cheques and forms through the program. When you **Confirm Printing of** the various forms, the program warns you if you forget to print before you post the transaction. If you are not printing the forms, you should leave the boxes unchecked to avoid receiving the warnings unnecessarily.

The last section gives you the option to **Print** the **Company Address** on the various forms. If you use your own customized preprinted forms that already include the address, you should uncheck the boxes. If you use generic forms, you can include the address. If you have some of each, add the address only to the ones you need.

The cursor is in the Next Number on Invoices field with the contents already selected. In the source documents in Chapter 3, the last sales invoice number used was 103 for Vindri Estates. Therefore we need to begin the sequence with 104. Sales Quote forms begin with number 2001. Instead of using the automatic numbering for cash receipts (the Receipts number), Play Wave will use this field to record the customer's cheque number so that it will be added to the journal reports. There have been no customer deposits yet so the sequence will begin with 1. All of these numbers can be edited in the journals.

◆   Type **104**

◆   Click **the Sales Quotes number field** to skip the Purchase Orders number.

◆   Type **2001**

◆   Press ⌨tab⌨ to advance to the Receipts number field.

◆   Press ⌨del⌨ to leave the Receipts number field blank and prevent the automatic updating of the receipt number.

The Customer Deposits number is correct.

If you are printing invoices and cheques, click the appropriate check boxes in the next section to activate the warning. If you have preprinted forms with addresses included, click the appropriate check boxes in the Print Address section to remove the checkmarks. Since we will use generic forms or plain paper for Play Wave, leave the option to print the address on the forms checked.

Comments Settings

We want to add default comments to the invoices.

◆   Click the **Comments tab** to show the Comments Settings:

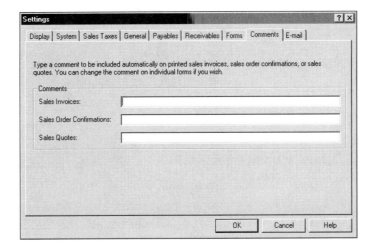

Comments Settings

Simply Accounting allows you to add a default comment to each of the sales forms that a customer receives. You may include a standard Comment on **Sales Invoices**, on **Sales Order Confirmations** and on **Sales Quotes**. You may use the same comment on each, such as a company motto, or a different one for each type of form. Again, you can modify the comment on individual invoices if you need to.

The cursor is in the Comment on Sales Invoices field.

- ◆ Type **Thank you for playing with us.**

- ◆ Press `tab` to move to the next comment field.

- ◆ Type **Thank you for playing with us.**

- ◆ Press `tab` to advance to the comment field for Sales Quotes.

- ◆ Type **Come play with us.**

- ◆ Click **OK** to save the settings and return to the Home window.

> **Y**ou can copy the comment from one field to the next. Highlight the entire text (Thank you for playing with us.). Then press `ctrl` + C (copy). Click the second comment field and press `ctrl` + V (paste).

Linked Accounts for the Receivables Ledger

The next step is to identify the accounts we want to use as the linked accounts. Most of the necessary accounts are already in the Chart of Accounts. However, one more account is needed.

☐ Create a new Group account: 4100 Sales Discounts (G)

As they do in other ledgers, linked accounts for the Receivables Ledger identify the accounts that the program will use for its automatic functions to ensure that the correct General Ledger accounts are updated. As in the Payables Ledger, you do not have to enter all of the accounts for many routine journal transactions because the same ones, the linked accounts, are used. Because the program also updates the customer records after each transaction, you do not need to enter the customer activity separately in the Receivables Ledger.

You should be in the Home window to enter the linked accounts.

◆ Choose the **Setup menu**, then choose **Linked Accounts** and click **Receivables** (or right-click the Sales, Orders & Quotes Journal icon and then click the Setup tool) to access the Receivables Linked Accounts screen:

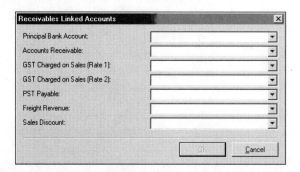

Receivables Linked Accounts

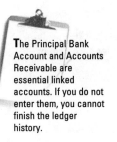

The Principal Bank Account and Accounts Receivable are essential linked accounts. If you do not enter them, you cannot finish the ledger history.

Principal Bank Account: This asset account is the postable Group or Subgroup account to which all cash receipts from customer sales are debited automatically by the Simply Accounting program. Cash sales are debited to this bank account at the time that the sales invoice is posted from the Sales Journal. Receipts from credit sales are processed through the Receipts Journal. Again, the bank account is debited automatically when the receipt is posted. You may use a single bank account for both cash receipts (Receivables Ledger) and cash payments (Payables Ledger), or you may use separate bank accounts. Accounts must be designated as Bank class before you can select them as principal linked bank accounts. When you use a second currency for sales, you can identify a separate default linked bank account for these transactions as well.

Accounts Receivable: You must choose an asset account. All credit sales to customers are automatically debited to *Accounts Receivable*. When customers make payments on account, this account is automatically credited for the amount of the payment entered in the Receipts Journal. The balance in this account reflects the sum of all amounts owed by all customers. You can view individual customer balances in the ledger records for the individual customers (Receivables Ledger).

Although this is a postable account, you cannot post directly to it when the Receivables Ledger is linked. It is selected by default by the Simply Accounting program whenever you enter credit sales in the Sales Journal or receipts in the Receipts Journal. The *Accounts Receivable* account portion of these journal entries is created automatically by the software.

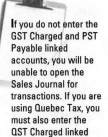

If you do not enter the GST Charged and PST Payable linked accounts, you will be unable to open the Sales Journal for transactions. If you are using Quebec Tax, you must also enter the QST Charged linked account.

GST Charged on Sales (Rate 1): If GST is applied to the goods and/or services provided by a business, the amount of GST entered in the GST fields in the Sales Journal is automatically credited to this linked account for sale transactions. *GST Charged* is a postable account that you can define as an asset or as a liability account, although you should use the same section as the *GST Paid* account. It is preferable to use a liability account because most of the time a business will owe GST to the Receiver General. Furthermore, if you choose Subgroup as the account type, the subtotal of this account and the other GST liability accounts will show the total amount of GST owing.

To make the GST remittance, the *GST Charged* is entered as a positive amount in the Payments or Purchases Journal to credit *Accounts Payable* and increase the amount owing to the Receiver General. GST refunds are processed in the Sales Journal, choosing the Receiver General as the customer and entering the *GST Paid* amount as a positive amount and *GST Charged* as a negative amount.

GST Charged on Sales (Rate 2): This linked account operates the same way as the previous one. It is used when different tax rates are applied to different types of goods or services. Presently, there is only one GST rate and this second linked account is not used. You might also use the second rate for interprovincial sales to enter the Harmonized Sales Tax rate.

PST Payable: Choose a postable liability account to define the *PST Payable* linked account, either a Group or Subgroup type. If PST is applied to the sale of goods or services, the amount charged is automatically credited to this linked account when the rate applicable to the sale is entered in the PST field of the Sales Journal. The balance in the *PST Payable* account reflects the total of all PST amounts collected from customers that must be remitted to the Minister of Finance. Make the remittance in the Purchases or Payments Journal by entering the *PST Payable* account balance from the General Ledger as a positive amount in order to reduce (debit) it and to increase (credit) *Accounts Payable*.

QST Charged on Sales (Rate 1): This linked account appears only when the option to Use Quebec Sales Tax is selected (Setup menu, Settings, Sales Taxes tab screen) and replaces the *PST Payable* linked account. It does not appear on the screen above because we did not choose to use Quebec Sales Tax. It operates very much like the *GST Charged* account but applies to the Quebec (Provincial) Sales Tax collected from customers on applicable sales. Again, when the settings are entered correctly, the Simply Accounting program automatically credits the account for the amount of tax collected. Like *GST Charged*, *QST Charged* is a postable account that you should define as a liability account because most of the time a business will owe QST to the Minister of Revenue. Furthermore, by choosing Subgroup as the account type, you can subtotal this account with other QST liability accounts to show the total amount owing. When a remittance is made through the Purchases or Payments Journal, the amount of *QST Charged* is entered as a positive amount to debit it and to increase or credit the *Accounts Payable* balance.

QST Charged on Sales (Rate 2): This linked account operates the same way as the previous one. It is used only when different tax rates are applied to different types of goods or services.

Freight Revenue: Choose a postable revenue account, type Group or Subgroup, as the *Freight Revenue* linked account. If customers pay freight for the delivery of their merchandise, the amount charged for freight is credited to this account automatically when the amount is entered in the Freight field of the Sales Journal.

Sales Discount: You may choose either a revenue or an expense account for the *Sales Discount* linked account. It is more reasonable to use a revenue account — contra-revenue, to be exact — because the discount relates to the sales revenue from conducting business (reducing the revenue). This postable account may be a Group or Subgroup account. It may be subtotalled with revenue to create net revenue.

When a business offers a discount for early settlement of an account, the amount of the discount is calculated automatically if the payment terms are included with the invoice and the customer makes the full payment before the discount offer expires. When the receipt is posted, the discount amount is debited to *Sales Discount*, and *Accounts Receivable* is credited for the amount of the payment plus the amount of the discount. The linked account *Bank Account: Chequing* is debited for the amount of the payment.

Play Wave has one bank account that is used for all the ledgers. The cursor should be in the Principal Bank Account field.

♦ Click the **Principal Bank Account field arrow** to see the accounts that can be selected. Notice that only Bank class accounts are included in the list.

♦ Click the account *1080 Bank Account: Chequing* to select it.

♦ Press (tab) to advance to the Accounts Receivable account field.

♦ Click *1200 Accounts Receivable* from the drop-down list to select it.

♦ Press (tab) to advance to the GST Charged on Sales (Rate 1) account field.

If you do not enter the Freight Revenue linked account, you cannot access the Freight fields in the Sales Journal. If you do not enter the Sales Discount linked account, you cannot post a Sales Journal entry with a discount. The missing discount portion of the journal entry leaves the debits and credits unequal.

Notice that accounts already used as linked accounts in other ledgers do not appear on the lists of available accounts. Only the Bank linked account may be selected more than once.

◆ Scroll down and click *2650 GST Charged on Services* from the drop-down list.

◆ Click the **PST Payable list arrow** to skip the GST Rate 2 field and to see the liability accounts available. Notice that the GST accounts are removed from the list because you have already used them.

◆ Click *2640 PST Payable*.

◆ **Skip the Freight Revenue field** because we do not use this account. When Play Wave adds inventory, it will charge customers for delivery. At that time, we will create and link the appropriate account.

◆ Click the **Sales Discount list arrow** to skip the Freight Revenue field and to see the accounts available.

◆ Click *4100 Sales Discounts*.

Check your accounts carefully. If you have entered a wrong account, reselect from the drop-down list. If you have an account in a field that should be blank, click the account number and press ⌐del⌐ to remove it.

◆ Click **OK** to save the new linked accounts.

Simply Accounting advises you that the account class for *Accounts Receivable* will change because of its designated linking status:

◆ Click **Yes** to accept the change and return to the Home window. (Click OK if you are using Version 8.0A.)

Setting Print Forms

Instead of printing sales invoices and customer statements on plain paper, you can use the custom forms that accompany the Simply Accounting program. If you chose the typical program installation, the Crystal Reports forms needed to print the forms should be installed in the Forms folder under Winsim. Also, remember that you need to select a form and printer for each type of printed document.

◆ Choose the **Setup** menu and click **Reports & Forms** in the Home window to open the Report & Form Options window for Reports & Graphs (the selected tab).

◆ Click the **Invoices tab** to open its screen as shown:

You can also install the Crystal Reports program from the Simply Accounting program CD-ROM.

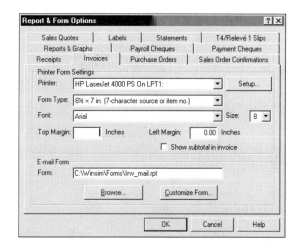

- ◆ Click the **Form Type field drop-down list** and choose **Custom**.

The name of the form file appears in the Form Type field. Accept this default generic form. To customize the form, you must have the Crystal Reports program.

- ◆ Click the **Statements tab**.

- ◆ Choose **Custom** from the Form Type drop-down list. Accept the default form file.

- ◆ Click **OK** to save the changes and return to the Home window.

Once you select the form for a type or report or document, it will apply as the default for that report or document for all your Simply Accounting files. You do not need to reselect for Live Links unless you want to change the settings.

Entering Customer Records

Accounts Receivable customer records are entered in the Receivables Ledger that is accessed with the Customers icon shown here:

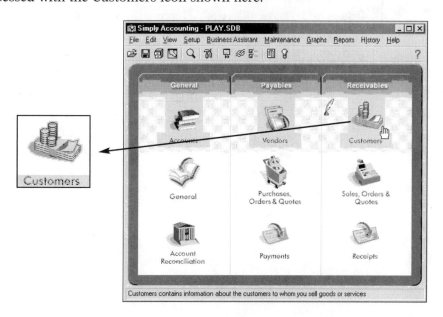

◆ Click the **Customers icon** to open the Customers window:

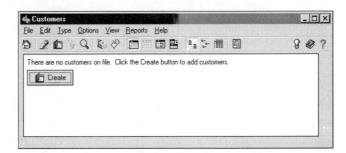

The Customers Window

The tool buttons are the same as those in the Accounts and the Vendors windows with the exception of the two new journal tools. Clicking the journal tool will open the journal window. The journals are also provided as options in the Type menu in the Customers window.

 Open the Sales, Orders & Quotes Journal.

Open the Receipts Journal.

The Customers window above displays the message that there are no customers on record yet. The first customer is MegaCity Parks & Rec. Complete details for the customer, including historical transactions, are provided below.

Customer (Contact)	Address	Phone, Fax, Terms	E-mail, Web, Year-to-Date Totals
MegaCity Parks & Rec (Marcus Fairplay) Credit Limit: $10 000	82 Greenfield Pl. Megacity, ON M2G 4G1	Tel: (416) 392-8123 Fax: (416) 372-9119 Terms: 2/10, n/30	E-mail: CityParks@govcity.ca Web: www.govcity.ca/parks YTD Sales: $6 420.00

Historical Information

Date	Invoice/Cheque	Terms	Pretax Amount	Tax	Total
Mar. 2/02	101	2/10, n/30	$6 000.00	$420.00	$6 420.00
Mar. 2/02	Chq #19882				$1 000.00
				Balance Owing	$5 420.00

◆ Click the **Create button** ⬛ Create (or click the Create tool ⬛ , or choose the File menu and click Create) to open the Receivables Ledger:

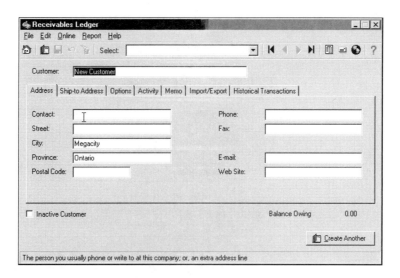

Customer Address Details

The Receivables Ledger, like the Payables has several parts that you access using the tabs. The Address tab input form is the first to appear. The input fields are the same as those in the Payables Address form. Refer to that description (Chapter 4, page 113) for a review if needed. The program calculates the Balance Owing based on the historical invoices and payments you will enter at the next stage, and from ongoing sales and receipt transactions.

◆ Type **MegaCity Parks & Rec**

◆ Press ⓣⓐⓑ to advance to the Contact field.

◆ Type **Marcus Fairplay**

◆ Press ⓣⓐⓑ to advance to the Street address field.

◆ Type **82 Greenfield Pl.**

◆ Click the **Postal Code field** to skip the City and Province field and accept the default information.

◆ Type **m2g4g1**

◆ Press ⓣⓐⓑ.

◆ Type **4163928123** in the Phone field.

◆ Press ⓣⓐⓑ.

◆ Type **4163729119**

◆ Press ⓣⓐⓑ to advance to the E-mail field.

◆ Type **CityParks@govcity.ca** (type the e-mail address exactly as you would enter it from your Internet account).

◆ Press ⓣⓐⓑ.

◆ Type **www.govcity.ca/parks** (type the Web site address exactly as you would enter it from your Internet account).

Ship to Address Tab Options

◆ Click the **Ship-to Address tab** to view the next input screen for the customer:

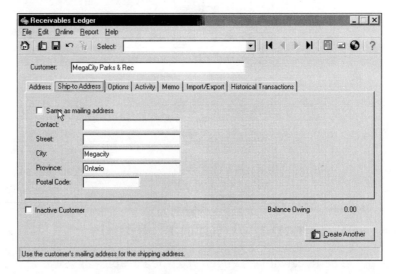

All of the customers for Play Wave have a single location so the shipping address is the same as the mailing address. If the addresses were different, you could enter the second address on this screen in the same way that you entered the primary address, or add it directly to the sales invoice. Both addresses will appear on sales invoices.

◆ Click the **Same as mailing address check box.**

Customer Options

◆ Click the **Options tab** to see the next group of input fields:

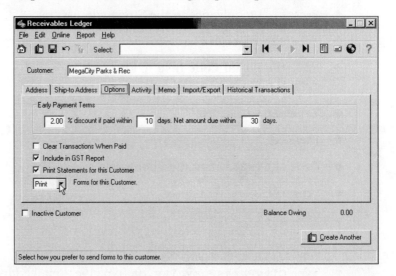

You do not need to make any changes to this screen. The default payment terms are correct. You can edit them for the customer on this ledger page. You can also edit the terms for individual sales invoices. We do not want to clear paid transactions. If you clear the invoices after they are paid, Invoice Lookup will be unavailable for them. Instead we will clear them on a regular basis after making backup copies. The option to print statements should be left checked so that you have this option. Including the customer in GST Reports ensures that all of the GST codes will be available for sales to the customer and that the customer's sales are added to the GST Reports. And finally, if both the business and the customer have e-mail, you may choose to send forms via e-mail. For now, leave the option set at print.

Historical Activity

◆ Click the **Activity tab** to see the next group of input fields:

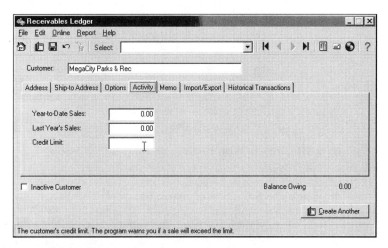

Activity Tab Screen

Year-to-Date Sales refers to the total for the current year, and **Last Year's Sales** refers to the total sales for the previous fiscal year. These totals are updated from journal transactions. We need to record only the Year-to-Date Sales that occurred before using the Receivables journals.

The **Credit Limit** is a pre-authorized limit, the amount that a customer can purchase on account without requiring special management approval. When a sale will cause the customer to exceed the credit limit, the program will warn you before posting or accepting the transaction. You may then proceed with the sale or ask for a down payment. The warning may also be a signal to re-examine the credit limit policy to determine whether the customer's limit should be raised or whether the customer is delinquent in making payments.

◆ Click the **Year-to-Date Sales field** to move the cursor and select the amount.

◆ Type **6420**

◆ Press `tab` twice to advance to the Credit Limit field.

◆ Type **10000**

Memos and Import/Export

◆ Click the **Memo tab** to advance to the next information screen.

The customer memo form is like the vendor memo form. You can type a memo, add it to the To-Do List to ensure that you will be reminded and indicate the reminder date.

◆ Click the **Import/Export tab** to advance to the next information screen.

Again, the input fields are the same as those in the Payables Ledger for vendors.

Historical Customer Invoices

◆ Click the **Historical Transactions tab** to open the final screen:

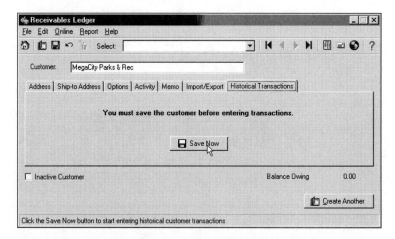

As with vendors, you must save the record before you can add outstanding invoices and payments.

◆ Click the **Save Now button** to access the Invoices and Payments options:

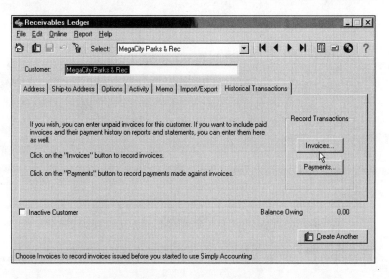

Notice that the Invoices and Payments buttons are added to the forms. These are used for the historical transactions. Simply Accounting also uses open-invoice accounting for the Receivables Ledger. (Refer to Chapter 4, page 119, for a review if necessary.)

◆ Click **Invoices** to see the Historical Invoices screen:

If your discount is calculated after taxes, or if no discount is offered, a single field for the total invoice amount appears on the Historical Invoices form, just as it does for historical purchases from vendors.

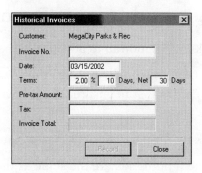

The input fields have the same functions for customers that they do for vendors. Because we chose the option to calculate discounts before taxes, the invoice amount field is divided into Pre-tax Amount, Tax and Invoice Total. The total amount is calculated by the program. You should enter the sales Invoice Number, the Date of the invoice, and the amounts for the sale. If the payment terms for the sale were different from the default, they can be edited too.

◆   Click the **Invoice No. field.**

◆   Type **101**

◆   Press ⒯ to advance to the Date field and select the default entry.

◆   Type **mar 2** to replace the Session date.

◆   Click the **Pre-tax Amount field** to skip the Terms. The defaults are correct.

◆   Type **6000**

◆   Press ⒯ to advance to the Tax field.

◆   Type **420**

◆   Press ⒯ to enter the amount and allow the program to enter the total.

◆   Click **Record** to save the invoice. A new invoice form appears.

If there are other invoices for the customer, enter and record each one on a separate invoice form. After recording the last invoice,

◆   Click **Close** to close the invoice and return to the ledger page.

Notice that the Balance Owing has changed to $6 420 to include the invoice you just added.

Historical Customer Payments

◆   Click **Payments** to open the Historical Payments screen:

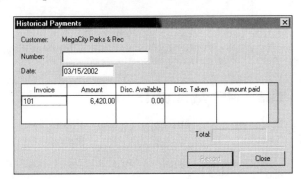

The Payments input fields serve the same purpose as they do for vendors. Each invoice appears on a separate line in the statement portion of the screen. As for vendors, the discount is calculated automatically based on the date of the invoice and the date of the payment.

MegaCity Parks & Rec made one payment towards this invoice on the day of the sale. Because they did not pay the full amount, they cannot take the discount.

Enter historical down payments or deposits from customers as invoices with negative amounts. Use the customer's cheque number or a memo number to replace the invoice number. Do not try to enter deposits as historical payments.

If you click Close before you click Record, you will not save the invoice.

◆ Click the **Number field**, the field for the customer's cheque number.

◆ Type **19882**

◆ Press ⑂ᵗᵃᵇ⑁ to advance to the Date field and select the default entry.

◆ Type **mar 2** to replace the Session date.

◆ Click the **Amount paid field** to skip the discount fields. The full amount appears by default. Be sure to delete any amount that appears in the Discount Taken field.

◆ Type **1000**

◆ Press ⑂ᵗᵃᵇ⑁ to update the total.

◆ Click **Record** to save the payment. The payment form reappears with the invoice amount reduced to $5 420.

If you click Close before you click Record, you will not save the payment.

If the customer has made more than one payment, record each cheque as a separate payment. After recording the last payment,

◆ Click **Close** to close the invoice and return to the ledger page.

Notice that the Balance Owing on the Ledger screen has changed to $5 420.

Discounts and Multiple Payments

When a customer makes a payment for the full amount of the invoice within the discount period, accept the discount taken amount and the default payment amount in the Amount paid column. Pressing ⑂ᵗᵃᵇ⑁ to move through the fields will display the amounts. When a customer pays more than one invoice with a single cheque, click the amount for each invoice that is paid and then press ⑂ᵗᵃᵇ⑁ to accept the amounts. When one invoice is fully paid and another is partially paid, edit the amount for the partially paid invoice and accept the amount for the fully paid invoice. If an invoice is not paid, be sure that the amount paid for that line is zero or blank. If it is not, click the amount and press ⑂ᵈᵉˡ⑁ to remove the amount. Then press ⑂ᵗᵃᵇ⑁ to enter the change.

◆ Click the **Create Another button** on the Ledger page to open a new customer record.

◆ Click the **Address tab** to return to this input screen.

◆ Add the remaining customer records.

Remember to edit the default payment terms when necessary.

CUSTOMER ACCOUNTS			
Customer (Contact)	**Address**	**Phone, Fax, Terms**	**E-mail, Web, Year-to-Date Totals**
Central Nursery Schools (Peter Pan) Credit Limit: $10 000	29 Careful Circle Megacity, ON M4T 7B2	Tel: (416) 488-5133 Fax: (416) 488-9110 Terms: 2/10, n/30	E-mail: tinytots@netcom.ca Web: www.tinytots.com YTD Sales: $5 350.00
Chaplin Estates (Charlie Chaplin) Credit Limit: $10 000	39 Tinkerbell Rd. Megacity, ON M4P 8T3	Tel: (416) 523-5667 Fax: (416) 523-5555 Terms: net 1	

CUSTOMER ACCOUNTS CONTINUED

Customer (Contact)	Address	Phone, Fax, Terms	E-mail, Web, Year-to-Date Totals
Nirvana Nursery School (Jack Horner) Credit Limit: $5 000	45 Corner Rd. Megacity, ON M9M 3C3	Tel: (416) 922-0135 Fax: (416) 972-6642 Terms: net 1	E-mail: nirvnursery@sympatico.ca
Vindri Estates (Kit Vindri) Credit Limit: $5 000	46 Funtime Rd. Megacity, ON M3F 5V5	Tel: (416) 772-6345 Fax: (416) 772-6642 Terms: net 1	E-mail: kvindri@cs.com Web: www.vindri.estates.com YTD Sales: $2 675.00

◆ Close the Receivables Ledger window to return to the Customers window.

An icon appears for the each customer record in the Customers window.

Correcting Customer Records

Accessing a Customer's Record

There are many ways to access the record for an individual customer. From the Customers window,

- Click the customer's icon and then click the Edit tool or choose the Edit menu and click Edit.

- Choose the Edit menu and click Find to open the Find Customer screen. Click the customer's name and then click Find.

- Click the Find tool to open the Find Customer screen. Click the customer's name and then click Find.

You can also access the customer's record from the Home window.

- Click the Customers icon to open the Customers window and choose one of the methods above.

- Click the Find tool to open the Select Record Type screen. Click Customers from the drop-down list and then click Select to open the Find Customer screen. Click the customer's name and then click Find.

- Right-click the Customers icon and then click the Find tool to open the Find Customer screen. Click the customer's name and then click Find.

- Choose the Edit menu, then choose Find and click Customer to open the Find Customer screen. Click the customer's name and then click Find.

Correcting Historical Information

Most of the customer information can be edited at any time. The Balance Owing, however, is updated directly from journal entries and cannot be edited. Once you finish the ledger history, you cannot change the YTD Sales amounts either.

It is important to enter the historical invoice details correctly. Even dates are important because they are used to calculate discounts. If you have entered historical amounts incorrectly, the total in the Receivables Ledgers may not match the General Ledger *Accounts Receivable* account balance. The program will not permit you to finish the ledger history unless these two amounts are in balance. The program will advise you that this is the error.

Once you have recorded an invoice or payment, you cannot edit it. To correct the error, you must remove the incorrect invoices. To do this, pay the outstanding balance by making a historical payment for the full amount of the incorrect invoice. Then clear the paid transactions for this customer. (From the Home window, choose the Maintenance menu, Clear Paid Transactions, and then click Clear Paid Customer Transactions. Select the customer from the list and enter the appropriate date. Click OK. When the warning appears, click Yes to proceed.) Then re-enter the customer's historical transactions carefully and correctly.

You should check your work by printing the relevant reports and correct mistakes by editing the customer record before you finish the ledger history.

Receivables Ledger Reports
Customer List

You can check the customer address details from the Customer List.

From the Customers window,

◆ Click the **Display tool** , click **Display Customer List** from the list and click **Select** (or choose the Reports menu and click Display Customer List).

From the Home window:

◆ Choose the **Reports** menu, then choose **Lists** and click **Customers**. (Or click the Display tool, click Customer List, and click Select. Or right-click the Customers icon and then click the Display Customer List tool.)

The customer address list is displayed immediately.

◆ Choose the **File** menu and click **Print** to print the Customer list and then close the displayed report.

Customer Aged Report

The Customer Aged Report provides the same information for customers that the Vendor Aged Report provides for vendors, that is, a record of customer sales, payments and balances for the aging periods defined in the Receivables Settings.

◆ Choose the **Reports** menu and click **Customer Aged** in the **Customers** window (or, in the Home window, choose the Reports menu, then choose Receivables and click Customer Aged) to display the report options:

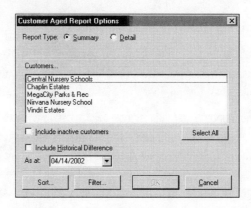

The Display tool label changes when you select a Home window icon first.

The Customer Aged Report can be shown in **Summary** or **Detail** form. The Summary option lists only the total outstanding balance for each customer, in aged columns according to the aging period entered for the Receivables Settings. The Detail Report provides the details for individual invoices and payments, again in aged columns. You may include payment terms as part of the Detail Report. You can select one or more customers to include in the report. To include some customers, press ⌷ctrl⌷ and click each name in turn. By default, the Session date is given for the report, but you may choose any date after the Fiscal Start date up to the Session date. Inactive customers may be included in the report or omitted. By default, they are omitted. Including the Historical Difference will show that the Customers Ledger history is balanced or show the amount of the discrepancy between the customer records and the *Accounts Receivable* account balance. As with vendor reports, you can sort and filter customer reports by name and balance owing.

To check the accuracy of the historical data for all customers at the Session date, you should include all the details, including terms. To do this,

◆ Click **Detail**. The option to include payment terms is added to the screen.

◆ Click **Select All** to select all customers.

◆ Click **Include Terms**.

◆ Click **Include Historical Difference**.

The April 14th date is correct.

◆ Click **OK** to display the report.

Drill-Down Reports

From the Customer List you can display the Customer Aged Report for the selected customer when you double click any item of information for that customer.

From the Customer Aged Detail Report you can view the Customer record by double clicking the customer's name. Entry line information in the Detail Reports will drill down to Invoice Lookup, showing a copy of the original journal invoice if the transaction was recorded in the Sales Journal. Invoice Lookup is explained in Chapter 8. From the Customer Aged Summary Report, you can go to the Customer Aged Detail Report for a customer by clicking any of the information for the customer you want.

◆ Print the report from the display by choosing the File menu and clicking Print.

◆ Close the display when finished.

Finishing the Receivables Ledger History

◆ Back up your data files before finishing the ledger history.

In this way, if you have made a mistake in one of the historical invoices, you can correct the customer record. Otherwise, you will have to start from scratch or with your most recent backup copy that does not include customer information. If you have made an error, like omitting a linked account or entering an incorrect customer outstanding balance, you must correct these before you can continue.

◆ Choose the **History** menu, then choose **Enter Historical Information** and click **Receivables**. If you see a message like the ones in the following section, you cannot continue before correcting the mistakes.

Finishing History Error Messages

When you try to finish the history for a ledger, Simply Accounting first checks the linked accounts for that ledger. If you have not defined one of the required linked accounts, as in the following message, you will be prevented from proceeding until you enter the missing accounts:

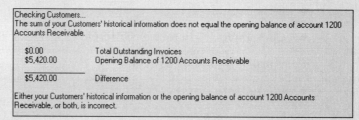

Checking Customers...
This module cannot leave history mode because the 'Receivable Bank Account' linked account is not defined.
This module cannot leave history mode because the 'Accounts Receivable' linked account is not defined.

Click OK. Make the corrections and then try finishing the ledger history again. If the essential linked accounts are defined, the program checks the *Accounts Receivable* control account balance. If you have entered amounts incorrectly, the total of the individual outstanding customer balances will be different from the balance in the *Accounts Receivables* control account and you will receive an error message like the one shown:

Checking Customers...
The sum of your Customers' historical information does not equal the opening balance of account 1200 Accounts Receivable.

$0.00	Total Outstanding Invoices
$5,420.00	Opening Balance of 1200 Accounts Receivable
$5,420.00	Difference

Either your Customers' historical information or the opening balance of account 1200 Accounts Receivable, or both, is incorrect.

Click OK. Make the corrections and then try finishing the ledger history again.

◆ Choose the **History** menu, then choose **Enter Historical Information** and click **Receivables**. If your work is correct, you will see the following warning message:

Simply Accounting - Warning

You are about to finish entering history.

THIS ACTION CANNOT BE REVERSED.

Make a backup of your company files before proceeding.

Proceed   Cancel   Backup

◆ Click **Proceed**.

◆ Close the Play Wave data file to prepare for setting up the Receivables Ledger for Live Links.

Practice: Live Links

You can now set up the Receivables Ledger for Live Links so that the Receivables Journals can be used to process customer transactions.

Receivables Ledger Setup

Instructions

If you have not completed the journal entries for Live Links in Chapter 5 and want to continue working on Chapter 6, you can use your copy of the Data Disk file — Ch06\links\linkch06.sdb — to continue this chapter.

1. Open the data files for Live Links. Accept August 8, 2002, as the Session Date.

2. Restore the icons for the Receivables Ledger (Home window, View menu, Modules, Receivables).

3. Set up the Receivables Ledger. Enter the following default settings:

Receivables Settings:
    Aging Periods: 10, 30 and 60 days
    Interest charged at 1% per month on accounts over 30 days
    No discount for early payment
    Do NOT calculate discount before taxes

Forms Settings:
    Next number on Invoices: 106
    Next number on Sales Quotes: 1
    Next number on Receipts: ⟨del⟩
    Next number on Customer Deposits: 1

Comments Settings:
    Sales Invoices: Interest charges on accounts over 30 days.
    Sales Order Confirmations: Prompt service is our rule.
    Sales Quotes: We honour our quotes.

---

4. Create the required new accounts and then enter the linked accounts for the Receivables Ledger:

Create New Accounts:
    4080 Sales Discount (A)
    4280 Freight Revenue (G)

Receivables Linked Accounts:

Principal Bank Account:	1080 Bank Account: Chequing
Accounts Receivable:	1200 Accounts Receivable
GST Charged on Sales (Rate 1):	2650 GST Charged on Services
GST Charged on Sales (Rate 2):	(leave blank)
PST Payable:	2640 PST Payable
Freight Revenue:	4280 Freight Revenue
Sales Discount:	4080 Sales Discount

---

5. Enter the customer records from the following page and add the historical invoice for City Hall Staff.

6. Print the Customer List and Customer Aged Detail Report to check your work.

7. Back up your data files.

8. Finish entering the Receivables Ledger history.

9. Close the data file for Live Links to prepare for making journal entries for Play Wave.

CUSTOMER ACCOUNTS

Customer (Contact)	Address	Phone, Fax, Terms	E-mail, Web, Year-to-Date Totals
Elsie Cordeiro	7003 Alberta St. Vancouver, BC V6G 3K9	Tel: (604) 789-8120 Terms: net 1	YTD Sales: $1 140
Credit Limit: $5 000			
Metro Credit Union (Odette Boreau)	55 Pacific Heights Dr. North Vancouver, BC V7Y 5R3	Tel: (604) 892-0346 Fax: (604) 887-9576 Terms: 2/10, n/30	YTD Sales: $1 605
Credit Limit: $5 000			
Prince College (Vi King)	72 Royal Road Burnaby, BC V7H 3B5	Tel: (604) 662-7719 Fax: (604) 663-7810 Terms: net 1	E-mail: VKing@prince.edu.net Web: www.princecoll.com YTD Sales: $1 605
Credit Limit: $5 000			
Pro-Career Institute (Able Staffer)	900 Folks Cres. Richmond, BC V7H 4F8	Tel: ((604) 821-7777 Fax: (604) 821-6712 Terms: net 30	E-mail: astaffer@netcom.net Web: www.jobfillers.com
Credit Limit: $5 000			
Prolegal Services Inc. (D. Fense)	54 Litty Gate Vancouver, BC V9T 4N4	Tel: (604) 558-8446 Fax: (604) 555-6119 Terms: net 30	Web: www.gofree. com YTD Sales: $2 280
Credit Limit: $5 000			
City Hall Staff (Inna Chambers)	1000 Central Ave. Vancouver, BC V6T 3E2	Tel: (604) 338-7711 Fax: (604) 339-8101 Terms: net 30	E-mail: ichamb@city.van.ca YTD Sales: $2 140
Credit Limit: $5 000			

Historical Information for City Hall Staff

Date	Invoice	Terms	Amount
Jul. 6/02	101	net 30	$2 140
		TOTAL	**$2 140**

All customers in this list are to be included in GST reports. Do not clear paid invoices. Sales discounts are all calculated after tax.

Review Questions

1. Why does Simply Accounting use the open-invoice method for recording customer invoices and payments?
2. What must you do before finishing the Receivables Ledger history?
3. What changes can you make to a customer record before finishing the Receivables Ledger history? What changes can you make after?
4. What role does the *Accounts Receivable* account serve in Simply Accounting before setting up the Receivables Ledger and after?
5. If you calculate discounts before tax, what additional historical invoice information is required compared with calculating discounts after tax?
6. Why might the Discount Available field be blank when you are entering historical customer payments?

CHAPTER 7

RECEIVABLES JOURNALS

Objectives

- *understand when to use the Receivables journals*
- *explain the components of Sales and Receipts Journals entry screens*
- *enter, review and correct credit and cash sales transactions*
- *prepare and fill sales quotes*
- *receive payments from customers*
- *enter sales discounts*
- *handle NSF cheques (reversing receipts)*
- *add new customers from journals*
- *print and adjust GST reports*
- *display and print Receivables Ledger reports*
- *complete additional entries for practice*

Introduction

Now that the Receivables Ledger is set up, you will begin to enter customer transactions for Play Wave Plus in the two journals for the Receivables Ledger, the Sales, Orders and Quotes (Sales) Journal and the Receipts Journal. By using these journals rather than the General Journal for routine customer transactions, the customer records are continually updated at the same time that the linked General Ledger accounts are updated. The two Receivables Ledger journals parallel the Payables journals. The Sales Journal for sales of all types, including sales on account, cash sales, sales orders and sales quotes, is the customer equivalent of the Purchases Journal, while the one for cash receipts from customers for payments on account is similar to the Payments Journal. You will continue to use the Payables and General Journals where appropriate for entries that occur between customer transactions.

If you have not completed the ledger setup in Chapter 6 and want to continue working on Chapter 7, you can use your copy of the Data Disk file — Ch07\play\playch07.sdb — to begin this chapter.

The Receivables Journals

The Sales Journal (Sales, Orders & Quotes) is used to enter all sales to customers. Sales transactions share common elements; they usually involve a revenue account, and they involve customers (Receivables Ledger). Sales orders and sales quotes are also entered through the Sales Journal. When the Receivables Ledger is set up, you cannot enter these transactions through the General Journal because you cannot access the *Accounts Receivable* control account. Although *Accounts Receivable* is a postable account, it does not appear on the Select Account lists for the Account fields in journals. The program automatically uses this account whenever you enter a credit sale transaction. Furthermore, using the Sales and Receipts Journals allows you to keep updated customer records without the double entry of information required in a manual accounting system when the ledgers are separate. Using the Sales Journal for all sales will also provide detailed GST reports and make remittances easier.

Receivables Journal Entries

Entering Sales Transactions

The first sales transaction is a regular credit sales invoice:

 Sales Invoice #104
Dated Apr. 8/02
To Nirvana Nursery School, $3 000 plus $210 GST charged for play centre completed. Invoice total $3 210. Terms: net 1 day.

◆ Start the Simply Accounting program and open your working copy of the Play Wave data files. Accept April 14, 2002, as the Session date.

We will use the term Sales Journal to refer to the Sales, Orders & Quotes Journal.

Sales invoices are entered in the Sales Journal (Sales, Orders & Quotes icon) shown here:

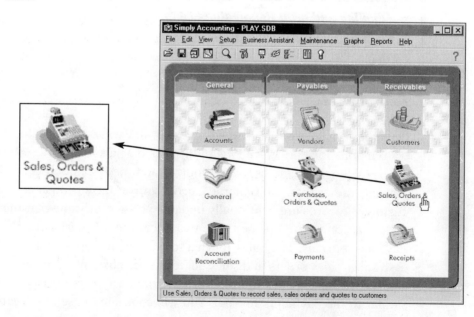

◆ Click the **Sales, Orders & Quotes icon** to open the Sales Journal:

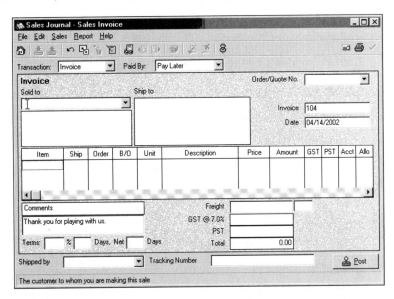

The Sales Journal Input Screen

Most of the components of the Sales Journal parallel those in the Purchases Journal described in Chapter 5, pages 133–135. There are no new tool buttons in this screen. All the tools should be familiar from previous journal input screens. Similarly, most of the menu options are the same as those in other journals. Only the Sales menu is shown here for the first time. Many of its options are, however, familiar from the Purchases Journal. The differences are simple — sales orders and quotes replace purchase orders and quotes.

The input fields too are mostly familiar. There are three types of **Transactions**. Select **Invoice** to enter normal sales transactions. Sales Quotes and Sales Orders are used for future sales. Sales **Quotes** provide a customer with a guaranteed sale price commitment for a limited time period. Customers may choose to accept the quote by making the purchase or not. **Sales Orders** usually imply that the customers have purchased the goods and will accept delivery at some agreed future date. Sales orders may be placed because the goods are out of stock, or because the customer wants to guarantee that the goods will be available when needed at a later time.

The **Paid By** options are the same as they are for purchases. **Pay Later** applies to customers who have established a credit account with the business. They are allowed to pay for their purchases at some agreed future time. When customers pay for their purchase at the time of the sale, choose **Cheque** or **Cash** (or **Credit Card** when these are set up) as the method of payment.

Sold to: Choose the customer's name from the selection list. The list includes all customers that you entered in the Receivables Ledger.

Ship to: Enter the address for shipping if it is different from the customer address on record.

Order/Quote No.: The next quote number in sequence from the automatic numbering in the Forms Settings or the order number. Sales orders often originate as a customer's purchase order and the customer's order number may be on the form.

Invoice: The invoice number from the invoice. Normally this number will be correct. You will want to change it for customer returns, or for other unusual entries that should not be part of the same numbering sequence.

Date: The date of the invoice/sale.

Item: Inventory code or item number.

Ship: The quantity, number of units of the item shipped, usually for inventory purchases. For non-inventory sales, the quantity is usually one.

Order: The quantity or number of units ordered.

B/O: The quantity that is backordered, not yet shipped.

Unit: Again for inventory, the unit of measurement for the item purchased (e.g., kit, dozen, tonne, item).

Description: The inventory item name or description, or a description that you type in for the sale.

Price: The price per unit for the goods.

Amount: If you have entered a quantity and a unit price, the software calculates a total amount before taxes for the invoice line and enters it in this column.

GST: The GST code that applies to the sale.

PST: The Provincial Sales Tax rate that applies to the sale, as a percentage.

Acct: The account that is to be credited for the sale. Normally a revenue account is credited and the *Accounts Receivable* account (or *Bank Account: Chequing*) is debited. Sometimes you will debit a revenue account or another type of account, such as when you receive GST rebates or when customers return goods. To debit an account, as for returns, you must enter a negative amount.

Allo.: If you are using project costing, you can use this column to allocate or distribute a revenue among the projects. Projects are discussed in Chapter 17.

Comments: The default comment that appears from the Comments settings, or a unique comment that you add to the invoice. You can edit the default comment.

Terms: The payment terms for this customer, according to the default Receivables settings or the entry in the customer's ledger record. You can edit the terms for an individual invoice if they are different from the default terms.

Freight: There are two freight fields. In the first field, enter the amount charged to the customer as the freight charge. The second field contains the GST code that applies to the freight amount.

Totals (GST @ 7%, PST and Total): The program automatically adds the GST applied to individual invoice line amounts and freight and all PST amounts and enters the totals in the corresponding total fields. The total of all amounts, the invoice total or the amount owed by the customer, appears in the Total field. You cannot edit these totals. They change automatically when you change the individual fields above. The total is automatically debited to *Accounts Receivable* (or *Bank Account: Chequing* for cash sales). For negative amounts, as in the case of returns, *Accounts Receivable* is credited.

Shipped by: Choose a shipping service from the drop-down list, if appropriate.

Tracking Number: Enter the shipper's tracking number for the delivery, if appropriate.

The transaction type and payment method are correctly selected by default as Invoice and Pay Later.

◆ Click the **Sold to field list arrow** to view the list of customers on record:

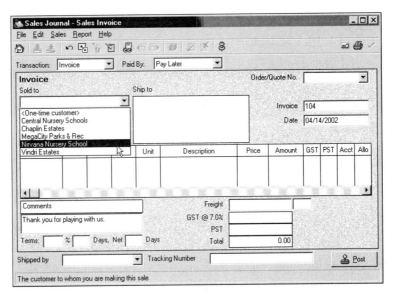

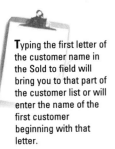

 Typing the first letter of the customer name in the Sold to field will bring you to that part of the customer list or will enter the name of the first customer beginning with that letter.

◆ Click **Nirvana Nursery School** to choose the customer.

The customer's name and address now appear on the invoice. They are taken from the customer's ledger record. The same information appears in the Ship to field. You can edit the shipping address if needed when the goods are to be sent to an address different from the customer's primary location.

The invoice number, 104, is correct, as it is updated from the Forms settings and this is a regular sale. You must change the Session date to the invoice date.

◆ Double click the **Date field**.

◆ Type **4-8**

We will skip the inventory fields that are not needed.

◆ Click the **Description field** to move the cursor.

◆ Type **play centre completed**

◆ Click the **Amount field** to move the cursor.

◆ Type **3000**

◆ Press (tab) to move to the GST code field.

◆ Press (enter) to display the Select GST code screen:

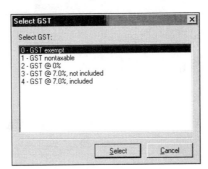

These codes are the same as the first five GST codes in the Purchases Journal, and they have the same applications. Play Wave does not include GST in its price.

◆ Click **3 – GST @ 7.0%, not included**.

◆ Click **Select** to add the code to the invoice.

The cursor moves to the PST rate field. Since the contract work is exempt from PST, leave the field blank.

◆ Press (tab) to move to the Acct field.

◆ Press (enter) to display the Select Account screen. Notice that you can add a new account if necessary using the Account Wizard described in Chapter 3.

◆ Type **4** to advance to the first 4000 account.

◆ Click *4020 Revenue from Contracting*.

◆ Click **Select** or press (enter) to add the account to the invoice.

The payment terms for Nirvana Nursery School should be set to net 1 from the customer's ledger. If necessary, change the terms on the invoice and then remember to edit the customer ledger (Options tab).

Editing Discount Terms

To remove or change default payment terms for an invoice,

• Click the % field, the first discount Terms field.

• Press (del) to remove the rate. Press (tab) to enter the change.

• Press (del) to remove the number of discount days and press (tab).

• Press (del) to remove the default entry and type 1 to add the new terms.

There is no freight charge and shipping information is not applicable. Your invoice is complete and should now look like the one shown here:

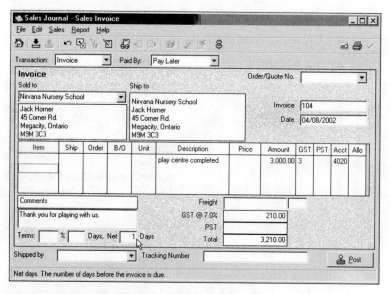

Check your work carefully. To review the journal entry,

◆ Choose the **Report** menu and click **Display Sales Journal Entry**:

Sales Journal Entry			
File Options Help			
04/08/2002 (J28)	Debits	Credits	Project
1200 Accounts Receivable	3,210.00	-	
2650 GST Charged on Services	-	210.00	
4020 Revenue from Contracting	-	3,000.00	
	3,210.00	3,210.00	

Linked Accounts for the Sales Journal

Routine credit sales have a number of common elements. They increase the balance in the *Accounts Receivable* control account, they increase the GST liability to the Receiver General (and the *PST Payable* liability when PST is applied to the sale). The principal linked accounts for credit sales are *Accounts Receivable* and *GST Charged on Services*. Although we did not enter either of these account numbers, the program uses them automatically because we identified them as the appropriate linked accounts for the Receivables Ledger. In addition to these General Ledger account changes, the transaction will increase the customer's balance owing by the total invoice amount.

◆ Close the display.

Correcting the Sales Journal Entry

It is important that all the invoice details are correct so that customers will be billed correctly. Even the date is important because it determines the eligible discount periods and interest charges.

Before Posting

You should always check your work carefully before posting because it is easier to correct mistakes before posting than after. You can edit any field for which you entered information by highlighting incorrect text and typing over it. You can reselect from the Select GST list or the Select Account list by double clicking the appropriate column to see the list, making the selection and clicking Select. The new selection automatically replaces the old one. If you have selected the wrong customer, reselect from the customer list. When you change an amount, you should press 〔tab〕 to ensure that the totals are correctly updated before you post the entry.

You can easily delete an entire line from the invoice. Click the incorrect line to select it and choose the Edit menu and then click Remove Line. In the same way, you can insert an additional line. Click at the point where you need to add an invoice line. Choose the Edit menu and click Insert line.

If you want to start over, click the Undo tool ⟲ or choose the Edit menu and click Undo Entry to delete the transaction. Confirm that you want to discard the transaction. A new blank journal form will appear.

After Posting

Sometimes you will find an error after you have already posted the transaction. At this point you must adjust the invoice or reverse it from the Sales Journal. You can adjust an invoice if you have turned on Invoice Lookup and if you have not cleared the invoice.

To adjust an invoice, click the Adjust invoice tool ▦ or choose the Sales menu and click Adjust Invoice. In the Adjust an invoice screen, enter the search options you need and click OK. Click the invoice you need to change on the Adjust an invoice screen. Click Select to open the Adjusting Invoice screen. Enter the necessary changes and post the adjusted transaction. Adjusting a sales invoice involves the same steps as adjusting a purchase invoice. Refer to Chapter 5, page 149, for further details.

You cannot adjust an invoice to correct for selecting the wrong customer. In this case, you must reverse the entry. Use Invoice Lookup to recall the posted transaction if you need to review the details you entered initially. Print the invoice. Open the Sales Journal and select the same customer, the incorrect one. Enter all the invoice details exactly as you did before, but add a minus sign to the Amount column. This will allow the program to reverse all the usual debit and credit amounts. Post the transaction. Enter the sales transaction again for the correct customer. Remember to pay the account for the incorrect invoice and its reversing entry. There will be no journal entry from this payment because the net amount paid is zero.

◆ Click the **Print tool** 🖨 to print the invoice. (Be sure that the printer is on.)

◆ Click **Post** 👤 Post to save the journal entry.

Sales with Payments (Cash Sales)

The next transaction is a cash sale, or sale that is accompanied by immediate payment. You should still be in the Sales Journal.

> ✔ Cash Sales Invoice #105
> Dated Apr. 8/02
> To Chaplin Estates, $1 000 plus $70 GST charged for repairs and building work on play centre. Invoice total $1 070. Payment in full by Cheque #47211.

◆ Click the **Paid By field** to display the drop-down list of payment methods:

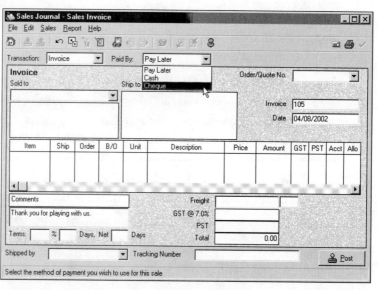

We will set up credit cards in Chapter 8. When you add them, all credit cards you set up will appear on the Paid By list.

◆ Click **Cheque** to add the necessary fields as shown:

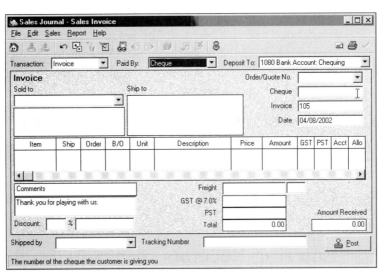

When you close the journal and re-open it, the date will return to the Session date by default.

The Sales Invoice now has a Cheque number field and a Deposit To drop-down list of bank accounts. The fields for discount terms have also changed, showing only fields for the percentage discount and the discount amount. An Amount Received field is added as well. The Cheque number field is not included for payments by cash or credit card.

◆   Choose **Chaplin Estates** from the customer list in the Sold to field.

◆   Click the **Cheque field**. Enter the number from the customer's cheque in this field.

◆   Type **47211**

The invoice number is correctly updated. The date is unchanged from the previous entry and correct. You may type a description for the transaction in the Description field. This information will appear on the printed invoice but not in the journal entry.

◆   Click the **Amount field**.

◆   Type **1000**

◆   Press ⟨tab⟩ to advance to the GST code field.

◆   Double click the **GST field**, choose code **3** from the list and press ⟨enter⟩.

◆   Click the **Acct field**.

◆   Press ⟨enter⟩, choose account **4020** from the list and press ⟨enter⟩.

The terms should be correct from the customer's ledger. If necessary, delete the discount on the invoice and press ⟨tab⟩ to enter the change and update all totals.

The invoice is now complete, and you can check your work.

◆   Choose the **Report** menu and click **Display Sales Journal Entry** to review the journal entry:

Sales Journal Entry			
File Options Help			
04/08/2002 (J29)	Debits	Credits	Project
1080 Bank Account: Chequing	1,070.00	-	
2650 GST Charged on Services	-	70.00	
4020 Revenue from Contracting	-	1,000.00	
	1,070.00	1,070.00	

Notice that this entry is different from the previous one. *Bank Account: Chequing* is the debited account because Cheque is the selected payment method. Again we see the operation of the linked accounts. In addition, the cash sale will be stored in the customer's ledger as a sale and payment for the same date. In this way, the customer's year-to-date purchases are updated.

◆ Close the display.

◆ Make corrections if necessary. You may print the invoice if you wish.

◆ Click **Post** [👤 Post] to save the journal entry.

◆ Close the Sales Journal to return to the Home window because the next transaction is not a sale.

Entering Receipts from Customers

Enter each cheque received from a customer as a separate transaction. A single cheque may, however, be used for a partial payment of a single invoice or to pay more than one invoice.

The next transaction is a payment on account from Nirvana Nursery School.

> ✔ Cash Receipt #4
> Dated Apr. 9/02
> From Nirvana Nursery School, cheque #124 for $3 210 in full payment of account.
> Reference invoice #104.

When a customer makes a payment to reduce an account balance, you enter the transaction in the Receipts Journal shown here with the arrow pointer:

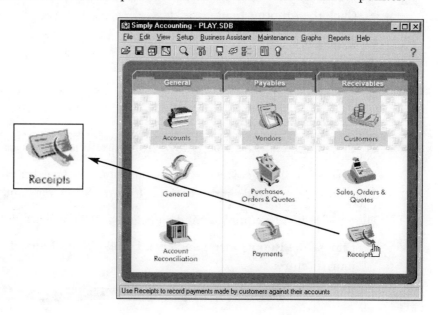

◆ Click the **Receipts icon** to open the Receipts Journal:

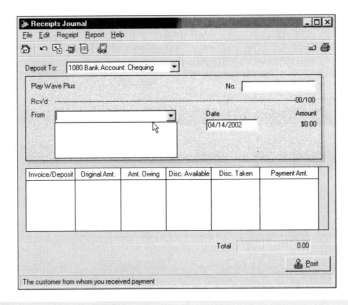

The Receipts Journal Input Fields

The Receipts Journal is similar to the Payments Journal with a cheque portion and a statement portion.

The default linked bank account is selected in the **Deposit To** field. When other bank accounts are set up and defined as Bank class accounts, they will appear on the Deposit To list and you may select one of them.

A complete list of customers on record is available in the **From** field. You can use the **No.** field to record the Receipt number (updated automatically by the program from the Forms Settings) or for the number from the customer's cheque. The number you enter becomes part of the recorded journal entry. Enter the date of the cheque, the date that payment is received, in the **Date** field.

The statement portion includes any outstanding invoices, one invoice for each statement line. The **Invoice** number, the full **Original Amount** from the original invoice, and the **Amount** or balance **Owing** appear in the first three columns. When the invoice includes a discount and the discount period has not expired, the amount of the discount is displayed in the **Disc. Available** column. When the discount is actually taken, as for a full payment within the discount period, the amount is added to the **Disc. Taken** field and the **Payment Amt**. is reduced accordingly. The program automatically calculates the total of all payment amounts for the individual invoices and adds it to the **Total** field and to the **Rec'd** line of the cheque portion.

Two other options appear as tool buttons. Click **Include fully paid invoices** to add all invoices that have not been cleared. The second tool, to accept customer deposits, will be used in Chapter 8.

The cursor is in the From (Customer) field.

◆ Click the **From list arrow** to display the list of customers.

When the customer is identified as a foreign currency customer and a linked foreign currency bank is set up, the foreign currency linked bank will be the default account for the transaction.

◆ Click **Nirvana Nursery School** to select this customer and add it to the form along with the outstanding invoice:

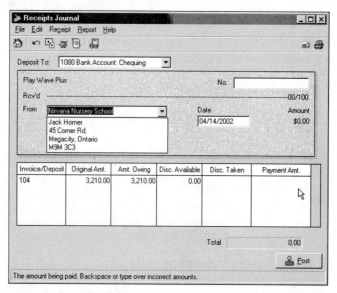

◆ Click the **No. field**. Remember that we are using this field for the cheque number.

◆ Type **124**

◆ Press ⟨*tab*⟩ to advance to the Date field and select the default Session date.

◆ Type **April 9**

◆ Press ⟨*tab*⟩ to advance to the first line of the invoice column.

If any discounts are still available, they will be listed at this point.

◆ Click the **Payment Amt. field** for the first invoice line to reveal the full amount.

◆ Press ⟨*tab*⟩ to accept the amount.

The Total is updated and the cheque amount in the upper portion of the form is entered. The completed payment form should look like the one below:

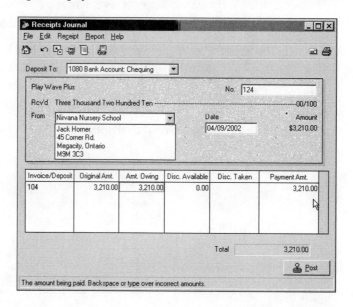

Remember that we are not using the automatic receipt number sequence because we want to record the customers' cheque numbers in the journal entries.

Discounts and Partial Payments

When a discount is offered with the sale and the discount period has not expired, the program calculates the discount and shows it in the Disc. Available column. To accept the discount, click the Disc. Taken column and then the Payment Amt. column. Remember that discounts are usually available only when an invoice is fully paid within the discount period.

To enter a partial payment, replace the default highlighted Payment Amt. with the amount of the payment. To pay more than one invoice with a single cheque, click the Payment Amt. column for each invoice that is paid, or enter the actual amount that is being paid towards each invoice if it is different from the balance owing.

Before posting the transaction, you should display and review the journal entry.

◆ Choose the **Report** menu and click **Display Receipts Journal Entry**:

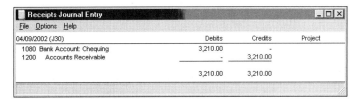

The program automatically chooses the correct accounts that we identified as linked accounts for the ledger in the previous chapter. Because all receipt entries follow the pattern of debiting *Bank Account: Chequing* and crediting *Accounts Receivable*, it is not necessary to enter the account numbers in the transaction. Furthermore, the program prevents you from entering an amount that exceeds the balance owing. The customer's ledger is also updated by the receipt entry. These automatic procedures reduce the opportunity to make a mistake.

◆ Close the display to return to the Receipts Journal.

Correcting the Receipts Journal Entry

To correct a cheque number, date or amount, double click the field's contents and type the correction. After changing an amount, press ⌧tab⌧ or click elsewhere on the form to update the Total. If you have selected the wrong customer, choose again from the customer list and press ⌧tab⌧ to enter the change. When asked to confirm that you want to discard the transaction, click Yes.

Making corrections after posting is explained in the section NSF Cheques — Reversing a Receipt (pages 208–209).

When you are certain that the information is correct,

◆ Click **Post** ⌧🔨 Post⌧ to save the entry.

If you have not deleted the automatic receipt number, the customer's cheque number, the entry 124, will be greater than the receipt number. You will see the following warning advising you of the change in the numbering sequence:

This message will appear each time you enter a receipt if you have not deleted the Forms Setting entry for Receipts (Home window, Setup menu).

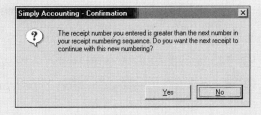

Click **No** so that the numbering does not change. Delete the Receipts number (edit the Forms Settings, refer to page 171) so that you do not receive the message again.

◆ Close the Receipts Journal to return to the Home window.

◆ Enter the following payment in the Payments Journal.

☐ Cheque Copy #111
Dated Apr. 13/02
To The Buildex Corp., $3 187.74 in full payment of account balance, including
$65.06 discount taken for early payment. Reference invoice #BC-612.

◆ Close the Payments Journal to return to the Home window.

◆ Back up your work.

◆ Advance the Session date to **April 22, 2002**.

◆ Enter the next two transactions in the Payments Journal as other payments.

☐ Cash Purchase Invoice #OH-214324
Dated Apr. 15/02
From Ontario Hydro, $100 for hydro services plus $7 GST paid. Invoice total $107.
Issued cheque #112 in full payment.

☐ Cash Purchase Invoice #BC-521142
Dated Apr. 15/02
From Bell Canada, $60 for telephone services plus $4.20 GST paid and $4.80 PST
paid. Invoice total $69. Issued cheque #113 in full payment. (Enter 8 in the P field
for the PST rate at 8%, enter 60 in the Amount field and allow the program to
allocate the tax payment automatically to the expense account.)

Sales Quote for a New Customer

Sales Quotes may be offered to customers in advance of the customer placing an order. The quote usually offers a guaranteed price for a fixed period of time. The quote may be sent to the customer by mail, fax or e-mail.

The following transaction includes two new features. A sales quote is provided to a customer not currently in the ledger records. We can add the customer directly from the Sales Journal where you enter sales quotes, just as you added a new vendor from the Purchases Journal.

☑ Sales Quote #2001
Dated Apr. 15/02
To Teddy Day Care Centres, $10 000 plus $700 GST for a play centre that will be
completed before the end of the month. Terms: 2/10, n/30.

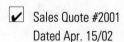

◆ Click the **Sales Journal icon** 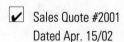 to open the Sales Journal.

◆ Choose **Quote** as the Transaction Type from the drop-down list.

The program enters the next quote number automatically from your Forms Settings and adds a Ship Date field as shown:

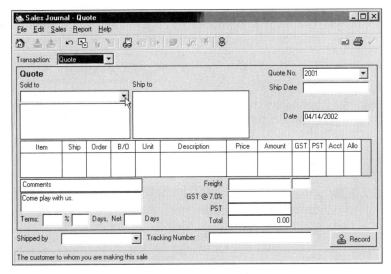

◆ Click the **Sold to (customer) field** to move the cursor.

◆ Type `Teddy Day Care Centres`

◆ Press ⟨tab⟩.

The program recognizes that the name is new and allows you to add the record:

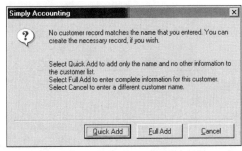

For Sales Invoices, you will see Continue as an additional option when you type in a new customer name. The Continue option will not create a customer record and will not include the new customer in Aged Reports.

The choices are almost the same as those for new vendors. You may choose to add the full record details (the Full Add option) or to add only the name at this stage (the Quick Add option). You can edit the record later to add the remaining information. Or if this is a customer who is unlikely to make additional purchases, you may leave the record with only the customer's name.

◆ Click **Quick Add**.

You have added an incomplete ledger record for the customer. The customer's name will appear in the customer field lists and complete invoice details will be part of the Receivables reports.

◆ Click the **Ship Date field**.

◆ Type `April 30, 2002`

◆ Press ⟨tab⟩ to advance to the Date field.

◆ Type `4 15`

◆ Click the **Order field**.

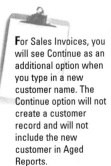

◆ Type `1`

You must enter an order quantity for both sales quotes and sales orders. The program will warn you if you try to leave this field blank.

◆ Click the **Description field**.

◆ Type `Contract to build playground`

◆ Press (tab) to advance to the Price field.

◆ Type `10000`

◆ Press (tab) twice to advance to the GST code field. The amount is calculated as the order quantity times the price.

◆ Double click to show the Select GST screen. Click **3** and click **Select** to return to the form.

◆ Press (tab) to skip the PST field, leaving it blank because PST is not applied to the sale.

◆ Press (enter) to display the Select Account screen. Notice that you can add a new account at this stage if necessary.

◆ Choose account *4020 Revenue from Contracting* and add it to the invoice.

The payment terms are correct and the quote is complete as shown here:

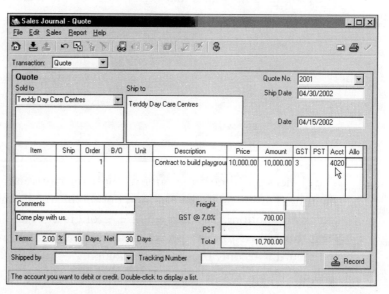

Because the sales quote does not generate a journal entry, there is no journal entry to review. When the quote is accepted and the order filled, the journal entry is generated. Check the information carefully. Make corrections in the same way you correct a Sales Invoice. When you are certain that the information is correct,

◆ Click **Record** ![Record button] to save the entry. Leave the Sales Journal open.

Converting Sales Quotes to Orders

Once a sales quote is accepted by a customer, it may be filled directly by making a sale, or it may be converted to a sales order. Teddy Day Care Centres accepted the sales quote before the work began, so the quote should be changed to an order.

> ✔ Sales Order #2001
>
> Dated Apr. 17/02
>
> To Teddy Day Care Centres, to confirm sales quote #2001, $10 000 plus $700 GST for a play centre that will be completed before the end of the month. Terms: 2/10, n/30.

◆ Choose **Sales Order** from the Transaction drop-down list to open the Sales Order screen.

◆ Choose quote **#2001** from the Order/Quote No. drop-down list.

◆ Press ⌜tab⌟ to see the sales quote for Teddy Day Care Centres presented as a sales order as shown here:

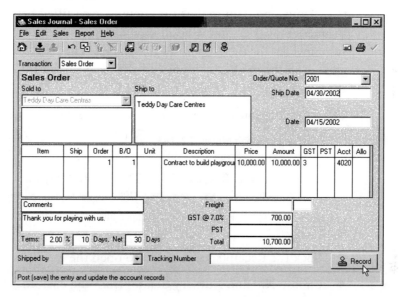

All fields, except the customer, may now be edited if necessary. The customer address fields are still blank because we used Quick Add to create an incomplete customer record. We need to change only the Date of the order. Frequently, customers will have their own order forms with their own sequence numbers. In this case, Play Wave's sales quote number will be used as the sales order number.

◆ Double click the **Date field**.

◆ Type **apr 17**

Check your work carefully because there is no journal display to review. Sales orders do not generate journal entries.

◆ Click **Record** [Record] to save the order.

Before the quote is removed, you are given a warning:

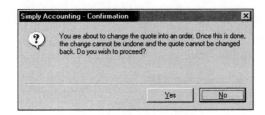

◆ Click **Yes** to confirm the change and proceed.

◆ Close the Sales Journal to return to the Home window.

NSF Cheques — Reversing a Receipt

Sometimes a bank will return a cheque because the account does not have sufficient funds to cover it. These cheques are NSF (not sufficient funds) and are entered as negative receipts in the Receipts Journal. Banks frequently charge a fee for processing the cheque and require that the cheque be certified before it can be resubmitted. A business may pass on the additional charge to the customer by creating a separate sales invoice for the amount of the charge. The NSF charges to the business will appear on the bank statement and will be processed through the Account Reconciliation Journal in Chapter 11.

The following source document provides the details of a customer NSF cheque.

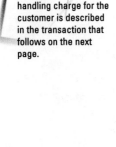The Sales Journal entry to record the handling charge for the customer is described in the transaction that follows on the next page.

 Bank Debit Memo #672147
Dated Apr. 18/02
From Royal Trust, $3 210 for NSF cheque #124 from Nirvana Nursery School plus a handling charge to process the NSF cheque. Nirvana Nursery has been notified of the outstanding balance. Reference invoice #104 and cash receipt #4.

◆ Click the Receipts icon 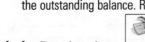 to open the Receipts Journal.

◆ Choose **Nirvana Nursery School** from the customer list.

◆ Click the **No. field**.

◆ Type **NSF124**

◆ Press `tab`.

◆ Type **4-18-02** in the Date field.

No invoices are listed because none are outstanding.

◆ Click the **Include fully paid invoices tool** ▤ .

◆ Invoice #104 paid with cheque #124 is now listed with no balance outstanding:

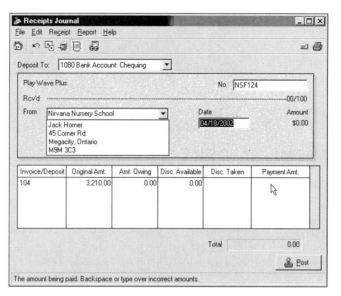

◆ Click the **Payment Amt. field.**

◆ Type **-3210** (add a minus sign to the amount) as the payment amount.

◆ Press 〔*tab*〕.

◆ Choose the **Report** menu and click **Display Receipts Journal Entry:**

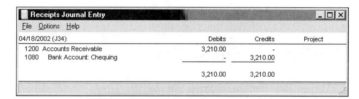

Explanation of Receipts Journal Entry

This journal entry is the opposite of the one for the payment on page 203 because it reverses that transaction. The *Accounts Receivable* balance owing is restored and the balance for *Bank Account: Chequing* is reduced.

◆ Close the display.

Check your work carefully and make corrections if necessary.

◆ Click **Post** 〔 ☚ Post 〕 to save the transaction.

◆ Choose Nirvana Nursery School again. The balance owing is restored.

◆ Close the Receipts Journal.

◆ Record the NSF service charges (Sales Journal) and then record the receipt that settles the account:

☐ Sales Invoice #106
Dated Apr. 18/02
To Nirvana Nursery School, $20 for handling charges for the NSF cheque. Terms: net 1. (Enter the charges as an invoice that is paid later and credit a new Group account, 4300 Other Revenue. Use the Add Account Wizard to create the new account.)

If a discount was taken, you also should reverse it by typing the amount of the discount with a minus sign in the Discount Taken column.

Remember that no GST is charged on the service fee and of course there is no discount on the handling charges.

☐ Cash Receipt #5
Dated Apr. 20/02
From Nirvana Nursery School, certified cheque #124 (CC-124) for $3 230 in full
payment of outstanding account. Reference invoices #104 and #106 and bank debit
memo #672147. (Type CC-124 in the No. field as the cheque number.)

☐ **Advance the Session date to April 30**

◆ Record the following Payment and Purchase Order:

☐ Cheque Copy #114
Dated Apr. 23/02
To Swede Steel, $2 097.20 in full payment of account, including $42.80 discount for
early payment. Reference invoice #SC-5019.

☐ Purchase Order #20003
Dated Apr. 24/02
Shipping date Apr. 29/02
From The Buildex Corp., $2 500 for plastics and fibreglass and $2 500 for lumber
plus $350 GST paid. A freight charge of $40 plus $2.80 GST will be added to the
invoice. Invoice total $5 392.80. Order is to be shipped within 5 days.
Terms: 2/10, n/30 days.

Filling a Sales Order

When the contract work for Teddy Day Care Centres was completed on April 28, the
sales order was filled. Filling a sales order by making a Sales Journal entry is similar
to filling a purchase order.

☑ Sales Invoice #107
Dated Apr. 28/02
To Teddy Day Care Centres, to fill sales order #2001, $10 000 for completion of play
centre plus $700 GST charged. Invoice total $10 700. Terms: 2/10, n/30 days.

◆ Return to the Home window if you have not already done so.

◆ Click the **Sales icon** to open the Sales Journal.

◆ Choose **Invoice** as the Transaction type and **Pay Later** as the payment method.

◆ Click the **Order/Quote No. field** list arrow.

◆ Choose **2001** from the list.

◆ Press *tab* to enter the information from the sales order recorded earlier:

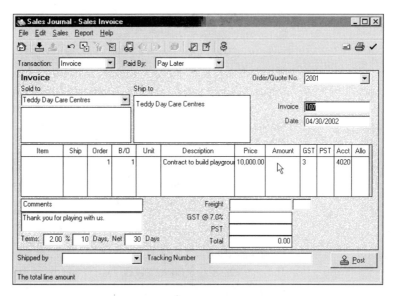

The invoice is incomplete because the order is unfilled, and the date is incorrect.

◆ Click the **Fill backordered quantities tool** 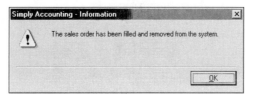 (or choose the Sales menu and click Fill Sales Order) to complete the sales invoice. The Order quantity becomes the quantity in the Ship field, and the total amounts are added.

◆ Change the invoice date to April 28.

◆ Choose the **Report** menu and click **Display Sales Journal Entry** to review your work.

◆ Close the display. When all the information is correct,

◆ Click **Post** 〔 Post 〕 to save the entry. The program advises you that the sales order will be deleted:

> **Simply Accounting - Information**
>
> ⚠ The sales order has been filled and removed from the system.
>
> [OK]

◆ Click OK to proceed.

Converting a Sales Quote into a Sale

Sometimes after receiving a quote, a customer will make the purchase from the business directly, without first placing an order. To turn a sales quote into a sale, choose Invoice as the Transaction type, choose the Quote number from the list and press 〔tab〕. When you post the entry, the program confirms that the quote will be removed. Click OK to proceed.

◆ Close the Sales Journal. Using the appropriate journals, complete the entries that follow.

☐ Purchase Invoice #CC-82
Dated Apr. 28/02
From Casual Contractors, $2 000 for subcontracted payroll expenses for the Teddy Day Care Centres project.

☐ Purchase Invoice #BC-811

Dated April 29/02

From The Buildex Corp., to fill purchase order #20003, $2 500 for plastics and fibreglass and $2 500 for lumber plus $350 GST paid. Freight charge of $40 plus $2.80 GST added to the invoice. Invoice total $5 392.80. Terms: 2/10, n/30 days.

☐ Purchase Invoice #GM-1092

Dated Apr. 29/02

To fill purchase order #20002

From Groundfos Machinery, $12 000 for hydraulic ground drill plus $840 GST paid. Invoice total $12 840. Terms: 2/20, n/30.

☐ Sales Invoice #108

Dated Apr. 29/02

To Central Nursery Schools, $1 000 for addition to playground completed in March plus $70 GST charged. Invoice total $1 070. Terms: 2/10, n/30 days.

☐ Sales Quote #2002

Dated Apr. 29/02

For Bayview Kindergarten Schools, $8 000 plus $560 GST, to build a play centre in front of main building. Work to be completed before May 15. Invoice total $8 560. Terms: 2/10, n/30 days.

☐ Bayview Kindergarten Schools (contact: Jackie O. A. Trades)

Address: 1244 Bayview Ave., Megacity, ON M5R 2J9

Tel: (416) 793-7399

Fax: (416) 793-6644

E-mail: JTrades@golden.net

Credit limit: $10 000

☐ Sales Order #2002

Dated Apr. 30/02

Convert sales quote #2002 for Bayview Kindergarten Schools to a sales order. All amounts, dates and terms are unchanged.

☐ Cheque Copy #115

Dated Apr. 30/02

To Casual Contractors, $2 000 in full payment of account. Reference invoice #CC-82.

☐ Bank Debit Memo #699143

Dated Apr. 30/02

From Royal Trust, $2 000 preauthorized withdrawal for mortgage payment. This amount consists of $1 890 interest and $110 for reduction of principal.

☐ Memo #9

Dated Apr. 30/02

Based on the end-of-the-month count of supplies remaining, it was determined that the following quantities of supplies were used during April. Make the necessary adjusting entry to account for the supplies used:

Fibreglass & Plastics	$3 200
Lumber	$3 300
Hardware	$2 100
Office Supplies	$120

☐ Memo #10

Dated Apr. 30/02

Gen One month of prepaid insurance worth $200, has expired. Recall the stored adjusting entry to debit the Insurance Expense account for this amount.

☐ Memo #11

Dated Apr. 30/02

Depreciation is calculated and recorded monthly for all depreciable assets. Recall *Gen* the stored depreciation entry to record the following depreciation amounts:

Portable Computer System	$75
Machinery & Tools	$125
Shop	$250
Truck	$400

☐ Edit the customer record for Teddy Day Care Centres by adding the following:

Contact: Goldi Locks

Address: 100 Dalmation Ave.

               Megacity, ON M4T 3D3

Telephone: (416) 632-7190

Terms: 2/10, n/30 (Options tab)

Credit Limit: $10 000 (Activity tab)

To open the record for editing, click the Customers icon in the Home window. Click the customer icon for Teddy Day Care Centres. Click the Edit tool.

◆ Close the ledger record and the Customers window to return to the Home window.

Receivables Ledger Reports

Customer Lists and Customer Aged Reports were described in the previous chapter. The Customer Sales Report will be discussed in Chapter 15 with the Inventory Reports.

Sales Journal

The Sales Journal Report includes only transactions posted through the **Sales Journal**.

◆ Choose the **Reports** menu, then choose **Journal Entries** and click **Sales** to see the report options:

Refer to pages 178–185 for complete details on Receivables Ledger fields and entering and editing customer records.

You can access all Receivables Ledger reports from the Customers window using the Reports menu or the Select a report tool

To see the journal entries for all journals in a single report, go to the Home window. Choose the Reports menu, then choose Journal Entries and click All.

The report options are the same as those for other journals. You can sort and filter the report by date, journal entry number, source or comment. You can report by posting date or by journal entry number. The Session dates are the defaults for both Start and Finish dates. The journal for the last three weeks of April will include all the Sales Journal entries to date.

- ◆ Type **4-8**

- ◆ Press (tab) to advance to the Finish date to highlight it for editing.

- ◆ Type **4-30**

- ◆ Click **OK** to display the report.

Drill-Down Reports

The same drill-down reports are available from both the Sales Journal and the Receipts Journal Report. Double click the journal entry number, the date or the invoice number to access the Invoice Lookup window for the journal entry. All of the usual lookup options are available. When you double click the customer name, the Customer Aged Report appears for the selected customer. Double clicking the account number, account name or the amount will lead you to the General Ledger (All Transactions) Report for the selected account. The date range for the drill-down report will match the dates for the journal report. You may print the drill-down report. When you close the drill-down report, you will return to the previous report window.

- ◆ Choose the **File** menu and click **Print** in the Report window to print the report.

- ◆ Close the display when you have finished viewing it.

Receipts Journal

The Receipts Journal Report includes only the transactions posted through the Receipts Journal.

- ◆ Choose the **Reports** menu, then choose **Journal Entries** and click **Receipts** to see the report options:

The familiar journal options screen appears with sort and filter buttons, and the posting date and the Session dates selected by default. To print the Receipts Journal for the last three weeks of April,

- ◆ Type **4 8** to replace the highlighted Start date.

- ◆ Press (tab) to advance to the Finish date to highlight it for editing.

- ◆ Type **4 30**

- ◆ Click **OK** to display the report.

The Lookup feature is introduced in Chapter 8.

214

Notice that the initial receipt from Nirvana, its reversing entry and the final payment are all included.

The drill-down reports available are the same as those described for Sales Journal Reports above.

◆ Print the report and then close the display.

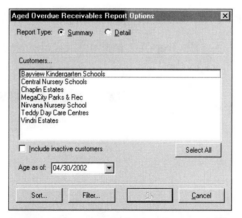

The Display tool label changes to match a selected icon.

Alternate Methods of Accessing Journal Reports

You can access the Sales and Receipts Journal Reports in several ways, both from the Home window and from the Customers window.

- From the Home window, click the Display tool button. Choose Sales Journal or Receipts Journal from the Select Report screen to indicate the report you want. Click Select to display the report options.

- From the Home window, right-click the Sales Journal icon to select it. Then click the Display Sales Journal tool to display the Sales Journal report options. To see the Receipts Journal report options, right-click the Receipts Journal icon and then click the Display Receipts Journal tool.

- From the Customers window, click the Select a report tool. Then choose Display Sales Journal or Display Receipts Journal to indicate the type of report you want and to display the report options. All Receivables Ledger Reports are included in this selection list. Click Select.

- From the Customers window, choose the Reports menu and click Display Sales Journal or Display Receipts Journal to display the corresponding report options. All Receivables Ledger Reports are included in this Reports menu.

Aged Overdue Receivables Report

The Aged Overdue Receivables Report is very similar to the Customer Aged Report discussed in the previous chapter, with the addition of a column for any accounts that are overdue.

◆ Choose the **Reports** menu, then choose **Receivables** and click **Aged Overdue Receivables** to see the report options:

The Aged Overdue Receivables Report and its options are like the Customer Aged Report discussed in the previous chapter. You may sort and filter the report by customer name and balance owing, and print the report for one or more customers or for all customers. Press ⌈ctrl⌉ and click the name of each customer to include in the report or click Select All to include them all.

The Detail and Summary options again offer you the choice to display only the total owing in each aging period, the Summary option, or the individual invoices in each aging period, the Detail option. If there are overdue accounts, they will be listed in a separate column based on the customer terms. Customers with no outstanding balance are excluded from the Aged Overdue Receivables Report.

To display the Detail Report for all Customers up to the Session date,

◆ Click **Detail**.

◆ Click **Select All**.

◆ Click the **Date field** to move the cursor and prepare the field for editing.

◆ Type **04-30-02** if this date does not appear.

◆ Click **OK** to display the report.

The report shows that the MegaCity Parks & Rec account is overdue.

Drill-Down Reports

From the Detail Report, double click the customer's name to display the Customer Aged Detail Report. Double click any other item in the report to access the Invoice Lookup window for the journal entry and the usual lookup options. Lookup is available only for invoices posted from the Sales Journal.

From the Summary Report, double click any item on the line for a customer to see the Aged Overdue Detail Report for the same customer. You may print the drill-down report. When you close the drill-down report, you will return to the previous report.

◆ Choose the **File** menu and click **Print** in the Report window to print the report.

◆ Close the display when you have finished viewing and printing the report.

Pending Sales Orders

The Pending Sales Orders Report shows all sales orders that have not been filled.

◆ Choose the **Reports** menu, then choose **Receivables** and click **Pending Sales Orders** in the Home window to see the report options:

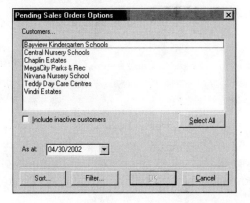

Again, you can include one or more customers or all customers. Only customers with outstanding orders will actually be added to the report. Others are omitted. The date for the report is always the Session date. You may sort and filter the report by order number, order date, shipping date or amount.

◆ Click **Select All**.

◆ Click **OK**.

Because there are no outstanding sales orders at this time, you will see the message that there is no data to report.

Drill-Down Reports

Again, drill-down reports are available when you have data to report. Double click the customer's name to display the Customer Aged Report. Double click any other item in the report to view the sales order. The order is in Lookup format, and cannot be adjusted from this window. When you close the drill-down report, you will return to the previous report.

◆ Click **OK** to return to the Home window.

Printing Customer Statements

Sort and filter options do not apply to customer statements.

You can print but not display customer statements. Any transactions within the period you selected in the Receivables Settings are part of the printed statement. Unpaid invoices are always included in the statement.

◆ Choose the **Reports** menu, then choose **Receivables** and click **Customer Statements** in the Home window to see the report options:

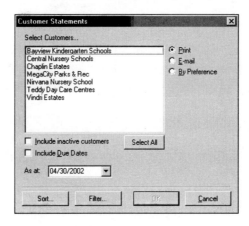

◆ Click **MegaCity Parks & Rec**. Then press *ctrl* and click **Nirvana Nursery School** to select these two customers. (You would click Select All to print statements for all customers.)

◆ Click **Include Due Dates** if you also want to inform customers when payment is due as part of the statements.

- Accept **Print** to send the statement by mail or fax, the default setting, or choose the method by which you are sending the statement, by E-mail or By the Preference indicated in the customer's record.

Be sure that you have the printer turned on and prepared with the appropriate forms. For practice, you can use the custom form we selected with ordinary printer paper.

- Click **OK** to print the statements or begin the e-mail procedure. Printing will begin immediately.

Printing Mailing Labels

If you have printer label forms, you can use the Simply Accounting program to prepare mailing labels for customers as well as vendors. Be certain that your print options are set up correctly for the label paper you are using. If you have set the printer settings for labels, they will still be saved.

Setting the Printer for Labels

The labels settings you entered in Chapter 5 will remain in effect for all labels for all your Simply Accounting files. Refer to page 162 for these procedures if you need to.

Printing the Labels

- Choose the **Reports** menu, then choose **Mailing Labels** and click **Customers** in the Home window to see the options:

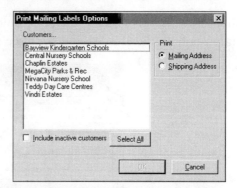

You can include one or more customers in the list or all the customers.

- Click **Select All**.

- Click **OK** to print the labels. Printing will begin immediately.

Management Reports

Management Reports are the Simply Accounting Advice reports that are customized for your data files. If you have the Crystal Reports program installed (from the Simply Accounting installation disk) you can further modify the report to suit your needs.

- Choose the **Reports** menu, then choose **Management Reports** and click **Receivables** in the Home window to see the topics in the Advice window:

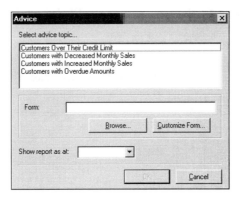

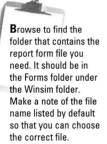

Browse to find the folder that contains the report form file you need. It should be in the Forms folder under the Winsim folder. Make a note of the file name listed by default so that you can choose the correct file.

The topics include reports that management can use to make decisions about credit limits or to analyze buying patterns over time. The Browse button allows you to find a report form file, while the Customize button allows you to modify a selected report form.

◆ Click **Customers with Increased Monthly Sales** as the advice topic.

◆ Click **OK** to see the customer report showing sales averaged over two months.

None of the customers were on record one year ago so all have increased sales since last year.

◆ Click the **Print tool**  to print the report.

◆ Close the report when finished.

GST Reports and Remittances

The GST Report may be used to help prepare the GST returns that are sent to the Receiver General. These returns may be requesting refunds or sending remittances.

◆ Choose the **Reports** menu and click **GST** in the Home window to see the options:

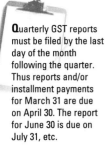

Quarterly GST reports must be filed by the last day of the month following the quarter. Thus reports and/or installment payments for March 31 are due on April 30. The report for June 30 is due on July 31, etc.

◆ Accept the Session date for the report. In the As at field, you should enter the date for the report, usually the end of the period for which you are preparing the return.

A Summary and a Detail Report are available. The Summary Report includes the total purchases, total sales, total GST paid and total GST charged.

The Detail Report has these totals as well as the dates, invoice numbers, purchase and sale amounts and GST amounts for individual transactions for each customer and vendor.

◆ Click **Detail** to change the report type.

◆ Click **OK** to see the report.

◆ Choose the **File** menu and click **Print**.

Comparing the GST Report with General Ledger Balances

Look at the GST Detail Report for April 30:

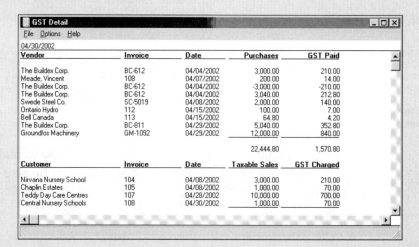

There is no GST Report for March 31 because all transactions in March were entered in the General Journal.

Only the GST amounts entered through the Purchases and Sales Journals and only customers and vendors for whom the option to Include in GST Reports was selected in the ledger record are part of the GST reports. Any GST amounts entered in General Journal entries are therefore not part of the report.

Now print the General Ledger reports for the two GST accounts, 2650 and 2670, for the period from March 15 to April 30. (Refer to Chapter 3, pages 94–95.) The report is shown here:

The balances for GST accounts are also available from the Balance Sheet for the end of the reporting period, usually the end of the previous month.

Compare the amounts for the two reports. The General Ledger balances are higher than the GST Report balances because we entered the first month of purchase and sale transactions through the General Journal. Normally, once the Receivables and Payables Ledgers are set up and used, the two balances will correspond. However, if there has been a General Journal adjusting entry for any reason involving these accounts, the balances will differ. As a precaution, therefore, the GST General Ledger account balances should always be compared with the GST Report amounts. The Ledger balances will always show the correct amounts for the purpose of submitting returns and should be used to prepare the remittance journal entry. The GST Report should be printed for reference as well.

☐ Memo #12

Dated Apr. 30/02

Record the GST refund for the period ending March 31 as a receivable from the Receiver General of Canada. Use the March 31, 2002, General Ledger balances. Use Full Add to add the Receiver General as a new customer. Record the GST refund as a Sales Invoice (Pay Later). Use the memo number as the invoice number. Enter the GST Paid ($1 951.40) as a positive amount and enter the GST Charged on Services ($1 015) as a negative amount. The net balance receivable is $936.40.

☐ New Customer: Receiver General of Canada

Address:	Summerside Tax Centre
	Summerside, PE C1N 6L2
	Tel: (902) 821-8186
*Web site:	www.ccra-adrc.gc.ca This is the Web site for Canada Customs and
	Revenue Agency (formerly Revenue Canada).
Terms:	net 60

Do not include in GST reports.

◆ Back up your data files.

◆ To follow good management practice, we recommend printing the following reports:
Journal Entries: All journals for April 8 to April 30
Trial Balance: As at April 30
Income Statement: From March 1 to April 30
Balance Sheet: As at April 30
Vendor Aged Detail Report: For all vendors as at April 30
Customer Aged Detail Report: For all customers as at April 30

◆ Close the Play Wave data files to prepare for entering journal transactions for Live Links.

Practice: Live Links

At this stage you are ready to use all the General, Payables and Receivables Journals to complete the accounting transactions for Live Links. Remember that some sales are subject to PST at 7 percent while others are not. Leave the PST field blank if PST is not applied. Type 7 in the PST (rate) field to allow the program to calculate the tax amounts automatically and credit the *PST Payable* account.

Receivables Journal Entries
Instructions

If you have not completed the ledger setup for Live Links in Chapter 6 and want to continue working on Chapter 7, you can use your copy of the Data Disk file — Ch07\links\linkch07.sdb — to continue this chapter.

1. Open the data files for Live Links.

2. Enter August 14, 2002, as the Session date.

3. Enter the following transactions using the appropriate journals. Remember to back up your work regularly.

☐ Add the following accounts:
4300 Other Revenue (G)
5084 Depreciation: Colour Laser (G)

☐ Sales Invoice #106
Dated Aug. 9/02
To Metro Credit Union, $1 000 plus $70 GST charged and $70 PST charged (7%) for memory upgrades on computers at Pacific Heights branch office. Invoice total $1 140. Terms: 2/10, n/30 days.

☐ Cash Sales Invoice #107
Dated Aug. 9/02
To Jerome Wiggles, $400 plus $28 GST charged (no PST charged) for consultation service. Invoice total $428. Paid in full by cheque #832. Use Quick Add for the new customer.

☐ Purchase Order #2
Dated Aug. 9/02
Shipping date Aug. 25/02
Convert purchase quote PUQ-222 to purchase order #2.
From Promo Uno, $450 plus $31.50 GST paid and $31.50 (7%) PST paid for design, printing and lamination of posters to advertise workshop series. Invoice total $513. Terms: net 30 days.

☐ **Advance the Session date to August 21, 2002**

☐ Cash Receipt #4
Dated Aug. 15/02
From Metro Credit Union, cheque #4433 for $1 117.20 in full payment of account, including $22.80 (2%) discount taken for early payment of account. Reference invoice #106.

☐ Bank Debit Memo #458378
Dated Aug. 17/02
From Learnx Bank, $1 117.20 for NSF cheque from Metro Credit Union plus a service charge to process NSF cheque. Reference invoice #106 and cheque #4433. Remember to reverse both the cheque amount and the discount taken.

☐ Sales Invoice #108
Dated Aug. 17/02
To Metro Credit Union, $20 for NSF service charges. Reference Bank Debit Memo #458378. Remove the discount and set the payment terms as net 1 day.

You must reverse both the payment and the discount for the NSF cheque. Type –1117.20 in the Amount field and type –22.80 in the Disc. Taken field. Check the journal entry carefully before posting to be sure that all amounts have been reversed correctly.

☐ Memo #7
Dated Aug. 17/02
Edit the customer record for Metro Credit Union. Remove the discount for early payment, change the net days to zero and reduce the credit limit to zero. This places the customer on cash payment terms.

☐ Cash Receipt #5
Dated Aug. 20/02
From Metro Credit Union, certified cheque #RB-4433 for $1 160 in full payment of account, including $20 handling charge. The customer included a letter of apology. Reference invoices #106 and #108 and bank debit memo #458378.

☐ Sales Quote #1
Dated Aug. 21/02
Completion (Shipping) date: August 30/02
To Pearson Publishing (new customer), $5 000 plus $350 GST charged and $350 PST charged for duplication services. Invoice total $5 700. Terms: 2/10, n/30 days.

☐ New customer information:
Pearson Publishing (contact: Addison Wesley)
      Address: 55 Booker Ave., Vancouver, BC V7R 2D2
      Tel: (604) 631-7444
      Fax: (604) 631-7500
      E-mail: AWesley@pearsoned.com
      *Web site: www.pearsoned.ca
      Include in GST reports.
      Credit limit: $10 000

☐ **Advance the Session date to August 28, 2002**

☐ Purchase Invoice #PU-2146
Dated Aug. 22/02
From Promo Uno, to fill purchase order #2, $450 plus $31.50 GST paid and $31.50 (7%) PST paid for design, printing and lamination of posters to advertise workshop series. Invoice total $513. Terms: net 30 days.

☐ Cheque Copy #23
Dated Aug. 23/02
To Business Depot, $102.60 in full payment of account balance. Reference invoice #BD-6972.

☐ Sales Invoice #109
Dated Aug. 24/02
To Prolegal Services, $1 200 plus $84 GST charged and $84 PST charged for memory upgrades. Invoice total $1 368. Terms: net 30 days.

☐ Cash Purchase Invoice #BCT-2866

Dated Aug. 28/02

From BC Telephone, $80 plus $5.60 GST paid and $5.60 PST paid for telephone services. Invoice total $91.20. Issued cheque #24 in full payment.

☐ Cash Purchase Invoice #BCH-3851

Dated Aug. 28/02

From BC Hydro, $50 plus $3.50 GST paid (no PST paid) for hydro services. Invoice total $53.50. Issued cheque #25 in full payment. Store as a recurring monthly entry because equal billing arrangements have been made.

☐ Sales Invoice #110

Dated Aug. 28/02

To fill sales quote #1

To Pearson Publishing, $5 000 plus $350 GST charged and $350 PST charged for duplication services. Invoice total $5 700. Terms: 2/10, n/30 days.

☐ Sales Quote #2

Dated Aug. 28/02

Shipping (First Workshop) date Sep. 5/02

To Pro-Career Institute, $500 plus $35 GST charged for technology awareness workshop presentation to career professionals. Invoice total $535. Terms: net 30 days. This will be a regular bi-weekly workshop for 3 months.

☐ **Advance the Session date to August 31, 2002**

☐ Bank Debit Memo #458743

Dated Aug. 30/02

From Learnx Bank,

Recall stored entry for monthly payroll and services for administrative assistant.

Wages	$3 000.00
Payroll Services fee	40.00
GST Paid @ 7%	2.80
Total	$3 042.80

Amount withdrawn from bank account as authorized by contract #3322888.

☐ Memo #8

Dated Aug. 31/02

Based on the end-of-the-month count of supplies remaining, the following quantities of supplies were used during August. Make the necessary adjusting entry to account for the supplies used.

Office Supplies	$150
Computer Supplies	$80
Memory Chips	$150

☐ Memo #9

Dated Aug. 31/02

One month of prepaid rent, $1 000, has expired. Recall the stored adjusting entry to debit the Rent Expense account for this amount.

☐ Memo #10

Dated Aug. 31/02

Recall the stored adjusting entry to recognize $50 as Interest Payable on the demand loan for the month of August.

☐ Memo #11

Dated Aug. 31/02

Recall the stored entry to record the following depreciation amounts. Edit the stored entry to add the depreciation for the Laser Colour Printer. Store the changed entry.

Computers & Peripherals	$150
Custom Tools	$50
Data Recovery Equipment	$200
Duplication Equipment	$100
DLP Projection Unit	$125
Motor Vehicle	$500
Laser Colour Printer	$200

To edit a stored entry, recall the stored entry. Edit the journal entry to add the new depreciation amount. Before posting, store the revised entry using the same name and frequency. Choose Yes when the program asks to confirm that you want to overwrite the recurring transaction in use.

4. To follow good management practice, we recommend printing the following reports:

Journal Entries: All journals for August 8 to August 31

Trial Balance: As at August 31

Income Statement: From July 1 to August 31

Balance Sheet: As at August 31

Vendor Aged Detail Report: For all vendors as at August 31

Customer Aged Detail Report: For all customers as at August 31

5. Back up your data files. Close the Live Links data files to prepare for the advanced entries for the Receivables and Payables Journals for Play Wave.

Review Questions

1. What happens in the Receipts Journal when you click the tool "Include fully paid invoices"? When do you need to use this option?

2. NSF cheques from customers are entered as negative receipts in the Receipts Journal. Why is this approach preferred over entering the NSF cheque as a new sales invoice?

3. If you repeatedly get the message that a Sales Journal entry will cause a customer to exceed the credit limit, what should you do?

4. How is a sales order different from a sales quote?

5. When would you see only the codes 0 and 1 in the Select GST screen? What should you do if this is an error?

6. What role does the *Accounts Receivable* account play after the Receivables Ledger history is finished and before when you are using only the General Journal?

7. Why might GST amounts in the General Ledger be different from the amounts in the GST Report, even if transactions are entered in the Sales and Purchases Journals?

8. How is a sale paid by cheque different from a sale that is paid later?

9. What reports could you use to decide about setting payment terms and credit limits for customers?

10. In the Receipts Journal, the Number field (No.) can be used for the customer's cheque number or for the receipt number. What difference does it make which one you choose?

11. How do you enter new customers?

12. How do you change the payment terms for a customer?

13. How is recording a sale in the General Journal different from recording a sale in the Sales Journal?

CHAPTER 8

ADDITIONAL A/R AND A/P FEATURES

Objectives

- *set up credit cards for purchases and sales*
- *set up shippers for tracking of shipments*
- *enter credit card sales and purchases*
- *make credit card bill payments*
- *enter customer deposits or advance payments*
- *enter invoices for interest charges to customers*
- *look up invoices to track shipments*
- *enter transactions with future dates*
- *complete additional transactions in all journals for practice*

Introduction

Play Wave Plus will continue to use the General, Payables and Receivables Ledgers at this stage, to take advantage of additional features for these ledgers in the software. In this chapter, you will set up the credit card and shipping features to prepare for entering credit card sales and purchases as well as tracking shipments from vendors and to customers. In addition, Play Wave will implement the interest charges for overdue accounts and begin to request deposits from customers on major contracts. Setting up the credit cards involves identifying the linked accounts and adding the rates for transaction fees. Shippers may be added with Web addresses to permit online tracking for purchases and for sales.

If you have not completed the journal entries in Chapter 7 and want to continue working on Chapter 8, you can use your copy of the Data Disk file — Ch08\play\playch08.sdb — to begin this chapter.

Additional A/R and A/P Features

Credit Cards

Play Wave accepts payments from customers by cash, cheque or credit card. Businesses normally pay a fee — a percentage of the total sale amount — to the credit card company for the service. Receipts are deposited directly into the bank account, after the credit card company has deducted the fees. To avoid setting up several additional accounts, we will create a single generic credit card named Chargit for Play Wave.

Credit Card Policies

Credit cards from different banks often carry different charges depending on the volume and type of business. Usually the transaction fee is worth the freedom from worrying about NSF cheques, credit checks or non-payment of accounts. Often a business accepts more than one type of card and has bank accounts set up for each card company. Different credit card issuers may have different fees and payment procedures. If a business uses the older manual credit card forms, the receipts are submitted to the credit card company in batches and the card company then pays the business the total of the receipts minus the transaction fee, either by cheque or by direct deposit. If the business uses an electronic sales terminal or cash register, the payments from the card company are deposited immediately to the linked bank account. The transaction fee, a percentage of the total sale, is withheld immediately to reduce the amount of the deposit. Because the card fees will be avoided when customers pay cash, discounts for cash payments may be offered.

Setting up Credit Cards

◆ Open the files for Play Wave Plus and change the Session date to **May 7, 2002**. You will see the following advice message:

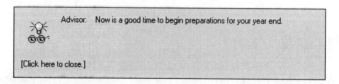

As soon as you start the last month of a fiscal period, the program reminds you about preparing for year-end.

◆ Close the advisor message. We will complete all year-end preparations in Chapter 13.

◆ Choose the **Setup** menu and click **Credit Cards** to see the Credit Card Information entry screen:

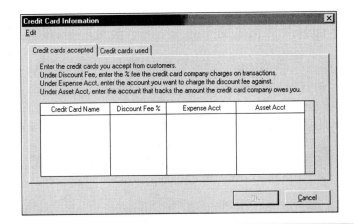

The Credit Cards Accepted Tab Screen

The first tab screen records the information about credit cards that the business accepts from customers in payment. The Credit cards used tab records information about the credit cards used by the business to make business purchases.

Credit Card Name: The name of the credit card (e.g., Visa, American Express, MasterCard). Each type of card appears on a separate line of the entry form.

Discount Fee %: The percentage of the total sales amount that is withheld by the credit card company as the service fee or commission for the use of the card.

Expense Acct: The expense account used to record the discount or transaction fees. This is a linked account. The program will automatically debit the fees to this account when you choose a credit card sale. A business may choose to use separate expense accounts for each credit card or a single account.

Asset Acct: The asset account to which credit card receipts are deposited. Simply Accounting requires you to choose an account that is not a Bank class account. Some card issuers may require the business to set up a separate bank account for the deposits. This is a linked account. The program will automatically debit the total sale, minus fees, to this bank account when you choose a credit card sale.

The cursor is in the Credit Card Name column. Play Wave has a single credit card account, Chargit, with discount or transaction fees at 2.5 percent. The linked bank account is used for deposits. You will create new linked accounts when needed.

◆ Type **Chargit**

◆ Press (tab) to move to the Discount Fee % column.

◆ Type **2.5**

◆ Press (tab) to move to the Expense Acct column.

◆ Press (enter) to display the account list.

◆ Click **Add** to begin the Account Wizard for the new account.

◆ Add the postable expense account

    ☐ 5020 Credit Card Fees
       Postable Group account
       Allocate amounts to projects

When you click Finish as the final stage of the Account Wizard, you will return to the Credit Card Information screen with the new account on the form.

◆ Press (tab) to move to the Asset Acct column.

◆ Press (enter) to display the account list. No bank accounts that are defined as **Bank** class accounts are included in this list, so we must add a new account. Credit cards require separate bank accounts.

◆ Click **Add** to begin the Account Wizard for the new account.

◆ Add the postable asset account

    ☐ 1090 Bank Account: Credit Card
       Postable Group account

When you click Finish as the final stage of the Account Wizard, you will return to the Credit Card Information screen with the new account on the form.

◆ Check your information carefully.

Play Wave also uses the Chargit card for some purchases. Again the linked accounts will be created as needed.

◆ Click the **Credit cards used tab** to display the setup for the cards used for purchases:

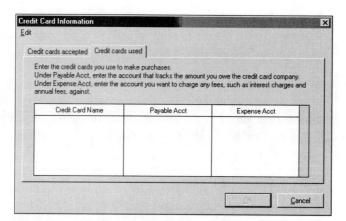

The Credit Cards Used Tab Screen

Credit Card Name: The name of the credit card (e.g., Visa, American Express, MasterCard). Each type of card appears on a separate line of the entry form. The business may use more than one credit card.

Payable Acct: The liability account to which credit card purchases are credited. Each time the card is used for a business purchase, the program will credit the linked payable account in the same way that *Accounts Payable* is credited for regular account purchases. When a card payment is made, the linked payable account is debited for the amount paid towards the accumulated purchases on the credit card bill.

Expense Acct: The expense account used to record the user fees attached to the card. These may include a fee per transaction or a flat monthly or annual fee. Interest charges accumulated on unpaid balances are also debited to this linked expense account. You may use the same linked expense account that you use for credit cards accepted, or choose a different account.

◆ Click the **Credit Card Name field**.

◆ Type **Chargit**

◆ Press (tab) to advance to the Payable Acct field.

◆ Press (enter) to display the account list.

◆ Click **Add** to begin the Account Wizard.

◆ Add the postable liability account

☐ 2250 Chargit Payable
Postable Group account

When you click Finish, you will return to the Credit Cards Used screen with the new account on the form.

◆ Press (tab) to advance to the Expense Acct field.

◆ Press (enter) to display the account list.

◆ Click *5020 Credit Card Fees*.

◆ Press (enter) to add the account and return to the information entry screen.

Check your information carefully. Make corrections by clicking the error and retyping the correct information or selecting a different account.

◆ Click **OK** to save the information. Simply Accounting displays a message about account classes:

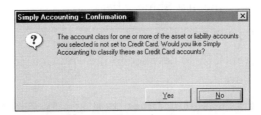

◆ Click **Yes** to accept the changes and return to the Home window. Both the linked asset and the liability account are assigned to the Credit Card class.

Setting up Shippers

Play Wave Plus occasionally receives raw materials via shipping companies or delivery companies. When inventory is sold directly to customers (Chapter 15), Play Wave will also use couriers and delivery companies to deliver goods to customers. At this stage, most of the shipping is done by the vendors since no finished goods are sent directly to customers. You must set up the shippers before you can track shipments from the Purchases and Sales Journals. You may enter up to 12 different shipping companies at once in Simply Accounting.

Shippers are added from the Home window. Play Wave may be using four different shipping companies or couriers. More may be added later if needed.

Shipper	Tracking Site
Purolator	*www.purolator.com
Federal Express	*www.fedex.com/ca
UPS	*www.ups.com/canada
ICS	*www.ics-canada.net

◆ Choose the **Setup menu** and click **Shippers** to open the Shipping Information screen:

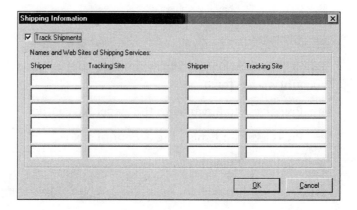

The Track Shipments option is turned on as the default setting. The Shipping Information consists of 12 pairs of fields for the name of the shipper and the Web site address.

◆ Click the first Shipper field.

◆ Type **Purolator**

◆ Press ⒯ to advance to the Tracking Site field for entering the shipper's Web site address.

◆ Type **www.purolator.com**

◆ Press ⒯ to advance to the second Shipper field.

◆ Add the remaining three shippers with their Web sites.

◆ Click **OK** to save the information and return to the Home window.

Interest Charges for Overdue Accounts

When we printed the customer statement for MegaCity Parks & Rec, the statement included an amount for interest charges on the unpaid overdue balance. Sending the statement notifies the customer of the additional charges. However, you must create an invoice in the Sales Journal for the late-paying customer to increase the Accounts Receivable balance for the customer and to allow the program to compound the interest charges for the following month. Simply Accounting calculates the interest charge as a simple interest rate. Thus, if you wait three months before preparing a statement and do not create the invoice, the interest charge on the statement will remain the same as it was when the account first became overdue. Interest charges should, therefore, be calculated and entered monthly. The source document for the interest transaction is usually an internal memo.

The following source document provides the details about the interest charge.

> ✔ Memo #13
> Dated April 30/02
> Charge MegaCity Parks & Rec $81.30 interest on the overdue balance (interest on $5 420 at 1.5%) for the month of April. Terms: net 1. (Interest charges are credited to Other Revenue.)

- ◆ Click the **Sales icon** to open the Sales Journal.

- ◆ Choose **Invoice** as the type of transaction and **Pay Later** as the method of payment.

- ◆ Choose **MegaCity Parks & Rec** as the customer.

- ◆ Type **Memo 13** in the Invoice field.

- ◆ Type **April 30** in the invoice Date field.

- ◆ Click the **Description field.**

- ◆ Type **Interest Charges**

- ◆ Click the **Amount field.**

- ◆ Type **81.30**

- ◆ Click the **GST field** and press ⏎ to see the codes. No tax is charged on the interest penalty.

- ◆ Double click **1 GST non-taxable** to add the GST code to the invoice.

- ◆ Click the **Acct field** and press ⏎ to see the Select Account screen.

- ◆ Double click *4300 Other Revenue* to add the account to the invoice.

- ◆ Click the default comment to select the text. The default is not appropriate for this invoice.

- ◆ Type **Interest on overdue account.** (Or type some other appropriate comment.)

- ◆ Press ⎇ to select the discount rate. No discount is applied to this invoice.

- ◆ Press ⌦ to remove the discount and then press ⎇ to select the discount Days entry.

- ◆ Press ⌦ to remove the entry and press ⎇ to select the Net Days field entry.

- ◆ Type **1**

Your completed invoice should look like the one shown here:

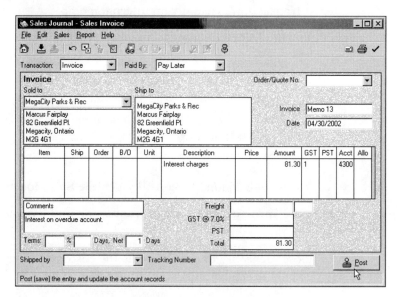

◆ Review the journal entry and when it is correct,

◆ Click **Post** 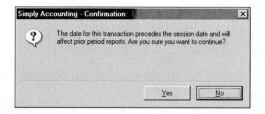 to save the transaction. You will be asked to confirm the posting date:

Because the invoice date is in the previous month, you will be advised that using the earlier date may affect previous period reports. Since we have not yet entered any transactions for May, we can proceed.

◆ Click **Yes** to confirm that the date is correct and that you wish to proceed.

◆ Close the Sales Journal to return to the Home window.

Entering Deposits from Customers

Sometimes customers are asked to provide a deposit when they order merchandise or sign a contract for work to be done. This enables the contractor to purchase some of the materials required for the job without cash flow problems. Because the deposits are frequently non-refundable, they also create a customer commitment to proceeding with the work. Advances or deposits are entered in the Receipts Journal as payments. In this way, the customer's ledger record is updated for the advance. Play Wave Plus will request a deposit of 25% of the contract amount before taxes. All customers with contracts over $1 000 will be asked to pay the deposit as soon as the sales order is confirmed or a quote is accepted.

The following source document provides the details about the deposit from Bayview.

✔ **Cash Receipt #6**

Dated May 1/02

From Bayview Kindergarten Schools, cheque #1373 for $2 000 as an advance (deposit #1) for a play centre in acceptance of contract offer. Reference sales order #2002.

◆ Click the **Receipts icon**  to open the Receipts Journal.

◆ Click the **Enter customer deposits tool** or choose the Receipt menu and click Enter Deposits. The Receipts Journal is revised:

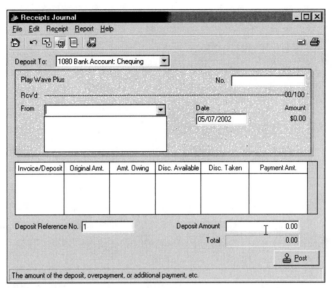

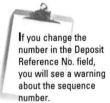

If you change the number in the Deposit Reference No. field, you will see a warning about the sequence number.

The Enter customer deposits tool acts as a toggle switch. It remains selected even after you close the journal until you click the tool again. Clicking the tool button adds two fields to the journal, a Deposit Amount field for the actual amount of the customer's cheque and a Deposit Reference Number field. If there is an invoice number or other document number, you can add it here. The program updates this number sequentially if you do not change the default entry. The usual receipt fields are blank and are not available.

◆ Choose **Bayview Kindergarten Schools** from the customer list.

◆ Click the **No. field** so that you can enter the customer's cheque number.

◆ Type **1373**

◆ Press (tab) to select the Date.

◆ Type **May 1**

◆ Click the **Deposit Amount field** (near the bottom right-hand corner of the screen).

◆ Type **2000**

◆ Press (tab).

◆ Choose the **Report** menu and click **Display Receipts Journal Entry**:

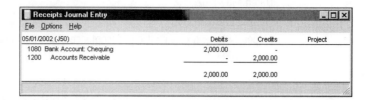

Explanation of the Deposit Journal Entry

The deposit amount leads to a credit for *Accounts Receivable*. The receipt of cash is recognized as a debit to *Bank Account: Chequing*. In most ways, this is a normal Receipts Journal entry. However, since there is no outstanding balance before the deposit, the customer has a negative balance owing or a credit balance. When the sale is completed and you add the full invoice, with taxes, the deposit is subtracted from the amount owing and the discount is calculated on the full invoice amount.

The approach to customer advances is different from the traditional manual entry (debit *Cash* and credit *Unearned Revenue*). The customer's ledger record must be updated separately to record the advance. However, in Simply Accounting, the General Journal entry made for this traditional approach would create no record for the individual customer. In Simply Accounting, you can update the customer record only through Sales or Receipts Journal entries. The deposit in the Receipts Journal is equivalent to entering a Pay Later invoice with a negative amount and choosing the bank account. By using the Receivables journals, the customer record is updated. The negative entry to *Accounts Receivable* generates the liability of unearned revenue.

◆ Close the journal display.

◆ Check your transaction carefully and make corrections if necessary.

◆ Click **Post** [Post] to save the entry.

◆ Click the **Enter customer deposits tool** again to close the Deposit Reference Number and Amount fields.

◆ Choose **Bayview Kindergarten Schools** again to see how the deposit is recorded:

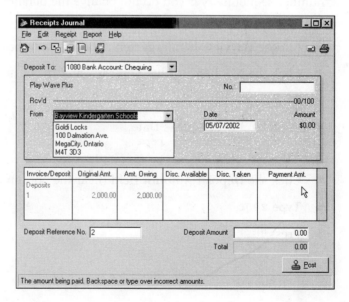

Entering Customer Receipts with Deposits on Record

When the customer pays the balance owing for an invoice and there has been a deposit, mark both the deposit and the invoice as fully paid. The deposit will be listed in red under the heading Deposits. Clicking the Amount field for the Deposit line will "pay" it. The cheque amount will then match the outstanding balance.

◆ Close the Receipts Journal to return to the Home window.

☐ Add the following new accounts and then complete the following General Journal transaction:

2230 Notes Payable (G)
2225 Interest Payable (G)
5192 Interest on Notes Payable (G)

☐ Memo #14
Dated May 1/02
Secured a privately arranged loan for $12 000 to pay for the hydraulic ground drill. Signed a note payable for 3 months at 10% interest. Principal and interest to be repaid in full on July 31, 2002. Money deposited into chequing bank account.

Credit Card Sales

On April 30, new safety guidelines were published for all playground equipment in parks and school grounds. Many public playgrounds were quickly demolished to prevent accidents. As an incentive for all customers to upgrade to the new standards, Play Wave is offering a discount to all of its customers. They will save 10% of the pretax amount if they pay for the work immediately upon completion, either by cash or by credit card. All customers have taken advantage of the offer and Play Wave will retrofit all recently constructed playgrounds in the first two weeks of May by adding additional hardware for strength and support. The contract for Bayview will incorporate the changes into the existing contract. Most of the customers have chosen to pay by credit card so that they can delay their own payments and still receive the discount.

☑ Credit Card Sales Invoice #109
Dated May 2/02
To Nirvana Nursery School, $600 plus $42 GST charged for installation of additional hardware to meet upgraded safety standards for playground. Terms: 10% discount for immediate payment. Total invoice amount paid by Chargit, $582.

◆ Click the **Sales icon** to open the Sales Journal. Accept **Invoice** as the type of transaction.

◆ Choose **Nirvana Nursery School** as the customer.

◆ Click the **Paid By list arrow** to see the payment methods:

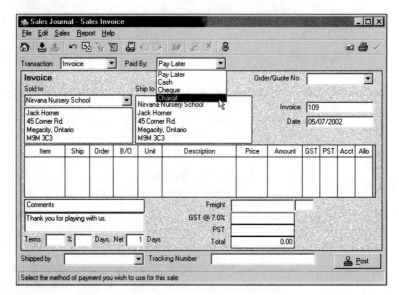

◆ Choose **Chargit** as the method of payment. All credit cards that you set up will be listed individually on the drop-down Paid By list.

◆ Enter **may 2** in the Date field.

◆ Enter **safety upgrades** in the Description field.

◆ Enter **600** in the Amount field.

◆ Enter **3** in the GST code field.

◆ Enter **4020** in the Acct field.

◆ Click the **Discount Terms % field**.

◆ Type **10**

◆ Press ⬛*tab* to update all totals and see the completed invoice:

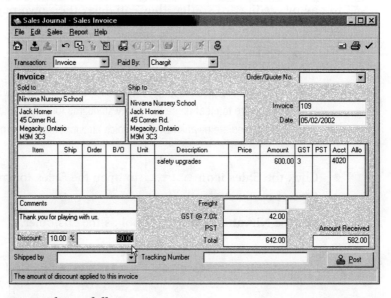

◆ Check your work carefully.

◆ Choose the Report menu and click Display Sales Journal Entry to review the transaction:

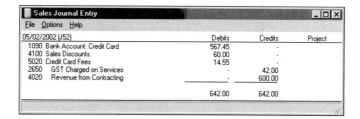

Explanation of the Credit Card Sale Entry

By default, the *Bank Account: Credit Card* is selected for the deposit instead of the *Bank Account: Chequing* because it was identified as the linked asset account for the credit card. To choose a different bank account, you must change the linked asset account on the Credit Card Information screen. In addition, the transaction fee, 2.5% of the total sale, is withheld by the credit card company, so the bank deposit is reduced by this amount. The program calculates this fee and charges it to the linked expense account *Credit Card Fees.* Most businesses that now accept credit card payments from customers have a direct link to the credit card company so that the transaction is immediately sent electronically to the credit card company and the deposit to the business's bank account is also immediate. Some businesses that use the charge plate and charge slips need to send these slips to the credit card company before they receive payment.

◆ Close the display and when you are certain that the entry is correct,

◆ Click Post  to save the transaction.

Credit Card Purchases

The following transaction involves two new features — payment by credit card and entering shipping details. Credit card purchases are similar to credit card sales. Once the credit cards are set up in the Credit cards used screen, the cards named are added to the Paid By drop-down list.

☑ Credit Card Purchase Invoice #SCI4423
  Dated May 4/02
  From Safe Computers Inc. $120 plus $8.40 GST paid and $9.60 (8%) PST paid for virus protection and utilities programs specializing in protection for e-mail and Internet. Order placed by telephone and paid by Chargit. Software to be shipped by Purolator and delivered in 5 days. Shipping costs $15 plus $1.05 GST. Invoice total $154.05. Shipping way bill and tracking number PCX75225. Use Quick Add for the new vendor.

◆ Click the **Purchases icon** to open the Purchases Journal.

◆ Accept **Invoice** as the type of transaction.

◆ Click the **Paid By list arrow** to see the payment options:

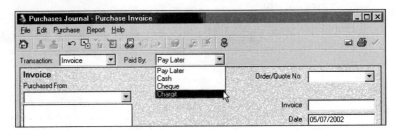

◆ Click **Chargit**.

◆ Type `Safe Computers Inc.` in the Purchased From field and press `tab`.

◆ Choose **Quick Add** for the new vendor.

◆ Enter `SCI4423` in the Invoice field.

◆ Enter `May 4` in the Date field.

◆ Enter `computer software` in the Description field.

◆ Enter `3` in the G (GST code) field.

◆ Enter `8` in the P (PST rate) field.

◆ Enter `120` in the Amount field.

◆ Enter `1360` in the Acct field.

◆ Click the **first freight field** (the GST code field).

◆ Type `3`

◆ Click the **last freight field** (the Freight amount field).

◆ Type `15`

Entering Shipping Information

Click the **Shipped by field list arrow** as shown:

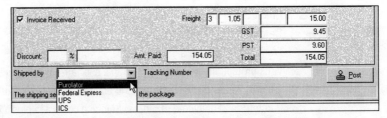

The shippers you entered earlier in this chapter are all listed.

◆ Click **Purolator** to select the shipper.

◆ Click the **Tracking number field**.

◆ Type `PCX75225` to complete the invoice as follows:

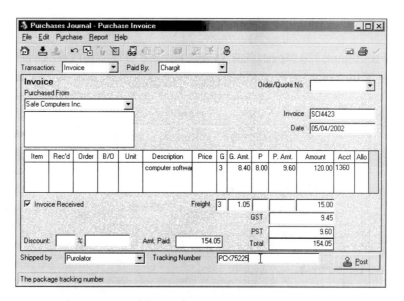

◆ Check your work carefully and review the journal entry:

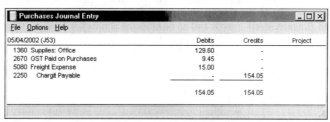

The only difference between this purchase entry and the previous ones is the credit to *Chargit Payable*, the linked liability account for the credit card used, instead of to *Accounts Payable*.

◆ Close the display and when you are certain that the entry is correct,

◆ Click Post [Post] to save the transaction.

◆ Enter the following transactions using the appropriate journals.

☐ Credit Card Purchase Invoice #SCI4424
Dated May 4/02
From Safe Computers Inc. $40 plus $2.80 GST paid and $3.20 (8%) PST paid for one year live upgrade offer to accompany virus protection and utilities program. Invoice total $46. Telephone order paid by Chargit. Internet access code for downloading upgrades: PW-664-3A. (Use Supplies: Office as the account.)

☐ Credit Card Sales Invoice #110
Dated May 4/02
To Vindri Estates $400 plus $28 GST charged for installation of additional hardware to meet upgraded safety standards for playground. Terms: 10% discount for immediate payment. Total invoice amount paid by Chargit, $388.

☐ Cash Receipt #7
Dated May 7/02
From Teddy Day Care Centres, cheque #79 for $10 500 in full payment of outstanding account including $200 discount taken. Reference invoice #107.

□ Cash Purchase Invoice #VM-140
Dated May 7/02
From Vincent Meade, $200 plus $14 GST paid for maintenance services rendered in shop and yard and for inventory maintenance. Invoice total $214. Issued cheque #116 in full payment. Recall the stored monthly entry.

□ **Advance the Session date to May 14, 2002**

□ Cheque Copy #117
Dated May 8/02
To Groundfos Machinery, $12 600 in full payment of account, including $240 discount taken for early payment. Reference invoice #GM-1092.

□ Cheque Copy #118
Dated May 9/02
To The Buildex Corp., $5 284.94 in full payment of account, including $107.86 discount taken for early payment. Reference invoice #BC-811.

□ Credit Card Purchase Invoice #GA-1209
Dated May 9/02
From Gasoline Alley, $130 plus $9.10 GST and $10.40 (8%) PST charged for truck repairs and $150 plus $10.50 GST and $12.00 (8%) PST charged for propane tank refill to fuel hydraulic drill. Total invoice amount paid by Chargit, $322.

Use Quick Add for new vendors and customers unless additional record details are provided.

□ Credit Card Sales Invoice #111
Dated May 9/02
To Central Nursery Schools $800 plus $56 GST charged for installation of additional hardware to meet upgraded safety standards for playground. Terms: 10% discount for immediate payment. Total invoice amount paid by Chargit, $776.

□ Cash Receipt #8
Dated May 9/02
From Central Nursery Schools, cheque #137 for $1 050, in full payment of account, including $20 discount taken. Reference invoice #108.

□ Sales Invoice #112
Dated May 14/02
To fill sales order #2002 for Bayview Kindergarten Schools, $8 000 for play centre contract completed plus $560 GST charged. Invoice total $8 560. Terms: 2/10, n/30.

Look up Invoices to Track Shipments

You can also look up invoices from many reports by using the drill-down feature.

Sometimes it is important to see an invoice that was posted so that you can review it or print it. Looking up invoices is similar to adjusting them. However, the entry you see on-screen cannot be edited. The procedure for looking up invoices is the same for all journals where the option appears.

✔ Memo #15

Dated May 14, 2002

The shipment from Safe Computers Inc. has not yet arrived. Look up the invoice to track the shipment. The vendor will be contacted if the shipment is not located.

Shipments are tracked by looking up the invoice and then connecting with the shipper's Web site. We will look up the invoices in the Payments Journal. From the Purchases Journal, you can look up all invoices posted from the Purchases Journal. From the Payments Journal, you can look up both Purchases Journal invoices and Payments Journal Other Payment invoices. To look up a posted invoice,

◆ Click the **Payments icon** 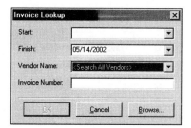 to open the Payments Journal.

◆ Click the **Look up an invoice tool** or choose the Payment menu and click Look up Invoice to see the Invoice Lookup screen:

The fields in this screen are identical to those for Adjust an invoice for Adjustments (see page 150). The Start field may be blank or may contain the calendar date.

◆ Click the **Start field**.

◆ Type **04-01-02** (no Purchases or Payments Journal entries precede this date).

The Session date is correct as the Finish date. If you know the invoice date, you can narrow the search parameters by typing the exact date in both the Start and Finish fields. We have the option of searching through the invoices for all vendors or we can select a specific vendor. If you know the invoice number, you can type it in the Invoice Number field and view it directly. Since we know the vendor, we can browse through only the invoices for this vendor.

◆ Click the **Vendor Name field** to see the list of all vendors.

◆ Click **Safe Computers Inc.** to select this vendor.

◆ Click **Browse** to open the Select An Invoice list:

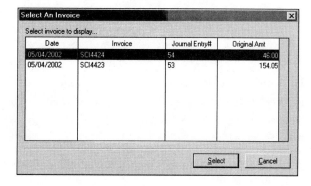

The two invoices from Safe Computers Inc. are on the list.

◆ Click **Invoice SCI4423** to select it.

◆ Click **Select** to open the Invoice Lookup screen:

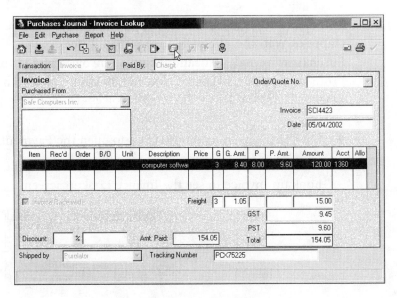

The invoice for the software purchase should be displayed.

By looking at the tools that are not dimmed, you can see what options are available. You can print the invoice, track shipments or store the invoice. If the invoice was already stored, you can recall it. To view other invoices, choose the tool to look up the next or the previous invoice. Although you cannot edit the invoice at this stage, the Adjust invoice tool is available. Selecting Adjust invoice will change the screen to the Adjusting Invoice screen.

The Look up previous invoice and Look up next invoice tools will allow you to search through the other invoices listed on the Select An Invoice screen (or choose the Purchase or Payment menu and click Previous Invoice or Next Invoice). If you want to be able to browse through all invoices, choose the default option in the Invoice Lookup window to Search All Vendors.

◆ Click the **Track shipments tool** or choose Track Shipments from the Purchase menu to see the following message:

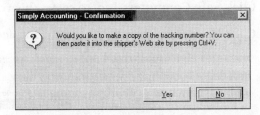

By copying the tracking number you can avoid making a typing mistake in the number when you are in the shipper's Web site and cannot view the Simply Accounting screen at the same time. However, we do not actually have an item to track.

◆ Click **No** to proceed to the next stage of launching your Internet program:

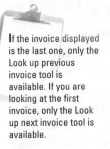

If the invoice displayed is the last one, only the Look up previous invoice tool is available. If you are looking at the first invoice, only the Look up next invoice tool is available.

If your Internet connection uses a network (e.g., Sympatico High Speed Edition), you will need to open your Internet connection before you click the Track shipments tool.

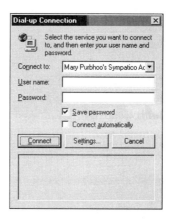

If your Internet program is set up to connect automatically, you will go directly to the shipper's Web site without seeing this connection screen. To access the information about a package that has been shipped, you will need an account and PIN number with the shipper.

◆ When you have finished, close your Internet connection. The Simply Accounting windows will be minimized to buttons on the Windows desktop task bar.

◆ Close the Purchases Journal Invoice Lookup window (right-click the Journal button on the task bar to see the pop-up menu and click Close).

Looking up Other Payment Invoices

To see invoices that were entered as Other Payments in the Payments Journal, you must be in the Payments Journal. Choose Make Other Payment from the Pay drop-down list. Click the Lookup tool. Enter April 1 as the Start date, search all vendors and click Browse. Invoices for Meade, the Minister of Finance, Ontario Hydro and Bell Canada should be listed. Click the invoice you want to view and click Select. The previous and next invoice tools are not available in the Other Payments Lookup window. Close the Invoice Lookup window to return to the Home window.

◆ Restore the Payments Journal (right-click the Payments Journal button and click Restore) so that you can continue with the next transaction.

Credit Card Bill Payments

Credit card statements are sent out to cardholders monthly. Generally, if the outstanding balance is paid in full before the statement due date, no interest is charged on previous purchases. Otherwise, interest charges accumulate from the date of purchase, so it is in the interest of the cardholder to pay the full balance if possible. Monthly interest rates vary from one card to another. In addition, some cards have user fees attached, usually at an annual rate. Some cards have a lower interest rate on outstanding balances in exchange for annual fees and some cards carry no fees. The monthly statement includes the accumulated purchases for the previous month, the interest charges or other fees, the total balance outstanding and the date on which payment is due.

The following source document describes the current credit card bill for Play Wave:

☑ Cheque Copy #119
Dated May 14/02
To Chargit $200.05 for purchases charged before May 7, the billing date, plus $45 annual card fees. Total payment submitted to avoid incurring interest charges $245.05 (paid from Bank Account: Chequing).

Credit card bill payments are entered in the Payments Journal.

◆ Open the Payments Journal if it is not already open.

◆ Click **Pay Vendor Invoices** to see the list of options:

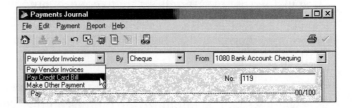

◆ Click **Pay Credit Card Bill** to select this type of payment. The journal fields change to match the selection:

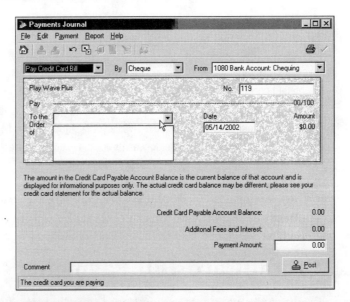

The Credit Card Bill Payment Screen

Credit cards may be paid by cheque from any account that has the Bank class assigned to it. All these accounts are available in the **From** list of accounts. The next cheque number is entered by default for the selected bank account in the **No.** field. Payments may also be made by cash by selecting Cash from list in the the **By** field. When Cash is selected, the cheque number field is removed. The upper portion of the journal window is the cheque. The **To the Order of** field has a list of all credit cards used that were set up.

The lower part of the journal window has the details relating to the credit card balance and payment. The **Credit Card Payable Account Balance** field has the General Ledger balance in the linked Payables credit card account as at the Session date. This balance will be different from the credit card bill or statement balance if there were purchases after the billing date. The **Additional Fees and Interest** field has the amount that you are including in this payment for charges that do not relate directly to purchases. Enter annual fees and interest on previous unpaid amounts or on cash advances in this field. In the **Payment Amount** field, enter the total of the payment remitted, or the cheque amount.

The next step is to select the card that is being paid.

◆ Click the **To the Order of list arrow** to see the list of credit cards set up for purchases.

◆ Click **Chargit**, the only card listed because it was the only one set up. Again the journal screen changes:

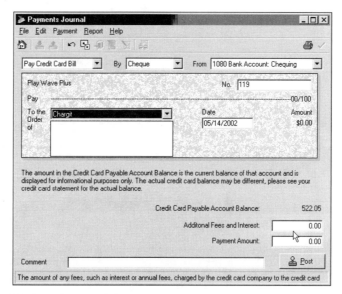

An amount is added to the Credit Card Payable Account Balance field. This amount is the General Ledger account balance for the linked payables account, and includes all unpaid purchases to date. Since the statement billing date was May 7 and the Session date is May 14, there were purchases after the billing date that are not yet due to be paid. In fact, only $200.05 of the amount currently due is for past purchases.

There are additional fees attached to this credit card; the annual fee of $45 is also due. This amount should be entered in the Additional Fees and Interest field.

◆ Click the **Additional Fees and Interest field** to select the amount.

◆ Type **45**

◆ Press ⟨tab⟩ to advance to the Payment Amount field where you should enter the total amount of the cheque, $245.05 ($45 for fees plus $200.05 for purchases).

◆ Type **245.05**

◆ Press ⟨tab⟩ to update the form amounts.

◆ Type an appropriate comment in the Comment field if you wish.

The completed journal entry is shown here:

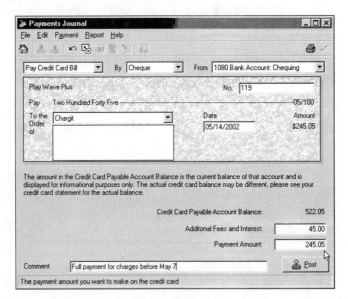

You are now ready to review your work.

◆ Choose the **Report menu** and click **Display Payments Journal Entry**:

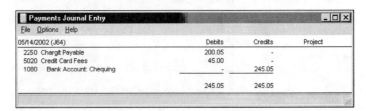

In the journal entry, we see the operation of the linked accounts again. The linked expense account, *Credit Card Fees*, is increased or debited for the fees and interest charges, if there are any. The linked payables account, *Chargit Payable*, is debited or decreased for the portion of the payment that applies to purchases. The bank account selected in the journal is credited or decreased for the total payment amount.

◆ Close the display and make corrections to the entry if necessary.

◆ Click **Post** ⟨ Post ⟩ to save the transaction.

◆ Click **Chargit** from the To the Order of List again to see the updated balance information. The Credit Card Payable account balance is now $322, the amount of the credit card purchase on May 9, after the billing date. Payment for this purchase, and any other purchases before June 7, will be due in June.

◆ Close the Payments Journal.

◆ Restore the Home window from the task bar if necessary (right-click the Simply Accounting button and click Restore).

Entering Postdated Transactions

There may be times when you want to enter a series of postdated transactions rather than waiting to record these transactions on their actual posting date. For example, when you write a series of cheques in advance to pay for rent, or insurance, etc., the cheques are numbered in sequence. If you wait to record individual cheques, you will have to edit the cheque numbers at the time of recording and there is a chance that you may forget to record them. By entering postdated transactions, you keep the cheque sequence in order.

Entering postdated transactions in Simply Accounting is very straightforward. Just prepare a normal journal entry with the future date and post. You can even store and recall the entry as often as needed so that the date will be correct automatically. You can use any future date up to the Fiscal End date. If you turn on the warning for future-dated transactions, you will see the following message:

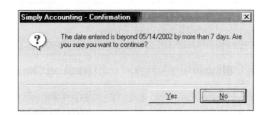

The warning helps you to avoid posting date errors so should be left on with a relatively short future period. If you click No, you will return to the journal so that you can edit the date.

◆ Click **Yes** to post the future-dated transaction.

◆ Back up your data files.

◆ To follow good management practice, we recommend printing the following reports:
Journal Entries: All journals for May 1 to May 14
Trial Balance: As at May 14
Income Statement: From March 1 to May 14
Balance Sheet: As at May 14
Vendor Aged Detail Report: For all vendors as at May 14
Customer Aged Detail Report: For all customers as at May 14

◆ Close the Play Wave data files to prepare for entering journal transactions for Live Links.

Practice: Live Links

At this stage you will continue to use all the General, Payables and Receivables journals to complete a variety of accounting transactions for Live Links after setting up credit cards.

Receivables Journal Entries
Instructions

1. Open the data files for Live Links. Accept August 31, 2002, as the Session date.

If you have not completed the journal entries for Live Links in Chapter 7 and want to continue working on Chapter 8, you can use your copy of the Data Disk file — Ch08\links\linkch08.sdb — to continue this chapter.

2. Set up the credit card accepted and used, creating new accounts as needed:

Credit Card Accepted Settings:

Name:	Credit Card
Discount %:	3%
Create New Expense Account:	5030 Credit Card Fees & Interest (G)
Create New Asset Account:	1090 Bank Account: Credit Card (G)

Credit Card Used Settings:

Name:	Credit Card
Create New Liability Account:	2150 Credit Card Payable (G)
Expense Account:	5030 Credit Card Fees & Interest (G)

---

3. Enter the following shippers:

Shipper	Tracking Site (Web) Address
Purolator	*www.purolator.com
Onestep	www.onestep.com
Speedy	www.fastest.com

---

4. Enter the following transactions using the appropriate journals. Remember to back up your work regularly.

☐ **Advance the Session date to September 7, 2002**

☐ Memo #12
Dated Aug. 31/02
Charge City Hall Staff $21.40 interest on the overdue balance (interest on $2 140 at 1%) for the month of August. Terms: net 1. (Interest charges are credited to Other Revenue.)

☐ Cash Receipt #6
Dated Sep. 1/02
From Pro-Career Institute, cheque #1127 for $200 down payment (deposit #1) on signing contract for delivery of bi-weekly workshops.

☐ Sales Order #2
Dated Sep. 1/02
First Workshop date Sep. 5/02
Convert sales quote #2 to Pro-Career Institute to sales order #2. The bi-weekly workshops will begin as soon as possible.

☐ Sales Invoice #111
Dated Sep. 2/02
To Pro-Career Institute, to fill sales order #2, $500 plus $35 GST charged for technology awareness workshop presentation to career professionals. Invoice total $535. Terms: net 30 days. This will be a regular bi-weekly workshop for 3 months. Store it as a recurring bi-weekly entry.

☐ Sales Invoice #112

Dated Sep. 16/02

To Pro-Career Institute, $500 plus $35 GST charged for technology awareness workshop presentation to career professionals. Invoice total $535. Terms: net 30 days. Recall stored bi-weekly entry and enter as postdated transaction.

☐ Sales Invoice #113

Dated Sep. 30/02

To Pro-Career Institute, $500 plus $35 GST charged (no PST charged) for technology awareness workshop presentation to career professionals. Invoice total $535. Terms: net 30 days. Recall stored entry and enter as postdated transaction.

☐ Credit Card Sales Invoice #114

Dated Sep. 4/02

To Valley Legal Services, $1 800 plus $126 GST charged and $126 PST charged for data recovery services. Invoice total $2 052. Paid by Credit Card. Use Quick Add.

☐ Credit Card Purchase Invoice #39346

Dated Sep. 4/02

From Petro Partners, $190 plus $13.30 GST paid and $13.30 PST paid for vehicle maintenance services. Invoice total $216.60. Paid by Credit Card.

☐ Cash Receipt #7

Dated Sep. 7/02

From Pearson Publishing, cheque #279 for $5 586 in full payment of account. This amount includes $114 discount for early payment. Reference invoice #110.

☐ **Advance the Session date to September 14, 2002**

☐ Add two new customers:

Insight PC (contact: Sophie Wise)

    Address: 80 Sharp Corner, Vancouver, BC V9E 2M2

    Tel: (604) 552-5678

    Fax: (604) 552-7522

    E-mail: sophiew@interlog.com

    Web site: www.insightpc.com

    Terms: 2/10, n/30

West Net Inc. (contact: Nettie West)

    Address: 79 West Pender St., Vancouver BC V6F 4G9

    Tel: (604) 259-8729

    Fax: (604) 259-8710

    E-mail: nwest@westnet.ca

    Web site: www.westnet.com

    Terms: 2/10, n/30

Both new customers are to be included in GST reports and have a credit limit of $10 000. Discounts are calculated after tax.

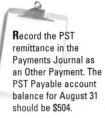

Record the PST remittance in the Payments Journal as an Other Payment. The PST Payable account balance for August 31 should be $504.

☐ Memo #13
Dated Sep. 8/02
Record the PST Payable account balance for Aug. 31, 2002, as a liability owing to the Minister of Finance, BC. This liability is reduced by the sales tax commission of 3.3% of the PST account balance. Issue cheque #26 for $487.37 in payment.

☐ Purchase Order #3
Dated Sep. 10/02
Shipping Date Sep. 18/02
From Business Depot, $600 plus $42 GST charged and $42 PST charged for 150 rewritable CDs and ten 100-MB zip disks. Invoice total $684. Terms: net 15. To be shipped by Onestep.

☐ Sales Invoice #115
Dated Sep. 13/02
To Insight PC, $4 000 plus $280 GST charged and $280 PST charged for CD-ROM and disk duplication services. Invoice total $4 560. Terms: 2/10, n/30 days.

5. To follow good management practice, we recommend printing the following reports:
Journal Entries: All journals for August 31 to September 14
Trial Balance: As at September 14
Income Statement: From July 1 to September 14
Balance Sheet: As at September 14
Vendor Aged Detail Report: For all vendors as at September 14
Customer Aged Detail Report: For all customers as at September 14

6. Close the Live Links files to prepare for setting up the Payroll Ledger for Play Wave.

Review Questions

1. What are the steps in setting up a credit card for customer sales? for purchases?
2. Why is interest on overdue Payables accounts not calculated automatically by the program as it is on overdue Receivables accounts?
3. How are sales with payments by credit cards different from payments by cash or cheque? How does Simply Accounting enter each of these payment methods?
4. When making a credit card payment, why is the amount shown on the credit card bill usually different from the balance in the *Credit Card Payable* account?
5. What amounts would you enter in the Additional Fees and Interest field?
6. Why might you be unable to find an invoice that you are trying to look up?
7. What options are available from the Lookup view of a journal entry?
8. Why are customer deposits processed through the Receipts Journal?
9. What are the advantages and disadvantages of accepting credit card payments from customers? Are there reasons for accepting a variety of cards?
10. How would you add a new shipper? How do you remove shippers?
11. Since you cannot use the credit card bank account to pay bills, how can you access this source of cash?
12. What are the advantages and disadvantages to using different linked expense accounts for credit cards used and credit cards accepted?

CHAPTER 9

PAYROLL LEDGER SETUP

Objectives

- *explain the components of Payroll Ledger entry screens*
- *enter settings for the Payroll Ledger*
- *understand and identify Payroll Ledger linked accounts*
- *enter employee address and tax information*
- *enter historical payroll information for employees*
- *enter additional employees for practice*
- *display and print Payroll Ledger reports*
- *finish the Payroll Ledger history*

Introduction

In May, Play Wave Plus will begin to use the Payroll Ledger to record employee wages and to write cheques rather than contracting out this service. All remittances are up to date at the time of the changeover. To use the Payroll module, you must set up the Payroll Ledger just as you set up the previous ledgers. After customizing the Payroll settings and identifying the linked accounts for the Payroll Ledger, you must enter the employee records. Employee information consists of address information, income tax information and other deductions, as well as the year-to-date historical data. There is no single control account for the Payroll Ledger that shows the total wages for all employees as the *Accounts Payable* and *Accounts Receivable* accounts do for the Payables and Receivables Ledgers, respectively. After finishing the ledger history, the Payroll Journal is ready for entering transactions.

If you have not completed the journal entries in Chapter 8 and want to continue working on Chapter 9, you can use your copy of the Data Disk file — Ch09\play\playch09.sdb — to begin this chapter.

Play Wave
Plus

The Payroll Ledger

The complexities of Payroll Journal entries and tax and deduction calculations often lead small businesses to contract out the administration of payroll to independent accountants, payroll service companies or banks. Simply Accounting makes it relatively easy for small businesses to manage their own payroll, although familiarity with tax legislation and accounting principles is still essential. The Payroll Ledger (Employees icon) contains all relevant information about employees. Most of this information is required for income tax reporting purposes so that T4 statements can be prepared at the end of the year. The program completes the calculations for required deductions automatically when you enter the Federal Tax Claim amount for each employee, because tax tables are built into the program. In addition, you can enter optional deductions, such as for company specific benefits or savings plans. Once these are set up, the program completes the appropriate calculations automatically and updates the corresponding accounts that are linked to the General Ledger.

Payroll Ledgers Settings

You must customize the default settings for the Payroll Ledger for Play Wave by identifying the payroll deductions and the methods of payment. The methods of payments and the deduction names are found in the Names screen.

PAYROLL PROFILE

Play Wave Plus took over the administration of its own payroll after the end-of-April paycheques were prepared. At that time, Casual Contractors had made the remittances for all deductions to the relevant companies or government agencies and provided complete historical records of previous transactions.

The two employees who worked part-time in March and April will both work full-time beginning in May. Peter Piper will be paid on an hourly basis and Rebecca Doolittle will switch from her hourly rate to a fixed monthly salary. Both employees assist with the building of playgrounds and Doolittle, because of her business experience, also assists with the accounting and bookkeeping. Child, the owner, plans to involve Doolittle in contract negotiations as well, and offer her a commission for any contracts that she is instrumental in acquiring. A third employee, Candie Rapper, was hired at the beginning of May to assist with the safety upgrades on previous installations.

For payroll, Play Wave Plus will use the chequing bank account that it uses for payments and receipts.

The Payroll for Play Wave is fairly basic. There are some compulsory payroll deductions and expenses. Employer expenses for health costs in Ontario at the rate of 0.98 percent of total payroll are remitted to the Minister of Finance of Ontario, employer contributions towards the Canada Pension Plan and Employment Insurance program are remitted to the Receiver General of Canada together with the employees' contributions to these programs, and income tax deducted. The employer deductions for the provincial Workplace Safety and Insurance program are remitted to the Ontario Workplace Safety and Insurance Board. In addition, Play Wave offers insurance and two payroll savings plans: purchase of Canada Savings Bonds (CSB) and contributions to a private Registered Retirement Savings Plan (RRSP). As members of a union, the hourly employees also pay union dues. The Group Insurance program is administered by CIBC Insurance and remittances of employee contributions are made quarterly. Quarterly remittances are also made to Fidelity Trust for CSB and RRSP, and to United Builders' Union for union dues.

Workplace Safety and Insurance Board (WSIB) is the name for Workers' Compensation Board (WCB) in Ontario.

Changing Payroll Deduction Names

◆ Open your working copy of the Play Wave files and accept the May 14 Session date.

◆ Choose the **View** menu, then choose Modules and click **Payroll** to restore the Payroll Ledger icons.

◆ Choose the **Setup** menu and click **Names** in the Home window:

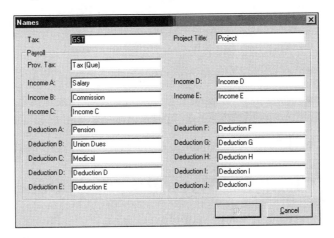

Names Screen Input Fields

All of the names on this screen, except Tax and Project Title, refer to Payroll settings.

Tax: The name for the federal Goods and Services Tax. In most provinces, this is the GST (Goods and Services Tax), which is the default name. In Nova Scotia, New Brunswick, Newfoundland and Labrador the federal tax is called the Harmonized Sales Tax (HST) because it combines the federal and provincial sales taxes into a single rate of 15 percent. When you change the name on this screen, the program will use the revised name in all GST fields and reports. Refer to Appendix C for more information on GST and HST.

Project Title: When amounts are allocated to different projects, you can enter the name for the project or job costing division in this field. For example, you may distribute among departments, divisions, groups, cities, sales persons, etc. The name you enter in this field will appear as the icon label in the Home window and on all project reports.

Prov. Tax: This field is reserved for the Quebec payroll taxes. If the province is not Quebec, the field may be left blank.

Income A through **E**: The usual names for different methods of paying employees. Most employees are paid a regular salary or an hourly wage rate. Sometimes they receive a bonus or commission that should be tracked separately from the regular pay.

Deduction A through **J**: These are the names of the regular deductions from the employees' wages. The default entries, Pension, Union and Medical are common deductions. Employees may also make regular contributions to a savings plan, private Registered Retirement Pension Plans, insurance or charitable organizations. You may enter up to 10 separate deduction names. Deduction names that are not needed may be left blank. New deductions may be added at any time.

For Play Wave, the tax name and and income names are correct. The deduction names must be changed to reflect the company's payroll profile.

◆ Double click the **Deduction A field** to select the entry for editing.

- ◆ Type **RRSP**

- ◆ Press ⌧*tab*⌧ to advance to Deduction B. The default, Union Dues, is correct.

- ◆ Press ⌧*tab*⌧ to advance to the next field.

- ◆ Type **CSB Plan** to replace Medical.

- ◆ Press ⌧*tab*⌧.

- ◆ Type **Gp Insurance** as the final deduction name.

- ◆ Press ⌧*tab*⌧ to advance to the next field.

- ◆ Press ⌧*del*⌧ to remove the entry (or type N/A for not applicable).

- ◆ Continue to delete the remaining deduction names, Deductions F through J. You may also delete the names for Income C, D and E since they are not used.

- ◆ Click **OK** to save the names and return to the Home window.

Changing Payroll Ledger Defaults

- ◆ Right-click the **Employees icon** in the Payroll column of the Home window as shown to select the icon:

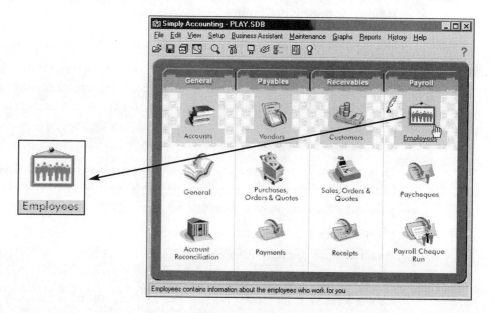

- ◆ Click the **Setup tool** ⌧⌧⌧ in the Home window to open the Payroll Settings screen. You can also choose the Setup menu and click Settings in the Home window and then click the Payroll tab to change to that screen:

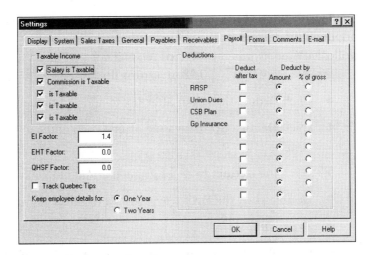

Incomes C, D and E, and Deductions E through J have been deleted for the screen illustrations in this chapter. Therefore, no names will appear for them.

Payroll Settings

Each type of income must be defined as **Taxable Income** or as non-taxable income.

Each of the payroll **Deductions** must be defined as a before-tax or after-tax deduction. Before-tax deductions are subtracted from gross pay before income tax is calculated. That means they qualify as deductions that reduce the taxable income. Pension plan, RRSP and union contributions are usually before-tax deductions. After-tax deductions are subtracted from income after income tax is calculated because they are not eligible as tax deductions. When the check box is marked (has a ✓ in it), the deduction is made after tax. Thus union dues, pension and RRSP contributions should not have the check box marked. The names that you entered in the Names screen appear as the deduction names for the Payroll Settings. Each deduction may be calculated as a percentage of gross income or as a fixed amount.

The **EI Factor** (formerly named UI) is used to calculate the employer's employment insurance obligation. The 1.4 factor means that the employer's contribution is 1.4 times as much as each employee's. The EI rate is set by the Federal Ministry of Finance for the employee contribution as a percentage of gross pay, and the employer's share is usually larger. The employer withholds the employee's contribution and makes regular remittances for both employer and employee contributions to the Receiver General.

The **EHT Factor** (Employer Health Tax) is the percentage of gross payroll that the employer must contribute for health costs in Ontario. The rate ranges from 0.98 percent for companies with total payroll less than $200 000 per year to 1.98 percent for companies with total payroll greater than $400 000. The EHT applies only in Ontario and provides basic medical insurance coverage for all legal residents of the province. In other provinces, when individuals pay medical insurance premiums for medical coverage directly through payroll deductions, you can set up one of the deductions for the amount of the premiums.

For employees in Quebec, you must also define the **QHSF factor** (Quebec Health Services Factor), the percentage of payroll that is contributed to the Quebec provincial health plan, and whether employees receive **tips** on the job that are to be **tracked** for provincial income tax.

You can **Keep employee details for** one or two years by choosing the corresponding setting. Keeping two years of data will also offer the flexibility of printing T4 statements after year-end because the information for the previous year is not deleted after moving into the next fiscal year. If you keep data for one year, you must use the backup copy of the data files that you prepared before closing routines to print T4s.

Two of the deductions for Play Wave, RRSP and union dues, are before-tax deductions, and CSB and Group Insurance are after-tax deductions. Union dues are calculated as a percentage of gross income. The EI factor is correct at 1.4. The EHT rate for Play Wave is 0.98.

◆ Click **Deduct CSB Plan after tax** to add a ✓ to the check box and change the setting.

◆ Click **Deduct Gp Insurance after tax** to add a ✓ to the check box and change the setting.

◆ Click the **Deduct by % of gross** income button for Union Dues.

◆ Double click the **EHT Factor field** to select the entry for editing.

◆ Type **.98**

◆ Click **Two Years** to indicate that you want to save two years of payroll data.

◆ Click **OK** to save the setting and return to the Home window.

You may see a warning advising you that tax calculation settings have changed:

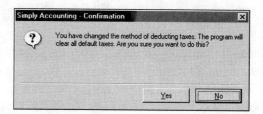

◆ Click **Yes** to continue.

Payroll Linked Accounts

Before entering the linked accounts for the Payroll Ledger, we must add the required General Ledger accounts. We will also create a new group for all the payroll related expenses.

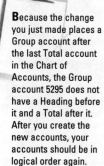

The Contracted Payroll Expenses account will remain inside the Payroll Expenses group after we change the account number for the Total account.

☐ Edit the account number for TOTAL OPERATING EXPENSES (T) account
From 5390 To 5285 to accommodate the new group of payroll expense accounts.

You may see a warning that the accounts are not in logical order. Click **OK** to proceed.

Because the change you just made places a Group account after the last Total account in the Chart of Accounts, the Group account 5295 does not have a Heading before it and a Total after it. After you create the new accounts, your accounts should be in logical order again.

☐ Create the following new accounts:

1240 Advances Receivable (G)	2300 Vacation Payable (G)
2310 EI Payable (A)	2400 RRSP Payable (G)
2320 CPP Payable (A)	2410 Union Dues Payable (G)
2330 Income Tax Payable (A)	2420 CSB Plan Payable (G)
2340 Receiver General Payable (S)	2430 Group Insurance Payable (G)
2390 EHT Payable (G)	2460 WSIB Payable (G)
5290 PAYROLL EXPENSES (H)	5300 Wage Expense (G)
5310 EI Expense (G)	5320 CPP Expense (G)
5330 WSIB Expense (G)	5360 EHT Expense (G)
5390 TOTAL PAYROLL EXPENSES (T)	

◆ Display or print the Chart of Accounts to review your account changes.

◆ Choose the **Setup** menu, then choose **Linked Accounts** and click **Payroll** from the Home window to see the first Payroll Linked Accounts screen:

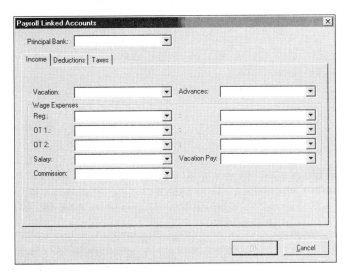

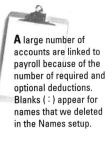
A large number of accounts are linked to payroll because of the number of required and optional deductions. Blanks (:) appear for names that we deleted in the Names setup.

The Bank account, EI, CPP and Tax Payable, EI, CPP and Wage Expense accounts are required in order to finish the Payroll Ledger history.

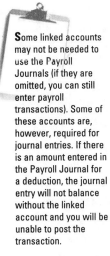
Some linked accounts may not be needed to use the Payroll Journals (if they are omitted, you can still enter payroll transactions). Some of these accounts are, however, required for journal entries. If there is an amount entered in the Payroll Journal for a deduction, the journal entry will not balance without the linked account and you will be unable to post the transaction.

Income Linked Accounts for Payroll

Principal Bank: This asset account is the postable Bank class account, Subgroup or Group, to which all wage-related payments to employees are credited automatically by the Simply Accounting program. All cheques issued through Payroll Journal transactions should be processed through this account. Again, the bank account is credited automatically when the Payroll Journal entry is posted. You may use a single bank account for payroll, cash receipts and cash payments, or you may use separate bank accounts for each ledger.

Vacation Payable: You must choose a postable liability account for Vacation Payable. This account records the total amount of vacation pay that is withheld from all employees. Frequently employers withhold vacation pay and make a single payment each year for the full amount. This enforced savings plan ensures that the employee will receive a cheque at vacation time. The Simply Accounting program automatically calculates the amount of vacation pay, based on the percentage in the employee ledger. If the vacation pay is retained, that is, it is not paid out with each paycheque, the amount of vacation pay owing to the employee is automatically credited to *Vacation Payable*. When the vacation pay is released to the employee by making the appropriate Payroll Journal entry, *Vacation Payable* is automatically debited. The opening *Vacation Payable* balance must equal the total vacation pay owed to employees before you can finish the payroll history.

Advances: The *Advances Receivable* linked account is the postable asset account for recording amounts given to employees in advance of their regular paycheques. Employees may receive advances for emergency purposes or for special purchases. When the amount of the employee advance is entered in the Advances field of the Payroll Journal, the amount is automatically debited to the linked Advances account. When the money is withheld from later paycheques to repay the advance, the negative amount in the Advances field is automatically credited to *Advances Receivable*. The opening balance in *Advances Receivables* must match the total of advances given to employees that are not yet recovered before you can finish the ledger history.

Wage Expenses Accounts: These postable expense accounts record the total or gross amount of each employee's paycheque for the different types of income before deductions. As such, they represent the employer's direct wage expense for hourly work and overtime work, salaries, commissions or bonuses and vacation pay. The Simply Accounting program automatically totals the relevant components from the Payroll Journal entry. You may choose different accounts for each of type of income, or you may use the same account.

- Click the Principal **Bank account field** list arrow. Only accounts defined as Bank class are listed.

- Choose *1080 Bank Account: Chequing* from the list.

- Press ⌨ to advance to the Vacation account field.

- Choose *2300 Vacation Payable* from the list.

- Press ⌨.

The cursor moves to the Advances account field.

- Choose *1240 Advances Receivable* from the list.

- Press ⌨.

- Choose *5300 Wages Expense* from the list for each Income linked account field.

- Click the **Deductions tab** to access the input screen for the next set of payroll linked accounts:

If a linked account field is blank, press ⌨ to keep it blank and advance to the next field. If there is an account in a field that should be blank, click the incorrect account, press ⌨ and then press ⌨ to leave it blank and advance to the next field.

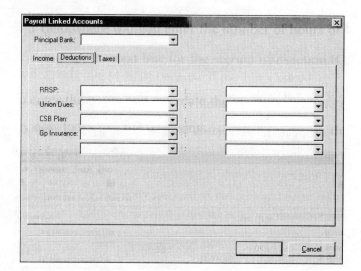

Linked Accounts for Payroll Deductions

The linked Principal Bank account appears at the top of each Payroll Linked Accounts tab screen.

Pension Payable, Union Payable, Medical Payable, etc.: These linked accounts are used for regular employee payroll deductions that are company-specific. They are all postable accounts, usually Group liability accounts (although Simply Accounting allows you to choose expense accounts). The deductions most commonly used are for pension plan contributions, medical plan payments, insurance, union dues, charitable contributions or payroll savings plans like the Canada Savings Bond plan. When you set up the deductions in the Payroll Ledger for each employee, the program will enter them automatically each time you complete a Payroll Journal entry for the employee. The amounts can be edited in the Payroll Journal for one-time changes to the amount of the deduction. Remittances are made as an Other Payment in the Payments Journal or through the Purchases Journal to the agency or company that administers the plan. The names of the deductions that appear in the Payroll Linked Accounts screen are the ones you defined in the Names settings from the Setup menu. The predefined deduction names are: Pension Payable, Union Payable, Medical Payable, etc.

- Enter the following linked accounts on this screen. Choose from the list in each account field and press $\boxed{tab}$ after each selection to move to the next account field. If you have an incorrect entry, click it to select it, then press $\boxed{del}$ to remove the incorrect account or to leave an account field blank. Press $\boxed{tab}$ to save the change.

PAYROLL DEDUCTION LINKED ACCOUNTS

RRSP	2400 RRSP Payable
Union Dues	2410 Union Dues Payable
CSB Plan	2420 CSB Plan Payable
Gp Insurance	2430 Group Insurance Payable

- Click the **Taxes tab** to access the final input screen for payroll linked accounts:

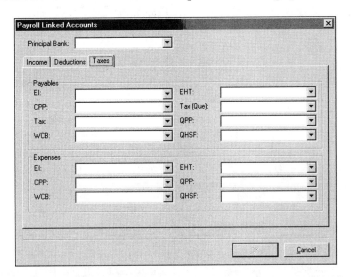

Linked Accounts for Payroll Taxes

The remaining Payables linked accounts must be postable liability accounts, either Group or Subgroup. They record the employee contributions, the amounts that are withheld from the employee paycheques, and the amounts that the employer contributes towards these taxes. Remittances are made to the appropriate government agency or organization as an Other Payment in the Payments Journal, or through a Purchases Journal invoice paid by cheque. Enter the General Ledger balance in the appropriate payables account in the amount field of the journal and enter the Payables account number in the account field. No taxes should be included. *Bank Account: Chequing* will be credited, and the Payables account will be debited to reduce the liability.

EI Payable: This postable Subgroup liability account records the amounts that are withheld as employee contributions plus the amounts that are owed as the employer's share of the contribution to the federal Employment Insurance program. Employment Insurance contributions by the employer and employee pay for the Employment Insurance benefits received by eligible unemployed workers. Again, the program calculates both these amounts automatically and credits the *EI Payable* account each time a Payroll Journal entry is completed. The employer's contribution, normally 1.4 times the employee's contribution, is debited to the *EI Expense* account. EI is remitted to the Receiver General by the employer. *EI Payable* is subtotalled with CPP and Income Tax, the other wage deduction amounts that are remitted to the Receiver General.

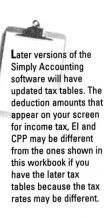

Later versions of the Simply Accounting software will have updated tax tables. The deduction amounts that appear on your screen for income tax, EI and CPP may be different from the ones shown in this workbook if you have the later tax tables because the tax rates may be different.

CPP Payable: This postable Subgroup liability account records the amounts that are withheld as employee contributions plus the amounts that are owed as the employer's share of the contribution to the Canada Pension Plan. Payments towards this federal plan pay for the pensions of retired workers. Again, the program calculates both amounts automatically and credits *CPP Payable* each time a Payroll Journal entry is completed. The employer's contribution, normally equal to the employee's contribution, is debited to *CPP Expense*. CPP is also remitted to the Receiver General. *CPP Payable* is subtotalled with EI and Income Tax, the other wage deduction amounts that are remitted to the Receiver General.

Tax Payable: This postable Subgroup liability account, *Income Tax Payable*, records the amount of income tax that is deducted from an employee's pay each period. The program calculates the amount of tax owing based on the employee's Federal Claim amount and the tax tables built into the software. These tables are updated every six months. Tax is remitted to the Receiver General. *Income Tax Payable* is subtotalled with EI and CPP, the other wage deduction amounts that are remitted to the Receiver General.

WCB Payable: This postable Group liability account records the amounts that are owed by the employer for Workers' Compensation Benefits. WSIB provides compensation (income replacement) for workers who are injured on the job. Again, Simply Accounting calculates the amount automatically as a percentage of the total wages and credits *WSIB Payable* each time a Payroll entry is completed. The employer expense is debited to *WSIB Expense*. WSIB is remitted to the Workplace Safety and Insurance Board. The actual amount is a provincial rate set for each industry and job classification, based on the work-related danger and the likelihood of worker injury and required compensation.

In January 1998, in Ontario, the WCB was renamed WSIB, Workplace Safety and Insurance Board, to emphasize worker safety rather than injury and compensation.

EHT Payable: This postable Group liability account records the amount that Ontario employers pay towards health costs, the Employer Health Tax. Again, the program calculates the amount automatically as a percentage of the total wages and credits *EHT Payable* each time a Payroll Journal entry is completed. The employer expense is debited to *EHT Expense*. EHT is remitted to the Minister of Finance. The actual amount is a function of total payroll for the business for the year, with larger companies being assessed at a higher percentage. The EHT rate is entered on the Payroll Settings screen.

Tax (Que.) Payable: This postable Subgroup liability account applies only to employees in Quebec. *Quebec Income Tax Payable* is the provincial equivalent of the *Income Tax Payable* linked account. The provincial government of Quebec collects its own income tax, while for other provinces, the federal government collects total income tax and then transfers the provincial portion to the province. The *Quebec Income Tax Payable* account records the amount of provincial income tax that is deducted from the employee's wages, and is calculated automatically based on the gross taxable income and the provincial tax exemption amount for the employee. Quebec Tax is remitted to the provincial Minister of Revenue. *Quebec Income Tax Payable* is subtotalled with QHSF and QPP, the other provincial wage deduction amounts that are remitted to the Quebec Minister of Revenue.

QPP Payable: For employees in Quebec, this postable Subgroup liability linked account replaces the *CPP Payable* account. Quebec administers the pension plan for its residents, while in other provinces, the federal government administers the pension plan. It is calculated in the same way as CPP and the contributions are similarly shared between the employee and the employer. The employer expense is debited to the *QPP Expense* account. Remittances are made to the Quebec Minister of Revenue. *QPP Payable* is subtotalled with QHSF and Quebec Income Tax, the other provincial wage deduction amounts that are remitted to the Quebec Minister of Revenue.

QHSF Payable: Again, this postable Subgroup liability account applies only to employees in Quebec. The *Quebec Health Services Factor Payable* linked account records the employer's liability for health care costs. The expense is debited to the *QHSF Expense* account. Remittances are made to the Quebec Minister of Revenue. *QHSF Payable* is subtotalled with QPP and Quebec Income Tax, the other provincial wage deduction amounts.

Linked Expense Accounts for Payroll

You must choose postable expense accounts, either Group or Subgroup, for these linked accounts. The program debits these accounts automatically for the employer's share of required deductions when you post the Payroll Journal entry, and reports the amounts on the Income Statement.

EI Expense: This is the employer's contribution to the Employment Insurance plan. The expense amount is included in the *EI Payable* amount for the journal entry. The Simply Accounting program automatically calculates this amount as 1.4 times (the EI factor you entered earlier in the Payroll Settings) the amount of the employee's contribution based on current payroll formulas.

CPP Expense: This is the employer's contribution to the Canada Pension Plan. The expense amount is included in the *CPP Payable* amount for the journal entry. The Simply Accounting program automatically calculates the expense amount equal to the amount of the employee's contribution based on current payroll formulas.

WCB Expense: This account records the employer's contribution to the Workplace Safety and Insurance Board plan (formerly WCB). The expense amount is the same as the *WSIB Payable* amount for the journal entry because there are no employee contributions. The Simply Accounting program automatically calculates this amount based on the percentage entered in the employee's (Payroll) Ledger.

EHT Expense: This is the employer's contribution to the Employer Health Tax. The expense amount is the same as the *EHT Payable* amount for the journal entry because there are no employee contributions to EHT. The Simply Accounting program automatically calculates this amount based on the percentage entered in the Payroll Settings under the Setup menu. EHT is applied only in Ontario.

QPP Expense: This account records the employer's contribution to the Quebec Pension Plan. The expense amount is included in the *QPP Payable* amount for the journal entry. The Simply Accounting program automatically calculates the expense amount equal to the amount of the employee's contribution based on current payroll formulas. It applies only in Quebec. (See QPP Payable above.)

QHSF Expense: This account records the employer's contribution to the Quebec Health Services Factor. The expense amount is equal to the *QHSF Payable* amount for the journal entry because there are no employee contributions to QHSF. The Simply Accounting program automatically calculates this amount based on the built-in tax formula. QHSF is used only in Quebec.

◆ Enter the remaining linked accounts from the following chart. Choose from the list in each account field and then press ⌧tab⌧ to move to the next account field. If you have an incorrect entry, click to select it and press ⌧del⌧ to remove the incorrect account. Reselect from the account list or leave the field blank. Press ⌧tab⌧ to save the change.

PAYROLL LINKED ACCOUNTS

Payables		Expenses	
EI	2310 EI Payable	EI	5310 EI Expense
CPP	2320 CPP Payable	CPP	5320 CPP Expense
Tax	2330 Income Tax Payable	WCB	5330 WSIB Expense
WCB	2460 WSIB Payable	EHT	5360 EHT Expense
EHT	2390 EHT Payable		

◆ Click **OK** to save the accounts and return to the Home window.

Creating Employee Records

Now that all the linked accounts are identified for the Payroll Ledger, you can begin to enter employee information in the ledger.

EMPLOYEE INFORMATION

Profile: **Peter Piper** began working on March 15, 2002, and has worked part-time for six weeks, averaging about 50 hours per month while he was still a full-time student. He will work full-time for the summer, starting in May. His pay, at the rate of $14 per hour for regular work hours and $21 per hour for overtime work (hours in excess of the normal 40 hours per week), is paid every two weeks. His studies in Landscaping Architecture fit well with his job at Play Wave. The community college tuition of $2 800 and education deduction of $200 per month provide additional claims over the basic claim of $7 131 for a single self-supporting individual. Vacation pay at the rate of 4 percent has been paid with each cheque for the previous pay periods. However, the amount will be retained while he works full-time for the summer and then released at the end of the summer.

Personal Information:

Employee Name	Peter Piper
Position	Assistant
Address	111 Man-in-the-moon Cres.
	Megacity, ON M5G 8G8
Telephone	(416) 772-9123
Social Insurance Number (SIN)	562 812 636
Date of Birth	March 31, 1974
Date of Hire	March 15, 2002

Taxes:

Tax Table	Ontario
Federal Claim (Tax Exemption)	
Basic Personal	$7 131
Other: Education & Tuition	$4 400
Total Federal Claim	$11 531
WSIB Rate (WCB)	3.13%
EI Eligible (EI Factor)	Yes (1.4)
Additional Federal Tax	0.00
CPP and Income Tax	calculations built into program

Income:

Regular Per Hour Wage Rate	$14/hour
Regular Hours Per Period	80 hours
Overtime Per Hour Wage Rate	$21/hour
Number of Pay Periods Per Year	26 (paid bi-weekly)
Vacation Pay Rate	4% Retained

Deductions:

RRSP	$25
Union Dues	2%
CSB Plan	$25
Group Insurance	$10

The minimum information required for employee records includes the date of birth, the tax table and the number of pay periods. You cannot create the record without these. The program will then substitute default information for the Federal Tax Claim. If you do not enter an hourly wage rate, you must use the Salary or Commission field in the Payroll Journal to process a paycheque for the employee.

◆ Click the **Employees icon** 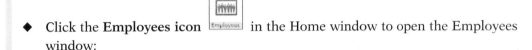 in the Home window to open the Employees window:

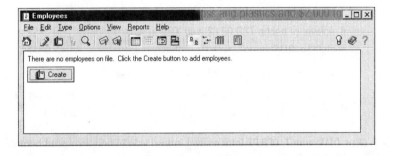

Employees Window

The Payroll journal tools are the only new tool buttons in the Payroll Ledger. They provide direct access to the Payroll journals. The same journal options appear under the Type menu.

 Open the Payroll Journal (Paycheques)

 Open the Payroll Run Journal (Payroll Cheque Run)

The Employees window is empty because there are no employee records yet.

◆ Click the **Create button** 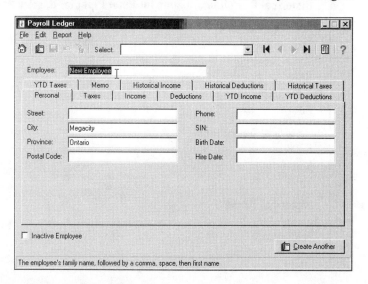 in the Employees window (or click ▣ , or choose the File menu and click Create) to open the Payroll Ledger:

Personal Tab Input Screen Fields

The Payroll Ledger entry screens are divided by several tabs, just like the Payables and Receivables Ledger screens. The first tab includes Personal identification information.

Employee: The name of the employee. Enter the last name first, followed by a comma and a space and then the first and middle names. This order will ensure correct alphabetization of the employee list.

Street, City, Province and Postal Code: Address information. The business city and province are the default entries from the Company Information you entered in Chapter 2. They can be changed. The program corrects the the postal code format when you type a Canadian postal code pattern.

Phone: The program corrects the format for the telephone number when you type ten or seven digits, that is, with or without the area code.

SIN: The nine-digit social insurance number for income tax reporting purposes. You must use a valid number.

Birth Date: Follow the usual format for dates. You must enter the date of birth to use the Payroll Ledger.

Hire Date: The date that the employee began working for the business, using the normal format for dates.

Employee Address Details

The Employee name field is selected, ready for editing.

◆ Type **Piper, Peter**

◆ Press ⌨ *tab* to move to the Street field.

◆ Type **111 Man-in-the-moon Cres.**

◆ Click the **Postal Code field** to skip the City and Province fields, accepting the default entries.

◆ Type **m5g8g8**

◆ Press ⌨ *tab* to move to the Phone number field.

Make corrections to any field by double clicking the error to select it and then typing the correct details.

- ◆ Type `4167729123`

- ◆ Press (tab) to move to the SIN (Social Insurance Number) field.

- ◆ Type `562812636`

- ◆ Press (tab) to move to the Birth Date field.

- ◆ Type `3-31-74`

- ◆ Press (tab) to move to the Hire Date field.

- ◆ Type `Mar 15`

Tax Details

- ◆ Click the **Taxes tab** to display these input fields:

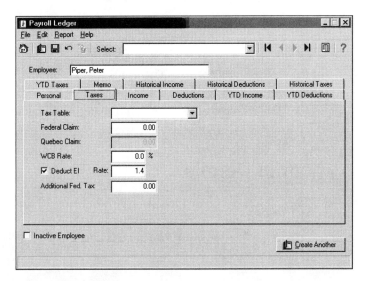

Taxes Tab Input Screen Fields

Employee: The name you entered previously stays on display in the screens for all tabs.

Tax Table: From the list, select the province in which the employee works. The program uses this entry to determine which rates and taxes apply. Different provinces have different rules for health taxes, income taxes, WSIB/WCB rates, etc.

Federal Claim: The amount that the employee claims as federal tax deductions on the TD-1 form. All employees have a basic personal claim. Some may have additional claims for a spouse, dependents, disability, tuition fees or age. The employee will not pay income tax if the annual pay is less than the Federal Claim amount. The program calculates the annual salary by multiplying the pay for the period times the number of pay periods to determine income taxes.

Quebec Claim: This equivalent of the Federal Claim amount for Quebec is used to assess the amount of provincial taxes owed. The claim amounts for the province are different from the federal amounts.

WCB Rate: The rate of tax for the Workers' Compensation (or Workplace Safety and Insurance) Board program. Each workplace is assigned a rate based on the safety record of the business, the industry and the specific occupation. For example, the rate for clerical retail workers is less than the rate for construction workers.

Remember that WSIB is the name for WCB in Ontario.

Deduct EI: If the employee is eligible to receive EI benefits when unemployed, the employee must make EI contributions. Not all workers are eligible for EI. Self-employed individuals do not receive EI benefits if they are out of work, but they do not pay EI premiums either. **Rate** defines the employer's contribution.

Additional Fed. Tax: This field allows you to indicate an additional amount of tax that should be withheld from each paycheque. Employees might choose to pay additional taxes if they have other sources of income that are not taxed. Paying additional taxes on a regular basis will help them avoid a large tax burden at income tax reporting time or even a penalty for not making tax installment payments on the additional income.

◆ Click the list field **arrow for Tax Table**.

◆ Click **Ontario** from the list.

◆ Press ⌨tab to move to the Federal Claim field.

◆ Type **11531**

◆ Press ⌨tab to move to the WCB Rate field to prepare for changing the entry.

◆ Type **3.13**

The EI settings are correct. The employee is eligible for Employment Insurance benefits and the rate is correct at 1.4. The employer's contributions are 1.4 times those of the employee. Piper has not asked to have additional tax deducted. You must now enter the income details for the employee.

Income Details

◆ Click the **Income tab** to display these input fields:

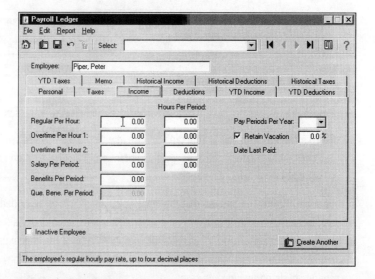

Income Tab Input Screen Fields

Employee: The name you entered previously stays on display in all tab screens.

Regular Per Hour: The amount of money the employee earns for each hour of work at the regular rate of pay.

Overtime Per Hour 1 and **2**: The amount of money the employee receives for each hour of overtime work, additional hours beyond the normal number of hours worked each pay period. There may be two different overtime rates, for example, one rate for regular evening overtime and a higher rate for statutory holidays.

Salary Per Period: The amount of money the employee receives as a fixed amount each pay period. The number of hours worked is not counted for determining pay for salaried workers. Salaried employees are not normally paid for overtime work either. Instead they may be given time off work in a later pay period.

Benefits Per Period: The amount the employee receives each pay period in taxable benefits.

Que. Benefits Per Period: For Quebec employees, the amount the employee receives in benefits.

Hours Per Period: The normal number of hours an employee works for each type of pay in each pay period.

Pay Periods Per Year: From the list, select the number of times the employee is paid in a normal year. Employees may be paid weekly (52 times), every two weeks or bi-weekly (26), every four weeks (13), every month (12), every month except summers (10), every six months (2) or annually (1).

Retain Vacation: When an employee receives vacation pay, the amount may be withheld or retained and paid out once a year, or it may be included with each paycheque (not retained). The default setting is to retain the vacation pay. The next field contains the rate of vacation pay calculated as a percentage of gross pay.

◆ Double click the **Regular Per Hour field** to prepare it for editing.

◆ Type **14**

◆ Press ⌐tab⌐ to move to the Hours Per Period field.

◆ Type **80**

◆ Press ⌐tab⌐ to move to the Overtime field.

◆ Type **21** (there is no regular number of overtime hours).

◆ Click the list field **arrow for Pay Periods Per Year**.

◆ Click **26**.

◆ Double click the **Retain Vacation field**. Leave the checkmark for the Retain setting.

◆ Type **4**

You are now ready to enter information about deductions.

Regular Deduction Amounts

◆ Click the **Deductions tab**:

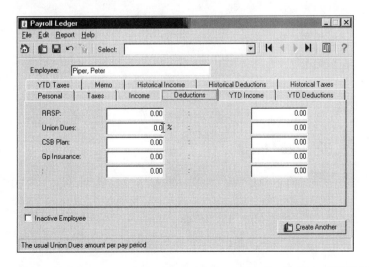

Default Deductions

In the Deductions tab screen, you can enter the amounts that should be deducted every pay period for the optional or company-specific deductions. The names you entered in the Names setup will appear on your ledger screen. These default deduction amounts can be changed for a specific pay period if necessary. If you have not changed the names, you will see the labels **Pension**, **Union Dues**, **Medical**, **Deduction D**, etc.

- ◆ Double click the **RRSP field** to select the default entry.

- ◆ Type **25**

- ◆ Press ⬚tab⬚ to advance to and highlight the Union Dues field contents. Enter the percentage of gross pay to be deducted.

- ◆ Type **2**

- ◆ Press ⬚tab⬚ to advance to and highlight the CSB Plan field contents.

- ◆ Type **25**

- ◆ Press ⬚tab⬚ to advance to and highlight the Gp Insurance field contents.

- ◆ Type **10**

There are currently no other deductions. The next step is to enter the historical payroll details. After entering the amounts paid and deducted so far this year, we will examine the YTD (year-to-date) tabs screens.

Historical Income Details

The historical payroll information needed to complete the Historical Income screen for Peter Piper is on page 265.

- ◆ Click the **Historical Income tab**:

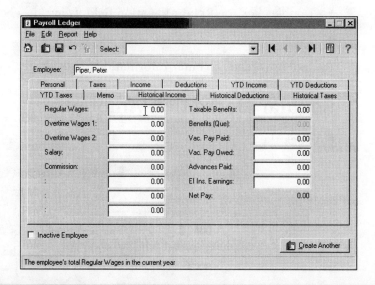

Historical Income

These fields record the total amounts earned by the employee so far this calendar year. The different types of income are separated, just as they are in the Income and Taxes screens. The historical information also becomes part of the T4 statements.

Regular Wages, **Overtime Wages**, **Salary** and **Commission**: Enter the total amounts received this year for each method of payment that applies to the employee. Any that do not apply have zero amounts or are left blank.

Taxable Benefits: If the employee has received taxable benefits, enter the total in this field. Taxable benefits are taxed as if they were income. Tuition paid by the employer for employee courses is an example of a taxable benefit.

Benefits (Que): The total benefits received that have Quebec Income Tax applied to them — for employees in Quebec.

Vac. Pay Paid: The total amount of vacation pay already paid out this year.

Vac. Pay Owed: The total amount of vacation pay that has been withheld and will be paid out at a later date.

Advances Paid: The payroll advances that an employee received this year and has not yet repaid. That is, the employee still owes this amount to the employer. The advance will be deducted from future paycheques.

EI Ins. Earnings: The total pay received so far this year that is eligible for EI. EI payroll deductions continue until the employee reaches the maximum wage on which EI benefits are calculated. After that, no further EI is deducted.

Net Pay: The amount of money that the employee actually received this year, after all deductions but including vacation pay paid and advances paid. The program automatically calculates the net pay and updates it regularly from Payroll Journal entries.

> The total amounts for Vacation Pay Owed and Advances Paid for all employees must equal the opening balances for these General Ledger accounts before you can finish the Payroll Ledger history.

Piper has received only regular wages since he started working, no overtime pay, benefits or advances.

- ◆ Double click the **Regular Wages field**.

- ◆ Type **1400**

- ◆ Double click the **Vac. Pay Paid field** to skip the fields that do not apply.

- ◆ Type **56**

- ◆ Double click the **EI Ins. Earnings field**.

- ◆ Type **1456**

At this point, the Net Pay will show only earnings because we have not yet entered the historical deductions. The next step is to enter the historical, year-to-date total deduction amounts for both the compulsory and the optional deductions.

Historical Deduction Amounts

◆ Click the **Historical Deductions tab**:

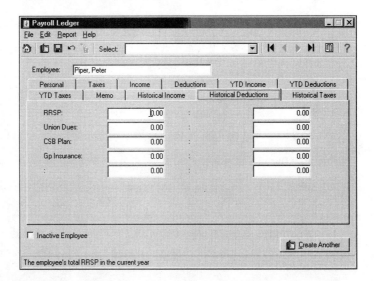

Historical Deductions

The totals for the optional or company-specific deductions are entered on this screen.

RRSP (Pension): The total deducted for the first optional deduction. In Play Wave, this is the Registered Retirement Savings Plan. The default name for Deduction A is Pension.

Union Dues: The total deducted for the second optional deduction. In Play Wave, this is the amount paid for Union Dues.

CSB Plan (Medical): The total deducted for the third optional deduction. In Play Wave, this is the Canada Savings Bond Plan. The default name for Deduction C is Medical.

Gp Insurance (Deduction D): The total deducted for the fourth optional deduction. In Play Wave, this is the Group Insurance Plan.

Deductions E through J: The total deducted for the remaining optional deductions. In Play Wave, these fields are blank.

◆ Double click the **RRSP field**.

◆ Type **50**

◆ Press ⒯ⒶⒷ. Piper has just joined the union and has not yet paid dues. Press ⒯ⒶⒷ.

◆ Type **50** to enter the CSB Plan contributions.

◆ Press ⒯ⒶⒷ

◆ Type **20** to enter the Group Insurance contribution amounts.

The next tab on the employee ledger form is for historical tax amounts.

Historical Taxes Amounts

◆ Click the **Historical Taxes tab**:

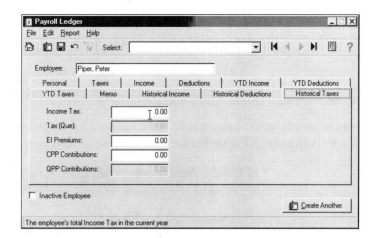

Historical Taxes

The totals for the legally required deductions are entered on this screen. These amounts are important because some deductions (e.g., EI and CPP) have a maximum. After this point, no further deductions are made.

Income Tax: The total income tax deducted from paycheques so far this year.

Tax (Que): This field name may be blank, as indicated earlier, if you removed the name for Prov. Tax in the Names settings (pages 255–256). It refers to the total Quebec Income Tax paid so far this year.

EI Premiums: The total EI premiums paid.

CPP Contributions: The total deducted for Canada Pension Plan contributions.

QPP Contributions: The total deducted for Quebec Pension Plan contributions (only for employees in Quebec).

◆ Double click the **Income Tax field**.

◆ Type **110.94**

◆ Press ⌈tab⌉ to move to the **EI premiums field**.

The program skips the fields related to Quebec because you selected Ontario as the province for tax tables. These fields are dimmed.

◆ Type **37.80**

◆ Press ⌈tab⌉ to advance to the **CPP Contributions field**.

◆ Type **49.90**

The next tab on the employee ledger form is for memos. There is no memo for the employee at this time.

Employee Memos

The employee **Memo** tab serves the same function as the customer and vendor memo tabs. You can enter a reminder Memo, such as a note to schedule a bonus cheque or vacation pay, with a **To-Do Date** that is **Displayed in the To-Do Lists**.

◆ Click the **Historical Income tab**.

The Net Pay amount should now correspond to the Historical Information on
page 265.

Checking Employee Historical Details

You can use the YTD tab screens to check the accuracy of your inputs. These fields
are updated directly by the program based on the historical information and on the
ongoing journal entries.

◆ Click the **YTD Income tab**:

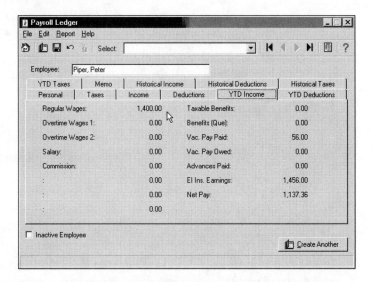

◆ Check the income amounts on this screen against the table on page 265. Return to
the Historical Income tab screen to make corrections.

◆ Click the **YTD Deductions tab**:

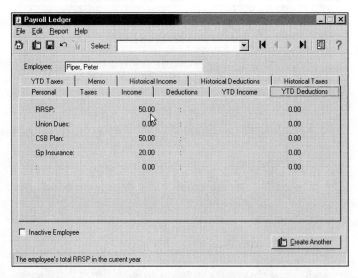

◆ Compare the deduction amounts on this screen with the amounts on page 265. If
there are errors, click the Historical Deductions tab and make corrections.

◆ Click the **YTD Taxes tab**:

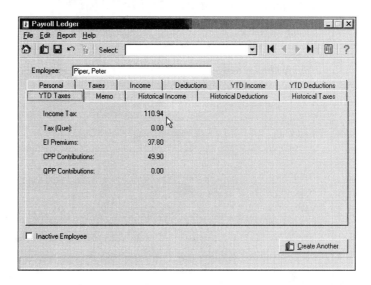

◆ Compare the tax amounts with the table on page 265. If there are errors, click the Historical Taxes tab and make corrections.

◆ Review each tab screen carefully to check your work. When you are certain that it is correct, you may save the record.

◆ Click **Create Another.**

◆ Now enter the information for the two remaining employees.

EMPLOYEE INFORMATION

Profile: **Rebecca Doolittle** started working part-time on March 9, 2002, at an hourly rate of $17 per hour. She has not worked any overtime hours. Beginning in April, she will receive a full-time salary of $41 600 per year. Since she is paid bi-weekly, she receives $1 600 in every two-week paycheque for an average of 75 hours work. As a salaried employee, she has no vacation pay. Instead, she is entitled to take three weeks vacation each year while receiving her regular salary. Doolittle, a single and self-supporting employee, claims the basic federal amount for income tax purposes.

Profile: **Candie Rapper** began working for Play Wave on May 1, 2002, to assist with the safety retrofit projects and will continue during the busier summer months. She is paid at an hourly rate of $14. Since she works part-time, no overtime rate is assigned. Her vacation pay rate is 4% and will be retained. Rapper has recently graduated from college and claims the basic federal amount for income tax purposes.

Personal Information:

Employee Name	Rebecca Doolittle	Candie Rapper
Position	Assistant	Assistant
Address	222 Pie-in-the-sky Ct.	16 Gumley St.
	Megacity, ON M2C 6H4	Megacity, ON M5R 2J4
Telephone	(416) 283-4629	(416) 338-7213
Social Insurance Number (SIN)	482 751 997	587 532 888
Date of Birth	April 17, 1969	June 4, 1978
Date of Hire	March 9, 2002	May 1, 2002

EMPLOYEE INFORMATION CONTINUED

Employee Name	Rebecca Doolittle	Candie Rapper
Taxes:		
Tax Table	Ontario	Ontario
Federal Claim (Basic Amount)	$7 131	$7 131
WSIB Rate (WCB)	3.13%	3.13%
EI Eligible (EI Factor)	Yes (1.4)	Yes (1.4)
Additional Federal Tax		
CPP and Income Tax	calculations built into program	

Income:		
Regular Per Hour Wage Rate		$14
Salary Per Period	$1 600 bi-weekly	
Hours Per Period	75 hours	50
Vacation	3 weeks (0%, do not retain)	4% retained
Number of Pay Periods	26 (every two weeks)	26 (every two weeks)

Default Deductions:		
RRSP	$25	
Union Dues		2%
CSB Plan	$25	
Group Insurance	$10	

Historical Payroll Information for the Pay Period Ending April 30, 2002

Historical Income:	
Regular Wages	$1 700.00
Vacation Pay Paid	$102.00
Gross Earnings	$1 802.00
EI Insurable Earnings	$1 802.00
Net Pay	$1 319.12

Historical Deductions:	
RRSP	$50.00
CSB Plan	$50.00
Group Insurance	$20.00

Historical Taxes:	
Income Tax	$254.54
EI Premiums	$45.90
CPP Contributions	$62.44

Payroll Ledger Reports

You should print the Employee List to check address information and the Employee Summary Report to check income, deduction and year-to-date details. You will be unable to correct errors in historical information after finishing the history. A backup is, therefore, essential.

Employee Lists

From the Employees window:

◆ Click the **Select a report** tool 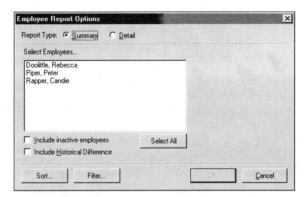, click **Display Employee List** and click **Select**. (Or choose the Reports menu and click Display Employee List.)

From the Home window:

The Display tool label changes when you select a Home window icon first.

◆ Choose the **Reports** menu, then choose **Lists** and click **Employees**. The employee address list is displayed immediately. (Or click the Display tool, choose Employee List and then Select, or click the Employees icon and click the Display Employee List tool.)

◆ Print the list or check your work from the on-screen display. Close the display.

Employee Reports

◆ Choose the **Reports** menu, then choose **Payroll** and click **Employee** in the Home window. (In the Employees window, choose the Reports menu and click Employee.)

Sort and Filter options do not apply to payroll reports.

Your options are to display a Summary report or a Detail report. The Summary report includes all the financial data entered in the ledger record, including deduction amounts, wage or salary amounts and all year-to-date totals. The Detail report is useful after you have made journal entries, because it shows the amounts paid and deducted for each paycheque.

◆ Click **Summary** to select this report option.

◆ Click **Select All** to include all three employees in the report.

◆ Click **OK** to display the report.

◆ Print the report or check your work from the on-screen display.

◆ Close the display. Return to the Home window.

Finishing the Payroll Ledger History

The final step in setting up the Payroll Ledger is to finish the history so that no changes to historical information may be made in error. Until the Payroll Ledger history is finished, you must enter all taxes manually. Without accurate historical amounts, the amounts calculated automatically may be incorrect. As usual, it is very important to make a backup copy of the file with the Payroll Ledger history unfinished.

◆ Back up your data files.

◆ Choose the **History** menu, then choose **Finish Entering History** and click **Payroll** in the Home window.

Errors in the Payroll Ledger

If you have omitted an essential linked account, you will see the message that a required linked account is not defined. Click OK to return to the Home window. Check your linked accounts carefully. Add the missing account and try finishing again. There is no single control account for the Payroll Ledger, but if there are advances or vacation pay owed and these account balances do not match the employee historical ledger information, you will see an account balance error message for these accounts. There is no similar control for the remaining historical data. Therefore, it is extremely important to check your work before proceeding and to make a backup with the Payroll Ledger history unfinished.

If you have entered the required details correctly, Simply Accounting displays the familiar warning:

◆ If you have backed up your files already, click **Proceed**.

◆ Close the Play Wave files so that you can set up the Payroll Ledger for Live Links.

Practice: Live Links

Live Links will begin managing its own payroll beginning in September. Live Links had one employee, Carrie Dell, throughout July and August and a new employee was hired at the beginning of September. Thus, historical information is provided only for Dell. Dell received her regular salary at the end of August so there were no wages outstanding on September 1. The bank has also made all remittances before turning the payroll management over to Live Links. In addition to the required payroll deductions, Live Links deducts medical premiums from employee paycheques so that they do not have to submit their own payments. Some large companies provide medical coverage as a taxable benefit to employees but Live Links cannot afford benefits at this early stage of company development. The remaining deductions — contributions to an RRSP program, to a CSB savings plan and to a group life insurance program — are optional. Remittances to the agencies administering these plans are made quarterly.

If you have not completed the journal entries for Live Links in Chapter 8 and want to continue working on Chapter 9, you can use your copy of the Data Disk file — Ch09\links\ linkch09.sdb — to continue this chapter.

Payroll Ledger Setup

Instructions

1. Open the data files for Live Links. Accept September 14 as the Session date.

2. Restore the icons for the Payroll Ledger (Home window, View menu, Modules Payroll).

3. Enter the following names for the payroll deductions:

Names Settings	
Incomes C to E	Press 〔del〕
Deduction A	Medical
Deduction B	RRSP
Deduction C	CSB
Deduction D	Group Insur
Deductions E to J	Press 〔del〕
Prov. Tax	Press 〔del〕

4. Change the Payroll Ledger default settings as follows:

> RRSP is deducted before tax (no ✓).
>
> Medical, CSB and Group Insur are after-tax deductions (add a ✓).
>
> Keep employee details for two years.

5. In the General Ledger, add the following new accounts required for the payroll:

New Accounts

1210 Advances Receivable (G)	2410 RRSP Payable (G)
2300 Vacation Payable (G)	2420 CSB Plan Payable (G)
2310 EI Payable (A)	2430 Group Insurance Payable (G)
2320 CPP Payable (A)	2460 WCB Payable (G)
2330 Income Tax Payable (A)	5310 EI Expense (G)
2340 Receiver General Payable (S)	5320 CPP Expense (G)
2400 Medical Payable (G)	5330 WCB Expense (G)

6. Enter the linked accounts for the Payroll Ledger:

PAYROLL LINKED ACCOUNTS

Principal Bank	1080 Bank Account: Chequing		
Income		**Deductions**	
Vacation	2300 Vacation Payable	Medical	2400 Medical Payable
Advances	1210 Advances Receivable	RRSP	2410 RRSP Payable
All Income	5300 Wages	CSB	2420 CSB Plan Payable
		Group Insur	2430 Group Insurance Payable
Taxes			
Payables		**Expenses**	
EI	2310 EI Payable	EI	5310 EI Expense
CPP	2320 CPP Payable	CPP	5320 CPP Expense
Tax	2330 Income Tax Payable	WCB	5330 WCB Expense
WCB	2460 WCB Payable		

To skip a linked account field that is not needed, press 〔tab〕 or if there is an account in the field that you do not need, select it and press 〔del〕.

7. Enter the employee records for the two employees and add historical payroll data for Carrie Dell from the following chart:

EMPLOYEE INFORMATION

Profiles:

Carrie Dell and Adrian Borland work as general assistants to Helen Lively. Both are single and self-supporting and have the basic Federal Claim amount for income tax purposes. In addition, Dell claims the spousal equivalence allowance for one of her daughters whom she supports fully. Dell, who began working for Lively in July, earns additional regular income and has, therefore, chosen to have additional federal taxes deducted from the paycheques she receives from Live Links. She also participates in all the payroll deduction plans and the payments for these plans are deducted automatically from each of her monthly salary cheques. She is paid $3 000 at the end of each month. As a salaried employee, she takes three weeks off each year with pay instead of vacation pay.

Borland started working for Live Links in September. He has the required medical premiums deducted from his paycheque and the optional RRSP payments. His bi-weekly pay is at the rate of $12 per hour for the first 40 hours each week and $18 per hour after that for overtime hours. He also receives vacation pay at the rate of 4 percent of his gross pay and this amount is retained until he takes his vacation. There is no historical pay information for Borland.

Personal Information:

	Carrie Dell	Adrian Borland
Employee Name	Carrie Dell	Adrian Borland
Position	Assistant	Assistant
Address	28 Next Ave.	386 Windows Blvd.
	Vancouver, BC V5R 6K8	Vancouver, BC V6D 2M9
Telephone	(604) 298-4929	(604) 772-6219
Social Insurance Number (SIN)	586 157 117	519 811 012
Date of Birth	May 21, 1968	August 8, 1972
Date of Hire	July 1, 2002	September 1, 2002

Taxes:

Tax Table	British Columbia	British Columbia
Federal Claim (Tax Exemption)		
Basic amount	$7 131	$7 131
Spousal amount	$6 661	
Total Federal Claim	$13 792	$7 131
WCB Rate	1.09%	1.09%
EI Eligible (EI Factor)	Yes (1.4)	Yes (1.4)
Additional Federal Tax	$50	
CPP and Income Tax	calculations built into program	

Income:

Regular Wage		$12.00/hour
Overtime Wage		$18.00/hour
Salary	$3 000 monthly	
Regular Hours Per Period	140 hours	80
Number of Pay Periods	12 (paid monthly)	26 (paid bi-weekly)
Vacation	0% not retained (3 wks/yr)	4% retained

Default Deductions:

Medical	$72	$18
RRSP	$50	$20
CSB	$25	
Group Insur	$20	

Historical Payroll Information for Carrie Dell for the Pay Period Ending August 31, 2002

Historical Income:		**Historical Deductions:**	
Salary	$6 000.00	Medical	$144.00
Gross Earnings	$6 000.00	RRSP	$100.00
EI Insurable Earnings	$6 000.00	CSB	$50.00
Net Pay	$4 159.52	Group Insur	$40.00

		Historical Taxes:	
		Income Tax	$1 171.14
		EI Premiums	$162.00
		CPP Contributions	$173.34

8. Print the Employee List and the Employee Summary to check your work.

9. Make a backup copy of the data files before finishing the Payroll Ledger history.

10. Finish the Payroll Ledger history.

11. Close the data files for Live Links.

Review Questions

1. What details can you change in the employee ledger record before you finish the Payroll Ledger history? What can you change after you finish the ledger history? Why are there restrictions? (Look at the record for Piper in the Play Wave Plus files if you are unsure.)
2. What information must you record as historical information for an employee when you set up the Payroll Ledger? Why?
3. How are deductions such as EI or CPP different from deductions such as RRSP contributions or insurance?
4. What reports can you print to check your input of employee information? What details do these reports provide?
5. Why are there two linked accounts related to EI but only one for RRSP contributions?
6. How do you change the name of an optional payroll deduction (e.g., change Deduction A to RRSP)? What other information must you add for each of these optional deductions before you finish the ledger history?
7. Why are there no overall control accounts (like Accounts Payable) for the Payroll Ledger?
8. What names appear on the Names setup screen that are not related to payroll?
9. Why might the linked accounts for Quebec Payroll not be dimmed in the Payroll Ledger even if you have Ontario employees?

CHAPTER 10

PAYROLL JOURNALS

Objectives

- *explain the components of the Payroll journal entry screens*
- *enter and recover payroll advances*
- *enter, review and correct Payroll journal transactions*
- *adjust Payroll journal entries after posting*
- *enter payroll for salaried and hourly employees*
- *complete payroll runs to prepare multiple paycheques*
- *complete additional entries for practice*
- *display and print Payroll Ledger reports*

Introduction

In this chapter, you will begin to process payroll transactions through the Simply Accounting program. As with the journal entries for the other subsidiary ledgers, the transactions in the Payroll journals are much simpler to prepare than the comparable General Journal entries, because of the linked accounts. Since not all transactions that occur in May require Payroll journal entries, you will continue to use the General, Payables and Receivables journals when they are appropriate.

If you have not completed the payroll setup in Chapter 9 and want to continue working on Chapter 10, you can use your copy of the Data Disk file — Ch10\playch10.sdb — to begin this chapter.

PlayWave Plus

If you make a payment to an employee for a non-wage item, you should use the Payables journals.

The Payroll Journals

The Payroll Ledger has two journals, one for paying a single employee and one for a payroll run to pay several employees at once. All payments to employees that are wage-related and that should be included as wage-related expenses should be processed through the Payroll journals. This includes payment of salaries, bonuses, hourly and overtime wages, vacation pay and commissions. From the employee's point of view, all of these are components of taxable income. Processing the payroll entry through the Payroll journals automatically debits the expense and liability accounts that are set up for deductions as well as *Bank Account: Chequing* for the net amount. The comparable manual General Journal entry is quite complex because of both the large number of accounts involved and the various tax deduction tables that are used.

Entering Payroll Transactions

◆ Open your working copy of the Play Wave files. Accept May 14 as the Session date.

The first payroll transaction is for Piper, an hourly employee.

> ✔ Employee Time Summary Sheet #1
> Dated May 14, 2002
> Pay Period Ending May 14, 2002
> Peter Piper worked 80 regular hours and 0 hours overtime. Piper requested an advance of $100 for personal reasons. Child, the owner, has approved the advance. Issue cheque #120.

Paycheques are prepared and processed in the Paycheques Journal.

◆ Click the **Paycheques Journal icon** [Paycheques] shown here:

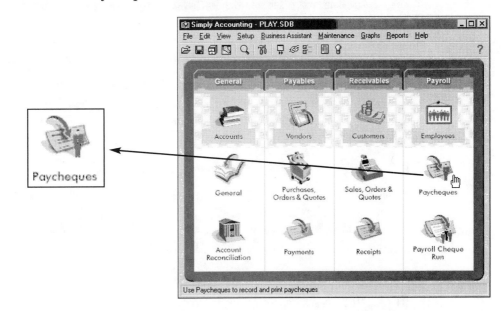

The Payroll Journal opens:

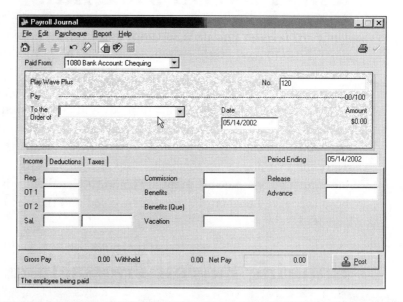

The Payroll Journal Screen

The Payroll Journal is divided into two parts — the upper part is a cheque and the lower part is the payroll stub. Payroll stub details are divided among three tab screens. The different tab screens show the amounts for all types of income, all automatic optional deductions and taxes, respectively. There are four buttons unique to the Payroll Journal. Two of the entries under the Paycheque menu, Adjust Cheque and Recalculate Taxes, duplicate the tool button functions.

 Adjust cheque can be used to correct a journal entry after posting.

 Calculate taxes automatically is the default setting. The program calculates deductions based on the built-in tax tables.

 Enter taxes manually is used to edit information in the automatic deduction fields (i.e., EI, CPP and Tax) for special paycheques like bonuses and commissions.

 Recalculate taxes is selected after you have adjusted a cheque in order to update the deduction amounts.

Paid From: You can pay from any Bank class account. All Bank class accounts are on the drop-down list.

No.: The next cheque number in sequence from the automatic numbering series.

To the Order of: Select the name of the employee from the drop-down selection list. As in the name fields of the Purchases and Sales Journals, you can add a new employee when you type in a new name. Since you must enter income tax-related information, you must enter the full employee record. You do not have the "Quick Add" option of entering only the name.

Date: The date of the payment to the employee.

Period Ending: The last day of the pay period covered by the cheque. This may be different from the date of the payment. Payroll cheques are frequently prepared before the pay period ends for salaried employees whose pay is not determined by the exact number of hours worked. For hourly employees who must finish working the hours before they are paid, the Period Ending date is often earlier than the transaction or pay date.

Reg.: The number of hours worked in the pay period that are paid at the regular hourly rate.

OT 1 and **OT 2**: The number of hours worked that will be paid at each overtime hourly rate.

Sal.: The regular salary for the pay period. The first field shows the number of hours worked in a regular pay period and the second shows the salary amount. The number of hours is required for EI, because employees who work less than the minimum required hours will not be eligible for EI.

Commission: The dollar amount received as a commission or bonus during the pay period. Payments for periodic bonuses should be prepared as separate cheques so that the income tax can be recalculated correctly. If the bonus is added to the normal pay, the income tax for that period will be excessive because the program assumes that the combined amounts are earned in every pay period.

Other Income: If other types of income are defined, they will be shown on the journal screen as well.

Benefits: The dollar amount of taxable benefits the employee received from the employer.

Benefits (Que): The dollar amount of benefits received that have Quebec tax applied.

Vacation: The amount of vacation pay earned in the pay period — the vacation pay rate times the gross pay.

Release: The amount of vacation pay released with this paycheque. To release vacation pay, change the setting for Retain Vacation in the Payroll Ledger (Income tab screen). Click the option to remove the ✓.

Advance: The amount received as an advance against future paycheques. After an advance is received, the Payroll Journal for the employee will show the amount of the advance not repaid as a negative amount in the Advance field. The negative amount indicates that the repayment reduces the amount of the cheque.

Gross Pay: The total amount of wages and taxable benefits received before deductions. The program calculates this amount automatically.

Withheld: The total amount of deductions from the gross pay. The program calculates this amount.

Net Pay: The actual amount received in the cheque, the amount shown in the Pay field on the upper cheque portion and the amount for which the selected bank account is credited.

◆ Click the **Employee (To the Order of) list arrow** to show the list of employees.

◆ Click **Piper, Peter** to select this employee.

◆ Press ⌨tab⌨ to see the updated journal window:

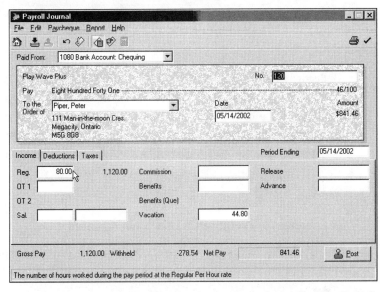

The employee information is added to the form, including all default information about hours worked and deduction amounts for the optional deductions. The Session date appears as the default for the cheque and for the Period Ending date, the last day of the pay period covered by the cheque. You can change either date. The Period Ending date may be later or earlier than the date of the cheque or posting date.

The linked bank account is selected as the default and the cheque number is updated from the cheque number sequence in the ledger record for the bank account. The default information is correct.

All the remaining default information is also correct. The regular number of bi-weekly hours from the ledger record is entered automatically but you may edit the number of hours worked. Vacation pay is also calculated automatically. We need to enter the payroll advance.

◆ Click the **Advance field** to move the cursor to that field.

◆ Type **100** to enter the advance.

◆ Press ⌨tab to enter the amount and update the totals. The screen is advanced to the Deductions tab information because Advance was the last input field on the Income screen:

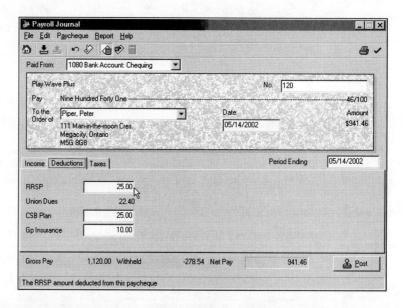

Deductions Tab Details: For **RRSP**, **Union Dues**, **CSB Plan** and **Gp Insurance**, the default deduction amounts for the optional payroll deductions are entered from the ledger record information. These amounts can be changed in the journal. However, if the employee requests a change in deduction amounts, you should change them in the employee's Payroll Ledger Deductions tab screen. Because Union Dues are calculated as a percentage, you cannot edit this amount directly. You must click the Enter taxes manually tool to access the field, or change the percentage in the ledger record. The names you entered in the Names setup appear on the screen.

No changes are required for the deductions.

◆ Click the **Taxes tab** to see the remaining payroll details:

A payroll entry for a salaried worker is completed the same way. Choose the employee and edit default amounts if necessary.

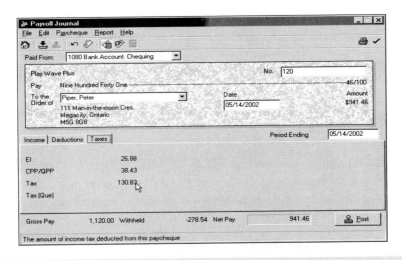

Taxes Details: **EI**, **CPP/QPP** and **Tax** are the required employee deductions built into the program. The amounts appear as soon as you enter the pay amounts. If you need to change the amounts, as for special bonus cheques, you must first turn on the option to Enter taxes manually by clicking this tool button. The fields will become available for editing.

Both the cheque and the pay stub portions of the journal are completed automatically. The pay stub shows all of the employee deductions. The advance does not affect deduction amounts because it is a temporary loan and not income. The income tax for the advance will be deducted from the regular pay amount in future pay periods when the advance is being repaid and the net pay is reduced. Before posting the transaction, you should review the journal entry.

◆ Choose the **Report** menu and click **Display Payroll Journal Entry** to see the entry:

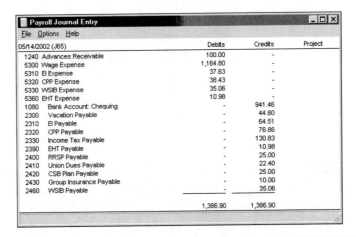

Linked Payroll Accounts

All the accounts in the journal entry are the linked accounts you entered when setting up the Payroll Ledger. *Bank Account: Chequing* is credited for the amount of net pay plus advances (*Advances Receivable*). *Wage Expense* is debited for the amount of gross pay plus vacation pay even though the vacation pay is retained. The credit entry for *Vacation Payable* shows that vacation pay is retained. The remaining expense accounts for EI, CPP, WSIB and EHT record the employer's contributions to these government programs. The payable accounts record the liabilities created by the payroll entry to the various agencies. Because contributions to EI and CPP are made by both the employee and the employer, these liabilities are larger than the expense portion. Income tax and the optional deductions, RRSP, Union Dues, CSB and Group Insurance, are paid solely by the employee so there is no corresponding expense entry for them. EHT and WSIB are funded solely by employers, so the liability and expense amounts are equal. Refer to Chapter 9 to review these linked accounts if necessary.

The journal entry shows the manual entry you would complete if you were not using the Payroll Journal. You can see that the manual journal entry is complex. It requires making many calculations as well as having access to current tax tables.

◆ Close the display when finished.

Review your work carefully and make corrections. As usual, making corrections before posting is preferred to making them afterward.

Correcting the Payroll Journal Entry

You can edit any field that is not dimmed, in the usual way — selecting the text to be changed and then typing over it. Pressing ⟨tab⟩ moves you forward to the next available field. Pressing ⟨shift⟩ and ⟨tab⟩ together moves you back to the previous field. When you select a different employee from the employee list and press ⟨tab⟩, the program will ask you to confirm that you want to discard the current transaction. Click Yes to confirm the change.

You can discard a payroll transaction by clicking the Undo tool ⟨↰⟩ or choosing the Edit menu and clicking Undo Entry. Again, you must confirm your intention to discard the entry by clicking Yes when prompted.

To make a change after posting the entry, you can use the Adjust Cheque feature described later in this chapter.

◆ Click **Print** 🖶 to print the cheque and stub directly from the journal.

◆ Click **Post** ⟨👤 Post⟩ to save the entry.

You will see the warning message:

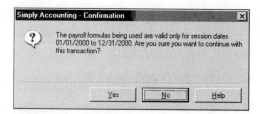

Because tax tables are updated regularly, the program warns you whenever you enter dates that are outside of the range for the tax tables in the program. When you use the program for your business payroll, you must have current tax tables. For instructional purposes, you can use tables that do not match the transaction dates.

◆ Click **Yes** to proceed.

◆ Close the Payroll Journal to return to the Home window.

Completing Payroll Cheque Runs

Frequently a business pays all or many of its employees at the same time and the payments are routine. That is, they do not change from one pay period to the next. You can complete these routine payroll runs in Simply Accounting from the Payroll

Cheque Run Journal. If there are any changes from a regular paycheque, such as giving advances, recovering advances, or changing the default deduction amounts, you must use the Paycheques Journal for a single employee. The following source document describes the payroll transactions.

> ✔ Memo #16
> Dated May 14, 2002
> Payroll Cheque Run Time Sheet for pay period ending May 14.
> Candie Rapper worked 45 hours at the regular hourly rate.
> Rebecca Doolittle should receive her normal bi-weekly salary.
> Issue cheques #121 and 122.

◆ Click the **Payroll Cheque Run Journal icon** shown here:

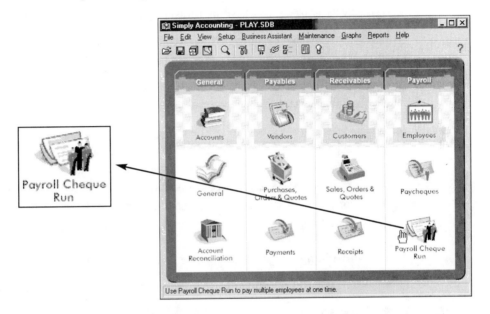

The Payroll Run Journal opens:

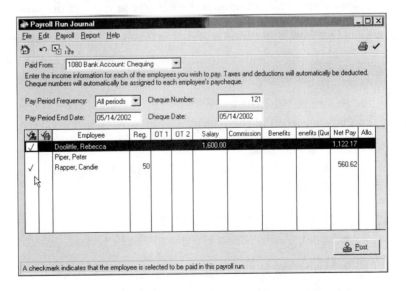

Although you can complete transactions in other journals before finishing the history for a ledger, you cannot use the Payroll Run Journal until the Payroll history is finished. Furthermore, you must enter taxes manually in the Payroll Journal if the history is unfinished. You cannot finish the Payroll history until the General Ledger history is finished.

The Payroll Run Journal

The Payroll Run Journal lists all employees because the **Pay Period Frequency** has the option to include All Periods selected. You may choose a specific pay period frequency instead, and complete a payroll run for only the employees usually paid on that cycle. The regular number of hours worked or the salary, and the net pay amounts are shown for each employee. The column headings refer to the same details as the field names in the Payroll Journal and calculations for deductions are made automatically based on the default ledger entries. The **Period End Date** and the **Cheque Date** (posting date) must be the same for all employees selected and must be the same as the Session date. The first two columns allow you to select employees for this pay run and to choose whether or not to print their cheques. Checkmarks in the **Post** (first) **column** indicate that the employee is selected. To deselect an employee (remove the checkmark) click the **Post column** for that employee. Initially, all employees who have not yet been paid in this period will be selected, therefore Piper is not selected to be paid in this run. **Cheque Numbers** are assigned in sequence to each employee, but you may change the starting cheque number. You may select any Bank class account from the **Paid From** drop-down list. To print a cheque for the employee, click the **Print column** beside the employee. Click again to remove a checkmark.

The tool for **Renumber Cheques** (also on the Payroll menu) is needed when you select different employees for the payroll run after printing the Cheque Run Summary.

The **Report menu** has two options: the usual one to display the journal entry and a new one to **Print the Cheque Run Summary**. The summary shows the pay stubs for each employee with all income amounts and deductions.

You can edit many of the fields in this journal. For hourly employees, you can change the number of regular or overtime hours worked, provided that you have entered an hourly rate for the employee. For salaried employees, you may change the salary amount. In addition, you may add amounts for commissions, bonuses or benefits. You cannot add an advance or change deductions. **Do not use** the Payroll Run Journal for any employee who is receiving an advance, repaying an advance, or who needs to change any of the deduction amounts.

The only change required is for the number of hours worked by Rapper.

◆ Click the **Reg. column** for Rapper to select the number of hours.

◆ Type **45**

◆ Press ⌐tab⌐ to update the net pay and tax deductions.

The remaining information is correct, so your journal entry is complete.

Review the journal entry. Journal entries are provided for both selected employees. Close the display to return to the journal. Make corrections if necessary.

Before posting the journal entries, you should print the payroll summary so that you have a record of the payroll transaction for your files. You cannot display this summary.

◆ Choose the **Report menu** and click **Payroll Run Cheque Summary**. Printing will begin immediately.

◆ Click **Post** [Post] to save the entry.

◆ Click **Yes** to accept the dates that lie outside the dates for the tax tables.

◆ Close the journal to return to the Home window.

◆ Change the Session date to **May 22, 2002.**

If the payroll run date is different from the Session date, you can change the Session date backwards or forwards to match the cheque date.

If you want to print cheques, select the appropriate cheque form in the Setup menu, Reports & Forms option. Choose Custom as the form (then accept the default selection) for Payroll Cheques. Printing cheques also provides a payroll summary because the cheque stub is printed in duplicate.

290

Adjusting Payroll Entries

You can adjust Payroll Journal entries after posting them just as you can adjust Purchases Journal entries. The paycheque for Peter Piper was posted with an incorrect amount.

> ✔ Memo #17
>
> Dated May 15, 2002
>
> Peter Piper brought his paycheque back because his overtime was not included. He worked 4 hours of overtime in addition to the 80 regular hours in the previous two weeks. Make the adjustment to the Payroll Journal entry.

◆ Click the **Paycheques icon** to open the Payroll Journal.

◆ Click the **Adjust cheque tool** or choose the Paycheque menu and click Adjust Cheque to open the Select Entry To Adjust screen:

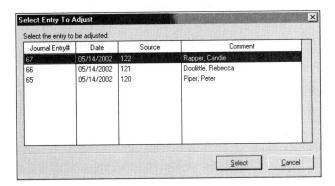

The three payroll transactions are listed. Notice that you can adjust paycheques completed in the Payroll Run Journal as well as regular Payroll Journal entries from the Adjust cheque feature in the Payroll Journal.

◆ Click anywhere on the line for **Peter Piper's entry** to select this transaction.

◆ Click **Select** to open the Adjusting Cheque screen. An advice message is displayed:

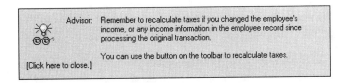

When you adjust a payroll entry, you can edit any of the income or deduction field amounts. You must recalculate taxes after the change so that these figures will also be correct. The taxes are not automatically updated as they are when you entered the original transaction because these amounts may be adjusted manually as well.

◆ Click the message as instructed to close the advisor.

The Adjusting Cheque screen appears:

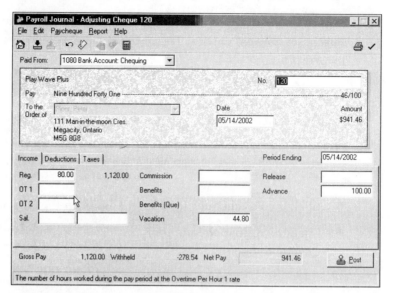

◆ Click the **OT 1 field** where you will enter the number of hours of overtime worked.

◆ Type **4**

◆ Press (tab) to enter the hours and calculate the overtime wages.

The revised entry now looks like the following:

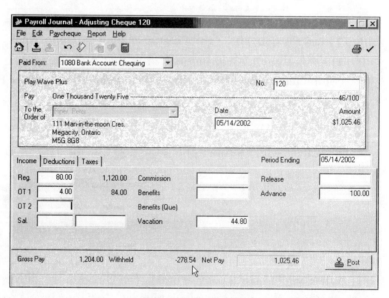

The Gross Pay and Vacation amounts are updated, but from the amount Withheld, you can see that the deduction amounts have not changed. Remember the advisor warning to recalculate taxes.

◆ Click the **Recalculate taxes tool** to update the tax amounts or choose the Paycheque menu and click Recalculate Taxes.

The entry is revised again as shown:

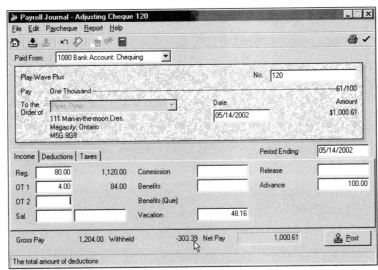

The Net Pay amount has changed. The EI, CPP and Income tax amounts are also updated. You should review the entry.

◆ Choose the **Report** menu and click **Review Payroll Journal Entry**:

When you print the Payroll Journal, you will see that the there are now five entries: the three original ones for Piper, Doolittle and Rapper, the reversing entry for Piper and the correction for Piper.

05/14/2002 (J68)		Debits	Credits	Project
1240	Advances Receivable	100.00	-	
5300	Wage Expense	1,252.16	-	
5310	EI Expense	40.46	-	
5320	CPP Expense	41.71	-	
5330	WSIB Expense	37.69	-	
5360	EHT Expense	11.80	-	
1080	Bank Account: Chequing	-	1,000.61	
2300	Vacation Payable	-	48.16	
2310	EI Payable	-	69.36	
2320	CPP Payable	-	83.42	
2330	Income Tax Payable	-	148.70	
2390	EHT Payable	-	11.80	
2400	RRSP Payable	-	25.00	
2410	Union Dues Payable	-	24.08	
2420	CSB Plan Payable	-	25.00	
2430	Group Insurance Payable	-	10.00	
2460	WSIB Payable	-	37.69	
		1,483.82	1,483.82	

◆ Close the display.

Reversing Payroll Entries — Correcting for an Incorrect Employee

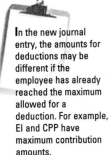

In the new journal entry, the amounts for deductions may be different if the employee has already reached the maximum allowed for a deduction. For example, EI and CPP have maximum contribution amounts.

If you have recorded payroll for the wrong employee, you cannot use the Adjust cheque tool. In this case, you must complete a reversing entry. You can take advantage of the Adjust cheque feature to review the payroll entry. Bring the original entry to the screen with the Adjust cheque tool. Print the Payroll Journal — Adjusting Cheque for this entry. Review the journal entry and print it. Click Undo [↶] to delete the adjustment **without posting** the entry or closing the journal. Choose the same employee and re-enter the same number of hours or salary. The amounts and deductions will be entered by the program.

Click the Calculate taxes manually tool [⬛]. This will make all the fields available for editing. The next step is to change the sign for all the original amounts. If the journal entry amounts are the same as the original amounts, add a minus sign in front of the original positive amounts and remove the minus sign from the original negative amounts. Check your work carefully. If the amounts on-screen are not the same, change the amounts to match the incorrect entry and then change the sign. Review the journal entry and compare it with the original. All the debit and credit entries should be reversed. Make any further corrections that are necessary so that the two journal entries will cancel each other out. When you are certain that this is the case, post the new entry.

◆ Click **Post** 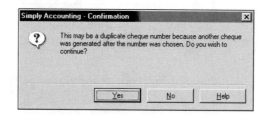 .

You will see the warning message:

This entry uses a duplicate cheque number. If the original cheque has been returned and not yet cashed, it is safe to leave the duplicate number. Otherwise, you should click No and update the cheque number to the next one in the sequence.

◆ Click **Yes** to save the entry using the duplicate cheque number.

◆ Close the Payroll Journal.

◆ Continue by entering the following transactions using the appropriate journals.

☐ Memo #18
Dated May 15/02
The manufactured cost of sales in April was $8 400. Complete a General Journal entry to record $672 ($8 400 x .08) as the PST Payable for April. Refer to Chapter 5, pages 154–158 for assistance if necessary.

☐ Memo #19
Dated May 15/02
Pay the PST amount owing for April to the Minister of Finance (Other Payment). The $672 liability is reduced by the sales tax compensation of $33.60 (5% of the PST account balance). Issue cheque #123 for $638.40 in payment.

☐ Credit Card Sales Invoice #113
Dated May 15/02
To MegaCity Parks & Rec, $800 plus $56 GST charged for installation of additional hardware to meet upgraded safety standards for playground. Terms: 10% discount for immediate payment. Invoice total $776, paid in full by Chargit.

☐ Purchase Order #20004
Dated May 16/02
Shipping date May 22/02
From Swede Steel Co., $2 500 plus $175 GST paid for nuts, bolts and steel rods. Invoice total $2 675. Order is to be shipped within 6 days. Terms: 2/15, n/30 days.

☐ Sales Quote #2003
Dated May 16/02
Completion (Shipping) date May 31/02
To Broadview Daycare Centre, $9 000 plus $630 GST charged for building play centre. Invoice total $9 630. Terms: 2/10, n/30 days. Work to be completed by May 31. Use Full Add for the customer.

☐ Broadview Daycare Centre (contact: Kid Powers)
Address: 99 Broadview Ave., Megacity, ON M7T 3B2
Tel: (416) 488-9023
Fax: (416) 488-9122
E-mail: kidpowers@kidsnet.ca
Include in GST reports.
Credit limit: $10 000

☐ Cash Purchase Invoice #OH-321423
Dated May 16/02
From Ontario Hydro, $90 for hydro services plus $6.30 GST paid. Invoice total
$96.30. Issue cheque #124 in full payment.

☐ Cash Purchase Invoice #BC-611729
Dated May 16/02
From Bell Canada, $80 for telephone services plus $5.60 GST paid and $6.40 PST
paid. Invoice total $92.00. Issue cheque #125 in full payment.

☐ Sales Order #2003
Dated May 18/02
Completion (Shipping) date May 31/02
To Broadview Daycare Centre, $9 000 plus $630 GST charged to accept sales quote
#2003. Invoice total $9 630. Terms: 2/10, n/30 days.

☐ Cash Receipt #9
Dated May 19/02
From Broadview Daycare Centre, cheque #348 for $2 250 as a down payment
(deposit #2) on acceptance of contract. Reference sales order #2003.

☐ Credit Card Sales Invoice #114
Dated May 20/02
To Chaplin Estates $200 plus $14 GST charged for installation of additional
hardware to meet upgraded safety standards for playground. Terms: 10% discount
for immediate payment. Invoice total $194, paid in full by Chargit.

☐ **Advance the Session date to May 28, 2002**

You will see the following message advising you of the need to complete year-end
adjustments:

> Advisor: See the Accounting Manual for information on making the following
> year-end adjustments: Writing off bad debts; Accounting for
> amortization; Accounting for prepaid expenses; Accounting for
> supplies used during the year; Adjusting inventory values.
>
> [Click here to close.]

◆ Click the Advisor to close the message. You will complete the necessary
adjustments in Chapter 13.

☐ **Purchase Invoice #SC-5410**

Dated May 22/02

From Swede Steel Co., to fill purchase order #20004, $2 500 plus $175 GST paid for nuts, bolts and steel rods. Invoice total $2 675. Terms: 2/15, n/30 days.

☐ **Cash Receipt #10**

Dated May 24/02

From Bayview Kindergarten Schools, cheque #1392 for $6 400 in full payment of account, including $160 discount. Reference invoice #112 and deposit #1.

☐ **Sales Quote #2004**

Dated May 26/02

Completion (Shipping) date Jun. 4/02

To Dr. Manga, $7 500 plus $525 GST charged for building play centre. Invoice total $8 025. Terms: net 1 day. (Choose Quick Add for this customer. Remember to edit the terms.)

☐ **Sales Order #2004**

Dated May 27/02

Completion (Shipping) date Jun. 4/02

From Dr. Manga, convert sales quote #2004 for $7 500 plus $525 GST charged for building play centre to a sales order. Invoice total $8 025. Terms: net 1 day.

☐ **Cash Receipt #11**

Dated May 28/02

From Dr. Manga, cheque #213 for $1 875 as a down payment (deposit #3) on accepting contract. Reference sales order #2004.

☐ **Employee Time Summary Sheet #2**

Dated May 28/02

Pay Period Ending May 28, 2002

Peter Piper worked 75 regular hours and 2 hours overtime.

Collect $50 to recover advances received. Recovered advances are entered with a minus sign in the Advance field. Issue cheque #126 for $771.74.

☐ **Memo #20**

Dated May 28, 2002

Payroll Cheque Run Time Sheet for pay period ending May 28.

Rapper worked 50 hours ar the regular hourly rate.

Doolittle should receive her normal bi-weekly salary.

Issue cheques #127 and #128 in payment.

☐ **Memo #21**

Dated May 28, 2002

Edit the Payroll Ledger for Candie Rapper. For the rest of the summer, she will work full-time (80 hours every two weeks) and will be entitled to overtime pay at the rate of $21 per hour for hours beyond 40 per week.

To edit the Payroll Ledger, return to the Home window. Click the Employees icon. Double click the icon for Rapper to open the ledger. Click the Income tab. Double click the field that needs to be changed and type the new details. (Reg. hours worked and OT 1 must be edited.)

☐ Memo #22
Dated May 28, 2002
Edit the vendor record (Payables Ledger) for Casual Contractors to include the vendor in GST reports.

☐ Purchase Invoice #CC-103
Dated May 28, 2002
From Casual Contractors, $180 plus $12.60 GST paid for two months of payroll services plus preparation of payroll summary statements. Invoice total $192.60. Terms: net 1.

☐ **Advance the Session date to May 31, 2002**

☐ Cheque Copy #129
Dated May 29, 2002
To Casual Contractors, $192.60 in full payment of account. Reference invoice #CC-103.

☐ Purchase Order #20005
Dated May 30/02
Shipping date Jun. 9/02
From The Buildex Corp., $1 500 for fibreglass and plastics and $2 000 for lumber plus $245 GST. Freight charge of $50, plus $3.50 GST added to invoice. Invoice total $3 798.50. Order is to be shipped within 10 days. Terms: 2/10, n/30 days.

☐ Sales Invoice #115
Dated May 30/02
To Broadview Daycare Centre, to fill sales order #2003, $9 000 plus $630 GST charged for completion of play centre. Invoice total $9 630. Terms: 2/10, n/30 days.

Payroll Ledger Reports

The Employee List and the Employee Summary Report were described in the previous chapter.

Payroll Journal

The Payroll Journal Report includes all transactions completed in the Payroll Journal and the Payroll Run Journal. Methods of accessing the report and the report options are similar to those of other journal reports.

You can access the Payroll Journal report both from the Home window and from the Employees window, just like the other journal reports. Refer to page 91 and substitute Payroll Journal for General Journal.

◆ Choose the **Reports** menu, then choose **Journal Entries** and click **Payroll** in the Home window to open the Report Options screen:

Again, you can list the journal report by date or by journal number, and sort and filter the journal. Both date fields show the Session date. This is correct for the Finish date. The Start date is selected for editing. We want to print the journal for May.

◆ Type **5-1**

◆ Click **OK** to see the report.

Notice that the initial paycheque for Piper, its reversing entry and the correcting entry are all included.

Drill-Down Reports

The drill-down reports available from the Payroll Journal parallel some of those for other journals. Double click the employee name, the journal entry number, the date or the invoice number to access the Employee Report. Double clicking the account number, account name or an amount will lead you to the General Ledger (All Transactions) Report for the selected account. The date range for the drill-down report will match the dates for the journal report. You may print the drill-down report. When you close the drill-down report, you will return to the previous report window. Invoice lookup is not available for the Payroll Ledger.

◆ Print the report if you want and then close the display.

Employee Reports

The Employee Summary Report includes the total amounts for all deductions from the paycheques, up to the Session date. It also includes information about wage rates, deduction rates and claim amounts.

Employee Detail Report

Sort and Filter are not available for the remaining Payroll Ledger reports.

The Employee Detail Report provides information about individual payroll entries and the details about the individual deductions from each paycheque. You can use this report to assist you with making reversing entries because it provides all the necessary details — hours worked, wages and employee deductions. You can choose which details to add to your report.

◆ Choose the **Reports** menu, then choose **Payroll** and click **Employee** in the Home window or, in the Employees window, choose the Reports menu and click Employee.

◆ Click **Detail** to expand the Report Options screen:

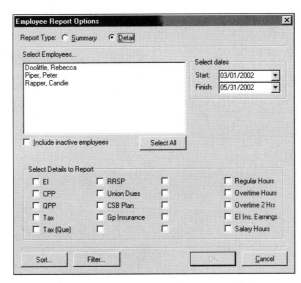

The Fiscal Start and the Session dates appear as the Start and Finish dates for the report.

◆ Select the employee for whom you want the report, or click Select All to include all employees. Press ⌐ctrl⌐ and click individual names to select more than one employee.

◆ Click each detail that you want in the report.

◆ Click **OK** to see the report.

The amount for each detail selected is given for each pay or journal entry up to the Session date. Totals for each detail and gross pay are also added to the reports.

◆ Print the report and then close the display.

Printing T4 Slips

T4 slips must be issued to all employees for income tax reporting purposes. Simply Accounting allows you to print them on the usual carbon paper preprinted forms, or using a laser printer. In either case, you should have the proper forms.

◆ Choose the **Reports** menu, then choose **Payroll** and click **Print T4 Slips** in the Home window to see the Options screen. (Or, in the Employees menu, choose the Reports menu and click Print T4 Slips.)

The Printed Summary has the totals with labels for the default deductions and any other deductions you choose to add. The T4s organize the information required to complete income tax forms in specific boxes according to the type of information.

◆ Select the employee for whom you want the T4, or click Select All to include all employees. Press ⌞ctrl⌟ and click employee names to select more than one employee.

◆ Click **Print Summary** to remove the checkmark. (Be sure that Print Employee T4s and Use Laser Printed T4s are checked.)

◆ Click **OK**.

You will now see the following screen:

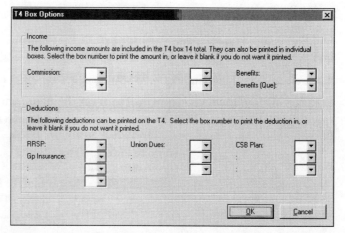

At this stage, you may designate which boxes on the form should be used to print additional or optional information. For each type of income and deduction, there is a list of box numbers to choose from. These box numbers are defined by Canada Customs and Revenue Agency, and you must follow the tax guidelines in selecting the numbers. If a deduction is not related to income tax, such as the Canada Savings Bond plan, you may omit it from the form by not selecting a box number.

◆ Click **OK** to proceed.

Printing Relevé 1 Slips

Relevé 1 Slips are comparable to T4s, but they apply only in Quebec.

◆ Choose the **Reports** menu, then choose **Payroll** and click **Print Relevé 1 Slips** in the Home window to see the options. (Or, in the Employees window, choose the Reports menu and click Print Relevé 1 Slips.)

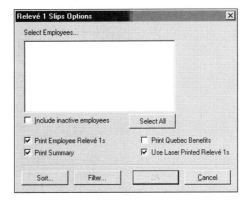

Since we have no Quebec employees, there are no names in the Select Employees box. The options are the same as those for T4s with the addition of printing Quebec benefits.

◆ Click **Cancel** to close the screen.

Printing Mailing Labels

You can prepare mailing labels for employees as you can for vendors and customers.

◆ Choose the **Reports** menu, then choose **Mailing Labels** and click **Employees** in the Home window. (Or, in the Employees window, choose the Reports menu and click Employee Labels.)

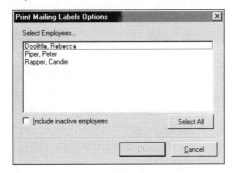

Be sure that your printer is on and has label paper loaded.

◆ Select the employee for whom you want labels, or click Select All to include all employees. Press *ctrl* and click individual names to select more than one employee.

◆ Click OK to begin printing.

Payroll Management Reports

There are management reports that deal entirely with payroll issues, just as there are reports for all the other ledgers.

◆ Choose the **Reports** menu, then choose **Management Reports** and click **Payroll** in the Home window to see the list of topics:

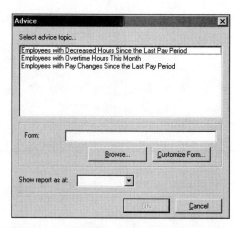

◆ Click **Employees with Overtime Hours This Month.**

◆ Click **OK**. The cursor advances to the Show report as at field. May is correct.

◆ Click **OK** again to view the report showing Piper's overtime work hours.

◆ Print the report and then close it to return to the Home window.

◆ Enter the following transactions in the appropriate ledgers and journals.

☐ Create a new group of General Ledger accounts for inventory assets as follows:
1400 INVENTORY ASSETS (H)
1420 Carousels (G)
1440 Jungle Gyms (G)
1450 Slides (G)
1460 Swings (G)
1470 Playground Kits (G)
1490 TOTAL INVENTORY ASSETS (T)

☐ Purchase Invoice #PF-1014
Dated May 31/02
From Playing Fields Inc., for inventory asset purchases as follows:

Carousels	$ 400
Jungle Gyms	400
Slides	2 200
Swings	900
Freight	100
GST Paid @ 7%	280
Invoice total	$4 280

Terms net 30 days. Use Full Add for the new vendor.

Record the purchase from Playing Fields as you recorded previous purchases. Do not use the inventory fields, but be sure to choose the correct asset accounts for the purchase. This purchase will create the historical information for the Inventory Ledger setup in Chapter 14.

☐ Playing Fields Inc. (contact: B. Gamely)
Address: 41 Parks Cres., Thornhill, ON L3H 8E9
Tel: (905) 492-9292
Fax: (905) 491-7222
Tax ID: 24365 2212
*E-mail: purbhoo.simply8@pearsoned.com
*Web site: www.pearsoned.ca/purbhoosimply8
Terms: net 30 days
Include in GST reports.

☐ Bank Debit Memo #714321
Dated May 31/02
From Royal Trust, $2 000 preauthorized withdrawal for mortgage payment. This
amount consists of $1 880 interest and $120 for reduction of principal.

☐ Memo #23
Dated May 31/02
Print the customer statement for MegaCity Parks & Rec to see the additional
interest charges accrued on the the overdue account. Prepare a sales invoice for
MegaCity Parks & Rec to charge $82.52, one month's interest on the overdue
account. Terms: net 1 day. (Credit Other Revenue.)

☐ Memo #24
Dated May 31/02
Based on the end-of-the-month count of supplies remaining, it was determined that
the following quantities of supplies were used during May. Make the necessary
adjusting entry to account for the supplies used.

Fibreglass & Plastics	$1 200
Lumber	$1 200
Hardware	$2 600
Office Supplies	$100

☐ Memo #25
Dated May 31/02
One month of prepaid insurance, $200, has expired. Recall the stored adjusting
entry to debit the Insurance Expense account for this amount.

☐ Memo #26
Dated May 31/02
One month of interest has accrued on the note payable. Although the note will not
be repaid until the end of the three-month term, the interest expense of $100 will
be recognized each month. Prepare the adjusting entry to debit Interest on Notes
Payable and credit Interest Payable. Since this entry will be required each month,
store it as a recurring monthly entry.

Memo #27

Dated May 31/02

Depreciation is calculated and recorded monthly for all depreciable assets. Recall the stored depreciation entry to record the following depreciation amounts:

Portable Computer System	$75
Machinery & Tools	$125
Shop	$250
Truck	$400
Hydraulic Drill	$150

Add a new depreciation account: 5160 Depreciation: Hydraulic Drill (G).

Add the new depreciation amount to the original journal entry. Store the revised entry and confirm that you want to overwrite the existing stored entry.

Memo #28

Dated May 31/02

Transfer $2 500 from Bank Account: Credit Card to Bank Account: Chequing.

It is not necessary to print any reports for this chapter because you will be asked to print a complete set of reports in Chapter 13 for this period as part of the preparation for closing the books.

◆ Close the data files for Play Wave.

Practice: Live Links

In this chapter, you will use all the journals in the General, Payables, Receivables and Payroll Ledgers to complete the transactions for Live Links.

Payroll Journal Entries
Instructions

1. Open the data files for Live Links.

2. Accept September 14, 2002, as the Session date.

3. Enter the following transactions using the appropriate journals. Remember to back up your work regularly.

Employee Time Summary Sheet #1

Pay Period Ending September 14, 2002

Adrian Borland worked 80 regular hours and 4 hours overtime.

Issue cheque #27.

Advance the Session date to September 28, 2002

☐ Purchase Invoice BD-9637

Dated Sep. 18/02

From Business Depot, to fill purchase order #3, $600 plus $42 GST charged and $42 PST charged for 150 rewritable CDs and ten 100-MB zip disks. Invoice total $684. Terms: net 15. Shipped by Onestep, way bill number OS-23398LL.

☐ Sales Quote #3

Dated Sep. 18/02

Completion (Shipping) Date Sep. 28/02

To West Net Inc., $5 000 plus $350 GST charged and $350 PST charged for duplication services. Invoice total $5 700. Terms: 2/10, n/30 days.

☐ Credit Card Sales Invoice #116

Dated Sep. 19/02

To Jerome Wiggles, $500, plus $35 GST charged and $35 PST charged for hard disk drive replacement and installation. Total invoice amount, $570, paid by credit card.

☐ Sales Order #3

Dated Sep. 19/02

Completion (Shipping) Date Sep. 28/02

Convert sales quote #3 for West Net Inc., to sales order #3. All amounts, terms and dates remain unchanged.

☐ Cash Receipt #8

Dated Sep. 20/02

From West Net Inc., cheque #1998 for $1 000 as deposit (#2) on accepting sales quote #3.

☐ Credit Card Purchase Invoice #46449

Dated Sep. 21/02

From Petro Partners, $160 plus $11.20 GST paid and $11.20 PST paid for vehicle maintenance services. Invoice total $182.40, paid in full by credit card.

☐ Cash Receipt #9

Dated Sep. 26/02

From Pro-Career Institute, cheque #1892 for $335 in payment of account. Reference invoice #111 and deposit #1 (cheque #1127 down payment).

☐ Sales Invoice #117

Dated Sep. 28/02

To West Net Inc., to fill sales order #3, $5 000 plus $350 GST charged and $350 PST charged for duplication services. Invoice total $5 700. Terms: 2/10, n/30 days.

☐ Cash Purchase Invoice #BCT-4119

Dated Sep. 28/02

From BC Telephone, $64 plus $4.48 GST paid and $4.48 PST paid for telephone services. Invoice total $72.96. Issue cheque #28 in full payment.

☐ Cash Purchase Invoice #BCH-4138
Dated Sep. 28/02
From BC Hydro, $50 plus $3.50 GST paid (no PST paid) for hydro services. Invoice total $53.50. Issue cheque #29 in full payment. Recall the stored monthly entry.

☐ Memo #14 (Credit Card Bill Payment)
Dated Sep. 28/02
Received monthly statement from Credit Card company for purchases up to and including September 15. Amount due is $216.60 for purchases plus $12 annual fee. Cheque #30 for $228.60 submitted in full payment.

☐ Memo #15
Dated Sep. 28/02
Helen Lively, owner, invested an additional $25 000 in the business from her personal funds. She deposited the money directly into the chequing bank account to prepare for the business expansion into the sale of computer systems.

☐ Employee Time Summary Sheet #2
Pay Period Ending September 28, 2002
Adrian Borland worked 80 regular hours and 2 hours overtime.
Issue cheque #31.

☐ **Advance the Session date to September 30, 2002**

☐ Memo #16
Dated Sep. 30/ 02
Pay salaried employee Carrie Dell for one month. Issue cheque #32.

☐ Create the following group of General Ledger asset accounts for inventory:
      1400 INVENTORY ASSETS (H)
      1420 Drives (G)
      1430 Hardware (G)
      1450 Monitors (G)
      1460 MMX System A (G)
      1470 MMX System B (G)
      1490 TOTAL INVENTORY ASSETS (T)

☐ Add the two new vendors who will supply inventory products:

CompuWorld Supplies (contact: Mitchell Dell)
1000 Zenith Heights Rd., Vancouver, BC V6T 3V2
Tel: (604) 934-7225
Fax: (604) 934-6236
Tax ID: 43624 6972
E-mail: mitchd@integra.com
Web site: www.compuworld.supplies.com
Terms: 2/10, n/30 (calculate discount after tax)
Include in GST reports.

Comtek Systems (contact: Margaret Tandy)
300 Novell Ave., Vancouver, BC V4F 2L9
Tel: (604) 462-8214
Fax: (604) 462-9186
Tax ID: 55431 8734
E-mail: mtandy@interface.com
Web site: www.computek.systems.com/resources
Terms: 2/10, n/30 (calculate discount after tax)
Include in GST reports.

Record the purchases of computer parts as you recorded previous purchases. Do not use the inventory fields, but be sure to choose the correct asset accounts in order to create the historical information for the Inventory Ledger setup.

Inventory items that are purchased for resale are exempt from PST.

☐ Purchase Invoice #CW-1471
Dated Sep. 30/02
From CompuWorld Supplies:

Drives	$ 800.00
Hardware	3 150.00
Monitors	6 800.00
GST paid	752.50
Invoice total	$11 502.50

Terms: 2/10, n/30

☐ Purchase Invoice #CS-2142
Dated Sep. 30/02
From Comtek Systems:

Drives	$2 100.00
Hardware	4 420.00
GST paid	456.40
Invoice total	$6 976.40

Terms: 2/10, n/30

☐ Memo #17
Dated Sep. 30/02
Print customer statements to determine interest charges. Prepare sales invoices for City Hall Staff for $21.40 (Invoice Memo #17A) and for Prolegal Services for $13.68 (Invoice Memo #17B) to charge one month's interest on the overdue accounts. Terms: net 1 day. (Credit Other Revenue.)

☐ Memo #18
Dated Sep. 30/02
Based on the end-of-the-month count of supplies remaining, the following quantities of supplies were used during September. Make the necessary adjusting entry to account for the supplies used.

Office Supplies	$170
Computer Supplies	$95
Memory Chips	$145

☐ Memo #19

Dated Sep. 30/02

One month of prepaid rent, $1 000, has expired. Recall the stored adjusting entry to debit the Rent Expense account for this amount.

☐ Memo #20

Dated Sep. 30/02

Recall the stored adjusting entry to recognize $50 as Interest Payable for the month of September.

☐ Memo #21

Dated Sep. 30/02

Recall the stored adjusting depreciation entry to record the depreciation amounts:

Computers & Peripherals	$150
Custom Tools	$50
Data Recovery Equipment	$200
Duplication Equipment	$100
DLP Projection Unit	$125
Motor Vehicle	$500
Laser Colour Printer	$200

☐ Memo #22

Dated Sep. 30/02

Transfer $2 000 from Bank Account: Credit Card to Bank Account: Chequing.

4. It is not necessary to print any reports for this chapter because you will be asked to print a complete set of reports in Chapter 13 for this period as part of the preparation for closing the books. Close the data files for Live Links to prepare for the closing routines for Play Wave.

Review Questions

1. How do you correct a Payroll Journal entry after you post it? a Payroll Run Journal entry?
2. How is preparing a payroll entry for salaried workers different from preparing the entry for hourly workers?
3. What fields can you edit in the Payroll Journal? in the Payroll Run Journal?
4. What do the different dates in the Payroll journals represent?
5. How are the Employee Summary and Employee Detail Reports different?
6. How can you change the amount an employee has deducted for an RRSP contribution?
7. When can you not use the Payroll Run Journal to complete an employee paycheque?

RECONCILING ACCOUNTS

Objectives

- print the General Ledger Report for a bank account
- compare bank statements with General Ledger Reports
- create linked accounts for reconciliation
- set up the account reconciliation feature
- reconcile bank statements
- mark journal transactions as cleared
- enter Account Reconciliation Journal entries
- display and print reconciliation reports

Introduction

At the end of each month, Play Wave Plus receives bank statements that must be reconciled because the statement balances do not match the balances in the Simply Accounting General Ledger Report for the bank account. Three bank statements must be reconciled for the principal bank account — the ones for March, April and May. The reconciliation is completed for one month at a time.

For this chapter, we recommend using the Data Disk file — Ch11\play\playch11.sdb — so that your amounts will match the ones we show in the screen illustrations and bank statements. You may want to complete the reconciliation again for additional practice with your own data file.

PlayWave
Plus

Account Reconciliation

For any bank account, the timing of monthly statements is usually not perfectly matched with the accounting entry for the corresponding transaction. Cheques written near the end of the month often do not appear on the statement, and interest earned on the account or bank charges are not yet recorded because they are unknown until receipt of the statement. Thus the balance on the bank statement most likely does not match the balance in the bank account. The process of identifying the differences to achieve a match is the process of account reconciliation.

Preparing for Account Reconciliation

Most bank statements include monthly bank charges, loan or mortgage payments and interest on deposits. That is, there are usually entries for income and some for expenses. Normally the only source document for these bank account transactions is the bank statement. To use Simply Accounting's account reconciliation feature, you must first create the accounts that link to these regular bank account transactions. When you examine the March bank statement for Play Wave on page 314, you will see that there is an interest deposit and a withdrawal for service charges. The business already has accounts for both of these items. In addition, you will need an account to enter adjustments related to the reconciliation. These are the accounts that will be linked to the account reconciliation process to identify the expenses and income related to the bank account.

The exact role of these accounts will be further explained as we proceed with the account reconciliation setup.

◆ Open your working copy of the data files for Play Wave with May 31 as the Session date. (Use Data Disk file **Ch11\play\playch11.sdb**.)

   ☐ Create a new Group account: 5175 Bank Reconciliation Adjustment

◆ Print the General Ledger Report for *Bank Account: Chequing* from March 15 to March 31, the period covering all transactions for the first statement to be reconciled.

Keep this report so that you can compare it with the bank statement.

◆ Make a backup of your data files before beginning the account reconciliation setup.

◆ Open your working copy of the data file.

Turning on the Account Reconciliation Feature

Before completing the reconciliation procedure, the General Ledger bank accounts required for the account reconciliation must be identified and modified.

You should be in the Home window.

◆ Right-click the **Accounts icon**.

◆ Click the **Find record tool** 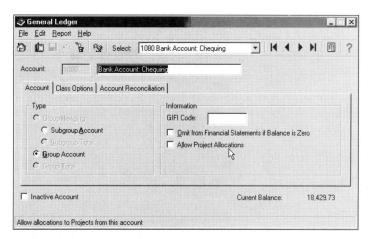 to display the Find Account screen.

◆ Click *1080 Bank Account: Chequing*.

◆ Click **Find** to open the ledger record for the account:

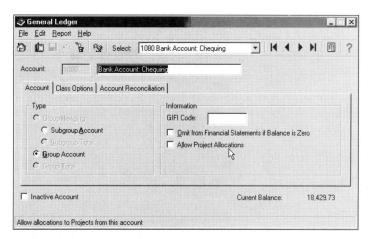

◆ Click the **Account Reconciliation tab**:

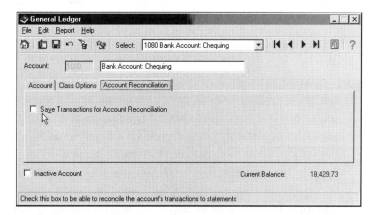

◆ Click **Save Transactions for Account Reconciliation** to display the additional option buttons shown in the following screen:

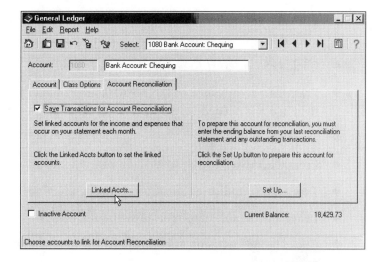

Naming and Linking Reconciliation Accounts

The next step is to identify the accounts that will be linked to the reconciliation of this bank account. Each account that you set up for reconciliation can have its own linked accounts. Therefore, they are identified in the ledger record for the account.

◆ Click **Linked Accts** to display the following screen:

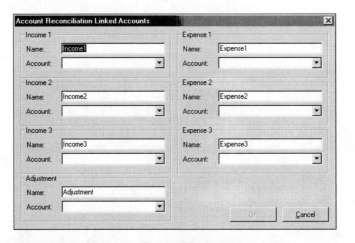

Reconciliation Linked Accounts

The fields on this screen are used to identify the appropriate General Ledger linked accounts for **income** (interest received) from bank deposits; for **expenses** associated with the account, such as service fees, NSF charges or interest paid on loans; and for **adjustments**, or small discrepancies between the accounting entries and the bank statements, such as for amounts entered incorrectly in journal transactions. You can identify up to three sources of income, three types of expenses and one adjustment account for each account that you want to reconcile. Each name may be up to 10 characters in length but you cannot leave these Name fields blank.

The first Income Name field is highlighted, ready for editing. The only source of income for this account is interest income.

◆ Type **Bank Int**

◆ Click the **Income 1 Account field arrow** to list the revenue accounts that are available.

◆ Click *4250 Interest Revenue*.

◆ Press (tab) to advance to the next Income field. This field and the third Income field are not needed, so you will indicate that they are not applicable.

◆ Type **n/a**

◆ Press (tab) twice to skip the Account field and advance to the third Income field.

◆ Type **n/a** to indicate that it too is not applicable.

◆ Leave the default name for adjustments unchanged.

◆ Click the **Adjustment Account field list arrow** to list the accounts that are available.

You can exit at any time and resume your work later. The work you have completed so far will be saved and you can begin from where you left off.

Either an expense or a revenue account can be used for adjustments because they can increase or decrease the account balance. Play Wave Plus will use the expense account created for this purpose.

◆ Click *5175 Bank Reconciliation Adjustment*.

◆ Press ⌐tab⌐ to advance to and highlight the first Expense Name field. There is one automatic expense related to the bank account, that is, bank charges.

◆ Type **Bk Charges**

◆ Click the **Expense 1 Account field list arrow** to display the list of expense accounts.

◆ Select *5170 Bank Charges* for this expense account.

◆ Press ⌐tab⌐ to advance to and highlight the second Expense Name field.

◆ Type **n/a**

◆ Press ⌐tab⌐ twice to skip the Account field and advance to the third Expense field.

◆ Type **n/a** to indicate that it is not needed.

◆ Check your work carefully. Edit the names and accounts numbers if needed.

◆ Click **OK** to save the new information and return to the *Bank Account: Chequing* account reconciliation screen.

Setting up for Reconciliation

The March General Ledger Report for *Bank Account: Chequing* is displayed here for reference, followed by the bank statement for March on page 314:

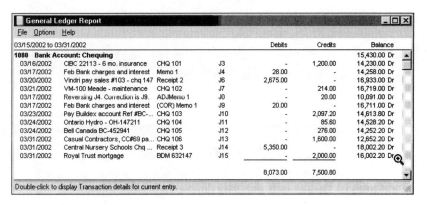

There are no account transactions for the period between March 1 and March 15, the date we started using the Simply Accounting program.

ROYAL TRUSTCO. BANK STATEMENT

2300 Yonge Street, Megacity, ON M7T 2F4

Account: Play Wave Plus
7310 Recreation Court
Megacity, ON M5E 1W6

Transit No. 06722
Account No. 45264-912
Statement Date March 31, 2002

Date	Transaction	Deposits	Withdrawals	Balance
02-28-02	**Balance Forward**			15,520.00
03-03-02	Deposit	1,000.00		16,520.00
03-15-02	CHQ #100		1,070.00	15,450.00
03-18-02	CHQ #101		1,200.00	14,250.00
03-20-02	Deposit	2,675.00		16,925.00
03-23-02	CHQ #102		214.00	16,711.00
03-25-02	CHQ #103		2,097.20	14,613.80
03-26-02	CHQ #105		276.00	14,337.80
03-27-02	CHQ #104		85.60	14,252.20
03-31-02	CHQ #106		1,600.00	12,652.20
03-31-02	Debit memo		2,000.00	10,652.20
03-31-02	Interest	37.30		10,689.50
03-31-02	Monthly fee		18.50	10,671.00
03-31-02	**Closing Balance**			**10,671.00**

Total Deposits   3,712.30
Total Withdrawals   8,561.30

Comparing the Reports

Look at the General Ledger Report you printed at the beginning of this chapter and the bank statement. You will notice these differences between them:

- The opening and closing balances are different.

- One deposit for $5 350 in the General Ledger Report on March 31 is not listed on the bank statement.

- One deposit for $1 000 and one withdrawal for $1 070 appear on the bank statement but not in the ledger report because they occurred before Play Wave began using the Simply Accounting program. These items were entered as historical transactions in the program and account for part of the difference in balances.

- Interest of $37.30 received on the deposit account does not appear in the General Ledger Report.

- Monthly bank charges of $18.50 have not been recorded in the General Ledger Report.

- The General Ledger debit on March 17 (Memo 1) and its original incorrect and adjusting entries do not appear on the bank statement. The $20 debit entry appeared on the bank statement for February and accounts for the part of the difference in opening balances.

- The sequence of the transactions differs for the two statements.

All of these items must be accounted for in order to have the bank statement match the bank balance in the General Ledger.

Correcting or reversing entries that you have made, such as the ones related to Memo 1, do not appear on the bank statement.

You should still be in the Account Reconciliation tab screen for *Bank Account: Chequing*.

◆ Click **Set Up** to display the following advisory screen:

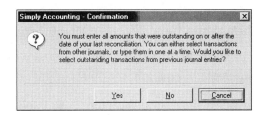

First you must enter all outstanding amounts according to the last reconciled statement. You must enter these amounts only once.

◆ Click **Yes**.

You must choose Yes in response to this advisory only the first time you open the Set Up screen. The following dialog box is displayed:

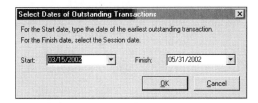

This screen asks you for the dates of the earliest and latest journal entries that have not yet been reconciled on your previous bank statement. For Play Wave, this will include all journal entries made during the months of March, April and May following the February bank statement. The default Start and Finish dates are correct, so do not change them.

◆ Click **OK** to display these outstanding transactions, as shown here:

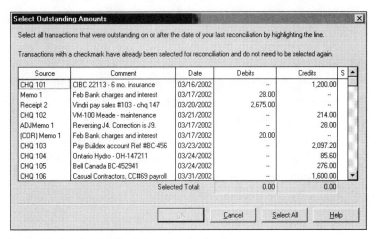

◆ Click **Select All** to select all of the journal entries.

All of the transactions are now selected or highlighted. However, one item is not outstanding, the debit entry for bank interest net of charges recorded on March 17. This journal entry was made from the February bank statement. You must deselect

If you exit after you enter all outstanding amounts, these entries will be saved. When you continue later, choose No so that you do not enter the same transactions twice. If you do enter the same transactions twice, choose the Edit menu and click Remove Line to remove the duplicate lines that should not be included.

Your screen will show the comments you added for transactions if you use your own data file. They will likely be different from the comments shown here.

this transaction. You should also deselect the incorrect and reversing entries related to this Memo.

◆ Click **(COR) Memo 1 Feb Bank charges and interest** (or your own comment or explanation for this transaction) to deselect it and remove the highlighting.

◆ Click **Memo 1** and click **ADJMemo 1** to deselect these two transactions.

This action leaves all other items selected while the ones you clicked are not selected. The unselected items are not outstanding according to the March bank statement.

◆ Click **OK** to advance to the next step and screen:

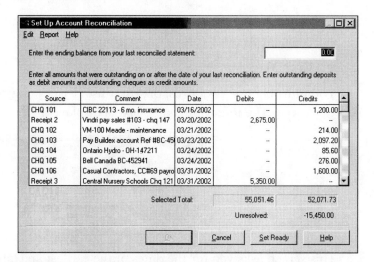

Unresolved Amount and Balances

The unresolved amount is normally the same as the opening bank balance. Calculating backwards gives us the formula: the closing General Ledger account balance less all outstanding deposits plus outstanding withdrawals equals the opening balance or last reconciled amount. Since the program has all these figures except the opening balance, this is considered the unresolved amount.

At this point you must enter the opening balance from the current bank statement as the Ending balance from your last reconciled statement. For Play Wave, this is the March 15 opening *Bank Account: Chequing* balance from the bank statement. To compare this with the March 15 General Ledger, add to the Ledger balance all withdrawals between the last statement and the starting date for Simply Accounting and subtract deposits for this period ($15 430 + $20 +1 070 – $1 000 = $15 520). Usually, if the earliest transaction date is the first of the month, all historical transactions are recorded through journal entries and the opening balance is the same as the unresolved amount.

The Last reconciled end balance field is highlighted, ready to be changed.

◆ Type **15520**

◆ Press ⌨(tab) to update the unresolved amount:

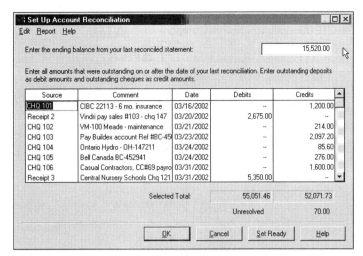

The unresolved amount is now set to $70, the difference between the deposits and the withdrawals that are not in the General Ledger. We must add these transactions manually.

◆ Click **CHQ 101** if the cursor is not on this line.

◆ Choose the **Edit menu** and click **Insert Line** as shown:

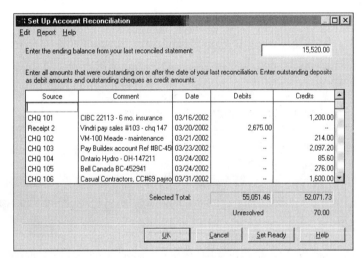

This step adds a blank line at the top of the transactions list with the cursor in the Source field. We can now add missing transactions.

◆ Type **Receipt 1**

◆ Press ⬚tab⬚ to move to the Comment field.

◆ Type **MegaCity chq #19882**

◆ Press ⬚tab⬚ to move to the Date field. You should enter the date that payment was received to replace the Session date.

◆ Type **Mar 2**

◆ Press ⬚tab⬚ to move to the Debits field.

◆ Type **1000**

These historical transactions were entered in the Payables Ledger setup, shown on page 112, and the Receivables Ledger setup, shown on page 178.

◆ Press ⌈tab⌋ to update the unresolved amount to $1 070, the amount of the historical payment. The cursor advances to the next line as shown:

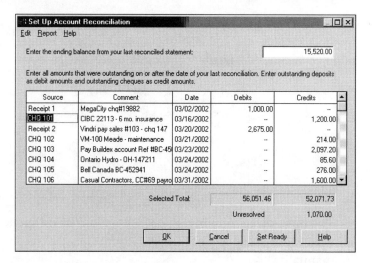

We can repeat the steps above to add the second historical transaction.

◆ Choose the **Edit menu** and click **Insert Line** to add another blank line.

◆ Type **CHQ 100** and press ⌈tab⌋ to move to the Comment field

◆ Type **Groundfos Machinery deposit** and press ⌈tab⌋ to move to the Date field.

◆ Type **Mar 13** to enter the date of the cheque and press ⌈tab⌋.

◆ Press ⌈tab⌋ again to move to the Credits field.

◆ Type **1070**

◆ Press ⌈tab⌋ to update the unresolved amount as shown:

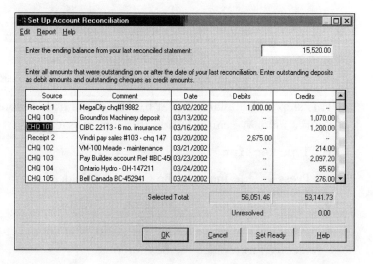

The unresolved amount is now zero. Do not set account reconciliation to Ready yet because we want to make a backup copy first.

◆ Click **OK**. This will save your changes without changing the status to Ready and return you to the *Bank Account: Chequing* Ledger window.

Setting Account Reconciliation Ready

You should make a backup copy of the data files before setting account reconciliation to Ready. In this way, you will be able to make changes later. If you made a backup before starting to set up account reconciliation, you can go back to it if you need to, but you will have to re-enter all the information in this chapter.

To make the backup, you must return to the Home window.

◆ Close the General Ledger window to return to the Home window.

◆ Make the backup.

◆ Return to the working copy of your data files if necessary.

◆ Open the General Ledger window for *Bank Account: Chequing*.

◆ Click the **Account Reconciliation tab**.

◆ Click **Set Up** to display the message about entering all outstanding amounts.

◆ Click **No** because you do not want to enter outstanding amounts again.

This should leave you where you left off, and you can proceed with setting Ready.

◆ Click **Set Ready**. A cautionary message appears on the screen:

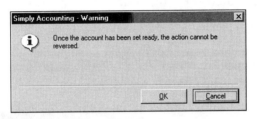

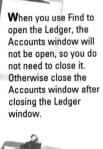

When you use Find to open the Ledger, the Accounts window will not be open, so you do not need to close it. Otherwise close the Accounts window after closing the Ledger window.

You must enter the outstanding amounts only once — the first time you choose the Set Up button and begin the setup procedures.

Warning

Simply Accounting is advising you that this step cannot be reversed. If you have not yet made a backup, click Cancel and then make the backup before proceeding.

If the unresolved amount is not zero, you can still set account reconciliation to Ready. However, the unresolved amount will be posted as an adjusting journal entry using the Adjustments linked account. The program will advise you that this step will be taken so that you can cancel the procedure and correct your work.

◆ Click **OK** to continue.

You will return to the bank account information window. The Set Up button has disappeared because the setup is complete. The Linked Accts button is still available because you can add more linked accounts later if they are needed.

◆ Close the *Bank Account: Chequing* ledger account information window to return to the Home window.

You are now ready to begin the reconciliation of the current bank statement.

The Account Reconciliation Journal

Reconciling the Bank Statement

Once you have completed the account reconciliation setup, you do not have to repeat it. To reconcile the bank statements in the following months, you can begin at this point, with the Account Reconciliation Journal entries.

The account reconciliation procedure consists of three steps to update the General Ledger. First, you record the bank statement account balance as the ending balance. Next, you identify all the deposits and withdrawals that have been processed by the bank. Finally, you must complete journal entries for any transactions for which the bank statement is the source document. All three steps are completed in the Account Reconciliation Journal. The result should be a match between the bank balances in two statements.

Accounts are reconciled in the Account Reconciliation Journal indicated with the arrow in the following screen:

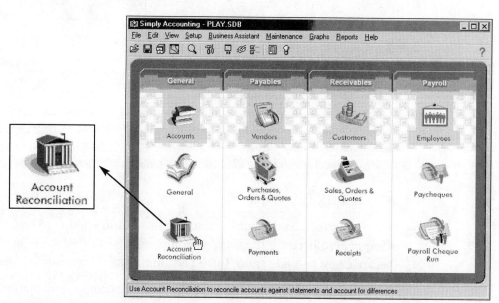

◆ Click the **Account Reconciliation Journal icon** to open the Account Reconciliation Journal entry form:

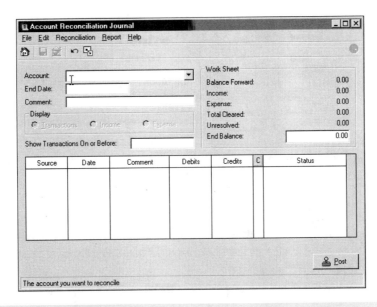

The Account Reconciliation Journal

Unlike other journals, the Account Reconciliation Journal has a **Save** tool that allows you to save your work and exit before completing the journal entry.

Two new tools, **Import Online Statements** and **Go to the financial institution's Web site**, allow direct Internet access to the bank.

Account: The account that you want to reconcile with a statement. All accounts set up for reconciliation will appear in the drop-down list. Click the Account field arrow to see the list of accounts.

End Date: The date of the account statement that you are reconciling. This will be the posting date for unresolved differences that are posted as a journal entry by the program.

Comment: A descriptive comment.

Display section: Use this area to choose the part of the reconciliation process you want to work on. The **Transactions** option allows you to mark individual journal entries as cleared. Initially, the Transactions screen is displayed. The **Income** option allows you to create journal transactions for the income sources that are identified during the setup and that are recorded on the bank statement. The **Expense** option allows you to enter journal transactions for account-related expenses that are identified during the setup and that appear on the bank statement.

Show Transactions On or Before: Allows you to limit the transactions shown by using an earlier end date. Use this option when you have statements for more than one month to reconcile.

Work Sheet section: The program completes most of the work sheet fields automatically as you enter information about transactions, income and expenses. The **Balance Forward** is the opening bank statement balance, or the last reconciled balance. The **Income** amount totals the debits to the account from income-related reconciliation journal entries, while the **Expense** amount shows the total credits to the account from expense-related journal entries. The next amount is the **Total Cleared**. This is the total amount of all transactions that you mark as cleared or already processed by the bank. After accounting for the Income, Expense and Total Cleared amounts, the Balance Forward should lead to the End Balance. If there is still a difference, it will appear in the **Unresolved** field. If the unresolved amount is zero, you have accounted for all the differences between the ledger balance and the statement. Before the program can complete its calculations, you must enter the **End Balance** from the account statement that you are reconciling. The

You cannot edit the Transactions table entries to remove or insert lines after setting Account Reconciliation Ready. If you have made a mistake, you must return to a backup from the not Ready stage.

program then uses the difference between the Balance Forward and the End Balance as the amount that must be accounted for in the Total Cleared, Income and Expense amounts.

Transactions Table: The first display area in the journal is the transactions list because Transactions is the Display option selected. Some of the columns refer to journal entry information. **Source** is the Source from the original journal entry. For cash purchases and sales (Payables and Receivables Ledgers) you have the option to use the cheque number or the invoice number as the source. You enter this choice in the Settings for System (from the Setup menu in the Home window). **Deposit No.** refers to the number from the deposit slip that you or the bank assigns when you make a deposit. If you have several cheques or cash amounts that you deposit at the same time but that were generated from separate invoices or journal entries, you can add the deposit number for all the items in the group and clear them at the same time. Deposit numbers are described later in this chapter in the Group Deposits reference information. The information for the **Date** and **Comment**, and for the amount of the **Debits** or **Credits** are all taken from the journal entry. In the final two columns, you must indicate whether the bank has cleared the transaction and what the status of the transaction is. If you mark the **C** column (**Cleared**), a checkmark appears and the amount is added to the total cleared in the work sheet. You can choose one of several different **Status** options to provide additional information about the transaction. Initially, all transactions are outstanding because you designated them as outstanding in the setup. Most of the transactions will be marked as Cleared, the basic status for items that have been processed normally by the bank. Other status options are discussed later in this chapter.

◆ Click the **Account field arrow** to display the available accounts for reconciliation.

The list displays the single bank account because it was the only one that was set up for account reconciliation.

◆ Select *1080 Bank Account: Chequing* to display the reconciliation information for this bank account:

Again, your screen will display the Source and Comment entries that you used when you completed the transactions.

The tools for Importing Online Statements and for connecting to the bank's Web site will be dimmed if you have not entered a Web address and login in the account's ledger record.

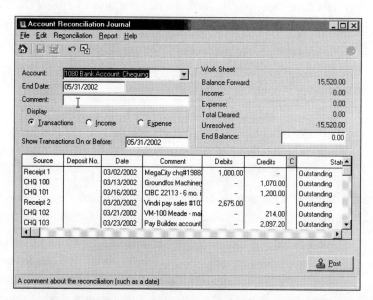

· The account is entered in the Account field and the Session date is entered automatically in the End Date field. The date is incorrect so we need to change it.

◆ Double click the **End Date field.**

◆ Type **mar 31**

◆ Press (tab) to advance to the Comment field.

◆ Type `March Bank Reconciliation`

◆ Double click the **Show Transactions On or Before date**. We will enter the bank statement date so that the entries we know are not cleared on this statement will not appear on-screen. This makes it easier to match the entries for the two statements. March 31 is the date we want.

◆ Type `3-31`

◆ Press ⌨tab⌨ to advance to and highlight the End Balance field in the Work Sheet area at the right-hand side of the screen. This field will be used for the ending bank balance as it appears on the bank statement on page 314.

◆ Type `10671`

◆ Press ⌨tab⌨ to update the Work Sheet amounts.

Marking Journal Entries as Cleared

You are now ready to begin processing individual journal entries to indicate whether they have been cleared in this bank statement. That is, the bank has processed the items and the amounts have been withdrawn from or deposited to the account. Your screen should now resemble the following:

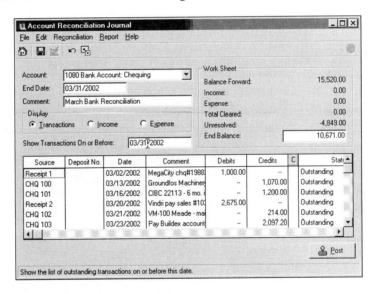

All outstanding items for the month are listed. These are the items that were left as outstanding during the setup stage. In addition, the unresolved amount has changed to reflect the new balance.

Group Deposits

Sometimes several cheques are deposited at the same time, as a group with a single deposit slip. These items will appear on the bank statement as a single entry. Each of these group deposits can also be cleared as a group. You must use the same deposit number for each deposit in the group. The Deposit No. column is used to clear these groups in the following way:

Click the Deposit No. column beside the entry for the first deposit. Type the deposit number.

Click the Deposit No. column beside the next transaction that was part of this group and type the same deposit number again. You can use the arrow keys to move up and down the column. Continue by entering the deposit number for each item of the same group in the Deposit No. column.

With one item in the group still selected, move to the C (cleared) column. Click the C at the top of the column. Your transactions list will now have a ✓ beside each item in the group in the C column and the status is changed to Cleared from Outstanding for all items in the group.

Repeat these steps for other group deposits.

You can enter the deposit numbers in the Account Reconciliation Journal at the time of the deposit and then save the information without posting until you are ready to reconcile the bank statement.

You are now ready to mark the transactions that have been cleared.

◆ Click the **C column** (Cleared) for Receipt 1 (or your own Source or Comment for this entry), the first entry on the list.

A checkmark ✓ appears in this column and the Status changes from Outstanding to Cleared. As you clear each item, the unresolved amount and the total amount cleared are updated in the Work Sheet section.

◆ Click the **C column** on the next line for the second transaction (CHQ 100 to Groundfos Machinery for $1 070) because it too has cleared.

If you clear an item by mistake, click the C column again to remove the checkmark.

◆ Continue to clear the remaining journal entries that appear on the bank statement and scroll as necessary to display additional items.

You should leave only one item as outstanding — the deposit from Central Nursery Schools that was not yet processed by the end of the month. After marking all the transactions, your Account Reconciliation Journal screen should look like the following:

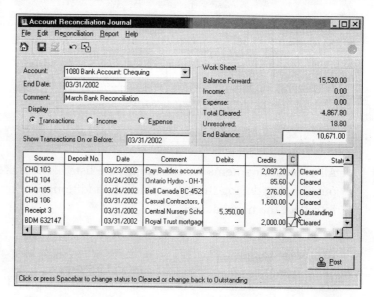

CHAPTER 11

Other Status Options

Not all bank transactions are cleared in the normal way. Sometimes there are errors and sometimes NSF cheques should be flagged. For these items, especially NSF cheques and their reversing entries, you may want to add further information. By marking their status correctly, you will have a more accurate picture of your business transactions. There are in fact six more status options that you can enter for any transaction. Double click the word Cleared in the Status column to see the list of Transaction Status options:

Cleared (C): for deposits and cheques that have been processed correctly.

Deposit Error (D): for the adjusting journal entry to account for the difference between the amount of a deposit that was recorded incorrectly and the bank statement amount for that deposit. Assign the Cleared status to the original entry for the deposit.

Payment Error (P): for the adjusting entry to account for a difference between the amount of a cheque recorded incorrectly and the bank statement amount for that cheque. Assign the Cleared status to the original entry for the cheque.

NSF (N): for customer cheques returned by the bank because there was not enough money in the customer's account. Assign the Adjustment status to the adjusting entry that reverses the NSF cheque.

Reversed (R): for the entries for cheques that are cancelled by posting reversing entries to the bank account for transactions involving cash. Assign the Adjustment status to the reversing entries that cancel the cheques.

Void (V): for the entries for cheques that are cancelled because of damage during printing. Assign the Adjustment status to the reversing entries that void the cheques.

Adjustment (A): for the adjusting or reversing entries that are made to cancel NSF, void or reversed cheques. (See the explanations for NSF, Reversed and Void above.)

Marking NSF Cheques

This section describes the procedure for clearing transactions that are different in some way, like NSF cheques. Read the following section. You will use it to mark the NSF cheques in the bank reconciliation for April.

To mark a cheque as NSF:

* Click the word Cleared in the Status column for the NSF cheque (the original entry for the cheque).

* Press *(enter)* to display the alternatives available for the Status of a journal entry.

* Click NSF to highlight this alternative.

* Click Select to enter it. The word Cleared changes to NSF for this item.

* Change the status of the journal entry that reverses the receipt entry to Adjustment.

* Enter Cleared as the status for the customer's cheque after the payment is properly cleared by the bank.

Adding Bank Statement Journal Entries

We recorded bank account interest and charges in the General Journal in the previous chapter because the Account Reconciliation Journal was not ready.

At this stage, the unresolved amount is still not zero; we have not accounted for all the differences between the General Ledger entries and the statement. We still must record the information for the interest received and for the bank charges. These journal entries are recorded in the Account Reconciliation Journal because they are part of the bank statement.

◆ Click **Income** in the list in the Display portion (above the transactions).

As shown here, a journal entry form now replaces the transactions portion of the Account Reconciliation Journal for entering the income transaction:

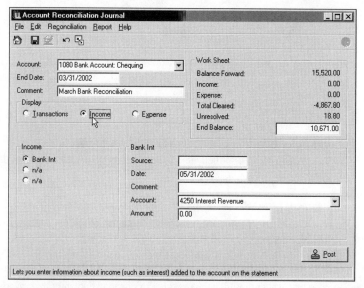

You can enter only one transaction for each type of income and expense. If there is more than one type of charge on a bank statement, such as regular monthly service fees and NSF cheque charges, you may combine all the amounts to create one journal entry, or create separate types of income or expense categories to record the different types of transactions. You can create three types of income and expense categories for each account. You may use the same linked account for more than one category.

Bank Int, the income source we named earlier, is selected in the Income group list.

◆ Click the **Source field** in the lower right-hand journal portion of the screen to advance the cursor.

◆ Type **Mar Bk-Stmt**

◆ Press (tab) to highlight the Session date.

◆ Type **3-31**

◆ Press (tab) to advance to the Comment field.

◆ Type **Interest earned on bank deposits**

◆ Press (tab) twice to skip over the correctly entered Account number. If necessary, you can select a different account for the transaction. The cursor advances to the Amount field. The field is highlighted, ready for editing. Check the bank statement for the correct amount.

◆ Type **37.30**

◆ Press (tab).

The unresolved amount has changed again. It is now –18.50, the amount of the bank charges. The income has also been added to the Income field in the Work Sheet portion of the screen.

◆ Choose the **Report** menu and click **Display Account Reconciliation Journal Entry**. If you were to post the entry at this intermediate stage, the program would make an adjustment for the unresolved amount by debiting the *Bank Reconciliation Adjustments* expense account and crediting *Bank Account: Chequing*.

◆ Close the display to continue.

If there are other income categories, click the income name in the Income group list to the left of the journal information. A new journal form will appear for this income.

◆ Click **Expense** in the Display portion of the window.

The expense Bk Charges is selected on the left-hand side of the screen and its journal form appears on the right-hand side.

◆ Click the **Source field** in the journal portion of the screen.

◆ Type **Mar Bk-Stmt**

◆ Press `tab`.

◆ Type **3 31**

◆ Press `tab` to advance to the Comment field.

◆ Type **Bank charges and service fee**

◆ Press `tab` twice to skip over the correctly entered account number and advance to the Amount field. The bank statement contains the amount for this expense.

◆ Type **18.50**

If there are other expense categories, click the expense name in the list to the left of the journal information. A new journal form will appear for this expense.

The Expense field in the Work Sheet is updated again as shown here:

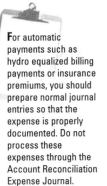

For automatic payments such as hydro equalized billing payments or insurance premiums, you should prepare normal journal entries so that the expense is properly documented. Do not process these expenses through the Account Reconciliation Expense Journal.

For one-time expense or income transactions, you may use one of the undefined categories to prepare a journal entry. In this case you must choose an account from the drop-down list in the Account field for the journal entry. This allows you to separate the unusual entries from the regular ones. NSF charges would be an example of this kind of expense.

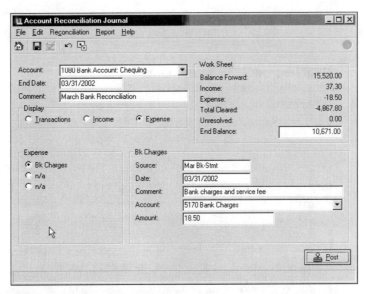

At this stage, the unresolved amount should be zero if everything is correct. If the unreconciled amount is not zero, check your journal entries to see whether you have made an error. Click each option in the Display box to show your work for the corresponding part of the reconciliation procedure. Make corrections if necessary.

You should also review the reconciliation journal entry before proceeding.

◆ Choose the **Report** menu and click **Display Account Reconciliation Journal Entry**. Your journal entry should appear as follows:

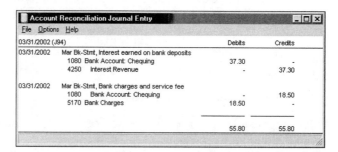

The income and expense journal entries are listed using the linked accounts that were designated for *Bank Account: Chequing*. In addition, an adjustment entry will be displayed if there is any unresolved amount.

◆ Close the report window when you have finished.

Adjustments

If you have made an error and the unresolved amount is not zero, the program will post the difference to the linked adjustment account you identified during the setup stage, or you can choose another postable account. The amount may be a credit or a debit, depending on the sign of the discrepancy. Before posting the adjustment, the program will warn you so that you can correct your mistakes. Only small amounts should be posted as adjustments of this sort. Large differences should be tracked and recorded with a proper journal entry and explanation. An example of the type of adjustment you might accept in this simulation is the difference that you may have in payroll cheques as a result of using a different version of the program with different income tax tables and amounts. These differences should be small.

If you cannot find the error immediately, save your work and return to it later. All the entries you have made in the journal can still be edited as long as you have not posted.

Handling Unresolved Amounts

Unresolved amounts will be posted as an adjustment to the linked reconciliation adjustments expense account you created earlier. Since this account should be used only for small amounts not significant enough to warrant a separate journal entry, you should try to correct the error first.

Double check that you have cleared all the items that should be cleared and that outstanding items are not cleared. Check your journal entries for errors in amounts. Also check that the amounts in your ledger statement match the amounts for the corresponding items in the bank statement. Was the error one you made or is the bank statement amount incorrect? If the bank made an error, contact the bank and notify them of the problem.

If you have an unresolved amount, you can save your work and try to sort out the details later. For work like this, it is sometimes easier to find mistakes after taking a short break.

Click the Save button. Close the Account Reconciliation Journal to return to the Home window.

Make a backup copy. Return to your working copy of the data file if necessary.

Open the Account Reconciliation Journal. The work will be displayed as you left it. You can now make the necessary corrections.

If your unresolved amount is zero, or you have identified the error and want to accept the adjustment entry,

◆ Click Post 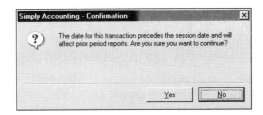 .

The program provides another warning message:

Since the month of the transaction precedes the month of the Session date, the program cautions you that the earlier reports will be affected by posting this transaction.

◆ Click **Yes** to proceed with posting the transaction.

The program will warn you before posting an unresolved amount, giving you an opportunity to correct any mistakes you may have made before posting the journal entries.

A blank Account Reconciliation Journal form appears. You can now complete the account reconciliation for April.

◆ Close the Account Reconciliation Journal to return to the Home window if you want to end your work session now.

◆ Complete the reconciliation for April and May using the Account Reconciliation Journal beginning with the instructions on page 320. You do not need to complete the setup again.

   ☐ Reconcile the bank statement for the month of April. Print the General Ledger for Bank Account: Chequing from April 1 to April 30.

     Remember to mark the first deposit for Nirvana Nursery School as NSF and the reversing entry (withdrawal of the cheque) as Adjustment. (First mark these items as cleared, then double click the word Cleared to access the list of Status Options and select the new status. Refer to page 325.)

     To record the NSF service charges, you can add the $20 charge to the other bank charges and process a single entry. Alternatively, you can record the NSF charges as a separate expense entry, choosing one of the N/A categories and including a separate comment. Choose Bank Charges as the expense account from the drop-down list in the Account field. Separating the two charges will create two journal entries with identifying comments, making it easier to track the different expenses.

ROYAL TRUSTCO. BANK STATEMENT

2300 Yonge Street, Megacity, ON M7T 2F4

Account: Play Wave Plus
7310 Recreation Court
Megacity, ON M5E 1W6

Transit No. 06722
Account No. 45264-912
Statement Date April 30, 2002

Date	Transaction	Deposits	Withdrawals	Balance
03-31-02	**Balance Forward**			10,671.00
04-01-02	Deposit	5,350.00		16,021.00
04-04-02	CHQ #107		3,170.00	12,851.00
04-10-02	CHQ #108		214.00	12,637.00
04-10-02	CHQ #110		535.00	12,102.00
04-09-02	Deposit	1,070.00		13,172.00
04-09-02	Deposit	3,210.00		16,382.00
04-15-02	CHQ #109		615.60	15,766.40
04-15-02	CHQ #111		3,187.74	12,578.66
04-15-02	CHQ #113		69.00	12,509.66
04-15-02	CHQ #112		107.00	12,402.66
04-18-02	Debit memo (NSF)		3,210.00	9,192.66
04-18-02	Debit memo - NSF charge		20.00	9,172.66
04-20-02	Deposit	3,230.00		12,402.66
04-25-02	CHQ #114		2,097.20	10,305.46
04-30-02	Debit memo		2,000.00	8,305.46
04-30-02	Interest	30.00		8,335.46
04-30-02	Monthly fee		18.50	8,316.96
04-30-02	**Closing Balance**			**8,316.96**

Total Deposits   12,890.00
Total Withdrawals   15,244.04

☐ May Bank Statement
Dated May 31/02
Reconcile the bank statement for May. Print the General Ledger for Bank Account:
Chequing from May 1 to May 31.

Remember to edit the End Date and the Show Transactions On or Before date to
May 31. If your payroll cheque amounts are different from the ones shown here
because you have different tax tables, mark the cheques as cleared and accept the
difference as a reconciliation adjustment. These differences should not be larger
than a few dollars.

Mark the first paycheque to Piper as Reversed and mark its reversing entry as
Adjustment. Refer to page 325.

ROYAL TRUSTCO. BANK STATEMENT

2300 Yonge Street, Megacity, ON M7T 2F4

Account: Play Wave Plus
7310 Recreation Court
Megacity, ON M5E 1W6

Transit No. 06722
Account No. 45264-912
Statement Date May 31, 2002

There is one group deposit for May 1. Two cheques for $2 000 and $12 000 were deposited together.

Date	Transaction	Deposits	Withdrawals	Balance
04-30-02	**Balance Forward**			8,316.96
05-02-02	CHQ #115		2,000.00	6,316.96
05-01-02	Deposit	14,000.00		20,316.96
05-07-02	Deposit	10,500.00		30,816.96
05-09-02	CHQ #116		214.00	30,602.96
05-09-02	Deposit	1,050.00		31,652.96
05-10-02	CHQ #117		12,600.00	19,052.96
05-10-02	CHQ #118		5,284.94	13,768.02
05-15-02	CHQ #119		245.05	13,522.97
05-15-02	CHQ #121		1,122.17	12,400.80
05-15-02	CHQ #122		511.33	11,889.47
05-16-02	CHQ #120		1,000.61	10,888.86
05-19-02	CHQ #125		92.00	10,796.86
05-20-02	Deposit	2,250.00		13,046.86
05-20-02	CHQ #123		638.40	12,408.46
05-20-02	CHQ #124		96.30	12,312.16
05-25-02	Deposit	6,400.00		18,712.16
05-29-02	Deposit	1,875.00		20,587.16
05-31-02	Debit memo		2,000.00	18,587.16
	Interest	40.00		18,627.16
	Monthly fee		18.50	18,608.66
05-31-02	**Closing Balance**			**18,608.66**

Total Deposits		**36,115.00**		
Total Withdrawals			**25,823.30**	

Reconciling the Credit Card Bank Account

Reconciling other bank accounts involves the same procedures as reconciling chequing accounts. No additional historical transactions need to be included.

◆ Make a backup copy of the data files.

◆ Print the General Ledger for account *1090 Bank Account: Credit Card* from May 1 to May 31.

◆ Set up the credit card account for reconciliation.
• Edit the account to save transactions for account reconciliation.
• Use the same linked account names and account numbers as for the chequing account. (Refer to pages 312–313.)

- Use the bank statement that follows to complete the remaining setup. All amounts are outstanding.
- The last reconciled balance is zero, the opening bank account balance.

◆ Make another backup copy and then set Account Reconciliation Ready. (Remember to respond No when prompted about entering outstanding amounts the second time.)

◆ Reconcile the account using the following statement.

ROYAL TRUSTCO. BANK STATEMENT

2300 Yonge Street, Megacity, ON M7T 2F4

Account: Play Wave Plus
7310 Recreation Court
Megacity, ON M5E 1W6

Transit No. 06722
Account No. 37662-771
Statement Date May 31, 2002

Date	Transaction	Deposits	Withdrawals	Balance
04-30-02	**Balance Forward**			0.00
05-02-02	Deposit	567.45		567.45
05-04-02	Deposit	378.30		945.75
05-09-02	Deposit	756.60		1,702.35
05-15-02	Deposit	756.60		2,458.95
05-20-02	Deposit	189.15		2,648.10
05-31-02	**Closing Balance**			**2,648.10**

Total Deposits 2,648.10
Total Withdrawals 0.00

Account Reconciliation Reports
Account Reconciliation Journal

◆ Right-click the **Account Reconciliation icon** to select it.

◆ Click the **Display Account Reconciliation Journal tool** 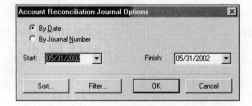 in the Home window. You will see the Report Options screen:

The journal can be prepared according to journal entry numbers or date. Like other journals, it may be sorted and filtered. By default, the report uses posting dates.

◆ Type **Mar 15** as the Start date and type **May 31** as the Finish date for the report to include all three bank statement periods.

 CHAPTER 11

◆ Click **OK**.

Drill-Down Reports

If you double click the date, journal entry number or comment, you will display the Customer Aged, Vendor Aged or Employee Summary Report if a customer, vendor or employee name is selected and if the report is available. When you double click an account name, number or amount, you will see the General Ledger (All Transactions) Report for the selected account.

◆ Print the report and then close the display when you have finished.

Account Reconciliation Status Report

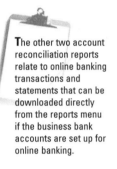

The other two account reconciliation reports relate to online banking transactions and statements that can be downloaded directly from the reports menu if the business bank accounts are set up for online banking.

◆ Choose the **Reports** menu, then choose **Account Reconciliation** and click **Account Reconciliation Status Report** to display the following Report Options:

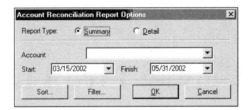

◆ Enter the chequing bank account number in the Account field or click the list arrow and choose it from the list.

◆ Click **Detail**. A list of Status categories is added:

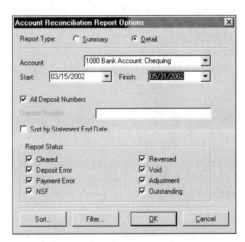

◆ Choose the Status categories to include in your reports. By default, all are included. Clicking a category will remove the ✓ from the check box and omit this category from your report.

The Detail Report lists all the bank account's journal entries with their status.

◆ Click **Summary**. The status list is removed.

◆ Type March 15 and May 31 as the Start and Finish dates if these do not appear, or choose them from the date field lists.

◆ Click **OK** to display the report.

The Summary Report provides totals for each type of Status, totals for income and expense categories and outstanding amounts that will reconcile the bank statement with the General Ledger account balance.

Drill-Down Reports

There are no drill-down reports available from the Account Reconciliation Summary Report.

From the Detail Report, you can double click the date or journal entry number to see the transaction details (journal entry) for the line. Double clicking the comment will lead to the Customer Aged, Vendor Aged or Employee Summary Report, if a customer, vendor or employee name is selected and if the report is available.

◆ Print the report and then close the displayed report when you have finished.

◆ Close the Play Wave file so you can complete the bank reconciliation for Live Links.

Practice: Live Links

After three month of transactions, Lively is ready to reconcile the bank account statements for July, August and September.

Account Reconciliation

Instructions

For this chapter, we recommend using the Data Disk file — Ch11\links\linkch11.sdb — so that your amounts will match the ones we show in the screen illustrations and bank statements. You may want to complete the reconciliation again for additional practice with your own data file.

1. Open the data file for Live Links and accept September 30 as the Session date.

2. Create new accounts:

   5025 Bank Reconciliation Adjustments (G)
   4240 Revenue from Interest (G)

3. Print the General Ledger for *1080 Bank Account: Chequing* from July 8 to July 31.

4. Make a backup copy of your files.

5. Edit account *1080 Bank Account: Chequing* to save transactions for account reconciliation.

6. Enter the linked accounts and the Names as follows:

   Income 1: Interest *4240 Revenue from Interest*

   Expense 1: Charges *5020 Bank Charges*

   Adjustment: Adjustment *5025 Bank Reconciliation Adjustments*

   Edit the names for Income 2, Income 3, Expense 2 and Expense 3 to N/A.

7. Set up the account reconciliation using the July bank statement together with the General Ledger report for *1080 Bank Account: Chequing* from July 8 to July 31. Make another backup before setting Account Reconciliation Ready.

   Accept all amounts from July 8 to September 30 as outstanding except the bank charges of $20 that applied to June and were not outstanding on July 1.

   The last reconciled balance on July 1, 2002, was $8 380. No historical transactions are missing from the General Ledger, so the last reconciled balance is the same as the initial unresolved amount.

8. Using the Account Reconciliation Journal, reconcile the bank statement for July.

Remember to edit the bank statement End Date and the date for Show Transactions On or Before.

LEARNX BANK STATEMENT   Pacific Heights Branch
                                 400 Pacific Blvd.,Vancouver, BC V7R 3W2

Account 554-66112   July 31, 2002

Date	Transaction	Deposits	Withdrawals	Balance
06-30-02	**Balance Forward**			8,380.00
07-09-02	CHQ #10		6,420.00	1,960.00
07-10-02	Credit memo	6,000.00		7,960.00
07-11-02	Deposit	1,605.00		9,565.00
07-14-02	CHQ #11		5,136.00	4,429.00
07-17-02	Deposit	1,140.00		5,569.00
	CHQ #13		100.00	5,469.00
07-21-02	CHQ #14		114.00	5,355.00
07-27-02	Deposit	2,280.00		7,635.00
07-28-02	Deposit	1,605.00		9,240.00
07-30-02	CHQ #15		68.40	9,171.60
	Debit memo		3,042.80	6,128.80
	Interest	15.00		6,143.80
	Monthly fee		20.00	6,123.80
07-31-02	**Closing Balance**			**6,123.80**

Total Deposits   12,645.00
Total Withdrawals   14,901.20

Account holder: Live Links
                       20300 Silicon Valley Rd. North
                       Burnaby, BC V5B 3A2

9. Complete the bank reconciliation for the chequing account for the months of August and September.

☐ Bank Statement
Dated Aug. 31/02
Print the General Ledger for August 1 to August 31.
Reconcile the following bank statement for August 31.

Mark the initial deposit for $1 117.20 as NSF, mark its reversing entry as Adjustment and the final deposit as Cleared. Remember to create an expense entry for the NSF charges. Refer to pages 325 and 326.

LEARNX BANK STATEMENT   Pacific Heights Branch
                                             400 Pacific Blvd., Vancouver, BC V7R 3W2

Account 554-66112   August 31, 2002

Date	Transaction	Deposits	Withdrawals	Balance
07-31-02	**Balance Forward**			6,123.80
08-02-02	CHQ #17		91.20	6,032.60
	CHQ #16		228.00	5,804.60
08-03-02	CHQ #18		53.50	5,751.10
08-05-02	CHQ #19		1,070.00	4,681.10
08-07-02	Deposit	10,000.00		14,681.10
08-10-02	Deposit	428.00		15,109.10
	CHQ #20		500.00	14,609.10
	CHQ #21		7,906.44	6,702.66
08-15-02	Deposit	1,117.20		7,819.86
	Debit memo (NSF)		1,117.20	6,702.66
	NSF Transaction fee		20.00	6,682.66
	CHQ #22		203.07	6,479.59
08-20-02	Deposit	1,160.00		7,639.59
08-27-02	CHQ #23		102.60	7,536.99
08-30-02	CHQ #25		53.50	7,483.49
08-30-02	Debit memo		3,042.80	4,440.69
	Interest	18.00		4,458.69
	Monthly fee		20.00	4,438.69
08-31-02	**Closing Balance**			**4,438.69**

Total Deposits   12,723.20
Total Withdrawals   14,408.31

Account holder: Live Links
                        20300 Silicon Valley Rd. North
                        Burnaby, BC V5B 3A2

☐ Bank Statement
Dated Sep. 30/02
Print the General Ledger for September 1 to September 30.
Reconcile the following bank statement for September 30.

10. Print the Account Reconciliation Journal and Summary Reports. Close the data files for Live Links to prepare for viewing the graphs for Play Wave.

Review Questions

1. How would you enter fixed mortgage payments in the Account Reconciliation Journal? What adjustments would you need to make at the end of the fiscal period?
2. How would you set up account reconciliation to use it for credit card accounts?
3. How could you enter fixed auto lease payments in the Account Reconciliation Journal? How else could you enter these payments? Which method is preferred?
4. What advantages are there to entering bank account transactions in the Account Reconciliation Journal compared with entering them in the General Journal?
5. What difference does it make whether you mark NSF cheques as Cleared or as NSF?
6. What entries appear in the Account Reconciliation Journal Report?
7. What safeguards are added to account reconciliation to help avoid mistakes during setup and in journal entries?
8. In addition to bank accounts, which accounts might you apply account reconciliation to? What information would appear on the statements for these accounts and how would you set them up for reconciliation?

GRAPHS

Objectives

- *display and print graphs*
- *customize the appearance of graphs*
- *understand the role and interpretation of graphs*

Introduction

The Simply Accounting program includes a variety of graphs that help you to analyze the performance of a business. Graphs are reports in a visual form. In addition to providing useful information for analysis, graphs can dramatically increase the effectiveness and impact of a written report or presentation when they are printed in colour.

There are no journal entries in this chapter.

If you have not completed the journal entries in Chapter 11 and want to display the graphs in Chapter 12, you can use your copy of the Data Disk file — Ch12\play\playch12.sdb — to complete this chapter.

Graphs

Instead of exporting data to a spreadsheet and then creating a graph, you can prepare graphs within the Simply Accounting program. Since the graphs are prepared directly from the data for the business, they are always current. For most graphs, the ability to change the report period provides even more flexibility. Furthermore, you can customize the graph in a number of ways — change its appearance, edit titles and export the graph as a bitmap file or export the graph data to other programs as text.

In addition to basic graphs showing payables and receivables information separately, other graphs show comparisons of payables and receivables information. Expense and revenue information is also available in graph format, both separately and together to show net profits. When the budgeting feature is used, there are graphs that show performance against budgets.

All graphs are displayed from the Home window.

Payables by Aging Period

The first graph provides the breakdown of payables according to the aging periods selected in the Payables Settings.

◆ Open the data files for Play Wave. The Session date is May 31 and you should be in the Home window.

◆ Choose the **Graphs** menu and click **Payables by Aging Period** to see the date window:

◆ Click **OK** to accept the date and to display the pie chart graph:

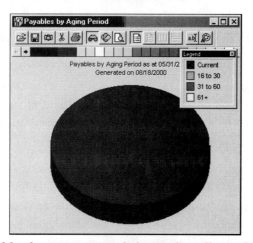

The pie chart for Payables by Aging Period shows that all payables accounts are current, due within the first period of 15 days. Generally, each section of the pie chart shows one aging period as defined in the Payables Settings.

You can still export other data from Simply Accounting to create customized graphs using other software programs. Exporting from Simply Accounting is explained in Appendix F.

Customizing the Graph

There is no menu bar for charts. All customization is handled through the tools. When you hold the mouse over a tool, the label for the tool appears. Right-click on any tool to see its function or label. The label will remain on-screen until you release the mouse. The tools are the same for all graphs, although some are used only for bar charts. These tools will be dimmed on the pie chart graphs.

The **tool buttons for graphs** provide a number of ways to customize or manipulate the format of the graph. Some of the tools lead to a second control or options screen for inputting specific details.

Import a chart from another program into Simply Accounting. Opens the Import Chart screen.

Export the chart displayed on-screen for use by another program. Opens the Export Chart screen.

Copy the chart on display to the clipboard as a bitmap file (graphics format). When you open the receiving graphics program, you can paste the graph.

Copy data from the chart to the clipboard as text for use in another software program.

Print the chart.

Switch between 3D and 2D views of the chart. The default setting is the 3D view. The tool operates like a toggle switch, changing back and forth between the two views.

Rotate the chart. Indicate the number of degrees of rotation for the X and Y axes in the options screen that opens when you click the tool.

Zoom.

Show or hide the legend. The tool operates as a toggle switch, changing back and forth between the two settings. The default setting shows the legend.

Show or hide the series legend showing the colour key for accounts or periods. Show is the default setting. The tool operates as a toggle switch, changing back and forth between the two settings.

Vertical grid adds vertical lines to the bar chart at each X-axis label. This option is not available for pie charts. The tool is like a toggle switch. The default setting omits the grid.

Horizontal grid adds horizontal grid lines to the bar chart at each Y-axis label. This option is not available for pie charts. The default setting omits the grid, and the tool acts as a toggle switch.

Edit the titles for the chart. You can edit the titles for all charts and the axis labels for bar graphs.

Change the font for the text in labels. You can choose the font for each label separately.

Use the **colour bar** to change the colours of any part of the chart, including the background and legend. To change a colour, just drag a colour from the bar to the area you want to "paint." When you double click any colour in the colour palette, you will see an expanded colour chart that includes the choice of adding custom colours.

The **legend** for the chart shows the key to interpreting the chart by linking a chart colour with an account or period. You can modify the legend on any chart. The default size for the legend is a small window that can include only a small part of an account list. You can extend the size of the legend by dragging its borders to the new size or you can reposition the legend by dragging the legend's title bar to the desired location. Double clicking the legend will expand its length, but not its width, to cover the entire length of the chart window. Account names appear with the numbers and colour keys in the expanded legend. Double click the legend again to restore its original size. When you right-click on the legend, you can choose the position for the legend from a menu list of options. And finally, you can close the Legend window like any other window.

◆ Double click the main section of the pie. A bubble appears with the period, the amount and the percentage of the total that is represented by this section of the chart.

To print this graph or any other graph, click the Print tool .

◆ Close the display when you have finished.

Payables by Vendor

The Payables by Vendor pie chart shows the proportion of outstanding payables for each vendor selected for inclusion in the chart. From this chart, you can determine whether you owe a larger share of the payables to any one vendor over the others.

◆ Choose the **Graphs** menu and click **Payables by Vendor** in the Home window to display the chart options:

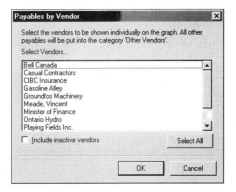

You can choose to include one or more vendors in the chart. Any amounts owing to vendors not selected will be combined into a category labelled "Vendors." Vendors with no accounts outstanding are not part of the chart.

◆ Click **Select All** to include all vendors to whom Play Wave owes money.

◆ Click **OK** to display the pie chart:

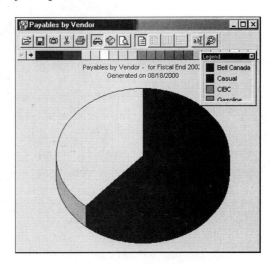

The fact that the graph is divided into two sections shows that Play Wave currently owes money to two vendors We know from the previous graph that both accounts are current.

◆ Double click the smaller portion of the pie. The bubble details inform us that this sector is the account with Swede Steel that accounts for 38 percent of the total owing.

◆ Close the display when you have finished.

Receivables by Aging Period

This graph is the customer equivalent of the Payables by Aging Period graph and shows the aging of receivables accounts in pie chart form according to the aging periods selected in the Receivables Settings. Customer deposits are included in this graph, too.

◆ Choose the **Graphs** menu and click **Receivables by Aging Period**:

◆ Click **OK** to accept the date and to display the chart:

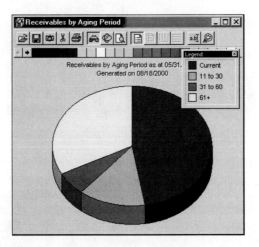

At present the receivables are divided into four periods, current (less than 11 days), 11 to 30 days, 31 to 60 days and overdue at more than 61 days. When you double click a section of the pie, you will see the period for that sector, the dollar amount and the percentage of the total receivables. When you click a pie sector and drag it away from the chart, that sector separates from the rest of the chart and the chart becomes smaller. Double clicking the sector for 61+ days shows that 45 percent of the total receivables amount is significantly overdue. The delinquent customer, MegaCity Parks & Rec, should be contacted.

◆ Close the display when finished.

Receivables by Customer

Again, this graph parallels the Payables by Vendor graph. Each selected customer with outstanding accounts will be included in the chart. Customer deposits are not included in this graph.

◆ Choose the **Graphs** menu and click **Receivables by Customer** in the Home window to display the chart options:

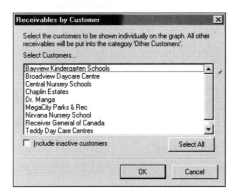

You can choose to include one or more or all customers in the graph. Only customers with outstanding balances will actually be included in the graph, and non-selected customers are combined into a category labelled "Customers."

◆ Click **Select All** to include all customers with outstanding balances.

◆ Click **OK** to display the pie chart:

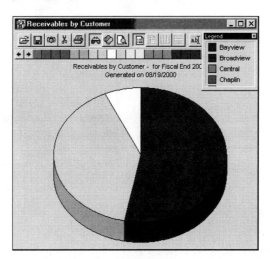

Three customers account for all of the receivables at present. The fourth customer with an outstanding receivable has a negative balance (deposit) and is omitted from the graph. The smallest sector represents the GST refund. When you double click a sector, you will see the customer's name, the dollar amount owing and the percentage of the total receivables that customer's account represents.

◆ Close the display when you have finished.

Sales vs Receivables

This graph compares the amounts in the *Accounts Receivable* account and revenue accounts on a monthly basis for the selected revenue accounts.

◆ Choose the **Graphs** menu and click **Sales vs Receivables** in the Home window to display the chart options:

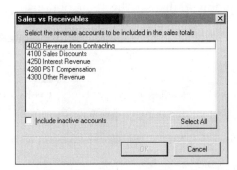

You can choose one or more revenue accounts to form the basis for comparison with the receivables category.

◆ Click **Select All** to include all the revenue accounts.

◆ Click **OK** to display the chart:

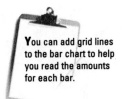

You can add grid lines to the bar chart to help you read the amounts for each bar.

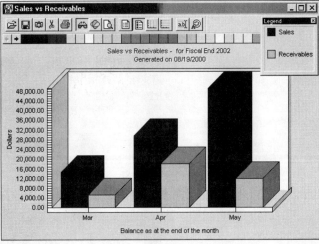

This bar chart shows the total *Accounts Receivable* balance at the end of each month and the total revenue for the same month. Using this graph can aid in deciding whether the payment terms for customers are appropriate and whether accounts are paid in a timely fashion. The dollar amounts are provided on the Y-axis and the months are shown on the X-axis. The increase in sales relative to receivables in May shows the influence of accepting credit card payments.

◆ Close the display when finished.

Receivables Due vs Payables Due

This chart can be a useful part of the cash management control system by comparing the amounts owed with receipts expected from customers.

◆ Choose the **Graphs** menu and click **Receivables Due vs Payables Due** in the Home window to display the chart options:

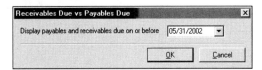

For this chart, you can indicate the term you want to show in the graph. By default, the Session date is provided.

◆ Type **Jun 30** to replace the date and include all accounts due in the next month.

◆ Click **OK** to display the chart:

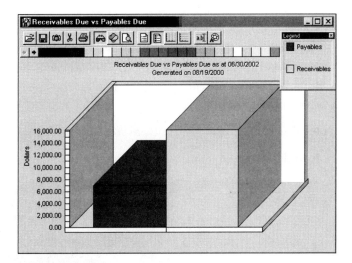

This bar chart may be useful in identifying potential cash flow problems based on current commitments. For example, the chart will show whether the money owed to vendors exceeds the amount coming in from customers. This chart can be used to supplement the Cash Flow Projection Report (Chapter 13). At present no problems are indicated since the payment obligations are substantially less than the expected receivables.

◆ Close the display when finished.

Revenues by Account

This graph provides a pictorial breakdown of the different sources of revenue.

◆ Choose the **Graphs** menu and click **Revenues by Account** in the Home window to display the chart options:

You can choose one or more revenue accounts to include in the graph or you can include them all. You can also choose the period for the report. By default, the Fiscal Start and the Session date are provided as the Start and Finish dates. We will use the default dates to provide a graph covering the entire fiscal period and include all the revenue accounts.

◆ Click **Select All** to include all revenue accounts.

◆ Click **OK** to display the pie chart:

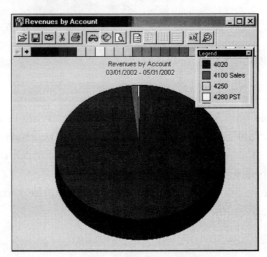

At present, by far the largest source of revenue, as expected, is the contracting revenue. Other sources contribute less than 1 percent of the total. When inventory sales are added in June, they should provide a second significant source of revenue.

◆ Close the display when finished.

Expenses by Account

This graph provides the expenses equivalent of the previous graph. It shows how expenses are broken down as a percentage of the total expenses.

◆ Choose the **Graphs** menu and click **Expenses by Account** in the Home window to display the chart options:

Again, you can choose to include one or more expense accounts in the graph, and you can choose the time frame for the graph. By default, the complete fiscal period up to the Session date is selected. We will use this period and include in the graph those accounts that we know form a significant share of the total, the supplies accounts and the wages accounts. Other expenses are combined into a category called "Other."

◆ Press ⌃ctrl⌄ and click the following accounts to include them in the chart:

5050 Fibreglass & Plastics Used
5060 Lumber Used
5070 Hardware Used
5295 Contracted Payroll Expenses
5300 Wage Expense

◆ Click **OK** to display the pie chart:

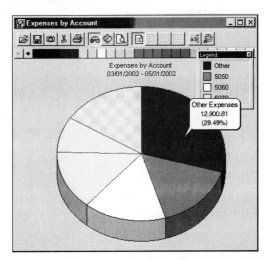

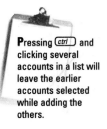

Pressing ⌃ctrl⌄ and clicking several accounts in a list will leave the earlier accounts selected while adding the others.

By double clicking the Other sector of the graph, as shown in the illustration above, you can see that all these expenses combined account for about 30 percent of the total expense, leaving 70 percent for the five selected expense categories. This graph permits you to identify the major costs of doing business. This can be useful in planning budgets and when you need to reduce expenses. By including all accounts in the graph, any expenses that form a significant part of the total will stand out. You can then analyze these items to see where changes can be made to reduce costs.

◆ Close the display when finished.

Expenses and Net Profit as % of Revenue

The final graph shows a graphic representation of the Income Statement.

◆ Choose the **Graphs** menu and click **Expenses and Net Profit as % of Revenue** in the Home window to display the chart options:

Again, you can choose the time period for the graph as well as the expense accounts that you want to identify separately. Other expenses are combined into the "Other" category. By default, all revenue accounts are used to determine the revenue amount, and the complete fiscal period up to the Session date is the default period. We will include the same expense items that we used in the previous chart and accept the default dates.

◆ Press ⌨*ctrl* and click the following accounts to include them in the chart:

5050 Fibreglass & Plastics Used
5060 Lumber Used
5070 Hardware Used
5295 Contracted Payroll Expenses
5300 Wage Expense

◆ Click OK to display the graph:

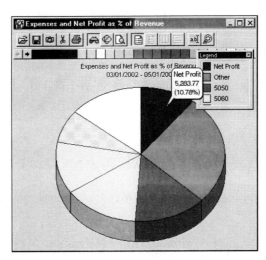

When you double click the Net Profit sector, as in the illustration above, you can see that the net profit in the illustrated graph is 10.8 percent of revenue. Significant expenses will also stand out in this chart when all accounts are included. The percentage net profit figure can be compared with industry standards to gauge overall performance as well.

◆ Close the display when finished.

Budgeting Graphs

When you turn on the budgeting feature, two additional graphs will become available: the Sales vs Budget and the Expenses vs Budget graphs. These graphs will be discussed in Chapter 16 when budgeting is introduced.

Review Question

For each graph described in this chapter, list the report or reports that provide the same details. If they are not comparable, what calculations must be performed on the report details to provide the information in the graphs?

CHAPTER 13

CLOSING ROUTINES

Objectives

- *make year-end adjusting entries*
- *print year-end reports*
- *clear paid invoices*
- *clear journal entries*
- *remove vendor and customer records that are not needed*
- *remove recurring transactions that are no longer needed*
- *advance the Session date to a new fiscal period*
- *compare trial balances for year-end and fiscal start*

Introduction

In this chapter, you will prepare the Play Wave company records for the new fiscal period that begins on June 1. Although the Simply Accounting program automatically closes the revenue and expense accounts when you advance the date into the new fiscal period, there are a number of preparations for this transition. These involve making adjusting entries, preparing backups of all the files, printing a complete set of financial reports and then clearing the data files of information that is no longer needed. If the history for any module is unfinished, you must finish it before advancing to the next fiscal period.

You can use your copy of the Data Disk file — Ch13\play\playch13.sdb — to work through this chapter. By using the Data Disk file, you can complete this chapter at any time after Chapter 3 since it uses only the General Journal. Omit any reports that you have not yet learned.

Preparing for Year-End

As soon as you advance the Session date into a new fiscal period, Simply Accounting automatically closes all revenue and expense accounts into the capital accounts so that the new period begins with zero balances for revenues and expenses. However, you must enter the details that the program does not know about before moving the date forward. Some adjusting entries may be completed at the end of each month, but others may occur only at the end of the fiscal period. For example, employees may have worked for several days since their last pay period. The entry for their accrued wages is an example of an adjustment that occurs only at the end of the fiscal period. The entry is required so that the wage expense will be matched with the corresponding revenue period. Another entry typically made at year-end is the adjustment for bad debts — writing off any accounts that are considered to be uncollectable. Adjusting entries may also be required for prepaid expenses, interest payable and depreciation, if these adjustments are not already entered.

In addition, it is important to prepare a complete set of financial reports for the fiscal period ending because this is the typical period for reporting to owners and investors or shareholders. If, for any reason, the computer data files are damaged, there will be a complete set of historical records available so that the necessary files may be re-created.

Clearing paid invoices, reports and journal entries is not a required step before proceeding to the next period. However, by reducing the amount of stored data, you can increase the program's operating speed. Furthermore, reports that include only data for the current fiscal period will be easier to interpret.

Adjustments

It is important that all expenses are allocated to the appropriate period, matching the period in which they helped to earn revenue. Most of the adjustments for Play Wave are completed monthly. These include the entries for depreciation, supplies used, accrued interest and prepaid expenses.

Some items remain, however, as expenses that are not fully allocated to the fiscal quarter. Accrued payroll is one of these. PST Payable is another expense that is normally recorded after the period to which it applies. We should record the sales tax on the manufactured cost of sales at the end of May rather than in the middle of June when the payment is remitted, in order to connect this expense with the sales for the same month (May). An adjustment for bad debts is not required at this time because all accounts are deemed to be collectable. A company's policy for handling bad debts may change at any time. The account for MegaCity Parks & Rec is overdue, but Tweedle, our contact there, has assured us that a cheque in full payment is en route.

All employees were paid on May 28. Piper and Rapper both worked 14 hours (two days) since then. They have each earned $196 gross pay for that time. Doolittle has earned $320 of her bi-weekly pay. Thus, $712 in wages has accrued by the end of May.

Refer to Chapter 3 for a detailed discussion of adjusting entries.

Entering the Adjustments

◆ Open the data files for Play Wave and accept May 31 as the Session date.

◆ Create a new General Ledger account for the payroll expenses accrued and then enter the two adjustments in the General Journal.

   ☐ Create new account: 2260 Wages Payable (G)

   ☐ Memo #29
   Dated May 31/02
   Prepare the adjusting entry to recognize $712 in payroll expenses accrued at the
   end of the fiscal period. (Debit Wage Expense and credit Wages Payable.)

   ☐ Memo #30
   Dated May 31/02
   The manufactured cost of sales for May was $14 000. In the General Journal,
   record $1 120, 8% of this cost, as the PST Payable.

Using the Checklists

Simply Accounting has a number of built-in features to assist you in routine business operations. We have seen some of these already in the form of advice, help topics, reports, etc. Checklists of procedures that should be carried out at various times are another useful guide to good business practice. Since there is a list for fiscal year-end activities, you should look at the checklists now.

◆ Choose the **Business Assistant menu** and click **Checklists** to see the lists available:

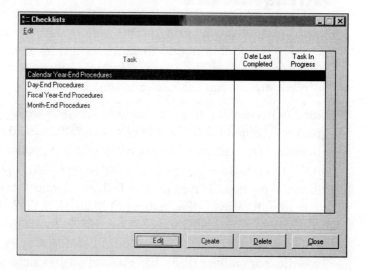

There are lists for four different time periods: the end of each business day or work session, the end of the month, the end of the fiscal period and the end of the calendar year. At each time, several activities should be completed. In addition, you can add your own checklists to suit your own business and you can edit the existing lists by adding and removing activities.

◆ Double click **Fiscal Year-End Procedures** to open this checklist:

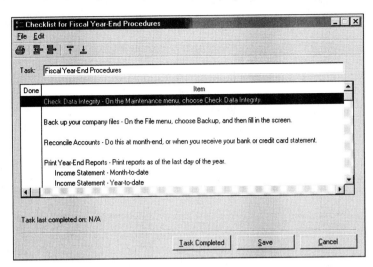

The Checklists Window

There are a number of tools for editing the lists in this window. The tools are duplicated in the Edit menu.

 Insert a new list item.

 Delete an item from the list.

 Move an item in the list up by one line.

 Move an item down one line.

You can use these tools to customize the checklist. For example, you can include a specific list of the adjusting entries that are needed at the end of a month or at the end of the year. If the business does not sell inventory, all references to inventory reports may be deleted. Items that are deemed to be more important may be moved to the top of a list. From the opening Checklists window, you can even create a new company-specific checklist. After completing an activity, you can click the Done column beside it, Save or record the completed activities and resume working on the items on the list. After all activities on the list are finished, click the Task Completed button.

◆ Click the **Print tool** ![printer icon] to print this list for reference.

Read the list carefully. Since we have already completed reconciling the bank accounts and entering year-end adjustments, we can check off these two items.

◆ Click the **Done column** beside Reconcile Accounts.

◆ Click the **Done column** beside Make year end adjustments. Notice that the steps for this item assume that you have already advanced the Session date to the new year.

Clicking an item a second time will remove the checkmark. After saving a list, you cannot remove checkmarks from the Done column.

◆ Click **Save** and then click ☒ to return to the opening Checklists screen:

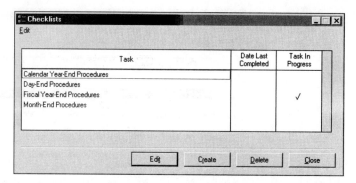

The checkmark in the Task in progress column beside Fiscal Year-End Procedures indicates that we have marked some of the items as completed. When we have finished all the items on the list, the Session date will be recorded in the Date Last Completed column.

Since May 31 is also the end of a work session and the end of a month, we should print these lists to be sure that no important procedures are omitted.

◆ Double click the list name to access it and then click the Print tool. Close the list window to return to the opening Checklists screen. Close the window to return to the Home window.

Reports

Print a complete set of reports for May 31. This should include the following:

> Journal Entries: All Transactions for Mar. 15 to May 31
> Balance Sheet as at May 31
> Trial Balance as at May 31
> Income Statement from Mar. 1 to May 31
> General Ledger Report for all accounts from Mar. 15 to May 31
> Account Reconciliation Status Report: Summary and Detail (all status types)
> Vendor Aged Detail Report
> Customer Aged Detail Report
> Employee Summary Report

These reports provide sufficient detail so that new company files could be created from scratch if necessary. They also provide the information usually required for income tax reports and the details found in the company's annual reports.

The Cash Flow Projection Report should also be printed at this time.

Cash Flow Projection Report

The Cash Flow Projection offers a forecast of cash flow for the next period based on recurring entries, payment commitments and customer receipts expected, according to the payment terms for previous purchases and sales. It does not include other sources, such as cash purchases and sales or future purchases and sales.

You should be in the Home window.

◆ Choose the **Reports** menu, then choose **Financials** and click **Cash Flow Projection** to see the Report Options:

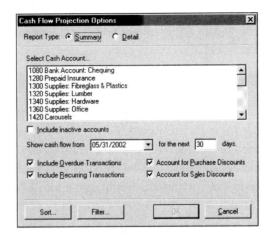

The Cash Flow Statement

Since it is common for a business to have more than one bank account, you can select which account to use in the statement. In addition, it may be useful to prepare the projection for different time periods to see what the short-term and longer-term financial commitments are.

Recurring entries show fixed commitments. These are helpful in planning payment schedules. The report can include the effects of sales and purchase discounts as well because it is useful to see how these influence payment schedules. It may even be useful to prepare separate statements, with and without discounts, to judge the cost of not taking advantage of discounts if cash flow becomes a problem. Overdue transactions may be included if it is likely that they will be resolved in the coming period. If they are more likely to become bad debts, it may be more prudent to omit them.

The **Summary** and **Detail** Reports are generally similar. Both include the current and ending balance, the net change in cash balance, the lowest and highest balance as well as any of the selected transactions categories. The Summary statement, however, adds all transactions of the same type to show the totals, while the Detail statement shows the transactions one at a time, like journal entries.

Drill-down reports are available only from the Detail statement. Double clicking an entry in the statement will load the journal transaction for that entry. If the entry you double click is a recurring entry, you will recall the stored entry and you can post it directly. Doing so may, however, place the journal entry out of sequence.

To print the Cash Flow Projection for the bank account for the next 15 days,

◆ Click *1080 Bank Account: Chequing* to select the bank account.

◆ Double click **30** in the Show cash flow for the next ___ days field.

◆ Type **15**

Leave the four options to include the details checked so that the report will be as complete as possible. To omit any category, click it to remove the checkmark. Including overdue accounts assumes that these will be paid in the near future.

◆ Click **Detail** as the statement type.

- Click **OK** to view the report. No cash flow problems are anticipated.
- Choose the **File** menu and click **Print** to print the report.
- Close the display after you have finished printing and viewing the report.

Backups
Checking Data Integrity

We used the Data Integrity Summary to check ledger balances before finishing the history. Refer to Chapter 6, page 126.

Simply Accounting includes a routine that checks the accuracy and completeness of the data you have entered. For example, the total of unpaid receivables and payables invoices must match the balances in *Accounts Receivable* and *Accounts Payable,* and the total number of credits must equal the debit entries. If these do not match, there are errors in the data files and you should return to a previous backup that has no data integrity problems. Check the data files from the Home window.

- Choose the **Maintenance** menu and click **Check Data Integrity**:

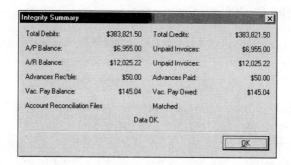

Your amounts on the Integrity Summary screen may be different from those shown if you have made additional entries or corrections.

The amounts in the left column must match the amounts in the right column and the final line should read Data OK. If it does not, use an earlier backup of the files and re-enter any transactions that occurred after the date of the backup.

- Click **OK** to close the summary and return to the Home window.

Making Backups

Once you are certain that your data files are complete and accurate, you should make a final backup of the files for the complete fiscal period.

- Make a backup copy of the files before proceeding!

Simply Accounting will warn you before completing most of the maintenance procedures and date advancements that follow. If you have made a backup copy of your year-end pre-closing data files, you can safely proceed.

Warning!

You may want to make two backup copies. Use one of them to practise clearing the journal entries, invoices, etc. Use the second copy as your working file to advance the Session date and continue working on the journal transactions in the following chapters without removing any data. This will provide you with complete records for both fiscal periods at the end of the simulation in a single data set.

◆ Return to your working copy of the data files for Play Wave.

Maintenance Procedures

In setting up the data files, we chose to store invoice lookup details and not to clear paid invoices. Both of these create additional storage demands and eventually can slow down the program's operating speed. Furthermore, we do not want to keep showing old vendor and customer invoices that are paid in the aged reports. Journal entries can also be removed to create more disk storage space. It is better to have extra backup copies with the old data than to keep the information in the active file indefinitely. Some reports, like GST reports, should be cleared every time a remittance is made so that the new report will show only GST charged and paid for the current remittance period. Therefore, it is important to know how to clear the information that is no longer needed.

Clearing Data

Clearing Journal Entries

Journal entries or transactions can be saved for two fiscal periods or they can be removed periodically. Removing journal entries does not change the availability of stored entries or financial reports. When you begin a new fiscal period, the program will automatically move the journal entries to the previous period. When you choose Journal Entries from the Reports menu, a Previous Year option is added to the Journal Report Options window. To remove journal entries,

◆ Choose the **Maintenance** menu and click **Clear Journal Entries** in the Home window:

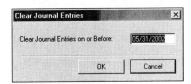

You can choose a date for the removal of old journal entries up to the current Session date. Once you remove the journal entries, you cannot restore them except from a backup copy, so do not proceed until you have made a backup copy.

◆ Click **OK** to proceed. Read the next warning carefully.

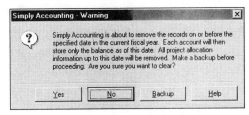

If you click No at this stage, there will be no changes to the data file.

◆ Click **Yes** to proceed. After a brief interval, you will return to the Home window.

The data files included with the text for the following chapters do not have the journal entries cleared so that you may print complete journal reports from any file.

Check with your instructor before clearing any data, or work with a spare backup copy.

Clearing Paid Vendor Invoices

You can clear paid invoices for some or all vendors for any period up to the current Session date. Once again, advancing to the new period does not remove the old information. Unpaid invoices are never removed.

◆ Choose the **Maintenance** menu, then choose **Clear Paid Transactions** and click **Clear Paid Vendor Transactions** in the Home window:

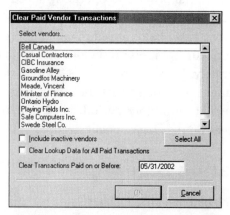

All vendors on record are listed in the Select vendors field. You can choose vendors individually by pressing ⒸⓉⓡⓛ and clicking their names or you can choose them all by clicking Select All. In the date field, you should enter the earliest date for which you want to keep complete records. Choosing to Clear Lookup Data will also remove all the stored invoices for the selected vendors. The Select An Invoice screen that you access from the Lookup tool will not list the paid invoices if you have removed them. If you want to keep this information, do not clear the Lookup Data. Remember that without the Lookup Data, you cannot make adjustments to posted invoices. You can also clear Lookup Data separately from another Maintenance menu option discussed below. The Session date is selected for immediate editing. We will keep paid invoices for the previous month.

◆ Type **4 30** to replace the Session date in the Clear Transactions Paid on or Before field.

◆ Click **Select All** to include all vendors in the selection.

◆ Click **Clear Lookup Data for All Paid Transactions**.

◆ Click **OK**. You will see the following warning:

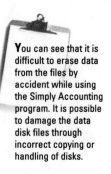

You can see that it is difficult to erase data from the files by accident while using the Simply Accounting program. It is possible to damage the data disk files through incorrect copying or handling of disks.

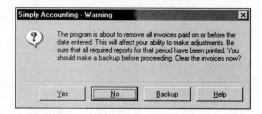

Since you have made a backup, you can safely proceed.

◆ Click **Yes**. The next warning message relates to the clearing of lookup data:

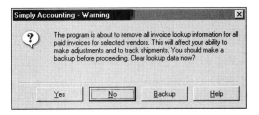

◆ Click **Yes** to continue. If you see an error message, click OK to return to the Home window.

Clearing Paid Customer Invoices

In the same way that you can clear vendor invoices, you can remove customer invoices. This step should not be taken before sending out the latest customer statements.

◆ Choose the **Maintenance** menu, then choose **Clear Paid Transactions** and click **Clear Paid Customer Transactions** in the Home window:

This screen has identical options as the Clear Paid Vendor Transactions screen, except, of course, that it lists customers. The same cautions apply. We will select the same time frame as we did before, keeping one month of information for all customers.

◆ Type **4 30** to replace the date in the Clear Transactions Paid on or Before field.

◆ Click **Select All** to include all vendors in the selection.

◆ Click **Clear Lookup Data for All Paid Transactions**.

◆ Click **OK** to see the following warning:

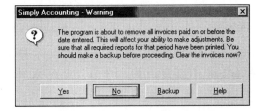

◆ Click **Yes** to see the warning about lookup data:

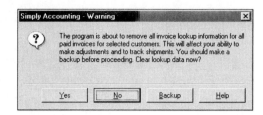

◆ Click **Yes** to proceed. If you see an error message, click **OK** to return to the Home window.

Clearing GST Reports

Old GST information that has already been filed with the Receiver General should be deleted so that new GST reports include only information related to the current filing period and required for the next report that is filed.

◆ Choose the **Maintenance** menu and click **Clear GST Report** in the Home window:

In the date field (Clear GST information on or before) you should enter the date of the most recent GST report you filed because these amounts should not be included in the next report.

◆ Click **OK** to proceed to the usual warning:

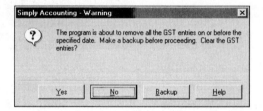

Since we have not yet filed the GST return for this period, we should **not** remove the entries.

◆ Click **No** to cancel the procedure and return to the Home window.

Clearing Account Reconciliation Data

You may want to clear account reconciliation data to create room on your data disk for future entries. The data for each account is cleared separately, so you can choose to keep reconciliation data for one account but not for another.

◆ Choose the **Maintenance** menu, then choose **Clear Account Rec.** and click **Clear Account Rec. Data** in the Home window:

You can select the account for which you want to clear data in the Account field. A drop-down list shows all the accounts that you set up for reconciliation. In the Clear Up To field, you can enter the date before which you want to remove data. Any information after that date will be retained. And finally, you can choose to remove all reconciliation information by selecting all Status Types or you can choose to keep the data for unusual Status Types, perhaps by removing only the items that cleared normally. Keeping the information for Status Types other than Cleared may provide useful information about the company's practices for writing and accepting cheques.

Be sure that *1080 Bank: Account Chequing* is displayed in the Account field. The Session date should appear in the Clear Up To field.

◆ Click **Clear by Statement End Date** to select this option.

We want to remove only the Cleared transactions. Leave this Status Type checked.

◆ Click **all other Status Types** individually to remove the checkmarks.

◆ Click **OK** to see the following warning:

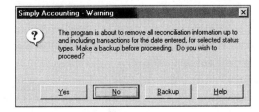

◆ Click **Yes** to proceed and return to the Home window.

◆ Clear all account reconciliation data for account *1090* up to May 31.

Clearing Invoice Lookup Data

By selecting the appropriate menu option, you can clear Invoice Lookup data for vendor invoices, for customer invoices or for both customer and vendor invoices at the same time. To clear both sets of data at the same time,

◆ Choose the **Maintenance** menu, then choose **Clear Invoice Lookup Data** and click **Clear Vendor & Customer Invoice Lookup Data** in the Home window:

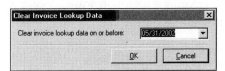

Once again, you must choose the date for clearing the information. The Session date is the default. Remember that you may need to use Lookup to adjust invoices so you should not clear these details without first making a backup.

◆ Click **OK** to see the following warning:

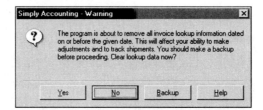

◆ Click **Yes** to proceed.

If you did not receive an error message earlier, you should see the following message because we already cleared the Invoice Lookup Data:

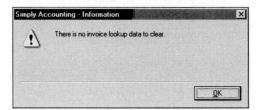

◆ Click **OK** to return to the Home window.

Clearing Lookup Data for Other Payments

Lookup data for other payments made in the Payments Journal are cleared separately from lookup data for vendors.

◆ Choose the **Maintenance** menu and click **Clear Lookup Data for Other Payments** in the Home window:

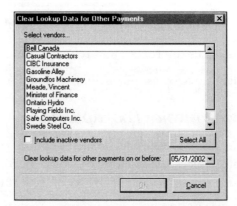

Again, you must choose the vendors for whom you want to remove transactions and the date beyond which you want to keep data. You can clear data up to the Session date, the default entry.

◆ Click **Select All** to choose all vendors.

◆ Click **OK** to see the following warning:

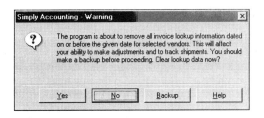

Be careful not to remove old invoices that you may need to adjust in the future.

◆ Click **Yes** to proceed and return to the Home window.

Removing Vendor and Customer Records

You cannot remove the record for a vendor to whom you still owe money.

Sometimes you want to remove the vendor and customer records of companies or clients that you no longer deal with. Sometimes customers move and you do not have a correct forwarding address, or a vendor may go out of business. You can remove the records for these vendors and customers so that they will not be included in mailing lists. Before removing a ledger record, the paid invoices must be cleared and there must be no outstanding invoices.

We will try to remove the record for Playing Fields, Inc. to observe the program's restrictions.

You can also remove a vendor record by opening the record for the vendor (viewing the ledger page) and clicking the Remove tool or choosing the File menu and clicking Remove.

◆ Click the **Vendors icon** in the Home window to open the Vendors window.

◆ Click **Playing Fields, Inc.** (click the vendor's icon or name) to select it.

◆ Click the **Remove tool** or choose the File menu and click Remove.

If you have not cleared the paid invoices for the selected vendor, or if there are outstanding invoices, you will see this warning:

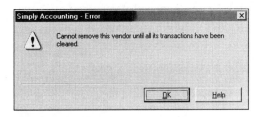

Instead of removing vendor and customer records, you can designate them as inactive in their ledger records and then omit them from reports.

Since there are outstanding invoices for Playing Fields, you cannot remove the vendor record. If the paid invoices are not cleared, the program displays the same warning.

◆ Click **OK** to return to the Vendors window.

We will remove the record for Casual Contractors because Play Wave now handles its own payroll. First we must clear all transactions for this vendor.

◆ Close the Vendors window to return to the Home window. (You cannot clear paid transactions while the ledger window is open.)

◆ Choose the **Maintenance menu**, then choose **Clear Paid Transactions** and click **Clear Paid Vendor Transactions**.

◆ Click **Casual Contractors**. Accept the Session date.

◆ Click **Clear Lookup Data for All Paid Transactions**.

◆ Click **OK**.

◆ Click **Yes** in response to the first warning.

◆ Click **Yes** in response to the warning about lookup data.

◆ Click the **Vendors icon** to open the Vendors window again.

◆ Click **Casual Contractors** (click the vendor's icon or name) to select it.

◆ Click the **Remove tool** or choose the File menu and click Remove.

If you have cleared the invoices, you will see this request for confirmation:

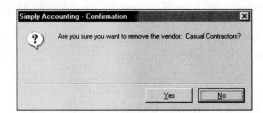

◆ Click **Yes** to proceed.

◆ The following additional confirmation request about the lookup data appears because we have turned on the Invoice Lookup feature:

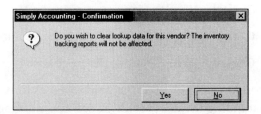

◆ Click **Yes** to proceed. Because you have already removed the lookup data, you will see the following message:

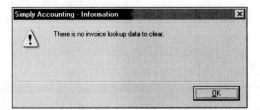

◆ Click **OK** to proceed and return to the Vendor's window.

You can remove only one vendor's record at a time. To remove another vendor, clear all transactions for the vendor, click its icon in the Vendors window and click the Remove tool.

◆ Close the Vendors window to return to the Home window.

Removing Customers

Removing customers follows the same steps as removing vendors:

- All invoices must be paid. Clear all transactions for the customer.
- Click  (the Customers icon) in the Home window to open the Customers window.
- Click the icon for the customer to select it.
- Then click the Remove tool ⬚ or choose the File menu and click Remove.
- Confirm that you want to remove the customer and then confirm that you want to remove lookup data.
- Click the next customer's icon and select Remove again.

Refer to page 359 if you need help with clearing transactions. In the list of customers, press ⟨ctrl⟩ and click each name in turn to select both names.

If you received an error message while clearing paid transactions, you will be unable to remove the records for Central Nursery Schools and Chaplin Estates.

◆ Clear paid transactions and lookup data up to May 31, the Session date, for the following two customers:

> Central Nursery Schools
> Chaplin Estates

◆ Remove the records for Central Nursery Schools and Chaplin Estates.

◆ Close the Customers window to return to the Home window.

Removing Stored Entries

When a recurring entry is no longer needed, you should remove it so that you can locate correct entries more easily and save disk space, and so that you cannot recall it by mistake. To remove a stored entry you must open the journal that has the stored entry.

We will work through the steps for removing an entry but we will cancel the procedure before finishing so that we do not actually delete it. All the recurring transactions for Play Wave are still needed. The following steps will remove a recurring transaction from the General Journal.

◆ Click the **General Journal icon** ⬚ in the Home window to open the General Journal.

◆ Click the **Recall recurring transaction tool** ⬚ or choose the Entry menu and click Recall to open the Recall Recurring Transaction screen:

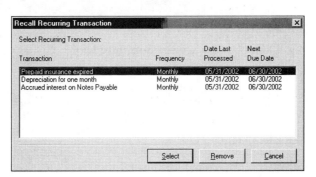

All the recurring entries for Play Wave are still needed in June, so they should **not** be removed. If you do remove an entry by mistake, you can re-enter the information and

If you remove a recurring transaction by mistake, re-enter it and then store it again. Your journal transactions will not be affected.

then store it again. You will not lose any data or transactions, but you will have to repeat the transaction entry the next time it recurs.

◆ Click the entry line for **Accrued interest on Notes Payable** to select it. (Your transaction may have a different name or comment.)

◆ Click **Remove** to see the warning:

◆ Click **No** to return to the Recall Recurring Transaction screen without removing the entry.

◆ Click **Cancel** to return to the General Journal.

◆ Close the General Journal to return to the Home window.

Advancing the Session Date

The actual timing of the appearance of these messages will depend on the Session dates that you choose.

Well before the new fiscal period begins, Simply Accounting advises you to make year-end preparations. The following message appears one month before the fiscal end:

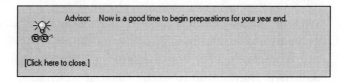

When the fiscal end is very close, you will see this advisory message:

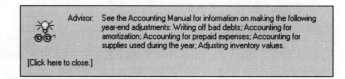

◆ Click the **Change session date tool**  (or choose the Maintenance menu and click Change Session Date in the Home window). Close the backup reminder screen if it appears.

◆ Type **June 6** to replace the current Session date.

◆ Click **OK**.

Simply Accounting shows the following warning:

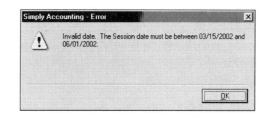

When you are ready to begin a new fiscal period, you must make the date change in two steps. First, you must advance to the first day of the new fiscal period. Then you can advance the Session date normally up to the end of the new fiscal period. This two-step process allows you to change your mind before proceeding, and gives the software a chance to complete all the closing journal entries.

◆ Click **OK** to return to the Change Session Date screen.

◆ Click **Cancel** to return to the Home window without advancing the date.

Beginning a New Fiscal Period

We are now ready to advance the date into the new fiscal period to prepare for further journal transactions. There are two different ways to move to a new fiscal period. The first is the one we have been using, advancing the Session date to the first date of the new period. The second method uses the Start New Year option on the Maintenance menu. Both methods result in the same Session date — the first day of the new fiscal period — and make the same changes to the data files. The screen messages are slightly different for the two methods, so we will show both. Of course you can use only one method at a time because you cannot start the new fiscal period more than once.

◆ Choose the **Maintenance menu** and click **Start New Year**. You will see the following message:

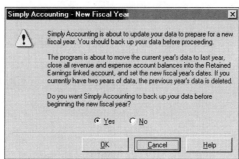

The transactions for two fiscal periods may be kept in your active file. Transactions before this are removed when you move to the next (third) fiscal period.

The option to make a backup before proceeding is selected as the default. If you continue, you will begin the backup procedure. Since you made a backup before clearing data, you do not need to do so now.

◆ Click **No**.

◆ Click **OK** to continue.

Starting the New Fiscal Period by Changing the Session Date

- Click the Change session date tool 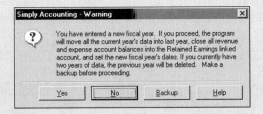 or choose the Maintenance menu and click Change Session Date to open the Change Session Date screen. Close the backup reminder screen, if it appears, because you made a backup before removing data.

- Type June 1 to replace the current Session date.

- Click OK to see the warning:

Simply Accounting - Warning

❓ You have entered a new fiscal year. If you proceed, the program will move all the current year's data into last year, close all revenue and expense account balances into the Retained Earnings linked account, and set the new fiscal year's dates. If you currently have two years of data, the previous year will be deleted. Make a backup before proceeding.

[Yes] [No] [Backup] [Help]

Read this message carefully because it explains the steps that the program follows in closing the revenue and expense accounts when you advance to a new fiscal period. Since we have completed the backup and maintenance procedures, we can proceed.

- Click Yes to advance the date and proceed.

After a brief interval, you will return to the Home window. The data files are now ready for journal transactions in the new fiscal period. You can now use any Session date up to the end of the new fiscal period.

Editing the Fiscal Dates

◆ Choose the **Setup** menu and click **Company Information**:

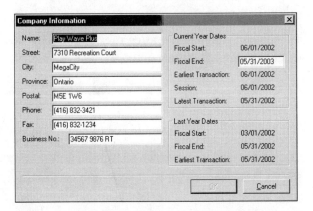

You will see that the company dates have changed to reflect the new fiscal period. The dates section has expanded. The dates for the new fiscal period are on top in the Current Year Dates section. A second set of dates — Last Year Dates — has been added for the period that has ended. The program assumes that the fiscal period is one year so the Fiscal End has advanced to May 31, 2003. We need to change this date so that the second period will be three months, or a quarter, just like the first one. You can change the Fiscal End date any time, but the new date must not be earlier than the Session date. Fiscal End is the only date that you can change on this screen.

◆ Double click **05-31-2003** (the date in the Fiscal End field in the Current Year Dates section) to select it.

◆ Type **08-31-02** to replace the current entry.

◆ Click **OK** to save the change and return to the Home window.

Comparing Financial Reports for the Two Periods

You should review the financial statements to see the other changes that result from closing the books and advancing to the new period. In particular, you should look at the Balance Sheet and Trial Balance for the previous Fiscal End and the new Fiscal Start dates.

◆ Choose the **Reports** menu, then choose **Financials** and click **Trial Balance** in the Home window.

◆ Choose **Comparative Trial Balance** from the Report Type drop-down list.

The default dates are correct at June 1 and May 31, the beginning of the new period and the end of the previous period. Dollar Amounts Only is the correct choice.

◆ Click **OK** to display the report:

If you prefer to see reports with the earlier date first, switch the two dates for the First and Second Periods.

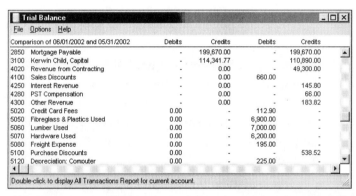

Comparison of 06/01/2002 and 05/31/2002	Debits	Credits	Debits	Credits
2850 Mortgage Payable	-	199,670.00	-	199,670.00
3100 Kerwin Child, Capital	-	114,341.77	-	110,890.00
4020 Revenue from Contracting	-	0.00	-	49,300.00
4100 Sales Discounts	-	0.00	660.00	-
4250 Interest Revenue	-	0.00	-	145.80
4280 PST Compensation	-	0.00	-	66.00
4300 Other Revenue	-	0.00	-	183.82
5020 Credit Card Fees	0.00	-	112.90	-
5050 Fibreglass & Plastics Used	0.00	-	6,900.00	-
5060 Lumber Used	0.00	-	7,000.00	-
5070 Hardware Used	0.00	-	6,200.00	-
5080 Freight Expense	0.00	-	195.00	-
5100 Purchase Discounts	0.00	-	-	538.52
5120 Depreciation: Computer	0.00	-	225.00	-

Double-click to display All Transactions Report for current account.

The partial Trial Balance shows some of the the revenue and expense accounts. The June 1 balances are in the left column and the right column has the May 31 balances. Notice that the revenue and expense amounts are all zero in the June 1 column. The asset and liability amounts are the same for both dates, but the capital account, *3100 Kerwin Child, Capital*, has been updated for June 1 to include the net income from the previous quarter.

◆ Print the report and then close the display.

◆ Choose the **Reports menu**, then choose **Financials** and click **Balance Sheet** in the Home window.

◆ Choose **Comparative Balance Sheet** from the Report Type drop-down list.

The default dates are correct at June 1 and May 31 and Dollar Amounts Only is the information we want.

◆ Click **OK** to display the report:

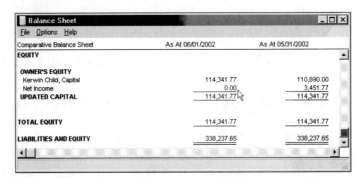

The partial Balance Sheet shown above focuses on the Equity section because it is the one that has changed. Notice that the *Net Income* for June has been reduced to zero. Its balance from May 31 has been closed to *Kerwin Child, Capital*.

◆ Print the Balance Sheet and then close the display to return to the Home window.

Reversing Adjusting Entries

One additional step is recommended as good accounting practice — reversing the closing adjusting entry that affects the next payroll journal transaction. This type of reversing entry is used for short-term payables and receivables, usually accruals. We need to remove the accrued payroll balance by creating a credit balance in *Wage Expense*. Remember that the starting balance for June 1 was zero. When the next Payroll Journal entry is completed, the portion that was accrued for the previous period will be removed from the expense for the new period. These entries are usually completed at the beginning of the new fiscal period to ensure that they will not be forgotten.

◆ Complete the following journal entry to record the wage expense adjustment.

> ☐ Memo #31
> Dated Jun. 1/02
> Prepare the adjusting entry to reverse the $712 in accrued wages payable for the
> beginning of the fiscal period (debit Wages Payable and credit Wage Expense).

◆ Close the data files for Play Wave. Complete the closing routines for Live Links.

Practice: Live Links

Live Links has reached the end of the first fiscal quarter and is ready to close the books in preparation for the second quarter.

Closing Routines
Instructions

You can use your copy of the Data Disk file — Ch13\links\linkch13.sdb — to work through the closing routines for Live Links.

1. Open the data files for Live Links. Accept September 30 as the Session date.

2. Enter the following transaction as an adjusting entry in the General Journal.

   ☐ Memo #23
   Dated Sep. 30/02
   Adrian Borland worked 15 hours since he was paid on September 28. Prepare the adjusting entry to recognize $180 in accrued wages payable for payroll expenses for the previous fiscal period. Create a new account: 2250 Accrued Wages Payable (G).

3. Check the data integrity for your files.

4. Print the following reports:

   Journal Entries: All Transactions for Jul. 8 to Sep. 30
   Balance Sheet as at Sep. 30
   Trial Balance as at Sep. 30
   Income Statement from Jul. 1 to Sep. 30
   General Ledger Report for all accounts from Jul. 8 to Sep. 30
   Cash Flow Projection for the next 30 days
   Account Reconciliation Status Report: Summary and Detail (all status types)
   Vendor Aged Detail Report
   Customer Aged Detail Report
   Employee Summary Report

5. Based on the Aged Vendor Report, two unpaid accounts are due or overdue. Enter the following transactions to make the payments.

   ☐ Cheque Copy #33
   Dated Sep. 30/02
   To Promo Uno, $513 in full payment of account. Reference invoice #PU-2146.

   ☐ Cheque Copy #34
   Dated Sep. 30/02
   To Business Depot, $684 in full payment of account. Reference invoice #BD-9637.

6. **Back up your data files. Return to your working copy of the data files.**

7. Clear the following information up to the Session date:
>   Journal Entries
>   Paid Vendor Invoices and Lookup Data for all vendors
>   Paid Customer Invoices and Lookup Data for all customers
>   Account Reconciliation Data — remove only Cleared Status transactions
>   Invoice Lookup Data

8. Remove the following customer records:
>   Elsie Cordeiro
>   Jerome Wiggles

9. Remove the following recurring entries (your entries may have different names):
>   General Journal: Learnx Bank Payroll Services
>   General Journal: Accrued Bank Loan Interest

10. Start the new year (advance the Session date to October 1, 2002).

11. Change the current year Fiscal End date in the Company Information screen to December 31, 2002.

12. Print the following reports:

>   Post-Closing Comparative Trial Balance for October 1 and September 30
>   Post-Closing Comparative Balance Sheet for October 1 and September 30

13. Enter the following transaction to reverse the payroll adjustment (a short-term accrued liability):

> ☐ Memo #24
>   Dated Oct.1/02
>   Prepare the adjusting entry to reverse the $180 in accrued wages payable for the beginning of the fiscal period (debit Accrued Wages Payable and credit Wages).

14. Close the data files for Live Links to prepare for setting up the Inventory Ledger for Play Wave.

Review Questions

1. Why are adjusting entries required before closing the books?
2. Why is it important to print all reports and make backups before advancing the Session date to the new fiscal year?
3. Why might you want to clear historical data from your files? Why might you choose not to clear the data?
4. If the Fiscal End is June 30 and the Session date is June 30, what date must you enter to advance the Session date?
5. What changes are made to your accounting data when you advance the Session date into a new fiscal period?
6. How is closing your accounting books manually different from closing them in Simply Accounting?
7. What information does the data integrity check provide?
8. What information do checklists provide?

CHAPTER 14

INVENTORY LEDGER SETUP

Objectives

- explain the components of the Inventory Ledger entry screens
- enter settings for the Inventory Ledger
- understand and identify Inventory Ledger linked accounts
- enter inventory item details
- enter additional inventory items for practice
- display and print Inventory Ledger reports
- finish the Inventory Ledger history

Introduction

In June, Play Wave Plus will begin to sell playground equipment sets directly to customers. The sets are therefore uninstalled and, like other retail sales, subject to both the Ontario Provincial Sales Tax at 8 percent and the federal Goods and Services Tax at 7 percent. In this chapter, you will enter inventory items into the Inventory Ledger and identify linked accounts to prepare for selling and buying inventory items. The purchase invoice from Playing Fields Inc. on May 31 provided the historical data that we will enter into the Inventory Ledger.

If you have not completed all the work from previous chapters and want to continue working on Chapter 14, you can use your copy of the Data Disk file — Ch14\play\playch14.sdb — to begin this chapter.

The Inventory Ledger

You can keep track of both goods and services using the Inventory Ledger in Simply Accounting. Once you identify the appropriate linked accounts for each item, the Inventory Ledger records are updated automatically each time you buy or sell inventory. Thus, Simply Accounting uses the perpetual inventory method with the average cost as the basis of cost. You can easily track the performance of individual items using margin or markup as your profit calculation method. While making sales or purchases, you can also tell how many items are left in stock.

Inventory Ledger Settings

Customizing the Inventory Ledger is relatively simple because there are few settings to enter.

◆ Open the data file for Play Wave. Accept June 1 as the Session date.

◆ Restore the icons for the Inventory Ledger (View menu, Modules, Inventory & Services).

The Inventory Ledger is represented by the Inventory & Services icon shown here:

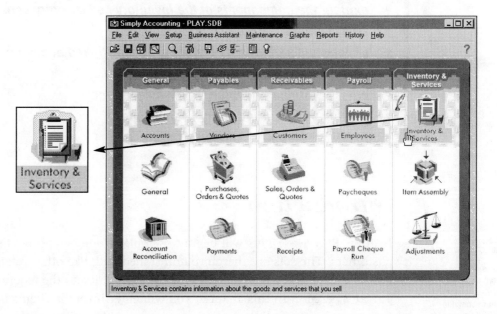

◆ Right-click the **Inventory & Services icon** in the Home window to select it.

You can also choose the Setup menu and click Settings in the Home window. Then click the Inventory & Services tab to change to the Inventory & Services Settings screen.

◆ Click the **Setup tool** to open the Inventory Settings screen:

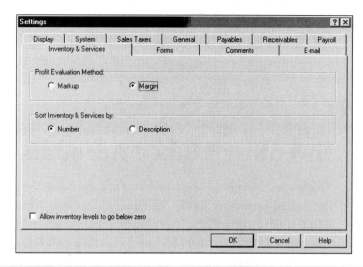

Inventory & Services Settings

Two different **Profit Evaluation Method** calculations are allowed: markup and margin.

Markup is calculated as
$$\frac{\text{Selling Price} - \text{Cost Price}}{\text{Cost Price}} \times 100\%$$

Margin is calculated as
$$\frac{\text{Selling Price} - \text{Cost Price}}{\text{Selling Price}} \times 100\%$$

You can change the setting any time. You can even print the inventory reports with one setting, change the setting and then print the same reports to get both calculations.

The second option allows you to **Sort Inventory & Services by** number or description. If you have item codes or numbers attached to the inventory, you can use them to sort the items for inventory lists and reports. If you sort by description, the items will be listed alphabetically by the descriptive name you entered in the description field. Again, you can change the setting any time.

When you **Allow inventory levels to go below zero**, you permit backorders, selling the item when it is out of stock and filling the order later. When you oversell, the new cost of the sold items may be different from the historical average cost of inventory items. If you then purchase inventory after the inventory has dropped below zero, the difference between this historical average cost of items available at the time of sale and the cost of the new purchase to fill the backorder is the variance. If this setting is not turned on, you will be warned when a sale exceeds the available stock and you will be unable to post the transaction.

The defaults for profit evaluation and sorting are correct.

◆ Click **Allow inventory levels to go below zero**.

◆ Click **OK** to return to the Home window.

Before defining the linked accounts in the next step, you must create a new expense subgroup of accounts for the Inventory Ledger, as well as a new revenue account that will track inventory sales separately from revenue generated by contract work.

☐ Add the following new General Ledger accounts for inventory setup:

5030 Cost of Goods Sold (A)
5032 Damaged Inventory (A)
5040 Assembly Costs (A)
5042 Variance Costs (A)
5045 Net Cost of Goods Sold (S)
4040 Revenue from Sales (G)

Inventory Linked Accounts

There are two sets of linked accounts for inventory: those for the ledger and those for individual inventory items. The linked accounts for the ledger are defined from the Setup menu. We will define these first. Linked accounts for items are defined in the Inventory Ledger records for the items. We will define these when we enter the inventory records.

◆ Choose the **Setup** menu, then choose **Linked Accounts** and click **Inventory Items** in the Home window to open the Inventory Linked Accounts screen:

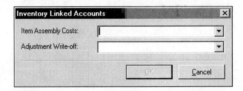

Inventory Linked Accounts

There are only two linked accounts for the Inventory Ledger as a whole, one for each inventory journal. The other linked accounts, for individual inventory items, are defined as part of the records for those items. These individual-item linked accounts are used for purchases and sales of inventory.

Item Assembly Costs: This linked account for the Item Assembly Journal records the expenses associated with transferring inventory from one inventory category to another or assembling several items to make a different item. For example, a store may offer a promotion that bundles several items at a special reduced price. There may be costs associated with this transfer (assembly) above the costs of the individual items. For example, packaging or shipping costs may be added. These additional costs are recorded in the *Item Assembly Costs* linked account. You must choose a postable expense account, either Group or Subgroup.

Adjustment Write-off: When inventory is damaged, lost or stolen, the asset account must be reduced by the cost of the loss. The linked account identifies the second half of this adjusting entry, the expense associated with the loss. Normally you would choose an expense account to record the expense, but the program also allows you to choose an asset account (contra-asset account). You may define the postable linked account as a Group or a Subgroup account.

◆ Click the **Item Assembly Costs field list arrow.**

◆ Click *5040 Assembly Costs* from the list.

◆ Click the **Adjustment Write-off field list arrow.**

◆ Click *5032 Damaged Inventory* from the list.

♦ Click **OK** to return to the Home window.

You can now begin to enter the individual inventory records.

Creating Inventory Records

The Inventory & Services icon provides access to the Inventory Ledger.

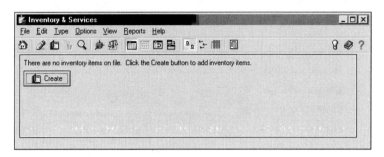

♦ Click the **Inventory & Services icon** in the Home window to open the Inventory & Services window.

The Inventory & Services Window

The only new tools in this window provide access to the Inventory journals. These journals are also available from the Type menu.

Open the Item Assembly Journal.

Open the Adjustments Journal.

There are no icons for inventory because no inventory items are on record yet.

♦ Click the **Create button** 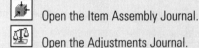, or click the **Create tool** , or choose the File menu and click Create to open the Inventory & Services Ledger record:

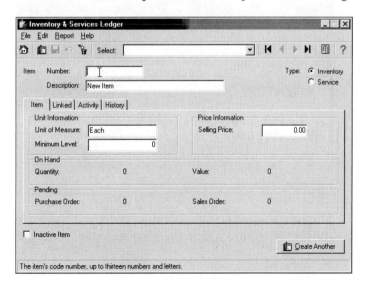

The Inventory & Services Ledger

The Inventory & Services Ledger has four tabs to record the inventory information. The Item Number and Description appear on all the input record screens for reference. The **Item Number** may be a numeric or alpha-numeric code containing up to 13 characters. The **Item Description** is the name of the item, up to 35 characters. You can sort the inventory records by either of these two fields. The second option common to all tab screens designates the item **Type** as a Service or an Inventory item. If you choose Service, some of the input fields will change to become suitable for this type of item. You may also define an item as Inactive.

The first Inventory & Services Ledger tab screen shows the Item information.

The Item Tab Input Screen

Many of the fields in this screen are familiar from the Purchases and Sales Journals.

The Item tab screen is further divided. The first group includes **Unit Information**. The **Unit of Measure** describes the way the item is sold (e.g., by tonnes, by dozens, by sets, by kits, each, by item, etc.). The **Minimum Level** is the re-order point. When inventory levels drop to this number, the program flags the item in reports to warn you that it is time to re-order. If a sale causes the level to drop to this number, the program warns you when you post the transaction. The **Selling Price** is the customer's price for the item. When you sell the item through the Sales Journal, the price appears automatically. You can still edit the price at the time of the sale.

Information about the items **On Hand**, or in stock, forms the middle group in the Item tab screen. The program updates these fields directly from the details you enter on the History tab screen (before finishing the history) and from journal transactions.

Information about items **Pending** comprises the final portion of the form. Quantities appear in the Pending section when the item is not in stock but commitments for purchases or sales already exist. This information is entered by the program as you complete purchase order and sales order transactions. You cannot enter these as historical information.

When you have **Service** inventory items, only the Unit of Measure portion appears on this screen. Because the business does not purchase the service, the cost and quantity are zero. There is also no minimum level. For services, you can indicate whether PST should be applied to the sale. For inventory items, PST is usually applied.

The first inventory record, for carousels, includes the following information:

Total Value represents the total cost of all units purchased, not the cost for each unit.

INVENTORY								
No.	Item Description	Min	Selling Price/Unit	Qty	Total Value	Asst	Rev	Exp	Var
01	Carousel	1	$410 each	2	$400	1420	4040	5030	5042

The cursor is in the Item Number field. We will enter the information for carousels, the first inventory item from the Inventory chart above.

◆ Type 01

◆ Press ⌜tab⌟ to advance to the Description field.

◆ Type **Carousel**

Inventory is the correct Type and the default entry, Each, is correct for the Unit of Measure.

◆ Double click the **Minimum Level** field.

◆ Type **1**

◆ Press ⌨(tab) to move to the Selling Price field and select the default entry.

◆ Type **410**

Note that the Selling Price refers to the price for a single unit while the Value refers to the cost price for the entire stock.

Inventory Item Linked Accounts

◆ Click the **Linked tab** to open this screen:

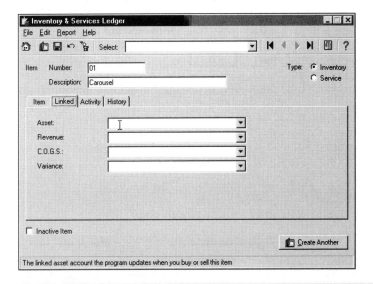

The Linked Tab Screen

The Linked tab screen provides information about the linked accounts for individual inventory items. You can use separate linked accounts for each item, you can group the items into asset groups or you can use a single set of accounts for all items. Or you might use separate asset and cost accounts but a single revenue and variance account for all items.

Asset: The asset account associated with the item. When you purchase the item, this asset account is debited for the unit purchase price times the quantity purchased. When you sell the item, this account is credited for the average cost of the items sold. You must choose a postable asset account, either a Group or Subgroup type.

Revenue: Each time you sell the inventory item, the postable linked revenue account is credited for the selling price times the quantity. You must choose a revenue account, either a Group or Subgroup type.

C.O.G.S. (Cost of Goods Sold): When you sell the inventory item, this linked expense account is debited for the unit purchase price or average cost of the items sold times the quantity. You must choose a postable expense account, but it may be a Group or Subgroup type of account.

Variance: The linked variance account is used whenever the inventory sold is on order, before the goods are in stock. At the time of the sale, the *Cost of Goods Sold* account is debited for the average cost of inventory on hand based on previous purchases. If there are no items in stock, the average cost is zero. When the goods are received, the actual purchase price may be different from this historical average. The price difference is charged

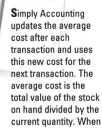

Simply Accounting updates the average cost after each transaction and uses this new cost for the next transaction. The average cost is the total value of the stock on hand divided by the current quantity. When the purchase price changes, the average cost also changes frequently.

to the linked variance account. You must allow inventory levels to go below zero in order to use the variance account. If you have not identified a linked variance account, the program will ask you to define one when you make a purchase that has a variance.

Service: These items have only revenue and expense linked accounts — the default revenue account for sales of the services and the default expense account for purchases of the services.

The linked accounts used for other ledgers are not available for selection as linked accounts for inventory items. They do not appear on the drop-down lists.

◆ Click the **Asset account field list arrow**. Only asset accounts may be used.

◆ Click *1420 Carousels*.

◆ Press (tab). An advisory message about the account class change appears:

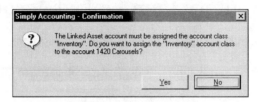

◆ Click **Yes** to accept the change and continue.

◆ Click the **Revenue account field list arrow**. The list includes only revenue accounts.

◆ Click *4040 Revenue from Sales*.

◆ Press (tab).

◆ Click the **Expense account field list arrow**. Only expense accounts are listed.

◆ Click *5030 Cost of Goods Sold*.

◆ Press (tab). Another message appears about changing the account class for this account:

◆ Click **Yes** to accept the change and continue.

◆ Click the **Variance account field list arrow**. Only expense accounts are listed.

◆ Click *5042 Variance Costs*.

◆ Press (tab) to see the message about changing the account class for the linked variance account:

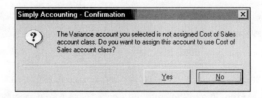

◆ Click **Yes** to accept the change and continue.

Activity Details

◆ Click the **Activity tab** to open the next information screen:

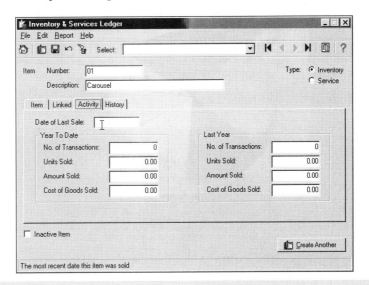

Activity Tab Screen

The Activity tab screen includes historical information for the item whose record is open. You can include information for the current year (Year To Date) and for the previous year (Last Year) for purposes of tracking the item. If the item has not previously been sold, you can leave this screen blank. If you have the information but choose not to include it, the inventory tracking will begin with the first journal entry involving the inventory item. If you want, you can add the information for the current year only. The more details you include, the more complete will be the tracking reports. The **Year To Date** details apply to all sales within the current fiscal period. The **Last Year** fields include the same details for the previous fiscal period.

Date of Last Sale: This is the date of the most recent sale of the inventory item. Use the usual date format.

No. of Transactions: The number of transactions refers to the total number of occasions on which the item was sold. For example, if one customer bought the item on three separate days, there are three transactions. If the customer bought three items on one day, there was one transaction. If four customers bought the item on one day, there were four transactions, regardless of the number of items each customer purchased.

Units Sold: The total number of units of the item sold over all transactions.

Amount Sold: The total sale price of all units sold in the relevant period, year-to-date or last year.

Cost of Goods Sold: The total cost or purchase price of all units sold in the relevant period.

Service items do not have the Cost of Goods Sold input fields on the Activity tab screen.

There is no historical information for the inventory because Play Wave is just starting to sell these items. Leave all the Activity fields blank.

History Details

◆ Click the **History tab** to open the next information screen:

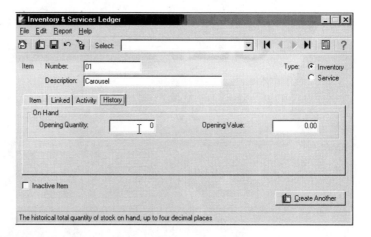

History Tab Screen

As for the other ledgers, the History tab details refer to the starting quantities — before the history is finished. You must enter the **Opening Quantity**, the number of units actually in stock. The **Opening Value** refers to the total cost price or value of the inventory in stock, not the unit cost. Unlike the General Ledger, the dates that the opening values refer to need not precede the Earliest Transaction Date for the company files.

◆ Click the **Opening Quantity field**.

◆ Type **2**

◆ Press (tab) to move to the Opening Value field. The cost of the two carousels was $400.

◆ Type **400**

◆ Review the details you have entered to make sure that they are correct. Correct mistakes by double clicking the error and retyping the information.

◆ Click **Create Another** to save the record and open a new ledger record.

◆ Enter the remaining inventory items from the following chart. Accept the account class changes for all linked asset accounts.

Notice that Play Wave uses separate asset accounts for each category but a single revenue account for all inventory. There is also only one expense account and one variance account.

INVENTORY

No.	Item Description	Min	Selling Price/Unit		Qty	Total Value	Linked Accounts Asst	Rev	Exp	Var
02	Jungle Gym	1	$410	each	2	$400	1440	4040	5030	5042
03	Slide: classic	1	510	each	2	500	1450	4040	5030	5042
04	Slide: wave	1	610	each	2	600	1450	4040	5030	5042
05	Swing Set: double	1	410	each	2	400	1460	4040	5030	5042
06	Swing Set: triple	1	510	each	2	500	1460	4040	5030	5042
07	Tube Slide: classic	1	510	each	2	500	1450	4040	5030	5042
08	Tube Slide: wave	1	610	each	2	600	1450	4040	5030	5042

◆ After creating the last inventory item, close the ledger record window and then close the Inventory & Services window to return to the Home window.

You may see the following message if all the amounts are correct:

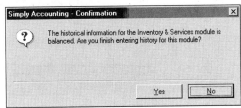

◆ Click **No** because we want to print reports, check the information carefully and make a backup before finishing the history.

Inventory Reports

You should check your work by printing the relevant inventory reports. Use the Inventory List to check the item numbers, descriptions and linked accounts, and the Inventory Reports to check the quantity and price details. You will be unable to change the quantity on hand and the total value after finishing the ledger history.

Inventory Lists

The Inventory List is also available from the Display tool and the Reports menu in the Inventory & Services window. From the Home window, the Display tool also provides access to the Inventory List.

From the Home window,

◆ Choose the **Reports** menu, then choose **Lists** and click **Inventory & Services** to immediately display the list of items with numbers, descriptions and linked accounts.

◆ Print the list or check your work from the on-screen display. Close the display.

Inventory Report

The Inventory Reports contain information about the quantities, prices and the cost of the inventory on hand.

◆ Choose the **Reports menu**, then choose **Inventory & Services** and click **Inventory** in the Home window (or, in the Inventory & Services window, choose the Reports menu and click Inventory) to see the Report Options:

When you click Select All, you will include all items in your report, whether you have selected by item or by asset.

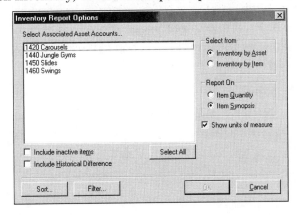

The first option, Select from, refers to how the inventory items are listed or selected. By default, the asset groups are listed. You may also choose Inventory by Item by clicking this option. If you have sorted by description, items will be listed alphabetically. If you sort by number, the items are listed by item code number. The following screen shows the Inventory by Item option with inventory sorted by number:

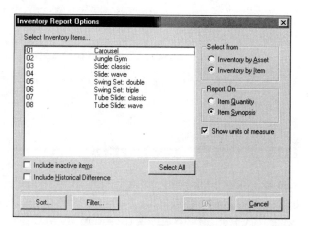

♦ Click **Select All** to include all the items in the report.

♦ Click **OK** to display the Item Synopsis Report, the default selection.

For each inventory item selected, the Inventory Synopsis Report includes the unit, the unit selling price, the quantity on hand, the cost per unit, the total value of the inventory on hand and the profit margin (or markup if you selected that method of profit evaluation in the Inventory Settings).

♦ Print the display to check your input and close the display when you have finished.

♦ Choose the **Reports menu**, then choose **Inventory & Services** and click **Inventory** in the Home window.

♦ Click **Select All**.

♦ Click **Item Quantity** as the Report type to display the Inventory Quantity Report.

♦ Click **OK**.

The Inventory Quantity Report includes the quantity on hand, the minimum quantity, the number of items on purchase orders and sales orders, and the number that should be ordered to restore the quantity to the minimum level if the quantity has dropped below the minimum level. You can use the Quantity Report to determine when to re-order inventory items.

♦ Print the display to check your input and close the display when you have finished to return to the Home window.

When you double click any detail on the inventory report, you will see the Inventory Transactions Detail Report.

Finishing the Inventory Ledger History

The final step is to finish the ledger history. First make a new backup of your work at this stage so that if you have made a mistake, you will be able to make corrections to the Inventory Ledger Not Finished version of the file. You must be in the Home window to finish the ledger history.

◆ Make a backup copy of the file before proceeding.

◆ Choose the **History** menu, then choose **Enter Historical Information** and click **Inventory & Services**. If you have made errors in your files you may be unable to finish the history for the Inventory & Services Ledger. You will see a screen like the one shown below in the section on Finishing History Errors.

Finishing History Errors

The linked accounts for inventory are not required for finishing the ledger history. They are needed for journal entries. However, if the opening values you entered in the individual item records do not match the totals in the linked asset accounts, you will see a message like the one in the following screen:

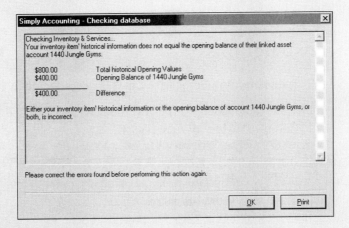

Correct the values in the inventory records and try finishing the history again.

◆ Choose the **History** menu, then choose **Enter Historical Information** and click **Inventory & Services** to see the familiar warning:

This message indicates that the history is balanced for the Inventory & Services Ledger.

◆ If you have backed up your work, click **Proceed**.

◆ Close the Play Wave data files to prepare for setting up the Inventory Ledger for Live Links.

Practice: Live Links

Live Links made two purchases of computer parts at the end of September to prepare for assembling and selling computer systems. These purchases provide the historical inventory information needed to create the Inventory Ledger records. You will now enter the Inventory Ledger settings for Live Links and then create the inventory records to prepare for selling these items. The computer systems and parts will have PST at 7 percent applied to the sales. Live Links does not pay PST on the purchases of these parts for resale and manufacture.

In addition to selling the computer systems, Lively wants to track the services she provides. By setting up consulting services and workshops as inventory, she can keep track of the number of hours she spends consulting and the total number of workshops she gives. For the time being, she will not include the remaining services she offers, such as repair work, duplication services and data recovery, in her inventory setup because she has not decided on a uniform pricing strategy for these activities.

Inventory Ledger Setup
Instructions

1. Open the data file for Live Links. Accept **October 1** as the Session date.

2. Restore the icons for the Inventory & Services Ledger (Home window, View menu, Modules, Inventory & Services).

3. Add the following General Ledger accounts that are needed for the Inventory Ledger setup:

    > 4070 Revenue from Sales (A)
    > 5130 Cost of Goods Sold (A)
    > 5140 Variance Costs (A)
    > 5150 Damaged Goods (A)
    > 5160 Item Assembly Costs (A)
    > 5190 Net Cost of Goods Sold (S)

4. Edit the following account from type G (Group) to type A (Subgroup):

    > 5135 Purchases Discounts

5. Enter the new default settings for the Inventory Ledger:

    > Profit Evaluation Method: Markup
    > Sort Inventory by Number
    > Allow inventory levels to go below zero

6. Enter the linked accounts for the Inventory Ledger:

    > Item Assembly Costs: 5160 Item Assembly Costs (A)
    > Adjustment Write-off: 5150 Damaged Goods (A)

If you have not completed all the work for Live Links in previous chapters and want to continue working on Chapter 14, you can use your copy of the Data Disk file — Ch14\links\linkch14.sdb — to work through the rest of this chapter.

7. Enter the following inventory items into the Inventory Ledger:

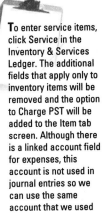

To enter service items, click Service in the Inventory & Services Ledger. The additional fields that apply only to inventory items will be removed and the option to Charge PST will be added to the Item tab screen. Although there is a linked account field for expenses, this account is not used in journal entries so we can use the same account that we used for inventory items.

INVENTORY

No.	Item Description	Min	Selling Price/Unit	Qty	Total Value	Asst	Rev	Exp	Var
01	CPU Cooler 2.3w Pentium III	1	$ 50 each	0	0	1430	4070	5130	5140
02	CPU Cooler x21 Pentium III	1	75 each	0	0	1430	4070	5130	5140
03	DVD-Rom 16x	2	150 each	8	$ 800	1420	4070	5130	5140
04	Enclosure - solid steel mini	1	250 each	4	720	1430	4070	5130	5140
05	Enclosure - solid steel tower	1	400 each	4	1 200	1430	4070	5130	5140
06	Hard Drive 3.5", 30GB IDE	1	300 each	4	900	1420	4070	5130	5140
07	Hard Drive 3.5", 40GB IDE	1	400 each	4	1 200	1420	4070	5130	5140
08	Memory 64 mb SDRAM	3	150 each	10	1 200	1430	4070	5130	5140
09	Modem 56kV.90 w/ethernet	2	225 each	8	1 200	1430	4070	5130	5140
10	Monitor 15" TFT Flat panel	1	900 each	4	2 400	1450	4070	5130	5140
11	Monitor 17" TFT Flat panel	1	1 500 each	4	4 400	1450	4070	5130	5140
12	Motherboard Pentium III at 1 GHz	2	660 each	0	0	1430	4070	5130	5140
13	Power Supply Turbo cool 400 slim	1	300 each	4	900	1430	4070	5130	5140
14	Power Supply Turbo cool 600 tower	1	550 each	4	1 600	1430	4070	5130	5140
15	Sound Card 64V Pro w/speakers	2	125 each	10	750	1430	4070	5130	5140
16	Video Card 32 mb nVIDIA	2	200 each	0	0	1430	4070	5130	5140

SERVICES

No.	Service Description	Selling Price /Unit	Charge PST	Rev	Exp
SRV-01	Consulting	$125/hour	No	4020	5130
SRV-02	Workshop - 3 hours	$500/wkshop	No	4060	5130
SRV-03	Workshop - 6 hours	$900/wkshop	No	4060	5130

8. Print the Inventory & Services List and the Inventory Synopsis and Quantity Reports to check your work.

9. Make a backup copy of the data files with the Inventory Ledger history not finished.

10. Finish the Inventory Ledger history.

11. Close the Live Links data files to prepare for making journal entries for Play Wave.

Review Questions

1. How do you enter linked accounts in the Inventory Ledger?
2. How are linked accounts for the ledger different from linked accounts for the inventory items? Why are they separated?
3. What historical information is required in an inventory record before you finish the ledger history?
4. What linked accounts serve as the control accounts in the Inventory Ledger? How do these accounts work as control accounts?
5. If inventory profit is measured by markup, how can you change it to margin? When can you make this change?
6. What reports can you print to check whether you entered the inventory record details accurately? What details can you check from each report?
7. What is the effect of selecting "Allow inventory levels to go below zero"?
8. Why might you want to create inventory records for services?
9. What is the difference between sorting the inventory records by number and sorting them by description?

INVENTORY JOURNALS

Objectives

- **explain the Item Assembly and Adjustments Journal entry screens**
- **complete inventory item assembly transactions**
- **complete inventory purchases and sales**
- **enter sales returns**
- **complete inventory adjustments**
- **complete additional entries for practice**
- **display Inventory Ledger Reports**

Introduction

If you have not completed the inventory setup in Chapter 14 and want to continue working on Chapter 15, you can use your copy of the Data Disk file — Ch15\play\playch15.sdb — to begin this chapter.

In this chapter, Play Wave Plus will purchase and sell playground equipment as inventory items. In addition, they will assemble these playground components, the raw materials, into kits for direct sale to customers. Customers who purchase these individual items and kits install and assemble them on their own. PST is charged on these sales. Play Wave will continue providing custom-built play centres through contract work as well.

Thus, the final set of journals are put to use in this chapter. You will now use all the journals in Simply Accounting to complete the variety of transactions that occur in a normal business.

Inventory Transactions

Purchases and sales of inventory are the most frequently occurring transactions involving inventory. These inventory transactions are entered in the Purchases and Sales Journals, just like the non-inventory purchases and sales in the previous chapters. The difference is that the program uses the default Inventory Ledger details to complete most of each journal entry when inventory items are involved in the transactions. Thus, most inventory transactions are not completed in the inventory journals. The two inventory journals are reserved for the remaining inventory transactions, those involving adjustments for lost, stolen or damaged goods, and those involving transfers from one inventory item to another, such as assembling finished goods from inventory raw materials. These two types of transactions are internal to the business; they do not involve customers or vendors.

Inventory Purchases

◆   Open your working copy of the Play Wave files.

◆   Advance the Session date to **June 7, 2002**.

The next transaction is a purchase of inventory.

> ✔   Purchase Invoice #PF-1032
> Dated Jun. 1/02
> From Playing Fields Inc.
>
> | | | | |
> |---|---|---|---|
> | two | 07 | Tube Slides: classic | $ 500.00 |
> | two | 08 | Tube Slides: wave | 600.00 |
> | | | Freight | 50.00 |
> | | | Total | 1 150.00 |
> | | | GST Paid | 80.50 |
> | | | Invoice total | $1 230.50 |
>
> Terms: net 30 days.

Inventory purchases, purchase orders and quotes are entered in the Purchases Journal, just like non-inventory purchases.

◆   Click the **Purchases Journal icon** to open the Purchases Journal:

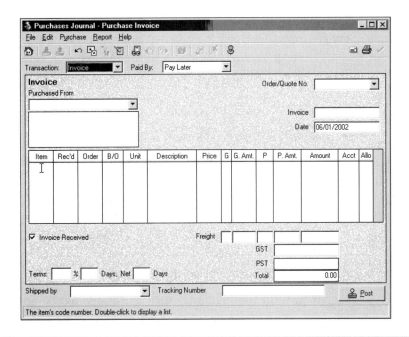

The Purchases Journal

None of the Purchases Journal fields, icons or menus has changed since we added the Inventory Ledger. You can see that the columns in the Purchases Journal correspond to the fields in the Inventory Ledger. **Item** refers to the item code or number, **Unit** is the unit of measurement, **Description** and **Price** are the item description and cost price per unit from the ledger record, and the **Acct** is the linked asset account for the item. As you complete the invoice, many of the fields are filled in with the default ledger information.

◆ Choose **Playing Fields Inc.** from the vendor list.

◆ Click the **Invoice field**.

◆ Type **PF-1032**

◆ Press ⬚ to advance to the Date field.

◆ Type **Jun 1**

◆ Press ⬚ to advance to the Item column.

A dotted box in the Item column indicates the cursor is in this position. If it is not, click the Rec'd column and then click the Item column again.

◆ Double click or press ⬚ to access the Select Inventory/service list:

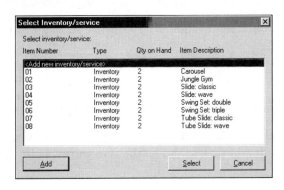

When you sort inventory by Description instead of by Number (Home window, Setup menu, Settings, Inventory & Services tab screen), item numbers are omitted from the inventory lists and items are listed in alphabetical order according to the item description.

This selection screen is similar to the Select Account screen that is available in all Account fields. The **Select Inventory/service screen** is available in all inventory Item fields. The quantity of each item in stock appears on this screen for reference. Notice that you can add a new inventory item from this screen by clicking Add new inventory/service and then clicking Select, or by clicking Add.

◆ Click **07 Tube Slide: classic** to highlight it.

◆ Click **Select** to add the item to the invoice (or double click 07 Tube Slide: classic) and advance to the Rec'd column.

The inventory unit, description, unit purchase price (cost), tax rates and account number have been added to the invoice. You cannot change the account number although you can edit the unit price.

◆ Type **2**

◆ Press ⌨tab⌨ to advance to the Unit field.

The amount for the inventory line, calculated as the quantity received times the unit price, is entered automatically. GST codes and PST rates and amounts are also added.

Since the inventory purchase is PST exempt, we must remove this tax entry.

◆ Click the **P (PST rate) field** to highlight 8.00, the Provincial Sales Tax rate.

◆ Press ⌨del⌨ to remove the entry.

◆ Press ⌨tab⌨ to advance the cursor, remove the PST amount and update the totals.

◆ Click the **Item column** on the second line.

◆ Double click to access the Select Inventory/service screen.

◆ Double click **08 Tube Slide: wave** to add this item to the invoice and advance to the Rec'd column.

◆ Type **2**

◆ Press ⌨tab⌨ to advance to the Unit field.

The new amount is added and the totals are updated.

Again, we must remove the tax entry for PST.

◆ Click the **P (PST rate) field** to highlight 8.00, the Provincial Sales Tax rate.

◆ Press ⌨del⌨ to remove the entry.

◆ Press ⌨tab⌨ to advance the cursor, remove the PST amount and update the totals.

◆ Click the **Freight GST code field**, the first Freight field on the left.

◆ Type **3** to enter the code.

◆ Click the **Freight amount field**, the final Freight field on the right.

◆ Type **50** to enter the freight charge.

◆ Press ⌨tab⌨ to update the GST total and the invoice total. Your completed invoice should now look like the one shown here:

Linked inventory asset accounts are not available for selection in Account fields once you have set up the Inventory Ledger.

If the GST code is not included automatically, click the G field (GST code field) and press ⌨enter⌨ to display the codes. Click Code 3 and click Select.

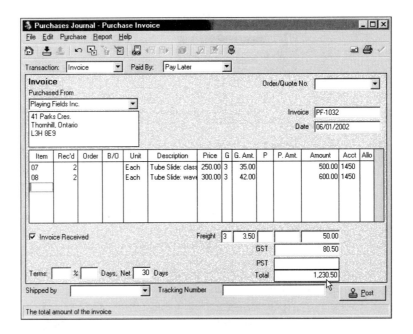

◆ Choose the **Report** menu and click **Display Purchases Journal Entry** to review the journal entry:

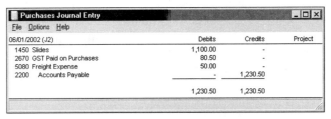

Although this journal entry looks just like the entry for previous purchase transactions, there is one important difference. For non-inventory purchases, you must enter the account number. For inventory purchases, you cannot enter or change the account number. The linked asset account must be used for inventory purchases. Thus, the only way to change the account number is to edit the Inventory Ledger record.

◆ Close the display to return to the Purchases Journal.

◆ Make corrections if necessary, just as you did for other purchase entries.

Correcting the Purchases Journal

Most of the corrections are the same as they are for non-inventory purchases. If the Item is incorrect, click the incorrect item in the Item field, press _enter_ and reselect from the selection list. Once you change the item, you must re-enter the quantity. Press _tab_ to update the totals.

When you are certain that the entry is correct,

◆ Click **Post** to save the transaction.

◆ Enter the next transaction, a purchase order, in the Purchases Journal.

Purchase Order #20006

Dated Jun. 2/02

Shipping Date: Jun. 7/02

From Playing Fields Inc.

one	05	Swing Set: double	$ 200.00
one	06	Swing Set: triple	250.00
		Freight	50.00
		Total	500.00
		GST Paid	35.00
		Invoice total	$535.00

Terms: net 30 days.

◆ Enter the following transactions in the appropriate journals.

Sales Invoice #116

Dated Jun. 3/02

To Dr. Manga, to fill sales order #2004, $7 500 plus $525 GST charged for completion of play centre. Invoice total $8 025. Terms: net 1 day.

Cash Receipt #12

Dated Jun. 4/02

From MegaCity Parks & Rec, certified cheque #21996 for $5 583.82 in full payment of account. Reference invoice #101, customer deposit cheque #19882 and Memos #13 and 23.

Cash Receipt #13

Dated Jun. 4/02

From Dr. Manga, cheque #268 for $6 150 in full payment of account. Reference invoice #116 and deposit #3.

Cheque Copy #130

Dated Jun. 4/02

To Swede Steel Co., $2 621.50 in full payment of account balance, including $53.50 discount taken for early payment. Reference invoice #SC-5410.

Purchase Invoice #BC-1121

Dated Jun. 6/02

From The Buildex Corp., to fill purchase order #20005, $1 500 for plastics and fibreglass and $2 000 for lumber plus $245 GST paid. Freight charge is $50 plus $3.50 GST. Invoice total $3 798.50. Terms: 2/10, n/30 days.

Cash Purchase Invoice #VM-160

Dated Jun. 7/02

From Vincent Meade, $200 plus $14 GST paid for maintenance services rendered in shop and yard, and for inventory maintenance. Invoice total $214. Issued cheque #131 in full payment. Recall stored monthly entry.

Purchase Invoice #PF-1048
Dated Jun. 7/02
From Playing Fields Inc., to fill purchase order #20006

one	05	Swing Set: double	$200.00
one	06	Swing Set: triple	250.00
		Freight	50.00
		Total	500.00
		GST Paid	35.00
		Invoice total	$535.00

Terms: net 30 days.

◆ Close the Purchases Journal to return to the Home window.

Inventory Item Assembly and Transfers

Sometimes a business wants to offer its inventory for sale in units other than those originally purchased. For example, a company may buy single units but sell in packages or sets of three. If the selling price for each set of three is less than the price for a single unit, a new inventory item created for the sets can reflect the new price. The transfer from the single units to sets allows the business to decide how many sets it will offer. Item assembly can also apply to the building of products from several different pieces of inventory. For example, assembling components to build a computer, packaging several different school supply products together for a back-to-school promotional special, combining earrings and necklaces to create a jewellery set, etc. Item assembly does not involve customers or vendors. The transaction is an internal transfer of inventory items for control purposes.

Play Wave will assemble different playground equipment pieces and sell them to customers as complete playground kits. Initially, they will provide two types of kits. The Tom Sawyer Kit comes complete with a picket fence, paint and a brush so that children can practise their persuasion skills while they play. The Huck Finn Kit includes a ready-to-assemble river raft for the added excitement of river orienteering. Play Wave also sells individual playground pieces because customers often want an extra slide or swing with their units.

The kits do not yet exist as inventory items, so you must first create them.

◆ Click the **Inventory & Services icon** in the Home window to open the Inventory window.

◆ Click the **Create tool** (or choose the File menu and click Create to open the Inventory Ledger).

◆ Enter the following record information for the two new inventory items.

Create two new inventory items in the Inventory Ledger to prepare for inventory item assembly.

Item No:		KIT-A	KIT-B
Item Description:		Tom Sawyer Kit	Huck Finn Kit
Unit:		Kit	Kit
Selling Price:		$1 800	$2 100
Minimum Qty:		0	0
Linked Accounts:	Asset	1470	1470
	Revenue	4040	4040
	Expense	5030	5030
	Variance	5042	5042

Entering Item Assembly Journal Transactions

The first transaction involving item assembly creates one Tom Sawyer Kit by combining a Carousel, Classic Slide, Double Swing Set and Classic Tube Slide. The second item assembly transaction will create one Huck Finn Kit by combining a Jungle Gym, Wave Slide, Triple Swing Set and Wave Tube Slide. Additional lumber and hardware are also provided in the kit. The Inventory Item Assembly (IIA) form serves as the source document.

 Inventory Item Assembly #IIA-1

Dated Jun. 7/02

Assembly Components: transfer one (1) of each item

01	Carousel	$200	each
03	Slide: classic	250	each
05	Swing Set: double	200	each
07	Tube Slide: classic	250	each
Additional Costs		75	

Assembled Items: assemble one (1) kit

KIT-A Tom Sawyer Kit $975 each

Store the transfer as a recurring transaction with random frequency.

◆   Close any open windows to return to the Home window.

Item assemblies are completed in the Item Assembly Journal shown with the pointer in the following screen:

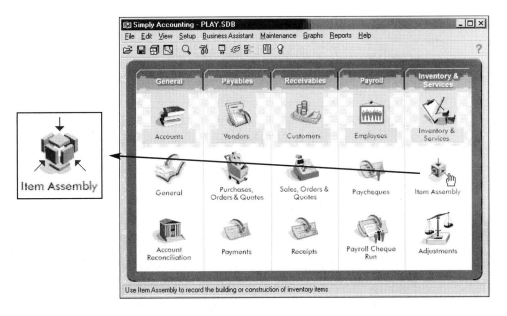

◆ Click the **Item Assembly Journal icon** to open the Item Assembly Journal:

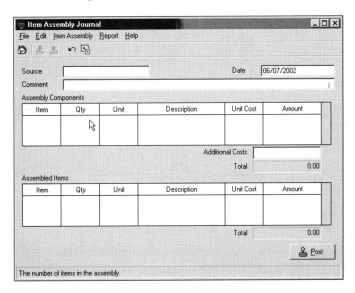

Item Assembly Journal Fields

The **Item Assembly menu** is new to this journal. It includes the familiar Store, Recall and Post menu options. The other menu items and the tools are the same as those found in other journals.

Source, **Date** and **Comment**: These fields serve the same purpose as they do in other journals. The Source may be an internal inventory assembly form or a memo. The Date of the assembly, or transfer of inventory items, becomes the transaction date, and the Comment provides a descriptive explanation of the transaction.

Assembly Components: These are the inventory items that are being removed from inventory to create the new items. The **Item** column contains the inventory number or code. The **quantity (Qty)** is the number of units being taken from inventory. The program enters the **Unit**, **Description** and **Unit Cost** from the ledger record and calculates the **Amount** as the quantity times the unit cost. You can edit the costs.

Additional Costs: Sometimes there are additional costs incurred as part of the assembly process. For example, there may be shipping costs for physically moving the items, there may be packaging costs associated with the new item, or additional material may be used, etc. These costs are entered in the Additional Costs field. These item assembly costs are recorded in the associated linked account. They should be viewed as a contra-expense; they add to the value or cost of the new asset, so the item assembly linked account is credited. Usually these costs are small compared with the component costs of the new inventory.

Assembled Items: These are the new inventory items that have been created or assembled. The columns have the same meaning that they do in the Assembly Components part of the journal. The Unit Cost field cannot be completed automatically until a cost is on record from a previous purchase or item assembly. The total amount for each assembled item must be the same as the total of its assembly components plus its share of the additional costs.

Total: The program calculates the totals automatically. Additional costs are added to the assembly component amounts to create the total for the upper portion of the journal. The total for the assembled items is the total of each item amount plus additional costs. The two totals must match before you can post the transaction.

The Item Assembly Journal is not intended as a cost accounting journal. Cost accounting usually involves a significant labour component as well as other fixed costs and overhead expenses. In Simply Accounting, labour costs are entered in the Payroll Journal. Entering them through the Item Assembly Journal would require complex additional adjusting entries.

Resizing the Journal Window

There may not be enough space in the default journal window to see all of the item lines at once. You can enlarge the window by using the mouse to drag the lower edge of the journal window down to increase the available space in the Assembly Components and the Assembled Items portions of the journal. You can also enlarge the window to full screen size by clicking the Maximize button ☐ or by choosing the Control menu and clicking Maximize. Later you can restore the window to its default size by clicking the Restore button 🗗 or by choosing the Control menu and clicking Restore.

The cursor is in the Source field.

◆ Type **IIA-1**

◆ Press ⌧ *(tab)* to advance to the Date field. The Session date is correct.

◆ Press ⌧ *(tab)* again to advance to the Comment field.

◆ Type **Assemble Tom Sawyer Kit for sale**

◆ Press ⌧ *(tab)* to advance to the Item field.

◆ Double click to see the Select Inventory screen.

◆ Double click **01 Carousel** to enter the item and advance to the Qty field.

◆ Type **1** to enter the quantity for this component item.

◆ Press ⌧ *(tab)* to update the Amount for this item line and advance to the Unit field. If necessary, you can edit either the Unit Cost or the Amount.

◆ Press ⌧ *(tab)* repeatedly to move to the Item column in the next line.

◆ Press ⌧ *(enter)* to see the Select Inventory list. The quantity for Carousels is updated.

◆ Double click **03 Slide: classic** to enter the item and advance the cursor.

◆ Type **1** to enter the quantity.

Services are not involved in inventory transfers and therefore are not part of the selection lists in this journal.

◆ Click the **Item column** in the next line. This will update the amount for the previous line.

◆ Press (enter).

◆ Double click **05 Swing Set: double**.

◆ Type **1**

◆ Click **the Item column** in the next line to update the previous line.

◆ Press (enter).

◆ Double click **07 Tube Slide: classic**.

◆ Type **1**

◆ Press (tab) to update the amount and total.

The additional costs associated with this assembly are for lumber and other materials for the picket fence.

◆ Click the **Additional Costs field**.

◆ Type **75**

◆ Press (tab) to update the total. Your journal should now look like the following:

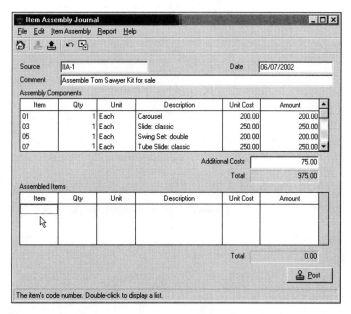

◆ Click the first line in the Item column of the Assembled Items part of the journal.

◆ Press (enter).

◆ Double click **KIT-A Tom Sawyer Kit**. The cursor moves to the Quantity field.

◆ Type **1**

◆ Click the **Amount field**.

No cost is associated with this item yet because it has not been purchased or assembled, so the program leaves the Amount field blank. The amount is the total of the costs of the assembly components plus any additional costs. When you are assembling only one type of item at a time, this amount will be the same as the Total in the upper portion of the journal. By entering the amount, you do not need to calculate the cost for individual units when more than one unit is assembled. The program calculates the unit cost automatically. The next time you assemble this item, the previous cost will become the default entry. You can change either the Unit Cost or the Amount if necessary (the other one will be updated automatically).

◆ Type **975**

◆ Press ⌐tab⌐ to update the Unit Cost and the Total.

Your journal entry is complete and should look like the one shown here:

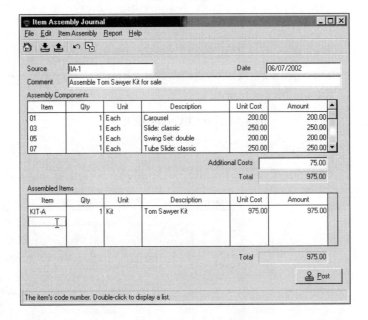

The next step is to review the journal entry.

◆ Choose the **Report** menu and click **Display Item Assembly Journal Entry**:

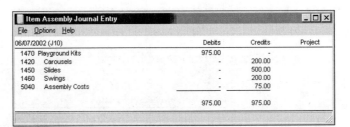

The journal entry shows that you have transferred the assets from one account to another to reflect the new inventory. When you use the same asset account for both the assembly components and the assembled item, there will be no journal entry. In this case, only the inventory ledgers will be updated for the quantity changes. The credit to *Assembly Costs* reflects the increased value of the new inventory item by crediting this expense (contra-expense) account. When we adjust for supplies used at the end of the month, the materials expenses will be recognized.

◆ Close the display.

Check your work carefully. After you post the transaction, you must complete a reversing entry to make corrections. There is no option to adjust the Item Assembly Journal entry after posting as you can adjust entries in the other journals.

Correcting the Item Assembly Journal Entry before Posting

Edit the Source, Date, Comment, Unit Cost (or Amount) and Additional Cost fields by selecting the text you want to change and retyping the correct information. To edit an item, click the incorrect item number or code, press ⟨enter⟩ and reselect from the inventory list. Re-enter the quantity. You can move forward through the fields by pressing ⟨tab⟩ and back to a previous field by pressing ⟨shift⟩ and ⟨tab⟩ together. Using the ⟨tab⟩ key will highlight the field contents so you can retype immediately.

If you need to add a line to the journal, click the line below the one you want to add and choose the Edit menu and click Insert Line. You can delete a line by choosing the Edit menu and clicking Remove Line.

If you want to start over, click ⟨↰⟩ or choose the Edit menu and click Undo Entry. Confirm that you want to discard the current entry.

Correcting the Item Assembly Journal Entry after Posting

After posting, you must make a complete reversing entry to correct an error. Print the journal to view the details that were posted. Recall the originally posted entry if you have stored it. Change the Source and Comment and then edit all the quantities by adding a minus sign.

If you did not store the entry, you must begin again. In a new blank journal entry, enter an appropriate Source and Comment for the reversing entry. Enter the items as they were in the incorrect entry, but replace all positive quantities with negative quantities. You can review the Inventory Transaction Report for the Item Assembly Journal (see page 419) to determine what information you entered originally.

Check your work carefully. Review the journal entry and compare it with the one you printed to be certain that everything is reversed. Post the entry when you are certain that it is correct.

There is no lookup feature for the Item Assembly Journal. Therefore you should store the Item Assembly Journal entry. Then, if you have made a mistake, you can recall the entry to see exactly how you entered the original transaction.

◆ Click **Store** ⟨⬇⟩ to save the transaction.

◆ Choose **Random** as the frequency because the transfer will be repeated at irregular intervals. Choosing a random frequency will enter the Session date as the transaction date when you recall the stored item.

◆ Click **Post** ⟨🖈 Post⟩ to save the transaction.

◆ Enter the next Item Assembly transaction.

☐ Inventory Item Assembly #IIA-2

Dated Jun. 7/02

Assembly Components: transfer one (1) of each item

02	Jungle Gym	$200	each
04	Slide: wave	300	each
06	Swing Set: triple	250	each
08	Tube Slide: wave	300	each

Additional Costs (lumber for raft)   80

Assembled Items: assemble one (1) kit

KIT-B Huck Finn Kit $1 130 each

Store the transfer as a recurring transaction with random frequency.

◆ Close the Item Assembly Journal.

◆ Advance the Session date to **June 11, 2002**. Enter the following transactions using the appropriate journals.

☐ Cash Receipt #14

Dated Jun. 9/02

From Broadview Daycare Centre, cheque #411 for $7 200 in full payment of account including $180 discount for early payment. Reference invoice #115 and deposit #2.

☐ Employee Time Summary Sheet #3

Pay Period Ending Jun. 11, 2002

Peter Piper worked 80 regular hours and 2 hours overtime.

Recover $50 advance. Issue cheque #132.

☐ Memo #32

Dated Jun. 11/02

Payroll Cheque Run Time Sheet for pay period ending June 11.

Rapper worked 80 hours ar the regular hourly rate.

Doolittle should receive her normal bi-weekly salary.

Issue cheques #133 and 134 in payment.

☐ Credit Card Purchase Invoice #GA-1459

Dated Jun. 11/02

From Gasoline Alley, $60 plus $4.20 GST and $4.80 (8%) PST charged for gasoline for truck and $50 plus $3.50 GST and $4 (8%) PST charged for propane gas. Total invoice amount paid by Chargit, $126.50.

◆ Advance the Session date to **June 18, 2002**. Enter the following transactions.

☐ Memo #33

Dated Jun. 14/02

In the Payments Journal, record the PST Payable for May 31, 2002, as a liability owing to the Minister of Finance. This liability is reduced by the sales tax compensation of 5% of the PST account balance (5% of $1 120 is $56). Issue cheque #135 for $1 064 in payment.

Do not advance the Session date beyond June 11. If you do, you should use the Payroll Journal instead of the Payroll Cheque Run Journal. Or you can change the Session date back to June 11 before completing the Payroll Cheque Run Journal transaction. Remember that for the Payroll Cheque Run Journal, you must use the Session date as the cheque date.

Remember that you already posted the General Journal entry to record the PST Payable in Chapter 13. Memo #33 describes the remittance (Make an Other Payment in the Payments Journal).

☐ Cheque Copy #136
Dated Jun. 14/02
To Chargit $322 for purchases charged before June 7, the billing date. Total payment submitted to avoid incurring interest charges, $322.

◆ Close the journal to return to the Home window.

Sales of Inventory Items

Inventory sales, like other sales, are entered in the Sales Journal. Unlike the contracting services provided by Play Wave, the inventory sales are subject to the Provincial Sales Tax as well as the federal GST. Since the PST rate has been entered in the Sales Taxes settings already, and the PST Payable account is already linked to the Receivables Ledger, no further setup is required. The program automatically enters the tax rate for inventory sales and credits *PST Payable*. If tax should not be applied, the rate can be deleted.

Play Wave's owner, Child, has decided to charge customers for delivery. This charge is credited to a *Freight Revenue* account that must be linked to the Receivables Ledger.

Adding a Linked Account

First we must create the new account and then add its linking function.

☐ Create the new Group account   4200 Freight Revenue

◆ Close any windows that are open to return to the Home window.

◆ Choose the **Setup** menu, then choose **Linked Accounts** and click **Receivables** to open the Receivables Linked Accounts screen.

◆ Click the **Freight Revenue field list arrow**.

◆ Click *4200 Freight Revenue* from the list.

◆ Click **OK** to save the change and return to the Home window.

Be careful not to change any of the other linked accounts in the Linked Accounts screen.

The first inventory sale is to a new customer who is paying by credit card.

✔ Credit Card Sales Invoice #117
Dated Jun. 14/02
To Robinson Crusoe (Use Quick Add for this customer)

one	KIT-A	Tom Sawyer Kit	$1 800.00
one	08	Tube Slide: wave	610.00
		Freight	50.00
		GST Charged (7%)	172.20
		PST Charged (8%)	192.80
		Total received	$2 825.00

Paid by credit card.

Inventory sales, sales orders and quotes are all completed in the Sales Journal.

◆ Click the **Sales Journal icon** to open the Sales Journal:

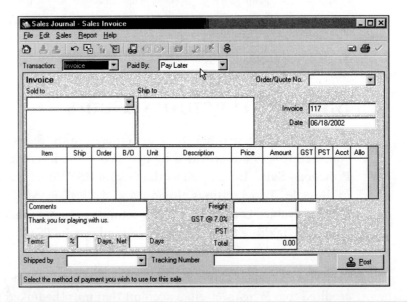

The Sales Journal Fields

The appearance of and options for the Sales Journal do not change when you add the Inventory Ledger. The column headings correspond to the Inventory Ledger record fields. Most of the fields are completed automatically based on the default information. You can change the selling price for individual sales. Unlike inventory purchases, the account number for sales can also be edited. Thus, for sales returns, you can use a different account such as *Sales Returns and Allowances*.

Invoice is correct as the type of transaction.

◆ Choose **Chargit** as the payment method in the **Paid By** field.

◆ Press ⓣ to advance to the Sold to (Customer) field.

◆ Type **Robinson Crusoe**

◆ Press ⓣ.

◆ Click **Quick Add** to add only the customer's name to the Receivables Ledger.

◆ Double click the **Date field**.

◆ Type **6 14**

◆ Press ⓣ to advance the cursor to the **Item column**.

◆ Press ⓔ to see the familiar Select Inventory/service screen.

◆ Click **KIT-A Tom Sawyer Kit** from the list.

◆ Click **Select** to add it to the invoice and move to the Ship column.

Some of the inventory fields are already completed with the default record details.

◆ Type **1** to enter the quantity purchased and shipped.

◆ Press ⓣ to advance to the Unit column.

The default selling price is correct. The program calculates the amount and enters it. The GST code and PST rate are added, as are the tax amounts and the revenue account. The defaults are correct.

◆ Click the **Item column** on the second invoice line.

◆ Press (enter) to see the selection list. Notice that the quantity for KIT-A is now zero.

◆ Double click **08 Tube Slide: wave** to enter the item.

◆ Type **1** to enter the quantity in the Ship field.

◆ Press (tab) to advance to the Unit column and update the invoice line.

Again, the default information is correct. You still need to remove the discount and enter the freight charge.

◆ Double click **2.00** in the Discount % field to select it.

◆ Press (del) to remove the amount.

◆ Press (tab) to update the invoice.

◆ Click the **first Freight field**, the amount field.

◆ Type **50**

◆ Press (tab) to advance to the Freight GST code field.

◆ Type **3**

◆ Press (tab) to update all the totals.

Your invoice is complete as shown:

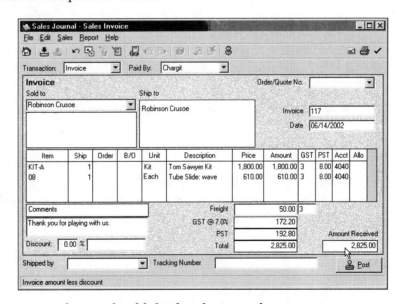

To review your work, you should display the journal entry.

◆ Choose the **Report** menu and click **Display Sales Journal Entry**:

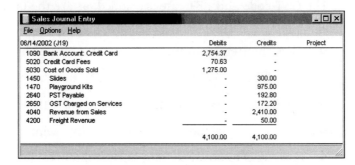

Notice that the journal entry consists entirely of linked accounts. The Receivables Ledger linked accounts seen in previous credit card sales transactions are repeated here, with the addition of *PST Payable* and *Freight Revenue*. The inventory asset accounts, *Slides* and *Playground Kits*, are each credited for the sale because the inventory is reduced. The *Cost of Goods Sold* is debited to recognize the cost of the merchandise sold and the linked revenue account, *Revenue from Sales*, is credited. Thus, both the Balance Sheet and the Income Statement are updated by the transaction. The Inventory Ledger is also updated by reducing the quantity on hand. The only account that you can edit in this transaction is the revenue account. The linked revenue account for the inventory item is entered as the default.

◆ Close the display when you have finished to return to the Sales Journal and make any corrections necessary.

Correcting the Sales Journal

Most of the corrections are the same as they are for non-inventory sales. If the item is incorrect, click the item number or code to move the cursor, press *enter* and reselect from the selection list. Once you change the item, you must re-enter the quantity. Press *tab* to update the totals.

◆ Click **Post** ⬚ *Post* to save the transaction.

Sales Returns

Customers may return goods for a variety of reasons. They may have received the wrong items, they may have received damaged goods or the items may be the wrong size or colour. Sometimes the customer is just generally not satisfied with the merchandise. Stores have different policies for returns. Some stores allow no returns or exchanges while others guarantee satisfaction and offer returns without question. In some cases, there may be a handling charge for returns.

Normally a business records sales returns in a separate revenue account, a contra-revenue account often named *Sales Returns and Allowances*.

The next transaction shows a sales return. Crusoe received the wrong items and has returned them. The correct invoice follows the keystroke instructions for the return.

✔ Credit Card Sales Return #117-R
Dated Jun. 15/02
To Robinson Crusoe
Crusoe returned the tube slide and KIT-A.

–one	KIT-A	Tom Sawyer Kit	–$1 800.00
–one	08	Tube Slide: wave	–610.00
		Freight	–50.00
		GST Charged (7%)	–172.20
		PST Charged (8%)	–192.80
		Total Credit	–$2 825.00

Total credited to credit card.

Charge the return to a new Group account, 4080 Sales Returns and Allowances.

◆ Click the **Sales Journal icon** to open the Sales Journal.

◆ Choose **Invoice** as the transaction type.

◆ Choose **Chargit** as the method of payment.

◆ Choose **Robinson Crusoe** as the customer.

◆ Double click the **Invoice field** to highlight the default invoice number.

We do not want this invoice to be part of the automatic numbering sequence. Adding R to the original invoice number will help to connect the two invoices.

◆ Type **117-R** as the invoice number.

◆ Press ⌨*tab* to advance to the Date field.

◆ Type **June 15**.

Because no discount is applied to the credit card sale, the discount entry must be deleted.

◆ Double click the **Discount field** contents to select it.

◆ Press ⌨*del* to remove the entry.

◆ Click the **Item field** to move the cursor.

◆ Press ⌨*enter* to access the Select Inventory/service list.

◆ Click **KIT-A Tom Sawyer Kit** to select it.

◆ Click **Select** to add the item to the invoice and advance to the Ship field.

◆ Type **-1** (minus one) as the quantity to indicate that the merchandise is returned.

◆ Press ⌨*tab* to advance the cursor and update the amounts.

Since this is not a sale, we must change the default revenue account.

◆ Double click the **Account field** to access the Select Account list.

◆ Choose **Add** and use the Account Wizard to add the new Group account *4080 Sales Returns and Allowances*.

◆ Press ⌨*tab* to advance the cursor to the Item field on the second line.

◆ Click **08 Tube Slide: wave** to select it.

◆ Click **Select** to add the item to the invoice and advance to the Ship field.

◆ Type **–1** (minus one) as the quantity to indicate that the merchandise is returned.

◆ Click the **Account field** and enter account **4080** for the returned item. The Amount and totals are updated again.

The next step is to reverse the freight charge.

◆ Click the **first Freight field** (the freight amount field).

◆ Type **–50**

◆ Press `tab` to advance the cursor to the Freight GST code field.

◆ Type **3**

◆ Press `tab` to update the totals.

The transaction is complete, and your journal should look like the following:

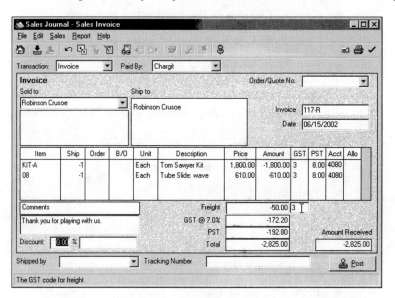

◆ Choose the **Report** menu and click **Display Sales Journal Entry** to view the completed journal entry:

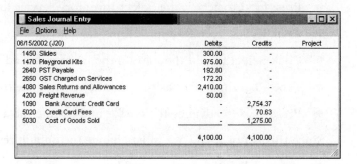

Notice that this reverses the original sale by reversing all the normal debit and credit entries. The negative quantity leads to this result automatically. When multiplied by the unit cost, all the amounts become negative, including the taxes calculated on the negative amount. The program interprets these negative amounts as the switch between debits and credits.

◆ Close the display to return to the journal.

◆ Check your work carefully, and make corrections if necessary. Refer to Correcting the Sales Journal Entry on page 197 if you need help.

◆ Click the **Use the same customer next time tool** 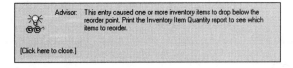 to keep the customer name selected.

◆ Click **Post** ▣ Post to save the transaction.

◆ Enter the correct sales transaction for Crusoe. Currently only one wave slide is in stock. Edit the default comment to indicate that one of the slides is still on order.

☐ Credit Card Sales Invoice #118
Dated Jun. 15/02
To Robinson Crusoe
Crusoe ordered 2 regular wave slides, and KIT-B.

two	04	Slides: wave	$610 each	$1 220.00
one		KIT-B Huck Finn Kit		2 100.00
		Subtotal		3 320.00
		GST @ 7%		232.40
		PST @ 8%		265.60
		Total received		$3 818.00

Because of the previous mistake in the order, there is no freight charge.
Paid by credit card.

When you post sales invoice #118, you will see the following message advising that one or more inventory item levels have dropped below the re-order point:

> Advisor: This entry caused one or more inventory items to drop below the reorder point. Print the Inventory Item Quantity report to see which items to reorder.
>
> [Click here to close.]

Close the advisor window. At this stage, you could view the Inventory Quantity Report to see what items should be re-ordered. Since we have chosen to allow inventory levels to go below zero in the Inventory Ledger settings, we can oversell the item. If you have not selected this option, the program will not permit you to enter the quantity larger than the existing stock. You will see a message that the quantity exceeds the stock on hand. Close the message, close the journal — discard the entry — and change the Inventory Ledger settings (see page 375). Re-enter the sales invoice. A comment about the backordered items should be included on the invoice when the customer does not receive all the goods purchased.

◆ Click the **Use the same customer next time tool** 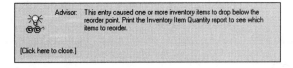 to deselect this customer.

◆ Close the Sales Journal to return to the Home window and continue entering the following transactions.

It is possible to complete the sales return on the same invoice as the sale by adding the items sold to the invoice after entering the items returned. This is the procedure used for exchanges. Most stores, however, have a separate form for returns.

☐ Cash Purchase Invoice #OH-411421
Dated Jun. 15/02
From Ontario Hydro, $100 for hydro services plus $7 GST paid. Invoice total $107.
Issued cheque #137 in full payment.

☐ Cash Purchase Invoice #BC-714323
Dated Jun. 15/02
From Bell Canada, $80 for telephone services plus $5.60 GST paid and $6.40 PST
paid. Invoice total $92.00. Issued cheque #138 in full payment.

☐ Sales Quote #2005
Dated Jun. 15/02
Completion date June 28/02
To York Recreational Centre, $8 000 plus $560 GST charged for completion of play
centre. Invoice total $8 560. Terms: 2/10, n/30 days. Use Quick Add for the new
customer.

☐ Cheque Copy #139
Dated Jun. 15/02
To The Buildex Corp., $3 722.53 in full payment of account, including $75.97
discount taken for early payment. Reference invoice #BC-1121.

☐ Sales Order #2005
Dated Jun. 16/02
Completion date June 28/02
Convert sales quote #2005 for York Recreational Centre to a sales order. All
amounts, dates and terms are unchanged.

☐ Cash Receipt #15
Dated Jun. 17/02
From York Recreational Centre, cheque #264 for $2 000 (customer deposit #4) to
accept sales order #2005.

Inventory Adjustments

When the business uses its inventory in the store, it must pay PST on the transferred merchandise since the goods were purchased for resale and were exempt at the time of purchase. The PST obligation should be entered in the General Journal. The Retail Sales Tax remittance form includes a category for this type of inventory transfer.

Sometimes a business loses inventory as a result of theft, breakage, loss or other damage. These decreases in inventory and their associated expenses are recorded in the Inventory Adjustments Journal. Losses may be discovered during periodic inventory inspections or checks, or when an item is retrieved for sale or assembly. The expense is recorded at the average cost price for the inventory. A business might also use the Adjustments Journal to record a transfer of merchandise from inventory for internal store or business use. Instead of selling the item to customers, the store sells the item to itself. Using the historical cost principle, the item should be transferred at cost price. Inventory adjustments are internal to the business, that is, they do not involve customers or vendors, and the transactions are at the historical average cost price.

On June 18, one of the employees damaged a slide beyond repair while constructing a playground kit, as described in the following source document.

✔ Memo #34
Dated Jun. 18/02
One Tube Slide: classic (item #07), valued at $250 was damaged during construction.
Since the plastic slide cannot be repaired, the loss should be written off completely.

Inventory adjustments are entered in the Inventory Adjustments Journal shown by the pointer in the following screen:

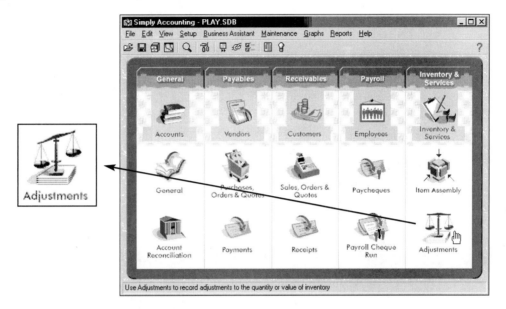

◆ Click the **Adjustments Journal icon** to open the Adjustments Journal:

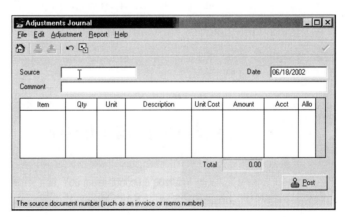

The Adjustments Journal

The tool buttons and most of the menu items in the Adjustments Journal are the same as those found in previous journals. The **Adjustment menu** is the only new menu, but its options, Store, Recall, Allocate and Post, are familiar.

Source, **Date** and **Comment**: These fields are familiar from other journals. Often the source for an adjustment is an internal memo written when the loss or damage is discovered.

Item: The inventory's item number or code. As in other Item fields, an inventory selection list is available from which to select the item or to add a new item.

Qty: The number of units involved. Usually the quantity is negative because the inventory has decreased. If lost merchandise is later recovered, the unit can be restored to inventory with an additional adjustment using a positive quantity.

Unit and **Description**: The unit of measurement and the item description are entered as defaults from the ledger record.

Unit Cost: The average cost per unit based on previous purchases. The cost can be edited if the actual cost for the unit involved is known to be different from this average.

Amount: The total cost amount of the inventory involved, calculated as the quantity times the unit cost. If the quantity is negative, the amount is also negative. The program calculates the amount.

Acct: The default linked account for adjustment write-off. You can change the account if necessary, for example, when inventory is removed from stock for store use. In this case, you would use a store supplies or a fixed asset account. The program automatically supplies the inventory asset account for the journal entry.

Allo: If you want to allocate or distribute an expense amount, you will use this column.

Total: The total of all amounts in the Amount column. The program calculates and enters this total.

The cursor is in the Source field.

◆ Type **Memo 34**

The Session date is correct at June 18. You can change the date if necessary.

◆ Click the **Comment field** to advance the cursor.

◆ Type **Slide damaged during construction**

◆ Press ⌨tab⌨ to advance to the Item column.

◆ Press ⌨enter⌨ to access the Select Inventory screen.

◆ Double click **07 Tube Slide: classic** to enter the item and advance to the quantity field.

The journal entry now resembles the one shown here:

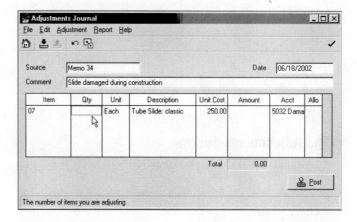

The program supplies the default record information. Since this is correct for the item, you do not need to change these entries. If necessary, you can edit the unit cost and the account number.

◆ Type **-1** to indicate that inventory is decreased by the transaction.

◆ Press (tab) to update the amount and total.

The entry is complete as shown here:

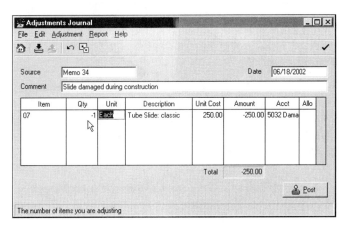

Notice that the amount and the total are negative because the quantity was negative. You should review the journal entry before proceeding.

◆ Choose the **Report** menu and click **Display Adjustments Journal Entry**:

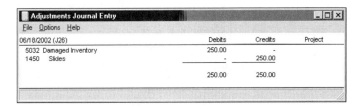

Typing a negative quantity has the desired effect of crediting (reducing) the asset account and debiting (increasing) the expense account. The default Inventory Ledger linked account, *Damaged Inventory*, is used whenever you want to record inventory losses that should be charged as expenses. For other types of adjustments, you can choose a different account. The default linked asset account is always used for inventory adjustments. You cannot change this account.

◆ Close the display to return to the journal and make any corrections to your work.

Correcting the Adjustments Journal Entry before Posting

Edit the Source, Date, Comment and Quantity fields by selecting the text you want to change and retyping the correct information. To edit an Item, click on the error, press (enter) and reselect from the inventory list. Re-enter the quantity and press (tab) to update the totals. To correct an Account, click the error, press (enter) and reselect from the account list. You can move forward through the fields by pressing (tab) and back to a previous field by pressing (shift) and (tab) together. Using the (tab) key will highlight the field contents so you can retype immediately.

If you need to add a line to the journal, click on the line below the one you want to add and choose the Edit menu and click Insert Line. You can delete a line by choosing the Edit menu and clicking Remove Line.

If you want to start over, click [↶] or choose the Edit menu and click Undo Entry. Confirm that you want to discard the current entry.

Correcting the Adjustments Journal Entry after Posting

After posting, you must make a complete reversing entry to correct an error. Print the original journal entry from the Reports menu. Recall the originally posted entry if you have stored it. Change the Source and Comment and then edit all the quantities by deleting the minus signs or adding a minus sign if the original was positive.

If you did not store the entry, create a new journal entry for the correction. Enter an appropriate Source and Comment for the reversing entry. Enter the items as they were on the incorrect entry, but replace all negative quantities with positive quantities, and all positive quantities with negative quantities.

Check your work carefully. Review the journal entry and compare it with the one you printed to be certain that everything is reversed. Post the entry when you are certain that it is correct.

◆ Click **Post** [⚒ Post] to save the journal entry. Close the advisor warning.

◆ Close the Adjustments Journal to return to the Home window.

◆ Advance the Session date to **June 25, 2002**, and continue by entering the next group of transactions in the appropriate journals.

   ☐ Sales Order #1001
   Dated Jun. 23/02
   Shipping Date Jun. 28/02
   To Laura Secord (Use Quick Add)

one	KIT-A	Tom Sawyer Kit	$1 800.00
one	05	Swing Set: double	410.00
		Freight	50.00
		GST Charged (7%)	158.20
		PST Charged (8%)	176.80
		Invoice Total	$2 595.00

   Terms: 2/10, net 30.

   ☐ Purchase Invoice #SC-6107
   Dated Jun. 23/02
   From Swede Steel Co., $2 000 plus $140 GST paid for nuts, bolts and steel rods.
   Invoice total $2 140. Terms: 2/15, n/30.

   ☐ Memo #35
   Dated Jun. 25, 2002
   Payroll Cheque Run Time Sheet for pay period ending June 25.
   Peter Piper worked 78 regular hours and 4 hours overtime.
   Candie Rapper worked 80 regular hours and no overtime.
   Rebecca Doolittle should receive her regular bi-weekly salary.
   Issue cheques #140, 141 and 142.

♦ Advance the Session date to **June 30, 2002**, and continue by entering the next group of transactions in the appropriate journals.

☐ Cash Sales Invoice #119
Dated Jun. 28/02
To fill sales order #1001
To Laura Secord

1	KIT-A	Tom Sawyer Kit	$1 800.00
1	05	Swing Set: double	410.00
		Freight	50.00
		GST Charged (7%)	158.20
		PST Charged (8%)	176.80
		Discount (2%)	(45.20)
		Invoice Total	$2 549.80

Paid in cash.

☐ Sales Invoice #120
Dated Jun. 29/02
To York Recreational Centre, to fill sales order #2005, $8 000 plus $560 GST charged for completion of play centre. Invoice total $8 560. Terms: 2/10, n/30 days.

☐ Cheque Copy #143
Dated Jun. 29/02
To Playing Fields Inc., $6 045.50 in full payment of account. Reference invoices #PF-1014, PF-1032 and PF-1048.

♦ Close the journal to return to the Home window.

Inventory Ledger Reports

The Inventory List and Inventory Report were discussed in the previous chapter. All the reports described below, except the journals, are related to inventory tracking. All Inventory Reports are available from the Home and the Inventory & Services windows.

Item Assembly Journal

The Item Assembly Journal Report includes all the transactions that were entered in the Item Assembly Journal, but not the transactions that were made in other journals.

♦ Choose the **Reports** menu, then choose **Journal Entries** and click **Item Assembly** in the Home window to see the report options:

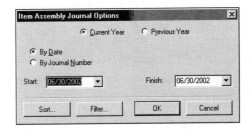

The default report lists journal transactions By Date for the Session date. As in other journal reports, you can sort and filter the report. The Start date is selected. We will display the entries for the month of June.

◆ Type **06 01** to enter the Start date.

◆ Click **OK**.

Drill-Down Reports

The same drill-down reports are available from both the Item Assembly Journal and from the Adjustments Journal Reports. Double click the account number, account name or the amount to access the General Ledger (All Transactions) Report for the selected account. The date range for the drill-down report will match the dates for the journal report. You may print the drill-down report. When you close the drill-down report, you will return to the previous report window.

◆ Choose the **File** menu and click **Print** in the Report window to print the report.

◆ Close the display when you have finished viewing and printing the report.

Adjustments Journal

The Adjustments Journal lists all transactions entered in the Adjustments Journal.

◆ Choose the **Reports** menu, then choose **Journal Entries** and click **Adjustments** in the Home window to see the report options:

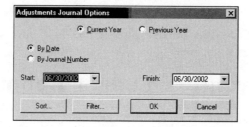

Again, the By Date option is selected as the default and you may choose to sort and filter the reports. The Session date is highlighted in the Start date field. To display the entries for June,

◆ Type **Jun 1** as the Start date.

◆ Click **OK**.

◆ Choose the **File** menu and click **Print** in the Report window to print the report.

◆ Close the display when you have finished viewing and printing the report.

Alternate Methods of Accessing Journal Reports

You can access the Item Assembly and Adjustments Journal Reports using the Reports menu or the Display tool, both from the Home window and from the Inventory & Services window, just like other journal reports. Refer to page 91, substituting Item Assembly or Adjustments for General in the instructions provided.

Inventory Activity Report

The Inventory Activity Report is one of the inventory tracking reports that monitors the sales of inventory items or groups. The Session date is used for the report.

◆ Choose the **Reports** menu, then choose **Inventory & Services** and click **Activity** in the Home window to see the report options:

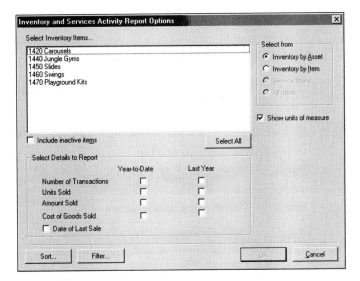

Activity Report Options

You can **Select** one or more Asset groups, inventory Items, Service Items or All Items for the report. If you select by Item, the selection list changes to list individual inventory items. Choosing Select All will automatically include all items from all asset groups. Inactive inventory items may be included or omitted from the report.

You must also choose which details to include in the report. There are four categories. The **Number of Transactions** refers to the total number of individual transactions in all journals that involved the selected item. The **Units Sold** and **Amount Sold** are the total number of individual units of the item and the total sale value for these items, and the **Cost of Goods Sold** is the total cost or purchase price for the items sold. You can report these details both for the **Year-to-Date** and for the **Last Year**. In addition, you can add the **Date of Last Sale** — the date that the item was most recently sold — and you can Sort and Filter the report by item number, by description or by any of the details you selected.

We will include all details for all items for the current year.

◆ Click **Inventory by Item** in the Select from list.

The display list should now include all the inventory by item number and description.

◆ Click **Select All** to highlight all items. (Pressing *ctrl* and clicking each item in turn will also highlight them all.)

◆ Click the **check boxes** in the Year-to-Date column for Number of Transactions, Units Sold, Amount Sold and Cost of Goods Sold to add a ✓.

◆ Click the **Date of Last Sale check box**.

◆ Click **OK** to display the report.

For each item you selected, the requested details are presented in columns.

Drill-Down Reports

Double click any item to access the Inventory and Services Sales Detail Report.

You may print the drill-down report. When you close the drill-down report, you will return to the previous report.

◆ Choose the **File** menu and click **Print** in the Report window to print the report.

◆ Close the display when you have finished viewing and printing the report.

Inventory Sales Report

The Inventory Sales Report is also part of the inventory tracking system. It reports the sales activity for the selected inventory items.

◆ Choose the **Reports** menu, then choose **Inventory & Services** and click **Sales** in the Home window to see the Report Options:

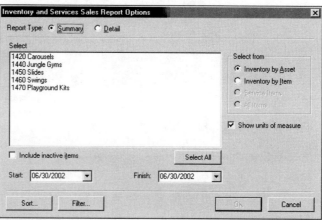

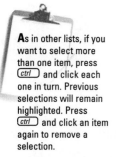

As in other lists, if you want to select more than one item, press *ctrl* and click each one in turn. Previous selections will remain highlighted. Press *ctrl* and click an item again to remove a selection.

Sales Report Options

The options are similar to those for the Activity Report. You can **Select** the report items by Asset group or by Item; you can select Service Items or you can select All Items. Choosing Select All automatically selects all the items, both service and inventory. Inactive inventory items may be included or omitted from the report. You must also indicate the date range for the report with the **Start** and **Finish** dates. The Session date is provided as the default for both. The other default setting is the Summary Report. For each selected item, the **Summary Report** includes the totals for the number of transactions, the quantity sold, the revenue from sales, the cost of the goods sold and the profit, either markup or margin according to the Inventory Ledger settings. The **Detail Report** includes the same information but adds the detail for individual transactions, including the customer's name, the journal entry number, source and date. You can Sort and Filter the report by most of the fields in the report.

We will print the Detail Report for the asset group Slides for the month of June.

◆ Click **Detail** to select the report type.

◆ Click **Slides** in the Select list.

◆ Click the **Start date field** to highlight the Session date.

◆ Type **6-1**

◆ Click **OK** to display the report.

Drill-Down Reports

From the Detail Report, there are several drill-down reports. Double click the Date or Customer name to see the Customer Aged Report. Double click the Source to access Invoice Lookup for the transaction with all of the usual lookup options. Double click the inventory item name to see the Inventory Ledger record and double click any other detail to see the journal entry for the transaction. From the Summary Report, double click any item to see the Detail Report for the line. You may print the drill-down report. When you close the drill-down report, you will return to the previous report.

◆ Choose the **File** menu and click **Print** in the Report window to print the report.

◆ Close the display when you have finished viewing and printing the report.

Inventory Transaction Report

The third inventory tracking report lists the inventory items according to the journals in which the original transaction was made.

◆ Choose the **Reports** menu, then choose **Inventory & Services** and click **Transaction** in the Home window to see the Report Options:

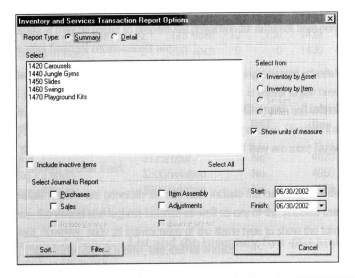

Transaction Report Options

Select the items by Asset group or by Item; choose Service Items or All Items. Choosing Select All will automatically select all service and inventory items. Inactive inventory items may be included or omitted. You can enter **Start** and **Finish** dates to indicate the reporting period. The four **Journals** listed are those that show inventory transactions. Choose one or more journals for the report. The final option is to include the **Balance forward** or the **Variance** for each item. As for many other reports, there is a Summary and a Detail version of the report. The **Summary** Report shows the totals for the quantity in and out and the amounts for these quantities. The quantity in reflects additions to inventory from purchases, sales returns, assembled items and losses restored. The quantity out is a total of decreases in inventory from sales, purchase returns, assembly components and adjustments. The **Detail** Report shows the same information for individual transactions together with the quantity on hand, the opening balance and balance forward (the quantity at the Finish date) or the variance. Journal details are also added — the date, the type of transaction (the journal used), journal entry number and date. You can Sort and Filter reports by date, source, journal number and quantity.

In the report, the journals are abbreviated as follows:
• ASM Item Assembly
  Journal
• ADJ Adjustments
  Journal
• PUR Purchases
  Journal
• SAL Sales Journal

To print the Transaction Detail Report for all items and journals for June,

◆ Click **Select All** below the Select from list to include all the items.

◆ Click **Detail** to select the report type.

◆ Click the **Start date field**.

◆ Type **June 1**

◆ Click the **check boxes beside each of the four journals** to include them all.

◆ Click the **check box for Balance Forward**.

◆ Click **OK** to see the report.

Drill-Down Reports

From the Detail Report, double click the inventory item name to access the ledger record. Double click the Date, Journal Entry number or Journal type to display the journal entry for the transaction and double click the Source or other details to access Invoice Lookup for the transaction for sales and purchases. From the Summary Report, double click any item to see the Detail Report for the line. You may print the drill-down report. When you close the drill-down report, you will return to the previous report.

◆ Choose the **File** menu, and click **Print** in the Report window to print the report.

◆ Close the display when you have finished viewing and printing the report.

Vendor Purchases Report

Although this report is included with the Payables Ledger because it can include non-inventory purchases, it is primarily an inventory tracking report. It links the vendors with inventory items to show which vendors supply most of the inventory purchased.

◆ Choose the **Reports** menu, then choose **Payables** and click **Vendor Purchases** in the Home window to see the Report Options:

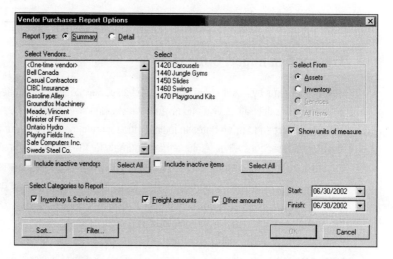

Vendor Purchases Report Options

You can **Select the items** for the report by Asset or by Item; choose Services or All Items. Choose items by pressing (ctrl) and clicking the names. When you choose Select All for the inventory items or assets, you automatically select all the items. You can also choose one or more vendors for the report from the **Select Vendors** box by pressing (ctrl) and clicking the names. Clicking the Select All button beneath the vendor list will include all vendors. Inactive inventory items and vendors may be included or omitted from the report. The range of dates for the report is provided by the **Start** and **Finish** dates. As usual, the Session date is given as the default. You can also choose the type of purchase to include in the report by including one or more kinds of amounts: **Inventory & Services**, **Other** (non-inventory purchases) and **Freight**. Thus, the report is organized according to vendor, type of purchase and inventory item.

Again, there are two reports. The **Summary** Report shows the totals for the number of transactions, the number of units purchased (quantity), the cost per unit and the total cost for each vendor for each selected item and type of purchase. The **Detail** Report has these same column headings but shows the information for individual transactions as well as the journal details — date, source and journal entry number. Reports may be sorted and filtered by date, item number, journal number, source, quantity and unit or total cost.

We will display the Detail Report for all vendors for all inventory items for June.

- ◆ Click **Detail** as the report type.
- ◆ Click the **Select All button** below the Select Vendors list box.
- ◆ Click the **Select All button** below the Select (inventory) list box.
- ◆ Click the **Start date field**.
- ◆ Type **06-01-02**
- ◆ Click the **check box for Other amounts** to remove the ✓.
- ◆ Click the **check box for Freight amounts** to remove its ✓.
- ◆ Click **OK** to see the report.

There is only one vendor in the report because all inventory purchases were from Playing Fields Inc.

Drill-Down Reports

From the Detail Report, double click the vendor's name to display the Vendor Aged Report. Double click the date, item or source to access the Invoice Lookup window for the transaction and all the usual lookup options. Double click any other item in the report to access the journal entry for the transaction. From the Summary Report, double click any item on the line for a vendor to see the Purchases Detail Report for the same vendor. You may print the drill-down report. When you close the drill-down report, you will return to the previous report.

- ◆ Choose the **File** menu and click **Print** in the Report window to print the report.
- ◆ Close the display when you have finished viewing and printing the report.

Customer Sales Report

The Customer Sales Report is the Receivables Ledger parallel to the Vendor Purchases Report. It is a joint Receivables and Inventory Ledger report as it combines information about sales to customers for specific items. You can see how well each inventory item is selling and which customers account for most of the sales.

◆ Choose the **Reports** menu, then choose **Receivables** and click **Customer Sales** in the Home window to see the Report Options:

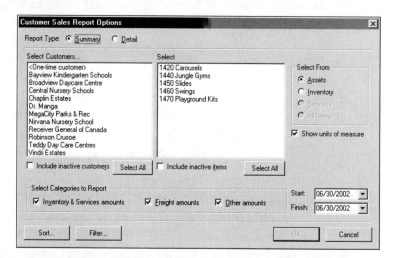

Customer Sales Report Options

This is the customer report that parallels the Vendor Purchases Report. You can **Select the items** for the report in the same ways as for other inventory reports, including one or more or all inventory and service items or asset groups. You can also choose one or more customers for the report from the **Select Customers** box by pressing ⌐ctrl⌐ and clicking the names. Clicking the Select All button beneath the customer list will include all customers. Inactive inventory items and customers may be included or omitted from the report. The range of dates for the report is provided by the **Start** and **Finish** dates, with the Session date given by default for both. You can also choose the type of sale to include in the report. The options are to include any one or more of **Inventory & Services**, **Other amounts** (non-inventory purchases) and **Freight amounts**. The report then is organized according to customer, sale category and inventory item.

As with several other reports, both **Summary** and **Detail** Reports are available. The Summary Report shows the totals for the number of transactions, the number of units sold (quantity), the revenue, the cost of goods sold and the profit (either markup or margin as selected in the Inventory settings) for each customer, for each selected item and type of sale. The Detail Report has these same column headings but shows the information for individual transactions as well as the journal details — date, source and journal entry number. You can sort and filter these reports by date, item number, journal number, source, quantity, cost, revenue or profit.

We will display the Detail Report for all inventory items for all customers in June.

◆ Click **Detail** as the report type.

◆ Click the **Select All button** below the Select Customers list box.

◆ Click the **Select All button** below the Select (inventory) list box.

◆ Click the **Start date field**.

◆ Type **06-01-02**

◆ Click the **check box for Other amounts** to remove the ✓.

◆ Click the **check box for Freight amounts** to remove the ✓.

◆ Click **OK** to see the report.

Drill-Down Reports

From the Detail Report, double click the customer's name to display the Customer Aged Report. Double click the date, item or source to access the Invoice Lookup window for the transaction and all of the usual lookup options. Double click any other item in the report to access the journal entry for the transaction. From the Summary Report, double click any item on the line for a customer to see the Sales Detail Report for the same customer. You may print the drill-down report. When you close the drill-down report, you will return to the previous report.

◆ Choose the **File** menu, and click **Print** in the Report window to print the report.

◆ Close the display when you have finished viewing and printing the report.

◆ Enter the remaining transactions for June using the appropriate journals.

☐ Bank Debit Memo #7434493
Dated Jun. 30/02
From Royal Trust, $2 000 preauthorized withdrawal for mortgage payment. This amount consists of $1 870 interest and $130 for reduction of principal.

☐ Memo #36
Dated Jun. 30/02
Based on the end-of-the-month count of supplies remaining, it was determined that the following quantities of supplies were used during June. Make the necessary adjusting entry to account for the supplies used.

Fibreglass & Plastics	$1 200
Lumber	$1 200
Hardware	$1 300
Office Supplies	$230

☐ Memo #37
Dated Jun. 30/02
One month of prepaid insurance, $200, has expired. Recall the stored adjusting entry to debit the Insurance Expense account for this amount.

☐ Memo #38
Dated Jun. 30/02
One month of interest has accrued on the note payable. Recall the stored adjusting entry to recognize $100 as the interest expense for June.

☐ Memo #39
Dated Jun. 30/02
Depreciation is calculated and recorded monthly for all depreciable assets. Recall the stored depreciation entry to record the following depreciation amounts:

Portable Computer System	$75
Machinery & Tools	$125
Shop	$250
Truck	$400
Hydraulic Drill	$150

June Bank Statement

Dated Jun. 30/02

Reconcile the chequing bank account with the following bank statement for June.

Be sure that you enter June 30 as the Statement End date. If you have small differences in payroll cheque amounts as a result of using different tax tables, accept the differences as a reconciliation adjustment entry.

The receipts from MegaCity Parks & Rec ($5 583.82) and from Dr. Manga ($6 150) were deposited together as a group on June 4. The total deposit amount was $11 733.82.

ROYAL TRUSTCO. BANK STATEMENT

2300 Yonge Street, Megacity, ON M7T 2F4

Account: Play Wave Plus
7310 Recreation Court
Megacity, ON M5E 1W6

Transit No. 06722
Account No. 45264-912
Statement Date June 30, 2002

Date	Transaction	Deposits	Withdrawals	Balance
05-31-02	**Balance Forward**			18,608.66
06-01-02	Deposit	2,500.00		21,108.66
	CHQ #128		560.62	20,548.04
06-02-02	CHQ #126		771.74	19,776.30
	CHQ #127		1,122.17	18,654.13
06-03-02	CHQ #129		192.60	18,461.53
06-04-02	Deposit	11,733.82		30,195.35
06-07-02	CHQ #130		2,621.50	27,573.85
06-09-02	CHQ #131		214.00	27,359.85
	Deposit	7,200.00		34,559.85
06-13-02	CHQ #133		1,122.17	33,437.68
06-14-02	CHQ #134		856.39	32,581.29
	CHQ #132		821.04	31,760.25
	CHQ #136		322.00	31,438.25
06-17-02	Deposit	2,000.00		33,438.25
	CHQ #138		92.00	33,346.25
06-18-02	CHQ #139		3,722.53	29,623.72
	CHQ #137		107.00	29,516.72
06-20-02	CHQ #135		1,064.00	28,452.72
06-27-02	CHQ #142		856.39	27,596.33
	CHQ #140		1,122.17	26,474.16
06-28-02	CHQ #141		880.90	25,593.26
	Deposit	2,549.80		28,143.06
06-30-02	Debit memo		2,000.00	26,143.06
	Interest	48.00		26,191.06
	Monthly fee		18.50	26,172.56
06-30-02	**Closing Balance**			**26,172.56**

Total Deposits	26,031.62	
Total Withdrawals		18,467.72

- Print the following reports to monitor performance and keep complete records of your work as part of good management practice:

  Journal Entries: All journals for June 1 to June 30

  Trial Balance: As at June 30

  Income Statement: From June 1 to June 30

  Balance Sheet: As at June 30

  Account Reconciliation Status Report: As at June 30

  Vendor Aged Detail Report: For all vendors as at June 30

  Customer Aged Detail Report: For all customers as at June 30

  Inventory Synopsis Report

- Close the data files for Play Wave Plus to prepare for making the journal entries for Live Links.

Practice: Live Links

Live Links will sell computer systems to customers after assembling them from parts purchased from Comtek Systems and CompuWorld Supplies. Most of the customers are groups of professionals, such as lawyers and doctors who share office space. Sometimes these same customers purchase extra monitors or disk drives to update their other office equipment. Lively continues to provide training workshops and consulting services. Her two assistants, in addition to assembling computer systems in the shop, provide the remaining services to customers.

Therefore, to complete the transactions for Live Links for October, you will use all of the journals in Simply Accounting.

Inventory Journal Entries
Instructions

If you have not completed the inventory setup for Live Links in Chapter 14 and want to continue working on Chapter 15, you can use your copy of the Data Disk file — Ch15\links\linkch15.sdb — to continue with this chapter.

1. Open the data files for Live Links. Advance the Session date to **October 7, 2002**.

2. Enter the following transactions using the appropriate journals.

    ☐ Credit Card Purchase Invoice #69923

    Dated Oct. 2/02

    From Petro Partners, $60 plus $4.20 GST paid and $4.20 PST paid for gasoline for vehicle. Invoice total $68.40. Paid in full by Credit Card.

    ☐ Purchase Invoice #CS-2155

    Dated Oct. 2/02

    From Comtek Systems

four	01	CPU Cooler 2.3w Pentium III	$120.00
four	02	CPU Cooler x21 Pentium III	200.00
		GST Paid	22.40
		Total	$342.40

    Terms: 2/10, n/30.

Since there is no quantity on hand for the items purchased from Comtek Systems and CompuWorld, there is no cost on record. You must enter the amount in the amount field. Remember to delete the PST for the inventory purchases.

☐ Purchase Invoice #CW-1482
Dated Oct. 2/02
From CompuWorld Supplies

eight	12	Motherboard Pentium III at 1 GHz	$4 000.00
ten	16	Video Card 32 mb nVIDIA	1 000.00
		GST Paid	350.00
		Total	$5 350.00

Terms: 2/10, n/30.

☐ Sales Quote #4
Dated Oct. 2/02
Delivery Date: Oct. 29/02
To Westmount Institute (use Quick Add for this new customer)

one	SRV-03	Workshop - 6 hours	$900 each	$900
		GST (7%)		63
		Invoice total		$963

Terms: 2/10, n/30 days.

☐ Create two new inventory items in the Inventory Ledger to prepare for inventory item assembly.

Item No:		SYS-A	SYS-B
Item Description:		800 MMX System A	800 MMX System B
Selling Price:		$2 800 each	$3 700 each
Minimum Qty:		0	0
Accounts:	Asset	1460	1470
	Revenue	4070	4070
	Expense	5130	5130
	Variance	5140	5140

☐ Inventory Item Assembly #IIA-1
Dated Oct. 2/02
Assembly Components: transfer two (2) of each item

01	CPU Cooler 2.3w Pentium III	$ 30 each
03	DVD-Rom 16x	100 each
04	Enclosure - solid steel mini	180 each
06	Hard Drive 3.5", 30GB IDE	225 each
08	Memory 64 mb SDRAM	120 each
09	Modem 56kV.90 w/ethernet	150 each
10	Monitor 15" TFT Flat panel	600 each
12	Motherboard Pentium III at 1 GHz	500 each
13	Power Supply Turbo cool 400 slim	225 each
15	Sound Card 64V Pro w/speakers	75 each
16	Video Card 32 mb nVIDIA	100 each

Assembled Items: assemble two (2) computer systems

| SYS-A | 800 MMX System A | $2 305 each |

Store the Item Assembly Journal entries as recurring entries with random frequency.

☐ Inventory Item Assembly #IIA-2

Dated Oct. 2/02

Assembly Components: transfer two (2) of each item

02	CPU Cooler x21 Pentium III	$ 50	each
03	DVD-Rom 16x	100	each
05	Enclosure - solid steel tower	300	each
07	Hard Drive 3.5", 40GB IDE	300	each
08	Memory 64 mb SDRAM	120	each
09	Modem 56kV.90 w/ethernet	150	each
11	Monitor 17" TFT Flat panel	1 100	each
12	Motherboard Pentium III at 1 GHz	500	each
14	Power Supply Turbo cool 600 tower	400	each
15	Sound Card 64V Pro w/speakers	75	each
16	Video Card 32 mb nVIDIA	100	each

Assembled Items: assemble two (2) computer systems

SYS-B   800 MMX System B $3 195 each

☐ Bank Debit Memo #562719

Dated Oct. 5/02

From Learnx Bank, $6 150 authorized withdrawal from account to repay the $6 000 demand loan secured on July 5, 2002. Remember to debit Interest Payable for $150, the accrued amount.

☐ **Advance the Session date to October 14, 2002**

☐ Sales Invoice #118

Dated Oct. 8/02

To Westmount Institute, $1 000 plus $70 GST charged and $70 PST charged for memory upgrades to computers in labs. Invoice total $1 140. Terms: 2/10, n/30 days.

☐ Memo #25

Dated Oct. 8/02

Record the PST Payable account balance for Sep. 30, 2002, as a liability owing to the Minister of Finance, BC. This liability is reduced by the sales tax commission of 3.3% of the PST account balance. Issue cheque #35 in payment.

☐ Cheque Copy #36

Dated Oct. 10/02

To CompuWorld Supplies, $16 515.45 in full payment of account, including $337.05 discount taken for early payment. Reference invoices #CW-1471 and CW-1482.

☐ Cheque Copy #37

Dated Oct. 10/02

To Comtek Systems, $7 172.42 in full payment of account, including $146.38 discount taken for early payment. Reference invoices #CS-2142 and CS-2155.

☐ **Cash Receipt #10**

Dated Oct. 11/02

From Pro-Career Institute, cheque #2489 for $535 in payment of account. Reference invoice #112.

☐ **Employee Time Summary Sheet #3**

Pay Period Ending October 12, 2002

Adrian Borland worked 80 regular hours and no overtime. Helen Lively has approved his request for an additional $100 as an advance. He will repay the advance at $50 per pay over the next two pay periods. Issue cheque #38.

Paycheques

☐ **Memo #26**

Dated Oct. 12/02

Enter the GST account balances for Sep. 30, 2002, to record the quarterly GST refund as a receivable from the Receiver General of Canada (Sales Invoice – Pay Later). Use Full Add for the Receiver General as a new customer. The refund amount is $4 465.98.

look in Trial Balance at Sept. 30 for GST Paid & GST charged

☐ New Customer: Receiver General of Canada

Address	Summerside Tax Centre
	Summerside, PE C1N 6L2
	Tel: (902) 821-8186
*Web site:	www.ccra-adrc.gc.ca
Terms:	net 60

Do not include in GST reports.

Remember that the * before the Web site address indicates that this is an actual site.

☐ **Credit Card Sales Invoice #119**

Dated Oct. 14/02

To Pair O' Legals (Use Quick Add for the new customer.)

one	SYS-A	800 MMX System A	$2 800 each	$2 800
two	SYS-B	800 MMX System B	3 700 each	7 400
		GST (7%)		714
		PST (7%)		714
		Total received		$11 628

Paid by Credit Card. (There is no discount.)

☐ **Sales Invoice #120**

Dated Oct. 14/02

To Pro-Career Institute, bi-weekly technology awareness workshop

one	SRV-02	Workshop - 3 hours	$500 each	$500
		GST (7%)		35
		Invoice total		$535

Terms: net 30 days. Recall the stored transaction. Edit the entry to record the sale as Inventory. Store the changed entry.

☐ Sales Invoice #121

Dated Oct. 28/02

To Pro-Career Institute, bi-weekly technology awareness workshop

one	SRV-02	Workshop - 3 hours	$500 each	$500
		GST (7%)		35
		Invoice total		$535

Terms: net 30 days. Recall the stored entry. Postdate the transaction.

☐ Sales Invoice #122

Dated Nov. 11/02

To Pro-Career Institute, final bi-weekly technology awareness workshop

one	SRV-02	Workshop - 3 hours	$500 each	$500
		GST (7%)		35
		Invoice total		$535

Terms: net 30 days. Recall the stored entry. Postdate the transaction.

☐ **Advance the Session date to October 26, 2002**

☐ Sales Invoice #123

Dated Oct. 16/02

To Pearson Publishing, $4 000 plus $280 GST charged and $280 PST charged for duplication services. Invoice total $4 560. Terms: 2/10, n/30 days.

☐ Credit Card Purchase Invoice #821776

Dated Oct. 18/02

From Petro Partners, $50 plus $3.50 GST paid and $3.50 PST paid for gasoline for vehicle. Invoice total $57. Paid in full by Credit Card.

☐ Cash Receipt #11

Dated Oct. 21/02

From West Net Inc., cheque #2432 for $4 700 in payment of account. Reference invoice #115 and deposit #2.

☐ Sales Order #10-24-1

Dated Oct. 23/02

Delivery date: Oct. 29/02

To West Coast Health Services (Use Quick Add for the new customer.)

two	SYS-A	800 MMX System A	$2 800 each	$ 5 600
one	SYS-B	800 MMX System B	3 700 each	3 700
		GST (7%)		651
		PST (7%)		651
		Total		$10 602

Terms: Cash on delivery.

☐ Cash Receipt #12

Dated Oct. 24/02

From West Coast Health Services, cheque #4112 for $2 000 as down payment (deposit #3) for sales order #10-24-1.

☐ Cash Receipt #13

Dated Oct. 24/02

From Pro-Career Institute, cheque #3581 for $535 in payment of account. Reference invoice #113.

☐ Cash Receipt #14

Dated Oct. 25/02

From Pearson Publishing, cheque #329 for $4 468.80 in full payment of account, including $91.20 discount for early payment. Reference invoice #123.

☐ Memo #27 (Credit Card Bill Payment)

Dated Oct. 26/02

Received monthly statement from Credit Card company for $250.80 for purchases up to and including October 15. Cheque #39 for $250.80 submitted in full payment.

☐ Employee Time Summary Sheet #4

Pay Period Ending October 26, 2002

Adrian Borland worked 80 regular hours. Recover $50 advance. Issue cheque #40.

☐ Purchase Invoice #CW-2211

Dated Oct. 26/02

From CompuWorld Supplies

four	03	DVD-Rom 16x	$ 400.00
four	08	Memory 64 mb SDRAM	480.00
four	09	Modem 56kV.90 w/ethernet	600.00
two	10	Monitor 15" TFT Flat panel	1 200.00
two	11	Monitor 17" TFT Flat panel	2 200.00
four	12	Motherboard Pentium III at 1 GHz	2 000.00
four	15	Sound Card 64V Pro w/speakers	300.00
two	16	Video Card 32 mb nVIDIA	200.00
		GST Paid	516.60
		Invoice Total	$7 896.60

Terms: 2/10, n/30.

☐ Purchase Invoice #CS-3081

Dated Oct. 26/02

From Comtek Systems

four	01	CPU Cooler 2.3w Pentium III	$ 120.00
four	02	CPU Cooler x21 Pentium III	200.00
four	04	Enclosure - solid steel min	720.00
four	05	Enclosure - solid steel tower	1 200.00
four	06	Hard Drive 3.5", 30GB IDE	900.00
four	07	Hard Drive 3.5", 40GB IDE	1 200.00
four	13	Power Supply Turbo cool 400 slim	900.00
four	14	Power Supply Turbo cool 600 tower	1 600.00
		GST Paid	478.80
		Invoice Total	$7 318.80

Terms: 2/10, n/30.

Advance the Session date to October 31, 2002

Cash Purchase Invoice #BCT-4123

Dated Oct. 28/02

From BC Telephone, $70 plus $4.90 GST paid and $4.90 PST paid for telephone services. Invoice total $79.80. Issued cheque #41 in full payment.

Cash Purchase Invoice #BCH-5139

Dated Oct. 28/02

From BC Hydro, $50 plus $3.50 GST paid (no PST paid) for hydro services. Invoice total $53.50. Issued cheque #42 in full payment. Recall the stored entry.

Credit Card Purchase Invoice #852216

Dated Oct. 28/02

From Petro Partners, $208 plus $14.56 GST paid and $14.56 PST paid for vehicle maintenance services. Invoice total $237.12. Paid by Credit Card.

Sales Invoice #124

Dated Oct. 29/02

To West Coast Health Services, to fill sales order #10-24-1

two	SYS-A	800 MMX System A	$2 800 each	$ 5 600
one	SYS-B	800 MMX System B	3 700 each	3 700
		GST (7%)		651
		PST (7%)		651
		Invoice Total		$10 602

Terms: Cash on receipt.

Inventory Item Assembly #IIA-3

Dated Oct. 29/02

Assembly Components: transfer three (3) of each item

01	CPU Cooler 2.3w Pentium III	$ 30	each
03	DVD-Rom 16x	100	each
04	Enclosure - solid steel mini	100	each
06	Hard Drive 3.5", 30GB IDE	225	each
08	Memory 64 mb SDRAM	120	each
09	Modem 56kV.90 w/ethernet	150	each
10	Monitor 15" TFT Flat panel	600	each
12	Motherboard Pentium III at 1 GHz	500	each
13	Power Supply Turbo cool 400 slim	225	each
15	Sound Card 64V Pro w/speakers	75	each
16	Video Card 32 mb nVIDIA	100	each

Assembled Items: assemble three (3) computer systems

SYS-A   800 MMX System A $2 305 each

Recall the stored item assembly transactions and edit the quantities. Do not store the changed entries. When you post the transaction, confirm that you will overwrite the entry when prompted that the entry is in use. This procedure will not change the stored entry.

☐ Inventory Item Assembly #IIA-4

Dated Oct. 29/02

Assembly Components: transfer three (3) of each item

02	CPU Cooler x21 Pentium III	$ 50 each
03	DVD-Rom 16x	100 each
05	Enclosure - solid steel tower	300 each
07	Hard Drive 3.5", 40GB IDE	300 each
08	Memory 64 mb SDRAM	120 each
09	Modem 56kV.90 w/ethernet	150 each
11	Monitor 17" TFT Flat panel	1 100 each
12	Motherboard Pentium III at 1 GHz	500 each
14	Power Supply Turbo cool 600 tower	400 each
15	Sound Card 64V Pro w/speakers	75 each
16	Video Card 32 mb nVIDIA	100 each

Assembled Items: assemble three (3) computer systems

SYS-B	800 MMX System B	$3 195 each

☐ Cash Receipt #15

Dated Oct. 29/02

From West Coast Health Services, cheque #4771 for $8 602 in payment of account. Reference invoice #124 and deposit #3.

☐ Sales Invoice #125

Dated Oct. 29/02

To Westmount Institute, to fill sales quote #4

first of five bi-weekly Windows workshops

one	SRV-03	Workshop - 6 hours	$900 each	$900
		GST (7%)		63
		Invoice total		$963

Terms: 2/10, n/30 days.

Store the invoice with a bi-weekly frequency because the workshop will be offered every two weeks, five times over the next two months.

☐ Edit the customer record for Westmount Institute to add the following details.

Contact:	Sydney Trayner
Address:	5000 College Ave., 4th floor
	Burnaby, BC V6E 2N9
Tel:	(604) 386-8319
Fax:	(604) 388-7311
E-mail:	Strayner@westmount.ca
Web site:	www.westmount.institute.com/business

Terms: 2/10, net 30

Include in GST reports.

Credit Limit: $5 000

Memo #28

Dated Oct. 31/ 02

Pay Carrie Dell, the salaried employee, for one month. Issue cheque #43.

Memo #29

Dated Oct. 31/02

Based on the end-of-the-month count of supplies remaining, the following quantities of supplies were used during October. Make the necessary adjusting entry to account for the supplies used.

Office Supplies	$145
Computer Supplies	$105
Memory Chips	$95

Memo #30

Dated Oct. 31/02

One month of prepaid rent, $1 000, has expired. Recall the stored adjusting entry to debit the Rent Expense account for this amount.

Memo #31

Dated Oct. 31/02

Recall the stored depreciation entry to record the following depreciation amounts:

Computers & Peripherals	$150
Custom Tools	$50
Data Recovery Equipment	$200
Duplication Equipment	$100
DLP Projection Unit	$125
Motor Vehicle	$500
Laser Colour Printer	$200

Memo #32

Dated Oct. 31/02

Print customer statements to determine interest charges. Prepare three sales invoices for one month's interest charges as follows:

Memo 32A: Insight PC $45.60

Memo 32B: City Hall Staff $21.83

Memo 32C: Prolegal Services $13.82

Terms: net 1.

☐ October Bank Statement

Dated Oct. 31/02

Reconcile the chequing bank account with the following bank statement for October.

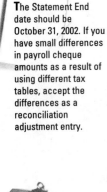

The Statement End date should be October 31, 2002. If you have small differences in payroll cheque amounts as a result of using different tax tables, accept the differences as a reconciliation adjustment entry.

The deposit on Oct. 24 for $7 003.80 is a Group deposit of three cheques, the ones for $2 000, $535 and $4 468.80.

LEARNX BANK STATEMENT

Pacific Heights Branch
400 Pacific Blvd.,Vancouver, BC V7R 3W2

Account 554-66112

October 31, 2002

Date	Transaction	Deposits	Withdrawals	Balance
09-30-02	**Balance Forward**			34,205.31
10-01-02	Deposit	2,000.00		36,205.31
10-02-02	CHQ #28		72.96	36,132.35
10-03-02	CHQ #32		2,149.40	33,982.95
10-04-02	CHQ #33		513.00	33,469.95
	CHQ #34		684.00	32,785.95
10-05-02	Debit memo		6,150.00	26,635.95
10-11-02	Deposit	535.00		27,170.95
	CHQ #35		764.90	26,406.05
10-13-02	CHQ #36		16,515.45	9,890.60
10-14-02	CHQ #37		7,172.42	2,718.18
10-16-02	CHQ #38		811.61	1,906.57
10-21-02	Deposit	4,700.00		6,606.57
10-24-02	Deposit	7,003.80		13,610.37
10-28-02	CHQ #39		250.80	13,359.57
10-29-02	Deposit	8,602.00		21,961.57
	CHQ #40		661.61	21,299.96
10-31-02	Interest	22.00		21,321.96
	Monthly fee		20.00	21,301.96
10-31-02	**Closing Balance**			**21,301.96**

Total Deposits   22,862.80
Total Withdrawals   35,766.15

Account holder: Live Links
20300 Silicon Valley Rd. North
Burnaby, BC V5B 3A2

---

3. To follow good management practice, we recommend printing the following reports:

Journal Entries: All journals for October 1 to October 31

Trial Balance: As at October 31

Income Statement: From October 1 to October 31

Balance Sheet: As at October 31

Account Reconciliation Status Report: As at October 31

Vendor Aged Detail Report: For all vendors as at October 31

Customer Aged Detail Report: For all customers as at October 31

Inventory Synopsis Report

4. Close the data files for Live Links to prepare for the next chapter.

Review Questions

1. How can you change the cost or value of inventory items recorded in the Inventory Ledger? How can you change the selling price? What other details can you change and not change in the Inventory Ledger record after the ledger history is finished?

2. How are entries in the Inventory Journals (Item Assembly and Adjustments) different from other inventory transactions such as sales and purchases?

3. How do you add a linked account? How do you change a linked account for a ledger? Are there any linked accounts that you cannot change?

4. What information could you use from the various inventory tracking reports to assess the performance of different inventory items?

5. How can you edit the asset account that appears in the Purchases Journal for inventory items?

6. How would you enter purchase returns? How are they different from sales returns?

7. How do you correct Item Assembly Journal transactions after posting?

8. What changes result from entering an Item Assembly Journal transaction? What changes occur from the same entry if a single asset account is used for all inventory items? Why might you still go to the trouble of completing the assembly transaction?

BUDGETS AND TO-DO LISTS

Objectives

- *activate the budgeting feature*
- *understand how budgets are set*
- *choose a budget period frequency*
- *enter budget amounts for revenue and expense accounts*
- *complete recurring entries from To-Do Lists*
- *enter payments and receipts from To-Do Lists*
- *prepare vacation paycheques for employees*
- *display and print budget reports and graphs*
- *analyze budget reports*

Introduction

If you have not completed the journal entries in Chapter 15 and want to continue working on Chapter 16, you can use your copy of the Data Disk file — Ch16\play\playch16.sdb — to begin this chapter.

In July, Play Wave Plus will begin to use the budgeting feature. The four months of historical data should be sufficient for creating a reasonable and realistic budget. By setting a budget as a target for performance, Child hopes to improve the performance of the business. The analysis that goes into preparing the budget figures should also improve his understanding of how his costs and revenues are fluctuating. As an additional attempt to improve cash flow management, he will review the To-Do Lists regularly and use them to make payment decisions and journal entries. Once budget information is added, journal entries are completed as usual. Only the reports are different. You will continue to use all the journals to complete the transactions in this chapter.

Budgets

It is important for a business to gauge its performance against some standards. These standards can be provided through comparisons with other companies that are in the same kind of business or by comparing the same company over several periods. It is common for a business to set goals for future performance based on the past. For example, there may be an expectation that profits will increase by 10 percent over the previous year or that expenses will be reduced because of the introduction of new technology. If a business waits until the end of the year to assess its progress toward its goals, it may be too late to make necessary corrections if things are not proceeding according to plan. Budgets serve the purpose of offering a realistic financial plan for the future that can be used as a standard for assessing performance.

The process of setting a budget may itself be a useful exercise for a business. Examining historical patterns of income and expenses can reveal persistent problems, patterns or potentials. Banks frequently use a company's forecast of its income or budget to assess the risk of granting a loan to the business.

Activating the Budgeting Feature

Before entering budget amounts and analyzing reports, you must turn on the budgeting feature. Budgeting is activated in the settings for the General Ledger.

◆ Open the data files for Play Wave Plus. Accept June 30 as the Session date.

You should be in the Home window.

◆ Right-click the **Accounts icon**  to select it.

◆ Choose the **Setup** menu and click **Settings** (or click the Setup tool).

You should see the Settings window with the General tab selected. (Click the General tab if you have opened the settings for a different ledger by mistake.)

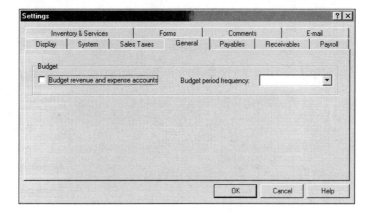

◆ Click **Budget revenue and expense accounts** to add a ✓ to the check box and select the feature.

◆ Click the **Budget period frequency list arrow** to see the frequency alternatives as shown:

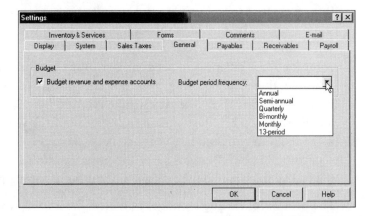

Budget Periods

The first decision after choosing the budgeting feature involves a budget period. Whether a business chooses to budget amounts yearly, quarterly or monthly depends on the needs and nature of the business. The purpose of a budget is to provide meaningful feedback, so the budget period must be matched to the business cycle. Monthly budget reports will be appropriate if the business cycle of buying and selling is short but not if long-term projects are involved. If the periods are too short, there may be insufficient information to judge performance; if the periods are too long, there may be no opportunity to correct problems because they are not detected soon enough.

The **Budget period frequencies** are the commonly used budgeting periods. The period you choose determines the number of budget amounts you enter. If you choose annual, you will have a single budgeted amount for the entire year — measured from the Fiscal Start to a full calendar year later. This allows you to compare performance against budget for the year as a whole. If there are seasonal or other business cycles throughout the year, it is better to choose a budget frequency that allows you to analyze these different parts of the cycle separately. The budget period should not be longer than the company's fiscal period. If the books are closed quarterly, quarterly budget periods are the longest period you can use because the Income Statements do not go beyond the three-month cycle. The shortest budget period allowed by the program is the 13-period option with 13 periods of four weeks each. The budget period can be changed at any time.

For now, we will choose a quarterly budget period to match the fiscal period.

◆ Click **Quarterly** from the list of periods.

◆ Click **OK** to save the settings and return to the Home window.

The next step is to enter the budget amounts for each revenue and expense account.

Budget Amounts

Setting a Budget

Budgets can be determined in several different ways. The most common methods are zero-based and incremental budgeting. With the zero-based method, a forecast is made for each revenue and expense account based on expectations about specific planned activities and expenditures. Each budget item usually must be justified. More commonly, last year's budgets and Income Statements are used as the starting point and a specific percentage change is anticipated. Thus, a company might expect to improve its performance over last year by 5 percent, either by increasing sales or by decreasing expenses. Planned special events such as annual month-long sales, new customer drives, peak holiday periods or slow periods for the product can be built into the changes in budgeted amounts from one period to the next. Whatever method is used, it is important that the budget be realistic. The projections must be high enough to motivate performance. If they are too high, they may be seen as impossible and even have a demotivating effect — "it's impossible so why even bother trying?" Performance-based incentives must also be linked with high realistic goals.

Kerwin Child examined previous Income Statements and business practices to see where he could make improvements and make a realistic forecast. He wanted a 10 percent growth rate. The corresponding expenses, sales discounts, cost of goods sold, etc. would increase by the same amount, but he hoped to reduce the costs that were not directly linked with sales. As the workers gained experience over the past few months, they worked more quickly and had less wastage of materials. Sales would not be divided evenly throughout the 12-month year. The winter quarter would be slow because the cold weather makes outdoor construction work difficult, and most customers begin to think about building outdoor play areas in the spring. To keep his staff fully employed, Child would have to find jobs that could be completed indoors. Until he has determined what these projects might be, he will limit his forecast to the next two quarters, up to November 30.

His detailed forecast is presented in the following budget rationale and chart:

2002 BUDGET FORECAST RATIONALE

Revenue Amounts
1. Contracting Revenue is expected to increase by 10 percent over the previous quarter. Sales Revenue was based on a prediction of selling four playground kits each month, plus some additional individual items. Both figures are realistic, based on the availability of staff and the time required in the past to complete each project.
2. Sales Returns and Allowances is estimated at 5 percent of Revenue from Sales, and Sales Discounts at 2 percent of Revenue from Contracting.
3. Freight Revenue, Interest Revenue and PST Compensation are estimated at three times the amount for June. Other Revenue is a best guess estimate.

Expense Amounts
1. Cost of Goods Sold is about 50 percent (based on markup) of Revenue from Sales. Assembly Costs are based on assembling four kits per month. The usage of building materials — fibreglass and plastics, lumber and hardware — has been declining since the previous quarter and is expected to be about 15 percent less than the amount used in the previous quarter.
2. The Sales Tax on Manufactured Cost is expected to increase about 10 percent over the previous quarter because it is calculated as a percentage of Revenue from Contracting.
3. Purchase Discounts are expected to remain at the same level as in the previous quarter.
4. Budgeted amounts for depreciation, insurance and interest expenses are based on actual amounts.
5. Many of the expense budget amounts were determined by multiplying the June amounts by three. All the wage expenses were determined in this way, as were Propane Gas Expense, Damaged Inventory, Freight, Hydro, Telephone, Maintenance and Bank Charges.
6. Variance Costs, with insufficient history to make a good forecast, is a best guess estimate. Truck Expenses are also estimated at $100 per month.

PLAY WAVE PLUS
INCOME AND BUDGET FORECAST FOR 2002

	Mar. – May Income	June Income	Quarter 1 Budget	Quarter 2 Budget
GENERAL REVENUE				
Revenue from Contracting	$49 300	$15 500	$55 000	$55 000
Revenue from Sales	0	7 940	27 000	27 000
Sales Returns and Allowances	0	–2 410	–1 350	–1 350
Sales Discounts	–660	–225	–1 000	–1 000
Freight Revenue	0	50	300	300
Interest Revenue	146	48	150	150
PST Compensation	66	56	150	150
Other Revenue	184	0	200	200
TOTAL REVENUE	**$49 036**	**$20 959**	**$80 450**	**$80 450**
EXPENSES				
Credit Card Fees	113	95	300	300
Cost of Goods Sold	0	2 905	14 000	14 000
Damaged Inventory	0	250	750	750
Assembly Costs	0	–155	–900	–900
Variance Costs	0	0	100	100
Fibreglass & Plastics Used	6 900	1 200	6 000	6 000
Lumber Used	7 000	1 200	6 000	6 000
Hardware Used	6 200	1 300	6 000	6 000
Freight Expense	195	150	500	500
Purchase Discounts	–539	–129	–500	–500
Depreciation: Computer	225	75	225	225
Depreciation: Mach & Tools	375	125	375	375
Depreciation: Shop	750	250	750	750
Depreciation: Truck	1 200	400	1 200	1 200
Depreciation: Hydraulic Drill	150	150	450	450
Bank Charges	94	19	60	60
Bank Reconciliation Adjustment	0	0	0	0
Hydro Expense	270	100	300	300
Insurance Expense	600	200	600	600
Interest on Notes Payable	100	100	100	100
Maintenance Expense	600	200	600	600
Mortgage Interest Expense	5 670	1 870	5 600	5 600
Office Supplies Used	320	230	450	450
Propane Gas Expense	162	54	150	150
Sales Tax on Manufactured Cost	2 440	0	2 500	2 500
Telephone Expense	410	86	300	300
Truck Expenses	140	65	300	300
Contracted Payroll Expenses	3 780	0	0	0
Wage Expense	7 683	7 249	22 000	22 000
EI Expense	229	261	800	800
CPP Expense	235	272	800	800
WSIB Expense	214	243	750	750
EHT Expense	67	76	250	250
TOTAL EXPENSES	**$45 584**	**$18 841**	**$70 810**	**$70 810**
NET INCOME	**$ 3 452**	**$ 2 118**	**$ 9 640**	**$ 9 640**

The Sales Tax on Manufactured Cost has not yet been recorded for June.

Entering Budget Amounts

Budget amounts are entered in the General Ledger for each account as part of the account's ledger record.

◆ Click the **Accounts icon** to open the Accounts window.

◆ Double click *4020 Revenue from Contracting* the first revenue account (double click the account name or icon) to open the ledger window:

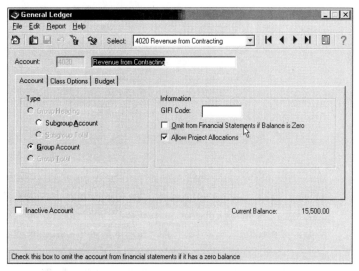

Notice that a Budget tab is added to the ledger window for the revenue account. As soon as you activate the budgeting feature, all revenue and expense accounts have the budget option added. You can enter budget amounts for each account or you can select a few accounts to budget. The more accounts you include in your budget setup, the more complete your Income Statements will be when performance is compared against budget.

◆ Click the **Budget tab** to open the next screen:

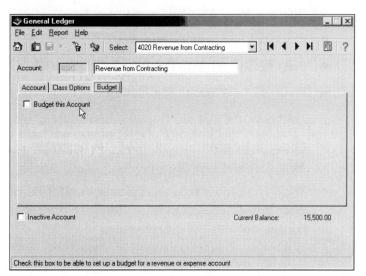

At this stage, you can choose whether to include budget information for the selected account. You must activate the budget feature for each account individually.

◆ Click **Budget this Account** to include budget information and proceed:

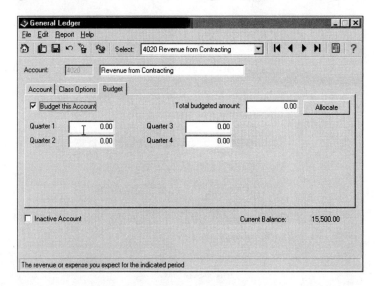

This screen allows you to enter budget amounts for the account. Because we chose quarterly periods, there are four input fields for amounts for each of the four quarters. There are two ways to enter amounts on this screen. If the same amount is budgeted for each period, you can enter the total amount for the year in the **Total budgeted amount** field and click **Allocate** to have the program enter the total divided by number of periods into each period field. If the amounts for each period are different, or you are entering the amounts for less than the full year, you must enter the amounts individually in the period fields.

Since we are entering budget amounts only for two quarters, we will enter amounts directly in the Quarter fields. From the budget we prepared, we can see that we are expecting $55 000 in revenue from contracting during the quarter.

◆ Click the **Quarter 1 field** to move the cursor.

◆ Type **55000**

◆ Double click the amount you just entered.

◆ Press ⌨ctrl⌨ + C (copy command).

◆ Press ⌨tab⌨ to move to the Quarter 2 input field.

◆ Press ⌨ctrl⌨ + V (paste command).

This will copy the amount from the first quarter to the second quarter.

◆ Click the **Next Account tool** ▶ to open the ledger window for *Revenue from Sales*, the next revenue account.

◆ The Budget tab screen should be open. If it is not, click the Budget tab. Choose Budget this Account and then enter the budget amounts. Continue by entering the budget amounts for the remaining revenue and expense accounts according to the preliminary budget on page 440. Remember to enter negative numbers for accounts such as *Sales Returns and Allowances* that have negative numbers in the budget chart.

Checking Your Budget Amounts

To check that you entered the amounts correctly, you can review each ledger account's Budget tab screen one at a time. Open the ledger record for *Revenue from Contracting*.

Click the Budget tab if this is not the screen that is open. Check the budget amounts. Double click an incorrect amount and type in the correction. Click ▶ to move forward to the next account. The Budget screen should be the one that is open. Continue checking the amounts in this way until you are certain they are all correct.

◆ Close the Ledger and Accounts windows to return to the Home window.

Changing the Budget Frequency

Sometimes you may want to change the budget frequency, either because more frequent feedback on performance is required or because the feedback is more frequent than the business cycle warrants. Simply Accounting allows you to change the frequency at any time by returning to the Settings for the General Ledger and choosing a new frequency. Click OK to save the change. The program will show you the following warning:

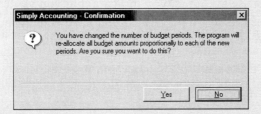

It is important to understand how the software re-allocates budget amounts for the new periods you select. The total budgeted amount for the year will be re-divided according to the new number of budget periods. If the amounts for the periods are different, the new budget will not retain these differences.

For example, a quarterly budget may allow for larger sales in the fourth quarter, perhaps from higher sales before the holidays than in other months. When changed to a monthly period, the monthly amounts will be equal.

	Initial period selection	Second period selection	Third period selection
Budget period	Quarterly (4 per year)	Monthly (12 per year)	Annual (1 per year)
Amounts	Quarter 1 $20 000	Month 1 $10 000	Year $120 000
	Quarter 2 20 000	Month 2 10 000	
	Quarter 3 20 000	Month 3 10 000	
	Quarter 4 60 000	etc.	
		Month 12 10 000	
Total budget for the year	$120 000	$120 000	$120 000

The variation in budget amounts among different periods is lost.

Changing Budget Amounts

If you discover that your budget forecasts are incorrect, you can update the amounts. You can change budget amounts at any time by editing the amounts in the Budget tab screen of the General Ledger window for the account. If you want to modify only some of the accounts, this is the approach you should use.

If, however, you want to change all the budget amounts by a fixed percentage, you can make the change globally. You must be in the Home window.

◆ Choose the **Maintenance** menu and click **Update Budget** in the Home window to see the Update Budget input screen:

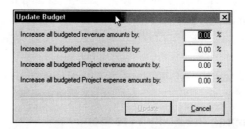

You can indicate a percentage change for revenue and expense accounts separately. You might want to increase the revenue forecast by 10 percent while predicting that expenses will increase by only 5 percent. If you anticipate that expenses will decrease, you can indicate this by typing a minus sign with the amount. Thus, by typing –10 for expense accounts, you indicate that you want to decrease all budget amounts for expenses by 10 percent. If you have entered budget amounts for projects, these may also be changed globally from this window. (Projects are explained in Chapter 17.)

The Increase all budgeted revenue amounts by field is selected so you can change it.

◆ Type **10**

◆ Click **Update** to enter the change.

The following warning gives you a chance to confirm the change or to cancel the update:

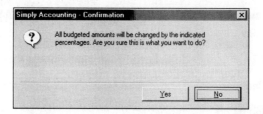

◆ Click **No** to cancel the update and return to the Update Budget screen.

◆ Click **Cancel** to return to the Home window without making any changes.

Before printing the budget reports, we will complete the transactions for July so that we will have an Income Statement for two months to compare against our new budget.

Additional Transaction Types

Some of the following transactions introduce important new topics. Keystroke instructions and explanations are included for these topics.

◆ Enter the transactions for July using the appropriate journals.

◆ Advance the Session date to **July 9, 2002.**

444

Editing a Purchase Price

◆ Open the Purchases Journal for the following purchase order:

    ☑ Purchase Order #20007
       Dated Jul. 1/02
       Shipping Date Jul. 2/02
       From Playing Fields Inc.

three	01	Carousels	$540.00
three	02	Jungle Gyms	540.00
three	03	Slides: classic	750.00
three	04	Slides: wave	960.00
three	05	Swing Sets: double	540.00
three	06	Swing Sets: triple	690.00
three	07	Tube Slides: classic	720.00
three	08	Tube Slides: wave	840.00
		GST Paid	390.60
		Invoice total	$5 970.60

    Terms: net 30.

◆ Choose Purchase Order as the Transaction Type. Choose Playing Fields as the vendor, and enter the shipping and transaction dates.

◆ Select the first inventory item (01 Carousel) and enter 3 as the quantity ordered.

◆ Delete the entry for **PST rate**.

The previous purchase price is used as the default, but it is now incorrect.

◆ Click the **Amount field** to highlight the entry.

◆ Type **540** to replace the old amount.

◆ Press ⌨️ tab .

The unit price is updated and the totals and taxes are also updated.

◆ Now add the remaining items from the purchase order, updating the amounts as necessary. Check the amounts carefully.

◆ Click Record 🖋️ Record to save the order.

Cost Variances

When we sold the wave slides to Robinson Crusoe on June 15, we had insufficient inventory to fill the order. We sold one item more than we had in stock and the inventory level dropped below zero. Because the new price is different from the old purchase price, a cost variance is created at the time of purchase. The following purchase will replenish the inventory and create the variance.

◆ Prepare the purchase invoice to fill the purchase order but **do not post** the entry yet.

> **B**y typing the amount and the quantity, you do not need to know or calculate the unit price.

Purchase Invoice #PF-1310

Dated Jul. 2/02

From Playing Fields Inc., to fill purchase order #20007

three	01	Carousels	$540.00
three	02	Jungle Gyms	540.00
three	03	Slides: classic	750.00
three	04	Slides: wave	960.00
three	05	Swing Sets: double	540.00
three	06	Swing Sets: triple	690.00
three	07	Tube Slides: classic	720.00
three	08	Tube Slides: wave	840.00
		GST Paid	390.60
		Invoice total	$5 970.60

Terms: net 30.

◆ Choose the **Report** menu and click **Display Purchases Journal Entry**. Your journal entry should look like the one shown:

Variances

The variance expense resulting from this purchase is $20 because the new unit cost for the wave slide is $20 higher than the old cost. At the time of the sale, the actual cost of goods sold is unknown if the inventory is out of stock. The cost entered for the sales transaction is the average cost of the goods on hand. When the new price is different, the difference becomes the cost variance. Two conditions usually occur when you have a variance — the inventory level drops below zero, and the new price is different from the old price. If the new price were lower than the old price, the variance would create a credit entry to the variance expense account because the actual cost of goods sold had decreased.

◆ Close the journal display and post the transaction (click **Post**).

◆ Enter the following transactions using the appropriate journals.

Purchase Invoice #PF-1311

Dated Jul. 2/02

From Playing Fields Inc.

one	03	Slide: classic	$250.00
two	04	Slides: wave	640.00
		GST Paid	62.30
		Invoice total	$952.30

Terms: net 30.

If there is no inventory in stock at the time of the sale, the entire unit cost is allocated to the variance account at the time of purchase. In that case, the purchase price may be the same as the former price. Because there is no current inventory on which to base a cost estimate, the cost at the time of sale is zero, and the program fills in the difference as a variance at the time of purchase.

Notice that the most recent purchase price becomes the new default unit price on the purchase invoice.

Sales Invoice #121

Dated Jul. 4/02

To Cathy Scott, $2 000 plus $140 GST charged for redesigning and refurbishing home recreation centre. Invoice total $2 140. Terms: net 30 days. No deposit was requested because she is a family friend. Use Quick Add for this new customer.

Purchase Return #PF-1311-R

Dated Jul. 4/02

To Playing Fields Inc., returning damaged inventory for credit

Remember to type minus one as the quantity for the purchase return. Delete the terms for the credit invoice.

−1	03	Slide: classic	$250.00
		GST Paid	17.50
		Total Credit	$267.50

Cheque Copy #144

Dated Jul. 5/02

To Swede Steel Co., $2 097.20 in full payment of account, including $42.80 discount taken for early payment. Reference invoice #SC-6107.

Purchase Invoice #BC-1349

Dated Jul. 6/02

From The Buildex Corp., $2 500 for plastics and fibreglass and $2 500 for lumber plus $350 GST paid. Freight charge is $40 plus $2.80 GST. Invoice total $5 392.80. Terms: 2/10, n/30.

Cash Purchase Invoice #VM-180

Dated Jul. 7/02

From Vincent Meade, $200 plus $14 GST paid for maintenance services rendered in shop and yard and for inventory maintenance. Invoice total $214. Issued cheque #145 in full payment. Recall the stored entry.

Purchase Invoice #PF-1323

Dated Jul. 9/02

From Playing Fields Inc.

one	03	Slide: classic	$250.00
		GST Paid	17.50
		Invoice Total	$267.50

Terms: net 30.

Sales Order #1002

Dated Jul. 9/02

Shipping Date Jul. 14/02

To MegaCity Parks & Rec

one	KIT-A	Tom Sawyer Kit	$1 800.00
one	KIT-B	Huck Finn Kit	2 100.00
		Freight	50.00
		GST Charged (7%)	276.50
		PST Charged (8%)	312.00
		Invoice Total	$4 538.50

Terms: 2/10, n/30.

For IIA-3 and IIA-4, recall the stored item assembly entry. Edit the quantities and the unit costs where necessary. The unit costs of the assembly component items are updated because the purchase prices have changed. The program uses the average cost method. Edit the unit cost of the kits, the assembled items. If you forgot to store the entry before, you can store it now for future use.

☐ Inventory Item Assembly #IIA-3
Dated Jul. 9/02
Assembly Components: transfer two (2) of each item

01	Carousel	$185	each
03	Slide: classic	250	each
05	Swing Set: double	185	each
07	Tube Slide: classic	244	each

Additional Costs (material for fence)   150

Assembled Items: assemble two (2) kits
   KIT-A Tom Sawyer Kit $939 each

☐ Inventory Item Assembly #IIA-4
Dated Jul. 9/02
Assembly Components: transfer two (2) of each item

02	Jungle Gym	$185	each
04	Slide: wave	320	each
06	Swing Set: triple	238	each
08	Tube Slide: wave	290	each

Additional Costs (lumber for raft)   160

Assembled Items: assemble two (2) kits
   KIT-B Huck Finn Kit $1 113 each

☐ Cash Receipt #16
Dated Jul. 9/02
From MegaCity Parks & Rec, cheque #20013 for $1 000 as down payment (deposit #5) for sales order #1002.

☐ Cash Receipt #17
Dated Jul. 9/02
From York Recreational Centre, cheque #314 for $6 400 in full payment of account including $160 discount taken for early payment. Reference invoice #120 and deposit #4.

☐ Memo #40
Dated July 9, 2002
Payroll Cheque Run Time Sheet for pay period ending July 9.
Peter Piper worked 80 regular hours and 2 hours overtime.
Candie Rapper worked 80 regular hours and 2 hours overtime.
Rebecca Doolittle should receive her regular bi-weekly salary.
Issue cheques #146, 147 and 148.

☐ **Advance the Session date to July 15, 2002**

☐ Credit Card Purchase Invoice #GA-4657
Dated July 11/02
From Gasoline Alley, $50 plus $3.50 GST and $4.00 (8%) PST charged for gasoline
for truck and $50 plus $3.50 GST and $4 (8%) PST charged for propane gas. Total
invoice amount paid by Chargit, $115.

☐ Sales Invoice #122
Dated Jul. 14/02
To MegaCity Parks & Rec, to fill sales order #1002

one	KIT-A	Tom Sawyer Kit	$1 800.00
one	KIT-B	Huck Finn Kit	2 100.00
		Freight	50.00
		GST Charged (7%)	276.50
		PST Charged (8%)	312.00
		Invoice Total	$4 538.50

Terms: 2/10, n/30.

☐ Memo #41
Dated Jul. 14/02
The manufactured cost of sales in June was $9 000. Complete a General Journal
entry to record $720 (.08 x $9 000) as PST Payable for June.

☐ Memo #42
Dated Jul. 14/02
PST Payable for June consists of the $442.40 PST charged on sales and $720 as the
sales tax on the manufactured cost of goods. Record $1 162.40, the combined
amount, as a liability owing to the Minister of Finance as an Other Payment in the
Payments Journal. This liability is reduced by $58.12 for the sales tax compensation
of 5%. Issue cheque #149 for $1 104.28 in payment.

☐ Cash Purchase Invoice #OH-521471
Dated Jul. 14/02
From Ontario Hydro, $90 for hydro services plus $6.30 GST paid. Invoice total
$96.30. Issued cheque #150 in full payment.

☐ Cash Purchase Invoice #BC-814324
Dated Jul. 14/02
From Bell Canada, $70 for telephone services plus $4.90 GST paid and $5.60 PST
paid. Invoice total $80.50. Issued cheque #151 in full payment.

☐ Cheque Copy #152
Dated Jul. 15/02
To The Buildex Corp., $5 284.94 in full payment of account, including $107.86
discount taken for early payment. Reference invoice #BC-1349.

☐ Cheque Copy #153

Dated July 15/02

To Chargit $126.50 for purchases charged before July 7, the billing date. Total payment submitted to avoid incurring interest charges, $126.50.

☐ Sales Quote #2006

Dated Jul. 15/02

To Teddy Day Care Centres, $10 000 plus $700 GST charged for fully redesigning and refurbishing recreation centres at two day-care sites. Invoice total $10 700. Work to be completed by July 30. Terms: 2/10, n/30 days.

☐ **Advance the Session date to July 23, 2002**

☐ Sales Order #2006

Dated Jul. 16/02

Convert sales quote #2006 for Teddy Day Care Centres to sales order #2006. All amounts, terms and dates are unchanged.

☐ Cash Receipt #18

Dated Jul. 16/02

From Teddy Day Care Centres, cheque #129 for $2 000 as advance (deposit #6) on project in acceptance of sales quote #2006.

☐ Purchase Invoice #SC-6714

Dated Jul. 22/02

From Swede Steel Co., $1 100 plus $77 GST paid for nuts, bolts and steel rods. Invoice total $1 177. Terms: 2/15, n/30.

☐ Sales Quote #2007

Dated Jul. 23/02

To Bronte Residence, $3 600 plus $252 GST charged for a play centre to be completed under contract. Invoice total $3 852. Work to be completed by August 1. Terms: net 1 day. Use Full Add for the new customer.

☐ New customer information

Bronte Residence (contact: Emily Bronte)

Address: 69 Wuthering Heights Dr.

Megacity, ON M4T 3V2

Tel: (416) 734-8123

Terms: net 1

Include in GST reports.

Credit Limit: $5 000

☐ Memo #43

Dated July 23, 2002

Payroll Cheque Run Time Sheet for pay period ending July 23.

Peter Piper worked 80 regular hours and 2 hours overtime.

Candie Rapper worked 80 regular hours and no overtime.

Rebecca Doolittle should receive her regular bi-weekly salary.

Issue cheques #154, 155 and 156.

☐ Memo #44

Dated Jul. 23/02

Piper took one day as personal leave and worked only 72 hours at the regular pay rate and 2 hours overtime. He has returned his cheque. Adjust the paycheque for Peter Piper for the pay period ending July 23 (cheque #155). Remember to recalculate taxes. (Refer to pages 291–293 for assistance.)

Vacation Pay

When vacation pay is retained, it must be released or paid out at the agreed time. The next transaction involves releasing vacation pay for Piper. You can add vacation pay to a regular paycheque or prepare a separate cheque for it.

Calculating Income Tax on Special Payments to Employees

If you add vacation pay to the regular pay, the income tax for that pay period will be higher than it should be. The program assumes that the vacation plus regular pay is the amount that will be received in each pay period throughout the year. The taxes owing are calculated based on that assumption. Since the vacation pay is a one-time increase, the tax for it should be calculated as if the amount were spread over the entire year. That is, divide the vacation pay by the number of pay periods and add that amount to the regular pay. Then, determine the tax on the combined amount for one period and take the difference between that tax and the tax amount for a regular paycheque. Multiply the tax increment by the number of pay periods to determine the actual tax owing. The tool to calculate taxes manually should be selected so that the income tax amount can be edited. A simpler approach is to prepare a separate cheque for the vacation pay. In this case, depending on the amount of the cheque, you can enter the minimum tax required to replace the default amount entered by the program.

Paycheques for bonuses can also be handled by preparing a separate cheque. Commissions that are received regularly can be added to the regular paycheque.

The next memo describes the vacation pay transaction.

☑ Memo #45

Dated Jul. 23/02

Release the vacation pay owing for Peter Piper because he is taking vacation time.

Issue cheque #157.

Before paying out the vacation pay that has accrued for an employee, you must change the Employee Ledger setting for the employee so that vacation pay is not retained.

◆ Close any journal window that you have open to return to the Home window.

◆ Click the **Employees icon** 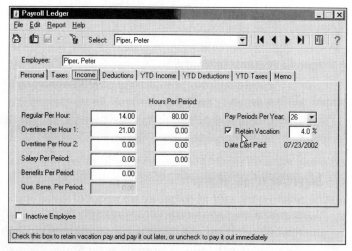 to open the Employees window.

◆ Double click the **icon for Peter Piper** to open the Payroll Ledger for Piper.

◆ Click the **Income tab** to open that window:

◆ Click the **Retain Vacation check box** to remove the ✓.

◆ Close the Ledger window to return to the Employees window.

You are now ready to prepare the cheque for vacation pay. By working from the Employees window, you are more likely to remember to reset the option to Retain Vacation after preparing the paycheque.

◆ Click the **Payroll Journal tool** in the Employees window (or choose the Type menu and click Payroll Journal) to open the Payroll Journal.

If Piper's icon is still selected, the Payroll Journal opens with Piper already selected as the employee. If it is not, choose Piper, Peter as the employee and press (tab). Your journal now looks like the one shown:

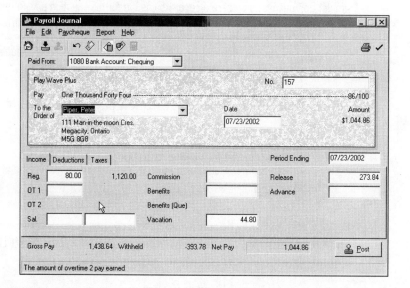

Notice that the total vacation pay retained to date is displayed in the Release field. We need to remove the automatic entries for regular hours worked and deductions. RRSP, Union dues, CSB and Insurance should not be deducted from the vacation pay.

◆ Double click **80.00** in the Reg field.

◆ Press ⌐del⌐ and then press ⌐tab⌐ to update the totals.

◆ Click the **Deductions tab**.

◆ Click the **Enter taxes manually tool** to make all the deduction and tax fields available for editing as shown:

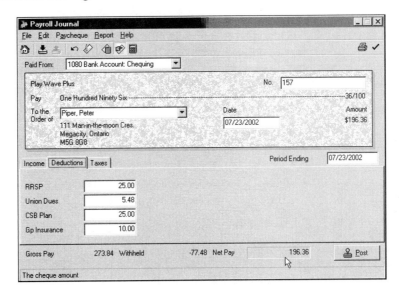

This makes all the deduction fields available for editing.

◆ Double click the **RRSP field contents (25.00)**.

◆ Press ⌐del⌐ to remove the deduction.

◆ Press ⌐tab⌐ to advance to and select the Union Dues field.

◆ Press ⌐del⌐ to remove the entry.

◆ Press ⌐tab⌐ to advance to the CSB Plan field and select the amount.

◆ Press ⌐del⌐ to remove the default entry and press ⌐tab⌐ to advance to the Gp Insurance field.

◆ Press ⌐del⌐ to remove the default entry and press ⌐tab⌐ to update the totals.

If you clicked the Calculate taxes manually tool before deleting the number of hours, your tax amounts will be wrong. Click the Recalculate taxes tool to correct the amounts for EI and CPP.

The Taxes tab screen opens with access to the tax fields:

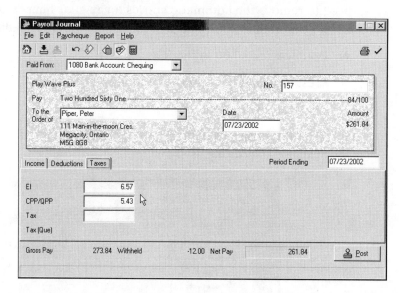

No income tax is withheld because the amount is too small to generate a taxable income (if this were the regular pay). A minimum of 10 percent income tax must be withheld on extra payments to employees (such as bonuses, etc.). We will deduct 10 percent of the vacation pay as income tax.

◆ Click the **Tax field** to move the cursor.

◆ Type **27.38** (10% of 273.84).

◆ Press (*tab*) to update the totals.

The journal entry is complete and ready for review.

◆ Choose the **Report** menu and click **Display Payroll Journal Entry** to review the entry:

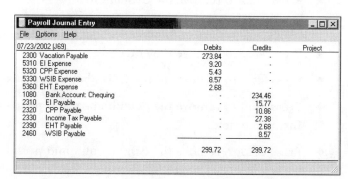

The accrued vacation payable has been debited to remove the liability. The remaining account entries are the same as they are for regular pay.

◆ Check your work carefully.

◆ Close the display when you have finished.

◆ Click **Post** [🔖 Post] to save the journal entry.

Before closing the journal you must turn on the automatic tax calculation again.

◆ Click the **Calculate taxes automatically tool** [icon].

- Close the Payroll Journal. You should still be in the Employees window.

It is important to reset the option to retain vacation pay before proceeding.

- Double click the **icon for Peter Piper** to open the ledger again.

- Click the **Income tab** if this window is not the one displayed.

- Click **Retain Vacation** to turn on the option again (add the ✓).

- Close the Ledger for Piper to return to the Employees window.

- Close the Employees window to return to the Home window.

- Advance the Session date to **July 31**.

- Enter the following transactions using the appropriate journals.

　Sales Order #2007
　Dated Jul. 24/02
　Convert sales quote #2007 for Bronte Residence to sales order #2007. All amounts, terms and dates are unchanged.

　Cash Receipt #19
　Dated Jul. 24/02
　From Bronte Residence, cheque #58 for $750 as advance (deposit #7) on project in acceptance of sales quote #2007.

　Sales Invoice #123
　Dated Jul. 28/02
　To fill sales quote #2006
　To Teddy Day Care Centres, $10 000 plus $700 GST charged for fully redesigning and refurbishing recreation centres at two day-care sites. Invoice total $10 700. Terms: 2/10, n/30 days.

　Credit Card Sales Invoice #124
　Dated Jul. 28/02
　To Nirvana Nursery School

one	KIT-A	Tom Sawyer Kit	$1 800.00
one	KIT-B	Huck Finn Kit	2 100.00
one	06	Swing Set: triple	510.00
one	08	Tube Slide: wave	610.00
		Freight	50.00
		GST Charged (7%)	354.90
		PST Charged (8%)	401.60
		Invoice Total	$5 826.50

　Paid by Chargit.

　Credit Card Purchase Invoice #GA-6765
　Dated July 28/02
　From Gasoline Alley, $120 plus $8.40 GST and $9.60 (8%) PST charged for gasoline for truck and truck repairs, and $40 plus $2.80 GST and $3.20 (8%) PST for propane gas. Total invoice amount paid by Chargit, $184.

Purchase Order #20008
Dated Jul. 30/02
Shipping Date Aug. 2/02
From Playing Fields Inc.

two	01	Carousels	$ 360.00
two	02	Jungle Gyms	360.00
two	03	Slides: classic	500.00
two	04	Slides: wave	640.00
two	05	Swing Sets: double	360.00
two	06	Swing Sets: triple	460.00
two	07	Tube Slides: classic	480.00
two	08	Tube Slides: wave	560.00
		GST Paid	260.40
		Invoice total	$3 980.40

Terms: net 30 days.

Sales Order #1003
Dated Jul. 30/02
Shipping date Aug. 14/02
To Vindri Estates (deliver to Vindri's cottage @ RR #2, Huntsville)

one	KIT-A	Tom Sawyer Kit		$1 800.00
two	07	Tube Slides: classic	$510 each	1 020.00
		Freight		100.00
		GST Charged (7%)		204.40
		PST Charged (8%)		225.60
		Invoice Total		$3 350.00

Terms: net 1 day.

Remember to edit the Ship To address for Vindri's sales order.

Cash Receipt #20
Dated Jul. 30/02
From Vindri Estates, cheque #333 for $500 as deposit #8 to confirm sales order #1003.

Cash Receipt #21
Dated Jul. 31/02
From MegaCity Parks & Rec, cheque #39112 for $2 000 in partial payment of account. Reference invoice #122.

Cheque Copy #158
Dated Jul. 31/02
To Yuping Manga, $12 300 in full payment of interest of $300 and principal of $12 000 for note payable. Reference memo #14. Use Quick Add for the new vendor.

Enter the repayment of the Note as an Other Payment with the following debit entries: Interest Payable ($200), Interest on Notes Payable ($100) and Notes Payable ($12 000).

✔ Memo #46
Dated Jul. 31/02
Update memos in the ledger records from the To-Do Lists if the messages or dates are no longer accurate.

CHAPTER 16

To-Do Lists

To-Do Lists provide an additional tool for internal control by including reminders about payments due, recurring transactions, etc. They can be displayed with any future date so you can choose the time frame that you want for viewing the lists. Because the lists include an aging column (the number of days remaining) with the earliest events listed first, they provide a summary for planning upcoming transactions that is easier to use than the aged reports. Furthermore, a variety of lists can be accessed from the same screen; you do not need to use separate reports.

For the next group of transactions we will access the journals from the To-Do Lists.

Accessing and Using To-Do Lists

◆ Click the **To-Do Lists tool** 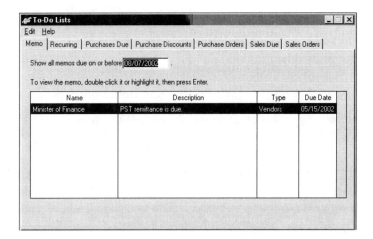 or choose the Business Assistant menu and click To-Do Lists.

You will see the first To-Do Lists screen — the one for memos:

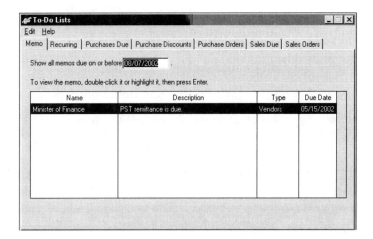

To-Do List for Memos

The first To-Do Lists screen shows the memos that you entered as part of customer, vendor or employee records. The memo displayed is the one that we entered in the ledger record for the Minister of Finance. All To-Do Lists are dated automatically for one week past the Session date. This is a reasonable working calendar for making payments, etc. If you advance the Session date by one week at a time, all reminders will appear. If you want to show a different list date or reminder period, you can change the date in the Show all memos due on or before date field, the list date. Each To-Do Lists screen has a similar list date field.

Memo Details

The Memo screen has four columns of information. The **Name** lists the name of the vendor (or customer or employee) in whose record you entered the memo. The **Description** column shows the contents of the memo. The Ledger is listed in the **Type** column and the date you entered for the To-Do Lists reminder with the memo appears in the **Due Date** column.

The Due Date has passed for this memo. We will update it so that we can use it as a reminder for future payments. The July payment has been made, so the next payment is due in August.

◆ Double click **any memo detail** (anywhere on the line for the memo).

The Payables Ledger window for the vendor opens at the Memo tab screen:

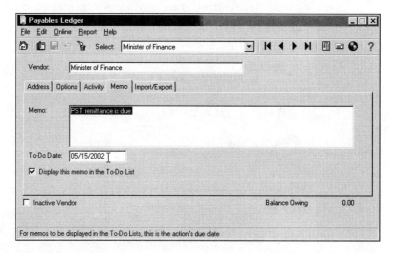

We can edit the memo now.

◆ Double click the **To-Do Date field contents (05/15/2002)**.

◆ Type **08-15** to enter the next Due Date.

◆ Close the Ledger window to return to the To-Do Lists screen.

The memo no longer appears on the screen because the Due Date is after August 7. If you type a later list date, the memo will be included again.

We will view and use the Recurring entries tab later.

To-Do List for Purchases Due

◆ Click the **Purchases Due tab**. The To-Do List for Purchases Due appears:

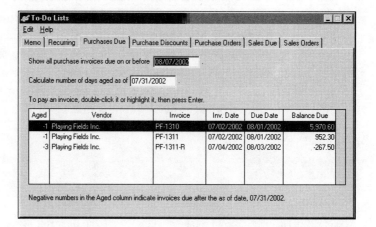

Purchases Due Details

As a short-cut, you can pay invoices directly from the To-Do Lists screen. Since all invoices from Playing Fields are due shortly, we will pay them now.

The following source document describes the payment.

> ✔ Cheque Copy #159
> Dated Jul. 31/02
> To Playing Fields Inc., $6 922.90 in full payment of account. Reference invoices
> #PF-1310, PF-1311, PF-1311-R and PF-1323.

◆ Double click **Invoice # PF-1310** for Playing Fields (click anywhere on the line) to open the Payments Journal for the selected vendor:

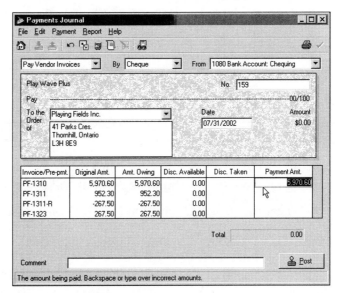

The Payments Journal entry is complete except for the amounts. The default cheque number and Session date are correct.

◆ Press ⓣ to accept the amount and then continue to complete the payment for all four invoices by accepting the full amounts.

◆ Check the entry.

◆ Click **Post** [🖥 Post] to save it.

You will see the advisor warning that the bank account is overdrawn:

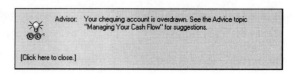

◆ Close the advisor. The Payments Journal stays open for paying other invoices.

◆ Close the Payments Journal to return to the To-Do Lists. The Playing Fields invoices have been removed from the screen because they are now paid.

We will now look up the advice about managing cash flow as recommended.

◆ Click anywhere on the Home window, if it is showing, or click the Simply Accounting button on the task bar to restore the Home window as the active window.

◆ Choose the **Business Assistant menu**, then choose **Business Advice** and click **All Modules** to see the complete list of topics.

◆ Double click **Managing Your Cash Flow** to open this information window:

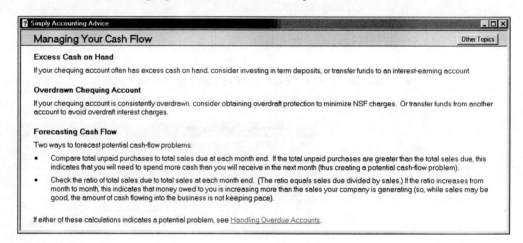

◆ Read the advice window.

◆ Close the advice window to return to the Home window. An immediate transfer of funds from the second bank account will cover the cheque to Playing Fields.

◆ Open the General Journal to complete the transaction for the transfer of funds.

> ☐ Memo #47
> Dated Jul. 31/02
> Transfer $8 000 from the Credit Card bank account to the Chequing bank account.

◆ Close the General Journal to return to the Home window.

◆ Click any part of the To-Do Lists window, or click the To-Do Lists button on the task bar to restore the To-Do Lists window.

To-Do List for Purchase Discounts

◆ Click the **Purchase Discounts tab** to see this To-Do Lists screen:

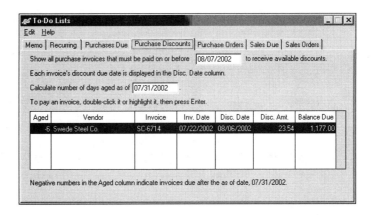

Purchase Discounts Tab Screen

The details on the Purchase Discounts tab screen are similar to the Purchases Due screen. Discounts available on or before the list date are shown in order according to their discount date. The Aged column shows the countdown to the date that the discount expires. Negative numbers show how many days the discount will remain available. The final date of discount availability is displayed in the **Disc. Date** column and the amount of the discount is listed in the **Disc. Amt.** column. The remaining columns provide additional information from the original invoice — **Vendor**, **Invoice number**, **Invoice Date** and the **Balance Due**.

Because all discounted invoices will appear together on this screen, the information is useful for cash flow projections. Purchase discounts can be seen as an interest penalty for later payments and where possible should be taken by making prompt payments. The interest rate, when calculated in this way, is usually quite high. However, when cash flow is a concern, it may be prudent for a business to take advantage of discounts for larger invoices and forgo the discount on smaller invoices. It may even be advantageous to take out a short-term loan to cover the payments, using customer receipts to repay the loan. The To-Do Lists screens can help in making some of these decisions by providing the relevant details in summary form. If you double click any invoice detail, you will access the Payments Journal for the vendor directly. When you close the Payments Journal, you will return to the To-Do Lists.

The screen displays a single discount available within the next week. Since the discount will remain available for six more days, we can delay the payment.

To-Do List for Purchase Orders

◆ Click the **Purchase Orders tab**:

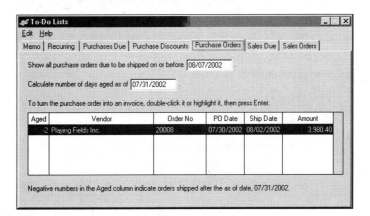

Purchase Orders Tab Screen Details

The details on this screen are similar to the ones we saw earlier. The **Aged** column in this screen refers to the number of days remaining till the **Ship Date**, also shown in a separate column. Again, you can work directly from this screen to access the purchase order and fill it if the shipment has arrived. Double clicking any of the purchase order details will open the Purchases Journal with the order displayed and ready to be filled. When you close the Purchases Journal, you will return to the To-Do Lists.

One outstanding purchase order is due in the next week — the one from Playing Fields. The order has not arrived yet, so there is nothing to do yet for this order.

To-Do List for Sales Due

◆   Click the **Sales Due tab** to open its To-Do Lists screen:

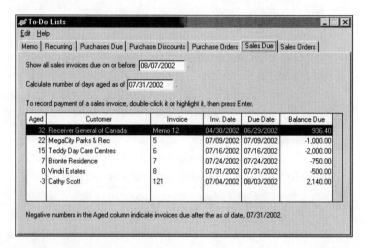

Sales Due Tab Screen Details

The Sales Due list is the customer equivalent of the Purchases Due list. It also has the same details, including aging, customer name, invoice number and date, invoice due date according to the payment terms on the invoice and the balance outstanding. If you have received a payment from the customer, you can access the Receipts Journal for the customer directly by double clicking any detail for the invoice, just as we did for Purchases Due. When you close the Receipts Journal, you will return to the To-Do Lists.

Two sales invoices are on the Sales Due list — Cathy Scott should pay within the week and the GST refund from the Receiver General is overdue. The remaining four entries are customer deposits. Expecting the GST rebate within 60 days should have been reasonable, and it is now time to follow up to make sure that the payment is being processed.

The cheque from Cathy Scott has arrived and is described in the following source document.

   Cash Receipt #22
Dated Jul. 31/02
From Cathy Scott, cheque #39 for $2 140 in full payment of account. Reference invoice #121.

◆ Double click **Sales Invoice #121**, the entry for Scott, to open the Receipts Journal with the invoice displayed for the chosen customer:

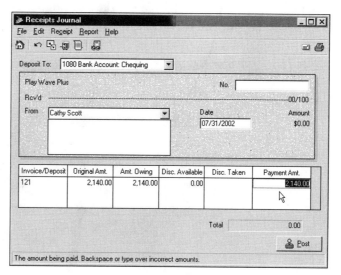

The amount is highlighted but not yet entered — the Total is still zero.

◆ Press ⌈tab⌉ to accept the amount and complete the Total and the cheque portion.

◆ Click the **No. field** so that you can enter the customer's cheque number.

◆ Type **39**

◆ Check the information and review the journal entry to be sure that all the details are correct.

◆ Click Post ⌈ Post ⌉ to record the receipt.

◆ Close the Receipts Journal.

To-Do List for Sales Orders

◆ Click the **Sales Orders tab** to open the next list:

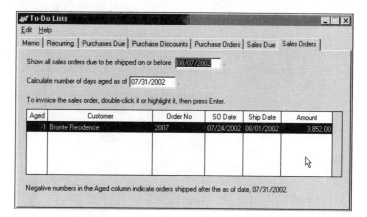

Sales Order Tab Screen Details

This screen shows any outstanding sales orders for customers that have shipping dates on or before the date of the list. If the order is ready to be filled, double click any of its details to open the Sales Journal with the order ready to be filled. When you close the Sales Journal, you will return to the To-Do Lists.

At present one sales order is due within the week. If you want to see the second order, the one from Vindri Estates, you must change the time frame so that a longer period is included in the list. Change the date to August 14 in the date field (Show all sales orders to be shipped on or before) and press ⬚tab⬚ to include both orders.

To-Do List for Recurring Transactions

◆ Click the **Recurring tab** to open its screen:

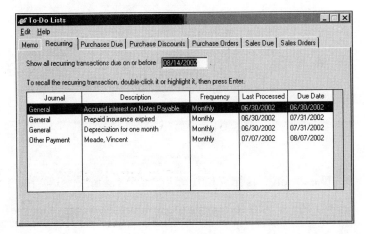

The date remains at August 14 after we changed it for the previous list.

All the recurring transactions due within the next two weeks are displayed on the screen. The details that help to identify the transaction include the journal, the description for the entry, the frequency, the last processing or posting date and the next due date. Three General Journal transactions are due on the current Session date. We will process them from the Recurring entries To-Do List. The details for the first of these transactions follows.

> ☑ Memo #48
> Dated Jul. 31/02
> One month of prepaid insurance, $200, has expired. Recall the stored adjusting entry to debit the Insurance Expense account for this amount.

◆ Click **Prepaid insurance expired** to select it if it is not already selected (or click the description you entered for this transaction).

◆ Press ⬚enter⬚ to display the General Journal with this transaction already on-screen:

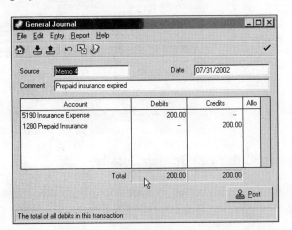

The journal entry is complete except for the Source. We need to change the memo number. The source is selected so you can edit it immediately.

◆ Type **Memo 48**

◆ Click Post $\boxed{\text{▲ Post}}$.

A new journal opens. The next memo requires that we remove a recurring transaction. The note has been repaid so the recurring entry is no longer needed.

> ☑ Memo #49
>
> Dated Jul. 31/02
>
> Remove the recurring transaction for interest accrued on the note because the note has been fully paid. Remove the entry from the General Journal Recall Recurring Transaction screen.

◆ Click the **Recall recurring transaction tool** $\boxed{\text{▲}}$ to open the Recall Recurring Transaction window:

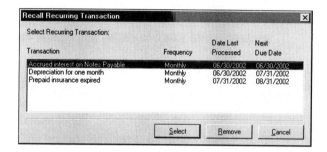

◆ Click the entry **Accrued interest on Notes Payable** if it is not already selected (or click the comment or description you used for this transaction).

◆ Click **Remove**.

You will see the familiar confirmation warning that Simply Accounting shows whenever you try to delete or remove information:

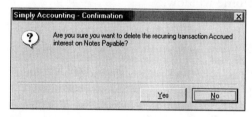

After removing the stored entry, you can close the General Journal to return to the To-Do Lists and select the recurring entry from that list. Since the next entry is also a General Journal transaction, it is easier to remain in the General Journal.

◆ Check that you have selected the correct entry. If you have not, click No to return to the Recall Recurring Transaction screen, select the correct journal entry and click Remove again.

◆ Click **Yes** to confirm that you want to remove the entry.

You will return to the Recall Recurring Transaction screen.

◆ Complete the next journal entry for depreciation directly from this window.

☑ Memo #50

Dated Jul. 31/02

Depreciation is calculated and recorded monthly for all depreciable assets. Recall the stored adjusting depreciation entry to record the depreciation amounts:

Portable Computer System	$75
Machinery & Tools	$125
Shop	$250
Truck	$400
Hydraulic Drill	$150

◆ Click **Depreciation for one month** if this entry is not selected (or click the description you used for this transaction).

◆ Click **Select** to display the General Journal entry for depreciation on-screen.

◆ Type **Memo 50** in the source field to replace the old memo number.

◆ Check your work to be sure the entry is correct.

◆ Click **Post** 🖳 Post to save the transaction.

◆ Close the General Journal to return to the To-Do Lists screen.

Only the Purchase Invoice for Meade remains in the upcoming transactions list. It is too early to process this invoice, because Meade has not yet finished the contracted work.

◆ Close the To-Do Lists to return to the Home window.

Turning on To-Do Lists

We will now activate the To-Do Lists so that they will be displayed automatically each time we start the program or advance the Session date.

◆ Choose the **View** menu, then choose **To-Do Lists** and click **At Startup** in the Home window.

◆ Choose the **View** menu, then choose **To-Do Lists** and click **After Changing Session Date** in the Home window.

◆ Check the To-Do Lists option in the View menu again to be sure that both options have a ✓ beside them. Do not click the options again because this will remove the ✓.

◆ Now process the transactions for the remainder of the month, using the appropriate journals.

☐ Memo #51

Dated Jul. 31/02

Based on the end-of-the-month count of supplies remaining, it was determined that the following quantities of supplies were used during July. Make the necessary adjusting entry to account for the supplies used.

Fibreglass & Plastics	$1 900
Lumber	$1 800
Hardware	$1 100
Office Supplies	$150

Complete the GST payment in the Payments Journal as an Other Payment to the Receiver General. Enter the GST Paid as a negative amount and enter GST Charged on Services as a positive amount. Use Full Add to enter the vendor record details (from page 221) so that you can choose not to include the Receiver General in GST reports.

Edit the dates for the statement to July 31. There is one group deposit on July 9 for $7 400 — a group of two cheques for $6 400 and $1 000.

Remember that if you have small differences in payroll cheque amounts as a result of using different tax tables, accept the differences as a reconciliation adjustment entry.

☐ Bank Debit Memo #801432

Dated Jul. 31/02

From Royal Trust, $2 000 preauthorized withdrawal for mortgage payment. This amount consists of $1 860 interest and $140 for reduction of principal.

☐ Memo #52

Dated Jul. 31/02

Pay the GST owing to the Receiver General for the period ending June 30. Use the the General Ledger balances and the GST Report for June 30. Issue cheque #160 for $1 277.15. After posting the payment, clear the GST report up to June 30.

☐ July Bank Statement

Dated Jul. 31/02

Reconcile the chequing bank account with the following bank statement for July.

ROYAL TRUSTCO. BANK STATEMENT

2300 Yonge Street, Megacity, ON M7T 2F4

Account: Play Wave Plus
7310 Recreation Court
Megacity, ON M5E 1W6

Transit No. 06722
Account No. 45264-912
Statement Date July 31, 2002

Date	Transaction	Deposits	Withdrawals	Balance
06-30-02	**Balance Forward**			26,172.56
07-02-02	CHQ #143		6,045.50	20,127.06
07-09-02	Deposit	7,400.00		27,527.06
	CHQ #144		2,097.20	25,429.86
07-10-02	CHQ #145		214.00	25,215.86
07-11-02	CHQ #146		1,122.17	24,093.69
	CHQ #147		871.04	23,222.65
	CHQ #148		885.96	22,336.69
07-16-02	Deposit	2,000.00		24,336.69
07-17-02	CHQ #152		5,284.94	19,051.75
	CHQ #150		96.30	18,955.45
	CHQ #151		80.50	18,874.95
	CHQ #153		126.50	18,748.45
07-25-02	CHQ #156		856.39	17,892.06
	CHQ #157		234.46	17,657.60
	CHQ #149		1,104.28	16,553.32
	CHQ #154		1,122.17	15,431.15
	CHQ #155		792.17	14,638.98
	Deposit	750.00		15,388.98
07-31-02	Debit Memo		2,000.00	13,388.98
	Interest	28.00		13,416.98
	Monthly fee		18.50	13,398.48
07-31-02	**Closing Balance**			**13,398.48**

Total Deposits 10,178.00
Total Withdrawals 22,952.08

◆ Close any journals that are open to return to the Home window.

Budgeting Reports and Graphs
Income Statement

◆ Choose **Financials** and then **Income Statement** from the **Reports** window to display the Income Statement Options.

◆ Click the **Report Type field list arrow** to see the expanded list of report options:

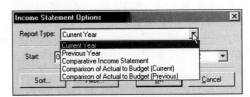

There are now two fiscal periods of financial data and we can display reports for either fiscal period or a comparative report for the two periods. We can also show budget comparisons in the report, again either for the current period or for the previous fiscal period. We want to see the budget comparisons for the current year.

◆ Click **Comparison of Actual to Budget (Current)** to choose this report. The Options screen changes again as follows:

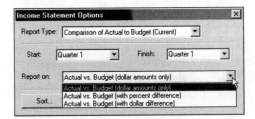

A new set of report types is added to include budget information. All the options now compare actual results to budgeted amounts with the three choices we saw earlier for comparative reports — dollar amounts only, dollar differences and percent differences. The Start and Finish dates now show the budget periods instead of the actual dates. The default time periods are correct because we have financial information only for the first budget quarter.

Three types of reports are available. The first, **Actual vs. Budget (dollar amounts only)**, lists the amounts that were budgeted for the revenue and expense accounts for the period indicated and the revenues and expenses actually obtained for the same period. The second, **Actual vs. Budget (with percent difference)**, gives these two amounts as well as the percentage that the actual amount is above or below the budgeted amount. The third option, **Actual vs. Budget (with dollar difference)** provides the same two base amounts, budget and actual, as well as the difference between them as a dollar amount.

◆ Click **Actual vs. Budget (with percent difference)** as the report type.

◆ Click **OK** to display the report. Print the report.

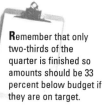

Analyzing the Budget Report

For the dollar difference and the percent difference reports, a positive difference means that the budget was exceeded and a negative difference indicates that the results came in under budget. Remember that for revenues, a positive difference means results were better than expected, but for expenses, a positive difference means that results were poorer than expected (expenses were higher than budgeted). Negative differences are favourable for expenses but not for revenues.

The effective use of budget reports involves more than merely observing whether budgeted targets were met or not. Sometimes more information is gained when targets are not met because the differences can lead to asking important questions:

- Were the targets realistic? What items were not on target and why?

- If performance exceeds the targets, how can we repeat the success?

- If performance did not meet the targets, were there factors that we failed to anticipate?

- Should we revise future budgets based on the new information?

In other words, the problem-solving cycle is set in motion. Even an Income Statement that is on target should be reviewed carefully. There may be room for improvements if the budget was a conservative estimate. There may be new information that will affect future performance that was unknown when the budget was drawn up.

◆ Close the report to return to the Home window.

Sales vs Budget Graph

Additional graphs become available once the budgeting feature is activated and budget amounts are entered. The graphs show sales and expenses separately as compared with budgets.

◆ Choose the **Graphs** menu and click **Sales vs Budget** to see the graph options:

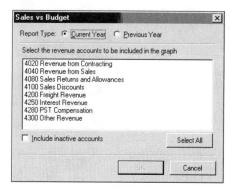

You must choose the revenue accounts that you want to include in the graph. All revenues for the selected accounts will be added together and all the budgeted amounts for these accounts will be added to form the basis for comparison.

You can also choose to show the budget for the current or the previous year if you have budget information for both periods. You can include all the accounts or select accounts individually. We will include the single account for the current year — *4020 Revenue from Contracting*.

◆ Click *Revenue from Contracting*.

◆ Click **OK** to display the bar chart graph:

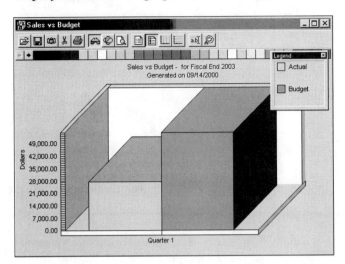

You can see that the revenue is less than half of the budgeted total and the quarter is two-thirds over. Performance is clearly below the predicted levels for this account. At this stage, the analysis should begin again to determine why revenues were not higher.

◆ Close the graph when you have finished to return to the Home window.

Expenses vs Budget Graph

◆ Choose the **Graphs** menu and click **Expenses vs Budget** to see the graph options:

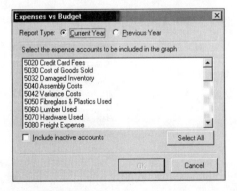

You must choose the expense accounts that you want to include in the graph. All expenses selected will be added together and all the budgeted amounts for these accounts will be added to form the basis for comparison.

You can also choose to show the budget for the current or the previous year if you have budget information for both. You can include all the accounts or select accounts individually. We will include the three accounts for the materials and supplies used in contracting jobs.

◆ Click *5050 Fibreglass & Plastics Used*.

◆ Press ⌷ctrl⌷ and click *5060 Lumber Used*.

◆ Press `ctrl` and click *5070 Hardware Used.*

◆ Click **OK** to display the graph:

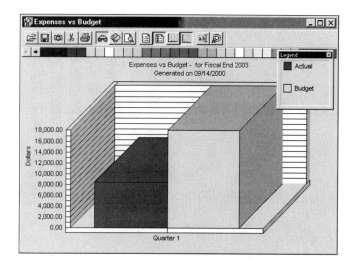

The graph shown here has horizontal grid lines added to make the amounts easier to read. The expenses selected, like the revenue, are significantly less than the budgeted amounts, indicating that less work was completed than anticipated since the supplies tend to be used proportionately to the work.

◆ Close the graph when you have finished.

One graph remains that we did not see earlier, the one comparing the performance for the two fiscal periods.

Current Revenue vs Last Year Graph

◆ Choose the **Graphs** menu and click **Current Revenue vs Last Year** to see the options:

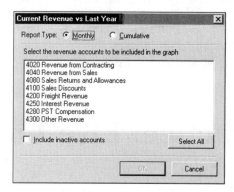

Again, you can choose one or more revenue accounts individually or you can include all the accounts at once. All amounts for the selected accounts will be added. The second option is to show the revenue amounts for each month separately or to show cumulative amounts for the two periods on a monthly basis.

◆ Click **Cumulative** to add the totals for the months.

◆ Click **Select All** to include all the revenue accounts.

If you deleted journal entries for the previous quarter, only the total for the first quarter appears in the graph.

◆ Click **OK** to display the graph:

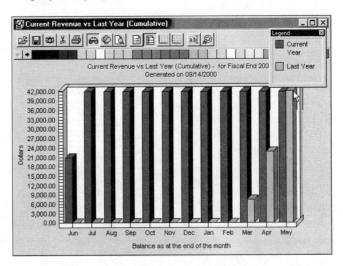

The graph begins with June, the beginning of the current fiscal period. The previous period is at the end of the series of months. If you look at these last three months, you can see that the total revenue in the current two months has almost matched the total for the previous quarter. This is largely the result of adding the sales of the playground equipment.

◆ Close the graph when you have finished.

◆ To continue good management practice, we recommend printing the following additional reports to monitor performance:
Journal Entries: All journals for July 1 to July 31
Trial Balance: As at July 31
Balance Sheet: As at July 31
Bank Reconciliation Status Report: As at July 31
Vendor Aged Detail Report: For all vendors as at July 31
Customer Aged Detail Report: For all customers as at July 31
Inventory Synopsis Report

◆ Close the data files for Play Wave Plus so that you can complete the next month of transactions for Live Links.

Practice: Live Links

Helen Lively is adding budget information to her Simply Accounting company files so that she can continue to improve her company's performance. After consulting with her employees, she has set budget targets that are high but realistic. She has discussed an employee incentive program with her two assistants as well, believing that they deserve a bonus if they reach their budget targets.

Budget Setup and To-Do Lists
Instructions

1. Open the data files for Live Links and accept October 31 as the Session date.

2. Turn on the budgeting feature. Choose quarterly budget periods.

3. Enter the budget amounts from the following chart.

LIVE LINKS
RATIONALE FOR BUDGET AMOUNTS

Revenue

Lively wants to increase Revenue from Workshops and Services by 10 percent over the previous quarter. She wants to increase her consulting time to at least one-half day per month and she expects to sell about six computer systems each month. Sales Tax Compensation is a percentage of sales; discounts and interest are budgeted at three times the amount for October. Other Revenue is a best guess estimate.

Expenses

Cost of Goods Sold is about 80 percent of Sales, based on the markup. Purchases Discounts are a percentage of COGS. Supplies Used and Telephone and Vehicle Expenses should remain constant from the previous quarter. Depreciation, Rent, Interest and Hydro Expenses are actual amounts. Bank Charges, Wages and wage-related expenses should be three times the October amounts, and the remaining expenses are best guess estimates.

INCOME AND BUDGET FORECAST

	Jul.–Sep. Income	October Income	Quarter 1 Budget	Quarter 2 Budget
REVENUE				
Revenue from Consulting	$ 2 400	$ 0	$ 2 700	$ 2 700
Revenue from Services	20 500	5 000	23 000	23 000
Revenue from Workshops	4 500	1 900	6 000	6 000
Revenue from Sales	0	19 500	55 000	55 000
Sales Discount	−114	−91	−300	−300
Sales Tax Compensation	23	26	150	150
Revenue from Interest	58	22	120	120
Freight Revenue	0	0	0	0
Other Revenue	76	81	100	100
TOTAL REVENUE	**$27 443**	**$26 438**	**$86 770**	**$86 770**
EXPENSES				
Advertising & Promotion	546	0	150	150
Bank Charges	100	20	60	60
Bank Reconciliation Adjustments	0	0	0	0
Credit Card Fees & Interest	91	349	1500	1500
Hydro Expense	150	50	150	150
Interest Expense	150	0	150	150
Loss on Sales	200	0	500	500
Depreciation: Computers	450	150	450	450
Depreciation: Custom Tools	150	50	150	150
Depreciation: Data Recovery Equip	600	200	600	600
Depreciation: Duplication Equipment	300	100	300	300

....continued on next page

INCOME AND BUDGET FORECAST CONTINUED

	Jul.–Sep. Income	October Income	Quarter 1 Budget	Quarter 2 Budget
EXPENSES Cont'd				
Depreciation: DLP Projection Unit	375	125	375	375
Depreciation: Motor Vehicle	1500	500	1500	1500
Depreciation: Colour Laser	400	200	600	600
Supplies Expense: Computer	275	105	300	300
Supplies Expense: Office	520	145	500	500
Memory Chips Used	895	95	900	900
Rent Expense	3 000	1 000	3 000	3 000
Telephone Expense	240	75	240	240
Vehicle Expenses	589	340	600	600
Cost of Goods Sold	0	16 500	44 000	44 000
Purchases Discounts	−161	−483	−900	−900
Variance Costs	0	0	200	200
Damaged Goods	0	0	500	500
Item Assembly Costs	0	0	100	100
Freight Expense	40	0	100	100
Payroll Services	80	0	0	0
Wages	11 289	4 817	15 000	15 000
EI Expense	169	165	450	450
CPP Expense	174	170	520	520
WCB Expense	55	54	180	180
TOTAL EXPENSE	**$22 175**	**$24 727**	**$72 175**	**$72 175**
NET INCOME	**$5 268**	**$1 711**	**$14 595**	**$14 595**

4. Enter the following transactions using the appropriate journals.

☐ **Advance the Session date to November 9, 2002**

☐ Purchase Order #4
Dated Nov. 1/02
Shipping Date Nov. 3/02
From Business Depot, $300 plus $21 GST paid and $21 (7%) PST paid for office supplies. Invoice total $342. Terms: net 15.

☐ Cash Sales Invoice #126
Dated Nov. 3/02
To Pacific Trust (Use Quick Add for the new customer.)

The sale to Pacific Trust combines inventory and non-inventory sales.

		Data recovery services	$ 800.00
four	11	Monitors 17" TFT Flat panel	6 000.00
		GST (7%)	476.00
		PST (7%)	476.00
		Invoice total	$7 752.00

Received cheque #317 in full payment. There is no discount.

☐ Purchase Order #5
Dated Nov. 4/02
Shipping Date Nov. 6/02
From CompuWorld Supplies

six	03	DVD-Rom 16x	$ 600.00
six	08	Memory 64 mb SDRAM	720.00
six	09	Modem 56kV.90 w/ethernet	900.00
three	10	Monitor 15" TFT Flat panel	1 800.00
six	11	Monitor 17" TFT Flat panel	6 900.00
six	12	Motherboard Pentium III at 1 GHz	3 000.00
six	15	Sound Card 64V Pro w/speakers	450.00
ten	16	Video Card 32 mb nVIDIA	1 000.00
		GST Paid	1 075.90
		Total	$16 445.90

Terms: 2/10, n/30.

☐ Purchase Order #6
Dated Nov. 4/02
Shipping Date Nov. 6/02
From Comtek Systems

three	01	CPU Cooler 2.3w Pentium III	$ 90.00
three	02	CPU Cooler x21 Pentium III	150.00
three	04	Enclosure - solid steel mini	540.00
three	05	Enclosure - solid steel tower	900.00
three	06	Hard Drive 3.5", 30GB IDE	675.00
three	07	Hard Drive 3.5", 40GB IDE	900.00
three	13	Power Supply Turbo cool 400 slim	675.00
three	14	Power Supply Turbo cool 600 tower	1 200.00
		GST Paid	359.10
		Total	$5 489.10

Terms: 2/10, n/30.

5. Open the To-Do Lists from the Home window and complete the next group of transactions from the To-Do Lists windows. Complete the cash receipt transactions from the Sales Due list, payments from the Purchase Discounts list (because the payments are not due yet), and purchases from the Purchase Orders list.

☐ Cash Receipt #16
Dated Nov. 5/02
From Westmount Institute, cheque #729 for $1 140 in payment of account.
Reference invoice #118.

☐ Cheque Copy #44
Dated Nov. 5/02
To Comtek Systems, $7 172.42 in full payment of account, including $146.38 discount taken for early payment. Reference invoice #CS-3081.

☐ Cheque Copy #45
Dated Nov. 5/02
To CompuWorld Supplies, $7 738.67 in full payment of account, including $157.93
discount taken for early payment. Reference invoice #CW-2211.

☐ Purchase Invoice #BD-12775
Dated Nov. 5/02
From Business Depot, to fill purchase order #4, $300 plus $21 GST paid and $21
(7%) PST paid for office supplies. Invoice total $342. Terms: net 15.

☐ Purchase Invoice #CW-3111
Dated Nov. 6/02
From CompuWorld Supplies, to fill purchase order #5

six	03	DVD-Rom 16x	$ 600.00
six	08	Memory 64 mb SDRAM	720.00
six	09	Modem 56kV.90 w/ethernet	900.00
three	10	Monitor 15" TFT Flat panel	1 800.00
six	11	Monitor 17" TFT Flat panel	6 900.00
six	12	Motherboard Pentium III at 1 GHz	3 000.00
six	15	Sound Card 64V Pro w/speakers	450.00
ten	16	Video Card 32 mb nVIDIA	1 000.00
		GST Paid	1 075.90
		Total	$16 445.90

Terms: 2/10, n/30.

☐ Purchase Invoice #CS-3711
Dated Nov. 6/02
From Comtek Systems, to fill purchase order #6

three	01	CPU Cooler 2.3w Pentium III	$ 90.00
three	02	CPU Cooler x21 Pentium III	150.00
three	04	Enclosure - solid steel mini	540.00
three	05	Enclosure - solid steel tower	900.00
three	06	Hard Drive 3.5", 30GB IDE	675.00
three	07	Hard Drive 3.5", 40GB IDE	900.00
three	13	Power Supply Turbo cool 400 slim	675.00
three	14	Power Supply Turbo cool 600 tower	1 200.00
		GST Paid	359.10
		Total	$5 489.10

Terms: 2/10, n/30.

6. Close the To-Do Lists window and complete the next group of transactions.

☐ Credit Card Purchase Invoice #902331
Dated Nov. 7/02
From Petro Partners, $50 plus $3.50 GST charged and $3.50 PST for gasoline for
vehicle. Invoice total $57 paid by Credit Card.

Recall the stored item
assembly transactions.
Remember to edit the
unit price for SYS-B
when necessary.

☐ Inventory Item Assembly #IIA-5

Dated Nov. 7/02

Assembly Components: transfer two (2) of each item

01	CPU Cooler 2.3w Pentium III	$ 30 each
03	DVD-Rom 16x	100 each
04	Enclosure - solid steel mini	180 each
06	Hard Drive 3.5", 30GB IDE	225 each
08	Memory 64 mb SDRAM	120 each
09	Modem 56kV.90 w/ethernet	150 each
10	Monitor 15" TFT Flat panel	600 each
12	Motherboard Pentium III at 1 GHz	500 each
13	Power Supply Turbo cool 400 slim	225 each
15	Sound Card 64V Pro w/speakers	75 each
16	Video Card 32 mb nVIDIA	100 each

Assembled Items: assemble two (2) computer systems

SYS-A   800 MMX System A $2 305 each

☐ Inventory Item Assembly #IIA-6

Dated Nov. 7/02

Assembly Components: transfer two (2) of each item

02	CPU Cooler x21 Pentium III	$ 50 each
03	DVD-Rom 16x	100 each
05	Enclosure - solid steel tower	300 each
07	Hard Drive 3.5", 40GB IDE	300 each
08	Memory 64 mb SDRAM	120 each
09	Modem 56kV.90 w/ethernet	150 each
11	Monitor 17" TFT Flat panel	1 150 each
12	Motherboard Pentium III at 1 GHz	500 each
14	Power Supply Turbo cool 600 tower	400 each
15	Sound Card 64V Pro w/speakers	75 each
16	Video Card 32 mb nVIDIA	100 each

Assembled Items: assemble two (2) computer systems

SYS-B   800 MMX System B $3 245 each

☐ Memo #33

Dated Nov. 7/02

Edit the inventory ledger item SYS-B to increase the selling price to $3 750 to
reflect the increased cost of the monitors.

☐ Memo #34

Dated Nov. 8/02

Record the PST Payable account balance for Oct. 31, 2002, as a liability owing to
the Ministry of Finance, BC. This liability is reduced by the sales tax commission of
3.3% of the PST account balance. Issue cheque #46 in payment
(PST Payable = $1 715, compensation = $56.60, net paid = $1 658.40).

☐ Employee Time Summary Sheet #5

Pay Period Ending November 9, 2002

Adrian Borland worked 80 regular hours and 2 hours overtime.

Recover $50, the last of the advance. Issue cheque #47.

☐ Cash Receipt #17

Dated Nov. 9/02

From Pro-Career Institute, cheque #4255 for $535 in payment of account. Reference invoice #120.

7. Turn on the To-Do Lists At Startup and After Advancing Session Date from the View menu.

☐ **Advance the Session date to November 24, 2002**

8. Work from the To-Do Lists to complete the next three transactions.

☐ Sales Invoice #127

Dated Nov. 12/02

To Westmount Institute, second in the series of five bi-weekly Windows workshops

one	SRV-03	Workshop - 6 hours	$900 each	$900
		GST (7%)		63
		Invoice total		$963

Terms: 2/10, n/30 days. Recall the stored invoice.

☐ Memo #35

Dated Nov. 12/02

The contract with Pro-Career Institute for a series of workshops is completed. Remove the stored entry for Pro-Career Institute from the Sales Journal Recall Recurring Transaction screen. (See the note for instructions about removing the entry from the To-Do Lists screen.)

☐ Cash Receipt #18

Dated Nov. 14/02

From Insight PC, cheque #423 for $4 605.60 in full payment of account. Reference invoice #115 and memo #32A.

9. Close the To-Do Lists window and continue with the next group of transactions.

☐ Credit Card Sales Invoice #128

Dated Nov 14/02

To Nature's Remedies (Use Quick Add for the new customer.)

two	SYS-A	800 MMX System A	$2 800 each	$ 5 600.00
one	SYS-B	800 MMX System B	3 750 each	3 750.00
		GST (7%)		654.50
		PST (7%)		654.50
		Total received		$10 659.00

Paid by Credit Card #4422 712 982 812. There is no discount.

To remove the Pro-Career recurring entry, recall the Pro-Career sales invoice from the To-Do Lists screen. Then choose the Edit menu and click Undo to discard the entry. Confirm that you want to discard the entry. This will leave the Sales Journal open. Now Click the Recall tool to open the Recall Recurring Transaction screen. Select the Pro-Career entry and click Remove. Confirm that you want to remove the entry. Close the Recurring Transaction screen. Close the Sales Journal to return to the To-Do Lists screen.

☐ Cash Sales Invoice #129
Dated Nov. 15/02
To Fraser Institute (Use Quick Add for the new customer.)

eight	SRV-01	Consulting	$125/hour	$1 000
		GST (7%)		70
		Total payment received		$1 070

Received cheque #93 in full payment. There is no discount.

☐ Cheque Copy #48
Dated Nov. 15/02
To CompuWorld Supplies, $16 116.98 in full payment of account, including $328.92 discount taken for early payment. Reference invoice #CW-3111.

☐ Cheque Copy #49
Dated Nov. 15/02
To Comtek Systems, $5 379.32 in full payment of account, including $109.78 discount taken for early payment. Reference invoice #CS-3711.

☐ Memo #36
Dated Nov. 15/ 02
Transfer $20 000 from the Credit Card bank account to the Chequing bank account.

☐ Sales Invoice #130
Dated Nov. 21/02
To Island Press, $2 000 plus $140 GST charged and $140 PST charged for duplication services. Invoice total $2 280. Terms: 2/10, n/30 days. Use Quick Add for the new customer.

☐ Cash Receipt #19
Dated Nov. 21/02
From Westmount Institute, cheque #798 for $1 906.74 in full payment of account, including $19.26 discount for early payment. Reference invoices #125 and #127.

☐ Employee Time Summary Sheet #6
Pay Period Ending November 23, 2002
Adrian Borland worked 80 regular hours and 2 hours overtime.
Issue cheque #50.

☐ Cash Receipt #20
Dated Nov. 24/02
From Pro-Career Institute, cheque #5377 for $535 in payment of account. Reference invoice #121.

☐ Memo #37 (Credit Card Bill Payment)
Dated Nov. 24/02
Received monthly statement from Credit Card company for $294.12 for purchases up to and including November 15. Cheque #51 for $294.12 submitted in full payment.

☐ **Advance the Session date to November 30, 2002**

10. Use the To-Do Lists for the next two recurring transactions.

    ☐ Sales Invoice #131

    Dated Nov. 26/02

    To Westmount Institute, third in the series of five bi-weekly Windows workshops

one	SRV-03	Workshop - 6 hours	$900 each	$900
		GST (7%)		63
		Invoice total		$963

    Terms: 2/10, n/30 days. Recall the stored invoice.

    ☐ Cash Purchase Invoice #BCH-6128

    Dated Nov. 28/02

    From BC Hydro, $50 plus $3.50 GST charged for hydro services. Invoice total $53.50. Issued cheque #52 in full payment. Recall the stored entry.

11. Close the To-Do Lists window and continue with the transactions for the remainder of the month.

    ☐ Sales Invoice #132

    Dated Nov. 28/02

    To Valley Legal Services

1	SYS-A	800 MMX System A	$2 800 each	$ 2 800.00
2	SYS-B	800 MMX System B	3 750 each	7 500.00
		GST (7%)		721.00
		PST (7%)		721.00
		Invoice total		$11 742.00

    Terms: 2/10, n/30.

    ☐ Cash Purchase Invoice #BCT-5881

    Dated Nov. 28/02

    From BC Telephone, $70 plus $4.90 GST charged and $4.90 PST charged for telephone services. Invoice total $79.80. Issued cheque #53 in full payment.

    ☐ Credit Card Purchase Invoice #1022

    Dated Nov. 28/02

    From Petro Partners, $210 plus $14.70 GST charged and $14.70 PST for vehicle maintenance services. Invoice total $239.40 paid by Credit Card.

    ☐ Purchase Invoice #MP-361

    Dated Nov. 30/02

    From Mega Pro Suppliers, $8 000 plus $560 GST charged (no PST charged) for CD and disk duplicator. Invoice total $8 560. Terms: 2/10, n/30. Use Full Add for the new vendor.

The duplicator is expected to have a value of $800 at the end of its useful life of three years. Therefore, it will be depreciated at the rate of $200 per month using the straight-line method.

☐ New vendor information

Mega Pro Suppliers (Contact: E.E. Prom)

8086 Atari Blvd.

North Vancouver, BC V6R 3E3

Tel: (604) 721-7127

Fax: (604) 721-9101

Web site: www.megapro/great.ideas/products

Terms: 2/10, n/30. Calculate discounts after taxes.

Include in GST reports.

☐ Memo #38

Dated Nov. 30/ 02

Pay Carrie Dell, the salaried employee, for one month. Issue cheque #54.

☐ Memo #39

Dated Nov. 30/02

Based on the end-of-the-month count of supplies remaining, the following quantities of supplies were used during November. Make the necessary adjusting entry to account for the supplies used.

Office Supplies	$205
Computer Supplies	$105
Memory Chips	$95

☐ Memo #40

Dated Nov. 30/02

One month of prepaid rent, $1 000, has expired. Recall the stored adjusting entry to debit the Rent Expense account for this amount.

☐ Memo #41

Dated Nov. 30/02

Recall the stored depreciation entry to record the following depreciation amounts:

Computers & Peripherals	$150
Custom Tools	$50
Data Recovery Equipment	$200
Duplication Equipment	$100
DLP Projection Unit	$125
Motor Vehicle	$500
Laser Colour Printer	$200

☐ Bank Credit Memo #1297721

Dated Nov. 30/02

Secured a new three-month demand loan for $8 000 at 9% interest to purchase new CD and disk duplicating equipment. The loan will be repaid in full with interest at the end of the three-month period.

Memo #42

Dated Nov. 30/02

Print customer statements to determine interest charges. Prepare sales invoices for
one month's interest charges as follows:

    Memo 42A: City Hall Staff $21.83

    Memo 42B: Prolegal Services $13.82

Terms: net 1 day.

Reconcile the chequing bank statement for November 2002. Remember to edit the
End Date to November 30.

LEARNX BANK STATEMENT

Pacific Heights Branch
400 Pacific Blvd., Vancouver, BC V7R 3W2

Account 554-66112

November 30, 2002

Date	Transaction	Deposits	Withdrawals	Balance
10-31-02	**Balance Forward**			21,301.96
11-01-02	CHQ #41		79.80	21,222.16
11-02-02	CHQ #42		53.50	21,168.66
11-03-02	Deposit	7,752.00		28,920.66
	CHQ #43		2,149.40	26,771.26
11-05-02	Deposit	1,140.00		27,911.26
11-08-02	CHQ #45		7,738.67	20,172.59
11-09-02	Deposit	535.00		20,707.59
	CHQ #44		7,172.42	13,535.17
	CHQ #46		1,658.40	11,876.77
	CHQ #47		686.78	11,189.99
11-14-02	Deposit	4,605.60		15,795.59
11-15-02	Deposit	1,070.00		16,865.59
	Transfer	20,000.00		36,865.59
11-17-02	CHQ #49		5,379.32	31,486.27
11-18-02	CHQ #48		16,116.98	15,369.29
11-21-02	Deposit	1,906.74		17,276.03
11-24-02	Deposit	535.00		17,811.03
11-26-02	CHQ #50		736.78	17,074.25
11-27-02	CHQ #51		294.12	16,780.13
11-30-02	CHQ #52		53.50	16,726.63
	CHQ #53		79.80	16,646.83
	Credit Memo	8,000.00		24,646.83
	Interest	29.00		24,675.83
	Monthly fee		20.00	24,655.83
11-30-02	**Closing Balance**			**24,655.83**

Total Deposits   45,573.34

Total Withdrawals   42,219.47

Account holder: Live Links
20300 Silicon Valley Rd. North
Burnaby, BC V5B 3A2

Remember that if you have small differences in payroll cheque amounts as a result of using different tax tables, accept the differences as a reconciliation adjustment entry.

12. To follow good management practice, we recommend printing the following reports:
    Journal Entries: All journals for November 1 to November 30
    Trial Balance: As at November 30
    Comparative Income Statement: Actual vs Budget (with percentage difference)
    From October 1 to November 30
    Balance Sheet: As at November 30
    Bank Reconciliation Status Report: As at November 30
    Vendor Aged Detail Report: For all vendors as at November 30
    Customer Aged Detail Report: For all customers as at November 30
    Inventory Synopsis Report

13. Close the data files for Live Links to prepare for setting up projects for Play Wave.

Review Questions

1. How do you enter a budget for a company in Simply Accounting?
2. What differences are there in using the program after you have set up the budget details?
3. What reports are affected by adding budget details? How are the reports different? What reports are unchanged and why?
4. How do you change budget amounts?
5. What will happen if you change the budget frequency for Play Wave or Live Links when budget amounts were entered for only two quarters?
6. What is a cost variance? How and when is cost variance created?
7. What happens when you buy new inventory items at a price that is different from the old price?
8. How do you prepare a vacation paycheque for an employee who has had vacation pay retained?
9. How can you use the To-Do Lists as part of regular accounting procedures? What are the advantages of having the To-Do Lists turned on?

CHAPTER 17

PROJECTS AND ALLOCATIONS

Objectives

- **enter settings for the Project Ledger**
- **create projects**
- **allocate revenues and expenses to projects**
- **set up a new payroll deduction**
- **add new employees**
- **add a new project from a journal**
- **enter one-time payroll deductions**
- **display and print project reports**

Introduction

In this chapter, Play Wave Plus will begin to use the Project Ledger. This feature of the program is another tool for understanding, predicting and controlling the costs associated with the different aspects of the business. No new journals are connected with the Project Ledger, but you will continue to use all the journals to complete the transactions for the final month, and add the allocation details.

If you have not completed the journal entries in Chapter 16 and want to continue working on Chapter 17, you can use your copy of the Data Disk file — Ch17\play\playch17.sdb — to begin this chapter.

PlayWave
Plus

The Project Ledger

Many businesses have revenue from more than one source. To help determine the profitability of these different parts of the business, some form of project costing is often used. Project costing separates the business into different groups or parts and then allocates expenses or costs to these different groups in proportion to the costs actually incurred by the different units. The divisions in the business may be determined in many ways. Some stores or companies use departments as the different projects, some use product lines or divisions. Contracting companies may use the actual individual projects. Choosing a realistic method of allocating costs to the groups or divisions is critical if project reports are to be meaningful. Accurate tracking of costs can help with making decisions about expanding a business, eliminating parts of the business or just controlling costs more effectively. When combined with budgeting information, cost tracking can offer a very powerful tool for analyzing performance trends.

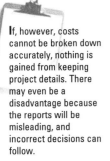
If, however, costs cannot be broken down accurately, nothing is gained from keeping project details. There may even be a disadvantage because the reports will be misleading, and incorrect decisions can follow.

Project costing can also be used to track the performance of individual employees. By attributing revenue to the appropriate individual (project), the project data can be used to determine sales commissions. Costs can be omitted from the tracking or can be assigned in proportion to the hours worked by each salesperson. When employees are paid on the basis of performance, they must be able to control their performance.

Setting up the Project Ledger is similar to setting up the other ledgers. After entering settings for the ledger and creating projects in the ledger, you can add historical project data. However, there are no linked accounts or journals for projects.

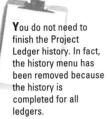
You do not need to finish the Project Ledger history. In fact, the history menu has been removed because the history is completed for all ledgers.

Project Settings

◆ Open the data file for Play Wave. Accept July 31 as the Session date.

◆ Close the To-Do Lists.

◆ Restore the Project Ledger icon (View menu, Modules, Project).

◆ Choose the **Setup** menu and click **Settings** in the Home window.

◆ Click the **Project tab** to open the Settings screen for Projects:

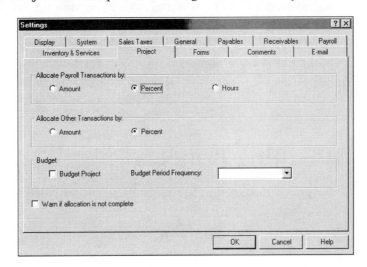

Project Settings Options

The settings options for projects involve choosing the method of allocating costs and revenue. You can **Allocate Payroll Transactions** on the basis of the dollar **Amount** spent, the **Percent** of time spent working on each project, or the actual number of **Hours** worked on each project. Obviously, the choice will be influenced by the data available and the ease of determining the amounts. Since the allocation for payroll transactions includes the wage expense and all the wage-related expenses, such as EI and CPP expense, the exact amount may be difficult to determine for regular employees. If the labour is contracted out and these expenses are not included, the amounts may be more readily available. Usually, it is easier to track the number of hours worked on a project, or the percentage of time, because you can record the number of hours employees actually work on each site. For salaried workers, the number of hours is less useful because they are not paid on an hourly basis. And finally, there is the choice about how to allocate time that is spent between projects.

For **Other Transactions**, the options are to allocate on the basis of dollar **Amount** or **Percent**. When the amounts are not simple numbers, allocation by percent is easier because the program takes care of the calculations. Other transactions include all sources of revenue and all non-payroll costs and expenses.

There is also an option to **Budget Projects**. When you select this option and enter a **Budget Period Frequency**, you can enter the total amounts budgeted for revenues and for expenses in the Project Ledger window. The budget period selections in the drop-down list are the same as those for the overall budget settings.

The final option in the Settings is extremely important as a control technique. If you choose to let the program **Warn if allocation is not complete**, you will see a warning screen whenever you try to post a transaction without completing the allocation. This reminder is useful because it is easy to forget to allocate an amount or to omit a project resulting in an incomplete distribution. If you want to leave the distribution incomplete, you can choose to proceed. The warning is helpful for those other times when you do not intend to omit an allocation.

The default settings are for percentage distributions, the setting Play Wave will use.

◆ Click **Warn if allocation is not complete** to activate the warning.

◆ Click **OK** to save the change and return to the Home window.

Project Names

You can change the name of the Project Ledger at any time. Choose the Setup menu and click Names. Double click the name in the Project field and type in the name you want. For example, you might use Division or Department instead of Project. The name you use will appear in the Home window to replace Project as the icon label, and all other references will change as well. For example, if you change the project name to Division, the Reports menu will include Division instead of Project. All reports will be renamed; the Project Allocation screen will be titled Division Allocation; the Select Project screen will be named Select Division, etc.

Creating Projects

Projects are created in the Project Ledger indicated with the arrow pointer in the following screen:

◆ Click the **Project icon** to open the Project window:

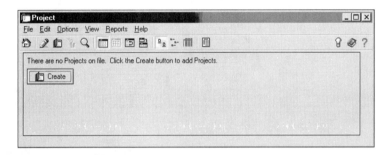

The window has no project icons, because there are no projects yet.

◆ Click the **Create button** [🗐 Create], or click the Create tool [🗐], or choose the File menu and click Create to open the Project Ledger, the input window for creating projects:

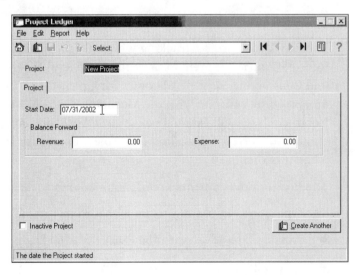

The Project Ledger Screen

The Project Ledger has a single input screen and the details are very straightforward. The name of the project appears in the **Project** field. The date that you want to start tracking amounts for projects is the **Start Date**. If you enter a Start Date that is earlier than the Session date, you can add **Balance Forward** information. This historical information includes the total in accumulated **Revenue** for the project and the total **Expense** incurred on the project from the Start Date to the Session date. You can leave the balance fields blank if you start tracking the project revenue and costs from the Session date. The tools, menu options and Select list are the same as those found in other ledgers.

Project Budgeting

When you select the option to enter budget amounts for projects, a Budget tab is added to the Project Ledger. Clicking the Budget tab and then clicking Budget this Project will open an input screen for budget amounts. The number of budget periods will match the selection made in the Project Settings screen. The following screen shows the input screen when Quarterly budgets periods were selected:

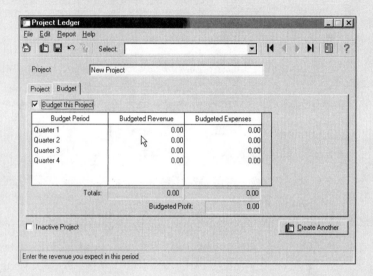

For each period, you should enter a total amount for budgeted revenue and budgeted expenses. You may then produce project budget reports that compare project performance against these budgeted amounts.

For Play Wave, project tracking will begin in August, so there is no historical information. There are two projects — General Sales for sales of inventory products, and Contracting for general contracting projects. A third project will begin shortly for an upcoming contract with the Megacity Board of Education. Because the School Board contract will extend over several work sites and several weeks, it is large enough to warrant separating the project details for it. This project will be added when it is first used.

The Project field contents are highlighted, ready for editing.

◆ Type `General Sales` to enter the project name.

◆ Press (tab) to advance to the Start Date field.

◆ Type `Aug 1`

◆ Click **Create Another** to save the new project and open a new ledger input form.

- Type **Contracting** as the project name and **Aug 1** as the Start Date.

- Click **Create Another** to save the second project and open a new ledger page.

- Close the Project Ledger to return to the Project window.

- Choose the **Reports** menu and click **Display Project List** in the Project window to check that you entered the project names and dates correctly.

- Close the report and then close the Project window to return to the Home window.

Allocating Amounts

The option to allocate is available whenever an account for which you have allowed project allocation is part of a journal entry. We have allowed project allocations for all revenue and expense accounts, so these accounts should make the allocation available. When you create new accounts in the Accounts window, the allocation option is selected by default. When you create new accounts in a journal window using the Wizard, you must change the default setting for this option. To be certain that all the accounts you need will allow allocation projects, check the General Ledger records.

Checking Account Allocation Settings

- Click the **Accounts icon** to open the Accounts window.

- Double click *4020 Revenue from Contracting*, the first revenue account, to open its ledger.

- If there is no checkmark in the box for Allow Project Allocations, click the check box.

- Click the **Next account tool** to move to the ledger window for the *Revenue from Sales* account.

- Continue in this way to check all the revenue and expense accounts, adding the checkmark when it is missing.

- Close the General Ledger window.

- Close the Accounts window to return to the Home window.

Allocating Expenses

Whenever an expense or revenue, or any other account for which you have allowed project allocations, is part of a journal transaction, you can distribute the amount for that account among the projects that you created. The following purchase has two expenses that should be allocated.

If you followed the instructions in the text, you created the following accounts using the New Account Wizard:
4080
4250
4300
5020
5100
5160
5170
5210
These accounts may not have selected the option to Allow Project Allocations. To be certain that you can allocate correctly, check all accounts.

Credit Card Purchase Invoice #GA-7818

Dated Aug. 1/02

From Gasoline Alley, $60 plus $4.20 GST and $4.80 (8%) PST charged for gasoline for truck and $40 plus $2.80 GST and $3.20 (8%) PST for propane gas. Total invoice amount paid by Chargit, $115. Allocate 50% of the truck expenses to the General Sales Project and 50% to the Contracting Project. Allocate 100% of the propane gas expense to the Contracting Project.

◆ Click the **Purchases icon** to open the Purchases Journal.

◆ Enter the transaction as usual but do not post it.

◆ Click **5260**, the account number on the first line of your journal entry as shown:

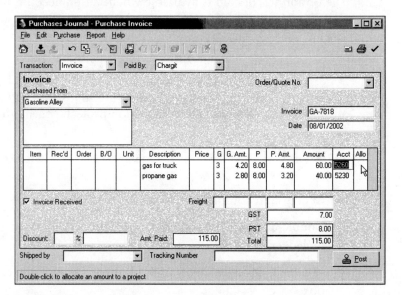

There are three different ways to begin the allocation procedure:

- Select the account by clicking anywhere on its journal line. Click the Allocate tool button,
- Select Allocate from the Purchase (or other journal name) menu, or
- Double click the Allo column beside the account for which you want to allocate an amount.

If the cursor is on a blank line, or on a line for an account that does not Allow Project Allocations, the Allocate tool and menu option will be dimmed.

When there is no account number in the journal, as in the Payroll Journal, you may use the Allocate tool or select Allocate from the Paycheque menu.

◆ Click the **Allocate tool** (or double click the Allo column beside the account, or choose the Purchase menu and click Allocate) to open the Project Allocation screen:

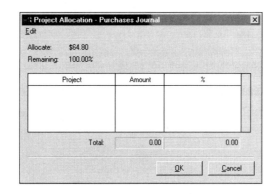

The Project Allocation screen has the total amount that is to be divided among the projects and the percentage of the total amount that is not yet distributed or allocated. Initially, 100 percent is Remaining or not allocated. The three columns in the input portion of the screen show the name of the project, the amount that is allocated to that project and the percentage of the total that the amount represents.

The cursor is in the Project column. (If it is not, click this column.) As usual, an entry list is available from which to choose.

◆ Press ⌜enter⌝ to display the list of projects:

The alphabetized list includes the two projects we created earlier in the chapter and the option to add a new project.

◆ Click **General Sales**, the first project for which we have information.

◆ Click **Select** to add the project name to the Project Allocation screen:

Since we have chosen to allocate on a percentage basis, the cursor moves to the % field. The percentage of the amount that remains to be allocated is entered and highlighted. Initially, of course, that is 100 percent of the amount. The correct allocation is 50 percent.

◆ Type **50** to replace the default entry.

◆ Press ⌧tab⌧ to accept the entry and update all amounts as shown:

Notice the changes in the screen that have taken place. The percent Remaining has decreased to 50 percent (100 – 50). The program calculates 50 percent of the full amount to be allocated and places that amount in the Amount column. The Totals at the bottom of the Amount and % columns are the sums of the entries in each column. When you choose to allocate by amount, the procedure is reversed. You type the amounts in the Amount column, and the program calculates and enters the percentages.

The cursor should be in the Project column again.

◆ Double click to see the Select Project screen.

◆ Double click **Contracting** to enter this project name.

The highlighted percent is now 50, the percent that is unallocated.

◆ Press ⌧tab⌧ to accept the entry, update the totals and advance the cursor to the next line in the Project column.

Your screen should now look like the one shown here:

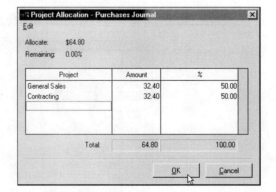

When the total expense has been allocated, the percent remaining is zero, the Total of the Amount column entries equals the Allocate amount and the Total for the % column entries is 100. From the numbers in the Amount column, you can see that allocating an expense like this one by amount is more difficult than by percent.

Check your percent entries to be sure that they match the ones shown here. To change an entry, double click the error and type the correct information. If the project is incorrect, reselect from the Select Project screen. You can change the project information any time before you post the transaction. After that, you must make changes by completing an adjusting entry.

◆ Click **OK** to save the distribution information and return to the Journal window.

You are now ready to allocate the amount for the *Propane Gas Expense*. You must allocate the amount for each account separately, even if the allocation percentages are the same. You must also allocate an amount when 100% is allocated to a one project.

◆ Double click the **Allo column** beside 5230 to open the Project Allocation window.

◆ Press ⓔⓝⓣⓔⓡ to see the project list.

◆ Double click **Contracting** to select and enter this project.

◆ Press ⓣⓐⓑ to accept the default and update the totals. Because the full amount is allocated to one project, you can accept the default percentage.

◆ Click **OK** to save the distribution information and return to the Purchases Journal window.

Your Purchases Journal should now look like the following:

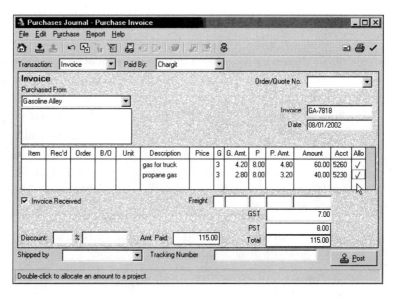

The only difference in the journal is the addition of the checkmarks in the Allo column beside the account numbers. You will see the effects of the distribution when you review the journal entry.

◆ Choose the **Report** menu and click **Display Purchases Journal Entry:**

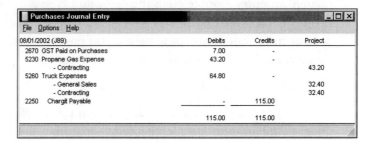

You can see that the program has allocated all expenses according to the percentages we entered. These amounts are displayed in the Project column of the report.

◆ Close the display.

If you have made an error, either in the journal portion or the allocation part, correct them before posting. Return to the allocation window by clicking the Allo tool again or by double clicking the Allo column.

◆ Click **Post** to save the transaction.

Allocating Expenses in Other Journals

If account numbers appear on-screen, you can choose the account for which you want to complete an allocation. Most journals that allow you to enter account numbers have a separate column for allocation beside the account number. For the Payroll Journal, no account number appears on-screen, so you must use the Allocate tool or the Allocate option in the Paycheque menu. In the Payroll Run Journal, the Allocate column applies to individual employees that you select instead of selecting accounts. For all payroll allocations, the program will automatically distribute all wage-related expenses for an employee according to the one distribution you enter. The amount allocated in the Project Allocation screen represents the total of all the wage-related expenses.

The next transactions for Play Wave in August do not involve any revenue or expense accounts, so there will be no allocation or distribution. There are no more allocations until the Payroll Journal entries for August 6.

◆ Advance the Session date to **August 7**.

◆ Work from the To-Do Lists (Purchase Orders and Purchase Discounts) to enter the next two transactions.

☐ Purchase Invoice #PF-1499

Dated Aug. 2/02

From Playing Fields Inc., to fill purchase order #20008

two	01	Carousels	$ 360.00
two	02	Jungle Gyms	360.00
two	03	Slides: classic	500.00
two	04	Slides: wave	640.00
two	05	Swing Sets: double	360.00
two	06	Swing Sets: triple	460.00
two	07	Tube Slides: classic	480.00
two	08	Tube Slides: wave	560.00
		GST Paid	260.40
		Invoice total	$3 980.40

Terms: net 30 days.

☐ Cheque Copy #161

Dated Aug. 5/02

To Swede Steel Co., $1 153.46 in full payment of account, including $23.54 discount taken for early payment. Reference invoice #SC-6714.

◆ Close the To-Do Lists and complete the next two transactions:

☐ Purchase Invoice #BC-1911

Dated Aug. 5/02

From The Buildex Corp., $3 000 for plastics and fibreglass and $2 000 for lumber plus $350 GST paid. Freight charge is $40 plus $2.80 GST. Invoice total $5 392.80. Terms: 2/10, n/30 days.

☐ Sales Quote #2008

Dated Aug. 5/02

Completion date for Phase One Aug. 31/02

To Megacity Board of Education, for 4 school mini-play centres to replace the recently demolished playgrounds. Each play centre will cost $4 000 plus GST. Invoice total for Phase One, $17 120. Terms: net 30 days. Use Full Add for the new customer. (Hint: type 4 in the Order field.)

☐ New customer information:

Megacity Board of Education (Contact: Constance Learner)
155 College St. W.
Megacity, ON M5T 2R4
Tel: (416) 393-0287
Fax: (416) 393-0221
E-mail: CLearner@schools.infonet.com
Web site: www.toronto.schools.com
Terms: net 30 days.
Include in GST reports.
Credit limit: $20 000

When you close the To-Do Lists, you may see an advisor message telling you to begin preparing for year-end. Close the advisor message.

You cannot allocate amounts for quotes and orders. When the invoice is completed to fill the order, you must add the allocation details.

☐ Sales Order #2008
Dated Aug. 5/02
Completion date Aug. 31/02
Convert sales quote #2008 for Megacity Board of Education to a sales order. All
contract amounts, dates and terms are unchanged.

☐ Cash Receipt #23
Dated Aug. 6/02
From Megacity Board of Education, cheque #1143 for $4 000 as an advance
(deposit #9) on Phase One contract for four school play centres.

◆ Close the journal to return to the Home window.

The next memo provides details of the final payment to Peter Piper. Since this is
Piper's last paycheque, vacation pay should be included. Because the amounts are
relatively small, the taxes should not be distorted significantly by the addition of the
vacation pay to the regular cheque.

◆ Turn off the option to retain vacation pay for Piper in the Payroll Ledger. Refer to
Chapter 16, page 452, for assistance if necessary.

Prepare the following payroll cheque for Piper but **do not post** it yet.

☐ Memo #53
Dated Aug. 6/02
Piper will not return to work after his vacation because he is starting a new college
program in August. Piper worked 24 hours before resigning. Prepare the final
paycheque for him and include the vacation pay with the cheque. Issue cheque
#162. Because Piper's last day of work was in July, his wage expenses will not be
allocated.

◆ Choose the **Report** menu and click **Display Payroll Journal Entry** to see the
transaction details:

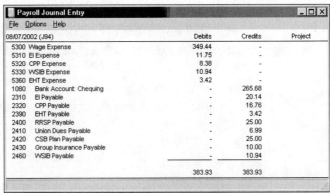

08/07/2002 (J94)	Debits	Credits	Project
5300 Wage Expense	349.44	-	
5310 EI Expense	11.75	-	
5320 CPP Expense	8.38	-	
5330 WSIB Expense	10.94	-	
5360 EHT Expense	3.42	-	
1080 Bank Account: Chequing	-	265.68	
2310 EI Payable	-	20.14	
2320 CPP Payable	-	16.76	
2390 EHT Payable	-	3.42	
2400 RRSP Payable	-	25.00	
2410 Union Dues Payable	-	6.99	
2420 CSB Plan Payable	-	25.00	
2430 Group Insurance Payable	-	10.00	
2460 WSIB Payable	-	10.94	
	383.93	383.93	

Remember, your
screen may show
different amounts for
EI, CPP and Income Tax
(and therefore also for
Bank Account:
Chequing).

Notice that there is no entry for *Vacation Payable* because the vacation pay is not
retained.

◆ Click **Post** 　 to save the transaction.

You will see the following warning because the expenses were not allocated:

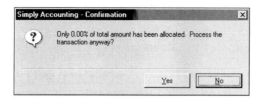

Simply Accounting provides the warning because we turned on the option to warn about incomplete allocations. This warning, or one similar to it, will appear whenever you do not allocate 100% of an expense or revenue amount. You must complete an allocation even if the amount is assigned fully to a single project (accept the default 100% for the project).

◆ Click **Yes** to accept the incomplete allocation and return to the Payroll Journal.

◆ Close the Payroll Journal.

The Payroll Journal transaction that follows includes a payroll deduction for contributions to a United Way campaign that we have not yet set up. Before completing the payroll entry, we must change the Payroll Ledger setup to accommodate the new deduction.

Adding a New Payroll Deduction

We want to add a payroll deduction for contributions to a United Way campaign so that these contributions can be included automatically in the Payroll Journal, just like the other deductions we set up in Chapter 9. This requires creating a new General Ledger account for the deduction, adding the name of the new deduction, identifying the tax status of the deduction and then linking the new account to the deduction.

☐ Create a new General Ledger Group account 2440 United Way Payable (G).

Entering a Name for a New Deduction

◆ Choose the **Setup** menu and click **Names** (Home window) to open the Names screen:

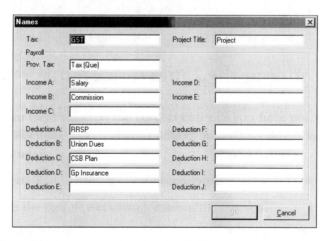

◆ Double click the **Deduction E field** to highlight the N/A entry (or click the field to move the cursor if the field is blank).

◆ Type **United Way**

◆ Click **OK** to save the name and return to the Home window.

Entering the Tax Status for a New Deduction

Once we have entered the name of the deduction, we must indicate whether it is a before-tax or after-tax deduction. This status is selected in the Settings for the Payroll Ledger.

◆ Choose the **Setup** menu and click **Settings**.

◆ Click the **Payroll tab** to open the Payroll Settings screen:

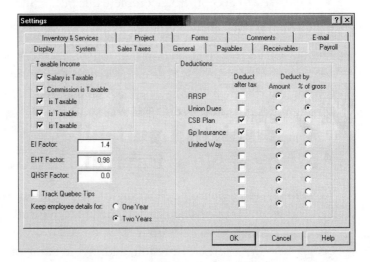

The new deduction, United Way, is now listed by name. Charitable donations reduce income tax by creating refundable tax credits on the income tax return. This deduction is different from pension contributions, which are subtracted from gross income before determining income tax, that is, they reduce taxable income. Thus, charitable donations, like the contributions to the United Way, are deducted after tax.

◆ Click the **Deduct after tax check box** beside United Way to add a ✓.

◆ Click **OK** to save the change and return to the Home window.

Adding the Linked Account

The final step involves linking the new account to the new deduction.

◆ Choose the **Setup** menu, then choose **Linked Accounts** and click **Payroll** in the Home window to open the first Payroll Linked Accounts screen.

◆ Click the **Deductions tab** to open the linked accounts screen for deductions:

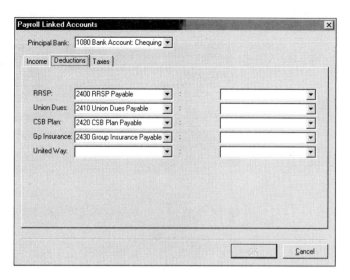

Again, the new deduction name appears in the Payables accounts section, below Gp Insurance.

◆ Click the **United Way account list arrow** to see the drop-down list of accounts.

◆ Click *2440 United Way Payable* to choose the new account and link it.

◆ Click **OK** to save the new link and return to the Home window.

◆ Complete the following two payroll transactions in the Payroll (Paycheques) Journal because you cannot change deduction amounts in the Payroll Cheque Run Journal.

◆ Review the journal entry display before posting to see how payroll expenses are allocated.

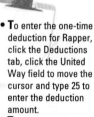

• To enter the one-time deduction for Rapper, click the Deductions tab, click the United Way field to move the cursor and type 25 to enter the deduction amount.
• To allocate payroll expenses, click the Allocate tool. Refer to pages 490–493 if you need assistance.
• Click Add new project in the Project Allocation screen and click Add to open the Project Ledger.

☐ Memo #54
Dated Aug. 6, 2002
Payroll Time Sheet for pay period ending Aug. 6
Candie Rapper worked 80 regular hours and 2 hours overtime.
Add a deduction of $25 for the United Way campaign. Since this is not a permanent deduction, do not change the ledger record; make the change directly in the Payroll Journal.
Allocate 20% of the expenses to the General Sales Project, 60% to the Contracting Project and 20% to the School Board Project. Create the new School Board Project from the Journal by using the Add New Project option in the Project Allocation screen. The new project should have August 1 as the Start Date.
Issue cheque #163.

The Payroll Journal entry for Rapper should look like the following:

Payroll Journal Entry			
File Options Help			
08/06/2002 (J95)	Debits	Credits	Project
5300 Wage Expense	1,208.48	-	
- General Sales			241.70
- Contracting			725.09
- School Board Project			241.69
5310 EI Expense	39.05	-	
- General Sales			7.81
- Contracting			23.43
- School Board Project			7.81
5320 CPP Expense	40.07	-	
- General Sales			8.01
- Contracting			24.04
- School Board Project			8.02
5330 WSIB Expense	36.37	-	
- General Sales			7.27
- Contracting			21.82
- School Board Project			7.28
5360 EHT Expense	11.39	-	
- General Sales			2.28
- Contracting			6.83
- School Board Project			2.28
1080 Bank Account: Chequing	-	860.96	
2300 Vacation Payable	-	46.48	
2310 EI Payable	-	66.94	
2320 CPP Payable	-	80.14	
2330 Income Tax Payable	-	184.84	
2390 EHT Payable	-	11.39	
2410 Union Dues Payable	-	23.24	
2440 United Way Payable	-	25.00	
2460 WSIB Payable	-	36.37	
	1,335.36	1,335.36	

- **N**otice that each expense account amount is distributed among the three projects according to the percentages entered.
- **R**emember, your screen may show different amounts for EI, CPP and Income Tax (and therefore also for the bank account).

☐ Memo #55

Dated Aug. 6, 2002

Prepare the regular bi-weekly salary for Doolitle. Add a deduction of $50 for the United Way. Since this is not a permanent deduction, make the change directly in the Payroll Journal. Allocate 20% of the expense to the General Sales Project, 30% to the Contracting Project and 50% to the School Board Project. Issue cheque #164.

Adding a New Employee from the Payroll Journal

Peter Piper resigned at the end of July after returning from his vacation. Play Wave needed to replace him immediately because of the commitment to the Megacity School Board to build several new playgrounds. Rebecca Doolittle recommended two people who had relevant experience and were available immediately. After interviewing both candidates and checking their references, Child hired both individuals because the new contract will generate additional work. Both employees began working on August 1.

The payroll transaction that follows involves these two new employees. We will add their records from the Payroll Journal, just as we added customer and vendor records from the Sales and Purchases Journals. You cannot add employees from the Payroll Cheque Run Journal.

The pay dates will continue on the bi-weekly cycle started for Piper. Thus, on Aug. 6, their first pay date, Muffet and Uphill have worked only one week.

☑ Memo #56

Dated Aug. 6, 2002

Payroll Time Sheet for pay period ending Aug. 6

Mitzy Muffet worked 40 regular hours and 0 hours overtime.

Jack Uphill worked 40 regular hours and 0 hours overtime.

Issue cheques #165 and #166.

For both employees, allocate 20% of the expenses to the General Sales Project, 60% to the Contracting Project and 20% to the School Board Project.

✓ New Employee Information

Mitzy Muffet is single and studies part-time at the University of Toronto. She will work full-time throughout the year assisting on construction projects and assembling kits. Because her tuition deduction is offset by the income she has from other sources, she has chosen not to have her tuition fees included in her federal claim amount. Muffet earns $14 per hour for the first 40 hours each week and $21 for each hour after that. In addition to the regular pay, she receives vacation pay at the rate of 4%. Vacation pay is retained. Her regular contributions to a Registered Retirement Savings Plan and to the United Way campaign are deducted automatically from her bi-weekly pay. She has chosen to join the union and pays dues.

Jack Uphill, the second new employee, will also assist with construction projects and assembly work. As a single father, his basic federal claim for income taxes is supplemented by the spousal equivalent claim for his son. (The spousal amount is reduced because his son has a small income.) Uphill is paid at the same rate as Muffet but participates in the Canada Savings Bond (CSB) Plan and the Group Insurance program as well as the RRSP program and United Way campaign. As a union member, he also pays union dues.

Ledger record details for both employees are provided in the following chart.

PAYROLL LEDGER INFORMATION FOR NEW EMPLOYEES

Personal Information

Name	Mitzy Muffet	Jack Uphill
Address	49 Curds-n-Whey Blvd.	40 Tumbledown Hill
	Megacity, ON	Brampton, ON
	M6G 3C3	L7R 4F1
Phone	(416) 489-9128	(905) 398-5100
SIN	538 910 811	672 619 624
Birth Date	May 21/72	Aug. 8/69
Date of Hire	Aug. 1/02	Aug. 1/02

Taxes

Tax Table	Ontario	Ontario
Federal Claim	$7 131	$13 186
WSIB (WCB) Rate	3.13	3.13
EI Eligible (EI Factor)	Yes (Factor = 1.4)	Yes (Factor = 1.4)

Income

Regular Per Hour Wage Rate	$14 per hour	$14 per hour
Regular Hours Per Period	80	80
Overtime Per Hour Wage Rate	$21 per hour	$21 per hour
Number of Pay Periods	26	26
Vacation Pay	4% Retained	4% Retained

Deductions

RRSP Contributions	$25	$25
Union Dues	2%	2%
CSB Plan Contributions	–	$20
Gp Insurance Premiums	–	$10
United Way Contributions	$20	$10

- Click the **Paycheques icon** 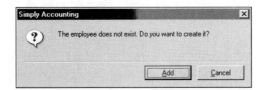 to open the Payroll Journal.

- Type **Muffet, Mitzy** in the name field.

- Press `tab` to see the warning:

The program recognizes that the name is new and gives you a chance to add the record or to change the name. We want to add the record. Adding a record from the journal for payroll requires the same information as entering the record from the Payroll Ledger. There is no Quick Add option because many of the information fields are required for federal tax reporting purposes.

- Click **Add** to open the Payroll Ledger input form:

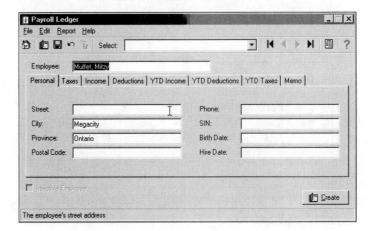

The Personal Information screen appears first with the employee name included.

- Enter the personal details required from the Payroll Ledger Information chart.

- Click the **Taxes tab** to open the next screen:

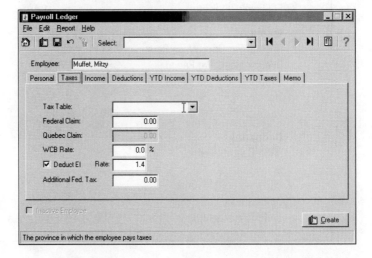

◆ Enter the details for taxes from the Payroll Ledger Information chart.

◆ Click the **Income tab** to open the next screen:

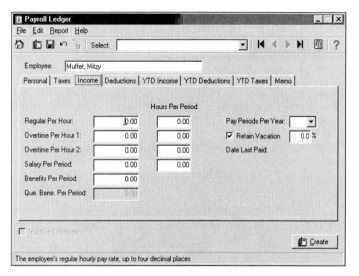

◆ Enter the details for income from the Payroll Ledger Information chart.

◆ Click the **Deductions tab** to open the next screen:

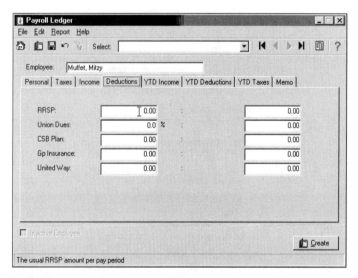

◆ Enter the deductions for **RRSP**, Union Dues and United Way. Leave the fields for the other deductions blank.

WARNING!

Check the employee information on each screen carefully because it will be used immediately in the journal entry that you are working on.

◆ Click **Create** to save the record and return to the journal.

◆ Press (tab) to continue with the journal entry. The cheque number should be correct.

◆ Type **Aug 6** in the Date field and in the Period Ending field.

- Click the **Reg. field** to move the cursor.

- Type **40** to enter the number of hours worked.

- Press ⌨tab to update all the amounts and taxes.

- Continue by entering the allocation.

- Review the journal entry, and when it is correct, post it.

- Complete the Payroll Journal entry for Uphill by adding the new employee.

- Close the Payroll Journal to return to the Home window.

- Now continue with the remaining transactions.

☐ Bank Debit Memo #811291
Dated Aug. 6/02
From Royal Trust, notification that cheque #39112 from MegaCity Parks & Rec for
$2 000 is NSF. Reverse the receipt. Prepare a sales invoice using the debit memo
number for the $20 NSF handling charges. Allocate 100% of Other Revenue to
General Sales Project. Terms: net 1. Reference cash receipt #21.

☐ Inventory Item Assembly #IIA-5
Dated Aug. 6/02
Assembly Components: transfer two (2) of each item

01	Carousel	$182.50 each
03	Slide: classic	250.00 each
05	Swing Set: double	182.50 each
07	Tube Slide: classic	242.40 each
Additional Costs		150.00

Assembled Items: assemble two (2) kits

| KIT-A | Tom Sawyer Kit | $932.40 each |

Recall the stored recurring entry and edit the unit costs if necessary. You can enter up to four decimals for the unit cost. The component prices have changed because the program applies average cost pricing. You cannot post the Item Assembly Journal entry until the total amount for the assembled items is equal to the total for components.

☐ Inventory Item Assembly #IIA-6
Dated Aug. 6/02
Assembly Components: transfer two (2) of each item

02	Jungle Gym	$182.50 each
04	Slide: wave	320.00 each
06	Swing Set: triple	234.00 each
08	Tube Slide: wave	286.00 each
Additional Costs (lumber for raft)		160.00

Assembled Items: assemble two (2) kits

| KIT-B | Huck Finn Kit | $1 102.50 each |

Double click the Allo column beside the account to open the Project Allocation screen.

☐ Sales Invoice #125
Dated Aug. 6/02
To fill sales order #2007
To Bronte Residence, $3 600 plus $252 GST charged for a play centre completed
under contract. Invoice total $3 852. Terms: net 1 day. Allocate 100% of the
revenue to the Contracting Project.

☐ **Cash Receipt #24**

Dated Aug. 6/02

From Teddy Day Care Centres, cheque #148 for $8 500 in full payment of account including $200 discount for early payment. Reference invoice #123 and deposit #6.

◆ Advance the Session Date to **August 14, 2002**. Use the To-Do Lists to complete the next group of transactions.

☐ **Cash Purchase Invoice #VM-200**

Dated Aug. 8/02

From Vincent Meade, $200 plus $14 GST paid for maintenance services rendered in shop and yard and for inventory maintenance. Invoice total $214. Issued cheque #167 in full payment. Recall the stored monthly entry and edit it to add allocation. Allocate 40% of the expense to General Sales, 20% to Contracting and 40% to the School Board Project.

Do not save the changes in the stored entries because the allocation percentages will change every month.

☐ **Cash Receipt #25**

Dated Aug. 8/02

From Bronte Residence, cheque #68 for $3 102 in full payment of account. Reference invoice #125, and deposit #7.

☐ **Cash Receipt #26**

Dated Aug. 12/02

From Receiver General, cheque #12774 for $936.40 in payment of GST refund. Reference memo #12.

☐ **Cheque Copy #168**

Dated Aug. 12/02

To The Buildex Corp., $5 284.94 in full payment of account, including $107.86 discount taken for early payment. Reference invoice #BC-1911.

☐ **Sales Invoice #126**

Dated Aug. 13/02

To Vindri Estates (deliver to cottage), to fill sales order #1003

one	KIT-A	Tom Sawyer Kit		$1 800.00
two	07	Tube Slides: classic	$510 each	1 020.00
		Freight		100.00
		GST Charged (7%)		204.40
		PST Charged (8%)		225.60
		Invoice Total		$3 350.00

Terms: net 1. There is no discount.

Allocate 100% of the revenue to the General Sales Project.

You must allocate each revenue amount (invoice line) separately.

☐ **Cash Receipt #27**

Dated Aug. 13/02

From Vindri Estates, cheque #374 for $2 850 in full payment of account. Reference invoice #126 and deposit #8.

◆ Close the To-Do Lists and enter the next group of transactions.

☐ Sales Invoice #127

Dated Aug. 13/02

To Megacity Board of Education, to partially fill sales order #2008, $8 000 plus $560 GST charged for a completion of 2 recreational play centres completed at Forest Hill and Landsdowne Public Schools. Invoice total $8 560. Terms: net 30 days. Allocate 100% of the revenue to the School Board Project. (Hint: To partially fill the order, type 2 in the Ship column and press ⟨tab⟩.)

☐ Cash Purchase Invoice #OH-612742

Dated Aug. 14/02

From Ontario Hydro, $100 for hydro services plus $7 GST paid. Invoice total $107. Issued cheque #169 in full payment. Allocate 20% of the expense to the General Sales Project, 15% to the Contracting Project and 15% to the School Board Project. Accept the incomplete allocation.

☐ Cash Purchase Invoice #BC-904721

Dated Aug. 14/02

From Bell Canada, $80 for telephone services plus $5.60 GST paid and $6.40 PST paid. Invoice total $92.00. Issued cheque #170 in full payment. Allocate 20% of the expense to the General Sales Project, 15% to the Contracting Project and 15% to the School Board Project. Accept the incomplete allocation.

☐ Cheque Copy #171

Dated Aug. 14/02

To Chargit, $414 for purchases charged before Aug. 7, the billing date. Total payment submitted to avoid incurring interest charges, $414.

We allocate only 50 percent of the hydro and telephone expenses because only this portion applies to the month of August.

Project Reports

Project reports may be viewed from the Home window or from the Projects window.

◆ Close the journal window to return to the Home window.

◆ Choose the **Reports** menu, then choose **Project** and click **Income** in the Home window to see the Project Reports Options:

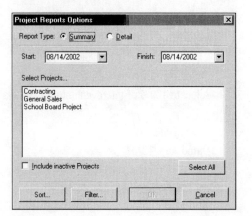

As usual, you can enter the Start and Finish dates for the report, and the Session date is the default entry. You can also choose to include one or more or all projects in the report. The report is available in the Summary and the Detail format. The Summary Report has only the totals for each account for each project, while the Detail Report will show each transaction for each selected account for the project as a separate entry line. Sorting and filtering are available for projects reports. You can sort and filter by date, comment, source, journal number or amount per transaction. We will display the unsorted Detail Report for all projects for the first half of August.

◆ Click **Detail**.

◆ Click the Start date to select it for editing.

◆ Type `Aug 1`

◆ Click **Select All**.

◆ Click **OK** to proceed to the next stage:

> Press `ctrl` and click individual projects and accounts to select them for the report.

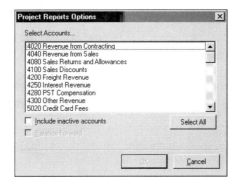

You can choose any or all of the revenue and expense accounts for the report. For a complete project report, you should select all accounts. Accounts without transactions related to the project are not displayed.

◆ Click **Select All**.

◆ Click **OK** to see the report.

The Detail Report has the amounts for each transaction for each selected account as well as a cumulative total for revenues and one for expenses for each project. The profitability of the project is calculated as the total revenue minus the total expense and is presented in the final line for each project.

Drill-Down Reports

Several **drill-down reports** are available from the Detail Project Report. When you double click an account number or name, the General Ledger Report for the account is displayed. If you double click a date or name, you will see the Customer (or Vendor or Employee) Aged Report for the customer (or vendor or employee) named in the transaction. Double clicking the invoice number will lead to the Invoice Lookup window for the transaction, and double clicking a journal entry number or an amount will show you the journal entry.

From the Summary Report, you will see the Project Detail Report for the line that you double click. When you close the drill-down report, you return to the previous report.

◆ Print the report.

◆ Close the displayed report when you have finished to return to the Home window.

Project Allocation Report

The Project Allocation Report is similar to the Project Income Report, but allows you to include in the report all accounts for which you have allowed allocations, not only the revenue and expense accounts. Amounts are reported for each account for each project, but project income is not calculated. To see the allocation report, choose Allocation instead of Income from the Project Reports submenu.

Project Budget Report

When you have set up budget information for each project, you can also generate project budget reports that compare the project's performance against budget. If no budget details are provided for the projects, the report is not available. We have added some budget information for the projects to generate the next screen.

Choose the Reports menu, then choose Project and click Budget in the Home window to see the Project Budget Report Options:

You will not see this screen unless you have added budget amounts for projects.

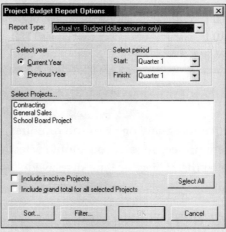

Like other budget income reports, you can choose to display the report with dollar amounts only, with dollar differences or with percent differences, for the current year or for the previous year, and for one or more projects. You may also request a total for all projects to provide a global budget income summary.

Select the projects and report options you want and then click OK to see the report. Close the report display when finished to return to the Home window.

Journal Reports with Project Allocations

Once you begin to use projects, you can display Journal Reports with or without the project breakdown.

◆ Choose the **Reports** menu, then choose **Journal Entries** and click **All** in the Home window to see the modified Journal Options screen:

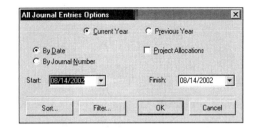

Since the default is to omit Project Allocations from Journal Reports, you must remember to check the option to see project details. All Journal Reports have the Project Allocation check box added once you set up project information.

◆ Type **8 1** as the Start date for the report to replace the Session date.

◆ Click **Project Allocations** to add a ✓ and include the allocations in the report.

◆ Click **OK** to see the report. Notice that the project amounts are added in a separate column for each transaction that has a revenue or expense allocation.

◆ Close the report when you have finished to return to the Home window.

Management Project Reports

◆ Choose the **Reports** menu, then choose **Management Reports** and click **Projects** in the Home window to see the project-related topics:

◆ Click the topic you want.

◆ Accept the report form or choose a different form from the list if necessary.

◆ Click **OK** to see the report.

◆ Close the report to return to the Home window.

◆ To continue good management practice, we recommend printing the following additional reports to monitor performance:

Journal Entries: All journals for August 1 to August 14

Trial Balance: As at August 14

Comparative Income Statement: Actual vs Budget from June 1 to August 14

Balance Sheet: As at August 14

Vendor Aged Detail Report: For all vendors as at August 14

Customer Aged Detail Report: For all customers as at August 14

Inventory Synopsis Report

Practice: Live Links

In December, Lively wants to include project information for her company to supplement the detailed information she already has about performance. She believes that the extra record keeping involved in determining the percentage of time and dollars spent for each project or division will pay off. She will use the information to decide about expanding some parts of her business and perhaps reducing others.

Projects and Allocations

Instructions

1. Open the data files for Live Links. Accept November 30 as the Session date.

2. Restore the icon for the Project Ledger (View menu, Modules, Project).

3. Change the Project settings to turn on the warning for incomplete allocations. Accept the default settings to allocate by percent.

4. Change the Project Title to Division. (Choose the Setup menu and click Names in the Home window.)

5. Create two divisions with December 1, 2002, as the Start date for both. There is no historical data for either division. The two divisions are:

   Service Division
   Sales Division

6. Check all revenue and expense accounts in the General Ledger to be sure that you have allowed allocation.

7. Advance the Session Date to **December 7**. Close the To-Do Lists and complete the first group of transactions.

   ☐ Add new accounts in the General Ledger
   1660 Digital Video Equipment (A)
   1670 Accum Deprec: Digital Video Equip (A)
   1675 Net Digital Video Equipment (S)
   5086 Depreciation: Digital Video Equip (G)

☐ Purchase Order #7

Dated Dec. 2/02

Shipping Date Dec. 8/02

From CompuWorld Supplies

two	03	DVD-Rom 16x	$ 200.00
two	08	Memory 64 mb SDRAM	240.00
two	09	Modem 56kV.90 w/ethernet	300.00
two	10	Monitor 15" TFT Flat panel	1 200.00
three	11	Monitor 17" TFT Flat panel	3 450.00
two	12	Motherboard Pentium III at 1 GHz	1 000.00
two	15	Sound Card 64V Pro w/speakers	150.00
two	16	Video Card 32 mb nVIDIA	200.00
		GST Paid	471.80
		Total	$7 211.80

Terms: 2/10, n/30.

☐ Purchase Order #8

Dated Dec. 2/02

Shipping Date Dec. 8/02

From Comtek Systems

two	01	CPU Cooler 2.3w Pentium III	$ 60.00
two	02	CPU Cooler x21 Pentium III	100.00
two	04	Enclosure - solid steel mini	360.00
two	05	Enclosure - solid steel tower	600.00
two	06	Hard Drive 3.5", 30GB IDE	450.00
two	07	Hard Drive 3.5", 40GB IDE	600.00
two	13	Power Supply Turbo cool 400 slim	450.00
two	14	Power Supply Turbo cool 600 tower	800.00
		GST Paid	239.40
		Total	$3 659.40

Terms: 2/10, n/30.

☐ Cash Receipt #21

Dated Dec. 6/02

From Westmount Institute, cheque #839 for $943.74 in full payment of account, including $19.26 discount taken for early payment. Reference invoices #131.

☐ Credit Card Purchase Invoice #4127

Dated Dec. 6/02

From Petro Partners, $70 plus $4.90 GST charged and $4.90 PST for vehicle maintenance services. Invoice total $79.80 paid by credit card. Allocate 80% of the expense to Service Division and 20% to Sales Division.

☐ Sales Invoice #133

Dated Dec. 6/02

To Pacific Video Inc., $3 000 plus $210 GST charged and $210 PST charged for CD-ROM duplication services. Invoice total $3 420. Terms: 2/10, n/30 days. Allocate 100% of revenue to Service Division. Use Quick Add for the new customer.

☐ Employee Time Summary Sheet #7

Dated Dec. 7/02

Pay Period Ending December 7, 2002

Adrian Borland worked 80 regular hours and 2 hours overtime.

Issue cheque #55.

Allocate 60% of wage expenses to Service Division and 40% to Sales Division.

8. Advance the Session date to **Dec. 14**, and work from the To-Do Lists for the next group of transactions. Advance the To-Do Lists date to Dec. 28 so that Sales Discounts will be included.

☐ Purchase Invoice #CW-3314

Dated Dec. 8/02

From CompuWorld Supplies, to fill purchase order #7

two	03	DVD-Rom 16x	$ 200.00
two	08	Memory 64 mb SDRAM	240.00
two	09	Modem 56kV.90 w/ethernet	300.00
two	10	Monitor 15" TFT Flat panel	1 200.00
three	11	Monitor 17" TFT Flat panel	3 450.00
two	12	Motherboard Pentium III at 1 GHz	1 000.00
two	15	Sound Card 64V Pro w/speakers	150.00
two	16	Video Card 32 mb nVIDIA	200.00
		GST Paid	471.80
		Total	$7 211.80

Terms: 2/10, n/30.

☐ Purchase Invoice #CS-5013

Dated Dec. 8/02

From Comtek Systems, to fill purchase order #8

two	01	CPU Cooler 2.3w Pentium III	$ 60.00
two	02	CPU Cooler x21 Pentium III	100.00
two	04	Enclosure - solid steel mini	360.00
two	05	Enclosure - solid steel tower	600.00
two	06	Hard Drive 3.5", 30GB IDE	450.00
two	07	Hard Drive 3.5", 40GB IDE	600.00
two	13	Power Supply Turbo cool 400 slim	450.00
two	14	Power Supply Turbo cool 600 tower	800.00
		GST Paid	239.40
		Total	$3 659.40

Terms: 2/10, n/30.

☐ Cash Receipt #22

Dated Dec. 8/02

From Valley Legal Services, cheque #49120 for $11 507.16 in full payment of account, including $234.84 discount for early payment. Reference invoice #132.

☐ Cheque Copy #56

Dated Dec. 9/02

To Mega Pro Suppliers, $8 388.80 in full payment of account including $171.20 discount taken for early payment. Reference invoice #MP-361.

☐ Sales Invoice #134

Dated Dec. 10/02

To Westmount Institute, fourth in the series of five bi-weekly Windows workshops

one	SRV-03	Workshop - 6 hours	$900 each	$900
		GST (7%)		63
		Invoice total		$963

Terms: 2/10 n/30 days. Recall the stored invoice. Allocate 100% to Service Division. Store the recurring entry again after adding the allocation.

9. **Close the To-Do Lists and continue entering the next group of transactions.**

Record the PST liability and payment in the Payments Journal as an Other Payment.

☐ Memo #43

Dated Dec. 10/02

Record the PST Payable account balance for Nov. 30, 2002, as a liability owing to the Minister of Finance, BC. This liability is reduced by the sales tax compensation of 3.3% of the PST account balance ($1 991.50 – $65.72). Issue cheque #57 in payment. Do not allocate this revenue because it applies to the previous month.

Recall the stored entries to complete the item assembly transactions.

☐ Inventory Item Assembly #IIA-7

Dated Dec. 10/02

Assembly Components: transfer two (2) of each item

01	CPU Cooler 2.3w Pentium III	$ 30 each
03	DVD-Rom 16x	100 each
04	Enclosure - solid steel mini	180 each
06	Hard Drive 3.5", 30GB IDE	225 each
08	Memory 64 mb SDRAM	120 each
09	Modem 56kV.90 w/ethernet	150 each
10	Monitor 15" TFT Flat panel	600 each
12	Motherboard Pentium III at 1 GHz	500 each
13	Power Supply Turbo cool 400 slim	225 each
15	Sound Card 64V Pro w/speakers	75 each
16	Video Card 32 mb nVIDIA	100 each

Assembled Items: assemble two (2) computer systems

SYS-A   800 MMX System A $2 305 each

Inventory Item Assembly #IIA-8

Dated Dec. 10/02

Assembly Components: transfer three (3) of each item

02	CPU Cooler x21 Pentium III	$ 50 each
03	DVD-Rom 16x	100 each
05	Enclosure - solid steel tower	300 each
07	Hard Drive 3.5", 40GB IDE	300 each
08	Memory 64 mb SDRAM	120 each
09	Modem 56kV.90 w/ethernet	150 each
11	Monitor 17" TFT Flat panel	1 150 each
12	Motherboard Pentium III at 1 GHz	500 each
14	Power Supply Turbo cool 600 tower	400 each
15	Sound Card 64V Pro w/speakers	75 each
16	Video Card 32 mb nVIDIA	100 each

Assembled Items: assemble three (3) computer systems

SYS-B   800 MMX System B $3 245 each

Cash Receipt #23

Dated Dec. 10/02

From Pro-Career Institute, cheque #6412 for $535 in payment of account. Reference invoice #122.

Purchase Invoice #AC-117

Dated Dec. 13/02

From Acculink Memory, $800 plus $56 GST paid for memory chips. Invoice total $856. Terms 2/15, n/30.

Credit Card Sales Invoice #135

Dated Dec. 14/02

To Prince College

two	SYS-A	800 MMX System A	$2 800 each	$ 5 600.00
one	SYS-B	800 MMX System B	3 750 each	3 750.00
		GST (7%)		654.50
		PST (7%)		654.50
		Total received		$10 659.00

Paid by Credit Card # 4210 573 710 662. There is no discount. Allocate 100% of revenue to Sales Division.

10. To follow good management practice, we recommend printing the following reports:

Journal Entries: All journals for December 1 to December 14

Trial Balance: As at December 14

Comparative Income Statement: Actual vs Budget from October 1 to December 14

Balance Sheet: As at December 14

Vendor Aged Detail Report: For all vendors as at December 14

Customer Aged Detail Report: For all customers as at December 14

Inventory Synopsis Report

Division Income Report: All divisions, all accounts

11. Close the data files for Live Links.

Review Questions

1. Why are there no special journals or linked accounts for projects?
2. How do you set up projects?
3. How do you enter project allocation information?
4. Why would a company want to set up projects?
5. What is the effect of choosing "Warn if allocation is not complete"?
6. Why might you choose not to complete an allocation for a revenue or expense amount?
7. What information do project reports provide?
8. What happens if you forget to allocate an expense or revenue amount?
9. If one project is not profitable, does it necessarily mean that the project should be discontinued? Why or why not?
10. What are some alternative methods, that is, decision criteria, for allocating costs among projects?
11. Why might the project allocation option not be available for an account in a journal transaction?

CHAPTER 18

DUAL CURRENCY AND INTERNET CONNECTIONS

Objectives

- *set up a second currency and exchange rates*
- *identify linked accounts for exchange rate differences and import duties*
- *enter vendors and customers for second currency transactions*
- *enter and track import duties*
- *set up a bank account for second currency transactions*
- *set inventory prices in a second currency*
- *enter sales and purchases in a second currency*
- *pay foreign vendors*
- *receive payments from foreign customers*
- *track exchange rate differences*
- *connect to a vendor's Web site*
- *e-mail orders and quotes*

Introduction

In this chapter, Play Wave Plus will carry out transactions with vendors and customers in the United States. The second currency feature in Simply Accounting allows sales and purchases directly in the second currency, including the tracking of import duties, if there are any. No new journals or ledgers are involved for dual currency transactions, but changes to the bank account, vendor, customer and inventory ledger records are required. You will continue to use all the journals to complete the transactions for the final month, including the allocation details.

If you have not completed the journal entries in Chapter 17 and want to continue working on Chapter 18, you can use your copy of the Data Disk file — Ch18\play\playch18.sdb — to begin this chapter.

Dual Currency Transactions

Today's economy is increasingly a global one. International agreements are reducing restrictions on trade between countries and the volume of Internet shopping is increasing rapidly. Many businesses, regardless of size, now deal with suppliers and customers in different countries. They may accept customer payments in a second currency, or require payment in their home currency. Products may be priced in more than one currency. Similarly, businesses may deal with suppliers who require payment in the second currency. Simply Accounting allows you to set up the information for a second currency for these kinds of transactions. Play Wave will set up the program for transactions with customers and vendors in the United States.

◆ Open the files for Play Wave Plus and accept August 14 as the Session Date.

◆ Close the To-Do Lists window.

◆ Create the following new Group accounts that will be needed as linked accounts:

> 5010 Exchange Rate Differences (G)
> 5015 Import Duties (G)
> 1100 Bank Account: USD Chequing (G)

Entering a Second Currency

◆ Choose the **Setup menu** and click **Currencies** to see the Currency Information window:

Once you have set up a second currency, reports may be shown with or without the second currency information.

◆ Click **Allow Transactions in a Foreign Currency** to expand the input screen:

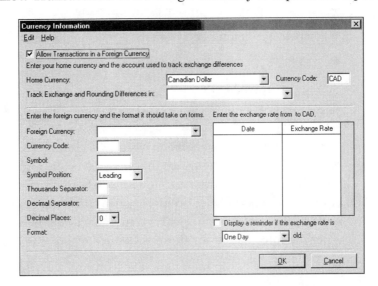

The Home currency is correctly defined as Canadian by default. We need to identify the linked account, choose a second currency and enter exchange rates.

Exchange rates vary from day to day and often even within a day. They often change from the time a purchase or sale is completed to the time that payment is made or received. Therefore, the amounts recorded for payables and receivables will be different from the amounts actually paid or received. These differences in exchange rates are tracked in a linked account.

◆ Click the **Track Exchange and Rounding Differences in** list arrow.

◆ Choose *5010 Exchange Rate Differences* from the drop-down list.

◆ Click the **Foreign Currency list arrow** to see the currencies available.

◆ Scroll down the list and click **United States Dollar** to select this currency.

The remaining currency definition details affect the appearance or formatting of the second currency. Code, symbol, symbol position and separator details are entered by default and are correct. The option to enter one or more exchange rates for different dates is the final one. Entering an exchange rate as part of the currency information does not prevent you from changing the rate in the journals. You can also ask the program to warn you if the rate you are using is out of date relative to the transaction date. We will enter one rate for the Session date and ask to be warned if the rate is one day old.

◆ Click the **Date column**. The usual date format options are available.

◆ Type **8 14**

◆ Press (tab) to move to the Exchange Rate column.

The rate you enter is the number of home currency (Canadian) dollars that one second currency (United States) dollar will purchase. These rates are published daily in newspapers and are also available from numerous Web sites. For our instructional purposes, we will enter an approximate rate.

◆ Type **1.48**

◆ Click **Display a reminder if the exchange rate is** to activate the warning.

◆ Accept the default entry of One Day.

◆ Click **OK** to save the settings.

Setting up Import Duty Tracking

Import Duties are frequently charged by a country to offset significant price differences between countries that may adversely affect the home economy by encouraging foreign transactions. In North America, free trade agreements have eliminated import duties on most goods travelling between Canada, the United States and Mexico. However, we will set up import duty information to illustrate how to enter the information for those situations where it is needed.

◆ Choose the **Setup menu** and click **Import Duty Information** to see the activation window:

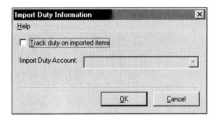

◆ Click **Track duty on imported items** to make the linked account field available.

◆ Click the **Import Duty Account list arrow**.

Notice that accounts in all sections are available for linking. Normally import duties are expenses. However, duties could be associated with an asset if the same item were routinely imported, in much the same way that freight expenses may be assigned to a specific item or to a *Freight Expense* account.

◆ Scroll down the list and click *5015 Import Duties* to select this account.

◆ Click **OK** to save the new settings and return to the Home window.

International Vendors and Customers

Vendors must be set up for a second currency before you can enter foreign currency purchases. Once you have allowed foreign currency transactions, ledger records include the option to buy from a vendor in either currency. Information for the first vendor in the United States follows:

Name:	International Building Supplies
Contact:	Jack Hammer
Address:	8073 Lumbering St.
	Buffalo, New York 14202
Phone:	(716) 866-7800
Fax:	(716) 865-9811
E-mail:	jack.hammer@ibs.com
Web site:	www.ibs.com
Terms:	net 10
Include in GST reports.	

◆ Click the **Vendors icon**  to open the Vendors window.

◆ Click the **Create tool** 🗐 to open a new ledger record.

◆ Enter the vendor's name, address and contact details on the Address tab screen. Notice that the program does not reformat the zip code as it does the Canadian postal codes.

◆ Click the **Options tab** to access the next information screen:

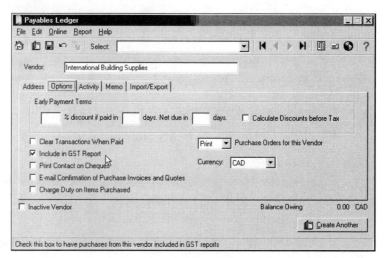

Two new fields have been added to this information screen. One allows you to select a Currency for the vendor, a selection that will appear in the Purchases and Payments Journals for the vendor. The second new option, Charge Duty on Items Purchased, will open the duty rate and amount fields in the Purchases Journal for the vendor.

◆ Click the **Currency list arrow.**

There are two currency options — CAD, the code for Canadian dollars, and USD, the code for United States dollars — in the Currency Information screen.

◆ Click **USD.** The Balance Owing now has two amounts, one for each currency.

We will activate the option to charge duty so that we can illustrate how duties are entered even though there is no duty on the items imported from the United States.

◆ Click **Charge Duty on Items Purchased.**

◆ Click the **Activity tab** to view the changes to this screen:

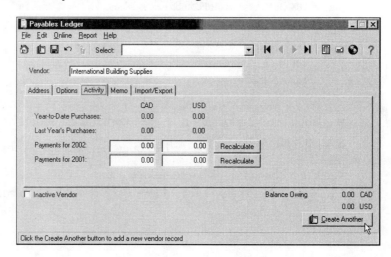

A column for payments and purchases in the second currency has been added.

◆ Click **Create Another** to save the record.

◆ Close the Ledger and the Vendors windows to return to the Home window.

After you enter transactions for a customer or vendor in one currency, you cannot change the Ledger setting for Currency.

Purchases and payments in US dollars will be recorded in the ledger and converted to Canadian dollars using the exchange rate for the day of the transaction.

The changes in customer records for foreign currency transactions are similar to those for vendors. The new customer information follows:

Name:	Tiny Tots Play Care
Contact:	Mary Contrary
Address:	24 Blackbirds Place
	Niagara Falls, New York 14301
Phone:	(716) 732-1090
E-mail:	mary_contrary@tinytots.com
Web site:	www.tinytots.com
Terms:	net 1
	Do not include in GST reports.
Credit Limit:	$10 000 USD

◆ Click the **Customers icon** to open the Customers window.

◆ Click the **Create tool** to open a new ledger record.

◆ Enter the customer's name, address and contact details on the Address tab screen.

◆ Click the **Options tab** to access the next information screen:

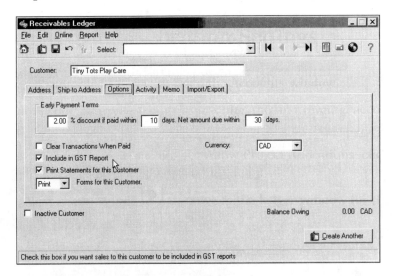

The currency field allows you to select a currency for the customer. This selection will later appear in the Sales and Receipts Journals for the customer.

◆ Click the **Currency list arrow**.

The same two currency options are available — CAD and USD.

◆ Click **USD**. The customer's Balance Owing is shown in both currencies.

◆ Enter the payment terms for the customer as net 1.

◆ Click the **Activity tab** to view the changes to this screen:

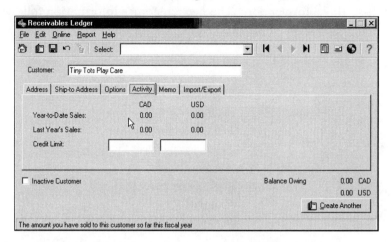

A column for sales in the second currency has been added.

◆ Click **Create Another** to save the record.

◆ Close the Ledger and the Customers windows to return to the Home window.

Inventory Prices in a Second Currency

Once a second currency is in use, you can set up the inventory records to price items in both currencies, or you can use the home currency only. The switch for this option is added to the Settings screen for Inventory and Services.

◆ Choose the **Setup menu** and click **Settings**.

◆ Click the **Inventory & Services tab** to see the revised Settings screen:

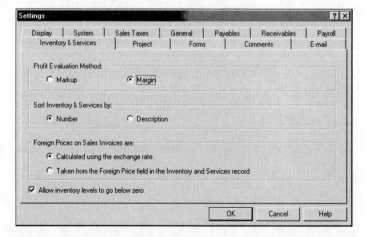

You have two options for pricing inventory. Foreign prices on sales invoices may be calculated using the exchange rate or taken from the Foreign Price field in the Inventory and Services Ledger record. If you choose the first option, the program will calculate the foreign currency amount required from the customer based on the current exchange rate for the home price. If you choose the second option, the foreign price is fixed, and the cash received is converted according to the current exchange rate. We will set a fixed price for inventory in United Sates dollars.

◆ Click **Taken from the Foreign Price field in the Inventory and Services record**.

◆ Click **OK** to save the new setting and return to the Home window.

Entering Inventory Prices

The following chart has the inventory prices in United States dollars (USD) for Play Wave. These new prices are approximately two-thirds of the inventory prices in Canadian dollars. Canadian prices are shown for comparison.

INVENTORY PRICE CHART

Item No.	Description	CAD Price/Unit	USD Price/Unit
01	Carousel	$ 410/each	$ 270/each
02	Jungle Gym	410/each	270/each
03	Slide: classic	510/each	340/each
04	Slide: wave	610/each	405/each
05	Swing Set: double	410/each	270/each
06	Swing Set: triple	510/each	340/each
07	Tube Slide: classic	510/each	340/each
08	Tube Slide: wave	610/each	405/each
KIT-A	Tom Sawyer Kit	1 800/kit	1 200/kit
KIT-B	Huck Finn Kit	2 100/kit	1 400/kit

◆ Click the **Inventory & Services icon** to open the Inventory & Services window.

◆ Double click item **01 Carousel** to open its ledger record:

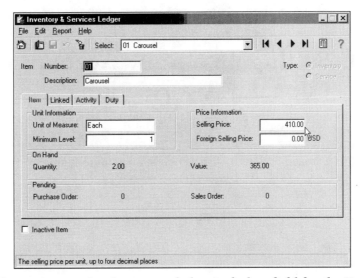

The price information section has expanded to include a field for the Foreign Selling Price. We will use this field to enter the prices in US dollars (USD). A new tab for import duties has been added as well. If you had selected "Calculated using the exchange rate" as the inventory setting, the Foreign Selling Price field would not appear. If you had selected not to track import duties, the Duty tab would not appear.

◆ Double click the **Foreign Selling Price field** to select the current entry.

◆ Type **270**

◆ Click the **Duty tab** to open the new information screen:

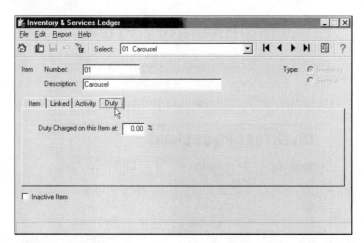

If the import duty rate is fixed for an inventory item, you may enter the rate in the field for Duty Charged on this Item at __ %. Since duties do not apply to purchases from the United States, leave the rate set at zero. You can still enter or change the duty rate in the journals.

◆ Click the **Item tab** to return to this information window.

◆ Click the **Next tool** [▶] to access the ledger for Jungle Gym.

◆ Continue in this way to enter the USD prices for the remaining items.

◆ Check the prices by returning to each record in turn with the **Previous tool** [◀].

◆ Close the Ledger window.

◆ Close the Inventory & Services window to return to the Home window.

Setting up a Bank Account for Second Currency Transactions

The next step is to modify the bank account ledger record. Since this is a USD chequing account, we must identify it as a Bank class account so that it is available as a linked account for payments, enter a next cheque number and, finally, identify the currency for the account.

◆ Click the **Accounts icon** [Accounts] to open the Accounts window.

◆ Double click account *1100 Bank Account: USD Chequing* to open its ledger record.

◆ Click the **Class Options tab**.

◆ Choose **Bank** from the Account Class list to open the fields related to bank accounts as shown:

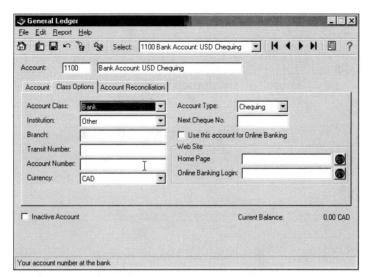

A Currency field is added to the ledger with a drop-down list of currencies.

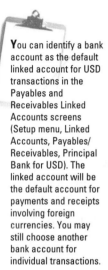

You can identify a bank account as the default linked account for USD transactions in the Payables and Receivables Linked Accounts screens (Setup menu, Linked Accounts, Payables/ Receivables, Principal Bank for USD). The linked account will be the default account for payments and receipts involving foreign currencies. You may still choose another bank account for individual transactions.

◆ Click the **Currency list arrow**.

◆ Click **USD** to select the second currency for this account.

◆ Click the **Next Cheque No. field**.

◆ Type **200**

◆ Close the Ledger window.

◆ Close the Accounts window to return to the Home window.

Entering Purchases from a Foreign Vendor

Purchases from foreign vendors are entered in the Purchases Journal, just like regular purchases. Most of the changes are handled automatically by the program.

The following invoice describes the purchase from the new foreign vendor:

✔ Purchase Invoice #IS-34499

Dated Aug. 15/02

From International Building Supplies

4	01	Carousels	$ 400.00 USD
4	02	Jungle Gyms	400.00 USD
4	03	Slides: classic	560.00 USD
4	04	Slides: wave	720.00 USD
4	05	Swing Sets: double	400.00 USD
4	06	Swing Sets: triple	480.00 USD
4	07	Tube Slides: classic	480.00 USD
4	08	Tube Slides: wave	600.00 USD
		Freight: shipped by ICS	200.00 USD
		GST Paid	296.80 USD
		Invoice total	$4 536.80 USD

Terms: net 10.

◆ Click the **Purchases icon** [Purchases, Orders & Quotes] to open the Purchases Journal.

◆ Choose **International Building Supplies** from the list of vendors to modify the journal for the foreign currency transaction:

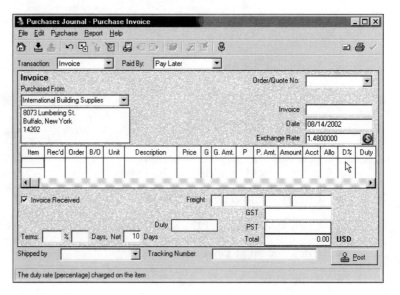

The journal is modified to accommodate the foreign currency and import duties. The exchange rate on the date of the invoice appears in the Exchange Rate field, according to the Currency Information settings. You may enter a different rate at any time. Two columns for the duty rate and amount are added when you choose to track duty information. You may need to scroll to the right to see these extra columns. All amounts are in United States dollars as indicated by the USD code for this currency beside the Total field.

◆ Enter the invoice number and the transaction date as usual.

◆ Press (tab) to advance the cursor and see the warning about the exchange rate:

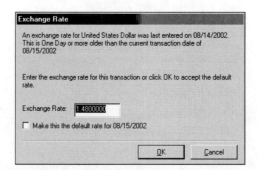

Since we asked to be advised when the exchange rate was at least one day old, the warning appears. At this point, you may enter a new rate and apply this rate to the new date, maintain the old rate for the new date or cancel the message. If you cancel the message, you will see the warning again when you use August 15 or a later date as the transaction date. The exchange rate is unchanged so we can accept the rate from the previous day.

◆ Click **Make this the default exchange rate for 08/15/2002** to accept the rate and apply it to the new date.

◆ Click **OK** to return to the journal.

◆ Enter the first item from the invoice and the quantity received.

◆ Press (tab).

Notice that the amounts and tax fields are not completed automatically. The Canadian costs cannot be used for reference.

◆ Click the **GST field** and press (enter) to see the codes. They are the same as before. GST is charged on imported goods whenever they are consumed or used in Canada. The tax is collected at the same time as the Customs or Excise Taxes.

◆ Double click **code 3**.

◆ Click the **Amount field**. All prices are entered in United States dollars.

◆ Type **400** and press (tab) to update the unit price.

◆ Enter the remaining items purchased.

◆ Enter **200** as the Freight charge, **3** as its tax code, and choose **ICS** as the shipper.

The journal entry is complete and you are ready to review it. The finished journal entry should look like the one shown here:

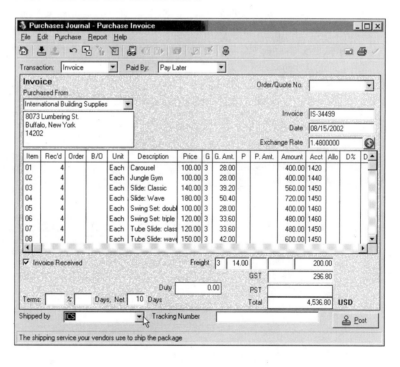

In practice, the business would pay GST on imported goods directly to the Receiver General rather than to the vendor who exported the goods. Furthermore, the GST would be calculated on the cost of goods plus excise taxes. A General Journal entry would be completed to record the GST Paid.

◆ Choose the **Report menu** and click **Display Purchases Journal Entry:**

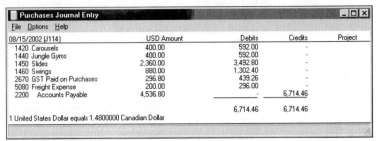

An extra column appears in the journal for US dollar amounts. The Canadian dollar amounts are shown in the Debits and Credits columns. These are the amounts that will be posted to the accounts. Otherwise, the journal entry is the same as before.

◆ Close the display when you have finished reviewing it.

◆ Make corrections to the journal entry if necessary.

◆ Click **Post** [Post] to record the transaction.

◆ Close the Purchases Journal.

Import Duties

When import duties are charged, enter the rate in the D% column. The program will calculate and enter the amount in the Duty column and assign the total duty amount — the amount in the Duty field at the bottom of the journal — to the linked duty tracking account that you identified. The following journal display shows a duty rate of 5% charged for all inventory items. Remember that if the rate is constant, you can enter it as part of the Inventory Ledger record.

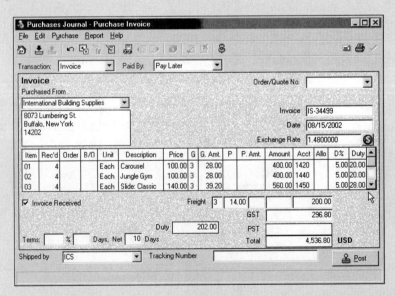

You can see that the duty amount does not affect the GST. In the journal entry for this transaction that follows, you can see that the duty is credited to the linked duty tracking account. The tracking account acts as a contra-expense account. The duty amounts are debited to the corresponding inventory asset accounts (e.g., *1420 Carousels* is debited for $420 when duty applies, instead of $400 in the previous journal display).

```
Purchases Journal Entry                                                    _ □ ×
File  Options  Help
08/15/2002 (J115)              USD Amount        Debits      Credits     Project
     1420 Carousels              420.00          621.60        ·
     1440 Jungle Gyms            420.00          621.60        ·
     1450 Slides               2,478.00        3,667.44        ·
     1460 Swings                 924.00        1,367.52        ·
     2670 GST Paid on Purchases  296.80          439.26        ·
     5080 Freight Expense        200.00          296.00        ·
     2200   Accounts Payable   4,536.80            ·         6,714.46
     5015   Import Duties        202.00            ·           298.96
                                                _____      _____
                                               7,013.42      7,013.42
1 United States Dollar equals 1.4800000 Canadian Dollar
```

◆ Advance the Session date to **August 20, 2002**, and use the To-Do List for the next transaction.

☐ Memo #57
Dated Aug. 15/02
From To-Do Lists, edit the To-Do List date for the Memo in the ledger record for the Minister of Finance to Sep. 15/02.

◆ Close the To-Do Lists and complete the next group of transactions.

Notice that a Currency field is added to the General Journal so that you can enter transactions in either currency.

☐ Memo #58
Dated Aug. 15/02
The manufactured cost of sales in July was $9 000. Complete a General Journal entry to record $720 ($9 000 x .08) as the PST Payable for July. Do not allocate the sales tax expense because it applies to July.

☐ Memo #59
Dated Aug. 15/02
PST Payable for July consists of the $713.60 PST charged on sales and $720 as the sales tax on the manufactured cost of goods. Record $1 433.60, the combined amount, as an Other Payment to the Minister of Finance in the Payments Journal. This liability is reduced by $71.68 for the 5% sales tax compensation. Issue cheque #172 for $1 361.92 in payment. Do not allocate the PST compensation because it applies to July.

Ignore any messages you see about backorders. Also, if you see a warning about an incomplete allocation for the Cost of Goods Sold, click Yes to ignore it and proceed. (The average cost has changed since the original sale to Vindri. The new prices in the US purchase caused the reversing entry to use a different amount for the Cost of Goods Sold.)

☐ Memo #60
Dated Aug. 15/02
The shipment to Vindri Estates was incorrect. Vindri should have received 1 Swing Set: triple (#06) and 1 slide instead of 2 slides. KIT-A has been accounted for correctly. Adjust the original invoice (#126) for the exchange. Because there is no price difference, no payment is required from the customer. The Swing Set will be shipped immediately at no extra charge. Allocate 100% of the revenue from the sale of the Swing Set to General Sales.

☐ Inventory Item Assembly #IIA-7
Dated Aug. 15/02
Assembly Components: transfer four (4) of each item

01	Carousel	$159.50	each
03	Slide: classic	225.5429	each
05	Swing Set: double	159.50	each
07	Tube Slide: classic	205.3717	each

Additional Costs   300.00

Assembled Items: assemble four (4) kits
    KIT-A   Tom Sawyer Kit $824.9150   each

☐ Inventory Item Assembly #IIA-8
Dated Aug. 15/02
Assembly Components: transfer four (4) of each item

02	Jungle Gym	$159.50	each
04	Slide: wave	284.2667	each
06	Swing Set: triple	196.40	each
08	Tube Slide: wave	249.4286	each

Additional Costs (lumber for raft)   320.00

Assembled Items: assemble four (4) kits
    KIT-B   Huck Finn Kit $969.595   each

☐ Credit Card Purchase Invoice #GA-9338
Dated Aug. 15/02
From Gasoline Alley, $80 plus $5.60 GST and $6.40 (8%) PST charged for gasoline for truck. Total invoice amount paid by Chargit, $92. Allocate 30% of the expenses to General Sales, 30% to Contracting and 40% to the School Board Project.

Entering Sales to a Foreign Customer

Sales to foreign customers are entered in the Sales Journal, just like other sales. The following invoice describes a sale to the new foreign customer:

☑ Sales Invoice #128
Dated Aug. 16/02
To Tiny Tots Play Care

four	KIT-A	Tom Sawyer Kit	$1 200.00 USD	each
four	KIT-B	Huck Finn Kit	1 400.00 USD	each
		Kit installation work	800.00 USD	
		Freight	200.00 USD	

Allocate 100% of the revenue from inventory to the General Sales Project.
Allocate 100% of the revenue from installation to the Contracting Project.
Terms: net 1.

◆ Click the **Sales icon**  to open the Sales Journal.

◆ Choose **Tiny Tots Play Care** as the customer to see the modified journal:

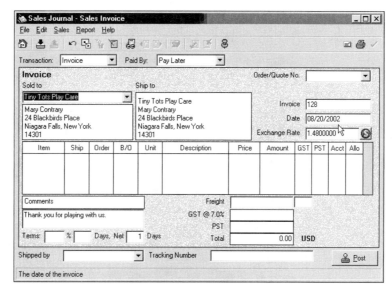

The only change in the journal is the addition of the Exchange Rate field and the USD currency code beside the Total amount.

◆ Type **Aug 16** in the Date field and press <u>tab</u>.

You will see the Exchange Rate warning screen because the exchange rate is one day old. The rate on record for the previous date closest to the transaction date is selected.

◆ Type **1.485** as the new rate.

◆ Click **Make this the default rate for 08/16/2002**.

◆ Click **OK** to return to the journal.

◆ Enter the inventory items sold and the contract installation work.

GST and PST do not apply to exported goods. They are zero-rated for purposes of GST. Because we selected not to include the customer in GST reports, the remaining GST codes are not available.

◆ Delete the entries for PST.

◆ Complete the allocations for the three revenue account lines.

After deleting taxes for foreign customer sales, you may need to re-enter the tax rates and codes for Canadian customers.

Your completed journal entry should look like the following one:

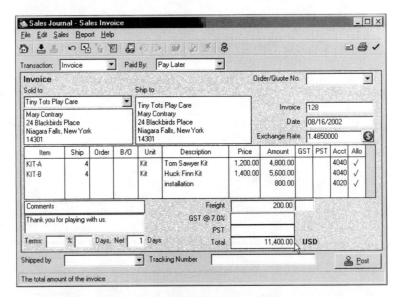

◆ Choose the **Report menu** and click **Display Sales Journal Entry:**

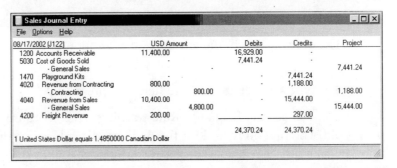

The accounts are all debited and credited in Canadian dollars according to the exchange rate for the transaction. US dollar amounts are provided for reference.

◆ Close the display and correct the journal entry if necessary.

◆ Click **Post** [& Post] to record the transaction.

◆ Allow the customer to exceed the credit limit because they have already given a cheque in full payment.

Entering Receipts from Foreign Customers

◆ Enter the receipt from Tiny Tots Play Care in the Receipts Journal.

> ✔ Cash Receipt #28
> Dated Aug. 17/02
> From Tiny Tots Play Care, cheque #765 for $11 400 USD in full payment of account. Reference invoice #128. The exchange rate on Aug. 17 is 1.482. Amount deposited to 1100 Bank Account: US Chequing. Review the entry before posting.

◆ Click the **Receipts icon** [Receipts] to open the Receipts Journal.

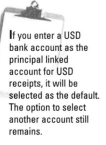

If you enter a USD bank account as the principal linked account for USD receipts, it will be selected as the default. The option to select another account still remains.

◆ Choose **Tiny Tots Play Care** from the customer list. Notice that the receipt is now recorded in US dollars.

◆ Choose *1100 Bank Account: US Chequing* from the Deposit to list to select the US dollar bank account.

◆ Type **765** in the Number field to enter the customer's cheque number.

◆ Type **Aug 17** in the Date field and press ⌨*tab* to see the Exchange Rate screen.

◆ Type **1.482** as the exchange rate and make this the default exchange rate for that date.

◆ Accept the full invoice amount as the payment amount.

The completed journal should look like the one shown here:

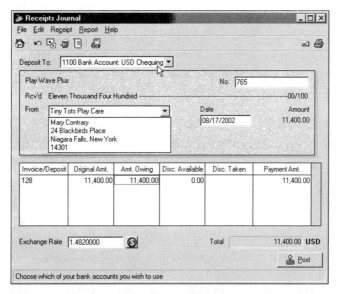

◆ Choose the **Report menu** and click **Display Receipts Journal Entry**:

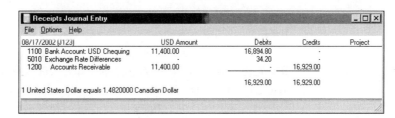

Because the exchange rate was lower on the day money was received than on the day the invoice was posted, the difference creates an expense that is posted to the *Exchange Rate Differences* account. If the exchange rate increases before payment is received, the expense account is credited.

◆ Close the display. Make corrections if necessary.

◆ Post the receipt.

◆ Enter the next group of transactions using the appropriate journals.

If you choose a Canadian currency bank account for the receipt, Simply Accounting will warn you that the bank account does not use the same currency as the customer. You may proceed with the transaction or choose a different account.

☐ Memo #61
Dated Aug. 20/02
Payroll Time Sheet for pay period ending Aug. 20/02
Candie Rapper worked 80 regular hours and 2 hours overtime. Add a deduction of
$25 for the United Way campaign. This is her final United Way contribution so you
should make the change directly in the Payroll Journal. Allocate 20% of the
expenses to the General Sales Project, 60% to the Contracting Project and 20% to
the School Board Project. Issue cheque #173.

Pay Rebecca Doolittle, the salaried employee, her regular salary for the pay period
ending August 20. Add a final deduction of $50 for the United Way campaign.
Allocate 20% of the wage expenses to the General Sales Project, 30% to the
Contracting Project and 50% to the School Board Project. Issue cheque #174.

Mitzy Muffet worked 80 regular hours and 2 hours overtime.
Jack Uphill worked 80 regular hours and 2 hours overtime.
Issue cheques #175 and #176.
Allocate 10% of the wage expenses to the General Sales Project, 10% to the
Contracting Project and 80% to the School Board Project.

You may use the
Payroll Cheque Run
Journal to complete the
paycheques for Muffet
and Uphill.

☐ Cash Receipt #29
Dated Aug. 20/02
From Nirvana Nursery School, cheque #165 for $500 as an advance (deposit #10) on
a contract to upgrade the outdoor recreational playgrounds. Work will begin
immediately and should be completed by September 20. Terms: net 30.

◆ Advance the Session date to **August 31/02**. Close the To-Do Lists.

Entering Payments to Foreign Vendors

☑ Cheque Copy #200
Dated Aug. 22/02
To International Building Supplies., $4 536.80 USD, in full payment of account.
Reference invoice #IS-34499. Account paid from 1100 Bank Account: USD Chequing.
The exchange rate is 1.486.

◆ Click the **Payments icon** to open the Payments Journal.

◆ Choose **International Building Supplies** from the customer list. Notice that the
payment will be recorded in US dollars.

If you enter a USD
bank account as the
linked account for USD
payments, it will be
selected as the default.
The option to select
another account still
remains.

◆ Choose *1100 Bank Account: US Chequing* from the From list to select the US
dollar bank account. The cheque number changes to match the next cheque
number we entered for the bank account.

◆ Type **Aug 22** in the Date field and press ⌨ to see the Exchange Rate screen.

◆ Type **1.486** as the exchange rate and make this the default rate for August 22.

◆ Accept the full invoice amount as the payment amount.

The completed journal should look like the following one:

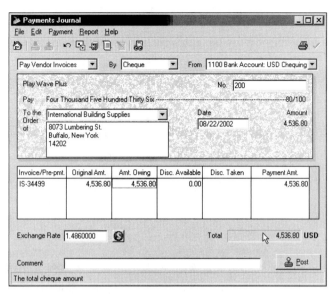

◆ Choose the **Report menu** and click **Display Payments Journal Entry**:

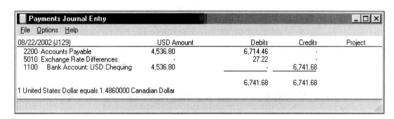

Because the exchange rate is higher on the day payment is made than on the day the invoice was posted, the difference creates an expense that is posted to the *Exchange Rate Differences* account — it cost more to buy the US dollars at the higher rate. If the exchange rate decreases before payment is received, the expense account is credited.

◆ Close the display. Make corrections if necessary, and then post the payment.

◆ Enter the next group of transactions using the appropriate journals.

☐ Purchase Invoice #SC-7143
Dated Aug. 22/02
From Swede Steel Co., $2 100 plus $147 GST paid for nuts, bolts and steel rods.
Invoice total $2 247. Terms: 2/15, n/30.

☐ Sales Invoice #129
Dated Aug. 28/02
To Megacity Board of Education, to complete sales order #2008, $8 000 plus $560
GST charged for two recreational play centres. The centres at Rosedale Public
School and Whitney Public School complete Phase One of the project. Invoice total
$8 560. Terms: net 30 days. Allocate 100% of revenue to School Board Project.
(Hint: Click the Fill backordered quantities tool.)

Check the tax fields carefully. After changing the taxes for foreign transactions, you may need to re-enter the tax rates and codes for Canadian vendors and customers.

The sale to Megacity Board of Education fills the remainder of the sales order.

☐ Credit Card Sales Invoice #130
Dated Aug. 28/02
To Dr. Manga

one	KIT-B	Huck Finn Kit	$2 100.00
one	05	Swing Set: double	410.00
one	08	Tube Slide: wave	610.00
		Freight	50.00
		GST Charged (7%)	221.90
		PST Charged (8%)	249.60
		Total Received	$3 641.50

Paid by Chargit. There is no discount.
Allocate 100% of the revenue to the General Sales Project.

☐ Credit Card Purchase Invoice #GA-1121
Dated Aug. 28/02
From Gasoline Alley, $50 plus $3.50 GST and $4.00 (8%) PST charged for gasoline for truck and $50 plus $3.50 GST and $4 (8%) PST charged for propane gas. Total invoice amount paid by Chargit, $115. Allocate 20% of the gasoline expenses to the General Sales Project, 60% to the Contracting Project and 20% to the School Board Project. Allocate 50% of propane expense to the Contracting Project and 50% to the School Board Project.

Accessing a Vendor's Web Site

In Chapter 8, we used Internet connections from Simply Accounting to track a shipment. You can also link to customers' and vendors' Web sites, and e-mail orders and quotes directly from the program.

Playing Fields, one of Play Wave's vendors, is having a liquidation sale. Details are available from the vendor's Web site. Play Wave will take advantage of the reduced prices on its regular inventory items to stock up and reduce the cost of goods sold over the next few months.

◆ Click the **Vendors icon** to open the Vendors window. (If your Internet access uses a network [e.g., Sympatico High Speed Edition], you will need to open your Internet connection before you click the Web site tool.)

◆ Double click **Playing Fields Inc.** (the vendor icon or name) to open the ledger for Playing Fields.

◆ Click the **Go to the vendor's Web site tool** or choose the Online menu and click Web site to access your Internet program.

The screens you see next will depend on how your Internet access is set up. If you have chosen to connect automatically, you may bypass the following screen and connect directly. If you have saved your user name and password, they will appear on the connection screen. The screen for a Sympatico connection with Netscape is shown here:

The Web address you need to complete this transaction is <www.pearsoned.ca/purbhoosimply8>. Edit the Web site in the ledger record, if necessary, before you click the Web tool.

◆ At this stage, you would enter your User name and Password, unless they already appear and click Connect to proceed.

◆ Click the Playing Fields Inc. link as indicated on-screen to access the Web page for this vendor.

◆ Print the page if you want.

◆ Close the Internet connection after you have found the information you need and continue with the Simply Accounting data entry.

We cannot anticipate the variety of Internet connection methods that users of this book may have. Some setups allow you to enter the Internet directly when you click the Web tool. Others may require passwords or other steps before the connection is established.

From the Web page, we learn that all merchandise is reduced to 50 percent of the last price. The quantities remaining are also listed on the page. Based on this information, we will place the following order at the sale prices and e-mail it directly to Playing Fields so that the order can be filled while the quantities we want are still available.

◆ Enter the purchase order for Playing Fields but do not post it.

Edit the amount for each inventory item.

> ☐ Purchase Order #20009
> Dated Aug. 31/02
> Shipping date Sep. 15/02
> From Playing Fields Inc.

ten	01	Carousels	$ 900.00
ten	02	Jungle Gyms	900.00
ten	03	Slides: classic	1 250.00
ten	04	Slides: wave	1 600.00
ten	05	Swing Sets: double	900.00
ten	06	Swing Sets: triple	1 150.00
ten	07	Tube Slides: classic	1 200.00
ten	08	Tube Slides: wave	1 400.00
		GST Paid	651.00
		Invoice total	$9 951.00

> Terms: Cash on delivery.

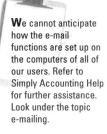

We cannot anticipate how the e-mail functions are set up on the computers of all of our users. Refer to Simply Accounting Help for further assistance. Look under the topic e-mailing.

◆ Click the **E-mail tool** [🖃] or choose the File menu and click E-mail to send the order immediately.

If you chose Print orders in the Vendor Ledger, you will see the following message advising you that you usually print the orders:

◆ Click **E-mail** to proceed. You will see the E-mail Information screen:

The e-mail address created for this book is <purbhoo.simply8 @pearsoned.com>. You will receive a reply automatically when you use this address. If you want, you can e-mail the orders and quotes in this book to a friend to test the e-mail functions.

◆ Type `purbhoo.simply8@pearsoned.com` as the e-mail address if this is not the address you have.

◆ Click the **Message text box.**

◆ Type `If you are unable to view the attached order, please contact us immediately.`

◆ Click **Send**. If you have changed the address, you will see another warning:

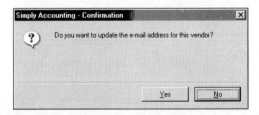

◆ When prompted, click **Yes** to update the vendor's e-mail address in the ledger record. You do not have to change the ledger record to continue.

You will see the Profile screen:

If necessary, create a new profile for your particular e-mail setup.

◆ From the list available, choose the profile for the e-mail.

◆ Click **OK** to proceed. You should connect with your e-mail provider.

- Close your e-mail program when the order has been sent, if necessary, to return to the Purchase Order.

- Click **Record** to save the order.

- Close the Purchases Journal to return to the Home window.

- Continue with the remaining transactions to complete the fiscal quarter.

To prepare the bonus cheque, delete the Salary amount. Type 400 in the Commission field. Click the Enter taxes manually tool. Edit the income tax amount to 40. Delete all the amounts in the Deductions tab fields (RRSP, CSB and Gp Insurance).

☐ Memo #62

Dated Aug. 31/02

Pay Rebecca Doolittle a bonus of $400 for her assistance in procuring the School Board projects. Issue cheque #177. Allocate 100% of the expense to the School Board Project.

☐ Memo #63

Dated Aug. 31/02

Candie Rapper plans to take a few days vacation at the beginning of September. Prepare a cheque for her retained vacation pay. Withhold 10% of the vacation pay amount for income tax. Issue cheque #178. Allocate 70% of the expense to Contracting and 30% to the School Board Project. Remove all Deductions tab field amounts, including Union Dues.

Refer to pages 451–455 for assistance with the vacation paycheque for Rapper.

☐ Cheque Copy #179

Dated Aug. 31/02

To Playing Fields Inc., $3 980.40 in full payment of account. Reference invoice #PF-1499.

☐ Bank Debit Memo #843217

Dated Aug. 31/02

From Royal Trust, $2 000 preauthorized withdrawal for mortgage payment. This amount consists of $1 850 interest and $150 for reduction of principal. Allocate 25% of the expense to the General Sales Project, 25% to the Contracting Project and 50% to the School Board Project.

☐ Memo #64

Dated Aug. 31/02

Based on the end-of-the-month count of supplies remaining, it was determined that the following quantities of supplies were used during August. Make the necessary adjusting entry to account for the supplies used.

Fibreglass & Plastics	$3 000
Lumber	$3 000
Hardware	$2 500
Office Supplies	$120

Allocate 5% of the above expenses to the General Sales Project, 35% to the Contracting Project and 60% to the School Board Project.

Do not save the changes in the stored entries because the allocation percentages will change every month.

☐ Memo #65
Dated Aug. 31/02
One month of prepaid insurance, $200, has expired. Recall the stored adjusting entry to debit the Insurance Expense account for this amount. Edit the entry to add the allocations. Allocate 20% of the expense to the General Sales Project, 20% to the Contracting Project and 60% to the School Board Project.

☐ Memo #66
Dated Aug. 31/02
Depreciation is calculated and recorded monthly for all depreciable assets. Recall the stored depreciation entry to record the following depreciation amounts:

Portable Computer System	$75
Machinery & Tools	$125
Shop	$250
Truck	$400
Hydraulic Drill	$150

Edit the entry to add the allocations.
Allocate 20% of the expense to the General Sales Project, 20% to the Contracting Project and 60% to the School Board Project.

☐ Memo #67
Dated Aug. 31/02
Accrued payroll for 11 days is $3 720. Prepare the adjusting entry to recognize the payroll expenses. Allocate 20% of the expense to the General Sales Project, 20% to the Contracting Project and 60% to the School Board Project.

☐ August Bank Statement
Dated Aug. 31/02
Reconcile the bank account with the following bank statement for August.

There are three group deposits: on Aug. 2, $10 640 was deposited as a group of three cheques for $500, $8 000 and $2 140; on Aug 6, $12 500 was deposited as a group of two cheques for $8 500 and $4 000; on Aug 13, $3 786.40 was deposited as a group of two cheques for $936.40 and $2 850. Remember that if you have different tax tables for your program, your paycheque amounts may be different. Clear your cheques and accept the differences as an adjustment. The amount should be small.

ROYAL TRUSTCO. BANK STATEMENT

2300 Yonge Street, Megacity, ON M7T 2F4

Account: Play Wave Plus
7310 Recreation Court
Megacity, ON M5E 1W6

Transit No. 06722
Account No. 45264-912
Statement Date August 31, 2002

Date	Transaction	Deposits	Withdrawals	Balance
07-31-02	**Balance Forward**			13,398.48
08-01-02	Deposit	2,000.00		15,398.48
08-01-02	Deposit	10,640.00		26,038.48
08-03-02	CHQ #158		12,300.00	13,738.48
	CHQ #159		6,922.90	6,815.58
	CHQ #160		1,277.15	5,538.43
	CHQ #161		1,153.46	4,384.97
08-06-02	Deposit	12,500.00		16,884.97
08-08-02	Deposit	3,102.00		19,986.97
	CHQ #163		860.96	19,126.01
	CHQ #164		1,072.17	18,053.84
	CHQ #165		422.83	17,631.01
	CHQ #166		453.77	17,177.24
	Debit Memo - NSF		2,000.00	15,177.24
	Debit Memo NSF charge		20.00	15,157.24
08-10-02	CHQ #162		265.68	14,891.56
	CHQ #167		214.00	14,677.56
08-13-02	Deposit	3,786.40		18,463.96
08-15-02	CHQ #168		5,284.94	13,179.02
08-18-02	CHQ #169		107.00	13,072.02
	CHQ #170		92.00	12,980.02
	CHQ #171		414.00	12,566.02
08-19-02	CHQ #172		1,361.92	11,204.10
08-20-02	Deposit	500.00		11,704.10
08-22-02	CHQ #173		860.96	10,843.14
	CHQ #176		880.81	9,962.33
08-23-02	CHQ #174		1,072.17	8,890.16
	CHQ #175		846.77	8,043.39
08-31-02	Debit Memo		2,000.00	6,043.39
	Interest	15.00		6,058.39
	Monthly Fee		18.50	6,039.89
08-31-02	**Closing Balance**			**6,039.89**

Total Deposits   32,543.40
Total Withdrawals   39,901.99

- To continue good management practice, we recommend printing the following additional reports to monitor performance. Show foreign amounts in reports:

  Journal Entries: All journals for August 15 to August 31

  Trial Balance: As at August 31

  Comparative Income Statement: Actual vs Budget for Quarter 1

  Balance Sheet: As at August 31

  Bank Reconciliation Status Report: As at August 31

  Vendor Aged Detail Report: For all vendors as at August 31

  Customer Aged Detail Report: For all customers as at August 31

  Inventory Synopsis Report

  Project Income Report: For all projects and all accounts from August 1 to August 31

Additional End-of-Period Transactions

The following end-of-period transactions will complete the fiscal period for Play Wave. We consider them to be challenge entries, so we have kept them apart from the others.

☐ Memo #68

Dated Aug. 31/02

A complete inventory inspection revealed that some of the items were damaged beyond repair or use. Prepare the Inventory Adjustments entry to recognize the loss of one Slide: wave (#04) costing $350 and one Tube Slide: classic (#07) costing $250. Edit the Amount for each item (these were the actual cost prices for the damaged units). An insurance claim will be made in September for these losses. Allocate 100% of the expense to the General Sales Project.

☐ Memo #69

Dated Aug. 31/02

The customer, Nirvana Nursery School, has decided not to proceed with the contracted work for financial reasons and will forfeit the deposit of $500. Prepare Sales Invoice #131 for the customer to credit Revenue from Contracting for the $500 deposit (debit Accounts Receivable). Choose GST code 4 (GST @ 7% included) to recognize GST as part of the revenue. Reference cash receipt #29 (deposit #10 and customer cheque #165). Allocate 100% of the revenue to the Contracting Project.

☐ Memo #70

Dated Aug. 31/02

Prepare a Receipts Journal entry to "pay" both the advance and the sales invoice for Nirvana Nursery School. Because the balance owing is zero, no journal entry results from this receipt, but it will remove the two outstanding invoices for the customer.

☐ Memo #71

Dated Aug. 31/02

At the end of August, the work on the second phase of the Megacity School Board project for $8 000 was 25% finished. Prepare a Sales Journal entry to recognize the revenue for the project in the fiscal quarter. GST for this portion should be added, and terms should be changed to 60 days. Allocate 100% of the revenue to the School Board Project.

☐ Memo #72

Dated Aug. 31/02

At the end of August, it was clear that the MegaCity Parks & Rec would be unable to pay its outstanding invoices. The balance owing was $3 558.50. Write off the balance owing by MegaCity Parks & Rec as a bad debt. The GST Charged portion of this was $216.60 and PST was $247.55. The tax accounts should be adjusted to reduce the amount payable. Thus the amount written off is $3 094.35 including freight and NSF charges. Use the direct write-off method. Create the General Ledger account 5025 Bad Debts Expense (G). Allocate 100% of the Bad Debts expense to the General Sales Project. Legal procedures will follow to recover the debt. The Last Man at City Hall will hear of this outstanding debt.

☐ Memo #73

Dated Aug. 31/02

Transfer $4 000 from the Bank Account: Credit Card to the Bank Account: Chequing (Memo 73A). Transfer $3 000 USD from the Bank Account: USD Chequing to the Bank Account: Chequing (Memo 73B). The exchange rate for August 31 is 1.485. (Hint: you must enter these transfers as separate journal transactions in order to use different currencies.)

☐ Memo #74

Dated Aug. 31/02

Make all remittances for payroll deductions for the previous quarter based on the General Ledger payable account balances for July 31. (You may want to print the Balance Sheet as at July 31 to include all the amounts in a single statement.)
The remittances include:
To the Receiver General: EI Payable, CPP Payable, Income Tax Payable
To the Minister of Finance: EHT Payable
To the Workplace Safety and Insurance Board: WSIB Payable (Use Full Add; Do not include in GST reports)
To CIBC Insurance: Group Insurance Payable
To Fidelity Trust: RRSP Payable and CSB Plan Payable (Use Full Add; Do not include in GST reports)
To United Builders Union: Union Dues Payable (Use Full Add; Do not include in GST reports)
Issue cheques #180, 181, 182, 183, 184 and 185.

☐ Memo #75

Dated Aug. 31/02

Using Web site information from Canada Customs and Revenue Agency, check for changes in the Federal Claim amount for income tax. Update all employee ledgers if there has been a change in basic or spousal claim amounts.

◆ Print the Journal Entries for this last group of transactions.

◆ Close the data file for Play Wave so that you can complete the dual currency setup and the final transactions for Live Links.

Practice: Live Links

In mid-December, Lively negotiated with a new vendor in the Seattle, Washington, United States, for the purchase of some computer parts. She has also negotiated a contract with a US branch of one of her Canadian customers.

Dual Currency Transactions

If you have not completed the journal entries for Live Links in Chapter 17 and want to continue working on Chapter 18, you can use your copy of the Data Disk file — Ch18\links\linkch18.sdb — to continue this chapter.

1. Open the file for Live Links and accept Dec. 14 as the Session date. Close the To-Do Lists window.

2. Create a new expense account in the General Ledger:

   5015   Exchange Rate Differences (Group)

3. Set up the currency information for transactions with customers and vendors in the United States. Enter exchange rates for dates in December as follows:

DATE	RATE
Dec. 15, 2002	1.446
Dec. 21, 2002	1.451
Dec. 23, 2002	1.479

4. Create a new bank account in the General Ledger:

   1100   Bank Account: USD (Group)
   Account Class: Bank
   Currency: USD
   Next cheque number: 400

5. Enter new vendor and customer records:

	Vendor Information	Customer Information
Name:	Computer Parts 'n More	Pacific Video, US
Contact:	Gig A. Bites	Seymore Flicks
Address:	42 IBM Way	390 Screenings Rd.
	Seattle, Washington 98115	Seattle, Washington 98102
Phone:	(206) 782-1190	(206) 342-8811
E-mail:	GigABites@partsnmore.com	Flicks@pacvideo.com
Web site:	www.partsnmore.com	www.pacvideo.com
Terms:	net 15	net 15
Currency:	USD	USD
	Include in GST reports.	Do not include in GST reports.

6. Calculate sales and inventory prices using the exchange rate (Inventory Ledger Settings).

7. Advance the Session date to **Dec. 21** and close the To-Do Lists.

☐ Sales Invoice #136

Dated Dec. 15/02

To Rupert College, $1 000 plus $70 GST charged for workshop presentations. Invoice total $1 070. Terms: net 30 days. Allocate 100% of revenue to Service Division. Use Quick Add for the new customer.

☐ Sales Invoice #137

Dated Dec. 15/02

To Pacific Video, US, $2 000 USD charged for DVD duplication services. Invoice total $2 000. Terms: net 15 days. Allocate 100% of revenue to Service Division. The exchange rate is 1.446.

☐ Purchase Invoice #CPM-6422

Dated Dec. 15/02

From Computer Parts 'n More, $500 USD plus $35 USD GST paid for memory chips. Invoice total $535 USD. Terms: net 15 days.

☐ Cheque Copy #58

Dated Dec. 15/02

To CompuWorld Supplies, $7 067.56 in full payment of account, including $144.24 discount taken for early payment. Reference invoice #CW-3314.

☐ Cheque Copy #59

Dated Dec. 15/02

To Comtek Systems, $3 586.21 in full payment of account, including $73.19 discount taken for early payment. Reference invoice #CS-5013.

☐ Cash Receipt #24

Dated Dec. 19/02

From Island Press, cheque #62 for $2 280 in full payment of account. Reference invoice #130.

☐ Cash Receipt #25

Dated Dec. 20/02

From Westmount Institute, cheque #862 for $943.74 in full payment of account, including $19.26 discount taken for early payment. Reference invoice #134.

☐ Cash Receipt #26

Dated Dec. 20/02

From the Receiver General, cheque #552721 for $4 465.98 in payment of GST refund. Reference Memo #26.

☐ Purchase Invoice #1121

Dated Dec. 20/02

From CyberTek Inc., $500 plus $35 GST paid for new custom tools. Invoice total $535. Terms net 30 days. The depreciation amounts will change in January.

☐ Cash Receipt #27
Dated Dec. 21/02
From Pacific Video, US, cheque #4229 for $2 000 USD in full payment of account.
Reference Invoice #137. Deposit to Bank Account: USD. The exchange rate is 1.451.

☐ Employee Time Summary Sheet #8
Pay Period Ending December 21, 2002
Adrian Borland worked 80 regular hours and 2 hours overtime. Issue cheque #60.
Allocate 60% of wage expenses to Service Division and 40% to Sales Division.

8. Advance the Session date to **Dec. 28** and complete the next group of transactions
    from the To-Do Lists.

☐ Cheque Copy #61
Dated Dec. 23/02
To Business Depot, $342 in full payment of account. Reference invoice #BD-12775.

☐ Cheque Copy #400
Dated Dec. 23/02
To Computer Parts 'n More, $535 USD in full payment of account. Reference invoice
#CPM-6422. Pay from Bank Account: USD. The exchange rate is 1.479.

☐ Sales Invoice #138
Dated Dec. 24/02
To Westmount Institute, final Windows workshop in the series

one	SRV-03	Workshop - 6 hours	$900 each	$900
		GST (7%)		63
		Invoice total		$963

Terms: 2/10, n/30 days. Recall the stored invoice. Allocate 100% of revenue to
Service Division.

☐ Cash Purchase Invoice #BCH-6964
Dated Dec. 28/02
From BC Hydro, $50 plus $3.50 GST paid (no PST charged) for hydro services.
Invoice total $53.50. Issued cheque #62 in full payment. Allocate 20% of expense to
Service Division and 80% to Sales Division. Recall and edit the stored entry.

☐ Cheque Copy #63
Dated Dec. 28/02
To Acculink Memory Inc., $840 in full payment of account including $16 discount for
early payment. Reference invoice #AC-117.

9. Close the To-Do Lists and continue entering the next group of transactions.

☐ Credit Card Purchase Invoice #7822
Dated Dec. 28/02
From Petro Partners, $140 plus $9.80 GST charged and $9.80 PST for vehicle
maintenance services. Invoice total $159.60 paid by credit card. Allocate 80% of the
expense to Service Division and 20% to Sales Division.

☐ Memo #44 (Credit Card Bill Payment)

Dated Dec. 28/02

Received monthly statement from Credit Card company for $376.20 for purchases up to and including December 15. Cheque #64 for $376.20 submitted in full payment.

☐ Purchase Invoice #2997

Dated Dec. 28/02

From Visual Technologies, $1 800 for SLR Camera and $4 000 for Digital Cam Recorder plus $406 GST paid. Invoice total $6 206. Terms 2/10, n/30 days. Edit the payment terms. (Both items are debited to the Digital Video Equipment account. Depreciation will commence in January.)

☐ Cash Purchase Invoice #BCT-6997

Dated Dec. 28/02

From BC Telephone, $70 plus $4.90 GST paid and $4.90 PST paid for telephone services. Invoice total $79.80. Issued cheque #65 in full payment. Allocate 60% of expense to Service Division and 40% to Sales Division.

☐ Credit Card Purchase Invoice #7877

Dated Dec. 28/02

From Petro Partners, $60 plus $4.20 GST paid and $4.20 PST paid for gasoline for vehicle. Invoice total $68.40 paid by credit card. Allocate 80% of expense to Service Division and 20% to Sales Division.

☐ Credit Card Sales Invoice #139

Dated Dec. 28/02

To Pro-Career Institute

one	SYS-A	800 MMX System A	$2 800 each	$2 800.00
one	SYS-B	800 MMX System B	3 750 each	3 750.00
five	16	Video Card 4mb VRAM	200 each	1 000.00
		GST (7%)		528.50
		PST (7%)		528.50
		Total received		$8 607.00

Paid by Credit Card #4101 589 510 529. There is no discount.

Allocate 100% of revenue to Sales Division.

10. Advance the Session date to **Dec. 31** and enter the next two recurring entries from the To-Do Lists.

☐ Memo #45

Dated Dec. 31/02

One month of prepaid rent, $1 000, has expired. Prepare an adjusting entry to debit the Rent Expense account for this amount. Recall the stored entry and edit it to add the project allocations. Allocate 50% of expense to Service Division and 50% to Sales Division.

□ Memo #46

Dated Dec. 31/02

Prepare the adjusting depreciation entry to record the following depreciation amounts:

Computers & Peripherals	$150
Custom Tools	$50
Data Recovery Equipment	$200
Duplication Equipment	$300
DLP Projection Unit	$125
Motor Vehicle	$500
Laser Colour Printer	$200

Allocate 100% of expenses to Service Division.

Recall the stored entry. Edit it to increase the depreciation for Duplication Equipment to include purchase in November and remember to add the allocations.

11. **Close the To-Do Lists and complete the remaining transactions for December.**

□ Memo #47

Dated Dec. 31/ 02

Pay Carrie Dell, the salaried employee, for one month. Issue cheque #66. Allocate 80% of salary expenses to Service Division and 20% to Sales Division.

□ Memo #48

Dated Dec. 31/02

Based on the end-of-the-month count of supplies remaining, the following quantities of supplies were used during December. Make the necessary adjusting entry to account for the supplies used.

Office Supplies	$95	Allocate 60% to Service & 40% to Sales
Computer Supplies	$205	Allocate 60% to Service & 40% to Sales
Memory Chips	$495	Allocate 100% to Service

□ Memo #49

Dated Dec. 31/02

Prepare an adjusting entry to recognize $60 as Interest Payable on Loan for the month of December. Allocate 100% of expense to Service Division.

□ Memo #50

Dated Dec. 31/02

Prepare bonus cheques for $300 for both employees. Include Borland's retained vacation pay with his bonus. Issue cheques #67 and 68. Deduct 10% income tax for both employees. Remember to delete the optional contribution amounts for both Dell and Borland. Recalculate taxes and then enter the 10% income tax amount. Allocate 60% of expense to Service Division and 40% to Sales Division.

The bonus amount for Borland should not have vacation pay added. Delete the amount (12.00) in the Vacation field.

☐ Memo #51
Dated Dec. 31/02
One SYS-B computer will be transferred out of inventory for business use. Prepare the Adjustments Journal entry to complete the transfer. The cost of the transferred computer is $3 236.66. Choose account 1520 instead of Damaged Goods.

☐ Memo #52
Dated Dec. 31/02
Prepare a General Journal adjusting entry to recognize the $226.57 as the PST on the computer transfer (7% of $3 236.66). Because Lively has purchased the computer for the business to use and not to sell, she must pay PST on the purchase.

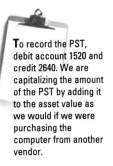

To record the PST, debit account 1520 and credit 2640. We are capitalizing the amount of the PST by adding it to the asset value as we would if we were purchasing the computer from another vendor.

☐ Memo #53
Dated Dec. 31/02
Prepare an adjusting entry to recognize $640 as accrued wages for Adrian Borland for the month of December. Allocate 60% of expense to Service Division and 40% to Sales Division.

☐ Memo #54
Dated Dec. 31/02
Print customer statements to determine interest charges. Prepare sales invoices for one month's interest charges as follows:

     Memo 54A: City Hall Staff $22.26
     Memo 54B: Prolegal Services $14.09

Terms: net 1. Credit Other Revenue account.
Allocate 100% of revenue to Service Division.
Read the advice topic on Handling Overdue Accounts.

☐ Purchase Order #9
Dated Dec. 31/02
Delivery Date Jan. 3/03
From Business Depot, $500 plus $35 GST paid and $35 PST paid for office supplies. Invoice total $570. Terms: Payment on receipt. (The terms have been changed because of frequent late payments.)

☐ Reconcile the bank statement for the CAD chequing account for December 2002.

Remember to edit the two dates to Dec. 31. There was one group deposit on Dec. 20 — $4 465.98 and $943.74 were deposited together. Remember that if you have different tax tables for your program, your paycheque amounts may be different. Clear your cheques and accept the differences as an adjustment. The amount should be small.

LEARNX BANK STATEMENT

Pacific Heights Branch
400 Pacific Blvd.,Vancouver, BC V7R 3W2

Account 554-66112   December 31, 2002

Date	Transaction	Deposits	Withdrawals	Balance
11-30-02	**Balance Forward**			24,655.83
12-03-02	CHQ #54		2,149.40	22,506.43
12-06-02	Deposit	943.74		23,450.17
12-08-02	Deposit	11,507.16		34,957.33
12-08-02	CHQ #55		736.78	34,220.55
12-10-02	Deposit	535.00		34,755.55
12-11-02	CHQ #56		8,388.80	26,366.75
12-15-02	CHQ #57		1,925.78	24,440.97
12-18-02	CHQ #58		7,067.56	17,373.41
12-18-02	CHQ #59		3,586.21	13,787.20
12-19-02	Deposit	2,280.00		16,067.20
12-20-02	Deposit	5,409.72		21,476.92
12-23-02	CHQ #60		736.78	20,740.14
12-25-02	CHQ #61		342.00	20,398.14
12-29-02	CHQ #64		376.20	20,021.94
12-30-02	CHQ #62		53.50	19,968.44
12-30-02	CHQ #65		79.80	19,888.64
12-31-02	CHQ #63		840.00	19,048.64
	Interest	35.00		19,083.64
	Monthly fee		20.00	19,063.64
12/31/02	**Closing Balance**			**19,063.64**

Total Deposits   20,710.62
Total Withdrawals   26,302.81

Account holder: Live Links
                           20300 Silicon Valley Rd. North
                           Burnaby, BC V5B 3A2

☐ Memo #55

Dated Dec. 31/02

Access the Web site for Rupert College at <www.pearsoned.ca/purbhoosimply8> to view the customer's announcement of a plan to computerize admissions procedures. Prepare two sales quotes for the 10 new computers that Rupert College will require, one quote for computer system A and one for system B. Include a generous 10% discount. E-mail the quote <purbhoo.simply8@pearsoned.com> so that they will receive the information immediately. The order will be shipped on Jan. 10, 2003.

Go to the Web site and then click the link for Rupert College.

Do not include the new vendors in GST reports. Leave the remaining ledger fields blank. Use Memo 56A, 56B, etc., as the source for these remittances.

☐ Memo #56

Dated Dec. 31/02

Make all remittances for payroll deductions for the previous quarter based on the General Ledger payable account balances for November 30. (You may want to print the Balance Sheet as at November 30 to include all amounts in one statement.)

The remittances include:

To the Receiver General: EI Payable, CPP Payable, Income Tax Payable

To the Minister of Finance: Medical Payable

To the Workers' Compensation Board: WCB Payable (Use Full Add)

To Faith Insurance: Group Insurance Payable (Use Full Add)

To Freedom Trust: RRSP Payable and CSB Plan Payable (Use Full Add)

Issue cheques #69, 70, 71, 72 and 73. (Do not include new vendors in GST reports.)

☐ Memo #57

Dated Dec. 31/02

An error was made in the count of office supplies used in December. Adjust the General Journal entry for Memo #48 to change the amount of office supplies used to $35. The allocation for the expense is unchanged.

12. To follow good management practice, we recommend printing the following reports:

Journal Entries: All journals for December 15 to December 31

Trial Balance: As at December 31

Comparative Income Statement: Actual vs Budget for Quarter 1

Balance Sheet: As at December 31

Bank Reconciliation Status Report: As at December 31

Vendor Aged Detail Report: For all vendors as at December 31

Customer Aged Detail Report: For all customers as at December 31

Inventory Synopsis Report

Division Report: For all divisions and all accounts from December 1 to December 31

Include foreign amounts in reports where possible.

13. Close the data files for Live Links.

Congratulations! You have completed all the transactions for two complete fiscal quarters for the principal companies in this text. For further practice, complete the simulations for Kindred Kitchenwares and Anderson Farm in Chapters 19 and 20. For additional challenge, complete the comparative Summary Case Analysis on the following page.

Review Questions

1. What must you do to enter and change exchange rates?
2. Why is important to enter exact exchange rates?
3. What are the advantages and disadvantages of setting inventory prices in the second currency rather than using the exchange rate to determine foreign prices?
4. Why might the duty fields not appear in the Purchases Journal?
5. Why might the foreign currency field not appear for a customer in the Sales Journal?

6. If you cannot change the currency setting for a customer after you enter transactions, how might you set up the accounts for a customer who has offices in both the home country and a foreign country?
7. Why is it helpful to have a separate bank account for foreign transactions? Are there any disadvantages?
8. Why should you turn on the reminder about exchange rates that are old?

SUMMARY CASE ANALYSIS

You now have six months of complete financial data, two fiscal quarters, for both Play Wave Plus and Live Links Computer Services. Both companies started as service and contracting businesses and expanded to include inventory sales in the second quarter. Both companies are still young, in their first year of operations.

Complete an evaluation of the two companies, comparing them where possible. Your analysis should address the following issues:

- Cash flow management: Look at the fluctuations in bank account balances and receipt and payment patterns.

- Budget: Discuss the success in meeting budget expectations.

- Addition of inventory sales: Was this a sound decision?

- Projects/divisions: Are all projects/divisions equally profitable or successful? Does it matter, that is, should all projects/divisions be continued?

- Are customer payment terms appropriate or working to the best advantage for each company?

- Outstanding business: Discuss the potential effect of the outstanding purchase order (Play Wave) and sales quote (Live Links) on future performance.

Looking ahead: Winter is approaching and outdoor building projects and sales of outdoor equipment will be restricted for Play Wave. What expansion opportunities should Child consider to keep the staff fully employed and the business profitable? For Live Links, how might technological changes influence the company? Consider both positive and negative effects.

Are there any other observations about the performance of either company?

As a summary, discuss whether or not you would invest in either or both companies. (Assume that you have the capital to do so.) Why or why not? What changes would you recommend or request before you invested in the companies?

CHAPTER 19

PRACTICE SIMULATION
KINDRED KITCHENWARES

Objectives

- create new company files
- enter settings for ledgers
- enter General Ledger accounts and balances
- set up bank accounts, credit cards and currencies
- enter ledger records and historical data for all ledgers
- enter linked accounts for all ledgers
- finish history for all ledgers
- complete transactions in all journals
- display and print reports for monitoring company performance

Introduction

Kindred Kitchenwares uses the General, Payables, Receivables, Payroll and Inventory Ledgers. After setting up the company files and entering the historical data for the five ledgers, you will enter accounting transactions for three months, a complete fiscal quarter.

There is no file on the Data Disk for Kindred Kitchenwares. You must create your own company files for this simulation.

Kindred Kitchenwares

Company Profile and Information

Kindred Kitchenwares, a restaurant equipment and supplies business, is owned and operated by Kyra Kindred in the city of Waterloo. She started the business in January 2002, after conducting thorough business research. Her studies revealed two very encouraging facts — her competition would come mostly from the Metropolitan Megacity region, and the restaurant industry in Kitchener-Waterloo was growing steadily with the increasing number of dual-career families who frequently eat in restaurants. To lure business away from these large out-of-town suppliers, she would have to price her inventory competitively and market her business aggressively.

She immediately hired three employees to assist with customer sales in the store, make deliveries to customers and receive shipments from vendors. This left Kindred free to handle marketing and sales. To find potential customers, she monitors applications for new restaurant licences and renovation permits and then contacts the owners of the business. At present, her customers include restaurants, hotels and small coffee shops. They buy large appliances such as industrial-standard ranges, cooktops and refrigerators, specialty equipment such as impingers and pizza ovens, and cooking and serving utensils. To encourage prompt payments, Kindred offers a 1 percent discount, after taxes, to all regular customers who have accounts if they pay within five days. Net payment is requested within 10 days. She has also negotiated a major contract with the head office of a chain of pizza restaurants to supply their expanding retail operations in the United States. In addition to these account customers who generally make large purchases, a few customers make smaller purchases with payment by credit card. These purchases are summarized twice a month as a single invoice and then deposited directly. All Canadian customers pay 7 percent GST and 8 percent PST on their purchases because they are the final customers for these products.

Kindred now has a number of regular suppliers with whom she has set up accounts. The payment terms with these vendors vary, but whenever possible, Kindred takes the discounts for early payments. She pays GST on all purchases, but no PST for her inventory purchases because she resells the merchandise. She does pay PST on other taxable purchases for regular business use.

Her GST registration, using the regular method, requires monthly reports and remittances of any excess of GST charged on sales over GST paid on purchases. She also makes monthly remittances of the PST she collects from customers.

On October 1, the time of converting her manual accounting system to Simply Accounting, Kindred has consolidated all her financial reports. The Income Statement for the previous quarter and the Balance Sheet are presented here. The remaining reports are presented in the pages that follow, along with the instructions for entering them.

KINDRED KITCHENWARES
INCOME STATEMENT

For the Quarter Ending September 30, 2002

Revenue

4000 GENERAL REVENUE		
4020 Revenue from Sales	$184 000.00	
4040 Sales Returns & Allowances	−2 500.00	
4060 Sales Discounts	−1 500.00	
4120 Net Sales		$180 000.00
4150 Interest Earned		370.00
4180 Sales Tax Compensation		630.00
4200 Freight Revenue		500.00
4390 TOTAL GENERAL REVENUE		$181 500.00
Total Revenue		**$181 500.00**

Expense

5000 OPERATING EXPENSES		
5010 Advertising & Promotion		$ 250.00
5020 Bank Charges		75.00
5025 Credit Card Fees	$ 450.00	
5050 COGS - Accessories	4 320.00	
5060 COGS - Professional Cookware	9 720.00	
5070 COGS - Service Equipment	93 960.00	
5080 Purchase Discounts	−800.00	
5090 Purchase Returns & Allowances	−500.00	
5105 Net Cost of Goods Sold		107 150.00
5110 Depreciation: Cash Registers	300.00	
5120 Depreciation: Comp & Peri	500.00	
5130 Depreciation: Equipment	250.00	
5140 Depreciation: Retail Premises	3 000.00	
5150 Depreciation: Vehicles	1 000.00	
5155 Net Depreciation		5 050.00
5160 Delivery Expense		100.00
5170 Freight Expense		200.00
5180 Hydro Expense		360.00
5190 Insurance Expense		300.00
5200 Interest on Loan		800.00
5210 Interest on Mortgage		6 100.00
5220 Maintenance Expense		150.00
5230 Office Supplies Used		150.00
5240 Property Taxes		750.00
5250 Uncollectable Accounts Expense		700.00
5260 Telephone Expense		160.00
5270 Truck Expenses		300.00
5290 TOTAL OPERATING EXPENSES		$122 595.00
5295 PAYROLL EXPENSES		
5300 Wages		33 852.00
5310 EI Expense		677.62
5320 CPP Expense		668.98
5330 WSIB Expense		1 625.19
5360 EHT Expense		320.46
5390 TOTAL PAYROLL EXPENSES		$ 37 144.25
5500 INCOME TAX EXPENSE		
5540 Business Income Tax Expense		6 000.00
5590 TOTAL INCOME TAX EXPENSE		$ 6 000.00
Total Expenses		**$165 739.25**
Net Income		**$ 15 760.75**

KINDRED KITCHENWARES
BALANCE SHEET

As at September 30, 2002

Assets

1000 CURRENT ASSETS

1070 Bank: Waterloo Trust Chequing	$ 23 002.88	
1080 Bank: Waterloo Trust Savings	5 000.00	
1090 Bank: Credit Card	2 500.00	
1100 Bank: USD Chequing ($335 USD)	500.00	
1120 Net Bank		$ 31 002.88
1200 Accounts Receivable	38 755.00	
1220 Allowance for Doubtful Accounts	−900.00	
1240 Advances Receivable	100.00	
1260 Interest Receivable	370.00	
1270 Net Receivables		38 325.00
1280 Office Supplies		200.00
1300 Prepaid Advertising		250.00
1320 Prepaid Insurance		1 500.00
1390 TOTAL CURRENT ASSETS		$ 71 277.88
1400 INVENTORY ASSETS		
1410 Accessories		7 980.00
1420 Professional Cookware		19 500.00
1430 Service Equipment		204 200.00
1490 TOTAL INVENTORY ASSETS		$231 680.00
1500 PLANT & EQUIPMENT		
1510 Cash Registers	5 000.00	
1520 Accum Deprec: Cash Registers	−900.00	
1525 Net Cash Registers		4 100.00
1540 Computers & Peripherals	6 000.00	
1550 Accum Deprec: Comp & Peri	−1 500.00	
1555 Net Computers & Peripherals		4 500.00
1570 Equipment	15 000.00	
1580 Accum Deprec: Equipment	−750.00	
1585 Net Equipment		14 250.00
1600 Retail Premises	300 000.00	
1610 Accum Deprec: Retail Premises	−9 000.00	
1625 Net Retail Premises		291 000.00
1630 Vehicles	40 000.00	
1640 Accum Deprec: Vehicles	−3 000.00	
1650 Net Vehicles		37 000.00
1800 TOTAL PLANT & EQUIPMENT		$350 850.00
Total Assets		**$653 807.88**

KINDRED KITCHENWARES
BALANCE SHEET CONT'D

Liabilities
2000 CURRENT LIABILITIES

2100 Bank Loan		$ 75 000.00
2200 Accounts Payable		33 500.00
2250 Credit Card Payable		200.00
2300 Vacation Payable		1 728.00
2310 EI Payable	$ 458.64	
2320 CPP Payable	342.88	
2330 Income Tax Payable	1 836.96	
2340 Receiver General Payable		2 638.48
2390 EHT Payable		320.46
2400 RRSP Payable		450.00
2410 CSB Plan Payable		450.00
2420 Group Insurance Payable		35.00
2460 WSIB Payable		1 625.19
2500 Business Income Tax Payable		0.00
2640 PST Payable		4 800.00
2650 GST Charged on Sales	4 200.00	
2670 GST Paid on Purchases	−2 800.00	
2750 GST Owing (Refund)		1 400.00
2790 TOTAL CURRENT LIABILITIES		$122 147.13
2800 LONG TERM LIABILITIES		
2850 Mortgage Payable		248 800.00
2890 TOTAL LONG TERM LIABILITIES		$248 800.00
Total Liabilities		**$370 947.13**

Equity
3000 OWNER'S EQUITY

3560 K. Kindred, Capital		267 100.00
3600 Current Earnings		15 760.75
3800 UPDATED CAPITAL		$282 860.75
Total Equity		**$282 860.75**
Total Liabilities and Equity		**$653 807.88**

Caution: Read This Note before You Start

As you finish entering accounts and balances for each ledger in the following sections, print the appropriate reports to check your work before proceeding. Do not begin the journal transactions if you see any error messages when you attempt to finish the history. You should also check the validity of accounts in the General Ledger and check the data integrity (Maintenance menu) as you proceed to monitor the accuracy of your work. Be sure to make backups regularly as no data disk files accompany this simulation.

1. Create a new folder named Kindred and a new set of company files.

2. Enter the fiscal dates and company information.

COMPANY INFORMATION

Business Name:	Kindred Kitchenwares
Address:	500 Appliance Rd., Waterloo, Ontario N4E 9X5
Phone:	(519) 263-4110
Fax:	(519) 264-4010
Business Number:	62991 6992
Fiscal Start:	October 1, 2002
Fiscal End:	December 31, 2002
Earliest Transaction Date:	October 1, 2002

---

3. Enter Names.

From	**To**
Income B	Bonus
Deduction A	RRSP
Deduction B	CSB Plan
Deduction C	Gp Insurance
Delete Incomes C to E and Deductions D to J	

---

4. Enter the settings for each module.

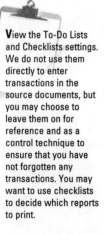

View the To-Do Lists and Checklists settings. We do not use them directly to enter transactions in the source documents, but you may choose to leave them on for reference and as a control technique to ensure that you have not forgotten any transactions. You may want to use checklists to decide which reports to print.

Display Settings
> Your choice for display font and size
> Use accounting terms
> Open records and transactions windows with a single click
> Show the Select Company window at startup

System Settings
> Store Invoice Lookup details
> Use cheque number as the source code for cash purchases and sales
> Allow transactions in the future and warn if they are 7 days in the future
> Warn if accounts are not balanced when entering a new month
> Choose semi-monthly as the backup frequency

Sales Taxes Settings
> GST Rate 1 at 7%
> PST Rate at 8%
> Do not apply PST to freight or to GST

Payables Settings
> Aging: 10, 30 and 60 days
> Do not calculate discounts before tax for one-time vendors

Receivables
> Aging: 10, 30 and 60 days
> No interest charges on overdue accounts
> Include paid invoices in last 31 days
> Payment terms: 1% discount in 5 days, net in 10 days
> Do not calculate discount before tax

---

5. Enter the General Ledger Accounts.

KINDRED KITCHENWARES CHART OF ACCOUNTS

Assets

1000 CURRENT ASSETS (H)	1430 Service Equipment (G)
1005 Test Balance Account (G)	1490 TOTAL INVENTORY ASSETS (T)
1070 Bank: Waterloo Trust Chequing (A)	
1080 Bank: Waterloo Trust Savings (A)	1500 PLANT & EQUIPMENT (H)
1090 Bank: Credit Card (A)	1510 Cash Registers (A)
1100 Bank: USD Chequing (A)	1520 Accum Deprec: Cash Registers (A)
1120 Net Bank (S)	1525 Net Cash Registers (S)
1200 Accounts Receivable (A)	1540 Computers & Peripherals (A)
1220 Allowance for Doubtful Accounts (A)	1550 Accum Deprec: Comp & Peri (A)
1240 Advances Receivable (A)	1555 Net Computers & Peripherals (S)
1260 Interest Receivable (A)	1570 Equipment (A)
1270 Net Receivables (S)	1580 Accum Deprec: Equipment (A)
1280 Office Supplies (G)	1585 Net Equipment (S)
1300 Prepaid Advertising (G)	1600 Retail Premises (A)
1320 Prepaid Insurance (G)	1610 Accum Deprec: Retail Premises (A)
1390 TOTAL CURRENT ASSETS (T)	1625 Net Retail Premises (S)
	1630 Vehicles (A)
1400 INVENTORY ASSETS (H)	1640 Accum Deprec: Vehicles (A)
1410 Accessories (G)	1650 Net Vehicles (S)
1420 Professional Cookware (G)	1800 TOTAL PLANT & EQUIPMENT (T)

KINDRED KITCHENWARES CHART OF ACCOUNTS

CONTINUED

Liabilities
2000 CURRENT LIABILITIES (H)
2100 Bank Loan (G)
2200 Accounts Payable (G)
2250 Credit Card Payable
2300 Vacation Payable (G)
2310 EI Payable (A)
2320 CPP Payable (A)
2330 Income Tax Payable (A)
2340 Receiver General Payable (S)
2390 EHT Payable (G)
2400 RRSP Payable (G)
2410 CSB Plan Payable (G)
2420 Group Insurance Payable (G)
2460 WSIB Payable (G)
2500 Business Income Tax Payable (G)
2640 PST Payable (G)
2650 GST Charged on Sales (A)
2670 GST Paid on Purchases (A)
2750 GST Owing (Refund) (S)
2790 TOTAL CURRENT LIABILITIES (T)

2800 LONG TERM LIABILITIES (H)
2850 Mortgage Payable (G)
2890 TOTAL LONG TERM LIABILITIES (T)

Equity
3000 OWNER'S EQUITY (H)
3560 K. Kindred, Capital (G)
3600 Current Earnings (X)
3690 UPDATED CAPITAL (T)

Revenue
4000 GENERAL REVENUE (H)
4020 Revenue from Sales (A)
4040 Sales Returns & Allowances (A)
4060 Sales Discounts (A)
4080 Exchange Rate Differences (A)
4120 Net Sales (S)
4150 Interest Earned (G)
4180 Sales Tax Compensation (G)
4200 Freight Revenue (G)
4390 TOTAL GENERAL REVENUE (T)

Expense
5000 OPERATING EXPENSES (H)
5010 Advertising & Promotion (G)
5020 Bank Charges (G)
5025 Credit Card Fees (G)
5030 Damaged Inventory (A)
5040 Assembly Costs (A)
5050 COGS - Accessories (A)
5060 COGS - Professional Cookware (A)
5070 COGS - Service Equipment (A)
5075 Cost Variance (A)
5080 Purchase Discounts (A)
5090 Purchase Returns & Allowances (A)
5105 Net Cost of Goods Sold (S)
5110 Depreciation: Cash Registers (A)
5120 Depreciation: Comp & Peri (A)
5130 Depreciation: Equipment (A)
5140 Depreciation: Retail Premises (A)
5150 Depreciation: Vehicles (A)
5155 Net Depreciation (S)
5160 Delivery Expense (G)
5170 Freight Expense (G)
5180 Hydro Expense (G)
5190 Insurance Expense (G)
5200 Interest on Loan (G)
5210 Interest on Mortgage (G)
5220 Maintenance Expense (G)
5230 Office Supplies Used (G)
5240 Property Taxes (G)
5250 Uncollectable Accounts Expense (G)
5260 Telephone Expense (G)
5270 Truck Expenses (G)
5290 TOTAL OPERATING EXPENSES (T)

5295 PAYROLL EXPENSES (H)
5300 Wages (G)
5310 EI Expense (G)
5320 CPP Expense (G)
5330 WSIB Expense (G)
5360 EHT Expense (G)
5390 TOTAL PAYROLL EXPENSES (T)

5500 INCOME TAX EXPENSE (H)
5540 Business Income Tax Expense (G)
5590 TOTAL INCOME TAX EXPENSE (T)

6. Enter account balances.

KINDRED KITCHENWARES
POST-CLOSING TRIAL BALANCE

October 1, 2002

1070 Bank: Waterloo Trust Chequing	$ 23 002.88	
1080 Bank: Waterloo Trust Savings	5 000.00	
1090 Bank: Credit Card	2 500.00	
1100 Bank: USD Chequing ($335 USD)	500.00	
1200 Accounts Receivable	38 755.00	
1220 Allowance for Doubtful Accounts		$ 900.00
1240 Advances Receivable	100.00	
1260 Interest Receivable	370.00	
1280 Office Supplies	200.00	
1300 Prepaid Advertising	250.00	
1320 Prepaid Insurance	1 500.00	
1410 Accessories	7 980.00	
1420 Professional Cookware	19 500.00	
1430 Service Equipment	204 200.00	
1510 Cash Registers	5 000.00	
1520 Accum Deprec: Cash Registers		900.00
1540 Computers & Peripherals	6 000.00	
1550 Accum Deprec: Comp & Peri		1 500.00
1570 Equipment	15 000.00	
1580 Accum Deprec: Equipment		750.00
1600 Retail Premises	300 000.00	
1610 Accum Deprec: Retail Premises		9 000.00
1630 Vehicles	40 000.00	
1640 Accum Deprec: Vehicles		3 000.00
2100 Bank Loan		75 000.00
2200 Accounts Payable		33 500.00
2250 Credit Card Payable		200.00
2300 Vacation Payable		1 728.00
2310 EI Payable		458.64
2320 CPP Payable		342.88
2330 Income Tax Payable		1 836.96
2390 EHT Payable		320.46
2400 RRSP Payable		450.00
2410 CSB Plan Payable		450.00
2420 Group Insurance Payable		35.00
2460 WSIB Payable		1 625.19
2640 PST Payable		4 800.00
2650 GST Charged on Sales		4 200.00
2670 GST Paid on Purchases	2 800.00	
2850 Mortgage Payable		248 800.00
3560 K. Kindred, Capital		282 860.75
	$672 657.88	**$672 657.88**

The opening balance in the USD Chequing account is entered in Canadian dollars.

Remember to use the Test Balance account for any out-of-balance difference if you must close the Accounts window before finishing or if you have made a data entry error. Do not finish the history until the Test Balance account balance is zero.

Print the Chart of Accounts and the Trial Balance to check your data entry for the General Ledger accounts and balances.

7. Set up the company file to allow transactions in US dollars as the second currency. Do not enter exchange rates at this time. Since there are only sales to US customers initially, the linked account for rate differences is a revenue account: *4080 Exchange Rate Differences*.

Although account 1080 is a savings account, it does have cheque-writing privileges. Therefore we define it as a chequing account and enter a next cheque number.

8. Modify the account class for bank accounts. Enter currencies and cheque numbers.

Account	Account Class	Currency	Next Cheque Number
1070 Bank: Waterloo Trust Chequing	Bank Class Chequing	CAD	300
1080 Bank: Waterloo Trust Savings	Bank Class Chequing	CAD	400
1090 Bank: Credit Card	Credit Card	CAD	
1100 Bank: USD Chequing	Bank Class Chequing	USD	200

9. Enter linked accounts for all ledgers.

General Linked Accounts

Retained Earnings	3560 K. Kindred, Capital
Current Earnings	3600 Current Earnings

Payables Linked Accounts

Principal Bank Account	1070 Bank: Waterloo Trust Chequing
Principal Bank Account for USD	1100 Bank: USD Chequing
Accounts Payable	2200 Accounts Payable
GST Paid on Purchases	2670 GST Paid on Purchases
Freight Expense	5170 Freight Expense
Purchase Discount	5080 Purchase Discounts

Receivables Linked Accounts

Principal Bank Account	1070 Bank: Waterloo Trust Chequing
Principal Bank Account for USD	1100 Bank: USD Chequing
Accounts Receivable	1200 Accounts Receivable
GST Charged on Sales (Rate 1)	2650 GST Charged on Sales
PST Payable	2640 PST Payable
Freight Revenue	4200 Freight Revenue
Sales Discount	4060 Sales Discounts

Payroll Linked Accounts

Principal Bank Account	1070 Bank: Waterloo Trust Chequing
Vacation	2300 Vacation Payable
Advances	1240 Advances Receivable
Wage Expenses and Vacation Pay	5300 Wages
RRSP Payable	2400 RRSP Payable
CSB Plan Payable	2410 CSB Plan Payable
Gp Insurance Payable	2420 Group Insurance Payable
Deduction D through J	not used
EI Payable	2310 EI Payable
CPP Payable	2320 CPP Payable
Tax Payable	2330 Income Tax Payable
WCB Payable	2460 WSIB Payable
EHT Payable	2390 EHT Payable
EI Expense	5310 EI Expense
CPP Expense	5320 CPP Expense
WCB Expense	5330 WSIB Expense
EHT Expense	5360 EHT Expense

Tax (Que), QPP & QHSF Payable; QPP & QHSF Expense linked accounts are not used

Inventory Linked Accounts

Item Assembly Costs	5040 Assembly Costs
Adjustment Write-off	5030 Damaged Inventory

10. Set up the files for accepting and using credit cards.

Credit Cards Accepted

Credit Card Name	Discount Fee %	Expense Account	Asset Account
VISA	2.75	5025 Credit Card Fees	1090 Bank: Credit Card
MasterCard	2.50	5025 Credit Card Fees	1090 Bank: Credit Card

Credit Cards Used

Credit Card Name	Payable Account	Expense Account
VISA	2250 Credit Card Payable	5025 Credit Card Fees

11. Enter Payables Ledger records and historical transactions.

All vendor discounts are calculated after tax.

KINDRED KITCHENWARES
VENDOR INFORMATION

Vendors with Historical Transactions

Vendor (Contact)	Address	Phone, Fax	E-mail, Web, Terms
Koolhouse Refrigeration (I. C. Box)	902 Frost St. Burlington, ON L4C 2Z4	Tel: (905) 446-3465 Fax: (905) 462-7194	E-mail: box@koolhouse.com Web: www.keep-all-cool.com 2/10, n/30
Restek Equipment Mfg. (May Tagge)	790 Woods Rd. Mississauga, ON L5F 2D5	Tel: 905) 279-1927 Fax: (905) 279-7611	E-mail: mtagge@restek.com Web: www.restek.mfg.com 2/10, n/30
Ronson Ranges (Rocky Range)	11 Stover Cres. Hamilton, ON L3B 2E5	Tel: (905) 523-7200 Fax: (905) 522-1924	E-mail: rrange@ronson.com Web: www.ronson.com net 30
Sheffield Steel Products (Rusty Cutter)	45 Lagostina Ave. Etobicoke, ON M9B 2D6	Tel: (416) 297-8273 Fax: (416) 298-6299	Web: www.sheffield.steel.com net 10

Vendor	Date	Invoice/Cheque #	Terms	Amount
Koolhouse Refrigeration	09/29/02	KR-114	2/10, n/30	$9 600
Restek Equipment Mfg.	09/28/02	RE-103	2/10, n/30	$9 600
Ronson Ranges	09/24/02	R-321	net 30	$3 900
	09/25/02	R-330	net 30	9 000
	09/25/02	Chq #294 (payment)		2 900
		Balance		$10 000
Sheffield Steel Products	09/25/02	1211	net 10	$4 300
		Grand total		**$33 500**

KINDRED KITCHENWARES
ADDITIONAL VENDORS

Vendor (Contact)	Address	Phone, Fax	E-mail, Web, Terms
Bell Canada (Colle Wayting)	39 Ring Road Kitchener, ON N2H 7F4	Tel: (519) 886-2347 Fax: (519) 888-6129	*Web: www.bell.ca net 1
Cuisine Pro Inc. (Olive Oyle)	599 Cook St. Hamilton, ON L5G 4B2	Tel: (905) 532-1245 Fax: (905) 525-1900	E-mail: Oyle.cuisine@foodscape.com Web: www.chop.it.up.com net 30
Kitchener Record (Dayley Ragge)	99 Nues Ct. Kitchener, ON N5M 7B7	Tel: (519) 521-8299 Fax: (519) 522-6399	Web: www.kitch.record.ca net 1
Laurier Insurance (Max Dollar)	28 Protector Ave. Waterloo, ON N6C 6B6	Tel: (519) 884-8844 Fax: (519) 884-1188	Web: www.laurier.international.com net 1
Metropolitan Investors Group (Monty Carlow)	55 Funding Ave. Waterloo, ON N4C 8K8	Tel: (519) 882-1019 Fax: (519) 882-2927	Web: www.metro.invest.group.com net 1
Minister of Finance	48 Pecuniary Ct. Oshawa, ON L7B 3V3	Tel: (905) 533-3344	net 1
Northland Gas Equipment (Jenn Aire)	38 Consumers Rd. Collingwood, ON L9Y 3F2	Tel: (705) 621-8643 Fax: (705) 621-7194	E-mail: JAire@NLGas.com Web: www.all.gas.appliances.com net 30
Receiver General of Canada	Summerside Tax Centre Summerside, PE C1N 6L2	Tel: (902) 821-8186	*Web: www.ccra-adrc.gc.ca net 1
Waterloo Hydro (Alec Trishan)	10 Watts Road Waterloo, ON N6F 3V9	Tel: (519) 629-1918 Fax: (519) 628-7162	E-mail: atrish@wnhydro.on.ca *Web: www.wnhydro.on.ca net 1
Waterloo Region Treasurer (Noel Cash)	55 Finance St. Waterloo, ON N3R 6B8	Tel: (519) 593-8712 Fax: (519) 599-7192	net 23
Workplace Safety & Insurance Board (N. Jured)	75 Ombuds Rd. Waterloo, ON N9N 4B7	Tel: (519) 699-8192 Fax: (519) 689-8811	net 1

Print the Vendor List and the Vendor Aged Detail Report including terms and historical differences to check the accuracy of your work.

12. Enter Receivables Ledger records and historical transactions.

KINDRED KITCHENWARES CUSTOMER INFORMATION

Customers with Historical Transactions

Customer (Contact)	Address	Phone, Fax, Terms	E-mail, Web, (Credit Limit)
Cornerhouse Cafe (Kappu Cheeno)	29 Spadina Ave. Kitchener, ON N5R 2N4	Tel: (519) 885-4578 Fax: (519) 885-5880 1/5, n/10	E-mail: kc@chc.com Web: www.chc.com ($20 000)
Lotus Gardens (Ida Blossom)	410 Dundas St Waterloo, ON N3P 8X1	Tel: (519) 622-8299 Fax: (519) 623-9018 1/5, n/10	E-mail: lda@istar.com Web: www.lotus.gardens.com ($20 000)
Palmleaf Restaurant (Orange Groves)	350 Tropicana Ave. Waterloo, ON N2M 1S1	Tel: (519) 775-9988 Fax: (519) 775-9980 1/5, n/10	E-mail: groves@palmwork.com Web: www.palmleaf.foodsinc.com ($20 000)

Historical Transactions

Customer	Date	Invoice/Cheque #	Terms	Amount
Cornerhouse Cafe	09/29/02	693	1/5, n/10	$14 720
Lotus Gardens	09/24/02	679	1/5, n/10	$12 190
Palmleaf Restaurant	09/23/02	667	1/5, n/10	$11 845
		Grand total		**$38 755**

NEW CUSTOMERS

Customer (Contact)	Address	Phone, Fax, Terms	E-mail, Web, (Credit Limit)
Ambassador Convention Centre (Claire Envoy)	40 Meeting Place Kitchener, ON N6H 5K9	Tel: (519) 289-9289 Fax: (519) 289-8098 1/5, n/10	E-mail: sales@ambassadors.com Web: www.ambassadors.com ($10 000)
Chico's Coffee Bar (Chico Mortadello)	400 Columbia Rd. Waterloo, ON N6G 6F6	Tel: (519) 884-1379 Fax: (519) 884-1370 1/5, n/10	E-mail: CM@chicos.com Web: www.good-coffees.com ($10 000)
Kaiser King Restaurants (Wilhelm Kaiser)	555 Bagel Cres. Kitchener, ON N4H 7F8	Tel: (519) 623-7555 Fax: (519) 625-8332 1/5, n/10	E-mail: wkaiser@kaiser.king.com Web: www.kaiser.king.com ($10 000)
Planet Pizza (Pan Zerroti)	63 Primavera Rd. Augres, Michigan 48640	Tel: (517) 837-9751 Fax: (517) 837-9700 1/5, n/10	E-mail: pizzas@planet.com Web: www.more-cheeses.com ($10 000 USD)
Rivers Edge Restaurant (Tira Misu)	9 Riverbank Rd. Waterloo, ON N4J 5C5	Tel: (519) 732-8339 Fax: (519) 732-8900 1/5, n/10	E-mail: TMisu@foodscape.com Web: www.foods.fish.com ($10 000)
The Russell Hotel (Russell Resorte)	699 Russell Hill Dr. Waterloo, ON N3D 2K8	Tel: (519) 882-8881 Fax: (519) 882-8001 1/5, n/10	*E-mail: purbhoo.simply8@ pearsoned.com *Web: www.pearsoned.ca/ purbhoosimply8 ($10 000)

Print the Customer List and the Customer Aged Detail Report including terms and historical differences to check your data entry work for the ledger.

Note that Planet Pizza is a US customer with transactions in US dollars.

The Russell Hotel addresses are set up for the transactions in this simulation. Use <www.pearsoned.ca/ purbhoosimply8> as the Web site address and use <purbhoo.simply8@ pearsoned.com> as the e-mail address.

13. Enter Payroll Ledger records and historical employee information.

KINDRED KITCHENWARES
EMPLOYEE INFORMATION

Personal Information

Name	Tracy Moffat	Terence Inglis	Hendrik Siemens
Position	Sales Rep/ Manager	Sales/Shipping Assistant	Shipping/Receiving Clerk
Address	51 Kenmore Ave. Waterloo, ON N7G 3K9	88 Viking Rd. Waterloo, ON N0R 1T0	11 Denby St. Waterloo, ON N2B 4C3
Telephone	(519) 772-9106	(519) 883-4517	(519) 289-6196
Social Insurance Number (SIN)	597 610 450	482 640 620	401 722 012
Date of Birth	12-25-71	02-14-68	04-01-78
Date of Hire	01-01-02	01-01-02	01-01-02

Taxes

Tax Table	Ontario	Ontario	Ontario
Federal Claim (Tax Exemption)			
Basic amount	$7 131	$7 131	$7 131
Spousal amount	$6 661	$6 661	$6 661
Total Federal Claim	$13 792	$13 792	$13 792
WSIB Rate (WCB)	1.52	4.97	4.97
EI Eligible (EI Factor)	Yes (1.4)	Yes (1.4)	Yes (1.4)
CPP and Income Tax	calculations built into Simply Accounting program		
Additional Federal Tax	$50		

Income

Regular Wage		$20/hour	$20/hour
Regular Hours Per Period		80 hours	80 hours
Overtime Wage		$30/hour	$30/hour
Salary	$4 500		
Salary Hours Per Period	160		
Bonus	year-end	year-end	year-end
Vacation	4 weeks with pay	6% retained	6% retained
Number of Pay Periods	12 (monthly)	26 (bi-weekly)	26 (bi-weekly)

Default Deductions

RRSP (before tax)	$200	$50	$50
CSB Plan (after tax)	$200	$50	$50
Gp Insurance (after tax)	$10	$5	$5

Historical Payroll Information for the Pay Period Ending September 30, 2002

Historical Income

Regular		$30 400.00	$30 400.00
Overtime		$600.00	$ 600.00
Salary	$40 500.00		
Vacation Pay Paid			$1 728.00
Gross Earnings	$40 500.00	$31 000.00	$32 728.00
Vacation Pay Owed		$1 728.00	
Advances Paid		$100.00	
EI Insurable Earnings	$39 000.00	$28 500.00	$28 500.00
Net Pay	**$25 653.00**	**$21 589.49**	**$23 217.49**

Print the Employee List and the Employee Summary to check your work.

KINDRED KITCHENWARES
EMPLOYEE INFORMATION CONTINUED

Name:	Tracy Moffat	Terence Inglis	Hendrik Siemens
Historical Deductions:			
RRSP	$1 800.00	$950.00	$950.00
CSB Plan	$1 800.00	$950.00	$950.00
Gp Insurance	$90.00	$95.00	$95.00
Historical Taxes:			
Income Tax	$8 891.10	$5 643.40	$5 643.40
EI Premiums	$936.00	$751.20	$751.20
CPP Contributions	$1 329.90	$1 120.91	$1 120.91

KINDRED KITCHENWARES
EMPLOYEE PROFILES

Tracy Moffat performs a variety of tasks in her combined job as sales assistant and manager. As sales assistant, she works in the store selling to customers and assisting with maintenance duties as needed. As manager, she assists Kindred with the accounting tasks and decision making based on her accounting reports and sales experience. She is single and fully supports her mother who has no independent source of income. At the end of the year, she will receive a bonus proportional to the performance of the business. Moffat earns a monthly salary of $4 500 for about 160 hours of work. In lieu of vacation pay, she takes four weeks vacation each year with pay. Her regular payroll deductions consist of contributions to the Registered Retirement Savings Plan, the Canada Savings Bond plan and a group life insurance plan. She has asked Kindred to deduct an additional $50 per month in income tax because she has other income from which no tax is deducted.

Terence Inglis assists on the sales floor and helps with shipping duties and general maintenance. He is married and supports his wife and two sons. He is paid bi-weekly at the rate of $20 per hour and $30 for each hour of overtime work. Because he has not yet taken his yearly vacation, the full amount of vacation pay calculated at the rate of 6 percent of gross pay is still owing to him. He too will receive a bonus at the end of the year. He pays into his Registered Retirement Savings Plan through payroll deductions and participates in the Canada Savings Bond plan and group insurance plan. Inglis has received pay advances of which he still owes $100.

Hendrik Siemens is responsible for all incoming and outgoing inventory, loading and offloading shipments from vendors and to customers. He also counts inventory and maintains the premises. Siemens is a single parent and claims the spousal equivalent tax deduction for his young daughter. His pay terms are the same as those for Inglis — bi-weekly pay at $20 per hour, $30 for overtime and a year-end bonus. His vacation pay at 6 percent is retained, but since he has recently taken a vacation, his vacation pay is fully paid out. He also participates in the optional payroll plans, and has RRSP, CSB and group insurance premiums deducted from each pay.

14. Enter Inventory Ledger records. You do not need to enter the selling prices in US dollars since these will be based on current exchange rates.

KINDRED KITCHENWARES INVENTORY

Item No.	Description	Min	Selling Price/Unit	Qty	Total Value	Asst	Rev	Exp	Var
Accessories									
A01	Bowls: stainless steel - 20 qt	5	$ 15 each	20	$ 200	1410	4020	5050	5075
A02	Bowls: stainless steel - 10 qt	5	12 each	20	160	1410	4020	5050	5075
A03	Champagne/Wine Bucket	5	60 each	20	800	1410	4020	5050	5075
A04	Instant Dicer: variable cutters	3	250 each	10	1 500	1410	4020	5050	5075
A05	Kitchen Scoops: cast alum - var	5	10 each	20	120	1410	4020	5050	5075
A06	Knife Sharpener: heavy duty	3	500 / unit	10	3 000	1410	4020	5050	5075
A07	Mop Bucket & Wringer	3	60 / set	10	400	1410	4020	5050	5075
A08	Utility Cart	3	180 each	10	1 200	1410	4020	5050	5075
A09	White China: porcelain - dozen	5	50 / set	20	600	1410	4020	5050	5075
					$7 980				
Professional Cookware									
PC01	Fryer Baskets: full set	5	$ 200 / set	20	2 800	1420	4020	5060	5075
PC02	Frying Pans: full set	5	250 / set	20	3 000	1420	4020	5060	5075
PC03	Pasta Cooker: 4 sections	3	200 / unit	15	2 100	1420	4020	5060	5075
PC04	Steam Table Pans: full set	5	80 / set	20	1 000	1420	4020	5060	5075
PC05	Stock Pots: full set	5	250 / set	20	3 000	1420	4020	5060	5075
PC06	18/10 Stn Steel Pots: full set	5	400 / set	20	7 600	1420	4020	5060	5075
					$19 500				
Service Equipment									
SE01	Charbroiler: cast iron CB4	1	$1 700 / unit	3	$ 3 750	1430	4020	5070	5075
SE02	Charbroiler: cast iron CB6	1	2 300 / unit	3	4 950	1430	4020	5070	5075
SE03	Cooler: 22 cu ft 1 door visual	1	1 400 / unit	3	2 700	1430	4020	5070	5075
SE04	Cooler: 38 cu ft 2 door visual	1	1 900 / unit	3	4 200	1430	4020	5070	5075
SE05	Cooker/warmer/chafer 4"	1	140 / unit	3	300	1430	4020	5070	5075
SE06	Cooker/warmer/chafer 2.5"	1	75 / unit	3	150	1430	4020	5070	5075
SE07	Dishwasher: door type DTB	1	6 200 / unit	4	20 000	1430	4020	5070	5075
SE08	Dishwasher: under counter UC4L	1	3 500 / unit	4	11 200	1430	4020	5070	5075
SE09	Fryer: gas fryer - economy EGF15	1	1 000 / unit	5	3 000	1430	4020	5070	5075
SE10	Fryer: gas fryer - stn steel GF15	1	1 500 / unit	5	5 000	1430	4020	5070	5075
SE11	Ice Cube Machine: 250/IC-250	1	2 200 / unit	5	8 000	1430	4020	5070	5075
SE12	Ice Cube Machine: 300/IC-300	1	2 800 / unit	5	10 000	1430	4020	5070	5075
SE13	Impinger: countertop	1	4 800 / unit	3	11 400	1430	4020	5070	5075
SE14	Mega Tops: stn steel MT-12m	1	1 800 / unit	5	6 500	1430	4020	5070	5075
SE15	Mega Tops: stn steel MT-18m	1	2 800 / unit	5	10 000	1430	4020	5070	5075
SE16	Mixer/blender: 20 qt capacity	1	3 300 / unit	4	11 000	1430	4020	5070	5075
SE17	Mixer/blender: 30 qt capacity	1	4 800 / unit	4	15 200	1430	4020	5070	5075
SE18	Oven: convection - 5 racks CO60	1	4 000 / unit	5	15 000	1430	4020	5070	5075
SE19	Oven: pizza	1	1 600 / unit	5	5 500	1430	4020	5070	5075
SE20	Preparation Table: 2 shelves PT2	1	1 400 / unit	5	4 500	1430	4020	5070	5075
SE21	Preparation Table: 6 shelves PT6	1	2 200 / unit	5	8 000	1430	4020	5070	5075
SE22	Range: 36" stainless steel RI6	1	1 800 / unit	4	5 200	1430	4020	5070	5075
SE23	Range: 60" cast iron top RI8	1	4 000 / unit	4	12 000	1430	4020	5070	5075
SE24	Range: tempuraware TW2	1	800 / unit	4	2 000	1430	4020	5070	5075
SE25	Refrigerator: beer - stn steel	1	2 800 / unit	3	6 000	1430	4020	5070	5075
SE26	Refrigerator: 1-door stn steel	1	1 800 / unit	3	3 900	1430	4020	5070	5075
SE27	Refrigerator: 2-door stn steel	1	2 000 / unit	3	4 500	1430	4020	5070	5075
SE28	Toaster: conveyor 3" clearance	1	1 100 / unit	5	3 750	1430	4020	5070	5075
SE29	Toaster: conveyor 1.5" clearance	1	1 200 / unit	5	4 000	1430	4020	5070	5075
SE30	Waffle Maker: 120V model WM-L	1	800 / unit	5	2 500	1430	4020	5070	5075
					$204 200				

Print the Inventory List and the Inventory Synopsis Report to check the accuracy of your work.

15. Make a backup copy of the data files and finish entering the history.

Source Documents

☐ **Advance the Session date to October 14, 2002**

☐ Sales Order #10-1RUS
Dated Oct. 1/02
Shipping Date October 5/02
To The Russell Hotel

1	SE02	Charbroiler: cast iron CB6	$2 300	/ unit
2	SE08	Dishwasher: under counter UC4L	3 500	/ unit
1	SE13	Impinger: countertop	4 800	/ unit
2	SE26	Refrigerator: 1-door stn steel	1 800	/ unit
1	SE27	Refrigerator: 2-door stn steel	2 000	/ unit
		Freight	40	
		GST	7%	
		PST	8%	

Terms: 1/5, n/10.

☐ Cash Receipt #99
Dated Oct. 1/02
From The Russell Hotel, cheque #162 for $4 000 as down payment (deposit #31) to confirm sales order #10-1RUS.

☐ Purchase Order #1
Dated Oct. 1/02
Shipping Date Oct. 7/02
From Koolhouse Refrigeration

2	SE25	Refrigerator: beer - stn steel	$ 4 000.00
2	SE26	Refrigerator: 1-door stn steel	2 600.00
2	SE27	Refrigerator: 2-door stn steel	3 000.00
		Freight	100.00
		GST	679.00
		Total	$10 379.00

Terms: 2/10, n/30.

☐ Cash Receipt #100
Dated Oct. 2/02
From Cornerhouse Cafe, cheque #37 for $14 572.80 in full payment of account, including $147.20 discount. Reference invoice #693.

☐ Cheque Copy #300
Dated Oct. 3/02
To Sheffield Steel Products, $4 300 in full payment of account. Reference invoice #1211.

Unless otherwise stated, use 1070 Bank: Waterloo Trust Chequing account for deposits and payments.

☐ Cash Receipt #101

Dated Oct. 3/02

From Palmleaf Restaurant, cheque #117 for $11 845 in full payment of account. Reference invoice #667.

☐ Cash Receipt #102

Dated Oct. 4/02

From Lotus Gardens, cheque #832 for $12 190 in full payment of account. Reference invoice #679.

☐ Sales Invoice #700

Dated Oct. 5/02

To The Russell Hotel, to fill sales order #10-1RUS

1	SE02	Charbroiler: cast iron CB6	$2 300	/ unit
2	SE08	Dishwasher: under counter UC4L	3 500	/ unit
1	SE13	Impinger: countertop	4 800	/ unit
2	SE26	Refrigerator: 1-door stn steel	1 800	/ unit
1	SE27	Refrigerator: 2-door stn steel	2 000	/ unit
		Freight	40	
		GST	7%	
		PST	8%	

Terms: 1/5, n/10. (Allow customer to exceed credit limit.)

☐ Credit Card Purchase Invoice #KR-6421

Dated Oct. 6/02

From Kitchener Record, $400 plus $28 GST and $32 PST for advertising over the next 20 weeks. Purchase invoice total $460. Total invoice amount paid by VISA.

☐ Credit Card Purchase Invoice #BD-1124

Dated Oct. 6/02

From Business Depot, $200 plus $14 GST and $16 PST for office supplies. Purchase invoice total $230. Total invoice amount paid by VISA. Use Quick Add for the new vendor.

☐ Purchase Invoice #KR-211

Dated Oct. 7/02

From Koolhouse Refrigeration, to fill purchase order #1

2	SE25	Refrigerator: beer - stn steel	$ 4 000.00
2	SE26	Refrigerator: 1-door stn steel	2 600.00
2	SE27	Refrigerator: 2-door stn steel	3 000.00
		Freight	100.00
		GST	679.00
		Total	$10 379.00

Terms: 2/10, n/30.

☐ Memo #50

Dated Oct. 7/02

From Kyra Kindred

Re: Removal of damaged inventory

A utility cart, item A08, was damaged beyond repair. Adjust the inventory to recognize the loss.

☐ Cheque Copy #301

Dated Oct. 8/02

To Restek Equipment, $9 408 in payment of account, including $192 discount taken for early payment. Reference invoice #RE-103.

☐ Cheque Copy #302

Dated Oct. 9/02

To Koolhouse Refrigeration, $9 408 in full payment of account, including $192 discount taken for early payment. Reference invoice #KR-114.

☐ Sales Invoice #701

Dated Oct. 10/02

To Rivers Edge Restaurant

1	SE07	Dishwasher: door type DTB	$6 200	/ unit
1	SE11	Ice Cube Machine: 250/IC-250	2 200	/ unit
2	SE14	Mega Tops: stn steel MT-12m	1 800	/ unit
1	SE18	Oven: convection - 5 racks CO60	4 000	/ unit
1	SE19	Oven: pizza	1 600	/ unit
3	A08	Utility Cart	180	each
4	A09	White China: porcelain - dozen	50	/ set
2	PC06	18/10 Stn Steel Pots: full set	400	/ set
		Freight	40	
		GST	7%	
		PST	8%	

Terms: 1/5, n/10. (Allow customer to exceed credit limit.)

☐ Memo #51 (Credit Card Bill Payment)

Dated Oct. 14/02

Received monthly statement from VISA for $200 for past purchases up to and including October 5 plus $15 for annual renewal fee and $3.50 interest on previous unpaid balance. Cheque #303 for $218.50 submitted in full payment.

☐ Memo #52

Dated Oct. 14/02

From Kyra Kindred, re: Remittances

Refer to September 30 General Ledger balances to make the following remittances. Each remittance should be treated as a separate cash purchase.

☐ Record GST owing for September as a liability owing to the Receiver General of Canada. Issue cheque #304 for $1 400 in full payment.

Refer to the Balance Sheet or General Ledger reports for the balances to be remitted. Use Memo 52A, Memo 52B, etc. as the source codes.

☐ Record the EI, CPP and Income Tax Payable for September as a liability to the Receiver General of Canada. Issue cheque #305 for $2 638.48 in full payment.

☐ Record the PST Payable for September as a liability to the Minister of Finance. Remember to collect the 5% of the PST amount as the sales tax compensation. Issue cheque #306 for $4 560 in full payment.

☐ Record the EHT Payable for September as a liability to the Minister of Finance. Issue cheque #307 for $320.46 in full payment.

☐ Record the RRSP Payable for September as a liability to Laurier Insurance. Issue cheque #308 for $450 in full payment.

☐ Record the CSB Plan Payable for September as a liability to Metropolitan Investors Group. Issue cheque #309 for $450 in full payment.

☐ Record the Group Insurance Payable for September as a liability to Laurier Insurance. Issue cheque #310 for $35 in full payment.

☐ Record the WSIB Payable for September as a liability to the Workplace Safety & Insurance Board. Issue cheque #311 for $1 625.19 in full payment.

☐ Employee Time Summary Sheet #20
Pay Period Ending October 14, 2002
Using the Employee Information, prepare the payroll for the hourly employees.
Terence Inglis worked 80 regular hours and 0 hours overtime. Recover $50 advance.
Hendrik Siemens worked 80 regular hours and 0 hours overtime.
Issue cheques #312 and 313.

☐ Credit Card Sales Invoice #702
Dated Oct. 14/02
To VISA Customers (Sales Summary)

1	SE04	Cooler: 38 cu ft 2 door visual	$1 900 / unit	$ 1 900.00
2	SE15	Mega Tops: stn steel MT-18m	2 800 / unit	5 600.00
2	SE20	Preparation Table: 2 shelves PT2	1 400 / unit	2 800.00
2	SE21	Preparation Table: 6 shelves PT6	2 200 / unit	4 400.00
5	A02	Bowls: stainless steel - 10 qt	12 each	60.00
3	PC03	Pasta Cooker: 4 sections	200 / unit	600.00
		GST	7%	1 075.20
		PST	8%	1 228.80
		Total received and deposited		$17 664.00

Enter VISA Customers and MasterCard Customers as the new customers for the credit card sales. Use Full Add so that you can remove the discount and set the terms as net 1. Leave the remaining ledger fields blank.

☐ Credit Card Sales Invoice #703
Dated Oct. 14/02
To MasterCard Customers (Sales Summary)

2	SE09	Fryer: gas fryer - economy EGF15	$1 000 / unit	$2 000.00
2	A04	Instant Dicer: variable cutters	250 each	500.00
		GST	7%	175.00
		PST	8%	200.00
		Total received and deposited		$2 875.00

☐ **Advance the Session date to October 28, 2002**

☐ Credit Card Purchase Invoice #AS-7881
Dated Oct. 15/02
From All-Service Gas, $60 plus $4.20 GST and $4.80 PST for truck fuel. Purchase
invoice total $69. Total invoice amount paid by VISA. Use Quick Add for the vendor.

☐ Cash Receipt #103
Dated Oct. 15/02
From The Russell Hotel, cheque #183 for $18 697.80 in full payment of account.
Reference invoice #700 and deposit #31.

☐ Cash Receipt #104
Dated Oct. 15/02
From Rivers Edge Restaurant, cheque #47 for $21 833.26 in full payment of account,
including $220.54 discount. Reference invoice #701.

☐ Purchase Order #2
Dated Oct. 15/02
Shipping Date Oct. 21/02
From Sheffield Steel Products

5	A02	Bowls: stainless steel - 10 qt	$	40.00
4	A08	Utility Cart		480.00
4	A09	White China: porcelain - dozen		120.00
3	PC03	Pasta Cooker: 4 sections		420.00
		Freight		20.00
		GST		75.60
		Total		$1 155.60

Terms: net 10 days.

☐ Cheque Copy #314
Dated Oct. 16/02
To Koolhouse Refrigeration, $10 171.42 in full payment of account, including
$207.58 discount taken for early payment. Reference invoice #KR-211.

☐ Cash Purchase Invoice #WH-44212
Dated Oct. 20/02
From Waterloo Hydro, $110 plus $7.70 GST for hydro services. Purchase invoice
total $117.70. Terms: cash on receipt. Issued cheque #315 in payment.

☐ Cash Purchase Invoice #BC-21414
Dated Oct. 20/02
From Bell Canada, $50 plus $3.50 GST and $4 PST for telephone services. Purchase
invoice total $57.50. Terms: cash on receipt. Issued cheque #316 in payment.

☐ Sales Invoice #704

Dated Oct. 20/02

To Chico's Coffee Bar

1	SE07	Dishwasher: door type DTB	$6 200	/ unit
1	SE28	Toaster: conveyor 3" clearance	1 100	/ unit
1	SE30	Waffle Maker: 120V model WM-L	800	/ unit
		Freight	40	
		GST	7%	
		PST	8%	

Terms: 1/5, n/10.

☐ Cash Purchase Invoice #W2002-4

Dated Oct. 21/02

From Waterloo Region Treasurer, $680 in full payment of property tax assessment.
Terms: EOM. Issued cheque #317 in payment.

☐ Purchase Invoice #1509

Dated Oct. 21/02

From Sheffield Steel Products, to fill purchase order #2

5	A02	Bowls: stainless steel - 10 qt	$	40.00
4	A08	Utility Cart		480.00
4	A09	White China: porcelain - dozen		120.00
3	PC03	Pasta Cooker: 4 sections		420.00
		Freight		20.00
		GST		75.60
		Total		$1 155.60

Terms: net 10 days.

☐ Cash Receipt #105

Dated Oct. 24/02

From Chico's Coffee Bar, cheque #83 for $9 264.22 in full payment of account,
including $93.58 discount. Reference invoice #704.

☐ Cheque Copy #318

Dated Oct. 24/02

To Ronson Ranges, $10 000 in full payment of account. Reference invoices #R-321
and #R-330 and cheque #294.

☐ Sales Invoice #705

Dated Oct. 27/02

To Ambassador Convention Centre

1	SE03	Cooler: 22 cu ft 1 door visual	$1 400	/ unit
1	SE12	Ice Cube Machine: 300/IC-300	2 800	/ unit
		Freight	40	
		GST	7%	
		PST	8%	

Terms: 1/5, n/10.

☐ Employee Time Summary Sheet #21

Pay Period Ending October 28, 2002

Using the Employee Information, prepare the payroll for the hourly employees.

Terence Inglis worked 80 regular hours and 2 hours overtime. Recover $50 advance.

Hendrik Siemens worked 80 regular hours and 2 hours overtime.

Issue cheques #319 and 320.

☐ Credit Card Sales Invoice #706

Dated Oct. 28/02

To VISA Customers (Sales Summary)

1	SE10	Fryer: gas fryer - stn steel GF15	$1 500 / unit	$1 500.00
1	SE17	Mixer/blender: 30 qt capacity	4 800 / unit	4 800.00
2	A03	Champagne/Wine Bucket	60 each	120.00
2	A07	Mop Bucket & Wringer	60 / set	120.00
		GST	7%	457.80
		PST	8%	523.20
		Total received and deposited		$7 521.00

☐ Credit Card Sales Invoice #707

Dated Oct. 28/02

To MasterCard Customers (Sales Summary)

2	A06	Knife Sharpener: heavy duty	$500 / unit	$1 000.00
		GST	7%	70.00
		PST	8%	80.00
		Total received and deposited		$1 150.00

Enter the sales credit as a Sales Invoice (Pay Later). Enter the amount as a negative amount (–100) and choose Sales Returns & Allowances as the account. Remember to delete any sales tax amounts and discounts.

☐ Credit Invoice #19

Dated Oct. 28/02

To Ambassador Convention Centre, $100 allowance for scratched cooler unit. Reference invoice #705.

☐ Credit Card Purchase Invoice #AS-9889

Dated Oct. 28/02

From All-Service Gas, $70 plus $4.90 GST and $5.60 PST for truck fuel. Purchase invoice total $80.50. Total invoice amount paid by VISA.

☐ Cheque Copy #321

Dated Oct. 31/02

To Sheffield Steel Products, $1 155.60 in full payment of account. Reference invoice #1509.

Complete the three transactions for October 31 as post-dated entries.

☐ Memo #53

Dated Oct. 31/02

Using the Employee Information prepare the payroll for the salaried employee, Tracy Moffat, the store manager, for the pay period ending October 31, 2002. Issue cheque #322.

Since the Account Reconciliation Journal is not used, enter the bank charges in the General Journal.

☐ Bank Debit Memo #414412

Dated Oct. 31/02

From Waterloo Trust, the following authorized withdrawals were made from the chequing account:

$30 for bank service charges

$2 500 for monthly mortgage payment ($2 250 interest and $250 principal)

$2 400 for monthly loan payment ($300 interest and $2 100 principal)

☐ **Advance the Session date to November 12, 2002**

☐ Cash Receipt #106

Dated Nov. 1/02

From Ambassador Convention Centre, cheque #517 for $4 724.07 in full payment of account, including $48.73 discount. Reference invoice #705 and CR-19. Allow discount on original invoice.

☐ Sales Invoice #708

Dated Nov. 2/02

To Planet Pizza (US customer)

2	SE18	Oven: convection - 5 racks CO60	$4 000 CAD	/ unit	$5336.89 USD
5	SE19	Oven: pizza	1 600 CAD	/ unit	5336.89 USD
2	SE23	Range: 60" cast iron top RI8	4 000 CAD	/ unit	5336.89 USD
		Freight			140.00 USD

Terms: 1/5, n/10. (Allow customer to exceed credit limit.)

The exchange rate is 1.499.

In the sales invoice on-screen, you will see only unit prices and amounts in US dollars. Canadian prices are not displayed.

☐ Purchase Order #3

Dated Nov. 2/02

Shipping Date Nov. 4/02

From Ronson Ranges

2	SE18	Oven: convection - 5 racks CO60	$ 6 000.00
5	SE19	Oven: pizza	6 000.00
		Freight	50.00
		GST	843.50
		Total	$12 893.50

Terms: net 30 days. Remember to change the amount for item SE19.

☐ Memo #54

Dated Nov. 2/02

Change the inventory price of SE19 Oven: pizza to $1 700 to reflect higher cost price of this item.

☐ Cash Purchase Invoice #LI-4432

Dated Nov. 4/02

From Laurier Insurance, $500 for additional insurance on property and inventory. Purchase invoice total $500. Terms: cash on receipt. Issued cheque #323 in payment.

☐ Purchase Invoice #R-398

Dated Nov. 4/02

From Ronson Ranges, to fill purchase order #3

SE18 Oven: convection - 5 racks CO60	$ 6 000.00
SE19 Oven: pizza	6 000.00
Freight	50.00
GST	843.50
Total	$12 893.50

Terms: net 30 days.

☐ Employee Time Summary Sheet #22

Pay Period Ending November 11, 2002

Using the Employee Information, prepare the payroll for the hourly employees.

Terence Inglis worked 80 regular hours and 0 hours overtime.

Inglis received an additional $250 as an advance. $50 will be recovered from each of the next five paycheques.

Hendrik Siemens worked 80 regular hours and 0 hours overtime.

Issue cheques #324 and 325.

☐ Sales Order #11-1AMB

Dated Nov. 12/02

Shipping Date Nov. 17/02

To Ambassador Convention Centre

2	SE14	Mega Tops: stn steel MT-12m	$1 800	/ unit
2	SE15	Mega Tops: stn steel MT-18m	2 800	/ unit
2	SE25	Refrigerator: beer - stn steel	2 800	/ unit
1	SE27	Refrigerator: 2-door stn steel	2 000	/ unit
5	A03	Champagne/Wine Bucket	60	each
5	PC03	Pasta Cooker: 4 sections	200	/ unit
		Freight	40	
		GST	7%	
		PST	8%	

Terms: 1/5, n/10.

☐ Cash Receipt #107

Dated Nov. 12/02

From Ambassador Convention Centre, cheque #576 for $3 500 as down payment (deposit #32) to confirm sales order #11-1AMB.

☐ Cash Receipt #108

Dated Nov. 12/02

From Planet Pizza, cheque #141 for $16 150.67 USD in full payment of account. Reference invoice #708. The exchange rate is 1.511. Deposit to 1100 Bank: USD Chequing account.

☐ **Advance the Session date to November 30, 2002**

☐ Memo #55 (Credit Card Bill Payment)

Dated Nov. 14/02

Received monthly statement from VISA for $839.50 for past purchases up to and including November 5. Cheque #326 for $839.50 submitted in full payment.

☐ Credit Card Purchase Invoice #AS-10362

Dated Nov. 14/02

From All-Service Gas, $170 for truck repairs and $60 for fuel plus $16.10 GST and $18.40 PST. Purchase invoice total $264.50. Total invoice amount paid by VISA.

☐ Credit Card Sales Invoice #709

Dated Nov. 14/02

To VISA Customers (Sales Summary)

1	SE01	Charbroiler: cast iron CB4	$1 700 / unit	$1 700.00
1	SE22	Range: 36″ stainless steel RI6	1 800 / unit	1 800.00
5	A01	Bowls: stainless steel - 20 qt	15 each	75.00
5	A05	Kitchen Scoops: cast alum - var	10 each	50.00
5	PC05	Stock Pots: full set	250 / set	1 250.00
		GST	7%	341.25
		PST	8%	390.00
		Total received and deposited		$5 606.25

☐ Credit Card Sales Invoice #710

Dated Nov. 14/02

To MasterCard Customers (Sales Summary)

1	SE24	Range: tempuraware TW2	$800 / unit	$ 800.00
5	PC01	Fryer Baskets: full set	200 / set	1 000.00
		GST	7%	126.00
		PST	8%	144.00
		Total received and deposited		$2 070.00

☐ Memo #56

Dated Nov. 14/02

From Kyra Kindred, re: Remittances

Refer to October 31 General Ledger balances to make the following remittances. Each remittance should be treated as a separate cash purchase.

☐ Record GST owing for October as a liability owing to the Receiver General of Canada. Issue cheque #327 in payment.

☐ Record the EI, CPP and Income Tax Payable for October as a liability to the Receiver General of Canada. Issue cheque #328 in payment.

☐ Record the PST Payable for October as a liability to the Minister of Finance. Remember to collect 5% of the PST amount as the sales tax compensation. Issue cheque #329 in payment.

☐ Record the RRSP Payable for October as a liability to Laurier Insurance. Issue cheque #330 in payment.

☐ Record the CSB Plan Payable for October as a liability to Metropolitan Investors Group. Issue cheque #331 in payment.

☐ Record the Group Insurance Payable for October as a liability to Laurier Insurance. Issue cheque #332 in payment.

☐ Memo #57
Dated Nov. 15/02
Add the following new inventory item:
Item: PC07 18/10 Stn Steel Cutlery Set
Selling price: $200 / set
Minimum qty: 2
Accounts: Asset 1420   Revenue 4020   Expense 5060   Variance 5075

☐ Purchase Invoice #CP-1491
Dated Nov. 15/02
From Cuisine Pro Inc.

20	PC07	18/10 Stn Steel Cutlery Sets	$3 000.00
		Freight	15.00
		GST	211.05
		Total	$3 226.05

Terms: net 30 days.

☐ Sales Invoice #711
Dated Nov. 17/02
To Ambassador Convention Centre, to fill sales order #11-1AMB

2	SE14	Mega Tops: stn steel MT-12m	$1 800 / unit
2	SE15	Mega Tops: stn steel MT-18m	2 800 / unit
2	SE25	Refrigerator: beer - stn steel	2 800 / unit
1	SE27	Refrigerator: 2-door stn steel	2 000 / unit
5	A03	Champagne/Wine Bucket	60 each
5	PC03	Pasta Cooker: 4 sections	200 / unit
		Freight	40
		GST	7%
		PST	8%

Terms: 1/5, n/10. (Allow customer to exceed credit limit.)

☐ Cash Purchase Invoice #WH-49143
Dated Nov. 20/02
From Waterloo Hydro, $100 plus $7 GST for hydro services. Purchase invoice total $107. Terms: cash on receipt. Issued cheque #333 in payment.

☐ Cash Purchase Invoice #BC-28123
Dated Nov. 20/02
From Bell Canada, $50 plus $3.50 GST and $4 PST for telephone services. Purchase invoice total $57.50. Terms: cash on receipt. Issued cheque #334 in payment.

☐ Memo #58
Dated Nov. 21/02
Add Amex as a new credit card accepted from customers with a transaction fee of 3%. Link the same accounts as used by the other credit cards.

☐ Credit Card Purchase Invoice #X11471

Dated Nov. 21/02

From Xpress Delivery Service, $100 plus $7 GST for delivery of equipment. Purchase invoice total $107. Terms: payment on receipt. Total invoice amount paid by VISA. Use Quick Add for the new vendor.

☐ Cash Receipt #109

Dated Nov. 22/02

From Ambassador Convention Centre, cheque #629 for $17 149.22 in full payment of account, including $208.58 discount. Reference invoice #711 and deposit #32.

☐ Employee Time Summary Sheet #23

Pay Period Ending November 25, 2002

Using the Employee Information, prepare the payroll for the hourly employees.

Terence Inglis worked 80 regular hours and 2 hours overtime.

Recover $50 advance from Inglis.

Hendrik Siemens worked 80 regular hours and 2 hours overtime.

Issue cheques #335 and 336.

☐ Credit Card Sales Invoice #712

Dated Nov. 28/02

To VISA Customers (Sales Summary)

2	SE11	Ice Cube Machine: 250/IC-250	$2 200 / unit	$ 4 400.00
2	SE12	Ice Cube Machine: 300/IC-300	2 800 / unit	5 600.00
2	SE13	Impinger: countertop	4 800 / unit	9 600.00
2	SE16	Mixer/blender: 20 qt capacity	3 300 / unit	6 600.00
		GST	7%	1 834.00
		PST	8%	2 096.00
		Total received and deposited		$30 130.00

☐ Credit Card Sales Invoice #713

Dated Nov. 28/02

To MasterCard Customers (Sales Summary)

2	SE29	Toaster: conveyor 1.5" clearance	$1 200 / unit	$2 400.00
		GST	7%	168.00
		PST	8%	192.00
		Total received and deposited		$2 760.00

☐ Credit Card Purchase Invoice #AS-11982

Dated Nov. 30/02

From All-Service Gas, $50 plus $3.50 GST and $4 PST for truck fuel. Purchase invoice total $57.50. Total invoice amount paid by VISA.

☐ Memo #59

Dated Nov. 30/02

Using the Employee Information prepare the payroll for the salaried employee, Tracy Moffat, the store manager, for the pay period ending November 30, 2002. Issue cheque #337.

☐ Bank Debit Memo #521432

Dated Nov. 30/02

From Waterloo Trust, the following authorized withdrawals were made from the chequing account:

$32 for bank service charges

$2 500 for monthly mortgage payment ($2 225 interest and $275 principal)

$2 400 for monthly loan payment ($275 interest and $2 125 principal)

☐ **Advance the Session date to December 14, 2002**

☐ Cheque Copy #338

Dated Dec. 1/02

To Ronson Ranges, $12 893.50 in full payment of account. Reference invoice #R-398.

☐ Purchase Order #4

Dated Dec. 1/02

Shipping Date Dec. 5/02

From Restek Equipment Mfg.

3	SE13	Impinger: countertop	$11 400.00
4	SE14	Mega Tops: stn steel MT-12m	5 200.00
5	SE15	Mega Tops: stn steel MT-18m	10 000.00
		Freight	80.00
		GST	1 867.60
		Total	$28 547.60

Terms: 2/10, n/30.

☐ Purchase Order #5

Dated Dec. 1/02

Shipping Date Dec. 14/02

From Koolhouse Refrigeration

2	SE11	Ice Cube Machine: 250/IC-250	$3 200.00
2	SE12	Ice Cube Machine: 300/IC-300	4 000.00
		Freight	100.00
		GST	511.00
		Total	$7 811.00

Terms: 2/10, n/30.

☐ Purchase Invoice #RE-1311

Dated Dec. 5/02

From Restek Equipment Mfg., to fill purchase order #4

3	SE13	Impinger: countertop	$11 400.00
4	SE14	Mega Tops: stn steel MT-12m	5 200.00
5	SE15	Mega Tops: stn steel MT-18m	10 000.00
		Freight	80.00
		GST	1 867.60
		Total	$28 547.60

Terms: 2/10, n/30.

Sales Invoice #714

Dated Dec. 6/02

To Kaiser King Restaurant

1	SE01	Charbroiler: cast iron CB4	$1 700	/ unit
1	SE05	Cooker/warmer/chafer 4"	140	/ unit
1	SE06	Cooker/warmer/chafer 2.5"	75	/ unit
5	PC02	Frying Pans: full set	250	/ set
		Freight	40	
		GST	7%	
		PST	8%	

Terms: 1/5, n/10.

Employee Time Summary Sheet #24

Pay Period Ending December 9, 2002

Using the Employee Information, prepare the payroll for the hourly employees.

Terence Inglis worked 80 regular hours and 2 hours overtime.

Recover $50 advance from Inglis.

Hendrik Siemens worked 80 regular hours and 2 hours overtime.

Issue cheques #339 and 340.

Cheque Copy #341

Dated Dec. 12/02

To Cuisine Pro Inc., $3 226.05 in full payment of account. Reference invoice #CP-1491.

Cash Purchase Invoice #4345

Dated Dec. 14/02

From Ontime Cleaning Co., $200 plus $14 GST for maintenance of premises. Purchase invoice total $214. Terms: cash on receipt. Issued cheque #342 in payment. Use Quick Add for the new vendor.

Sales Order #12-1PLA

Dated Dec. 14/02

Shipping Date Dec. 16/02

To Planet Pizza

1	SE17	Mixer/blender: 30 qt capacity	$4 800 CAD	/ unit	$3 168.32 USD
1	SE18	Oven: convection - 5 racks CO60	4 000 CAD	/ unit	2 640.26 USD
2	SE19	Oven: pizza	1 700 CAD	/ unit	2 244.22 USD
1	SE26	Refrigerator: 1-door stn steel	1 800 CAD	/ unit	1 188.12 USD
		Freight			140.00 USD

Terms: 1/5, n/10. (Allow customer to exceed credit limit.)

The exchange rate is 1.515.

No deposit was requested from Planet Pizza because they are regular customers and have always settled their account on time.

Memo #60

Dated Dec. 14/02

From Kyra Kindred, re: Remittances

Refer to November General Ledger balances to make the following remittances.

Each remittance should be treated as a separate cash purchase.

☐ Record GST owing for November as a liability owing to the Receiver General of Canada. Issue cheque #343 in payment.

☐ Record the EI, CPP and Income Tax Payable for November as a liability to the Receiver General of Canada. Issue cheque #344 in payment.

☐ Record the PST Payable for November as a liability to the Minister of Finance. Remember to collect 5% of the PST amount as the sales tax compensation. Issue cheque #345 in payment.

☐ Record the RRSP Payable for November as a liability to Laurier Insurance. Issue cheque #346 in payment.

☐ Record the CSB Plan Payable for November as a liability to Metropolitan Investors Group. Issue cheque #347 in payment.

☐ Record the Group Insurance Payable for November as a liability to Laurier Insurance. Issue cheque #348 in payment.

☐ Credit Card Sales Invoice #715
Dated Dec. 14/02
To VISA Customers (Sales Summary)

1	SE11	Ice Cube Machine: 250/IC-250	$2 200 / unit	$ 2 200.00
1	SE12	Ice Cube Machine: 300/IC-300	2 800 / unit	2 800.00
1	SE13	Impinger: countertop	4 800 / unit	4 800.00
2	SE15	Mega Tops: stn steel MT-18m	2 800 / unit	5 600.00
2	SE19	Oven: pizza	1 700 / unit	3 400.00
5	A01	Bowls: stainless steel - 20 qt	15 each	75.00
5	PC04	Steam Table Pans: full set	80 / set	400.00
		GST	7%	1 349.25
		PST	8%	1 542.00
		Total received and deposited		$22 166.25

☐ Credit Card Sales Invoice #716
Dated Dec. 14/02
To MasterCard Customers (Sales Summary)

2	SE14	Mega Tops: stn steel MT-12m	$1 800 / unit	$3 600.00
1	SE25	Refrigerator: beer - stn steel	2 800 / unit	2 800.00
		GST	7%	448.00
		PST	8%	512.00
		Total received and deposited		$7 360.00

☐ Memo #61 (Credit Card Bill Payment)
Dated Dec. 14/02
Received monthly statement from VISA for $429 for past purchases up to and including December 5. Cheque #349 for $429 submitted in full payment.

☐ Cash Receipt #110
Dated Dec. 14/02
From Kaiser King Restaurant, cheque #78 for $3 682.55 in full payment of account. Reference invoice #714.

☐ **Advance the Session date to December 28, 2002**

☐ Cheque Copy #350

Dated Dec. 15/02

To Restek Equipment Mfg., $27 976.65 in full payment of account, including $570.95 discount taken for early payment. Reference invoice #RE-1311.

☐ Memo #62

Dated Dec. 15/02

Transfer $50 000 from the Credit Card bank account to the Waterloo Trust Chequing account immediately to cover cheque written to Restek Equipment Mfg.

☐ Purchase Invoice #KR-309

Dated Dec.15/02

From Koolhouse Refrigeration, to fill purchase order #5

2	SE11	Ice Cube Machine: 250/IC-250	$3 200.00
2	SE12	Ice Cube Machine: 300/IC-300	4 000.00
		Freight	100.00
		GST	511.00
		Total	$7 811.00

Terms: 2/10, n/30.

☐ Memo #63

Dated Dec. 16/02

From Kyra Kindred

Re: Income Tax for Business

Issue cheque #351 for $6 000 to pay quarterly business income tax installment. Make cheque payable to the Receiver General of Canada.

☐ Sales Invoice #717

Dated Dec. 17/02

To Planet Pizza, to fill sales order #12-1PLA

1	SE17	Mixer/blender: 30 qt capacity	$4 800 CAD / unit	$3 189.37 USD
1	SE18	Oven: convection - 5 racks CO60	4 000 CAD / unit	2 657.81 USD
2	SE19	Oven: pizza	1 700 CAD / unit	2 259.14 USD
1	SE26	Refrigerator: 1-door stn steel	1 800 CAD / unit	1 196.01 USD
		Freight		140.00 USD

Terms: 1/5, n/10.

The exchange rate is 1.505. Recalculate all inventory prices.

☐ Cheque Copy #352

Dated Dec. 19/02

To Koolhouse Refrigeration, $7 654.78 in full payment of account, including $156.22 discount taken for early payment. Reference invoice #KR-309.

☐ Purchase Order #6
Dated Dec. 19/02
Shipping Date Dec. 23/02
From Northland Gas Equipment

1	SE01	Charbroiler: cast iron CB4	$1 250.00
1	SE02	Charbroiler: cast iron CB6	1 650.00
1	SE22	Range: 36" stainless steel RI6	1 300.00
1	SE23	Range: 60" cast iron top RI8	3 000.00
1	SE24	Range: tempuraware TW2	500.00
		Freight	70.00
		GST	543.90
		Total	$8 313.90

Terms: net 30 days.

☐ Cash Sales Invoice #718
Dated Dec. 20/02
To Slyz Cafe

2	A09	White China: porcelain - dozen @ $50 / set	$100
		GST	7%
		PST	8%

Received cheque #11 for $115 in full payment. Use Quick Add for the new customer.

☐ Cash Purchase Invoice #WH-51012
Dated Dec. 20/02
From Waterloo Hydro, $90 plus $6.30 GST for hydro services. Purchase invoice total $96.30. Terms: cash on receipt. Issued cheque #353 in payment.

☐ Cash Purchase Invoice #BC-34121
Dated Dec. 20/02
From Bell Canada, $50 plus $3.50 GST and $4 PST for telephone services. Purchase invoice total $57.50. Terms: cash on receipt. Issued cheque #354 in payment.

☐ Cash Receipt #111
Dated Dec. 20/02
From Planet Pizza, cheque #192 for $9 347.91 USD in full payment of account, including $94.42 discount. Reference invoice #717. The exchange rate is 1.500. Deposit to 1100 Bank: USD Chequing account.

☐ Memo #64
Dated Dec. 23/02
From Kyra Kindred
Issue Vacation Pay cheques to Inglis and Siemens for all vacation amounts owing to date. Issue cheques #355 and 356. Withhold 10% income tax and delete other deductions.

☐ Bank Debit Memo #591321
Dated Dec. 21/02
From Waterloo Trust, $115 for NSF cheque from Slyz Cafe, plus service charge of $20 to handle the NSF cheque. Reference invoice #718 and cheque #11.
Terms: net 1.
Create a new Group account, 4290 Other Revenue, for bank handling charges passed on to the customer. Create a new sales invoice to charge the full amount of $135 ($115 + $20) to Slyz Cafe. Use the Bank Debit Memo number as the Source.

☐ Memo #65
Dated Dec. 23/02
From Kyra Kindred
Re: Write off of account
Write off the Slyz Cafe account in the Sales Journal because attempts to contact the cafe owner have been unsuccessful. The GST adjustment amount is $7 (the GST portion of the unpaid debt). Delete the payment terms.

To write off the Slyz Cafe account, enter –128 as the amount that is uncollectable (account #1220) and –7 as the GST adjustment amount (account #2650). This is the GST on the original sale and it must be debited to reduce the GST owing.

Remember to retain the vacation pay for the hourly employees.

☐ Employee Time Summary Sheet #24
Pay Period Ending December 23, 2002
Using the Employee Information, prepare the payroll for the hourly employees.
Terence Inglis worked 80 regular hours and 2 hours overtime.
Recover $50 advance from Inglis.
Hendrik Siemens worked 80 regular hours and 2 hours overtime.
Issue cheques #357 and 358.

☐ Purchase Invoice #AS-13004
Dated Dec. 23/02
From All-Service Gas, $80 plus $5.60 GST and $6.40 PST for truck fuel. Purchase invoice total $92. Terms: net 30 days.

☐ Purchase Invoice #NG-112
Dated Dec. 24/02
From Northland Gas Equipment, to fill purchase order #6

1	SE01	Charbroiler: cast iron CB4	$1 250.00
1	SE02	Charbroiler: cast iron CB6	1 650.00
1	SE22	Range: 36" stainless steel RI6	1 300.00
1	SE23	Range: 60" cast iron top RI8	3 000.00
1	SE24	Range: tempuraware TW2	500.00
		Freight	70.00
		GST	543.90
		Total	$8 313.90

Terms: net 30 days.

Delete the regular pay amounts. Enter the bonus amount in the Bonus field and press `tab`. After the tax amounts appear, click the Enter taxes manually tool. Then edit the income tax amount so that it is 10% of the bonus amount. Delete the optional deductions and vacation pay amounts.

☐ Memo #66

Dated Dec. 24/02

From Kyra Kindred

Re: Payroll bonuses

Issue bonus cheques to all employees for the following amounts. The minimum income tax of 10% of the bonus amount should be withheld. Delete the optional deductions and vacation pay.

Moffat	$800
Inglis	$600
Siemens	$600

Issue cheques #359, 360 and 361.

☐ Credit Card Sales Invoice #719

Dated Dec. 28/02

To MasterCard Customers (Sales Summary)

1	SE28	Toaster: conveyor 3" clearance	$1 100 / unit	$1 100.00
5	PC06	18/10 Stn Steel Pots: full set	400 / set	2 000.00
		GST	7%	217.00
		PST	8%	248.00
		Total received and deposited		$3 565.00

☐ Credit Card Sales Invoice #720

Dated Dec. 28/02

To VISA Customers (Sales Summary)

1	SE02	Charbroiler: cast iron CB6	$2 300 / unit	$ 2 300.00
1	SE07	Dishwasher: door type DTB	6 200 / unit	6 200.00
1	SE08	Dishwasher: under counter UC4L	3 500 / unit	3 500.00
4	A04	Instant Dicer: variable cutters	250 each	1 000.00
3	A06	Knife Sharpener: heavy duty	500 / unit	1 500.00
5	PC02	Frying Pans: full set	250 / set	1 250.00
5	PC07	18/10 Stn Steel Cutlery Sets	200 / set	1 000.00
		GST	7%	1 172.50
		PST	8%	1 340.00
		Total received and deposited		$19 262.50

☐ **Advance the Session date to December 31, 2002**

☐ Memo #67

Dated Dec. 31/02

Using the Employee Information prepare the payroll for the salaried employee, Tracy Moffat, the store manager, for the pay period ending December 31, 2002. Issue cheque #362.

☐ Bank Credit Memo #114321

Dated Dec. 31/02

From Waterloo Trust, $284 was deposited to the chequing bank account and $180 to the savings bank account as the semi-annual interest paid. Remember that the Interest Receivable balance is $370.

Bank Debit Memo #634721

Dated Dec. 31/02

From Waterloo Trust, the following authorized withdrawals were made from the chequing account:

$50 for bank service charges including charge for NSF cheque

$2 500 for monthly mortgage payment ($2 200 interest and $300 principal)

$2 400 for monthly loan payment ($250 interest and $2 150 principal)

Memo #68

Dated Dec. 31/02

From Kyra Kindred

Re: Depreciation and quarter-end adjustments

Prepare the adjusting depreciation entry to record the following depreciation amounts for the fiscal quarter ended December 31, 2002:

Cash Registers	$300
Computers & Peripherals	$500
Equipment	$250
Retail Premises	$3 000
Vehicles	$1 000

The amount of Office Supplies on hand is $150. Record $266 as the amount of supplies used.

Write off $800 of Prepaid Insurance for Insurance Expense.

Write off $520 of Prepaid Advertising for Advertising and Promotion expenses.

Payroll liabilities accrued at the end of December:

Inglis	$800
Siemens	$800

Prepare an adjusting entry to recognize $1 600 as accrued wages.

Create a new account: 2240 Accrued Payroll (G)

Increase the Allowance for Doubtful Accounts by $300 for the following year (Uncollectable Accounts Expense).

Memo #69

Date Dec. 31/02

Access the Web site for The Russell Hotel. Prepare a competitive sales quote for completely equipping the proposed new hotel kitchen. E-mail the sales quote.

Further Analysis

1. Evaluate as many aspects of the company as you can from the data in the simulation. Print reports that support your evaluations.
2. Why is there a net loss in one of the three months?
3. Set up a budget for the quarter based on the Income Statement amounts for the previous quarter so that you can compare the performance for the two quarters.
4. Recommend policy changes to improve overall performance.

CHAPTER 20

PRACTICE SIMULATION

ANDERSON FARM

Objectives

- **create new company files**
- **customize settings and linked accounts**
- **create a numbering system for General Ledger accounts**
- **enter historical account balances**
- **create vendor, customer and employee records**
- **enter historical invoices for vendors and customers**
- **enter historical payroll information**
- **finish entering history**
- **complete transactions from realistic source documents**
- **print reports and graphs to monitor performance**

Introduction

In this chapter, you will set up complete company files for a business from scratch, including choosing an account numbering system and structure. The farm uses four modules of the Simply Accounting program: General, Payables, Receivables and Payroll. After setting up the company accounts and records, and finishing the history for the ledgers, you will enter the transactions for three months from realistic source documents.

There is no Data Disk file for Anderson Farm. You must create your own company files for this simulation.

Anderson Farm

Company Profile and Information

Anderson Farm is family owned and operated. The farm, outside of Calgary, Alberta, has been in the family for several generations. Currently, Chris Anderson owns the business and runs the farm with the assistance of his wife, Anna, and their three children. The demands of the children's school programs and of Anna's job, teaching kindergarten every morning at a nearby primary school, allow them to help with the farm work only part-time. Anderson, therefore, hires two full-time assistants. This year, his employees are the tenants who rent houses located on the farm property.

The farm is actually a multi-faceted business. Pig farming forms the core of the farm's operations. Pigs are bred until they reach a certain weight and then sold to another farm to be raised to maturity. The sows used for breeding are artificially inseminated and kept for a few breeding cycles before being sold. Thus, income from pig farming comes from the sale of the piglets and from the sale of mature pigs. In addition to the pigs and the rental properties mentioned above, the farm has a large acreage planted with both grain crops and fresh garden vegetables. The sowing, weeding and harvesting of these crops are carried out from late spring to early fall. Income from these crops comes from the sale of vegetables and grains from midsummer to fall. A final source of farm revenue comes from the large stands of lumber that are cut for timber and then replanted. Occasionally, government grants are available to farmers to encourage reforestation.

The variety of income sources goes hand-in-hand with the variety of customers and vendors. The tax rules also vary for the different parts of the business. There is no PST in Alberta, but the GST applies at the rate of 7 percent on taxable goods and services. For the products and services Anderson supplies, the GST rate varies. Food and animal products are zero-rated for GST, rent from residential units is GST exempt and lumber is taxed at 7 percent. Because the combined farm income from zero-rated and taxable products exceeds $30 000 per year, Anderson is required to register his business for GST. This enables him to claim input tax credits for any GST he pays on business expenditures. Because GST is charged on a small share of his products, Anderson is frequently eligible for GST refunds.

On June 1, Anderson decided to convert his manual accounting records to Simply Accounting. He has the following information to set up the files and complete the conversion:

- Company Information
- Chart of Accounts
- Trial Balance as at May 31, 2002
- Vendor Records
- Customer Records
- Employee Records

COMPANY INFORMATION

Business Name: Anderson Farm
Address: RR #3 Calgary, Alberta T3N 2P4
Phone: (403) 284-9123
Fax: (403) 284-8120
Business Number: 52752 5527
Fiscal Start: January 1, 2002
Fiscal End: December 31, 2002
Earliest Transaction Date: June 1, 2002

Forms Settings (next number):   purchase orders 12
      sales invoice 100

ANDERSON FARM
CHART OF ACCOUNTS

Assets
Cash in Bank
Accounts Receivable
Advances Receivable
Farm Supplies
Fertilizers & Chemicals
Computer System
Harvester
Tractor
Trucks
Barns
Rental Property
Farmhouse
Land

Liabilities
Bank Loan
Accounts Payable
Vacation Payable
EI Payable
CPP Payable
Income Tax Payable
Medical Payable
WCB Payable
GST Charged on Sales
GST Paid on Purchases
Mortgage Payable

Equity
C. Anderson, Capital
C. Anderson, Drawings
Current Earnings

Revenue
Revenue from Rent
Revenue from Harvests
Revenue from Livestock
Revenue from Lumber
Other Revenue
Sales Returns & Allowances

Expense
Bank Charges
General Expense
Fuel Expense
Purchase Discounts
Interest Expense
Hydro Expense
Maintenance & Repairs
Telephone Expense
Wages
EI Expense
CPP Expense
WCB Expense

BANK INFORMATION

Account: Cash in Bank
Class Option: Bank
Bank Account Type: Chequing
Next Cheque Number: 101

ANDERSON FARM
TRIAL BALANCE

As at May 31, 2002

Cash in Bank	$ 50 000.00	
Accounts Receivable	1 500.00	
Advances Receivable	400.00	
Farm Supplies	2 800.00	
Fertilizers & Chemicals	1 800.00	
Computer System	5 000.00	
Harvester	150 000.00	
Tractor	50 000.00	
Trucks	100 000.00	
Barns	150 000.00	
Rental Property	300 000.00	
Farmhouse	200 000.00	
Land	200 000.00	
Bank Loan		$ 100 000.00
Accounts Payable		1 000.00
Vacation Payable		0.00
EI Payable		367.20
CPP Payable		399.76
Income Tax Payable		1125.95
Medical Payable		68.00
WCB Payable		306.76
GST Charged on Sales		0.00
GST Paid on Purchases	318.00	
Mortgage Payable		200 000.00
C. Anderson, Capital		886 143.68
C. Anderson, Drawings	5 000.00	
Revenue from Rent		22 500.00
Revenue from Harvests		0.00
Revenue from Livestock		32 500.00
Revenue from Lumber		0.00
Other Revenue		0.00
Sales Returns & Allowances		0.00
Bank Charges	50.00	
General Expense	2 000.00	
Fuel Expense	1 000.00	
Purchase Discounts	0.00	
Interest Expense	15 000.00	
Hydro Expense	800.00	
Maintenance & Repairs	1 500.00	
Telephone Expense	300.00	
Wages	6 222.40	
EI Expense	214.31	
CPP Expense	199.88	
WCB Expense	306.76	
	$1 244 411.35	$1 244 411.35

ANDERSON FARM
VENDOR ACCOUNTS

Vendors with Historical Transactions

Vendor (Contact)	Address	Phone, Fax	E-mail, Web, Terms
Leanne's Service Centre (Leanne)	3 Service Road Calgary AB T3N 2G3	Tel: (403) 788-0102 Fax: (403) 788-9000	E-mail: Leanne@hotmail.com Web: www.i-fix-cars.com net 5
Tenderbuds Nursery (Bud Shutes)	2 Cultivate Blvd. Lethbridge, AB T7B 2N6	Tel: (403) 821-5544 Fax: (403) 822-9099	E-mail: BShutes@tenderbuds.com Web: www.from-seedlings.com 2/10, n/15

Vendor	Date	Invoice/Cheque #	Terms	Amount
Leanne's Service Centre	May 31/02	#347	net 5	$400.00
Tenderbuds Nursery	May 18/02	#5873	2/10, n/15	$600.00

ADDITIONAL VENDORS

Vendor (Contact)	Address	Phone, Fax	E-mail, Web, Terms
Alberta Health Insurance (Betz Weller)	88 Hospital Rd. Calgary, AB T4P 4B9	Tel: (403) 886-9552 Fax: (403) 886-9890	E-mail: bw@healthways.com *Web: www.health.gov.ab.ca net 1
Alberta Hydro (Sol R. Rayze)	43 Power Road Calgary, AB T3N 2L6	Tel: (403) 746-2122 Fax: (403) 746-2000	E-mail: solrayze@abhydro.com *Web: www.enmax.com net 5
Alberta Oil & Gas (Ben Zene)	444 Gasoline Alley Calgary, AB T4P 2P3	Tel: (403) 458-5321 Fax: (403) 458-7522	E-mail: bzene@ao&g.com Web: www.tarsands.oil.com net 5
Alberta Telephone (Ima Tokker)	6 Calling Ave. Calgary, AB T4G 3N3	Tel: (403) 633-0329 Fax: (403) 633-0300	E-mail: ltokker@sympatico.ca *Web: www.bell.ca net 1
Foothills Embryology Inc. (Barbara Groen)	39 Culture Rd. Calgary, AB T4C 6N3	Tel: (403) 613-4271 Fax: (403) 613-4272	E-mail: bg@foothills.com Web: www.sperms.anon.com COD – net 1
Let It Rain Roofers (Rufus Leakie)	99 Fixit Avenue Calgary, AB T3N 2G4	Tel: (403) 456-6754 Fax: (403) 456-6542	E-mail: leakie@roofscape.com Web: www.staydry.com net 1
North West Trailers (Tran S. Ports)	121 Park Lane Calgary, AB T4N 2P4	Tel: (403) 924-8444 Fax: (403) 924-7800	E-mail: NWT@istar.com Web: www.flat.bed.trucks.com net 30
Prairie Fertilizers (Colme Poste)	RR #2 Red Deer, AB T4P 7T2	Tel: (403) 776-8221 Fax: (403) 776-8543	E-mail: cp@cowsends.com Web: www.grow.greener.com net 30

ANDERSON FARM
VENDOR ACCOUNTS CONT'D

Vendor (Contact)	Address	Phone, Fax	E-mail, Web, Terms
Receiver General of Canada	Summerside Tax Centre Summerside, PE C1N 6L2	Tel: (902) 821-8186	*Web: www.ccra-adrc.gc.ca net 1
WCB Alberta (Whip Lash)	55 Luckless Rd. Calgary, AB T3C 7G5	Tel: (403) 488-9966 Fax: (403) 487-9236	E-mail: wl@wcb.alberta.ca *Web: www.wcb.ab.ca net 1

ANDERSON FARM
CUSTOMER ACCOUNTS

Customer with Historical Transactions

Customer (Contact)	Address	Phone, Fax, Terms	E-mail, Web (Credit Limit)
Corral Farms (Ada Corral)	RR #4 Calgary, AB T8B 2N2	Tel: (403) 653-6532 Fax: (403) 653-6400 net 10	E-mail: ACorral@farmscape.com ($5 000)

Historical Transaction

Customer	Date	Invoice/Cheque #	Terms	Amount
Corral Farms	May 31/02	AF-99	net 10	$1 500.00

ADDITIONAL CUSTOMERS

Customer (Contact)	Address	Phone, Fax Terms	E-mail, Web (Credit Limit)
Paradise Preserves (M. Petras)	42 Pickle Avenue Calgary, AB T3N 4G3	Tel: (403) 923-2345 Fax: (403) 923-2466 net 10	E-mail: Petras@keepscape.com Web: www.keep-it-longer.com ($10 000)
Prairieland Meat Packers (Frieda Collins)	33 Roast Avenue Calgary, AB T4T 2N8	Tel: (403) 788-8110 Fax: (403) 788-4129 net 10	E-mail: fc@PLMP.ca Web: www.for-all-occasions.com ($15 000)
Rocky Mountain Shakes & Shingles (Larry McMaster)	43 Shaky Ave. Calgary, AB T3C 2N2	Tel: (403) 566-9112 Fax: (403) 566-9000 net 10	E-mail: larry@rocky.mtss.ca Web: www.trees-to-pieces.com ($15 000)
Western Co-operative (Will Cooper)	109 Friendship Way Calgary, AB T3N 2G5	Tel: (403) 288-9752 Fax: (403) 288-9879 net 10	E-mail: wc@westerncoop.ca Web: www.working.together.com ($50 000)

ANDERSON FARM
EMPLOYEE INFORMATION

Personal Information

Employee Name	Tomas Nygard	Melissa Ryder
Position	Farm Assistant	Farm Assistant
Address	RR #3	RR #3
	Calgary, AB	Calgary, AB
	T3N 2P4	T3N 2P4
Telephone	(403) 288-6019	(403) 283-1751
Social Insurance Number (SIN)	505 129 734	498 662 626
Date of Birth	04-01-78	12-15-75
Date of Hire	01-01-02	01-01-99

Taxes

Tax Table	Alberta	Alberta
Federal Claim: Basic Amount	$7 131	$7 131
Tuition & Education	$3 800	$3 800
Total Federal Claim	$10 931	$10 931
WCB Rate	4.93	4.93
EI Eligible (EI Factor)	Yes (1.4)	Yes (1.4)
CPP and Income Tax	calculations built into Simply Accounting program	

Income

Regular Wage	$16/hour	$18/hour
Regular Hours Per Period	160 hours	160 hours
Overtime Wage	$24/hour	$27/hour
Number of Pay Periods	12 (monthly)	12 (monthly)
Vacation	6% not retained	6% not retained

Default Deductions

Medical (after tax deduction)	$34	$34

Historical Payroll Information for the Pay Period Ending May 31, 2002

Year-to-Date Income

Regular	$10 240.00	$11 520.00
Overtime	$720.00	$729.00
Vacation Pay Paid	$614.40	$691.20
Gross Earnings	$11 574.40	$12 940.20
Advances Paid		$400.00
EI Insurable Earnings	$11 574.40	$12 940.20
Net Pay	$8 760.76	$9 916.36

Year-to-Date Deductions

Medical	$170.00	$170.00
Income Tax	$1 987.12	$2 516.68
EI Premiums	$293.92	$327.92
CPP Contributions	$362.60	$409.24

Employee Profiles

Tomas Nygard and **Melissa Ryder** assist with all aspects of farm work. Both employees are self-supporting and study part-time while they work full-time on the farm. Melissa earns a higher hourly rate, $18 per hour compared with $16 for Tomas, because she has worked on the farm longer than Tomas. After 40 hours of work in one week, both employees earn at the overtime rate of one-and-a-half times the regular pay. They also receive an additional 6 percent vacation pay with each monthly paycheque and pay $34 per month for medical insurance premiums, an after-tax pay deduction. There are no other deductions or company benefits. At the end of May, Melissa received a pay advance of $400, which she will repay at the rate of $100 per month over the next four months.

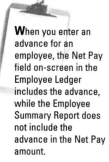

When you enter an advance for an employee, the Net Pay field on-screen in the Employee Ledger includes the advance, while the Employee Summary Report does not include the advance in the Net Pay amount.

Instructions

Set up the Company Files

1. Create company files for Anderson Farm in Simply Accounting. Create a new folder for the files.

2. Enter company information, names and ledger settings.

3. Assign account numbers and types to each account in the Chart of Accounts. Add Headings, Totals and Subgroups to organize the accounts.

4. Create accounts in the General Ledger and add account balances. Modify the bank account class and settings.

5. Enter the linked accounts needed for the General, Payables, Receivables and Payroll Ledgers.

6. Enter vendor, customer and employee information.

7. Enter historical balances for vendors, customers and employees.

8. Print the appropriate reports to check the accuracy of your work and make corrections if necessary.

9. Back up your files.

10. Finish entering the history.

Although you will not use the Inventory and Project Ledgers, it is not necessary to hide them in order to finish entering the history.

Source Documents

11. Enter the source documents from pages 597–616 using the appropriate journals. Create new accounts and vendor and customer records as needed. Advance the Session date as needed. Make regular backups.

Reports

12. After entering all the transactions, print the following reports:
    Journal Entries for all journals from June 1 to August 31, 2002
    Income Statement from January 1 to August 31, 2002
    Trial Balance as at August 31, 2002
    Balance Sheet as at August 31, 2002
    Vendor Aged Detail Reports (all vendors) at August 31, 2002
    Customer Aged Detail Reports (all customers) at August 31, 2002
    Employee Summary Report for all employees at August 31, 2002

Source Documents

Create new accounts as needed to complete the transactions for this simulation.

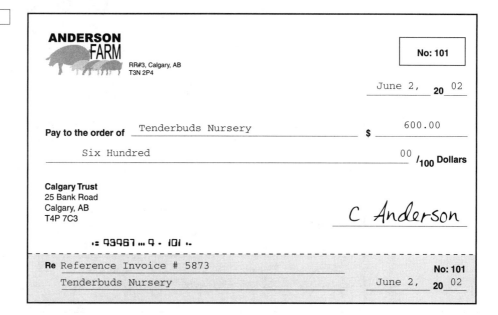

ANDERSON FARM
RR#3, Calgary, AB
T3N 2P4

No: 101

June 2, 20 02

Pay to the order of   Tenderbuds Nursery $ 600.00

Six Hundred   00 /100 Dollars

Calgary Trust
25 Bank Road
Calgary, AB
T4P 7C3

C Anderson

.: 93987 .. 9 - 101 .:

Re Reference Invoice # 5873   No: 101
Tenderbuds Nursery   June 2, 20 02

ANDERSON FARM
RR#3, Calgary, AB
T3N 2P4

No: 102

June 4, 20 02

Pay to the order of   Leanne's Service Centre $ 400.00

Four Hundred   00 /100 Dollars

Calgary Trust
25 Bank Road
Calgary, AB
T4P 7C3

C Anderson

.: 93987 .. 9 - 102 .:

Re Reference Invoice # 347, diesel fuel and repairs   No: 102
Leanne's Service Centre   June 4, 20 02

PURCHASE ORDER

PURCHASE ORDER NUMBER: 12
DATE: June 5/02

To:
Foothills Embryology Inc.
39 Culture Road
Calgary, AB
T4C 6N3

Ship to:
Anderson Farm
RR #3
Calgary, AB
T3N 2P4

PACKING INSTRUCTION

Mark cartons: **Deliver by:**
Handle with care   June 10/02

Bill to:
Anderson Farm
RR #3
Calgary, AB   T3N 2P4

Attention of: C. Anderson

**INCLUDE OUR PURCHASE ORDER NUMBER
ON ALL DOCUMENTS**

If undeliverable:
☑ Backorder   ☐ Substitute (specify)
☐ Cancel   ☑ Notify

Attention of: Barbara Groen

Ship via:
☑ UPS   ☐ Parcel post   ☐ Common carrier
☐ Air freight ☐ Other

Freight charges: ☑ Prepaid   ☐ Collect

Terms:
☑ COD   ☐ 1/10 EOM   ☐ other
☐ Net 30   ☐ 2/10 EOM

Quantity	Item no.	Description	Unit price		Amount	
1	SP-P33	Sperm - pig	2000	00	2000	00
		TOTAL ITEMS ORDERED	**GST**		Zero Rated	
			TOTAL COST		2000	00

Special instructions:
N/A

Signed: C Anderson
Date: June 5/02

Corral Farms
RR #4
Calgary, AB
T8B 2N2

No: 87

June 8, 20 02

Pay to the order of Anderson Farm $ 1500.00

Fifteen Hundred   00 /100 **Dollars**

Western Trust
35 Western Road
Calgary, AB
T2N 4N2

Ada Corral

⁙ 3921 ⑃ 1 - 8 - 87 ⑈

- -

Re Reference Invoice # AF-99, May transaction   **No: 87**
Anderson Farm   June 8, 20 02

FOOTHILLS EMBRYOLOGY INC.

39 Culture Road
Calgary, AB
T4C 6N3

Tel: 613-4271
Fax: 613-4272

Invoice: 642

To:

Anderson Farm
RR # 3
Calgary, AB
T3N 2P4

Date: June 10/02

Description		Amount	
SP-P33	Sperm - pig	2000	00
	Reference Purchase order #12		
	Subtotal	2000	00

Customer Signature: _C Anderson_

GST	Zero Rated	
GST # 612345361		
Total		
	2000	00

Terms: COD

ANDERSON FARM
RR#3, Calgary, AB
T3N 2P4

No: 103

June 10, **20** 02

Pay to the order of Foothills Embryology Inc. $ 2000.00

Two Thousand   00 /100 **Dollars**

Calgary Trust
25 Bank Road
Calgary, AB
T4P 7C3

C Anderson

⑈ 93987 ⑈ 9 - 103 ⑈

Re Reference Invoice # 642, pig sperm   **No: 103**
Foothills Embryology   June 10, **20** 02

SALES INVOICE

ANDERSON FARM
R.R. #3, Calgary, AB
T3N 2P4
Tel.: (403) 284-9123
Fax: (403) 284-8120

Invoice No: AF - 100

Date: June 20, 2002

Terms: Net 10 days
Overdue accounts are subject to interest at 15% per annum

Sold To:

Corral Farms
RR #4
Calgary, AB
T8B 2N2

Bus #: 527525527

Description	Unit Price	Charges	
Mature Female Pigs		800	00
Subtotal		800	00
GST		Zero Rated	

PLEASE PAY THIS INVOICE ➡ **AMOUNT OWING** | 800 | 00 |

Corral Farms

RR #4
Calgary, AB
T8B 2N2

No: 199

June 25, **20** 02

Pay to the order of Anderson Farm $ 800.00

Eight Hundred   00 /**100** Dollars

Western Trust
35 Western Road
Calgary, AB
T2N 4N2

Ada Corral

⑈ 3921 ⑈ 1 - 8 - 199 ⑈

Re Reference Invoice # AF-100, female pigs   **No: 199**

Anderson Farm   June 25, **20** 02

ANDERSON FARM
R.R. #3, Calgary, AB
T3N 2P4
Tel.: (403) 284-9123
Fax: (403) 284-8120

SUMMARY
RENTAL REVENUE
MONTH - June

June 30, 2002

Rental Unit # 1	1,200.00
Rental Unit # 2	1,500.00
Rental Unit # 3	1,800.00
AMOUNT DEPOSITED INTO BANK	$4,500.00

GST Exempt

ANDERSON FARM
R.R. #3, Calgary, AB
T3N 2P4
Tel.: (403) 284-9123
Fax: (403) 284-8120

TIME SUMMARY SHEET
JUNE 30, 2002

For period ending: June 30

Employee Name	Hours Regular	Hours Overtime
☐ Mellisa Ryder	160	4
☐ Tomas Nygard	160	6

*   Recover $100 from Mellisa Ryder, advanced in May.
** Issue cheques # <u>104</u> and # <u>105</u>

ALBERTA OIL & GAS

444 GASOLINE ALLEY, CALGARY, AB T4P 2P3

To:

Anderson Farm
RR # 3
Calgary, AB
T3N 2P4

GST # 343248373

Period:	Invoice date:
March-May 2002	July 2/02

Description	Amount	
Fuel oil delivery - March, April & May	500	00
Gas consumption - Flat Rate	300	00
	Subtotal	800	00
	GST	56	00

Terms: Net 5 days   #   31421

Total	
856	00

Customer Copy

ANDERSON FARM
R.R. #3, Calgary, AB
T3N 2P4
Tel.: (403) 284-9123
Fax: (403) 284-8120

SALES INVOICE

Invoice No: AF - 101

Date: July 3, 2002

Terms: Net 10 days
Overdue accounts are subject to interest at 15% per annum

Bus #: 527525527

Sold To:

Rocky Mountain Shakes & Shingles
43 Shaky Avenue
Calgary, AB
T3C 2N2

Description	Unit Price		Charges	
500 Cedar Logs	20	00	10,000	00
	Subtotal		10,000	00
	GST		700	00

PLEASE PAY THIS INVOICE ➡

AMOUNT OWING	
10,700	00

ANDERSON FARM

RR#3, Calgary, AB
T3N 2P4

No: 106

July 6, 20 02

Pay to the order of Alberta Oil & Gas Company $ 856.00

Eight Hundred Fifty-Six   00 /100 **Dollars**

Calgary Trust
25 Bank Road
Calgary, AB
T4P 7C3

C Anderson

⑈ 93967 ⑈ 9 - 106 ⑈

Re Reference Invoice # 31421, Fuel, Oil and Gas   **No: 106**
Alberta Oil & Gas Company   July 6, 20 02

Rocky Mountain Shakes & Shingles

43 Shaky Avenue
Calgary, AB
T3C 2N2

No: 124

July 8, 20 02

Pay to the order of Anderson Farm $ 10,700.00

Ten Thousand Seven Hundred   00 /100 **Dollars**

Nova Bank
39 Nova Road
Calgary ABT
T4N 2G7

Larry McMaster

⑈ 21932 ⑈ 35 ⑈ 124 ⑈

Re Reference Invoice # AF-101, cedar logs   **No: 124**
Anderson Farm   July 8, 20 02

ALBERTA HYDRO

43 Power Road, Calgary, AB T3N 2L6

SERVICE NAME AND ADDRESS

Statement Date: July 10, 2002

No: 342162

Anderson Farm
RR # 3
Calgary, AB
T3N 2P4

CUSTOMER COPY

Description	Billing Period	Rate /KWH	Energy Consumption	Amount	
Commercial Consumption 10,000 kwh	01-05-02 TO 30-06-02	N/A	166 Kwh/day	400	00
	Before		GST (7%)	28	00
GST # 462434372	July 15/02 ☞		Total due	428	00
Business Office: 403-746-2122			If paid after	458	00

ANDERSON FARM

RR#3, Calgary, AB
T3N 2P4

No: 107

July 14, **20** 02

Pay to the order of   Alberta Hydro $ 428.00

Four Hundred Twenty-Eight   00 /100 **Dollars**

Calgary Trust
25 Bank Road
Calgary, AB
T4P 7C3

C Anderson

⑈ 93987 ⑈ 9 · 107 ⑈

- -

Re Reference Invoice # 342162, hydro services   **No: 107**

Alberta Hydro   July 14, **20** 02

ALBERTA TELEPHONE

6 Calling Avenue
Calgary AB
T4G 3N3

CUSTOMER COPY

July 15, 2002

Telephone : (403) 633-0329

Account: Anderson Farm
Address: RR # 3
Calgary, AB
T3N 2P4

GST # 614272374

SUMMARY			
	Service	180	00
	Equipment Rental	0	00
	Tax-Fed.	12	60
	Chargeable Calls		
	Tax-Fed		

INVOICE NO: 16341 | **PLEASE PAY THIS AMOUNT UPON RECEIPT** | **$192** | **60**

ANDERSON FARM

RR#3, Calgary, AB
T3N 2P4

No: 108

July 15, **20** 02

Pay to the order of Alberta Telephone   **$** 192.60

One Hundred Ninety-Two   60 /100 **Dollars**

Calgary Trust
25 Bank Road
Calgary, AB
T4P 7C3

C Anderson

⑆ 93987 ⑈ 9 - 108 ⑆

- -

Re Reference Invoice # 16341, telephone services   **No: 108**
Alberta Telephone   July 15, **20** 02

LET IT RAIN ROOFERS

99 Fixit Avenue, Calgary, AB T3N 2G4

TO:	Anderson Farm RR # 3 Calgary, AB T3N 2P4	Date: July 21, 2002	NO: 74

Item Description		Amount	
Repairs to Roof on Barn		500	00
on Rental Units		700	00
	Subtotal	1200	00
Terms: Cash on Receipt	**GST (7%)**	84	00
Signature *C Anderson*	**Total**	1284	00

ANDERSON FARM

RR#3, Calgary, AB
T3N 2P4

No: 109

July 21, **20** 02

Pay to the order of   Let It Rain Roofers $ 1284.00

Twelve Hundred Eighty-Four   00 /100 **Dollars**

Calgary Trust
25 Bank Road
Calgary, AB
T4P 7C3

C Anderson

⑈ 93987 ⑈ 9 - 109 ⑈

- -

Re Reference Invoice # 74, roof repairs   **No: 109**
     Let It Rain Roofers   July 21, **20** 02

TIME SUMMARY SHEET
JULY 31, 2002

ANDERSON FARM
R.R. #3, Calgary, AB
T3N 2P4
Tel.: (403) 284-9123
Fax: (403) 284-8120

For period ending: July 31

Employee Name	Hours Regular	Hours Overtime
☐ Mellisa Ryder	160	5
☐ Tomas Nygard	160	4

*   Recover $100 from Mellisa Ryder, advanced in May.
** Issue cheques # <u>110</u> and # <u>111</u>

ANDERSON FARM
R.R. #3, Calgary, AB
T3N 2P4
Tel.: (403) 284-9123
Fax: (403) 284-8120

SALES INVOICE

Invoice No: AF - 102

Date: July 31, 2002

Terms: Net 10 days
Overdue accounts are subject to interest at 15% per annum

Bus #: 527525527

Sold To:

Paradise Preserves
42 Pickle Avenue
Calgary, AB
T3N 4G3

Description	Unit Price		Charges	
600 bushels - Red & Green Peppers	10	00	6,000	00
Subtotal			6,000	00
GST			Zero rated	
PLEASE PAY THIS INVOICE ➡ **AMOUNT OWING**			6,000	00

ANDERSON FARM
R.R. #3, Calgary, AB
T3N 2P4
Tel.: (403) 284-9123
Fax: (403) 284-8120

SUMMARY
RENTAL REVENUE
MONTH - July

July 31, 2002

Rental Unit # 1	1,200.00
Rental Unit # 2	1,500.00
Rental Unit # 3	1,800.00
AMOUNT DEPOSITED INTO BANK	$4,500.00

GST Exempt

FORM G-111

ALBERTA REFORESTATION PROGRAM

ENVIRONMENT AND FORESTRY DEPARTMENT-AB

TO: C. Anderson

Anderson Farm
RR # 3
Calgary, AB
T3N 2P4

Dear Sir: Your grant for $8000 to reforest 500 hectares has been approved. A cheque will follow this notification.

APPROVED

July 31, 2002

Kevin Jones
Minister

Leanne's Service Centre

3 Service Road, Calgary, AB T3N 2G3

Invoice: 602

Date: August 1/2002

Customer & Address

Anderson Farm
RR # 3
Calgary, AB
T3N 2P4

Item Description	Qty	Amount	
Repairs to Harvester		500	00
Diesel Fuel		200	00
	Subtotal	700	00

Terms: Net 5 days

Reg#: 434658433

GST (7%): 49 00

Customer: *C Anderson*

Total 749 00

ANDERSON FARM

R.R. #3, Calgary, AB
T3N 2P4
Tel.: (403) 284-9123
Fax: (403) 284-8120

CREDIT SALES INVOICE

Invoice No: AF - 102D

Date: August 3, 2002

Terms: N/A

Bus #: 527525527

Sold To:

Paradise Preserves
42 Pickle Avenue
Calgary, AB
T3N 4G3

Description	Unit Price	Charges	
Damaged peppers during shipment. Account Credited		200	00
	Subtotal	200	00
		Zero rated	
	GST		
➤	**AMOUNT CREDITED**	200	00

Paradise Preserves

42 Pickle Avenue, Calgary, AB T3N 4G3

No: 212

August 4, 20 02

Pay to the order of   Anderson Farm $ 5,800.00

Five Thousand Eight Hundred   00 /100 Dollars

Royal Mbanx
4 Hefty Road
Calgary AB
T4N 2N2

M. Petras

Finance Manager

.: 93121 ..- 7 -- 212 ..

- -

Re Reference Invoice # AF-102; # AF-102D, peppers   **No: 212**

Anderson Farm   August 4, 20 02

ANDERSON FARM

RR#3, Calgary, AB
T3N 2P4

No: 112

August 5, 20 02

Pay to the order of   Leanne's Service Centre $ 749.00

Seven Hundred Forty-Nine   00 /100 Dollars

Calgary Trust
25 Bank Road
Calgary, AB
T4P 7C3

C Anderson

.: 93987 ... 9 - 112 ..

- -

Re Reference Invoice #602, repairs to harvester   **No: 112**

Leanne's Service Centre   August 5, 20 02

Environment and Forestry Department
Edmonton, AB
T2E 3G4

No: 5341

August 6, **20** 02

Pay to the order of Anderson Farm $ 8,000.00

Eight Thousand   00 /**100 Dollars**

National Bank
100 Regal Avenue
Calgary, AB
T5G 2P3

Trish Curran
_____
Finance Dept.

Re Reforestation Grant - Form G-111   **No: 5341**

Anderson Farm   August 6, **20** 02

Prairie Fertilizers

Red Deer, AB T4P 2T2

Invoice: PF-4721

Date: Aug 11/02

Customer: Anderson Farm

Address: RR # 3
Calgary, AB
T3N 2P4

Item Description		Qty	Amount	
Fertilizers	FT-34XT	25	750	00
Chemicals	CM-PV27	8	800	00
		Subtotal	1550	00

Terms: Net 30 days

GST Reg#: 372142345

GST (7%)	108	50

Customer:

C Anderson

Total	$1658	50

ANDERSON FARM
R.R. #3, Calgary, AB
T3N 2P4
Tel.: (403) 284-9123
Fax: (403) 284-8120

MEMO

From the desk of C. Anderson

August 14, 2002
For the 3 months ending July 31, 2002

☐ A) Remit to Receiver General of Canada
    EI, CPP, Income tax   Issue cheque #113

☐ B) Remit to Alberta Health Insurance
    Medical Payable   Issue Cheque #114

☐ C) Remit to Workers' Compensation Board
    WCB Payable   Issue Cheque #115

North West Trailers

Invoice #: NW-1172   **Date:** Aug 17/02

121 Park Lane
Calgary, AB
T4N 2P4

Tel : 691-2444
Fax: 691-2555

Sold to Address:	Anderson Farm RR # 3 Calgary, AB T3N 2P4	**Deliver to:** SAME	**Delivery Date:** Customer pick up Aug 17/02

Qty	Description	Amount	
1	Flatbed Trailer and Hauler	3000	00

Terms: Net 30 days		**Subtotal**	3000	00
GST Reg. No: 123567992		**GST**	210	00
Signed	C Anderson	**Total**	3210	00

PURCHASE ORDER

PURCHASE ORDER NUMBER: 13
DATE: August 17/02

To:
Tenderbuds Nursery
2 Cultivate Blvd
Lethbridge, AB
T7B 2N6

Ship to:
Anderson Farm
RR #3
Calgary, AB
T3N 2P4

PACKING INSTRUCTION

Mark cartons: **Deliver by:**
                                              Aug 21/02

Bill to:
Anderson Farm
RR #3
Calgary, AB   T3N 2P4

Attention of: C. Anderson

**INCLUDE OUR PURCHASE ORDER NUMBER
ON ALL DOCUMENTS**

If undeliverable:
[✓] Backorder   [ ] Substitute (specify)
[ ] Cancel   [✓] Notify

Attention of: Polly Sidhu

Ship via:
[ ] UPS   [ ] Parcel post   [ ] Common
[ ] Air freight   [✓] Other   carrier

Freight charges: [✓] Prepaid   [ ] Collect

Terms:
[ ] COD   [ ] 1/10 EOM   [ ] other
[ ] Net 30   [✓] 2/10 EOM

Quantity	Item no.	Description	Unit price		Amount	
50	S-142	Seeds	3	00	150	00
300	P-67	Plants & Seedlings	2	00	600	00
			SUBTOTAL		750	00
	TOTAL ITEMS ORDERED		GST		52	50
			TOTAL COST		802	50

Special instructions:
                      N/A

Signed: *C Anderson*
Date: *August 17/02*

PRAIRIELAND MEAT PACKERS

33 Roast Avenue,
Calgary, AB
T4T 2N8

No: 333

August 20, 20 02

Pay to the order of Anderson Farm $ 12,500.00

Twelve Thousand Five Hundred   00 /100 **Dollars**

Alberta Saving & Trust
33 Lakeside Avenue
Calgary, AB
T2C 3F4

Frieda Collins
Treasurer

⑈30219⑈1⑈92⑈⑈⑈333

- -

Re Reference invoice #AF-103, Sale of hogs   **No: 333**

Anderson Farm   August 20, 20 02

You can enter the cheque from Prairieland Meat Packers as a cash sale for invoice AF-103 or as a prepayment (deposit) in full for the sale.

ANDERSON FARM

R.R. #3, Calgary, AB
T3N 2P4
Tel.: (403) 284-9123
Fax: (403) 284-8120

SALES INVOICE

Invoice No: AF - 103

Date: August 20, 2002

Terms: Net 10 days
Overdue accounts are subject to interest at 15% per annum

Bus #: 527525527

Sold To:

Prairieland Meat Packers
33 Roast Avenue
Calgary, AB
T4T 2N8

Description	Unit Price	Charges	
Pigs delivered as per contract		12,500	00
Subtotal		12,500	00
		Zero Rated	
GST			
PLEASE PAY THIS INVOICE ➡ **AMOUNT OWING**		12,500	00

Tenderbuds Nursery

2 Cultivate Blvd, Lethbridge, AB T7B 2N6

To:	Anderson Farm RR # 3 Calgary, AB T3N 2P4	Date: Aug 21, 2002	No: 6191

Description of Service	Amount	
Seeds, Plants & Seedlings	750	00
as per purchase order #13		
Subtotal	750	00
Terms: 2/10 EOM **GST**	52	50
Signed *C Anderson* **Total**	802	50

ANDERSON FARM

RR#3, Calgary, AB
T3N 2P4

No: 116

August 30, 20 02

Pay to the order of _Tenderbuds Nursery_ $ 786.45

Seven Hundred Eighty-Six 45/100 Dollars

Calgary Trust
25 Bank Road
Calgary, AB
T4P 7C3

C Anderson

.= 93987 ... 9 - 116 .-

Re Reference Invoice # 6191, Discount taken—$16.05

Tenderbuds Nursery

No: 116

August 30, 20 02

ANDERSON FARM

R.R. #3, Calgary, AB
T3N 2P4
Tel.: (403) 284-9123
Fax: (403) 284-8120

SALES INVOICE

Invoice No: AF - 104

Date: August 30, 2002

Terms: Net 10 days
Overdue accounts are
subject to interest
at 15% per annum

Bus #: 527525527

Sold To:

Western Co-operative
109 Friendship Way
Calgary, AB
T3N 2G5

Description	Unit Price	Charges	
Corn, Wheat and Legumes delivered as per contract.		40,000	00
Subtotal		40,000	00
GST		Zero Rated	
PLEASE PAY THIS INVOICE ➡ **AMOUNT OWING**		40,000	00

ANDERSON FARM
R.R. #3, Calgary, AB
T3N 2P4
Tel.: (403) 284-9123
Fax: (403) 284-8120

TIME SUMMARY SHEET
AUGUST 31, 2002

For period ending: August 31

Employee Name	Hours Regular	Hours Overtime
☐ Mellisa Ryder	160	10
☐ Tomas Nygard	160	10

*   Recover $100 from Mellisa Ryder, advanced in May.
** Issue cheques # <u>117</u> and # <u>118</u>

ANDERSON FARM
R.R. #3, Calgary, AB
T3N 2P4
Tel.: (403) 284-9123
Fax: (403) 284-8120

SUMMARY
RENTAL REVENUE
MONTH - August

August 31, 2002

Rental Unit # 1	1,200.00
Rental Unit # 2	1,500.00
Rental Unit # 3	1,000.00
AMOUNT DEPOSITED INTO BANK	$3,700.00

GST Exempt

Note: Tenant in Unit #3 was given $800 allowance for cost of paint and decorating materials. Work done by tenant. Receipts provided.

WINDOWS BASICS

Windows and Mouse Basics

Skip this section if you are already familiar with Windows and the use of a mouse.

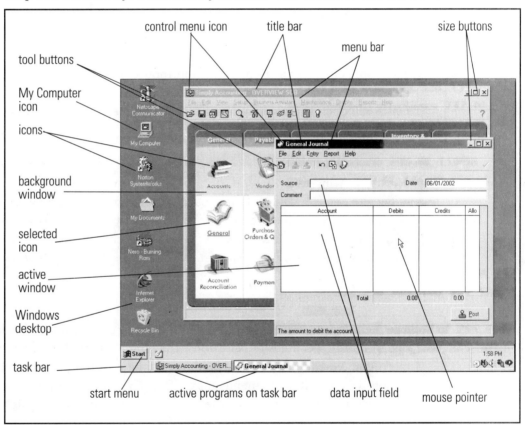

Terminology

The **mouse** is used to move the cursor. When you move the mouse, an arrow or pointer moves to indicate the cursor placement. If you **click** (press) the left mouse button, the cursor will move to the location of the arrow (if this is a legitimate location for the cursor). That is, you use the mouse to click (point to and click) a screen location, item on a list, command or icon.

The **arrow** or **pointer** changes shape, depending on what actions you may perform. When you are moving the mouse, it appears as an arrow or pointer. When you are in a field that can accept text, it appears as a **long I bar**. In a text field, clicking will change the cursor to a **flashing vertical line**, the insertion point for new text. When the computer is processing information and you are unable to perform any action, you will see an hourglass. This is your signal to wait.

Dragging refers to the method of moving the mouse while holding the left button down. Dragging through text will highlight it. Point to the beginning of the text to be highlighted. Then click and hold the mouse button down while moving through the entire area that you want to highlight. Release the mouse button when you reach the end of the area you want to highlight. You can highlight a single character or the entire contents of a field. The text will remain highlighted and can be edited by typing new text. It can be deleted by pressing the Backspace key or *del*. Clicking a different location will remove the highlighting.

You can tell when text is **selected** because the appearance has changed. Text that is normally dark on a light background appears in reverse-video mode as light text on a dark background. Selected icons or buttons have darker or thicker borders than usual and their labels appear in reverse-video mode. In Simply Accounting, labels for selected icons change colour and are underlined.

To **double click** means to press the left mouse button twice quickly. This action can be used as a shortcut for opening and closing windows. Double clicking an icon or file name will open it. Double clicking the control menu icon will close the window.

To **right-click** means to press the right mouse button once quickly. This will select an icon in Simply Accounting or will open a special menu.

The **active window** is the one you are currently working in. If you click an area outside the active window that is part of a background window, that window will become the one in the foreground. To return to your previous window, click any part of it that is showing. If the window you need is completely hidden, covered by another window, you can restore it by clicking its name on the **task bar**.

An **icon** is a picture form of your program, file name or item. **Buttons** are icons or commands surrounded by a box frame.

The **menu bar** is the line of options at the top of each window. Each menu contains one or more commands or selections (the pull-down menu) that can be accessed by clicking the menu name. Each window may have different menu selections, and the options in the pull-down menus may differ. To choose an option from the menu, click the menu name and then click the option you want in order to highlight and select it. If an option is dimmed, you will be unable to highlight or select it.

For example, to see the Trial Balance Report from the Simply Accounting Home window, click Reports on the menu bar, point to Financials, then point across to the submenu and click Trial Balance. In this text, we give this instruction as "Choose the Reports menu, then choose Financials and click Trial Balance."

The following screen shows the Reports pull-down menu with Financials and Trial Balance selected in the Simply Accounting Home window:

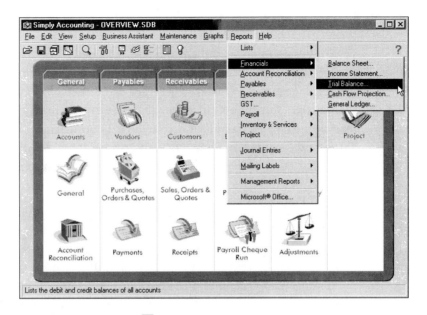

The arrow beside Financials (▇) indicates there is a second level of menu options.

The **control menu icon** is situated in the upper left-hand corner of each window. The icon is different for different programs and windows. It has its own pull-down menu, including the **Close** and size commands. To close a window, you can double click this icon and choose Close from its pull-down menu, or click the Close button ☒ in the upper right-hand corner of the window.

Size buttons are located in the upper right-hand corner of the window. Click a size button to change the window. Click ☐ to make the window larger (maximize to full screen size) or click ▭ to minimize the window (reduce it to a button on the task bar). If a window is full screen size, click the ▣ (restore) button to return to the default size.

The size of a window can also be changed by using the mouse to drag the side you want to move. When the pointer changes to a **two-sided arrow**, the window frame can be dragged to its new size.

When a window contains more information than can be displayed on-screen at once, the window will contain scroll arrows (▼ , ▲ , ▶ or ◀) in any corner or direction next to the hidden information. Scroll bars are located at the bottom or right sides of a window. Click the arrow and hold the mouse button down to scroll the screen in the direction of the arrow.

Input fields often include a **drop-down list** or **pop-up list** from which you can select a name or option. Whenever a list is available, there is a **list arrow** beside the field. These fields look like this:

When you click the arrow beside the field, the list appears. Click an item in the list to add it to the field directly. Sometimes these fields allow you to type in text and sometimes you must choose from the list. If you must choose from the list, clicking the field itself will often produce the list. Otherwise, clicking the field gives you the insertion point.

Working in Windows without a Mouse

All Windows software applications are designed to be used with a mouse. However, there may be times when you prefer to use keyboard commands to work with a program because it is faster. There are also times when you need to know the alternatives to using a mouse, as when the mouse itself is inoperative. It is not necessary to memorize all of the keyboard commands. A few basic principles will help you to understand how they work and over time you will use the ones that help you to work most efficiently. Some commands are common to more than one Windows software program. For example, (ctrl) (Control key) + C is commonly used as the copy command and (ctrl) + V as the paste command.

The menu bar and the menu choices can be accessed by pressing (alt). The first menu bar item will be highlighted. Use the arrow keys to move back and forth to other menu items or up and down through the pull-down menu choices of a highlighted menu item. Some menu choices have direct keyboard alternatives or shortcuts. If the menu item has an underlined letter, pressing (alt) together with the underlined letter will access that option directly. For example, (alt) + F (press (alt), and while holding down (alt), press F) accesses the File pull-down menu. Then pressing O (the underlined letter for Open) will give you the dialog box for opening a new file. Some tool buttons in Simply Accounting have direct keyboard commands and some menu choices also have shortcut keyboard commands. When available, these direct keystrokes appear with a button label or to the right of a menu choice. For example, (alt) + (f4) is the shortcut for exiting from the Simply Accounting program.

To cancel the menu display, press the (esc) (Esc or escape) key.

In the Simply Accounting Home window, you can use the arrow keys to move among the ledger and journal icons. Press (alt), (alt) and   to highlight the Accounts icon, and then use the arrow keys to change selections. Each icon is highlighted or selected as you reach it and deselected as you move to another icon.

Sometimes you need to select a command button, such as Yes, No, OK or Cancel. Press (tab) to select a different button until the one you need is selected or type the underlined letter for the command you need.

To choose or open a highlighted or selected item, press (enter).

When input fields are displayed in a Simply Accounting window, you can move to the next field by pressing (tab) or to a previous field by pressing (shift) and (tab) together. We frequently use the (tab) key in this workbook as a quick way to advance the cursor, highlight field contents to prepare for immediate editing and accept input. Using the mouse while you input information requires you to remove your hands from the keyboard, while the (tab) key does not.

Pressing (alt) + (f4) will close the active window. If the Simply Accounting Home window is the active window, you will therefore exit the program.

Copying Files onto a Hard Disk

Folders and files may be copied from the My Computer window; folders and files may also be copied using Windows Explorer. You should be in the Windows opening desktop screen and the Data Disk that came with this book should be in the CD-ROM drive.

To make a copy of the data files on your hard disk, use the Windows Explorer program. All of the instructions we show will copy the folders together with their contents. We do not encourage or show copying of individual files, to ensure that all the files required by the Simply Accounting program will stay together. If any file is missing from the folder, you will be unable to open the data files.

◆ Click **Start** on the desktop task bar.

◆ Choose (point to) **Programs** and then click **Windows Explorer**.

◆ Click the **CD-ROM** disk drive icon or name so that the contents of the Data Disk, all of the chapter folders, appear on the Contents side of the window under Name.

◆ Click **Ch01**, the first folder in the Contents list.

◆ Now press and hold _shift_ while you click **Ch18**, the last folder in the Contents list. (Or, you can choose the Edit menu and click Select All from the pull-down menu.) This will highlight all the folders (as well as the Basic Accounting Information file) on the Data Disk as shown:

There are no data files for Chapter 2 because you create new company files in that chapter.

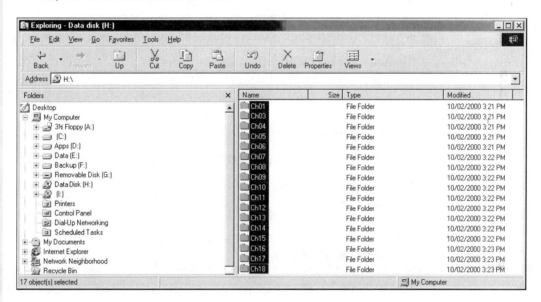

◆ Choose the **Edit menu** and click **Copy** or click the Copy tool. This creates a temporary copy of the files.

Now you need to open the folder into which you want to copy the data files. We show the files copied to the Data folder that was created as part of the Simply Accounting program installation. Of course, you may use another data folder.

◆ Click the ⊞ beside (C:) if its folders are not already listed.

◆ Scroll down the Folders side to the Program Files folder. Click the ⊞ beside the folder to see the folders under Program Files. Now click the ⊞ beside the Winsim folder to list the folders under Winsim. Click the Data folder to open it.

The Data folder name appears in the Address field above the listings of folders and files:

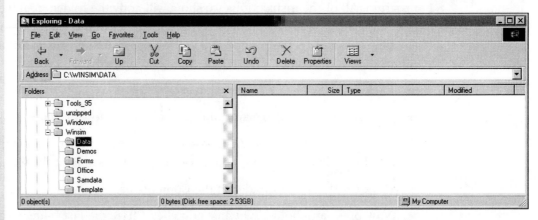

Once the files you want to copy are all selected, you may also drag them to the destination folder. We use the Copy and Paste method because it is easier to place the files in the correct folder.

The Winsim program is installed in the Winsim folder under (C:) in the screen displayed here, not in the Program Files folder. Choose the folder that you used for your own installation.

◆ Choose the **Edit menu** and click **Paste**, or click the Paste tool.

Your screen will show the files being copied. When the copying is complete, all the folders and files from the CD will be copied to the Data folder under Winsim that was created during installation. You will see the list of Chapter data folders in the Contents section under Name, and the Data folder will have a ⊞ beside it.

If you want to copy only the files for a single chapter, click the folder for the chapter you want (e.g., Ch01) to highlight it. Copy the folder (Edit menu or Copy tool), open the destination folder on the hard drive and Paste the folder into it (Edit menu or Paste tool).

Removing Read-Only File Restrictions

Before you can open the data files with Simply Accounting, you must remove the Read-Only file properties that all CD-ROM files have.

Read-Only Error Messages

If you try to open the files before changing the properties, you will see the following message:

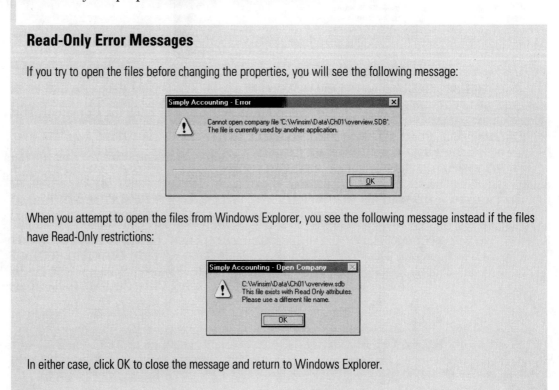

When you attempt to open the files from Windows Explorer, you see the following message instead if the files have Read-Only restrictions:

In either case, click OK to close the message and return to Windows Explorer.

622

After you copy the chapter folders, their names will appear in the large Contents box on the right-hand side of the Explorer window:

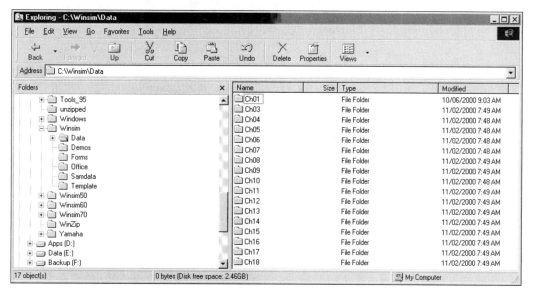

◆ Double click **Names** (in the title bar above the chapter folder names) to restore the alphabetical order if necessary.

◆ Double click **folder Ch01** to open it and see the two Simply Accounting files:

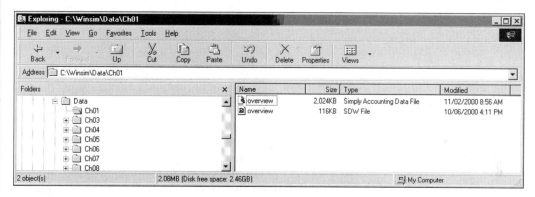

◆ Click **overview**, the Simply Accounting Data File, to select it. This first file is the primary data file, the .sdb file.

◆ Press shift and click **overview** (the second file, the .SDW file) so that both files remain selected as shown:

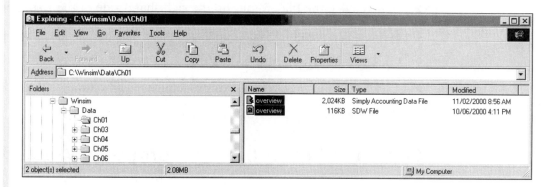

◆ Choose the **File menu** and click **Properties** as shown:

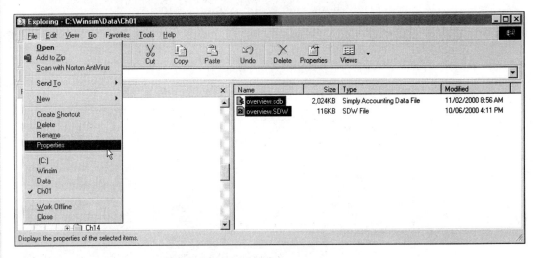

The Properties window for Overview will open:

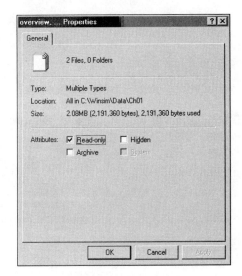

◆ Click **Read-only** to remove the ✓.

◆ Click **OK** to save the changes.

Now change the properties for the files you will need for Play Wave in Chapter 3.

◆ Double click the **Ch03 folder** on the left-hand side of the Explorer window.

◆ Double click the **Play folder** on the right-hand side of the Explorer window.

◆ Select **both Playch03 files**.

◆ Click Read-only to remove the ✓.

◆ Click **OK**. You must repeat this procedure for all data files that you want to use.

◆ Click ⊠ to close the Explorer window.

Copying Files in the My Computer Window

◆ Double click the **My Computer icon** ▦ on the desktop:

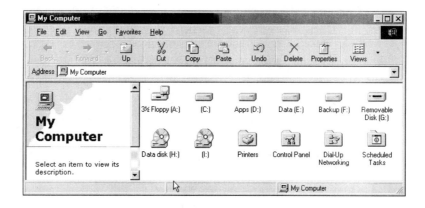

You can also use the Edit menu Copy and Paste commands from the My Computer window.

◆ Double click the **CD-ROM icon** 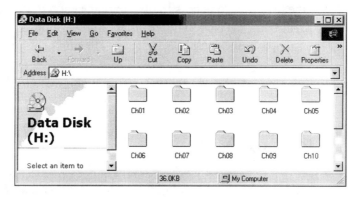 to display the folders on the CD.

◆ Click the **Ch01 folder** to select it and then drag it to the desktop area outside the Data Disk (CD-ROM disc) window.

◆ Click the **Back button** Back to return to the My Computer window.

◆ Double click the **(C:) icon** (C:) to open this drive and display the folders.

◆ Double click the **Program Files folder** and then double click the **Winsim** folder to display the files and folders in the Winsim folder. Double click the Data folder to open it. (Choose the folders that apply to your own installation.)

◆ Drag the **Ch01 folder** from the desktop into the Data folder:

The Winsim program is installed in the Winsim folder under (C:) in the screen displayed here. Choose the folder that you used for your own installation.

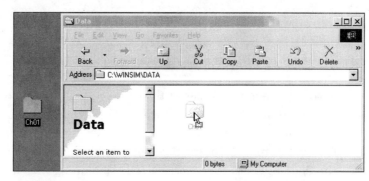

◆ Release the mouse button to begin copying. The Ch01 folder appears in the Data window when copying is complete. It no longer appears on the desktop area.

◆ Close all windows that are open when the copying is complete.

Copying All Folders

To copy all the folders and files at once, choose the Edit menu and click Select All in the CD-ROM window to highlight all the folders. When you drag, all the files will be included as a group. Drag the group of folders to the desktop. Then open the Data folder. To select the folders from the desktop, click the first folder you want to copy. Press *ctrl* and, while pressing *ctrl*, click the next folder you want to copy. The first folder remains selected. Keep the *ctrl* key down while you add more folders to the selected group and then drag the group to the new location, the Data folder. Release the mouse to begin copying. To change selected items, click the mouse elsewhere to remove the highlighting.

Working with Folders

Because each data set in Simply Accounting includes two files that must stay together for the program to access them, we place each data set in a separate folder as a way of organizing the files. Therefore, it is important to know how to create new folders as you are working with the Simply Accounting program. You can create folders directly in the Simply Accounting Open Company, Create Company or Save As windows without exiting the program. You can also create folders in the Windows Explorer window.

Creating New Folders

HINT: If you need to create a new folder, you can open a window such as the Save As window, and then create all the folders you want in a single session. Click Cancel to return to your working screen.

File extensions do not appear with the file names if your computer settings are to hide the extensions.

The Create Company, Save As and Open Company screens in Simply Accounting look very similar, and you use the same method to create folders in each of them.

◆ Start the Simply Accounting program and open the data files for Overview — the practice file for Chapter 1 (refer to Chapter 1 for instructions on opening a data file). You should be in the Home window.

◆ Choose the **File menu** and click **Save As** to see the Save As window:

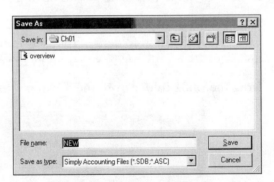

If you create a new folder at this stage, it will be placed inside the Ch01 folder because that is the folder named in the Save in field. Only files with the .sdb or .asc extensions are displayed in the central text area of the screen because these are the file types requested in the Save as type field. The only file with the .sdb extension in the Ch01 folder is overview.sdb. The remaining files in the folder are not displayed.

◆ Click the **Save in field drop-down list arrow**:

The Winsim program is installed in the Winsim folder directly under (C:) in the screen displayed here. Choose the folder that you used for your own installation.

If you click Save at this stage, you will save a file named new.asc (the name in the File name field) inside the Ch01 folder. When you have a folder selected, the Save button changes to Open.

If you click Winsim, you will go to this folder level. If you click (C:), you will list all the folders on the hard drive. To open a folder once you have changed levels, click it to select it and click Open, or double click the folder directly to open it. You may have to open several levels of folders to reach the one you want.

If you right-click on a folder or file, you will open a different menu. If you right-click on the desktop outside the Save As window, you will place the new folder on the desktop.

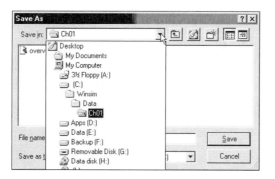

You will see the file path for the file that is open. The overview.sdb is in folder Ch01 in the Data folder, in Winsim in drive (C:). The open folder icon shows that Ch01 is the open folder. This list shows the other drives that you can use.

Changing Folders

You can switch to another drive by clicking the name of the new drive. The following steps will save the file in a new folder inside the Winsim\Data folder.

◆ Click **Data**. The folders inside this folder are now listed in the central text area.

This is the folder level you need so you can now add the new folder.

Sometimes the folder you want is one level up from the one you are using, as it was in this example. In this case, you can use the Up one level icon to change folders. For example, when you have the Data folder open,

Click the Up one level icon 🔼 to return to the Winsim folder. If you want to create the new folder in Winsim you can stop. If you want to continue to change levels,

Click 🔼 (Up one level icon) again to return to the Program Files folder. Once more will return you to (C:). Click once again to return to the My Computer level with all drives showing at once. Now you can select a different drive and begin opening the folders you want. Each time you click the icon, you will go up one level.

Creating the New Folder

◆ Right-click (click the right mouse button once) in a blank area of the text box to see a pop-up menu.

◆ Choose **New** and then **Folder** from this menu as shown:

◆ Click (the left mouse button) to create a new folder. Or,

◆ Click the **New Folder icon** 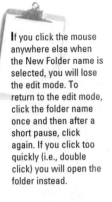 to create the folder directly without using the menu.

A folder labelled New Folder appears with the other folders that you may already have placed inside the Data folder.

The label is selected so you can change the name immediately.

◆ Type `practice`

◆ Click the folder icon or a blank portion of the central part of the screen to save the change. (If you skip this step, you may not have changed the name.)

◆ Now double click the **practice folder** to open it. The name practice should appear in the Save in field. You are now ready to type a new name for the file.

◆ Double click **NEW** in the File Name field.

◆ Type `practice`

◆ Click **Save** to return to the Home window for the new copy of the data file.

◆ Click ☒ to exit the program.

If you click the mouse anywhere else when the New Folder name is selected, you will lose the edit mode. To return to the edit mode, click the folder name once and then after a short pause, click again. If you click too quickly (i.e., double click) you will open the folder instead.

Creating Folders in Windows Explorer

Sometimes you may want to create a number of new folders before starting the Simply Accounting program. In this case, you can use Windows Explorer. You should be in the main Windows desktop to use this method.

Choose the Start menu, then choose Programs and click Windows Explorer on the Windows desktop.

Drive (C:) is the starting position in Windows Explorer. The new folder will be located as a separate folder on the selected drive (C:) if you do not open another folder first. You must open the folder that you want to use for the new folder (subfolder). To place the new folder inside the Winsim\Data folder, double click the Program Files folder, then double click the Winsim folder and then double click the Data folder.

Once the folder that will contain the new folder is open, right-click to view the pop-up menu. Choose New and then Folder (or choose the File menu, then choose New and click Folder). A folder labelled New Folder is added to the open folder or drive. The label is ready for editing, so you should type the new folder name immediately. Then click the mouse (left button) on a different location to save the new name.

Click ☒ to close Windows Explorer.

INSTALLING SIMPLY ACCOUNTING

Installing the Program

The Simply Accounting program is available in CD-ROM format.

◆ Start your computer.

◆ Close all other programs that you have running before beginning the installation. Disable virus protection programs.

◆ Insert the program CD into the CD-ROM drive. Installation may begin immediately. If it does, go to page 632 for the next step. If it does not, follow the steps below to start the installation.

◆ Choose **Run** from the **Start** menu on the Windows task bar as shown:

You can also click Browse to locate the file you want on the CD.

The Run screen opens:

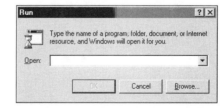

◆ Type **D:\launch.exe** (substitute the appropriate letter for your CD-ROM drive).

◆ Click **OK** to begin the setup.

Installation Using Add/Remove Programs

An alternative to using the Start – Run menu is the Add/Remove Programs option in the Control panel. You can access the Control Panel in two ways:

Double click the My Computer icon on the Windows desktop and then double click the Control Panel icon in the My Computer window, or

Choose the Start menu, then choose Settings, and click Control Panel on the Windows desktop as shown:

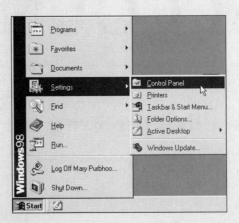

The Control Panel window appears:

Double click the Add/Remove Programs icon to use this feature:

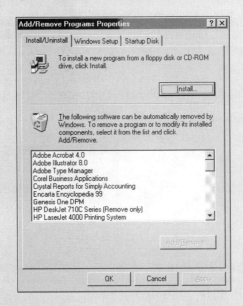

Since we want to install a program, we need the Install/Uninstall tab screen. If it is not selected by default, click the Install/Uninstall tab.

Click Install to advance to the next step:

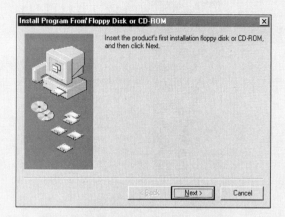

If you are installing a program from a CD, the installation usually begins automatically as soon as you insert the program CD without this Run Installation Program screen.

Insert the program CD as instructed, if you have not already done so.

Click Next:

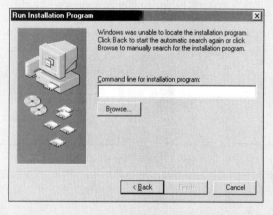

The launch.exe program you need may be selected already. If it is not, you can click Browse and choose it from the list of programs available. Click Open to choose the new folder. You may also type **D:\launch.exe** in the Command line field. (Substitute the CD-ROM drive letter from your own computer setup.)

Click Finish to begin the installation. The Simply Accounting logo and Setup Install Shield screen will appear next.

The Simply Accounting logo screen appears:

If you want to install the Crystal Reports program, begin the installation again and click Install Crystal Reports from this screen. Notice that the CD also contains manuals and demos for the program.

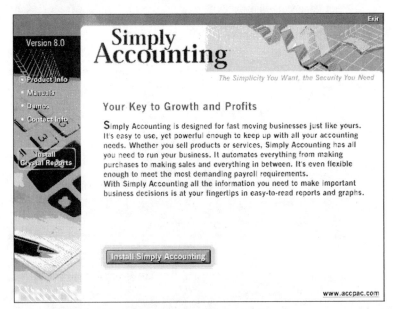

◆ Click **Install Simply Accounting** to begin running the Setup Install Shield.

The Simply Accounting Setup welcome screen appears next:

◆ Click **Next** to advance to the Licence Agreement screen. Read the information displayed.

◆ Click **Yes** to accept the licence conditions and advance to the Customer Information screen:

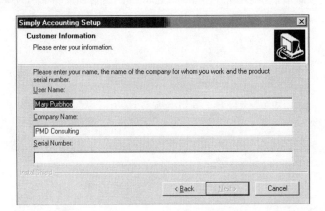

Your name and company name may appear already from previous programs that you installed.

- Type your name and company if you want. Click a field to move the cursor to the field you need.

- Type the product serial number from the software package.

- Click **Next** to proceed to the confirmation screen.

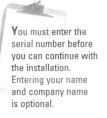

You must enter the serial number before you can continue with the installation. Entering your name and company name is optional.

- Check your information carefully, especially the serial number. If you made a mistake, click No to return to the Customer Information screen and make corrections.

- Click **Yes** to confirm that the identifying details are correct and to proceed:

In this screen, you must choose a location for your program files. The default location is your main hard disk drive (C:) in the Winsim folder, under the Program Files folder. To change the location, click Browse to choose a different folder and click OK. We recommend accepting the default location and program names unless you are an experienced user.

- Click **Next** to continue:

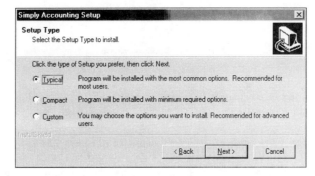

Now you must choose the type of installation. The default selection, Typical, will provide you with all the components you need. The Custom option allows you to include or omit individual components and the Compact option provides only the basics (if you are short of disk space). You can always add or change the missing components later by repeating the installation using the Custom mode and selecting the parts you want to add. Again we recommend the Typical installation unless you are an experienced user.

◆ Click **Next** to continue to the program folder name screen:

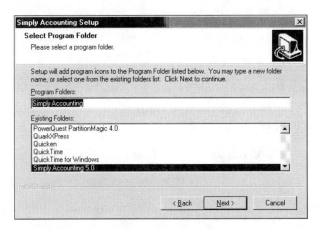

The installation will replace older versions of the programs that use the same folders and names. You will be prompted to replace some files as the installation proceeds. Data files are not normally removed in this procedure but you should make backups first to be sure your files are safe.

The name you enter here for the folder will appear on the Start menu Program Files list that you will use to run the program after installation. For example, if you have different versions of the Simply Accounting program, you may want to name this folder "Simply Accounting 8" to distinguish it from the others. This also reminds you which version you have installed, even if it is the only one you have on your computer. If you are unsure, accept the default settings and names.

◆ Click **Next**. Another confirmation screen appears with the selected settings:

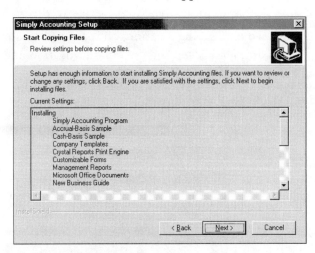

After you install the program, check the ACCPAC International Web site at <www.accpac.com> for any program updates or service packs that you can download and install. You can access the Web site from the Help menu in the Simply Accounting Home window. (From the Web site, search for service pack and find the updates for Simply Accounting.)

◆ Confirm that the settings you entered are correct. If you want to make any changes, click Back to return to the previous screen.

◆ Click **Next** to begin the installation of files.

When the installation is complete, you may see a number of messages advising you to register the program, restart your computer and view the ReadMe file. Choose to restart the computer to update the system settings on your computer. You should also view the Readme file for any product updates that came after the manuals were created. And you should register the product to be eligible for support.

◆ Choose **Finish** to complete the installation.

◆ Click **Exit** to return to the desktop. You are now ready to start using the program.

Components of Simply Accounting

The typical installation adds the following components to your hard drive:

Simply Accounting Program: This is the main program that allows you to create company files, enter accounting information and transactions and print reports.

Sample Data: Two sample company data sets are included with the installation. You can view these files to help you learn the software. Both accrual and cash based accounting methods are illustrated.

Starter Files and Templates: Templates for a large number of company types are provided as well as two generic starter files. In the templates, accounts, linked accounts and typical settings for the business type are preset, saving some setup time. You can change pre-defined accounts or settings to suit your own business needs.

Customizable Forms, Crystal Reports Print Engine, MS Office Files and Management Reports: These components work together to allow you to modify predefined printed forms such as sales invoices and to view management reports that combine data from your company with pre-defined report forms (e.g., a list of all customers with overdue accounts).

Conversion Utility: The conversion program updates older DOS-based versions of the program to the Windows format. The software automatically updates data files created with earlier Windows versions of the program.

New Business Guide: Checklists for different types of businesses for each province and territory are provided (Simply Accounting Home window, Business Assistant menu).

Simply Accounting Folders

Most of the program files are in the Winsim folder. Other components of the software are located in folders under Winsim that are also created with the installation. In addition to the main Winsim folder, several subfolders are created.

Data: This is an empty folder that you can use to store your own data files. By locating the data folder inside the Winsim folder, you can easily distinguish your accounting files from data for other programs.

Demos: This folder will store the demo programs that you install from the program CD.

Forms: The Forms folder has the customizable forms used for management reports and for working with the Crystal Reports program. You can also customize invoices and order forms.

Office: The files in this folder work with data that you export to MS Office programs.

Samdata: There are sample data sets for two companies in the Samdata folder, Universal Construction and Universal Crustacean Farms.

Template: The templates for a large number of business types are located in the template folder. You must use the Wizard for creating new company files to use templates. Two generic starter files that you can open like any other data file are also included — skeleton (General Ledger accounts only) and inteplus (a basic set of linked accounts for all ledgers).

SALES TAXES — FEDERAL AND PROVINCIAL

Goods and Services Tax

General Accounting Information
Definition of GST

The Goods and Services Tax (GST) is a compulsory tax levied by the federal government on most goods and services in Canada. The Goods and Services Tax rate of 7 percent applies at all levels. Manufacturers pay GST when they purchase raw materials; wholesalers pay GST to the manufacturers and retailers pay GST to wholesalers and other vendors. All these businesses are allowed to deduct the GST they pay from the GST they collect from their customers. They remit GST owing to the Receiver General of Canada or claim a refund on a monthly or quarterly basis.

Provinces may or may not include GST in the price on which they calculate Retail or Provincial Sales Tax (PST). Provincial tax rates vary from province to province.

GST Registration

A business with annual sales exceeding $30 000 per year must register to apply the Goods and Services Tax. Registration is optional for those businesses whose annual sales are less than $30 000. Registration allows a business to recover any GST paid on purchases made. Both taxable and zero-rated sales are included in the amount for registration.

Collecting the GST

Once a business registers for GST, it must collect GST for those goods and services sold that are not zero-rated or tax exempt. GST collected on sales is reduced by the GST on sales returns. The business must remit GST at regular intervals, filing GST returns monthly, quarterly, or annually with quarterly installments, depending on annual income and GST owing.

GST Rates and Codes

Not all goods and services are taxable, and there are options with respect to pricing goods that are taxable. These variations are covered by the GST codes built into the Simply Accounting program and are displayed in the following screen:

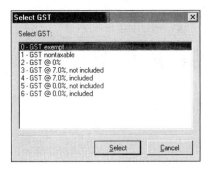

By selecting the correct GST code when you enter a sale or purchase, the software calculates the tax amounts automatically and debits or credits the appropriate accounts.

Tax-Exempted Goods and Services (Code 0 - GST exempt): Tax-exempted goods and services are those on which tax is not collected. These goods and services include health care, dental care, day-care services and rents on residential properties. Most educational and financial services are also included in this group. These businesses are not allowed to claim refunds for GST paid for any business purchases related to selling tax-exempted goods and services.

The **GST nontaxable code (Code 1)** is used for transactions such as remittance of taxes to government agencies.

Zero-Rated Goods and Services (Code 2 - GST @ 0%): Zero-rated goods and services are those on which the tax rate is zero. These goods include basic groceries, prescribed medical instruments and devices, prescribed drugs, exported goods and services, agricultural products and fish products. A business selling only zero-rated goods and services is not able to collect GST from customers, but it can still claim a refund for GST paid for any purchases made for selling these zero-rated goods and services.

Including GST in the Purchase Price: Some retailers or service providers choose to advertise their prices including GST to simplify the calculation on small sale amounts. For example, movie theatres, parking lots and some fast-food outlets include GST and post signs that prices include taxes. If taxes are included in the price already, entering the full amount of the sale and choosing code 4 - GST @ 7% included will lead to allocating the amount paid correctly between GST and the expense, asset or revenue accounts.

GST at Rates 1 and Rate 2: The program provides the option of entering two different tax rates for GST in the setup. If the government decides to apply different rates to different kinds of goods, you can indicate the appropriate rates. If some of the business is with a participating Atlantic province, the HST rate can be entered as 15% for GST Rate 2. This permits a business to track and report HST separately as required. HST is described later in this appendix.

In the Select GST screen above, the second GST rate is set at 0%, codes 5 and 6.

Paying the GST

The business must pay GST for purchases made specifically for business use unless the goods or services purchased are zero-rated or tax exempt. The business can use the GST paid as an input tax credit (ITC) by subtracting the amount of GST paid from the amount of GST collected, and remitting GST owing or claiming a refund. The input tax credit is reduced by the amount of GST for purchases returned. Purchases for personal use do not qualify as input tax credits.

Bank and Financial Institution Services

Most bank products and services are not taxable. Exceptions include safety deposit box rentals, custodial and safekeeping services, personalized cheques, fees for self-administrated registered savings plans, payroll services, rentals of night depository, rentals of credit card imprinters and reconciliation of cheques. Banks must remit the full amount of GST they collect from customers. They cannot claim input tax credits for GST they pay on business-related purchases.

Administering the GST

The federal government has approved different methods of administering the GST — the regular method and the quick method are the most common.

The Regular Method

The regular method of administering the GST requires the business to keep track of all GST paid for goods and services purchased from vendors (less returns) and of all GST collected for goods and services sold to customers (less returns). It then deducts the GST paid from the GST collected and files for a refund or remits the balance owing to the Receiver General on a monthly or quarterly basis.

Both GST Paid and GST Charged are liability accounts. GST Charged is credited for sales and GST Paid is debited for purchases. GST Paid is a contra-liability account.

Accounting Examples Using the Regular Method (without PST)

SALES INVOICE

Sold goods on account to customer for $200 plus $14 GST collected. Invoice total, $214.

Date	Particulars	Ref.	Debit	Credit
xx/xx	Accounts Receivable		214.00	
	GST Charged on Sales			14.00
	Revenue from Sales			200.00

PURCHASE INVOICE

Purchased supplies on account from vendor for $300 plus $21 GST paid. Invoice total, $321.

Date	Particulars	Ref.	Debit	Credit
xx/xx	Supplies		300.00	
	GST Paid on Purchases		21.00	
	Accounts Payable			321.00

The GST owing is further reduced by any GST adjustments — for example, GST that applies to bad debts that are written off. If the debt is later recovered, the GST liability is also restored as an input tax credit adjustment.

Simplified Accounting Methods

Certain small businesses may be eligible to use a simplified method of calculating their GST refunds and remittances that does not require them to keep a separate record for GST on each individual purchase or sale.

The Streamlined Accounting Method is available only to some grocery and convenience stores. The Quick Method is available to a wider range of businesses.

The Quick Method

Some small businesses may opt to remit a flat tax payment ranging from 1 percent to 5 percent of their sales. This simplified system is available to manufacturers and retailers with sales up to a maximum of $200 000 per year, to grocery and convenience stores with sales up to $500 000 per year and to some service businesses. The GST is calculated by multiplying the total sales for the filing period (monthly or quarterly) by the flat tax rate for the type of business under consideration. A business is still able to deduct any GST paid on capital expenditures from the GST liability calculated using the flat tax rate. Capital expenditures include purchases of plant and equipment such as cash registers, furniture, computers and other depreciable assets.

GST is included in the base revenue to which the flat tax rate is applied.

The quick method described above is not available to legal, accounting or financial consulting businesses. Businesses may change methods from year to year upon application for the change to the Canada Customs and Revenue Agency.

The quick method tax rate on the first $30 000 in sales is reduced by 1 percent.

Accounting Examples Using the Quick Method (without PST)

CASH SALES

Cash register tapes in a café for one week total $3 200 including GST collected for goods and services.

Date	Particulars	Ref.	Debit	Credit
xx/xx	Bank Account		3 200.00	
	Revenue from Services			3 200.00

PURCHASE INVOICES

1. Food Inventory

Purchased basic groceries for café services from vendor for $1 000 on account. Basic groceries are zero-rated goods.

Date	Particulars	Ref.	Debit	Credit
xx/xx	Food Inventory		1 000.00	
	Accounts Payable			1 000.00

2. Non-Capital Expenditures

Purchased gasoline, oil and repair services for delivery van from vendor on account for $428, including $28 GST.

Date	Particulars	Ref.	Debit	Credit
xx/xx	Van Maintenance		428.00	
	Accounts Payable			428.00

3. Capital Expenditures

Purchased pizza oven for café from vendor on account for $2 000 plus $140 GST paid. Invoice total, $2 140.

Date	Particulars	Ref.	Debit	Credit
xx/xx	Cafeteria Equipment		2 000.00	
	GST Paid on Capital Goods		140.00	
	Accounts Payable			2 140.00

Calculating GST Refunds or Remittances

The following examples are for a retailer who is filing quarterly and has maximum annual sales of $200 000.

THE REGULAR METHOD

Quarterly Total Sales	$50 000.00	
Quarterly Total Purchases	29 700.00	
GST Charged on Sales		$3 500.00
Less: GST Paid on Purchases		
Cash Register (cost $1 000)	70.00	
Inventory (cost $25 000)	1 750.00	
Supplies (cost $500)	35.00	
Payroll Services (cost $200)	14.00	
Store Lease (cost $3 000)	210.00	
Total GST Paid		− 2 079.00
GST Remittance		$1 421.00

THE QUICK METHOD WITH A FLAT RATE OF 2.5 PERCENT

Quarterly Total Sales (Including GST Charged)	$53 500.00
Multiply by 2.5%	$ 1 337.50
Less: GST Paid on Capital Goods Cash Register (cost $1 000)	− 70.00
GST Remittance	$ 1 267.50

The flat tax rate on the first $30 000 in sales is 1 percent less than the rate for remaining sales up to $200 000.

Generally the flat rate is set so that there is little difference between using the regular and quick methods. The quick method can save time if the business has a large number of purchases for small amounts.

GST Remittances and Refunds

GST Charged on Sales	>	GST Paid on Purchases	=	GST Owing
GST Charged on Sales	<	GST Paid on Purchases	=	GST Refund

The rules concerning the Goods and Services Tax may change periodically. Always refer to current GST guidelines.

GST Accounts

The GST accounts used in Simply Accounting should match the categories on the GST report that the business files. If there are two GST rates, there is an additional *GST Charged* and *GST Paid* account. Usually all GST accounts will be grouped so that the Subgroup total account *GST Owing (Refund)* shows the net of all the GST amounts.

GST Charged on Sales or Services: The GST collected from customers on taxable sales and services is credited to this account automatically when the account is linked.

GST Paid on Purchases: The GST paid on taxable purchases is debited to this account automatically when the account is set up as a linked account.

GST Adjustments and *ITC Adjustments*: These separate accounts may be used to reverse GST transactions that result from changes in purchases or sales already recorded, such as recording a bad debt or recovering a debt.

ITC is the abbreviation for Input Tax Credits, the amounts that reduce GST owing.

GST Payroll Deductions: Use this account to record GST collected from employees for taxable benefits. The account will normally be credited.

GST Owing (Refund): This Subgroup total account shows the net effect of all GST entries.

Remittances

The business must file a statement periodically that summarizes the amount of GST it has collected and the amount of GST it has paid. The business may file monthly, quarterly, or yearly with quarterly installments.

Most of the time a business will make GST remittances since sales usually exceed expenses — the business operates at a profit. The example below shows how the GST accounts are cleared and a liability (*Accounts Payable* account) is set up to remit GST owing to the Receiver General of Canada. In this case, the usual one, the Receiver General becomes a vendor for the business so that the liability can be entered and the payment made.

Date	Particulars	Ref.	Debit	Credit
03/31	GST Charged on Sales		2 500.00	
	GST Paid on Purchases			700.00
	A/P - Receiver General			1 800.00
03/31	A/P - Receiver General		1 800.00	
	Bank Account			1 800.00

The following screen shows the Payments Journal invoice for a GST remittance:

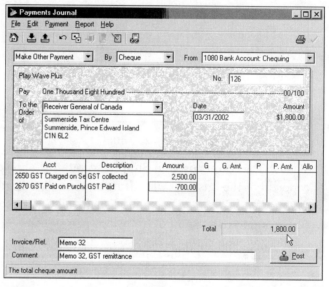

GST payments may be entered in the Purchases Journal as invoices paid by cheque. The account entries and amounts will be the same as shown here.

Make Other Payment is selected as the transaction type. Thus, in the journal entry display, the bank account is credited immediately instead of *Accounts Payable*:

03/31/2002 (J161)	Debits	Credits	Project
2650 GST Charged on Services	2,500.00	-	
1080 Bank Account: Chequing	-	1,800.00	
2670 GST Paid on Purchases	-	700.00	
	2,500.00	2,500.00	

Refunds

The example below shows how the GST accounts are cleared and a current asset account (*Accounts Receivable*) is set up for a GST refund from the Receiver General of Canada. In this case, the Receiver General owes money to the business; that is, it acts like a customer. A customer record is set up for the Receiver General, to record and collect the amount receivable.

642

Date	Particulars	Ref.	Debit	Credit
03/31	GST Charged on Sales		1 500.00	
	A/R - Receiver General		500.00	
	GST Paid on Purchases			2 000.00
04/15	Bank Account		500.00	
	A/R - Receiver General			500.00

In Simply Accounting, the refund request is processed as a Sales Invoice with Pay Later selected as the payment method, as in the following Sales Journal entry:

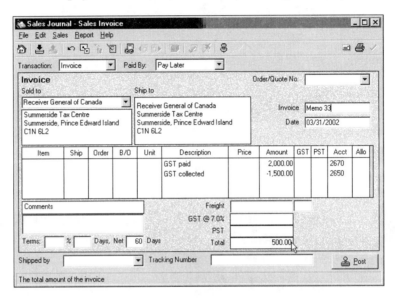

The journal entry produces an *Accounts Receivable* entry for the Receiver General:

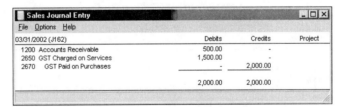

GST and Provincial Sales Taxes

The rules governing Provincial Sales Taxes vary from province to province, in terms of the rates of taxation, the goods and services that are taxed and whether or not PST is applied to the GST as well as to the base purchase price. The examples that follow assume that the item sold has both GST and PST applied.

Alberta has no Provincial Sales Tax. Therefore the examples provided above, without PST, illustrate the application of GST in Alberta.

Ontario, Manitoba, Saskatchewan, British Columbia

The provinces west of Quebec apply PST to the base price of the sale, the amount without GST included.

ONTARIO

Sold goods on account to customer for $500. GST charged is 7% and PST charged is 8%.

GST = (0.07 x 500) = $35
PST = (0.08 x 500) = $40
Total amount of invoice = $500 + $35 + $40 = $575

Date	Particulars	Ref.	Debit	Credit
xx/xx	Accounts Receivable		575.00	
	GST Charged on Sales			35.00
	PST Payable			40.00

The full amount of PST collected on sales is remitted to the provincial Minister of Finance (less any applicable sales tax commissions).

Nova Scotia, Newfoundland, New Brunswick, Labrador

Harmonized Sales Tax

The Harmonized Sales Tax model adopted in the Atlantic provinces is the one that the federal government would like to apply in all provinces across Canada.

In the participating Atlantic provinces, the GST and PST are harmonized at a single rate of 15 percent. The full 15 percent Harmonized Sales Tax (HST) operates much like the basic GST, with HST remittances equal to HST collected on sales less HST paid on purchases.

NEW BRUNSWICK

Sold goods on account to customer for $575, including HST at 15% ($500 base price).

HST = (0.15 x 500) = $75
Total amount of invoice = $575

Date	Particulars	Ref.	Debit	Credit
xx/xx	Accounts Receivable		575.00	
	HST Charged on Sales			75.00
	Revenue from Sales			500.00

A single remittance for the full 15 percent is made to the Receiver General; the provincial portion of the HST is not remitted separately.

Quebec Sales Tax (QST)

Provincial Sales Taxes in Quebec (QST) are also combined with the GST. The provincial tax rate applies to a broad base of goods and services, like the base that has GST applied. The QST is calculated on the base amount of the sale plus the GST. That is, QST is applied to GST — a piggy-backed tax or a tax on a tax.

QUEBEC

Sold goods on account to customer for $500. GST charged is 7% and QST charged is 7.5%.

GST = (0.07 x 500) = $35
QST = (0.075 x 535) = $40.13
Total amount of invoice = $500.00 + $35.00 + $40.13 = $575.13

Date	Particulars	Ref.	Debit	Credit
xx/xx	Accounts Receivable		575.13	
	GST Charged on Sales			35.00
	QST Charged on Sales			40.13
	Revenue from Sales			500.00

QST is remitted to the Quebec Minister of Revenue separately from GST. However, part of the QST is refundable and businesses can deduct some of the QST they pay on their purchases from the QST they collect on sales. The QST paid on items that are inputs to the business is refundable, the rest is not. Therefore, QST paid must be designated as refundable or non-refundable at the time of the purchase and when the purchase is recorded.

Prince Edward Island

Provincial Sales Taxes in PEI are applied to the base sale price plus GST. However, unlike Quebec, and like Ontario, some items have only GST applied and some have both GST and PST applied.

PRINCE EDWARD ISLAND

Sold goods on account to customer for $500. GST charged is 7% and PST charged is 10%.

GST = (0.07 x 500) = $35
PST = (0.10 x 535) = $53.50
Total amount of invoice = $500.00 + $35.00 + $53.50 = $588.50

Date	Particulars	Ref.	Debit	Credit
xx/xx	Accounts Receivable		588.50	
	GST Charged on Sales			35.00
	PST Payable			53.50
	Revenue from Sales			500.00

The full amount of PST collected on sales is remitted to the provincial Minister of Finance (less any applicable sales tax commissions).

PST Paid on Purchases

PST in Ontario is officially named the Retail Sales Tax. In BC, it is named the Social Services Tax.

PST is paid by the final customer of a taxable product or service. It is a retail sales tax. Thus, a business pays PST on the purchase of any goods that will be used within the business. If a business charges PST on sales, it can apply for PST exemption so that goods purchased for resale will be tax-exempt. In addition, equipment and tools used to manufacture taxable goods can be purchased without paying PST. Goods or services consumed by the business (office supplies, telephone or truck repairs) are taxable. Because PST paid by the business is not refundable (except for selected purchases in Quebec), it is added directly to the expense or asset cost associated with the purchase.

GST Adjustments for Bad Debt

If you have not created a separate ITC Adjustments account, you can debit GST Charged on Sales directly instead. Separate accounts show a direct correspondence of the amounts with the GST report.

Most businesses set up an allowance for doubtful accounts or bad debts, knowing that some of their customers will fail to pay. When the allowance is set up, a bad debts or uncollectable accounts expense account is debited. When a business is certain that a customer will not pay its account, the debt should be written off. In the past, the business would do this by crediting *Accounts Receivable* and debiting *Allowance for Doubtful Accounts*. When GST applies, an extra step is required. Part of the original sales invoice was entered as a credit (increase) to *GST Charged on Sales*. The amount of the GST liability can be reduced by the portion of the unpaid debt that was GST. A separate GST account, *ITC Adjustments*, may be used to record the GST for this transaction. The procedure for entering the transaction in Simply Accounting is to record the write-off of the debt in the Sales Journal using the following steps:

- Select the customer whose debt will not be paid.
- Enter a source document number to identify the transaction (e.g., memo).
- Enter the unpaid invoice minus GST as a negative amount in the Amount field.
- Enter the *Allowance for Doubtful Accounts* account number in the Account field.
- Advance to the next line of the invoice.
- Enter the GST that was charged on the invoice as a negative amount in the Amount field.
- Enter the *ITC Adjustments* account number in the Account field.

Review the transaction. The *Accounts Receivable* account is credited (reduced) by the full amount of the invoice to remove the balance owing by this customer. *Allowance for Doubtful Accounts* has been debited (reduced) by the amount of the invoice minus GST. The *ITC Adjustments* account has been debited for the GST portion of the invoice to reduce the liability to the Receiver General.

Manually you would complete the entry as follows:

---

1. Set up the Allowance for Bad Debts.

Date	Particulars	Ref.	Debit	Credit
xx/xx	Uncollectable Accounts Expense		1 000.00	
	Allowance for Doubtful Accounts			1 000.00

2. Customer G. Bell declares bankruptcy. Write off outstanding balance, $214, including GST.

Date	Particulars	Ref.	Debit	Credit
xx/xx	Allowance for Doubtful Accounts		200.00	
	ITC Adjustments		14.00	
	Accounts Receivable, G. Bell			214.00

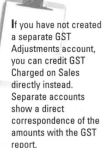

If you have not created a separate GST Adjustments account, you can credit GST Charged on Sales directly instead. Separate accounts show a direct correspondence of the amounts with the GST report.

Occasionally, a bad debt is recovered after it has been written off. When this occurs, the above procedure is reversed and the GST liability must also be restored. Another separate GST account, *GST Adjustments*, may be used to record the increase in the liability to the Receiver General. The recovery is entered as a non-inventory sale in the Sales Journal using the following steps:

- Select the customer and enter the date and source document number.
- Type an appropriate comment such as "Debt recovered" in the Description field.
- Enter the invoice amount minus GST as a positive amount in the Amount field.
- Enter the *Allowance for Doubtful Accounts* account number in the Account field.
- Advance to the next line of the invoice.
- Enter the GST that was charged on the original invoice as a positive amount in the Amount field.
- Enter the *GST Adjustments* account number in the Account field.

Review the transaction. You will see that *Accounts Receivable* has been debited for the full amount of the invoice. *Allowance for Doubtful Accounts* has been credited for the amount of the invoice minus GST. The *GST Adjustments* account has been credited for the amount of the GST to record the increase in the liability to the Receiver General.

As the final step, record the customer's payment using the Receipts Journal as you would record any other customer payment.

CORRECTING ERRORS AFTER POSTING

Reversing Entries

We all make mistakes. This appendix outlines briefly the procedures you need to follow for those rare occasions when you have posted a journal entry incorrectly.

Obviously, you should try to detect errors before posting. Reviewing the journal entry should become routine practice. The software has built in a number of safeguards that help you avoid mistakes. For example, outstanding invoices cannot be overpaid; employee wages and payroll deductions are calculated automatically, etc. Furthermore, names of accounts, customers, vendors, employees and inventory items appear in full, so that you may check your journal information easily.

Before making a reversing entry, consider the consequences of not correcting the error. For example, spelling mistakes in the customer name may not be desirable, but they will not influence the financial statements. After making the correction in the ledger, the newly printed customer statement will be correct (the journal will retain the original spelling). Sometimes, however, the mistake is more serious. Financial statements will be incorrect if amounts or accounts are wrong. Payroll tax deductions will be incorrect if the wage amount is incorrect. GST and PST remittances may be incorrect as a result of incorrect sales or purchase amounts. Discounts will be incorrectly calculated if an invoice or payment date is incorrect. Some errors also originate from outside sources. For example, purchase items may be incorrectly priced by the vendor.

For audit purposes, prepare a memo explaining the error and the correction procedure. A complete reversing entry is often the simplest way to make the corrections for a straightforward audit trail. With Simply Accounting's recall and lookup features, they are made easier because you can see an exact copy of the original entry that was incorrect. With invoice lookup turned on, you can automatically reverse and correct Sales and Purchases Journal entries by adjusting the original entry. Choose Adjust Invoice from the pull-down menu under Sale or Purchase or click the Adjust invoice tool in the journal (page 149). Payroll entries can be reversed and corrected in the Payroll Journal by choosing Adjust Cheque from the pull-down menu under Cheque, or by clicking the Adjust cheque tool (page 291). Similarly, General Journal entries can be adjusted automatically (page 80).

Under all circumstances, Generally Accepted Accounting Principles should be followed.

Reversing entries in all journals have several common elements. In each case, you should use an appropriate source number that identifies the entry as reversing (e.g., add ADJ or REV to the original source number). You should use the original posting date and add a comment. Make the reversing entry as illustrated on the following pages. Display the reversing journal entry, review it carefully and, when you are certain it is correct, post it. Next you must enter the correct version of the transaction as a new journal entry with an appropriate identifying source number (e.g., add COR to the original source number).

Reversing entries are presented below for each journal. Only the transaction portion of each screen is shown because the remaining parts of the journal screen do not change. The original and the reversing entry screens and most of the corresponding journal displays are included. Explanatory notes appear with each set of entries.

GENERAL JOURNAL: Original Entry

Account	Debits	Credits	Allo
1280 Prepaid Insurance	1,200.00	--	
1080 Bank Account: Chequing	--	1,200.00	
Total	1,200.00	1,200.00	

Reversing Entry
- Use the same accounts and amounts as in the original entry.
- Accounts that were debited should be credited, and accounts that were credited should be debited.
- Repeat the project allocation, if there is one, using the original percentages.
- The General Journal display is not shown because it looks basically the same as the journal input form.
- If you have invoice lookup turned on, you can use the Adjust a previously posted entry option instead (page 80).

Account	Debits	Credits	Allo
1080 Bank Account: Chequing	1,200.00	--	
1280 Prepaid Insurance	--	1,200.00	
Total	1,200.00	1,200.00	

PURCHASES JOURNAL (NON-INVENTORY): Original Entry

Item	Rec'd	Order	B/O	Unit	Description	Price	G	G. Amt.	P	P. Amt.	Amount	Acct	Allo
					truck expenses		3	21.00	8.00	24.00	300.00	5260	√

☑ Invoice Received   Freight [   ][   ][   ][   ]

GST	21.00
PST	24.00
Total	345.00

Terms: 1.00 % 20 Days, Net 30 Days

08/31/2002 (J160)	Debits	Credits	Project
2670 GST Paid on Purchases	21.00	-	
5260 Truck Expenses	324.00	-	
- Contracting			259.20
- School Board Project			64.80
2200 Accounts Payable	-	345.00	
	345.00	345.00	

Reversing Entry

- The only change you must make is that positive amounts in the original entry become negative amounts in the reversing entry (place a minus sign before the amounts in the Amount field and in the Freight amount field). GST and PST amounts will be reversed automatically.
- Similarly, change negative amounts, such as for GST Paid (in remittances) to positive amounts.
- Use the same amounts and accounts in the reversing entry as in the original entry.
- Repeat the project allocation, if there is one, using the original percentages.
- If you have invoice lookup turned on, you can use the Adjust invoice option, unless you are correcting for choosing the wrong vendor (page 149).

Item	Rec'd	Order	B/O	Unit	Description	Price	G	G. Amt.	P	P. Amt.	Amount	Acct	Allo
					truck expenses		3	-21.00	8.00	-24.00	-300.00	5260	√

☑ Invoice Received   Freight [   ][   ][   ][   ]

GST	-21.00
PST	-24.00
Total	-345.00

Terms: 1.00 % 20 Days, Net 30 Days

08/31/2002 (J161)	Debits	Credits	Project
2200 Accounts Payable	345.00	-	
2670 GST Paid on Purchases	-	21.00	
5260 Truck Expenses	-	324.00	
- Contracting			-259.20
- School Board Project			-64.80
	345.00	345.00	

PAYMENTS JOURNAL (OR RECEIPTS): Original Entry

Invoice/Pre-pmt.	Original Amt.	Amt. Owing	Disc. Available	Disc. Taken	Payment Amt.
GTS	345.00	345.00	3.00	3.00	342.00
				Total	342.00

08/31/2002 (J162)	Debits	Credits	Project
2200 Accounts Payable	345.00	-	
1080 Bank Account: Chequing	-	342.00	
5100 Purchase Discounts	-	3.00	
	345.00	345.00	

Reversing Entry

- Positive amounts in the original entry become negative amounts in the reversing entry.
- Click the Include fully paid invoices tool.
- In the Payment Amt. field, click the invoice line for the payment being reversed.
- Type a minus sign and the amount of the cheque.
- Click the Disc. Taken field. Type a minus sign and the amount of the discount.
- This will restore the original balance owing for the invoice and reverse the discount. Refer to page 208.
- If you have already cleared the paid invoice, make a Sales Journal entry for the amount of the payment and the discount taken (non-taxable) to restore the balance owing.

Invoice/Pre-pmt.	Original Amt.	Amt. Owing	Disc. Available	Disc. Taken	Payment Amt.
GTS	345.00	0.00	0.00	-3.00	-342.00
				Total	-342.00

08/31/2002 (J163)	Debits	Credits	Project
1080 Bank Account: Chequing	342.00	-	
5100 Purchase Discounts	3.00	-	
2200 Accounts Payable	-	345.00	
	345.00	345.00	

OTHER PAYMENTS: Original Entry

Acct	Description	Amount	G	G. Amt.	P	P. Amt.	Allo
5250 Telephone Expense	monthly phone service	120.00	3	8.40	8.00	9.60	√
					Total	138.00	

08/31/2002 (J166)	Debits	Credits	Project
2670 GST Paid on Purchases	8.40	-	
5250 Telephone Expense	129.60	-	
- Contracting			103.68
- School Board Project			25.92
1080 Bank Account: Chequing	-	138.00	
	138.00	138.00	

- Again, the only change you must make is that positive amounts in the original entry become negative amounts in the reversing entry. Place a minus sign before the amounts in the Amount field. GST and PST amounts will be reversed automatically.
- Similarly, change negative amounts, such as for GST Paid (in remittances) to positive amounts.
- Use the same amounts and accounts in the reversing entry as in the original entry.
- Repeat the project allocation, if there is one, using the original percentages.
- If you have invoice lookup turned on, you can use the Adjust a previously posted entry option, unless you are correcting for choosing the wrong vendor (page 149).

Acct	Description	Amount	G	G. Amt.	P	P. Amt.	Allo
5250 Telephone Expense	monthly phone service	-120.00	3	-8.40	8.00	-9.60	√

	Total	-138.00

08/31/2002 (J167)	Debits	Credits	Project
1080 Bank Account: Chequing	138.00	-	
2670 GST Paid on Purchases	-	8.40	
5250 Telephone Expense	-	129.60	
- Contracting			-103.68
- School Board Project			-25.92
	138.00	138.00	

CREDIT CARD BILL PAYMENT: Original Entry

Credit Card Payable Account Balance:	207.00
Additonal Fees and Interest:	20.00
Payment Amount:	227.00

08/31/2002 (J168)	Debits	Credits	Project
2250 Chargit Payable	207.00	-	
5020 Credit Card Fees	20.00	-	
1080 Bank Account: Chequing	-	227.00	
	227.00	227.00	

Reversing Entry

- Change the positive amounts in the original entry to negative amounts in the reversing entry. Place a minus sign before the amounts in the Additional Fees and Interest field and the Payment Amount field.
- Use the same amounts in the reversing entry as in the original entry.

Credit Card Payable Account Balance:	0.00
Additonal Fees and Interest:	-20.00
Payment Amount:	-227.00

08/31/2002 (J169)	Debits	Credits	Project
1080 Bank Account: Chequing	227.00	-	
2250 Chargit Payable	-	207.00	
5020 Credit Card Fees	-	20.00	
	227.00	227.00	

INVENTORY PURCHASE: Original Entry

Item	Rec'd	Order	B/O	Unit	Description	Price	G	G. Amt.	P	P. Amt.	Amount	Acct	Allo
07	3			Each	Tube Slide: classic	240.00	3	50.40			720.00	1450	

☑ Invoice Received   Freight | 3 | 2.80 | | | 40.00

GST   53.20
PST
Terms: ☐ % ☐ Days, Net 30 Days   Total   813.20

08/31/2002 (J170)	Debits	Credits	Project
1450 Slides	720.00	-	
2670 GST Paid on Purchases	53.20	-	
5080 Freight Expense	40.00	-	
2200 Accounts Payable	-	813.20	
	813.20	813.20	

Reversing Entry

- Place a minus sign before the quantity in the Rec'd field to change positive quantities in the original entry to negative in the reversing entry. GST and PST amounts will then be reversed automatically.
- Similarly, change negative quantities, such as for returns, to positive by removing the minus sign in the Rec'd field.
- Add a minus sign to the freight amount if freight is charged.
- Use the same accounts and amounts in the reversing entry as in the original entry.
- Repeat the project allocation, if there is one, using the original percentages.
- If you have invoice lookup turned on, you can use the Adjust invoice option, unless you are correcting for choosing the wrong vendor (page 149).

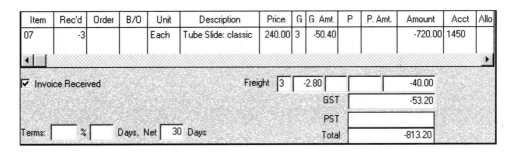

Item	Rec'd	Order	B/O	Unit	Description	Price	G	G. Amt.	P	P. Amt.	Amount	Acct	Allo
07	-3			Each	Tube Slide: classic	240.00	3	-50.40			-720.00	1450	

☑ Invoice Received   Freight | 3 | -2.80 | | | -40.00

GST   -53.20
PST
Terms: ☐ % ☐ Days, Net 30 Days   Total   -813.20

08/31/2002 (J171)	Debits	Credits	Project
2200 Accounts Payable	813.20	-	
1450 Slides	-	720.00	
2670 GST Paid on Purchases	-	53.20	
5080 Freight Expense	-	40.00	
	813.20	813.20	

SALES JOURNAL (INVENTORY & NON-INVENTORY): Original Entry

Item	Ship	Order	B/O	Unit	Description	Price	Amount	GST	PST	Acct	Allo
KIT-A	1			Kit	Tom Sawyer Kit	1,800.00	1,800.00	3	8.00	4040	✓
					Playground repairs		2,000.00	3		4020	✓

Comments		Freight	50.00	3
Thank you for playing with us.		GST @ 7.0%	269.50	
		PST	144.00	
Terms: 2.00 % 10 Days, Net 30 Days		Total	4,263.50	

08/31/2002 (J172)	Debits	Credits	Project
1200 Accounts Receivable	4,263.50	-	
5030 Cost of Goods Sold	847.41	-	
- General Sales			847.41
1470 Playground Kits	-	847.41	
2640 PST Payable	-	144.00	
2650 GST Charged on Services	-	269.50	
4020 Revenue from Contracting	-	2,000.00	
- Contracting			2,000.00
4040 Revenue from Sales	-	1,800.00	
- General Sales			1,800.00
4200 Freight Revenue	-	50.00	
	5,110.91	5,110.91	

Reversing Entry

- For inventory sales, place a minus sign before the quantity in the Ship field to change positive quantities in the original entry to negative in the reversing entry. Similarly, change negative quantities, such as for returns, to positive by removing the minus sign.
- For non-inventory sales, change positive amounts in the original entry to negative amounts in the reversing entry. Place a minus sign before the amount in the Amount column.
- Add a minus sign to the freight amount if freight is charged.
- Use the same accounts and amounts in the reversing entry as in the original entry.
- Repeat the project allocation, if there is one, using the original percentages.
- If invoice lookup is turned on, you can use the Adjust invoice option, unless you are correcting for choosing the wrong customer (page 149).

Item	Ship	Order	B/O	Unit	Description	Price	Amount	GST	PST	Acct	Allo
KIT-A	-1			Kit	Tom Sawyer Kit	1,800.00	-1,800.00	3	8.00	4040	✓
					Playground repairs		-2,000.00	3		4020	✓

Comments		Freight	-50.00	3
Thank you for playing with us.		GST @ 7.0%	-269.50	
		PST	-144.00	
Terms: 2.00 % 10 Days, Net 30 Days		Total	-4,263.50	

08/31/2002 (J173)		Debits	Credits	Project
1470	Playground Kits	847.41	-	
2640	PST Payable	144.00	-	
2650	GST Charged on Services	269.50	-	
4020	Revenue from Contracting	2,000.00	-	
	- Contracting			-2,000.00
4040	Revenue from Sales	1,800.00	-	
	- General Sales			-1,800.00
4200	Freight Revenue	50.00	-	
1200	Accounts Receivable	-	4,263.50	
5030	Cost of Goods Sold	-	847.41	
	- General Sales			-847.41
		5,110.91	5,110.91	

PAYROLL JOURNAL: Original Entry

Income	Deductions	Taxes				Period Ending	08/31/2002
Reg.	80.00	1,120.00	Commission			Release	
OT 1	4.00	84.00	Benefits			Advance	200.00
OT 2			Benefits (Que)				
Sal.			Vacation	48.16			

Income	Deductions	Taxes				Income	Deductions	Taxes
RRSP		25.00	United Way		10.00	EI		28.90
Union Dues		24.08				CPP/QPP		41.71
CSB Plan		20.00				Tax		138.00
Gp Insurance		10.00				Tax (Que)		

The Deductions and the Taxes tab amounts are shown together on this split Payroll screen illustration.

08/31/2002 (J174)		Debits	Credits	Project
1240	Advances Receivable	200.00	-	
5300	Wage Expense	1,252.16	-	
5310	EI Expense	40.46	-	
5320	CPP Expense	41.71	-	
5330	WSIB Expense	37.69	-	
5360	EHT Expense	11.80	-	
1080	Bank Account: Chequing	-	1,106.31	
2300	Vacation Payable	-	48.16	
2310	EI Payable	-	69.36	
2320	CPP Payable	-	83.42	
2330	Income Tax Payable	-	138.00	
2390	EHT Payable	-	11.80	
2400	RRSP Payable	-	25.00	
2410	Union Dues Payable	-	24.08	
2420	CSB Plan Payable	-	20.00	
2430	Group Insurance Payable	-	10.00	
2440	United Way Payable	-	10.00	
2460	WSIB Payable	-	37.69	
		1,583.82	1,583.82	

Reversing Entry

- Redo the original incorrect entry but DO NOT POST IT!
- Click the Enter taxes manually tool to open all the deduction fields for editing.
- Type a minus sign in front of the number of hours (regular and overtime) or in front of the Salary and Commission amounts. Press $\boxed{tab}$ to update the amounts, including vacation pay (i.e., change them to negative amounts).
- For the Advance field, change the sign for the amount. Advances should have a minus sign in the reversing entry and advances recovered should be positive amounts.
- Click the Deductions tab. Edit each deduction amount by typing a minus sign in front of the amount.
- Click the Taxes tab. Check the amounts for CPP, EI and income tax with the original journal entry because if the employee has reached the maximum contribution or has changed tax brackets since the original entry, these amounts may be incorrect. Change them to match the original if necessary.
- Repeat the project allocation, if there is one, using the original percentages.
- Remember to click the Calculate taxes automatically tool before you make the correct payroll entry.
- You can use the Adjust Cheque option in the Paycheques Journal to reverse and correct payroll transactions posted from the Paycheques Journal or the Payroll Cheque Run Journal, unless you are correcting for choosing the wrong employee (page 291).

Income	Deductions	Taxes			Period Ending	08/31/2002
Reg.	-80.00	-1,120.00	Commission		Release	
OT 1	-4.00	-84.00	Benefits		Advance	-200.00
OT 2			Benefits (Que)			
Sal.			Vacation	-48.16		

Income	Deductions	Taxes				Income	Deductions	Taxes
RRSP	-25.00	United Way	-10.00			EI		-28.90
Union Dues	-24.08					CPP/QPP		-41.71
CSB Plan	-20.00					Tax		-138.00
Gp Insurance	-10.00					Tax (Que)		

08/31/2002 (J175)	Debits	Credits	Project
1080 Bank Account: Chequing	1,106.31	-	
2300 Vacation Payable	48.16	-	
2310 EI Payable	69.36	-	
2320 CPP Payable	83.42	-	
2330 Income Tax Payable	138.00	-	
2390 EHT Payable	11.80	-	
2400 RRSP Payable	25.00	-	
2410 Union Dues Payable	24.08	-	
2420 CSB Plan Payable	20.00	-	
2430 Group Insurance Payable	10.00	-	
2440 United Way Payable	10.00	-	
2460 WSIB Payable	37.69	-	
1240 Advances Receivable	-	200.00	
5300 Wage Expense	-	1,252.16	
5310 EI Expense	-	40.46	
5320 CPP Expense	-	41.71	
5330 WSIB Expense	-	37.69	
5360 EHT Expense	-	11.80	
	1,583.82	1,583.82	

ITEM ASSEMBLY JOURNAL: Original Entry

Assembly Components

Item	Qty	Unit	Description	Unit Cost	Amount
01	1	Each	Carousel	200.00	200.00
03	1	Each	Slide: classic	250.00	250.00
05	1	Each	Swing Set: double	200.00	200.00
07	1	Each	Tube Slide: classic	250.00	250.00

				Additional Costs	75.00
				Total	975.00

Assembled Items

Item	Qty	Unit	Description	Unit Cost	Amount
KIT-A	1	Kit	Tom Sawyer Kit	975.00	975.00

				Total	975.00

06/07/2002 (J112)	Debits	Credits	Project
1470 Playground Kits	975.00	-	
1420 Carousels	-	200.00	
1450 Slides	-	500.00	
1460 Swings	-	200.00	
5040 Assembly Costs	-	75.00	
	975.00	975.00	

Reversing Entry

- Re-enter the item assembly as you did originally. Recall the entry if you stored it (check that unit costs have not changed for the recalled entry).
- Type a minus sign in front of each quantity in the Qty fields for both the Assembly Components and the Assembled Items sections.
- Also type a minus sign in front of the amount for Additional Costs.

Assembly Components

Item	Qty	Unit	Description	Unit Cost	Amount
01	-1	Each	Carousel	200.00	-200.00
03	-1	Each	Slide: classic	250.00	-250.00
05	-1	Each	Swing Set: double	200.00	-200.00
07	-1	Each	Tube Slide: classic	250.00	-250.00

				Additional Costs	-75.00
				Total	-975.00

Assembled Items

Item	Qty	Unit	Description	Unit Cost	Amount
KIT-A	-1	Kit	Tom Sawyer Kit	975.00	-975.00

				Total	-975.00

06/07/2002 (J113)	Debits	Credits	Project
1420 Carousels	200.00	-	
1450 Slides	500.00	-	
1460 Swings	200.00	-	
5040 Assembly Costs	75.00	-	
1470 Playground Kits	-	975.00	
	975.00	975.00	

ADJUSTMENTS JOURNAL: Original Entry

Item	Qty	Unit	Description	Unit Cost	Amount	Acct	Allo
06	-1	Each	Swing Set: triple	250.00	-250.00	5032 Dama	√
				Total	-250.00		

08/31/2002 (J176)	Debits	Credits	Project
5032 Damaged Inventory	250.00	-	
- General Sales			250.00
1460 Swings	-	250.00	
	250.00	250.00	

Reversing Entry

- Change the sign for the quantity in the Qty field (positive to negative or negative to positive).
- Repeat the project allocation, if there is one, using the original percentages.

Item	Qty	Unit	Description	Unit Cost	Amount	Acct	Allo
06	1	Each	Swing Set: triple	250.00	250.00	5032 Dama	√
				Total	250.00		

08/31/2002 (J177)	Debits	Credits	Project
1460 Swings	250.00	-	
5032 Damaged Inventory	-	250.00	
- General Sales			-250.00
	250.00	250.00	

SETTING SYSTEM SECURITY

Entering Passwords

In Chapter 1, we showed the restricted access symbols that result from adding passwords to a data file. Passwords may be needed when a company's computer is shared and files can be easily accessed by any of the users. It is very easy to remove and modify data in Simply Accounting, although it is not that easy to do it by accident because of all the built-in warnings. Nonetheless, security of confidential information is always important, and Simply Accounting's passwords offer an extra level of protection from unauthorized access or alteration.

Passwords are set from the Home window. To set passwords,

◆ Choose the **Setup menu** and click **Set Security** to display the User Maintenance control window:

If you want to practise setting passwords, work with a separate copy of your data file. For example save the file as Security.sdb and work with this new file. To be sure that you do not forget a password, choose a simple one such as your first name for the sysadmin password.

System Passwords

You can set passwords for different users and for access to different parts of the program. The highest level of access comes with the sysadmin password, which allows the system administrator to enter, use or modify any part of the data files, including adding and deleting other users and their passwords. The sysadmin password must be set before any other passwords can be set, so this password is selected initially.

To enter the password,

◆ Click **Edit** to open the password entry screen:

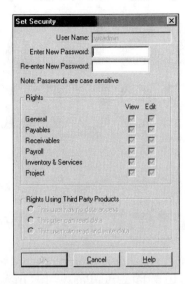

The user name "sysadmin" cannot be changed either.

Notice that most of the fields cannot be changed because the system administrator must have the right to control all aspects the program.

◆ Click the **Enter New Password field** to move the cursor.

◆ Type the word or code that you want as your password. You can use up to seven characters as the code, choosing any combination of letters and numbers.

◆ Press ⌨(tab) to advance to the next field, Re-enter New Password.

For security reasons, the password never shows on the screen — you will see an asterisk (*) for each letter or number you typed. As an additional precaution, Simply Accounting requires you to enter the code twice in exactly the same way.

◆ Type the password or code again.

If the two entries do not match, Simply Accounting will warn you:

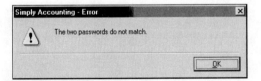

◆ Click **OK** and try re-entering the code again.

It is possible that you mistyped the first entry, so if you do not have a match, go back to the Enter New Password field and type in the code. Then re-enter the password in the Re-enter New Password field.

Passwords are case sensitive. If you create a password with uppercase letters, you must use uppercase letters to gain entry to the program.

◆ Click **OK** to return to the User Maintenance screen.

The Add button is now available for adding users with different passwords. You can return to the Home window or you can set passwords for additional users.

660

Second-Level Passwords and Rights

You can set a second password that restricts access to some of the ledgers and journals after adding a sysadmin (system level) password.

◆ Click **Add** to open the Set Security screen again:

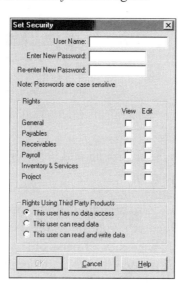

The rights of all additional users may be restricted regarding both access to different modules of the Simply Accounting program and to external programs that may be linked to the Simply Accounting data. For additional users, the system administrator must enter a name for the user and a unique password. User passwords must be different from the system password to serve the purpose of restricting access.

◆ Click the **User Name field**.

◆ Type the name of the first user and press ⌧tab to advance to the Enter New Password field.

◆ Type the word or code that you want as your restricted usage password. Again, you can use any combination of up to seven letters and numbers as the code.

◆ Press ⌧tab to advance to the next field, Re-enter New Password.

◆ Type the password or code again.

When the two entries match, you can continue by defining the rights for this user. For each of the six ledgers, you can allow viewing, editing or no access. Viewing access permits the users to see the reports and entries previously made but not to add to or change the information. Editing access allows the user to make journal entries and ledger changes but not to view reports.

To allow access, click the check box beside the ledger in the appropriate column. For example, to allow viewing access only for the General Ledger, click the box beside General in the View column. To allow no access, leave the check boxes empty. A ✓ indicates that access is provided.

◆ Click **OK** to save the details for this user and return to the User Maintenance screen.

You can continue to add users and to set passwords for them in the same way. After entering all the users and passwords,

◆ Click **Close** to return to the Home window. Nothing has changed yet.

However, the next time you open the file, the following dialog box will appear and you will be required to enter the password before you can open the data file:

◆ Type the user's name and password or code.

◆ Click **OK**.

If you enter an incorrect code, nothing happens — the Password dialog box remains open. If you enter sysadmin as the user and the system administrator password, you will have full access to all parts of the program, including the security settings. After you have set passwords, you must enter the program with the system password to change the security settings.

If you enter as another user, you will be shown a restricted view of the Home window similar to the following one:

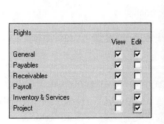

The Home window above shows the access rights definitions beside it. This user has no access to the Payroll Ledger or Journals — these icons do not appear. Full access to the General Ledger is available because these icons are shown in their normal manner. The Payables and Receivables Ledgers and Journals can be viewed but not edited (the pencil icon has an X above it). The Project and Inventory & Services Ledgers, with the X above the report icons, can be edited, but reports cannot be viewed. Several of the main menu options are also restricted, including the Set Security option.

Changing and Removing Passwords

To change or remove passwords, you must access the restricted files as the sysadmin user with the appropriate password.

Changing Passwords

To change a password, access the files with the sysadmin password.

◆   Choose the **Setup menu** and click **Set Security**:

All users are now listed on the User Maintenance screen.

◆   Click the name of the user whose details or password you want to change.

◆   Click **Edit** to open the Set Security screen.

◆   Type a new code or password in the Enter New Password field.

◆   Re-enter the same code in the Re-enter New Password field.

You may also change access privileges for this user from this screen by clicking in the View or Edit columns beside a module name to remove previously entered checkmarks or to add new ones.

◆   Click OK to save the changes and return to the User Maintenance screen.

To change other passwords, select the user's name, click Edit and repeat the step of entering the new code in the two password fields.

Removing Passwords

To remove a password, access the files with the system administrator password.

◆   Choose the **Setup menu** and click **Set Security**.

◆   Click **the User name**.

◆   Click **Delete**.

There is a Repair Security submenu option under Database Utilities on the Maintenance menu. Choosing this option will delete all passwords from the file except the one for sysadmin. User names will remain. Use this utility if you see a warning message that the security file is damaged. You can then re-enter passwords for the different users.

You will see a message asking you to confirm the deletion:

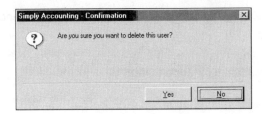

◆ Click **Yes**.

Repeat these steps to remove the other users.

◆ Click **Close** to return to the Home window.

If you wish to remove all passwords at once, you can do so by removing the system administrator password.

◆ Choose the **Setup menu** and click **Set Security**.

◆ Click **sysadmin** on the user name list.

◆ Click **Clear** to see the usual pre-deletion confirmation:

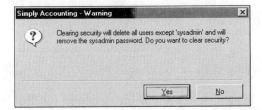

◆ Click **Yes** to confirm the deletion.

◆ Click **Close** to return to the Home window.

The sysadmin user name will not be removed, but all other users and all passwords will be removed. You should now be able to access your data files without a password.

INTEGRATION WITH OTHER SOFTWARE

Exporting Data and Reports

Simply Accounting includes a large number and variety of reports and graphs as part of the standard package. However, there may still be times when you want to work with the financial data of your company in ways that cannot be accommodated by the accounting software. Simply Accounting allows any report or graph that you can display to be exported to other kinds of software. Exporting is the ability to transfer information from one software application to another. These exported reports may then be used with a spreadsheet or wordprocessing application.

Simply Accounting allows files to be exported to the file and folder you specify. Exporting report files to other software applications allows the user to perform additional calculations and interpret reports for management decision making. Thus, integration is an important step in making the accounting process meaningful.

Integrated files can be used by businesses in a number of different ways as decision support tools. They include sales forecasting, determining implications of new taxes and tax increases and ratio analysis of financial statements. Reports gathered from Simply Accounting and spreadsheet applications can be brought together in a wordprocessing or presentation package to prepare comprehensive final documents.

Exporting Reports

Any report that you can display and print, you can also export to another software application. When you export a series of financial statements to a spreadsheet, you can reformat the statements and calculate any financial ratios that you need in order to analyze further the performance of the business.

◆ Open the Play Wave Plus file for August 31.

◆ Display the Comparative Balance Sheet for May 31 and August 31, the end dates for the two fiscal quarters. (Display any report you want to export.)

The data in the bank statements for account reconciliation in this text were created by exporting General Ledger reports, editing them and then pasting the spreadsheet data into the QuarkXPress files.

◆ Choose the **File menu** and click **Export** in the report window to view the export options:

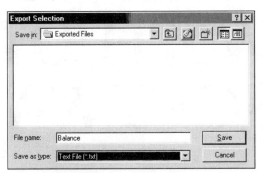

You may also see the My Documents folder as the default location.

By default, the folder you are currently using for your data files or, if you have exported files before, the folder you used most recently for exporting files, is selected. Only files with the selected format (.txt) are displayed in the File name box, so it may appear that the folder is empty. The file format you selected most recently is the selected file type.

◆ Click the **Save as type list arrow** to see the file format options:

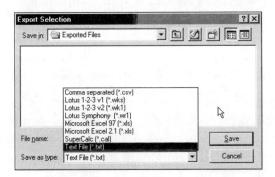

Exported File Formats

The available formats are compatible with wordprocessing, spreadsheet and database programs. If you want to use the report with a wordprocessing program, select the **Text File** format. To use the report in a database, choose the **Comma separated** format. The remaining formats are specialized for specific spreadsheet programs. They include two versions of **Lotus 1-2-3** (**v1** and **v2**), **Lotus Symphony**, **Microsoft Excel** (**97** and **2.1**) and **SuperCalc**. Simply Accounting adds a file name extension that is recognized by the program receiving the exported file. Thus, when you export a text file, .txt is the extension. For Excel files, the extension is .xls, etc. You must leave the file extension selected by Simply Accounting so that the receiving program will be able to recognize and open the exported file.

To save the Balance Sheet as a text file, click Text File as the File type. To save it as a Microsoft Excel file, click Microsoft Excel.

◆ Click **Microsoft Excel 97** to select this file type. Notice that the file extension has changed.

You can select the default folder for the new file or choose a different location. Click the list arrow for the Save in field to change folders just as you do for other file selection windows. Double click a folder in the text box area to open it. It is helpful to select the folder that contains your data files because this keeps all the files for your company together. You can also create a separate folder for your exported files as we have done in the illustrations above.

You can change the file name if you want. Simply Accounting automatically uses the report type as the file name, making recognition easy. You may want to add the company name. If you export the same type of report later, the same name will be used by default, and the first exported version will be overwritten, after your confirmation, so it is helpful to change the name before you export a report.

◆ Click **OK** to create the new file.

◆ Close the displayed report to return to the Home window.

◆ Close the Simply Accounting program.

◆ Start the Microsoft Excel program to access the new spreadsheet for the comparative balance sheet.

Exporting Data to MS Access

You can export reports to Microsoft Excel or you can export other parts of your data set directly to a Microsoft Access database. Since you do not have to choose a report, you can export a wide range of data in this way. To begin the export to MS Access,

◆ Click the **Export to Microsoft Access tool** or choose the File menu and click Export to Microsoft Access in the Home window. The introductory Wizard window appears:

◆ Click **Next** to proceed:

At this stage, you can choose whether to export all of the data set (Typical Export) or only the parts that you select. If you choose a typical export, you cannot select the file name and location for the exported file. Previously exported files are automatically replaced, so you should copy them to another file or location if you want to keep them. The custom export option will display all the data elements from which you can choose for the MS Access file. You can select one or more or all the data from the file and you can change the name of the exported file. The Wizard guides you through the steps of making these selections.

Leave the Typical Export option selected.

◆ Click **Next** to continue:

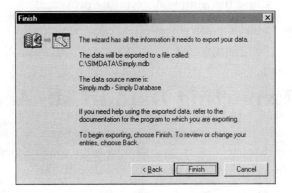

The file name and location are displayed for your reference.

◆ Click **Finish** to begin exporting the file. The Home window reappears when the file has been exported.

◆ Close the Simply Accounting program.

◆ Open the Microsoft Access program

◆ Open the file you just created (C:\SIMDATA\Simply.mdb).

You will see the parts of the database that you can now modify as needed:

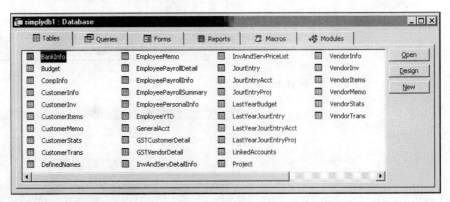

Data from all the ledgers is included, as well as budget details. Furthermore, since we have two complete fiscal periods in the file, data for the previous year is also available.

◆ Click the database you want to use to select it and click Open to see the data.

The MS Access version of the inventory and services price list is shown here:

You may be able to open and manipulate the Access database files with another database program if it can accept or convert the .mdb file.

You may be required to convert the .mdb file to a .db1 file if you have a more recent version of Microsoft Access than the one used by the Simply Accounting program.

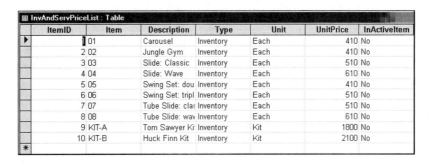

ItemID	Item	Description	Type	Unit	UnitPrice	InActiveItem
1	01	Carousel	Inventory	Each	410	No
2	02	Jungle Gym	Inventory	Each	410	No
3	03	Slide: Classic	Inventory	Each	510	No
4	04	Slide: Wave	Inventory	Each	610	No
5	05	Swing Set: dou	Inventory	Each	410	No
6	06	Swing Set: tripl	Inventory	Each	510	No
7	07	Tube Slide: clas	Inventory	Each	510	No
8	08	Tube Slide: wav	Inventory	Each	610	No
9	KIT-A	Tom Sawyer Ki	Inventory	Kit	1800	No
10	KIT-B	Huck Finn Kit	Inventory	Kit	2100	No

◆ Close the database files and MS Access when you have finished.

Exporting GIFI Reports

When you add the GIFI (General Index of Financial Information) codes to the General Ledger account records, you can export financial statements that use these codes to organize the reports. These are the account numbers or codes required for businesses filing their tax returns electronically with Canada Customs and Revenue Agency (CCRA). You can obtain more information about GIFI from the CCRA Web site at <www.ccra-adrc.gc.ca>.

The Canada Customs and Revenue Agency (formerly Revenue Canada) Web site included several documents about GIFI at the time this book was written. Search for GIFI on the Web site.

◆ Choose the **File menu** and click **Export GIFI** in the Home window:

◆ Choose a data set. You can export data for the current year or the previous fiscal year. Usually tax returns are prepared after a fiscal year has ended.

◆ Click **OK** to open the Export Selection screen:

At this stage, you can rename the exported file and choose a destination folder. You should not change the file extension because it is the format required by CCRA.

◆ Click **Save** to save the file and return to the Home window.

You can now open the newly created data file with a database program and print the report or send the file directly to CCRA.

DDE (Dynamic Data Exchange)

All the exported reports described so far provide a single or static file that you can integrate with other software programs. The next option, DDE or Dynamic Data Exchange, interacts dynamically with your data files. As the name DDE suggests, the link is interactive. As you make changes in Simply Accounting by entering transactions or changing records, the corresponding information in the linked file in the other program is also updated with the current information.

Data from each ledger must be exported separately, although you can easily combine information from two ledgers into a single external file by repeating the DDE selection process. We will add a list of vendors and the balance owing to a WordPerfect file.

◆ Choose **DDE** and then **Vendors** from the **Edit** menu in the Simply Accounting Home window:

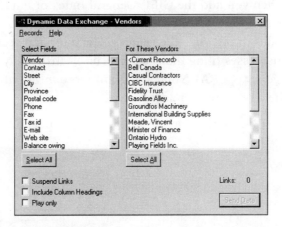

The data to be selected includes a set of fields and records. You can select one or more fields for one or more vendors. First, select the fields, the kind of information you want to link to the other program.

◆ Click **Vendor** in the Select Fields list.

◆ Press ⌐ctrl⌐ and click **Balance Owing** in the Select Fields list.

◆ Click **Select All** below the list For These Vendors to include all the vendors. You can include one or more of the vendor names individually.

To select more than one vendor from the list, press ⌐ctrl⌐ and click the name of each vendor you want to include.

DDE Options

There are three options in the DDE screen. You should choose to **Suspend Links** while exporting so that Simply Accounting does not attempt to update the linked program references until you have finished entering transactions. This speeds up the processing of data because the linked program is not updated continually as you work. Continual updating would have some pieces of information changed more than once in a work session because the link is dynamic, rather like the automatic recalculation in spreadsheets. If you have a large amount of data, continual updating can slow down the program.

The second option will **Include Column Headings** with the data, a good choice if you are sending a large number of fields of information that may look similar. Column headings are helpful when you create tables.

The third option applies if you have data for more than one company. The current file is named as **Play only** in the example. If you want to include only the current file in the DDE linkage, check Play only (your own file name will be substituted for Play). This will prevent the DDE link from updating references to other company files that you may have created elsewhere.

◆ Click **Include Columns**.

◆ Click **Play only** (or the name for your file) to prevent the link from affecting other data files.

◆ Click **Send Data**. After a brief delay, you will see the confirmation message:

The message advises you of the size of the data table you are linking. The one we selected contains all of the vendors in column one with the balance owing to each vendor in column two.

◆ Click **OK** to close the message and return to the DDE screen.

◆ Close the DDE window.

◆ Open the WordPerfect program (or another Windows wordprocessing program). You may want to leave the Simply Accounting program open in the background for this step so that you can add more data links.

◆ Choose **Paste Special** (or Paste Link) from the Edit menu. Do not use the Paste command as this will copy only the contents and not the link with the Simply Accounting data file. Paste Special will maintain the link.

You may see an intermediate screen advising you of the format of the data you are pasting.

◆ If Paste Link appears as a separate option at this stage, choose it as well.

◆ Click OK (or the appropriate command button) to continue.

This will place a copy of the data from the Simply Accounting program in your WordPerfect program.

Now when you add a new purchase invoice or make a payment to one of these vendors, the WordPerfect file will also remain current. If you add a new vendor, however, you must repeat the DDE procedure for the new vendor to add the new link.

Although a link may contain several fields and several records, each link will be treated as a single block of information. It is generally easier to manage the linked data if each link contains one piece of information. It may take longer to set up, but the end result is a more flexible file.

Clearly, using DDE takes more effort than exporting a report. However, you need to complete the setup only once and your final document will contain current information automatically whenever you need it. In addition, with DDE you can combine information from different ledgers or reports easily into a single document. For example, you can create form letters advising employees of their payroll deduction amounts. Another example might be a letter to all customers including an inventory list containing only item names and prices.

Importing Data to Simply Accounting

The ability to import external data adds further to the interactivity of the Simply Accounting program. Sales orders and purchase quotes may be received directly from customers and vendors by e-mail. If they use the same inventory codes and they also use Simply Accounting, these orders and quotes are incorporated directly as transactions. Bank statements may be imported directly from a financial institution and automatically reconciled. Journal entries and other transactions may also be brought into Simply Accounting.

Importing Bank Statements

When you import online bank statements into Simply Accounting by downloading from your financial institution's Web site, Simply Accounting automates the matching and clearing process. Simply Accounting changes the status of matched transactions to Cleared in the Account Reconciliation window by using the source number (such as the cheque number) and the amount to match transactions on your downloaded statement with transactions in your Simply Accounting records.

To import online statements, set up your bank account to use online banking on the Class Options tab screen in the account's ledger record.

◆ Open the ledger record for the bank account.

◆ Click the **Class Options** tab as shown here:

Your bank must be able to download statements in OFX (Open Financial Exchange) format, the file format used by Simply Accounting. Not all financial institutions supported this format at the time of writing this text.

If your bank requires you to enter a unique identifier instead of the bank's transit number in the Transit Number field in the bank's account, include the transit number at the beginning of the Account Number field. Contact your bank for more information.

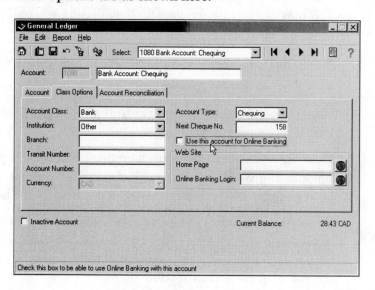

◆ Click **Use this account for Online Banking**.

◆ Type the bank's Web site address and login information.

◆ Close the ledger and Accounts windows to return to the Home window.

◆ Choose the **File menu** and click **Import Online Statements** to begin the downloading procedure:

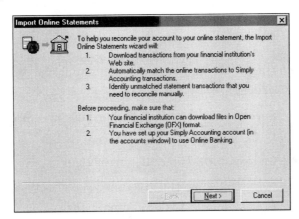

The opening screen advises you of what the program will do and the information you need to obtain. Follow the steps outlined in each screen to continue.

Importing Vendor and Customer Transactions

Vendors and Customers can e-mail you their sales invoices, sales quotes or purchase orders. When you import these transactions directly into Simply Accounting, your records are updated automatically. You can recall the imported quote or order to fill it. Similarly, you can e-mail (export) sales invoices, sales quotes, or purchase orders to vendors and customers. First you should enter the Import/Export tab information in the vendor/customer record.

◆ Open the ledger record for the vendor (or customer) you want to e-mail.

◆ Click the **Import/Export tab** to open this information screen:

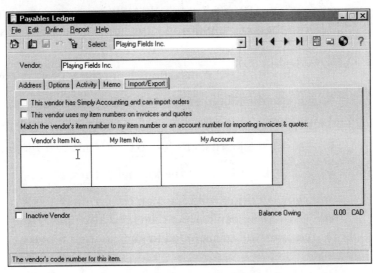

◆ Click **This vendor (or customer) has Simply Accounting and can import orders**.

If you and the vendor use the same inventory item numbers, click this option. The inventory matching boxes will be removed from the screen because they are not

Since the procedure for setting up and working with vendor and customer information is the same, we show only one.

Both you and your vendors or customers must use Simply Accounting version 7 or later and have MAPI-compatible e-mail programs (such as Lotus Domino or Microsoft Outlook Express) to use this feature.

A sales invoice or sales quote from a vendor becomes a purchase invoice or quote. A purchase order from a customer becomes a sales order when imported.

needed. If you do not use the same numbers, you can enter the matching information item by item. You may also do the matching when you import the transaction.

◆ Close the ledger window and the Vendors (Customers) window.

◆ Exit the Simply Accounting program before you attempt to import a form.

◆ Open your e-mail program.

◆ Open the e-mail message containing the Simply Accounting attachment. Then either

◆ Save the attached IMP file for later use, or double click the IMP file to use it immediately.

◆ Choose to Open the file rather than to save it.

◆ Enter the name (including the path, or location) of your company file, or click Browse to select your company file.

◆ Click OK.

◆ Open the transaction window for the transaction you imported. Use the Invoice Lookup feature to display the invoice, order or quote. Correct the details if necessary. Inform your vendor or customer if you make any changes. Proceed just as you do for other Simply Accounting transactions.

Importing General Journal Transactions

Simply Accounting can also import General Journal transactions from another program, such as a spreadsheet program. However, there are some limitations. You can import only transactions that you would normally enter in the General Journal. No linked Accounts Receivable, Accounts Payable, Payroll Advances, Vacation Payable or Inventory accounts may be used in the transactions after you have finished entering the history. Other modules are not updated as a result of the imported transactions. The file must be in text format and must follow a very specific format. Refer to the topic Importing miscellaneous transactions in Simply Accounting Help for details about the required text format.

Begin importing the transactions from the Simply Accounting Home window.

◆ Choose the **File menu** and click **Import General Journal Entries**. An open file window appears for you to choose the file from which to import the transactions.

◆ Choose the journal entries text file. Only text files are listed in this window.

◆ Click Open to import the journal entries.

Simply Accounting will report on the errors in the format of the text files, if there are any, so that you can correct them and attempt the import again. The imported transactions will be included in your journal reports.